SHRINES

SOUTH INDIAN SHRINES

P.V. Jagadisa Ayyar

Photographs by
Ajay Khullar

Rupa & Co

First in Rupa Paperback 2000

Published by
Rupa & Co.
15 Bankim Chatterjee Street, Calcutta 700 073
135 South Malaka, Allahabad 211 001
P.G. Solanki Path, Lamington Road, Bombay 400 007
7/16, Ansari Road, Daryaganj, New Delhi 110 002

ISBN 81-7167-410-0

Typeset by
Megatechnics
19A, Ansari Road,
New Delhi 110002

Printed in India by
Gopsons Papers Ltd.
A-14, Sector 60
Noida

Rs 195

CONTENTS

PREFACE

ANCIENT HINDU IDEALS

In introducing a work of this kind, which is as much intended for the instruction of the Western world as for the recording of traditions and memories which are dear to the heart of every pious Hindu, it is necessary to indicate briefly, for the benefit of European readers, something of the structure of the ideals and the beliefs of those who worship at the shrines which form the subject-matter of this work.

It is hardly necessary, however, to enter into a discourse on the history of the sacred land of Bharata Varsha — the land of Bharata, a famous and powerful emperor of this land. The legend of the Aryan invasion of India, from the days when the Aryans poured in through the Khyber Pass from their home in Central Asia till they crossed the Indus and commemorated this achievement by giving to the land the name of Hindustan, is too well-known, and from an ethnological point of view, too controversial to be discussed here. What, however, must be borne in mind is that it is the culture and tradition of these Aryan invaders, however differentiated in details by local conditions, that have influenced the whole of Hindu civilisation, even in provinces where the Aryan racial element has been comparatively small. It is not the purpose of the author to enter here into the heated controversies that have divided Ethnologists on the vexed question of the Aryan origin of the Indian people. All which is meant is that Hindu civilisation and particularly religious observances are, to this day, found influenced by the Aryanism typified in the code of Manu, very much as Christian Europe is still influenced by the Mosaic Law.

Popular and ceremonial Hinduism is a panorama of fasts and feasts and pilgrimages, and to give some idea it is sought of these in this introductory sketch. Those desirous of learning more about this subject can refer to my other work on the subject, viz., South Indian Festivities.

VEDAS AND DHARMA

The Vedas (derived from Sanskrit *vid* = to know) are the sacred writings of the Hindus, and present the entire Hindu theory of life. They present at once a philosophic theory of life, a social polity and a penal code. According to those ideals, man's present life is the net result of his Karma in a previous life. Dharma signifies duty, that is, the discharge of the duties enjoined on each man according to his Varṇa. The patriarchal ideal prevails throughout. A son must obey his father's commands, and a wife her husband's, without questioning their justice. Thus, Rama went into banishment at his father's command; and Sita followed him through the wilderness.

According to the Hindu Śāstras, Artha is the life of the temporal world. Charity, with a pure heart and a mind devoid of other expectations, is the ideal to be aimed at. Thus, Sri Rama pitied the wounded Jatayu (the Jatayu was not god!); thus he gave to the simian chief Sugriva the kingdom of Bali; and similarly he gave the boon of immortality, and the kingdom of Rāvaṇa to the pious Vibhishana.

It is laid down in the Hindu scriptures that legitimate desire is wholesome and good, but envy and avarice lead to destruction. So, the irresistible demand of Sita to get her the golden deer blinded Sri Rama's clarity of reason. He pursued the deer and lost his consort. Rāvaṇa's unlawful lust for Sita eventually cost him his life. Life, according to Hindu conception, is a theatre where each man plays an allotted part. Some recite the Vedas, some plough their lands, and others perform penance. But all must meditate on God.

Vratas, or observances of fasts and festivities formed an important part in the life of the ancient inhabitants of India. These consisted in the propitiatory worship of certain deities, and aimed at the attainment of certain ideals. The exact time for these occasions was fixed according to astronomical, or rather astrological, conditions. It was determined by astrological calculations regarding the relative position and aspect of the Hindu planetary system.

PURĀṆAS

The Purāṇas form the records of the ancient history of India interspersed with theology. A rationalistic study of these works is sure to be of great scientific importance. In olden days the sage Suta is said to have expounded them to the sages assembled in the Naimisaranya (Nimsar is situated in Oudh). Thereafter, it has become the practice for experts or scholars in the Sanskrit language, to read out these works to ordinary people and explain the meaning. Nowadays the idea has become a matter of ridicule for want of learned scholars who could explain the underlying meanings of the texts and for the dearth of an appreciative and sympathetic audience.

Purāṇas contain statements which require to be swallowed as they are. They are said to possess *panchalakshaṇas* or the five essential characteristics. These are, *sarga* (primary creation), *prati sarga* (secondary creation), *vamsa* (genealogy) of *devas, asuras*, kings and others, *manvantra* (marking the period of time), *vamsavalicharitra* (history of the royal dynasties). They also contain several moral stories which guide a man in leading a virtuous life.

In ancient India life and religion were so interturned that it was difficult to separate them. The Purāṇas are a curious blend of theology, history, and a moral code. These are amongst the oldest of Indian books and shed much light on Hindu religion and morals.

The Macenzie Collection on page 16 says: "There is one division of the Sanskrit books, which is in a great degree of local origin and interest, that of the Mahatmyas, the Sthala or local Puranas, the legendary histories of celebrated temples and objects of pilgrimage, and especially of those of the Dekkan, which are exceedingly numerous. These tracts describe the circumstances under which the place originally acquired its sanctity, the period of which is almost always in some former Yuga or great age; the foundation of the first temple or shrine, the different visits paid to it by gods and heroes, its discovery and renovation in the present age, the marvels which have resulted from its worship, and the benefactions made to it by modern sovereigns. In this latter portion some genuine history is occasionally preserved."

HINDU ERAS

The centuries in ancient India were divided into *Yugas*, or cosmic cycles, an arrangement popularly recognised even today. It is the conjunction of particular planets that forms the starting point of the various Yugas. There were four Yugas, the Krita Yuga, the Treta Yuga the Dwapara Yuga and the Kali Yuga (corresponding roughly, one supposes, to the golden, silver, bronze and iron ages of Augustan Chronology). The first of these four Yugas is named Krita Yuga (*kritam* means *srishti* or creation). The second is called Treta, or three sacrificial fires, so called because the great sacrifice in which these fires are used, was introduced during the period. The third is named Dwapara, which means that which followed the first two. The fourth, or the present age, is named Kali, which means vicious or sinful. The first three of the Hindu ages are said to have passed, and the present era is the fourth one. No doubt every generation, from time immemorial, has regarded its own time as the 'iron age.'

The Krita Yuga consisted of 1,728,000 years, and was the golden age when virtue prevailed and vice did not exist.

The Treta Yuga extended over 1,296,000 years, and was the beginning of what we now call decadence. In the previous Yuga the average life of a man was four hundred years, in the Treta Yuga the average came down to three hundred years.

The Dwapara Yuga covered eight lakhs sixty-four thousand years and was characterised by half virtue and half vice. People were heroic, polite and god-fearing. Man's age ranged up to two hundred years.

As for the present Kai Yuga, where virtue has diminished by 75 per cent., the averge life of a man has come down apparently to the proverbial three score and ten, or a little more. The only comfort is that this Yuga does not last longer than four lakhs two thousand years. And, after that comes the deluge, when Vishṇu reincarnates; and destroys the sinful races of the earth, and there begins a repetition of the cycle of Yugas.

The acquisition of merit appears to vary with the Yugas in which the person concerned happens to live. Thus, in the Krita Yuga it takes 10 years of virtuous living to acquire the merit which may be had in one year of the Treta Yuga, in one months of the Dwapara Yuga, and in one day in the Kali Yuga. The means by which the various Varṇas may acquire merit, differ equally. Thus, the Brahmin's duty is to study and recite

Vedas and to lead a religious life; the Sudra's salvation is
worked out by serving Brahmins.

The evils to come in our present Iron Age are set out
prophetically in the Puranas, which foreshadow changed
marriage customs, the rebellion of the pupil against his
preceptor, mammon worship, injustice and oppression, the
breaking of their vows by ascetics, immodesty of women,
irreligiousness, and finally drought, famine and pestilence.

In this connection Dubois in his *Hindu Manners, Customs
and Ceremonies* writes:

"This (Yuga) pretension to remote antiquity is a favourite
illusion amongst ancient civilized peoples, who, as they sank
into idolatry, soon forgot the traditions of their ancestors
regarding the creation of the world, and believed they could
add to their own glory by assuming an origin which was, so
to say, lost in the dim vista of mythical times. It is well-known
to what extremes the Chinese, the Egyptians and the Greeks
carried this mania, and it is characteristic of the Hindus that
they far excel these nations in their retensions.

"At the close of each of the Yugas there took place a universal
upheaval in nature. No trace of the preceding Yuga survived
in that which followed. The gods themselves shared in the
changes brought about by these great upheavals. Vishnu, for
instance, who was white in the preceding Yuga, became black
in the present one.

"But of all the Yugas the most dire is the Kali Yuga, in which
we now live. It is verily an Iron Age, an epoch of misrule
and misery, during which everything on earth has
deteriorated. The elements, the duration of life, the character
of mankind; everything in a word, has suffered, everything
has undergone a change. Deceit has taken the place of
justice, and falsehood that of truth. And this degeneration

must continue and go on increasing till the end of the Yuga.

From what I have just stated it will be seen that the commencement of the true era of the Hindus, that is to say, of their Kali Yuga, dates from about the same time as the epoch of the deluge, an event clearly recognized by them and very distinctly mentioned by their authors, who give it the name of the Jala pralayam, or the flood of waters.

"Their present era, indeed, dates specifically from the commencement of this Jala pralayam. It is definitely stated in the Markandeyapurana and in the Bhagavata that this event caused the destruction of all mankind, with the exception of the seven famus Rishis or Penitents whom I have often had occasion to mention, and who were saved from the universal destruction by means of an ark, of which Vishṇu himself was pilot. Another great personage, called Manu, who, as I have tried elsewhere to show, was no other than the great Noah himself, was also saved along with the seven great Penitents. The universal flood is not, to my knowledge, more clearly referred to in the writings of any heathen nation that has preserved the tradition of this great event, or described in a manner more in keeping with the narrative of Moses, than it is in the Hindu books to which I have referred.

"It is certainly remarkable that such testimony should be afforded us by a people whose antiquity has never been called in question; the only people, perhaps, who have never fallen into a state of barbarism; a people who, judging by the position, the climate and the fertility of their country, must have been one of the first nations to be regularly constituted; a people who from time immemorial have sufferd no considerable changes to be made in their primitive customs, which they have always held inviolable. And curiously enough, in all their ordinary transactions of life, in the promulgation of all their acts, in all their public monuments, the Hindus date everything from the subsidence of the Flood. They seem to tacitly acknowledge the other past ages to be purely chimerical and mythical, while they speak of the Kali Yuga as the only era recognized as authentic, Their public and private events are always reckoned by the year of the various cycles of sixty years which have elapsed since the Deluge. How many historical facts, looked upon as established truths, have a far less solid foundation than this!

"Another very remarkable circumstance is that the Hindu method of reckoning the age of the world agrees essentially with what we have in Holy Scrpiture. In Genesis viii. 13, for example, we read: 'In the six hundredth and first year, in the first month, the first day of the month, the waters were dried up from off the earth.' We read in Hindu works; 'On such a day of such a month of such a year of such a cycle, reckoning from the commencement of the Kali Yuga.'

"It is true that in the passage just quoted from Holy Scripture the date is reckoned from Noah's birth. He was then entering on his six hundred and first year. But according to many chronologists, it appears that in many times immediately succeeding the Deluge, the Scriptures reckon time by this patriarch, and that the annivesary of his birth commemorated the day on which the earth was restored to mankind — a momorable epoch from which they henceforth dated the years of the newly-restored earth, that is, of new era which they had just entered.

"The mighty changes which nations underwent entirely upset their calculations relating to those remote times; but the Hindus, settled as they were in a country long exempt from the revolutionary troubles that agitated other countries, have been able to preserve intact the tradition of those events.

"Their ordinary cycle is of sixty years, but they have also adopted another of ninety years, used in astronomical calculations. The latter is a much more recent invention, and was introduced at the time of the death of a famous king of India, named Salivahana, who reigned over a province then called Sagam, and who died at the end of the first century of the Christian era. It should be remarked that the use of these two rerent cycles could never occasion the least confusion in point of dates, since a period of three ordinary cycles corresponds to a period of two astronomical cycles, and they both start from the same epoch.

"The Chinese, likewise, have an ordinary cycle of sixty years in common with the Hindus; but there is this difference between the two : the Chinese, according to Du Halde, are ignorant as to when their era commenced, at least with reference to the epoch of the Flood. On the other hand, it is hardly likely that the two nations could have communicated with each other on this subject, seeing that they do not agree in their computations. According to the author just quoted, the birth of our Saviour falls on the fifty-eighth year of the Chinese cycle, while it coincides with the forty-second year of the Hindu cycle. But this coincidence, nevertheless, goes to confirm the high antiquity of the cycle of sixty years still in use with the two most ancient races on the face of the earth.

"It would be quite useless to inquire whether this cycle was adopted before the Flood, and whether it was from Noah or his immediate descendants that the Hindus and Chinese learned its use. We do not know for certain, however, that the weekly period was known prior to this remarkable event, and that the Hindu week agrees exactly with that of the Hebrews and with ours. Indeed, the days of their week corresponds exactly with those of ours, and bear similar names.

"One peculiar circumstance is that just as every day of the Hindu week has its own particular name, so has each of the sixty years of a cycle. Thus they do not say like us that a certain event happened, say, on the twentieth or thirtieth year before or after such an era. But they give the year its particular name, and say, for example, that such an event happened in the year Kilaka, in the year Bhava, in the year Vikari, and so forth.

"The only real difficulty is that the Hindu computation with regard to the epoch of the Flood does not appear to correspond with that of Holy Scripture.

"But it should be remembered that there is a difference of more than nine hundred years between the period supposed to have elapsed between the Flood and the Birth of Christ according to the Septuagint on the one hand, and according to the Vulgate on the other hand. Yet neither of these calculations is wholly rejected, and both of them are supported by able chronologists. The Catholic Church, which adheres to the Vulgate for the Old Testament, adopts the calculation of the Septuagint for the Roman Martyrology, which forms part of its liturgy. The difference, therefore, between the Hindu calculation and ours does not appear a sufficient reason for rejecting it, or even for supposing that it does not proceed from the same source.

"According to Hindu calculations, the time that elapsed between the Deluge and the Birth of Jesus Christ is 3,102 years. This period differs from that laid down in the Vulgate by about 770 years; but it approached much nearer to the calculations made in the Septuagint, which gives 3,258 years between the Deluge and the commencement of the Christian era. If we accept this last calculation, the epoch of the Hindu Jala pralayam does not differ from that of the Deluge of the Holy Scriptures by more than 156 years, a discrepancy of no great importance, considering the intricacy of a computation which dates from such remote times. I am, therefore, fully convinced that the Hindu computation serves to corroborate the accuracy of the event as narrated by Moses, and incontestable evidence to prove that most important event, the Universal Deluge.

"Some modern chronologists, with the learned Tournemine at their head, who based their calculations on the Vulgate, have professed to reckon between the Deluge and the Christian era, a period of 3,234 years, and they have supported their calculations with substantial arguments. Their learned investigations in this direction excited even in those days the admiration of competent critics. In relying, therefore, on this calculation, we have a difference of only 132 years between the Hindu computation and that of Holy Scripture as regards the Deluge.

"Deucalion's Flood does not approach so near the Universal Deluge of Scripture as the Jala pralayam of the Hindus. All the critics place the former so near the Birth of Jesus Christ that its comparative modernness alone is quite sufficient to prove that it has not even been borrowed from other ancient nations. The Flood of Ogyges, the occurrence of which is generally placed in the year 248 before that Deucalion, is, however, posterior, by more than twelve hundred years to the Universal Deluge, according to the Hindu calculations of the Jala pralayam. We have, therefore, fresh evidence that the Flood of Ogyges and that of Deucalion were only partial inundations, if indeed they are not altogether mythical."

DUTY OF WOMEN

It is laid down in the ancient Hindu scriptures that women should keep their tongue, mind and body pure, and serve their

husbands with devotion. The wife must regard her husband
as god; thus only they may reach heaven in company with
their husbands. Women should spend their time in the
chanting of sacred hymns and in the worship of their
husbands. This is the ideal of a Hindu woman.

VICE OR ADHARMA

This is regarded as the animating spirit of the *Rakshasas*
or demons. These demons are evil incarnate, and cannot
tolerate virtue in men. They are represented as eternally
tempting the virtuous, who, on the contrary, have their refuge
in Sri Krishna, who says in the Bhagavad Gita: "I take
incarnation in every Yuga to uphold the cause of virtue and
to destroy the element of vice."

HINDU PIETY

Nine aspects of piety are enjoined upon good Hindus: (i)
association with the virtuous; (2) recitation of sacred hymns
and songs; (3) love of God and His goodness; (4) homage done
in shrines and holy places; (5) worship of preceptors; (6)
solitary puja and purification; (7) worship of the devotees of
God; (8) constant recital of *Mantras*; (9) universal love and
respect for all created beings.

Bathing in the sacred rivers on auspicious occasions such as
the equinoxes (Vishnu Punyakala), Uttarāyana, Dakshiṇāyana
and the eclipses, is especially beneficial. Amongst the sacred
places which are said to possess peculiar merit are Sriparvata
(Srisailam), Kedar (in Himalayas), Prayag (Allahabad),
Benares, Kurushethra (near Delhi) and Kamalalaya (Tiruvarur.)

In the month of Arpisi or Tula the Nymphs of the river are
said to pay a visit to the sacred river Kaveri, and thence to
join their lord — the sea. A bath in the Kaveri at this period
is believed to be exceptionally beneficial.

Śraddhas are the annual ceremonies performed to propitiate the names of departed ancestors. It is considered a meritorious action on these occasions to provide money for education and for the feeding of the poor. Other means are through fasting on ceremonial occasions and giving gifts.

Everyone is enjoined to perform *puja* and observe seasonal vratas explained above. He who performs puja (ceremonial worship) to Brahmā acquires acuteness of intellect and long life; he who does similar honour to Vishnu attains great physical strength; while Śiva gives wisdom; Agni cures diseases and the serpent god ensures fruitfulness.

ARCHAEOLOGY

The only trace of many of the races, who have either colonised or exploited India from time to time, is now to be found only in archaeological remains, only a bare fringe of which has so far been touched by research work. In this province the problem presents less complexity, for it has been a Dravidian territory from time immemorial. Indian architecture is an ancient national art, bound up with the religion and tradition of the people, and nowhere has it been better preserved than in the religious edifices of the country. In the elaboration of minute, intricate and often, extremely fine ornamentation on stone, the Indian art is entirely sui generis.

The iconoclastic rule of the Mohammedans caused the artist families of the Hindus, who had previously enjoyed the patronage of the state, to be deprived of all state encouragement and be denounced as infidels and heretics. Many masterpieces of Indian sculpture were mutilated and defaced as being against the precepts of the faithful, and very few indeed have escaped the hands of the Mohammedans. For some time, after the Mohammedan power had begun to wane, anarchy and misrule prevailed over the greater part of

India. The images of gold and precious metals formed tempting booty, and marauders of this period melted and carried away the treasures. Under such insecurity of life and property, we cannot expect either literary or artistic culture to have flourished, and must be thankful for the few remains that are now to be seen. With foreigners at the head of the state, Indian master builders were deprived of their employment, and when the British began to adopt first the Palladian, then the Gothic and finally the Saracenic style of architecture, now in vogue, the noblest of the Indian arts was degraded to a common trade.

The Indian sculptor models the representation of the deity with attenuated waists and exhibits all the smaller anatomical details so as to obtain an extreme simplicity of contours. The hair, eyes, nose, mouth, sometimes even teeth and nails are executed nearly always with admirable care and fidelity as laid down in the ancient Śilpa Śāstras. In order that the form of the image may be brought out clearly, the sculptor is recommended to meditate on his model and told that his success will be proportionate to his meditation. No other way, not even seeing the object, will serve the purpose. To help him in his thoughts there are various descriptive and contemplative verses called the Dhyāna ślokas. The standard authorities on the subject state that the artist should learn to depict the image of the gods by means of spiritual contemplation only, as that is the best and truest standard for him. Indian art cares little for a very close study of facts or for anatomical detail.

According to the Śilpā Śāstras it is bad and even irreligious to make human figures. It is thought far better to present the figure of a god though it is not beautiful, than reproduce a remarkably handsome human figure. The image constructed fully according to the prescribed proportions is beautiful and yields virtue; otherwise, it takes away wealth and life and increases grief. The image, therefore, must be made according to the conventional proportions. The sanction that compels the artist is of a religious nature. The artist must not bungle with the work entrusted to him. The images of gods yield happiness to men and lead to heaven, but those of men lead away from heaven and produce grief. An image which is neither above nor below the fixed proportions, is beautiful. But the images of the gods, even if deformed, are for the good of men. There are many injunctions against the formation of human images.

Havell says:

"Spiritual contemplation is the key note of the Hindu art, as it was the art of Fra Angelico and the other great Christian masters; the whole philosophy of Indian art is in these two words, spiritual contemplation, and they explain a great deal that often seems incomprehensible and even offensive to Europeans."

Sir John Marshall, in his *Guide to Sanchi*, writes:

"The artists of early India were quick with the versatility of all true artists to profit by the lessons which others had to teach them; but there is no more reason in calling their creations Persian or Greek, than there would be in designating the modern fabric of St. Paul's, Italian. The art which they practised was essentially a national art, having its root in the heart and in the faith of the people, and giving eloquent expression to their spiritual beliefs and to their deep and intuitive sympathy with nature. Free alike from artificiality and idealism, its purpose was to glorify religion, not by seeking to embody spiritual ideas in terms of form, as the mediaeval art of India did, but by telling the story of Buddhism or Jainism in the simplest and most expressive language, which the chisel of the sculptor could command;

and it was good because of its simplicity and transparent sincerity that it voiced so truthfully the soul of the people, and still continues to make an instant appeal to our feelings."

Lawrence Binyon, in his *Painting in the Far East*, says:

"The Indian ideal claims everywhere its votaries and the chosen and recurrent theme is the beauty of contemplation, not of action. Not the glory of the naked human form, to western art the noblest and most expressive of symbols; not the proud and conscious assertion of human personality; but, instead of these, all thoughts that lead us out from ourselves into the Universal life, hints of the infinite, whispers from secret sources — mountains, water, mists, flowering trees, whatever tells of powers and presence mightier than ourselves; these are the themes dwelt on, cherished and preferred."

The French writer Taine, says that as one can only speak to another person in a language with which both are acquainted, so also you can appeal to man's artistic side by means of some common tradition, feeling and symbolism:

"The Indian art is, therefore, essentially idealistic, mystic, symbolic and transcendental and cannot as such be judged by the canons of Greek art, the Renaissance or the art of modern Europe, which are all in a greater or less degree naturalistic and realistic."

The *London Times* in, reviewing Vincent Smith's *History of Fine Art in India and Ceylon*, observes:

"The four-armed Śiva is not a whit more anatomically impossible than the winged angels or the centaurs which have been represented by the greatest artists of the west — not to mention those cherubs of Italian art whose anatomical deficiencies, from the school-master's point of view, gave an ever memorable opportunity to the humour of Charles Lamb.

The fact is, that no artist of genius, east or west, has ever cared a straw about anatomy when he had anything to gain by disregarding it. Extra limbs can be badly composed, just as the ordinary number can, but each case must be judged on its own merits; nor is it possible, in dealing with a definitely symbolic work of art, to separate the symbolism from the art so drastically as Mr. Vincent Smith is inclined to do. Nor, again, can the symbolism of one section of the Hindu mythology be justly separated from the rest and condemned as the product of a diseased imagination because it represents certain terrible aspects of Nature, which undoubtedly form a part of the whole and have to be taken into account in any deep and sincere conception of the Universe."

Ananda Coomaraswamy, in his *Arts and Crafts of India and Ceylon*, says:

"Sukracharya says 'Even a misshapen image of a god is to be preferred to an image of a man, however charming. Not only are images of men condemned, but originality, divergence from type, the expression of personal sentiment, are equally forbidden."

In the ancient sculptures, we see indications of the abnormally narrow waist and an expression of the muscular details which are characteristic of those days. At some later period, Indian artists may be said to have abandoned purely naturalistic aims and adopted an ideal of their own devising.

Again, no Hindu idol or image is considered worthy of worship until it has been consecrated by elaborate ceremonies known as *prāṇaprathishtha* or infusing life into the body and *avahana* or drawing the divine force and making it reside in the image. It is only after these necessary preliminaries have been gone through that daily service is rendered to the god. When either the daily services cease or the image becomes defiled by contact with unworthy hands, it must be consecrated again before worship. Great sanctity is attached to the Vedic mantras recited in the course of the ceremonies. It is only in the presence of such images, thus mesmerised by the force of mantras, that the sincere worshipper appears to be carried away so entirely as to identify the invisible object of his thought with that which is presented to him before his eyes. The Sthala Purāṇas of the various sacred shrines very reasonably and ingeniously furnish clues to the elucidation of several local peculiarities, though these valuable records are completely neglected, misinterpreted and abused in the present day.

HINDU TEMPLES

Temples are considered to be hallowed ground. They are the great teachers of piety to all classes of persons. They are the centres from which divine blessings issue to the deserving; hence they are said to promote justice throughout the land. It is also laid down that so long as these ancient institutions are duly maintained by the ruling race, there will be prosperity in the country and famine will not visit the land. These sacred shrines, by the splendour of their massive structure and the fine sculptures to be found therein, prompt the worshippers to lead a life of purity and devotion.

The Pope in his telegram to Emperor William on the destruction of Rheims Cathedral says:

"When you destroy the temples of God, you provoke the divine ire before which even the most potent armies lose all power."

The great temples of India are philanthropic as well as religious institutions. There the poor are fed; learning is promoted; and religion enjoins obedience even to a foreign ruler who maintains these heritages of all the ages.

The more famous of these shrines, built in ancient times in the busiest part of the village or town, are the greatest centres of activity. From early dawn till midnight, they attract large gatherings of people from various parts of the surrounding country. The preservation of temples is, therefore, considered an act of public service.

According to Hindu belief, there is no space which is not pervaded by god. Temples are the abode of wisdom, and are, therefore, the worthiest place of worship. Worshipping gods in temples infuses into our mind a feeling of divinity. Various minute rules have been laid down regarding temples, and the worship of the gods therein, such as the selection of site for the temple, the shape and beauty of the images to be installed therein, the time in which the puja is to be conducted, the kind of food to be offered to the idols, the qualifications of priests, and other details. Worshipping gods in temples is said to purify the heart, helps in the controlling of the passions, and enables the devotees to lead a pious and virtuous life.

The late Romesh Chunder Dutt says in his *Rambles in India*: "India is a land of recollections, and there is scarcely an ancient site of which does not open up a vista of ancient history and traditions. The Hindu lives in these traditions, and cherishes these recollections."

The famous sixty-three Saivaite devotees obtained the favour of Śiva, and their images are also to be seen in Saiva temples. Similarly, the representations of the twelve Alwars are to be found in the shrines dedicated to god Vishṇu. Sometimes temples are built over the tombs of the honoured dead to commemorate their deeds. This is supported by the authority of the Puraṇas, and their evidences are to be found to the present day.

The Historical Sketches of Ancient Dekkan states:

"One of the most important ancient customs of southern India revealed by the inscriptions, is the building of shrines and temples over the tombs or in honour of the dead. The literature of the Tamils contain a few references to this kind of practice which, as will be shown below, was generally prevalent in the Dekkan. Silappadigaram states that temples were erected in several parts of the Tamil country, nay even in Ceylon and northern India, to enshrine the image of Kannagi, and thus refers to an ancient custom. In the tenth idyll, Malaipadukadam of Pattupattu, Perungunrur Kousikanar of Iranyamuttam, writes that the country abounds in stones planted with inscriptions to celebrate the fame of military men, who have given their lives in fighting to the last with the enemy, even when the whole army was put to flight, thinking it better to die in battle-field than brook the ignominy attending a flight. Similar references to these kinds of monuments are found in Purapporul Venbamalai and Tolgappiyam. Inscriptions discovered in the Kanarese country amply bear testimony to the account given in the Tamil works just referred to. Some of these monuments belong to the tenth century A.D. Men of remarkable deeds, who had earned the admiration and respect of the people during their lifetime, such as the Saiva Nayanmars, the Vaishnava Alwars and a few of the kings of southern India came to be defied in later times. The earliest reference to a temple built on the tomb of a dead person is perhaps the one at Satyavedu in the Ponneri taluka of Chingleput district. Two of the inscriptions of this temple are dated in the fourth and fifth years of the region of the Ganga Pallava king Aparajita who appears to have flourished in the last quarter of the ninth century A.D. They call the temple Mattangan Palli and this is perhaps to be interpreted as the tomb of Matanga. The word 'Palli' occurring here cannot be taken to mean 'a Jaina temple', because it is still a Śiva shrine. Popular tradition connects the temple with the sage Matanga

Maharishi for which there is no warrant. At Tirunageswarem near Kumbakonam, there is a *mandapa* in front of the Nageswaraswamin temple and it contains an inscription of the time of Rajakesarivarman who has been identified with Aditya I. It mentions a shrine of Miladudaiyal Palli. The first part of this name might be connected with the Saiva saint Meypporul Nayanar, who was the lord of Miladu, the country of which the Capital was Tirukoilur. It may be seriously doubted if the Tirunageswarem inscription refers to a shrine built in honour of the saint, because there is ample evidence in the sculptures found all round the shrine of the goddess in the Śiva temple, that there was a big Jaina temple in the place from which these image should have been removed to the place where they are now found. Most of the images are certainly Jaina in their form. Besides, the people of Tirunageswarem say that the images were removed from a field near a ruined temple. The ruined temple should, therefore, have been a Jaina shrine and it might have borne the name Miladudaiyar Palli indicating that it was built by a Miladu chief, who was in all likelihood a feudatory of the Chola king of his time.

During the time of Rajaraja I (A.D. 985-1013), the images of the Saiva saints Tirunavukkarasu, Jnanasambandha, Sundaramurti and his two wives, Siruttonda and his father and son, and several others were set up in the big temple of Rajarajeswara built by him at Tanjore. The large number of images set up shows that the worship of the dead, had become quite common at the end of the tenth century A.D. and the beginning of the eleventh. One of the inscriptions of the Śiva temple at Tondamanad near Kalahasti in the Chittoor district, is very interesting in this connection. It registers the fact that the temple which bears the record under reference was erected as a pallipadai (a memorial over the remains) of the king who

died at Tondaiman Arrur. Since the place itself is called by
the name Tondaiman perarrur, there is little doubt that the
king on whose behalf it was built died in the place and the
temple was probably raised over the place of his burial. The
king here referred to is spoken of, in an inscription at
Tirumalperu, as the immediate predecessor of Parantaka I,
indicating clearly that he is identical with Aditya I. The
Melpadi inscription of Rajaraja I states that the temple of
Arinjeswara was erected as a pallipadai to the king who died
at Arrur. From the very fact that the temple was erected in
a place different from where died, it is certain that there is
a clear reference to the construction of a shrine in honour of
the dead king, not being on his tomb but far removed from
the place of burial."

Many of the great temples of southern India are of the
genuine ancient Hindu style of architecture. However, most
of them exhibit, more recent extensions and modern
construction, while the deity in the sanctum is invariably
allowed to remain as in the days of old. The local shrine of
the chronicle or Sthala Purana refers the original foundation
of each shrine to some remote period, usually to some
preceding yuga.

In the case of the Dravidian temples, the main shrine is
situated in the centre and the other accessory buildings stand
inside a long rectangular enclosure divided by a high cross
wall into two courts, which, according to the importance of
the shrine, may amount to as many as seven, and are in such
cases styled as the *sapta prakaras*. The eastern, or the entrance
court, is entered by a lofty *gopura* or tower which forms a
conspicuous feature at the outset. The lower portion of the
gopura up to the lintel and cornice over the high entrance
gateway is of stone ornamented with pilasters and niches or
projections from the main walls. An ornamental base runs

around a cornice surmounting the lower storey. The massive wooden gates, studded with large nails, are placed about a third of the depth of the passage from the front. The superstructure consists of several storeys, each of them being of smaller area. In early examples these are constructed of stone, but in later structures they are constructed invariably of brick. The lowest of these is entered by a narrow outer staircase from a chamber raised a few feet on each side of the gateway. In each of these chambers is to be found a massive square pier ornamented on the lower part by plaited bands, rosettes, pateras and other floral designs. Above this lower chamber is another similarly situated. The floors above the entrance are reached by ladders through a gangway on the floor. The gopura, or entrance leading to the court inside, is considerably lower in elevation than the eastern or one at the entrance. The tower or *vimana* on the shrine is almost to its very top ornamented with plaster figures. An ornamental base course, which runs round the open sides of the central shrine, raises the floor several feet above the court. This base is likewise ornamented with dancing figures, rows of elephants and other works of art. The floor is on three levels, the highest of which is the innermost. The piers, which in general are alternately square and polygonal, are surmounted by a deep circular moulded capital with a square abacus. The square portions are covered with mythological figures. A deep cornice runs round the exposed sides of the central shrine and the ceiling is plain with a flat stone terrace.

The principle shrine of the temple stands near the inner or the central court. Its plan consists of a small square or rectangular cell or chamber, called the *garbhagriha* or the sanctum, for the image, which is enclosed in a square building, leaving a covered *pradakshina* or space for the devotees to go round. In front is a passage or double chamber forming the *ardhamandapa*. This latter building is square or rectangular with a door on the sides and with lofty piers inside. In advance of the ardhamandapa is what is called the *mahamandapa*, consisting of a pillared building with entrance doors and steps on three sides. Besides these two mandapas in front of the central shrine, there are other and more spacious ones, with a dais in one end for the god to be placed on and decorated during festivals. On either side of the front entrance of the ardhamandapa are to be found two colossal figures of *dwarapalas* and the two side entrances have ornamental doors likewise. Closeby, the inner door of the shrine stand also similar figures of dwarapalas. An ornamental base surrounds all these buildings. Fine rectangular perforated stone windows of various designs are often seen on the sides of both the anti-chambers. In front of the sanctum is located the bull in the case of Śiva temple and the Garuda in the shrines of Vishṇu with the platform or *bali peetha* and the *dwajastambha* or the flag staff. The principal features of temples are the following:

(1) The garbhagriha, or the cell containing the sacred deity, with a vimana or tower over it.

(2) Mandapas, or pillared halls, in front of it.

(3) Gopuras, or the entrance towers, opening through the walls enclosing the vimanas on all sides generally, but with special reference to the east.

(4) The verandah, or the *tirumalapatti*, attached to the inside walls of the *pradakshina*,

(5) *Tirthas* (tanks and wells), held sacred for purposes of bathing.

(6) Subsidiary shrines dedicated to various other minor gods, each in its appropriate place.

According to the Agamas, in dealing with the repairs of temple buildings, extreme care has to be exercised when such ancient structures stand in need of repairs. If any stone happens to be broken, it should be replaced with the same quality of stone, having the same colour and architectural features as the original one. New works of art should not be introduced on any account. Under these circumstances, a building that has a broken pier or a lintel should not be dug out to its foundation, nor a new one put up in its place.

It is an admitted fact that temple building was a customary religious act amongst the ancient Hindu kings. There is a saying of the famous Tamil poetess Auvaiyar that men ought not to live in places where there are no temples; and the Tevaram also mentions that places without temples are unfit for purposes of residence, as they are merely deserts. The poet Narkkirar says, "God is pleased to preside in places where festivities are observed faithfully, where devotees pray earnestly for Him, in the confluence and banks of rivers, in the heart of towns, at the meeting place of 3 or 5 streets, under the shade of trees planted in the centre of the village, and in cow pens." Hence the popular saying 'No temple, no village'." This is why in ancient India each place of habitation, whether a hamlet or a city, had to maintain its own temple for the prosperity of the inhabitants.

With the Hindus, science appears to have gone hand-in-hand with religion and the religious dictates are full of sanitary principles though one has to take the trouble of going deeper to recognize them. Even an atheist cannot deny that the Hindu temples contribute to the health of the inhabitants of the place. Occupying the central part of the city and covering an immense area they contain a large quantity of fresh air which is so necessary for the health of the citizens. The time-honoured practice of fixing iron *trisulas* or tridents in front of the shrines, copper *kalasas* or pinnacles over the high towers, etc., is analogous to fixing a lightning conductor. Again the existence of tanks in the temples with a garden closeby affords an ample supply of good water. In some of the temples the tanks are surrounded with colonnades and spacious mandapas which afford ample room for the sojourn of the pilgrims visiting the shrine from distant places. In cases of the smaller temples, the tanks are situated on the outside but as close to the shrine as possibe. The preservation of the temple gardens and the rearing of large trees and flowering plants therein, purifies the air in the locality. Not to speak of the sanitary advantages, there is the additional beauty and elation of the spirit that is afforded to us in beholding such spacious and ornamental structures. Therefore in the formation of towns and villages, separate sites are set apart for the temple and even for its subsequent expansion.

Professor Geddes, who visited India under the patronage of the government of India, observes:

"That India, and particularly south India, was, and this up to a not so remote past, one of the greatest city-making regions of the world, is ever being more plainly re-established by the investigators of books and of buildings alike. In India cities have mostly grown around temples. The mutual attraction of temples to national surroundings, and of cities to temples have been the chief factors in the growth and development of city life in India."

The *Historical Sketches of Ancient Dekkan* mentions:

"Of all the institutions of southern India, the most important was the temple. During the early days i.e., long before the advent of the Muhammadans, each big village could boast of an excellent temple built in the old style and picturesquely situated within a radius of one or two miles from the village in a very fine and evergreen grove of plantains, coconuts and areca palms, with a tank of crystal water just in front of it. Novel as this idea may seem, it is not far from the truth. If we look at some of the most ancient temples of southern India such as the Vedaranyeswara, Vataranyeswara, Svetavaneswara, Madhyarjuneswara and the like, the fact will become quite evident. All these temples were so called because they were situated in groves adjoining villages — not in villages themselves. Even at the present day, after a lapse of several centuries, it will not fail to strike even a casual observer that the temples are at a little distance from the inhabited villages. I later times the size and capacity of the temple increased several-fold by the ever new additions of spacious halls. Innumerable shrines for minor deities were erected in the covered verandah, of the huge prakara walls built round the central shrine, one within the other, and of the towering gopuras attracted the traveller's eye even from a distance. The well-to-do persons loved to erect monuments by expending enormous sums of money and the original structures, shorn of all later improvements, modest as they were, were not without a history of their own, memorable enough to be sketched by the gifted.

The earliest form of a temple consisted of three parts viz., the garbhagriha, i.e., the innermost apartments of the central shrine with two mandapas, one in front of the other. The middle portion called the *antarala mandapa* is a passage leading from the more spacious outer *mukha mandapa* into the central shrine. While the worship was being conducted in the central shrine, the devotees gathered together in these two mandapas and outside of them. All round this temple structure of three stages which was known by the name of *traiyanga*, there were niches provided on the outside walls to accommodate some principal deities. The structure itself was built of five parts or *angas* called the *panchanga*. The five parts are known by technical names *kandeppadai*, *kumudappadai*, *jagadippadai*, *uttiram* and *vimanam*. In the central shrine of a Śiva temple, generally, a linga is found and this is sometime replaced by stone images of Śiva and Parvati comfortably seated together on a well-decorated pedestal. The linga and *avadei* within which it is fixed, represent the *purusha* or the universal spirit and the *prakriti* or primeval matter and thus establish the idea of the evolution of the manifested world by their combination, resulting in a variety of forms. It is this idea that is prominently brought into the minds of the innumerable devotees that stand before the shapeless image wrapt in silence, perceiving how inseparably soul and matter are united together in this world of changes. The spontaneous outburst of thousands of stirring hymns of the pious leaders of the Saiva creed embodied in the Tamil Devarem often refer to this aspect and amply bear testimony to the object with which the images were enshrined in temples. In the central shrines of Vishṇu temples, there are invariably placed huge sculptures of one form or another of the several manifestations of Vishṇu with a number of attendant deities with whom he is said to have been associated in the incarnations taken in order to put an end to the cup of misery or the misdoings of the wicked when unrighteousness reigned supreme in the world. The Puraṇic stories regarding them are picturesquely delineated in the images enshrined in these temples and the devotees are made to profit by them. The niches accommodate in them the various forms assumed by the Almighty and furnish a visible explanation of the fund of knowledge stored in ancient lore. Such are the Lingodbhava, Dakshinamurti, Ardhanariswara, Mahishasuramardini and the like. To these were added the images of the principal devotees themselves, who by their perfect abstinence from the worldly ways and search after the imperishable one, praised in the books, by a severe penance, had come to acquire a halo of divinity and regarded as the first servants of god. These are the Nandi, Bhringi, Chandesa and others. In this connection, it may be pointed out that all transactions connected with Śiva temples were done in the name of Chandesa, who is stated to be the first servant of god. It was in his name that the sale of temple lands took place. It was again he who purchased all lands for the temple, leased them out or received the money paid into the temple treasury. Not a single Hindu is unaware of the life of this sage as vividly portrayed in the Periyapuranam of Sekkilar. Various places of the Dekkan, connected with the lives of these sages, celebrate special festivals which keep alive their memory and the miracles popularly attributed to them. Thus at Kalahasti, Tiruvalangadu, Chidembaram, Tiruvarur, Shiyali, Tiruchchangattangudi and others, prominence is given to the devotees of Kannappa Nayanar, Karikkalammai, Nanda, Manu Chola, Jnanasambanda, Siruttonda among the Saivas; Poygaiyalwar, Budattalwar, Peyalvar, Tirumangai, Tirumalaisai, Nammalwar and others among the Vaishnavas.

Many more instances may be given, but it will suffice to point out how useful information could be collected from lithic records of what are recorded in books. To return to our subject, we may state that in the grandeur of the massive shrines and in the exquisite sculptures, which strike the imagination in a way that could not be done by any other means, the temples of southern India taught the people for centuries, lessons of purity and devotion.

*

The temple was in ancient times the busiest part of all the places in a village or town. From early dawn till midnight could see crowds of people, rich and poor gathered from far and near. A number of shepherds and other classes of men were left in charge of land, money or livestock, which formed the donations made to the temple. They brought to its courtyard, at fixed hours, ghee for burning lamps or for feeding Brahmans, flowers and garlands, rice for offerings, fruits and vegetables of various kinds, sandal pastes and incense, scents like *pachchaikarpuram*, musk, rose-water, etc., and in short all the requirements of the temple and gave them away to the authorities according to the terms of contract by which they were put in possession of temple holdings. In this connection, we may quote the words of one such contract which runs thus: "If he (the donee) dies, absconds or gets into prison, fetters or chains, we, all these aforesaid persons (the sureties of the donee) are bound to supply ghee for burning the holy lamp as long as the sun and the moon endure." The contents of two other similar documents may also be taken note of. The first of them is the Sirpur inscription which registers a grant of villages for the maintenance of almhouses, the repairer of cracks in the temple, the supporting of the servants of the sanctuary and for the Brahmans versed in the three Vedas: Rig, Yaju, and Sama. The record enjoins that the sons and grandsons who succeed the Brahman donees should offer sacrifice to fire and know the six supplements of the Vedas, should not be addicted to gambling or other bad associations, should have their mouth clean and not be servants. If they did not answer or possess the above qualifications or if one dies or was removed in their places they should be replaced by Brahmans possessing the stipulated qualifications. The substituted individuals should be chosen from among the relations of the unqualified men and should be advanced in age while being learned at the same time. They must be appointed by their consent alone and not by an order of the king. It further states that in place of those donees (of shares allotted for the performance of specified services in temples) who die or emigrate, the nearest relatives of such persons have to receive the grant and do the service. In case the nearest relatives of such individuals are not qualified themselves, they have to select others who are qualified and let them do the service receiving the remuneration provided for. And if there were no near relations to such individuals, the other incumbents of the service have to select qualified persons for doing the same and the person so selected shall receive the remuneration in the same way as the person whom he represented had received it before.

People who held temple lands on lease were bound by agreement to bring to the courtyard of the temple the stipulated quantity of paddy or rice, free from dust, chaff and unripe grains and give them in heaped measures. It can be gathered from the wording of the documents that they have to bear the incidental charges such as the wages of those who have to carry them to the temple and the tolls. In the temples, labour was divided; each one had to do a particular duty assigned to him and for which he received a remuneration. In a spacious mandapa so constructed as to accommodate a large concourse of people, sitting on a pedestal in a prominent place, a famous scholar chanted the hymns of the Vedas and expounded them to his ardent hearers. In another mandapa the great epic Mahabharata, which had moulded the life and character of the Hindus for ages, was read and explained to the people. The Dharmaśāstra embodying the rules of right conduct, the purāṇas, grammar, rhetoric, logic, astrology, astronomy, medicine and other special sciences were taught to those who thronged to learn them.

In the temple at Tiruvorriyur, Vyakarana, Somasiddhanta and Panini's grammar were taught. There are references also to the recital and teaching of Prabhakara, Rudra, Yamala, Puraṇa, Śivadharma, Panchanga, and Bharata. Lands were granted to learned scholars and their future generations as Vedavritti, Bhattavritti, Vaidyavritti, or Maruttuvapperu, Archanavritti and the like. From all these it would be clear that the temple was the seat of free learning in ancient times and it was also the place where charities of every description were conducted. A record of the twelfth century A.D. states that a big hospital existed at Tirumukkudal in the Chingleput district provided with a number of beds for the sick, with nurses to attend on them, with men to fetch fuel and medicinal herbs, with a good stock of many a patent remedy and with doctors, cooks and others. There is not the least doubt that other temples of the south had similar provisions. Among the Tamil hymns sung in temples, we may note that those of the Devaram, Nalayiraprabhandam, and Tiruchchalal, Tiruvembavai and Tiruppadiyam are often found in inscriptions. Among the musical instruments that were in use in ancient times, we may mention besides Mattalam, Karadigai, Segandi Kaimani, Parai and Sangu already noticed, Yal or Vinai, Kulal, Udukkai, Kudamula and Kalam. In the temples of southern India there was invariably a spacious ranga mandapa. On almost all days, dancing was practised and plays staged on special occasions. The latter were divided into acts and scenes and the former consisted of several varieties of popular amusement conveying religious instructions. Besides being the scene of all the aforesaid activities, the temple was the principal feeding house of the village. All strangers, ascetics and men of learning were fed sumptuously in the temple. Fruits, ghee and sugar were largely used and people were served with several kinds of boiled preparations from raw vegetables by the addition of condiments such as pepper, pulses, mustard, turmeric, cumin, salt and tamarind, along with a few others, fried in ghee. Chillies were not included in the preparations, but asafoetida was largely consumed. Ancient inscriptions reveal the method of preparing several varieties of special dishes. For festive occasions, ample provisions were made and a large number of people were fed. There were several of these occasions given below are some of those related to the Śiva temples:

1. Vishu in the months of Sittarai and Arpisi.
2. Visakha in the month of Vaigasi.
3. Puram in Adi.
4. Sravishtha in Avani.
5. Satabhishaj in Purattasi.
6. Krittika in Kartigai.
7. Arudra in Margali.
8. Pushya in Tai.
9. Makha in Masi.
10. Uttara Phalguni in Panguni.
11. Sankranti in the two Ayanas.
12. The hunting excursion of the god, the *rathotsava* or the car festival, the vasantotsava and the like.

Most of the festivals enumerated, continue to be observed even at the present day; but they appear to have been more elaborate in the past and that on these occasions a large number of men were fed free of cost.

The temple was also the place where ancient kings performed their *tulabhara* and *hiranyagarbha* ceremonies which attracted crowds of people from all parts of the kingdom. The greatest of the Chola kings, Rajaraja I had his tulabhara ceremony performed in the Sivayoganathaswamin temple at Tiruvisalur in his twenty-eighth year of his reign (A.D. 1013) On that very day, the queen Dantisaktivitanki or Lokamahadevi passed through a gold cow in the same place. It is stated in the Tamil work *Koyilolugu* that Jatavarman Sundara Pandya I (A.D. 1251-71), the greatest of the Pandya kings, built several tulapurusha mandapas in the Srirangam temple and had his tulabhara ceremony performed there, several times. Many of the Vijayanagara kings had the same ceremony performed in temples at Srirangam and Conjevaram. Almost in all the temples visited by the south Indian kings, special festivals, called after their own names, were ordered to be conducted annually on the asterism of their birthday and rich endowments were made for them. To secure merit for the dead, to get success in battle, to be rid of some sickness from which one was suffering or for obtaining prosperity, wealth and happiness in life, offerings were made to propitiate the god. On these occasions, images in temples were bathed in 108 pots of water to the accompaniment of the chanting of the Vedic hymns, were smeared with sandal-paste and taken in procession."

Dubois in his *Hindu Manners, Customs and Ceremonials* says:

"The structure of the large temples, both ancient and modern, is everywhere the same. The Hindus, devoted as they are to ancestral customs, have never introduced innovations in the construction of their public edifices. Their architectural monuments, such as they exist today, are probably better examples of building as practised by ancient civilized nations than the ruins of Egyptians and Greeks, concerning which European scholars have so much to say.

"The entrance gate of the great pagodas opens through a high, massive pyramidical tower, the summit of which is ordinarily topped by a crescent or halfmoon. The gate faces the east, a position which is observed in all their temples, great and small. The pyramid or tower is called the gopuram.

"Beyond the tower is a large court, at the farther end of which is another gate, opening like the first through a pyramid of the same form, but smaller. Through this you pass to a second and smaller court, which is in front of the shrine containing the principal idol.

"In the middle of this second court and facing the entrance to the shrine, you generally see upon a large pedestal, or within a kind of pavilion open all sides and supported by four pillars, a coarsely sculptured stone figure, either of a bull lying flat on its belly, or of a lingam, if the temple is dedicated to Śiva; or of the monkey Hanuman, or of the serpent Capella, if it is a temple of Vishṇu, or of the god Vigneswara; or may be of some other symbol of Hindu worship. This is the first object which the natives worship before entering the shrine itself.

"The door of the shrine is generally low and narrow, and it is the only opening which allows a free passage of air and light from outside, for the use of windows is entirely unknown in the Pebubsyka. The interior of the shrine is habitually shrouded in darkness, or is lighted only by the feeble flicker of a lamp which burns day and night by the side of the idol. One experiences a sort of involuntary shock on entering one of these dark recesses. The interior of the shrine is generally divided into two parts, sometimes into three. The first, which may be called the nave, is the largest, and it is here that the worshippers assemble. The second is called the *adytum*, or sanctuary, where the idol to whom the shrine is consecrated is placed. This chamber is smaller and much darker than the first. It is generally kept shut, and the door can be opened only by the officiating priest, who, with some of his acolytes, has alone a right to enter its mysterious precincts for the purpose of washing and dressing the idol and presenting the offerings of the faithful, such as flowers, incense of sandalwood, lighted lamps, fruit, butter-milk, rich apparel, and jewels.

"Some of the modern Hindu temples are vaulted, but most of

them have flat roofs supported by several rows of massive stone pillars, the capitals of which are composed of two heavy stones crossed, on which are placed the beams, also of stone, which extend through the length and breadth of the building. The beams again are covered horizontally with slabs of stone, strongly cemented to prevent leakage. Whether the object be to make these buildings more imposing and solid, or to preserve them from the danger of fire, wood is never employed except for the doors.

"The adytum, or sanctuary, is often constructed with a dome, but the building as a whole is generally very low, and this destroys the effect of its proportions in a striking degree. The low elevation; the difficulty with which the air finds a way through a single narrow and habitually closed passage; the unhealthy odours rising from the mass of fresh and decaying flowers; the burning lamps; the oil and butter split in libations; the excrement of the bats that take up their abode in these dark places; finally, and above all, the fetid perspiration of a multitude of unclean and maladorous people — all contribute to render these sacred shrines excessively unhealthy. Only a Hindu could remain for any length of time in their heated and pestilential precincts without suffocation." (Abbe nowhere remarks on the burning of camphor, which plays so conspicuous a part in all Hindu worship, and which acts at the same time as a disinfectant.)

MURTIS IN TEMPLES

According to orthodox Hindu philosophy, the God in temples is nameless and shapeless. As omnipotent, He is called Brahman; as all powerful, Paramesvara; as the destroyer of sins, Hari. Birthless He is, yet as the author of all, He is called Swayambhu. As the ultimate receptacle of the whole universe,

He is called Narayana; as the destroyer of samsara or the ties of the world, He is called Hara; and as omnipresent, Vishnu. As the life-giving force, He is known as Omkaresvara; as capable of knowing everything through intuition, He is called Sarva; and in tribute to His undisturbed mind, He is known as Śiva. As all pervading, He is known as Vibhu; and as remover of all grief as Taraka.

God is all-powerful and all-knowing. Worship of Him alone leads to eternal bliss. He is invisible, but such a conception of the deity transcends the mental horizon of the unlearned and unintelligent masses. It is for them that temples are built, with representations of God in His various aspects, each of which exhibits a definite phase of His infinite greatness. Most of the images in the Hindu temples represent the several *avataras* of God, each of which was assumed for a definite purpose.

The five elements are worshipped by Hindus as gods, especially in specified seasons of the year; the eighteenth Adi or Ashada (June-July) is the day for Appu or water; the fourth day after the full moon in the month of Avani or Sravana (July-August) for the earth; the Saraswati puja day for Vayu or the air; during the asterism of Krittika in the month of Karttika or Pausha (October-November) for Tejas or fire; and the Sankranti day for Akasa or ether.

The festival of burning Kama (the element of desire) is observed all over India. Figures of Manmatha and Rati (Adonis and Venus) are worshipped and then placed on a bonfire and burnt. The ashes are smeared on the brows by the devout. Manmatha was burnt to ashes by Śiva on the full moon day of the month of Panguni (March-April).

Festivals are also observed in honour of Mari, Kali and Sasta. The propitiation of these deities is regarded as a precaution against epidemics like cholera and small-pox.

The Agamas that treat the rituals and other ceremonies to

be observed in the temples, mention three requisites for a town or village, namely, *sthala* or soil, tirtha or water and *murti* or deity. Unless the place satisfies these three essentials, it is not recommended as a place of habitation. There are again, particular trees which are attached to the temples in different localities. These trees are known as stala *vrikshas*. Some of these features frequently contribute towards the naming of the place.

Offerings are made to the gods in the temples for the happiness and prosperity of the devotee and his family. It is laid down in the ancient books that those who erect or rebuild temples not only reap the benefit themselves for their virtuous actions but also help to liberate their deceased forefathers in the other world.

TEMPLES AS EDUCATIONAL INSTITUTIONS

That in the good old days the temples of southern India served the purpose of educational institutions is supported by inscriptions engraved on the walls of several temples and those so far noticed are made mention of in the annual reports of the Epigraphical Department. According to these reports, which contain a wealth of information on the subject, we find that not only did these institutions served a social and religious purpose but were also of educational value. The reading of epics and the recitation of other important hymns formed a part which enabled people to faithfully follow their religion without which any education imparted to Hindus could not be a success.

The sacred utterances of the Saiva saints that go by the name of Tevaram and those of the Vaishnava saints named Tiruvoimozhi acquitted the sanctity of the Vedas in the eyes of the Tamilians. These utterances had, during the course of a few centuries since the authors of the hymns sambhandar, appar and sundaramurti, passed away, went into oblivion and their rescue is attributed to a devotee named Nambiandarnambi of Tirunaraiyur, near Chidambaram. This young devotee belonged to the class of *archakas* or temple worshippers. His devotion was considered so great, that the Vinayaka of the place yielded to his request to eat a dish of rice offered by him! The then Chola king at Tiruvarur, Tanjore district, Rajaraja Abhayakula Sekara, identifiable with Kulottunga I, according to the researches of the Madras Epigraphical Department, hearing of this miraculous proceeding, went to this devotee and applied for his securing these Tamil scriptures of Tevaram songs through the blessings of that god. Accordingly he learnt that they were preserved on palm leaves in one of the rooms on the southwest corner of the second prakara of Sri Nataraja temple at Chidambaram. The king with his devotee proceeded there and had the room examined and found heaps of palm leaf manuscripts, much of which had been eaten by moths. When in anxiety for this serious loss of religious literature an aerial voice made it known that those valuable for that age alone were preserved i.e., out of 16,000, 49,000 and 37,000 songs of sambhandar, appar and sundarar only 384,312 and 100 were available then. These were subsequently printed. Again in 1918, eleven more were found engraved in the stone of the temple at Tiruvidavayil in the Nannilam Taluk of Tanjore district. The Epigraphical Report for the year 1917-18 says:

"This is the first instance in which the Tevaram verses are found engraved on the walls of a temple, whose existence was brought to my notice by Mr. Jagadisa Iyer, Manager, Office of the Archaeological Superintendent... The script in which the epigraph is incised may be roughly assigned to the 12th century A.D., just the time when the other Tevaram hymns were collected. The method adopted in the treatment of the subject matter of the hymn is quite characteristic of the saint

(Jnanasambandha) to whom it is attributed in the inscription inasmuch as one half of each verse describes the God and the other half furnishes a description of the place."

On the west wall of the central shrine of the Sundareswara temple at Sendalai (or Mannar Samudram) near Tanjore known in inscriptions as Chandrasekharachadurvedimangalam is an inscription relating to Chola king Ko Parakesarivarman or Rajendra Chola which provides for the recitation of the Bharata in a mandapa within the temple. The ancient name of the temple was Perundurai.

The north wall of the central shrine of Sri Nageswara in Kumbakonam bears a record dated in the third year of Parakesarivarman relating to the expounding of the Prabhakaram which is the name given to one of the famous commentaries on the *Purva Mimamsa Sutras*. It formed a new school of philosophy called Prabhakaramata after its expounder, the great Prabhakara, whom the Epigraphist to the Government of Madras infers should have lived early in the eighth century.

The west wall of the first prakara of the Adipuriswara temple at Tiruvottiyur near Madras bears an inscription of Chola king Tribhuvanachakravartin Konerimaikondan (Kulottunga III) providing for the maintenance of the pavilion called Vyakarnadanavyabhyanamandapa within the temple, for the upkeep of the teachers and pupils who studied grammar there, and for the worship of the god Vyakaranandana Perumal Śiva who is supposed to have appeared before Panini Bhagavan in this very mandapa for fourteen continuous days and to teach him the first fourteen aphorisms with which Panini's grammar begins.

On the east wall of the first prakara in the Venkatesaperumal temple at Tirumurkudal (Chingleput district) is a record of Chola king Rajakesarivarman or Virarajendra, dated in his fifth year, relating to the maintenance of a school in the Janana mandapa within the temple for the study of the Vedas, śāstras, grammar, Rupavatara etc., a hostel for students and another hostel (*atulasalalai*) or *aturasala*. The students (*śattirar*) were provided with food and bathing oil on Saturdays. The hospital was named Virasolan and was provided with fifteen beds for sick people. The items of expense set apart for their comforts were: rice, a doctor (in whose family the privilege of administering medicines was hereditary), a surgeon, two servants who fetched drugs, supplied fuel and did other services for the hospital, two maid servants for nursing the patients, a general servant for the school hospital and for the general hospital. The medicines required for one year were stored, water from Parambalur scented with cardamom and khas. Khas roots were supplied to the inmates of this institution.

On the north wall of the central shrine in the Alagia Narasingha Perumal temple at Ennayiram near Villupuram, south Arcot district, there is a record of Chola king Parakesarivarman or Rajendra Chola providing for the recitation of Tiruvoymozhi and for the maintenance of the educational institution in which the Vedas, Vyakarana, Mimamsa and Vedanta were taught.

On the west wall of the first prakara of the Bhuvaraha Perumal temple in Srimushnam, south Arcot district, is a Telugu record quoting from the *Srimushna Mahatmaya* or the local chronicle of the place, the merit to be obtained in performing the twelve monthly festivals to be conducted in a year, when the sun is in the different signs of the zodiac. This also prescribes the processional vehicles to be used and offerings to be made on these occasions.

On the second gopura of the Gramardhanatheswara temple at Elvanasur, south Arcot district, is a record dated the seventeenth year of Vikrama Chola (AD 1135) making provision for the recital of the hymn 'Tiruchchalal' of Saint Manikkavachakar every Sunday. According to the report of the Madras Epigraphical Department for the year 1906-1907 (page 68) this saint was a contemporary of Pandya king Varaguna who ascended the throne in AD 862. Elvanasur in the taluk of Tirukkoyilur was known in ancient days by the name Solakeralachadurvedimangalam or Irayanariyur.

On the south wall of the central shrine in the Karkotakeswara temple at Kamarasavalli in the district of Trichinopoly is an inscription dated in the thirteenth year of the reign of Chola king Raja Raja I relating to the recitation of Talavakarasamaveda during the night preceding the day of the Tiruvadirai festival in the month of Margali, before the god started for the second bath. Each reciter was fed and also paid one to four *kalanjus* of gold. Details of the method of recitation are also given.

That temple charities were not exclusively meant for the ceremonials alone but also for scientific (śāstric) and religious (Vedic) education is further proved by an inscription in the Varadaraja Perumal temple at Tribhuvani near Pondicherry of the French dominions. This place was called Tribhuvanamahadevichadurvedimangalam. It is dated in the thirtieth year of Rajadhiraja 1 (2nd March, 1048) for reciting the Tiruvoymozhi and for teaching the Rig Veda, Yajur Veda, Chandogosama, Talavakarasama, Apurva, Vajasaneya, Bodhayaiya Satyashtaadha Sutra and for the expounding of the Vedanta, Vyakarana, Rupavatara, Bharata, Ramayana, Manu-Śastra and Vaikanasa Śastra.

On the west and south walls of the mandapa in front of the central shrine in the Viswanadaswami Temple at Tenkasi (in Tinnevelly district) is record of the Pandya king Vira Pandyadeva, dated Saka 1384 (AD 1462), registering the gift of houses and shares in the village of Virapandyachadurvedimangalam to 24 Brahmans for reciting the Vedas, reading the Panchanga (the Indian calender) and Puraṇas.

On the south wall of the first prakara of the Natarajaswami shrine in the Vataranyesvara temple at Tiruvalangadu there is an inscription dated in the 1322nd year of Kulottunga III (Tribunavanaveradeva) AD 1178 to 1215, which registers an endowment by Aranilaivisagan Trailokyamallan Vatsarajan of Arumbakkam who rendered the Bharata into elegant Tamil and found out the path of Śiva (the Saiva creed). This translation of the epic Mahabharata does not survive to this day. Three Tamil versions of the epic are known viz., the earliest by Perundevanar called Bharatavenba. Perundevanar might have lived in the 9th century AD Villiputturalvar has also translated ten *parvas* of the epic. His date has been fixed to the 15th century. The latest standard Tamil translation is by Nallapillai, who is believed to have lived in the 18th century.

INSCRIPTIONS IN TEMPLES

The Madras Presidency is specially rich in inscriptions on stone and copper. There is scarcely a village of any size without at least one temple. Indeed, as according to the Sastras no village is complete without at least one temple. Almost every temple has one inscription, and the largest temples, such as those in the south have hundreds. The inscriptions recorded in temples supply us only with dates for the several charities made, and occasionally also for the construction of certain mandapas or halls, tanks, etc., subsequently put up. Some of them date from the earliest historical times, such as those at Conjeevaram, Srirangam, Tanjore, etc., south of the city of Madras. The greatest donors to religion who have left their mark in temples everywhere through the length and breadth of the Madras Presidency, and indeed much further beyond it, such as in Mysore and elsewhere, are the Cholas, the

Pallavas, and the Vijianagar kings. Almost every temple, of any size whatever, has one or more records of their acts of beneficence.

In the opinion of Doctor Burgess, "Inscriptions are of course most useful, but they have to be used with caution, for we do not always know whether they have not been added at some period of restoration or addition, long after the original work was finished, or whether they belong to some previous structure demolished to make room for that which may be under consideration."

These inscriptions are sometimes cut on the walls around the sanctum of the god on pillars of the temple, and in other instances are on detached stones set up in some prominent place in the courtyards. It can, therefore, be easily imagined what a wealth of historical information lies scattered throughout the whole of this part of the country. Early in the eighties, when the archaeological survey was formed and an epigraphical branch attached to it they took up the work of collecting these records. Since then, many thousands of inscriptions of all ages have been collected and stored in the Office of the Assistant Archaeological Superintendent for Epigraphy. Some of these records have been published in *South Indian Inscriptions*, in the *Epigraphica Indica* and elsewhere, but the great bulk have so far not been published.

The inscriptions recorded in temples generally supply us only with dates for the several charities made; and occasionally also for the construction of certain mandapas and tanks subsequently put up. They do not give us any clue as to the origin of the main shrines or of the connected structures. This is always the case with the majority of south Indian temples and the reason for omitting such an important piece of information regarding the foundation of the temple, is apparent. Every temple must recognize this as a tenet of

Hinduism that the gods worshipped inside are ancient (Puraṇa Dampati). There is also a common saying that the origin of gods, saints and rivers ought not to be investigated; for the enquiry may often lead to undesirable revelations; the temple may happen to be a tomb originally; a saint may be but a miserable man of low birth, and a sacred river may be only a dirty little pool at its source. Consequently, for securing great antiquity to the god, so old as to be even worshipped by the sun, the moon and the ancient sages, people deliberately avoid giving the date of consecration of the temples.

Chapter 1

MADRAS

TRIPLICANE

Among the shrines in Madras, the most important is the temple of Parthasarathi,[1] named after the charioteer of Arjuna, the great Pandava chief. The Sri Parthasarathi temple, in Triplicane (Tiruvallikkeni), contains some particularly fine carvings and images, among the most notable of which, in the inner sanctum of the temple, are the representations of Sri Parthasarathi with his consort Rukmini, Balarama[2] (the elder brother of Sri Krishna), Satyalki (the younger brother of Sri Krishna), Sankarshana[3] and Aniruddha.[4] The figure of Parthasarathi, scarred with the arrow-wounds he received in the epic battle of the Mahabharata, is moulded of some dark metal, evidently not the alloy of five metals (panchaloha) used for such sacred images. Within the temple, there are also shrines dedicated to Sri Ranganatha, Sri Rama (the hero-god of the Ramayana), and Varadaraja. No fish can live, it is believed, in the Kairaveni tank to the east of the temple, and this phenomenon is popularly attributed to the curse of a sage of olden time, whose *tapas*[5] (prayers and penances) on the banks of the tank were interrupted by the fish! The ancient name of the place, according to Puranas, was Brindavanam.[6]

Tirumangai-Alvar has spoken of this temple having been founded by a king of Tondaiyar i.e. Pallava.

From inscriptions found in the temple, it would appear that it was restored by a pious citizen somewhere about AD 1564 , when new shrines were set up and part of the temple was rebuilt. An early inscription of the eighth century has also been discovered in this temple. In later years endowments of villages and gardens have enriched the temple greatly.

RUKMINI KALYANAM

The wedding of Rukmini (Rukmini Kalyanam) forms an interesting episode and the following translation of the account narrated by sage Suka, the expounder of the Puranas to king Parikshit, appears in the *Indian Antiquary* (December, 1907, Volume XXXVI):

"O Parikshit, there lived a king, Bhishmaka by name, ruler of Kundina in Vidarbha. He had five sons, of which the eldest, Rukmi by name, was a spotless person. The last and most beloved of the lot was a daughter Rukmini by name.

"The house of Bhishmaka glowed with the growth of his daughter Rukmini, as the western horizon glows with the rising of the moon. She, growing day by day, indulged herself in performing make-believe marriages; in serving sweet-flavoured food to other girls of her own age, which pleased them very much; in the growth of creepers and flowers in the adjacent park; in rocking herself in golden cradles, in houses set with diamonds and other precious stones; in playing ball very elegantly with other girls of her own age; in teaching parrots; in teaching methods of walking to peahens and slowness of pace to fresh-bloomed swans. The growth of Rukmini's body varied with the growth of Krishna's love towards her; her lotus-face varied with the lotus of Krishna's mind; her breasts with Cupid's finely-pointed darts varied with Krishna's growth; her loins waved with the waving of Krishna's patience; her braided tresses increased with the increase of Krishna's love-chord towards her, so that her growth might keep pace with Krishna's pleasures. Thus Rukmini, the sister of Rukmi, Rukmaratha, Rukmabahu, Rukmakesa and Rukmanetra, being in her teens, heard of the accomplishments of Sri-Krishna from the hosts who came to her house, and came to a resolution in her mind that Krishna would be the best man to be her husband.

"After hearing of the beauty, intelligence, character, and general accomplishments of Rukmini, Sri-Krishna, thought that she would be the fittest woman for him to take as his wife. While all his relatives were holding consultations with the wise about giving Rukmini in marriage to Krishna, the foolish Rukmi came to a different conclusion and wanted to be married to Sisupala. Rukmini, after having ascertained her brother's intentions, called in a Brahman confidentially and told him that her hot-headed brother had come to a firm resolve to give her in marriage to Sisupala somehow, and that she wanted him to go to Dvaraka and inform Krishna of the affair. 'Best of Brahmans, as my father too cannot set aside the firm resolve of my brother, kindly go on this mission to Dvaraka, inform Krishna of the whole affair, and fetch him hither as soon as possible to baffle the endeavours of my brother.'

"The Brahman, after hearing these and some other secret words, proceeded to Dvaraka, informed Krishna of his coming through the guards stationed outside. He received Krishna's orders, entered the palace, and blessed him to become a bridegroom. Whereupon Krishna, ever bent upon observing Vedic ritual, vacated his seat smiling, requested the Brahman to sit on the same seat and worshipped him, as he is himself worshipped by the angels. He fed him sumptuously, approached him most heartily and slowly, and with his hands, which wield sway over the whole world, pressed his legs and addressed him thus:

"'Best of Brahmans, I see you are always contented. This dharma is acceptable to the elders. A Brahman, however wealthy he may be, should be contented and happy and should not be swayed by a feeling of pride. Whoever does not quit this swatharma, would have all his desires fulfilled. Whoever is not content with the little that he gets would always be crushed, even if he gets Indra's riches. Whoever is content with the little that he gets would be quite happy, even though he be a pauper. Therefore, I would prostrate before those who show signs of friendship to all beings, who are content with the little they get, who are patient, good and not proud. O intelligent and best of Brahmans, I like that king, under whose sway all the people live comfortably, in whose kingdom you are, and by whom you are protected. Kindly let me know what induced you to enter this impenetrable island home at this unusual hour. I promise to fulfil your desire.'

"Having heard these words from Krishna, the divine being in human form, the Brahman replied 'Lord, there lives a king in Vidarbha, Bhishmaka by name. He has a daughter whose name is Rukmini. She, being intent on serving you, requests you to marry her, and has sent some news to you through me which, if you be pleased to hear, I am ready to narrate in her own words: O killer of Kamsa, punisher of the vicious, plunderer of the wealth of beauty, robber of women's hearts. Krishna, by hearing whose name all the *tapas* (*adhyatmika, adhidaivik, adhibhautika*) would vanish; by seeing whose frame, the eye would derive the pleasure of seeing everything in the Universe; by always serving whom a man can attain eminence; by repeating whose name a man is freed from the trammels of *samsara* — to such a man is my mind united. You are the best witness to all this. Although the members of my sex feel generally shy of expressing such secrets, I, quitting aside all sense of shame, speak my heart before you, as the feeling of *bhakti* preponderates in me, for which I beg to be excused. Krishna, is there anyone among women who does not love you? Even Lakshmi, the best among women, has loved you. Say, has this love emanated from me alone?

"'Purushottama, you who have Lakshmi in your breast, the proud Sisupala, king of Chedi, intends to carry me off soon — me who always thinks of you and you alone, as the fox desires the food best adapted for the lion. The meanest of mortals knows not your wondrous valour. If, in my previous births, I had worshipped angels, Brahmans, gurus, pandits, and others, and if I had given gifts to the entire satisfaction of Vishnu, Krishna would now carry me off and marry me after slaying Sisupala and other such meanest of kings. Krishna, you who have the lotus in your navel which is the birthplace of Brahma, you who are the best of *purushas*, you have no reason to find a pretext. Tomorrow, if you come with your armies and slay Jarasandha, Sisupala, and others in battle and carry me off with your valour, I am ready to accompany you and marry you in the Rakshasa* form. Krishna, if you should think as to how best you can take me off from the palace, — for you will be labouring under the impression that in carrying me off you will be obliged to shed, unnecessarily, the blood of so many relatives, friends, and servants, who would offer resistance to you — I have devised a measure, which I shall carefully suggest to you if you be pleased to hear. My people are accustomed to send the bride, previous to the marriage proper, to worship the tutelary deities outside the town. I shall be sent on this occasion outside the town to worship Parvati and that will be most opportune moment when you can come and carry me off. Krishna, my protector, if you think I am not fit to receive your mercy, and if in consequence you do not choose to take me as your wife, I shall assume at the least one hundred rebirths, perform *vratas* in the meanwhile, always think about you and attain your mercy and then marry you. You may rest assured that this is truth and nothing but the truth. Do not, therefore, give a deaf ear to my entreaties but carry me off soon. My protector, the ears that do not hear your soothing word; the eyes that cannot see the one beloved by the world at large; the tongue that cannot drink the nectar which emanates from your lips; the nose that cannot smell the fragrance of your beautiful bunch of flowers; the life that cannot serve you — all these are next to useless, even though they live. They should be considered as dead rather than living. All the *jnanarthis* (seekers of wisdom), if they should live at all, should serve you and you alone and any other form of servitude is next to useless.'

"Having fulfilled his mission, the Brahman told Krishna of her exceeding beauty, and wanted him to do the best he could under the circumstances convincing him that she was best object for his love. 'O Krishna, Rukmini's feet are the best resorts for all tendrils; her thighs laugh at golden plantain trees; her hands are beautiful with a coating of redness; her neck is exceedingly beautiful, being turned a little and as white as a conch. There is a suspicion whether she possesses a waist or not. Her breasts give pleasure to the eye; her forehead laughs at the semi-circular moon; her braided tresses laugh at black wild bees; her sight resembles the finely-pointed darts of Cupid; her eye-brows resemble the branches of Cupid's arrows; her words invigorate the mind; her face resembles the moon. Krishna, you are the best person fitted for her and she for you. I tell you, on my guru, you should be married. Why do you make unnecessary delay? Take all people by whom you wish to be accompanied and come with me to fetch Rukmini. Slay your enemies, do good to the world and obtain fame.'

"When Krishna heard all that the Brahman had said, he took hold of the Brahman's hand, and laughing, said 'O Brahman, my thoughts are fully centred on Rukmini and that is why my nights are always sleepless. I know already of Rukmini's hindrance to this marriage. Therefore I shall bring Rukmini after slaying the armies of my enemies. I shall immediately go to Vidarbha, enter Bhishmaka's territory in a fitting manner and slay all my enemies who come across my path and tear open their bodies.'

"Krishna ascertained from the Brahman the auspicious moment of Rukmini's marriage and ascended with him to the chariot drawn by four of his best horses harnessed to it by the charioteer under his own instructions, and reached Vidarbha in a single night. There Bhishmaka, king of Kundina, who could not set his son aside, had resolved to marry his daughter to Sisupala and had made the necessary preparations for its performance. The public streets, lanes, and thoroughfares of the city were swept and kept scrupulously clean, excellent sandalwood water was sprinkled on them and they were adorned with beautiful flowers of various kind. All houses were repaired and kept in good order, incense and camphor were burnt. The men and women were in their best and appropriate attires and were adorned with beautiful flowers, the best jewels and excellent scents. Drums and instruments of all sorts were played. Thus the whole city presented a gay and lively appearance. Maharaja Bhishmaka first propitiated the *pitris*, fed the Brahmans, purified the city, had Rukmini bathed, adorned her with the best jewels and in the best attire possible, performed all observances in accordance with the strict injunctions of the Vedas, engaged Brahmans to chant the various mantras, and the *purohit* to perform *navagraha homa* and to give away gifts of sesame seeds, cows, silver, gold, and cloths.

"At this juncture the proud Sisupala came to the city with the object of marrying Rukmini, accompanied by various armies under his command, his innumerable relatives, friends, and others. Jarasandha, Dantavaktra, Salva, Biduratha, Paundraka, Vasudeva and other kings came to the firm resolution that they would defend Sisupala against Krishna and Balarama and all their innumerable armies, relatives, and friends and drive them off the field, and overcome any objection to making Sisupala marry Rukmini. Many other Rajas came to witness the marriage. Of these Sisupala was lodged by Bhishmaka in the best lodgings possible, and when Balarama heard this, he went to the place with a host, all the while thinking that Krishna went there single-handed. He thought that many kings were there to help Sisupala, and that when the girl was to be brought, a fight would necessarily ensue. At such a juncture Krishna would need assistance.

"When the host of Rajas were approaching the town, Rukmini entertained grave doubts about Krishna's coming there: Tomorrow is the auspicious moment and my mind is wavering as to why Krishna has not come as yet. I wonder if Krishna has given a deaf ear to my news. Why is it that the Brahman resembling the fire has not come here as yet? Would my attempts to marry Krishna be fulfilled? Has Brahma thought otherwise? Such were the thoughts passing in the mind of Rukmini. She wondered if the enlightened and best of Brahmans did repair to Krishna or not; whether he was fatigued on the way or found fault with her for having given unnecessary trouble to the Brahman? Would the Almighty help in her undertakings? Whether her tutelary deity, Parvati, protect her? Would fortune favour her? She said to herself 'The Brahman may not have gone to Dvaraka and therefore Krishna has not been able to come here. There is no confidential person whom I could hereafter send to fetch Krishna. There is not an atom

of justice to be got from my brother Rukmi. He intends to give
me to Sisupala, the staunchest enemy of my lover, Krishna.
Even my Parvati has lost her pity for me.'

"She would not communicate her thoughts even to her
mother. Her face had turned very pale. She would not even
smile, nor would she try to remove the wild bees which used
to sit on her face, thinking it to be a lotus. She would not unwind
the twisted pearl necklaces on her breast. She would ever be
bent on eagerly looking at Krishna's arrival. She would weep,
thinking she was not to be blessed by marrying him; she would
not drink water. She would not teach her pet parrot a song. She
would not play on the lyre and would shun society as much
as possible. As sorrow was great at her heart on account of
Krishna not having come to marry her as yet, Rukmini — the
lion-waisted, lotus-scented, mirror-faced, flower-bodied, lotus-
eyed, swan-gaited, creeper-framed, the jewel of jewels, the
flower of all women, with hands formed after the lotus —
would not daub her body with musk, would not bathe, would
not see a looking-glass, nor wear flowers, nor resort to parks,
nor tame swans, grow creepers, wear jewels, nor wear marks
on the forehead, or swim in water. Being unable to bear the
finely pointed darts of Cupid, she would shiver at sweet soft
winds, would be terrified at the noise of the wild bees and be
struck with horror at the song of nightingale. She would be
annoyed by parrots and run away from them and would avoid
moonlight shade of the sweet mango-tree. While thus eagerly
waiting for the coming of Hari and looking carelessly at all
other business, and being scorched by Cupid's arrows, she felt
her left eye and left shoulder tremble, which foreboded
something good. Then the Brahman, being sent by Sri Krishna,
arrived, when Rukmini went and stood before him with a
glowing face. The Brahman said: 'O Rukmini, Sri Krishna was
exceedingly pleased at your good character and has given me

immense wealth. He has also himself arrived here. He is at
present outside the town. He would marry you in the Rakshasa
form, even though the whole host of angels and Rakshasas
come and oppose him. You have this day reaped the fruit of
your labours.' Rukmini replied 'You have protected me by
carrying my news to Krishna and bringing him here. I live by
your mercy. There is in the whole world none other like you.
I cannot repay the good you have done to me except by a
prostration before you.' Thus saying, she prostrated before him
and dismissed him.

"Afterwards, Bhishmaka, having heard of the arrival of
Balarama and Krishna at his daughter's marriage, went to meet
them with beating of drums. He received them kindly,
presented them with clothes and ornaments, showed resting
places for their armies, friends, and relatives, showed
hospitality to all the other kings and supplied them with all
necessities. Then the townsfolk, having heard of the arrival of
Sri Krishna at Rukmini's marriage, came and saw him and
soliloquised thus: 'This Krishna must be the fittest man for that
Rukmini and she for him. Brahma can be called intelligent only
when such a pair are brought into unison with each other. If
we have done good deeds in our previous births, may Krishna
become the husband of Rukmini after slaying all those who offer
resistance to him in battle.'

"While the fully armed soldiers were accompanying the
dancing women and were advancing with offerings for god, the
Brahman women wearing flowers, sandalwood, cloths, and
jewels, proceeded with singing. There was a tremendous noise
caused by the beating of drums, the playing of different kinds
of music. Rukmini, with the utmost feminine modesty, with
ringlets falling on her forehead, proceeded from the palace to
worship Parvati. While a host of people of various sorts were
accompanying her, she was all the while thinking of Krishna

in her mind, and went to the temple of Gauri, washed her hands and feet, sipped water thrice, and with a pure heart approached and stood before her. Then the Brahman women bathed Gauri and Siva, applied sandalwood, worshipped them with flowers, offered various offerings which were brought for the purpose, and made Rukmini prostrate. Then Rukmini said: 'I fully believe in my mind the everlasting, time-honoured couple of Parvati and Mahesvara. I pray you to bless me. You are the chief and oldest of all mothers. You are the ocean of mercy. Whoever conscientiously and firmly believes in you will not suffer. Kindly, therefore, have mercy on me and bless me that I may have Krishna as my husband.'

"Rukmini then worshipped the Brahman couples with *paan supari*, salted cakes, fruits, and sugarcane, upon which they were exceedingly delighted and blessed Rukmini when she again prostrated before Parvati, and left the temple. As a spark of lightning in the wintry sky, as the animal in the orbit of the moon, as the mohini which appears on the scene when the curtain is drawn by Brahma, as Lakshmi who came out from the milky sky when it was churned by the angels and rakshasas with Mount Manthara as the churning staff and Vasuki as the chord, glittering with the rays of the finest ornaments, Rukmini came out of Gauri's temple. She walked with the pace of the fattened swans at Manasarovara. Her waist appeared to be troubled by the weight of her heavy breasts which resembled a pair of golden pots. Her diamond-ringed hands twisted round the hands of a maiden, with chins sparling with the lustre of diamond earrings, with ringlets covering the round forehead like fattened wild bees which encircle sweet-scented lotuses. Her smile shed a lustre of moonlight at an unseasonable moment, her lips red as ruby shed a ruddy lustre to the rows of teeth white as jasmine, with the upper garment resembling the flag of Cupid studded, with precious stones glittering in the gold belt as a rainbow out of season. Her sight resembled the glitter of arrows drawn by Cupid from his sheath which broke open the hearts of valorous kings. As she walked with measured steps waiting for the arrival of Krishna, she attracted the hearts of all brave Rajas.

"Rukmini passed by the post of kings who were confused when the smiling look, indicative of feminine bashfulness, fell upon them. They lost their valour, nobility, and honour, they lost their senses and let slip the weapons from their hands. They were not able to mount their elephants, horses, or chariots. They were so bewildered that they leaned towards the ground. Rukmini removed the ringlets from the forehead with the nails of her left hand, and, looking askance at this host, saw Sri Krishna whose face resembled the rays of the full moon. His waist resembled that of the lion, his eyes were broad as the lotus and his body shone like a newly-formed cloud. His shoulders resembled the trunk of Airavata bedecked with cloths of gold and best ornaments, and his neck turned like a conch. Rukmini saw this world-enchanter and was delighted with the beauty, age, character, nobility, valour, and glitter of Krishna, and being enraptured with love she intended to climb his chariot. When he saw her he approached and lifted her up and placed her in his chariot, not caring a straw for the host of kings who were viewing, as the lion carries off the piece of flesh lying amidst foxes. He then blew his conch and proceeded towards Dvaraka, while Balarama and others were following him with their armies. Jarasandha and his hosts were not able to brook this and questioned each other as to why they were seeing all this, so much perplexed. They thought: A crew of shepherds are robbing us of our honour and are carrying off the girl as the low animals rob the honour of the lion. When else can we show our valour if we cannot show it on this occasion? Are our bows and arrows fit to be thrown away into fire if we cannot use them now? Would the people of the world fail to laugh if we let slip this opportunity and let go of the girl? Thus reasoning with one another, they became exceedingly angry, put on mail armours, bore arrows and bows, joined the charioteers, infantry, and cavalry and went in pursuit of the Jadava forces, telling them to stop. They showered a volley of arrows on them which were returned by a similar shower from the Jadava leaders.

"While the troops of the enemy showered a volley of arrows and encircled Krishna and his armies, Rukmini, with a look indicative of extreme terror and shame, saw Krishna's face who siad 'My dear girl,' you may in a moment witness Yadava warriors opposing the enemy and they will be very much troubled and would either run away or die.' Thus did Krishna console Rukmini when Balarama and others of Yadava warriors showered a host of arrows, which resembled the heavy thunder and clouds that spread over the whole sky at the time of the deluge. The enemy's camp presented a ghastly sight. There were slaughtered horses, foot-soldiers, Mahawats, charioteers and horsemen. All that could be seen were hands, legs, broken skulls, extensive hair, severed feet, knees, calves of the legs, powdered teeth, thrown-off ornaments and other similar ones worn by the brave at the battle-field, broken pieces of instruments of war, umbrellas, tattered armour, dust raised to the skies caused by the trampling of horses, motionless chariots. One could hear the low cries of horses and elephants, the sounds of battle-drums, tattered host of kings, the noises of devils, foxes and other animals eating the flesh and drinking the blood of corpses. It seemed as if she-devils were feasting on skulls and flesh of carcases.

"Jarasandha and others, being unable to bear his attack turned their backs and fled, assembled at a certain spot, wept and soothed Sisupala who stood before them pale-faced as

one who had lost his wife, asking whether he was alive.
Jarasandha and others said to Sisupala: 'Man can live
anywhere, provided there is life in the body. If a man lives,
a wife will somehow come of her own accord. You are now
alive and therefore a wife can be secured from somewhere.
Do not, therefore, weep over this affair very often.'
Jarasandha again said to Sisupala, 'Sisupala, hear me. Man
is not the agent of any deed. He would do a deed being held
tight by the Almighty, as the puppet plays being led by the
leading strings of the puppeteer in a pantomine. I invaded
Mathura seventeen times, when my whole army was reduced
to nothing by Krishna and I was captured by Balarama,
whereupon Krishna, out of mercy, released me. I again
invaded Mathura the eighteenth time with twenty-three
akshauhinis, when I drove out my enemies, Krishna and
Balarama, and gained a complete victory. I neither felt sorrow
over a defeat, nor joy over a victory. If we should enquire
carefully into this day's proceedings we cannot vanquish
Krishna, even though we join Siva and wage a war against
him. Nor is this all. The whole world is pervaded by
omnipotent time. As this was a good day for the Jadavas, they
overcame us with the help of Krishna — us, whose valour is
recognized in the three worlds. We, too, can gain victories
over our enemy if fortune be in our favour. Weep not,
therefore, for this trifle.'

"Jarasandha and others thus consoled Sisupala and went
each his own way to his own country. Sisupala, too, went
home with his armies. Then Rukmi, the brother of Rukmini,
not agreeing to the carrying off of his sister by Krishna and
not reconciling himself with the state of affairs, pursued him
with an *akshouhini* and spoke thus to his charioteer: 'This
shepherd boy has slighted me and carried off my sister
Rukmini, as if he were a daring valiant soldier. He knows not

my prowess and descent. I must chase him swiftly, drive on the chariot so as to overtake him. I will, with my glittering arrows, put him down and sow my valour.' Having thus addressed the charioteers, oblivious of Krishna's prowess, drove near him and said: 'Stop a little, you butter-stealing shepherd boy. You shall very soon see your fate.' Having thus slighted him, he aimed three sharp arrows at him and spoke to him in a manner which irritated Krishna very much: 'Thou shepherd, you are not our compeer to carry off our child. What dharma do you follow? What caste do you belong to? Of what family are you? Where were you born? Where brought up? What is your calling? What is your *gotra*? Who knows you? You have no sense of shame or honour. Wherever you come you assume a disguise and do not appear at all in your true colours before your enemies. Moreover, you are no king. You are not tied to the world. Therefore leave our child and depart, otherwise I will put down your pride in battle by arrows which appear as flames of fire at the time of *pralaya*.'

"Sri Krishna laughed at Rukmi, tore asunder his bow with one arrow, with six others his body, with eight others his chariot horses, with two more his charioteer, with three pointed ones his banner, he broke another of his bows and arrows and reduced to pieces all his other weapons. Angered by this act Rukmi descended from his chariot, held a knife in his hand and came upon Krishna once more, when the latter powdered his knife and armour. Then Krishna grew exceedingly angry at the conduct of Rukmi and drew his knife from his sheath and was about to cut off his head when Rukmini interfered and fell upon her knees before Krishna and said: 'Enlightened and honourable being, seat of mercy, angelic god, my brother, not knowing your omniscience and omnipresence, has committed a grievous fault for which I intercede on his behalf and request you to excuse him. My preserver, I am not come here to say that my brother has committed no fault. Whatever may be the heinous nature of the crime he has committed, if you should kill him, my parents would weep over the death of their son and pine away instead of feeling glad at their being able to secure Vishnu as their son-in-law. Therefore you should excuse him.' Thus, with a shivering tone which showed extreme terror, with a convulsed frame and a great fallen countenance which dishevelled her, Rukmini prayed to Krishna. Krishna desisted from murdering Rukmi and went back intent on punishing him differently. He then tied him to his chariot and shaved him in the most awkward way possible. Meanwhile, the Yadava leaders drove the enemy's troops off the field and came near Krishna. Then Balarama, seeing the almost lifeless frame of Rukmi and being very much moved, untied the strings, liberated him, approached Krishna, and said: 'O Krishna, it is not proper of you to shave the head and face of a relative like Rukmi. If a relative should come to battle knowingly or unknowingly, instead of telling him t o away, committing such a deed is more shamefull then severing the head off the body. O Krishna, you make no difference between a friend and a foe. You neither show favour to one, nor disfavour to another. You treat all men equally. That you should now have thought otherwise and offered such a treatment to a relative is exceedingly bad in you.'

"He then turned round to Rukmini and said: 'Blame not our Krishna for the deed he has committed. We should not think that one ought to protect another for the good he has done and punish him for the evil committed. This depends entirely on the karma of our previous existence. Karmic law pervades through the whole universe. Therefore your brother has but suffered for the deed he has committed in a previous existence. We should not kill a relative, though he deserves death. To him a sense of shame should be more than death. When Brahma created the four castes and defined the *Varnasrama dharma* of each, he said that it was but proper to kill any person in battle, be he a brother, father, or son. That is why kings in their thirst for dominion slay any person in battle, irrespective of the relationship they bear. Those kings who want to earn a reputation of being great, being desirous of dominion, wealth, sustenance, women or honour, and not for a moment thinking of the troubles they would endure in the other world, always drag other people to quarrel for one reason or another. O Rukmini, hear me. To the ignorant one that makes a difference between God and man, being surrounded by the *maya* (the magical power) of Vishnu; to those that draw a distinction between *sthula*, *sukshma*, and *karana sariras*, and between *jnanendrias* and *karmendrias*, there exists a difference between friend, foe, and acquaintance. As the sun, moon and stars appear in mirrors, waters, and precious stones, as the horizon presents various shapes in the waters of pots, ponds, lakes, wells, and rivers, so the all-pervading Universal Soul (God) appears differently to different living beings. This sthula sarira, capable of undergoing life and death, assumes the form of the five elements and makes the *jiva* wander in this miserable samsara and undergo life and death in utter ignorance. As the eye and the objects of vision appear bright when sun is shining, the *jnanendrias* and *karmendrias* follow their own calling when the soul is shining. As there is no relation between the sun and the objects of vision, so no relation exists between the soul and the body. As waxing and waning disturb only the fifteen phases of the moon and not the nectar-phased moon itself, so birth and death disturb the body and not the soul. As the sleeping person enjoys the appearances presented to him in a dream, so the person who has no knowledge of the soul thinks the transient

pleasures of this world to be immortal. Therefore, think not
that Krishna has put your brother to shame and that he has
suffered from it. Put off, therefore, all sorrow from your heart.
O Rukmini, put off all your sorrow which arises out of
ignorance by your knowledge of self. It is not proper for you,
who knows the self, to weep like ignorant.'

"When Rukmini was thus taught by Balarama, she learnt
fully of the soul and stopped weeping. Rukmi, who was put
to shame by Krishna, suffered like one under the pangs of
death, sobbed over his disfigured frame and resolved that he
would not enter Kundinanagara without defeating Krishna.
He therefore stayed outside the town. Thus did Krishna take
Rukmini to his abode after slaying all his enemies.
Preparations for marriage were being made throughout the
town. There were dances, songs, and the beating of drums.
Men and women put on their best attire. Public thoroughfares
became damp from the perspirations of the elephants of the
kings who came to witness the marriage. Plantain and areca
trees were tied at the front of every house. Camphor and
incense were burnt. The walls, terraces, doorways, doors and
pillars of every house were beautifully adorned. Festoons and
cloths, flowers and precious stones were tied everywhere.

"On this occasion Sri Krishna married Rukmini
(Lakshmi), a woman best adapted to his tastes, possessing an
extreme sense of honour, capable of making others
exceedingly rich, honored by her relatives, and in turn
honouring them, of good character, capable of removing
immense poverty, and wearing the best jewels and putting on
the best cloths. By such a marriage Krishna obtained an
everlasting fame. Then the townsfolk, wishing for their
welfare, came to see the newly-married pair and gave them
valuable offerings. The kings of the various kingdoms of the
world were delighted and wondered at hearing of the marriage

of Rukmini and Krishna. O Parikshit, the people of the city were overjoyed by the happy union of Rukmini and Krishna."

INSCRIPTIONS[7]

It is an ancient temple. Its Chola and Pandya inscriptions were later on misplaced and scattered in the course of renovation in Vijayanagara times. There are fragments of tombstones in Roman characters near the garbhagriha, the presence of which is unaccountable.

234 of 1903 (Tamil) — On a stone built into the floor at the entrance into the garbhagriha of the Parthasarathisvamin temple. A record in the twelfth year of the Pallava king Dantivarma Maharaja shows that the temple priests mortgaged one of the fields of the temple, that the offerings to the god in consequence fell short and that a certain Pugalttunai Visaiyaraiyan redeemed the field and arranged for the usual quantity of rice offerings everyday. (The inscription corroborates the testimony of Tirumangai Alvar's Periatirumozhi which attributed the foundation of the temple to the Tonda king (Pallava). See Ep. Ind. Vol. VIII, pp. 290-6.

235 of 1903 (Tamil) — On the north wall of the central shrine in the same temple. A record of the Vijayanagara king Vira Venkatapatideva Maharaja (Venkata I) in S. 1527, Vikarin. Refers to the king as seated on a jewelled throne at the city of Perungondai.

236 of 1903 (Tamil) — On the south base of the same shrine. A record of the Vijayanagara king Vira Venkatapatideva Maharaya I (1586-1616), in S.1525, Sobhakrit. Refers to the king as seated on a jewelled throne at the city of Perungondai and to the consecration of an image of Tirumalisai Alvar and a gift of twenty *varahas* to this shrine.

237 of 1903 (Telugu) — On the same base. A record of the Vijayanagara king Rangarayadeva Maharaya I (1578-86), in S.1507, Tarana. Records the gift of the villages of Sembiyam and Nidambaram (Nadumbarai), besides a garden by Tirumala Nayaningaru the general of Ramaraja Venkatapatiraju (Venkata I). The revenue from these two villages was 180 rekha chakra gedyena and from the garden 20 chakra gedyena.

238 of 1903 (Tamil) — On the north base of the shrine. A mutilated record in the forty-ninth year of the Pandya king Maravarman or Tribhuvanachakravartin Kulasekharadeva. Records a sale of land and mentions god Telliyasinga Nayanar.

239 of 1903 (Tamil) — On the same base. A record of the Vijayanagara king Mahamandaleswara Virapratapa Sadasivadeva Maharaya (in S.1486, Raktakshin). Records that a private individual built certain portions of the temple (e.g., shrines of Pallikonda Perumal, Krishna, Vedavalli Nachchiyar) the Tiruvaymozhi mandapa, the kitchen and enclosure wall and set up a number of images and granted three villages, Pudupakkam, Vepery and Vesharuppadi (Vyasarpadi).

240 of 1903 (Tamil) — On the east and north bases of the mandapa in front of the same shrine. A record of the Vijayanagara king Virapratapa Vira Venkatapatideva. Maharaya I (1586-1616 in Krodhin i.e., S.1527).

241 of 1903 (Tamil) — On a stone built into the floor of the same mandapa. A fragmentary record of the Chola king Tribhuvanaviradeva (Kulottunga III), the date of which is lost, mentions Tiruvamiyur (i.e., Tiruvamur near Mylapore) in Kotturnadu.

242 of 1903 (Tamil) — On another stone built into the same place. A fragmentary record in the twenty-third year of the Chola king Rajarajadeva. Four other similar fragments are

built into this mandapa and a number of others in other portions of the temple.

243 of 1903 (Tamil) — The south and east walls of the Alagiyasinga Perumal shrine in the same temple. Records certain arrangements referring to temple servants made while Etirajanayakar was the manager.

MYLAPORE

Hardly less important than that of Triplicane is the great temple of Mylapore (Mayilappur) situated about a mile to the south of Triplicane. The suburb of Mylapore (the town of the Peacock) takes its name from a Puranic legend regarding the goddess Parvati, who, during her incarnation as a peacock (mayura)[8], worshipped the linga[9] there, to obtain deliverance from that incarnation. The legend is commemorated in a beautiful sculpture in the north prakara (courtyard) of the temple. In Vaishnavite, Saivite and Jaina religious manuscripts, the place is called Tirumayilai (*tiru* in Tamil means beautiful) while the early Portuguese settlers called it San Thome de Meliapore (still the name of the Roman Catholic Diocese) in commemoration of the traditional martyrdom of St. Thomas, whose sarcophagus the local cathedral enshrines.

A number of local legends are commemorated in the sculptured images within the temple. Thus we find in a shrine in the west courtyard a sculptured representation of a miracle performed by the Saiva saint Sambandar,[10] who restored out of her bones a cremated Chetti girl to life, by chanting a lyric in praise of the Lord of the temple !

There is also a shrine to Vayelar Nayanar, one of the 63 Saiva saints, on the south courtyard of the temple. Besides these sculptures, there are also bronze statues of the 63 Saiva devotees in this temple.

TIRUVALLUVAR SHRINE

Here too, at a distance of a few yards on the north side of Kapaliswarar temple is the shrine of another saint Tiruvalluvar, the author of *Kural*, who spent his last days in Mylapore; and besides the sculptural representation, there is also preserved a metal image of the saint. The Tamil poetess Auvaiyar's memory is commemorated by the aspect of the elephant-god Vinayaka of the central shrine, who is depicted with his trunk lifted up, as when he raised the poetess to heaven.

PEYALWAR

The Vaishnava saint Peyalwar[11] is also connected by legend with a sacred well in Mylapore.

TIRUVORRIYUR

This famous centre of pilgrimage, the name of which is derived from Adipura, i.e., 'mortgage village' which is the Sanskrit equivalent of Orriyur, about five miles to the north of Madras, does not belong to Madras proper and is situated in the Chingleput district. It owes its sanctity to the miracles said to have been worked in the locality by the Hindu ascetic Pattinattu Pillaiyar,[12] whose *samadhi* (sepulchre) still stands within the town. Another Hindu saint traditionally connected with the place, is Sundarar, who is said to have wooed and won one of his two consorts here. The local temple contains a shrine dedicated to Tyagaraja.

According to the Madras Government Epigraphist's[13] version, the deity in the central shrine is named Adipuriswarar. It is said that the linga therein is in the form of an anthill. It is in the presence of this god that saint Sundarar is said to have accepted Sangili as his consort, with whom he fell in love in this temple. The religious importance of this place is so great that even the Chola kings of the south attended its festivals as detailed below:

"Chola king Rajadiraja II has personally attended a festival in the temple in the 9th year of his reign, when the king in company with certain learned teachers heard the story of Aludaiyanambl. His successor Kulottunga III in the 19th year of his reign was present at the Rajarajantirumandapam, to witness the Ani festival. He also held a *durbar* therein attended by the temple servants and tenants of the village to enquire into a petition relating to the temple lands being laid waste.

The great Saiva teacher Sri Sankaracharya is said to have personally gone to this temple to secure the vital energy of an evil goddess who was then swallowing everything that came in her way, threw it into a well (pointed out even now) and closed its mouth with a huge stone! The goddess in consequence became powerless and assumed a calm countenance. This is similar to the incident connected with the goddess of the temple at Jambukeswaram. Even now the sculpture of Sri Sankaracharya is worshipped in this temple.

According to an inscription in the south wall of the central shrine, architect Ravi or Vira Chola, at the bidding of Chaturanana and under the patronage of Rajendra Chola I, (1012-42), built the central shrine.

"The following subordinate shrines are referred to in the inscriptions: (1) Pillai Subramaniyar (Kumaraswamideva), (2) Tiruvattapirai Pidariyar, (3) Karanaï Vitankadeva, (4) Padampakkadeva, (5) Kshetrapaladeva, (6) Surya, (7) Arinjiswaramudaiyar, (8) Kampiswaramudaiyar, (9) Videlvidugeswara, (10) Durgaiyar, and (11) Anukka Pillaiyar. Of these Nos.2 and 10 are perhaps the same and may be identical with the present Vattapirai Amman situated within the temple in the northern verandaha round the central shrine.

No.4 is evidently identical with Gaulisvara, for, an inscription
on that shrine states that the building for Padampakkadeva
was constructed in the 5th year of Virarajendradeva (i.e., in
A.D. 1067-68). Karanai Vitanka (No.3), like Tanjai Vitanka of
the Tanjore records, may have been the name given to this chief
deity of the temple. In this case, Karanai would be an earlier
name of Tiruvorriyur itself. Several charitable institutions
such as Rajendrasolan *matha* and Kulottungasolan matha,
called apparently after the Chola kings Rajendra Chola I
and Kulottunga Chola I, were situated within the temple.
The former was built by a certain Aryaminai, wife of
Prabhakarabhatta who came from Mergalapura in the
Aryadesa (perhaps, the northern country?) and dwelt at
Tiruvorriyur as a devotee of the temple. In the latter were fed
50 Saiva devotees everyday. Tirugyanasambanda matham is
mentioned in No.238 of Appendix B and Nandikeswara matha
in No.239. In the time of the Vijayanagar king Harihara II,
there was still another institution of the same kind named
Angarayan matham. Further, the existence of open pavilions
(mandapas) such as Vakkanikkum mandapa, 'the hall where
discussions were held' and Vyakaravadana Vyakhyana
mandapa, 'the hall where grammar was presented (to Panini)
and was commented upon' is eloquent testimony to the
impetus that was being given to literary culture through the
agency of this temple. In a later Chola record we find that
the god of the temple (Siva) himself received the name
Vyakaranadana Perumal, consistently perhaps, with the
tradition that the first 14 aphorisms of Panini's grammar were
produced from the kettle-drum no Siva. Names of other
mandapas such as Mannaikondasolan, Rajarajan and
Rajendrasolan, clearly indicate the origin of these pavilions
which were built under the patronage of the Chola kings who
bore the titles and proper names. The temple was very richly

embellished and owned a large number of *devadana* villages. A special man owned the hereditary right of watching the precincts of the temple (tiruvellaikaval). The items required for festive days generally comprised rice, vegetables, curd, ghee, plantain, fruits, pepper, mustard, arecanuts, betel leaves, unguents, camphor, red paint, scented dusk, sandal, flower garlands, oil, sesame, etc. On all special occasions new clothes (parisattam) were presented to the servants of the temple who, according to inscription No.131 of Appendix B, numbered 139. Kings, ministers, military officers, merchants, peasants, and Brahmanas were alike its devotees and made valuable gifts."

A record dated the 29th year of Parakesarivarman Parantaka I registers a grant by one Iravinili, daughter of the Chera king Vijayarayadeva thereby proving the friendly relations that existed between the Cholas and the Cheras at that time.

One of the 16th year of Parakesarivarman Uttama Chola refers to a scrutiny of the accounts of this temple made at that time.

INSCRIPTIONS[14]

The great religious and historical importance of this place, together with its temple, mathas, pavilions, mandapams, etc., is described in detail Ep. Rep. 1912, p.68, and Ibid. 1913, p.86.

366 of 1911 (Tamil) — The east wall of the second prakara in the Adhipuriswara temple. Records in the thirty-first year of the Chola king Tribhuvanachakravartin Tribhuvanaviradeva, 'who having been pleased to take Madurai (Madura), Ilam (Ceylon), Karuvur, and the crowned head of the Pandya, was pleased to perform the anointment of heroes' (i.e. Kulottunga III, 1178-1216) gift of a cow, a bull and a calf,

for a lamp to the temple of Tiruvorriyurudaiya Nayanar by
a devotee in the Kulandaiyandar matham at Kulattur in
Venkunrakottam. (See Ins. S. Dts., p. 105, No.6, where this
inscription is given.)

367 of 1911 (Tamil) — On the same wall. Dated in the
reign of the Vijayanagara king Virapratapa Devaraya II.
Records in Krodhin (S. 1346) gift of a salt-pan in the
village of Manali in Pularkottam, a sub-division of
Jayangondasolamandalam, by the residents of that village.
Mentions the salt-pan called Padampakkanayakapperalam
(Pulalnadu and Pulalkottam were evidently named after the
village Pulal near Madras on the road to Nellore. The deity
was so-called because he is on an anthill covered by a
metallic protector. The inscription is given in Ins. S. Dts.,
p.105, No.8)

368 of 1911 (Tamil) — On the same wall. Dated in
the reign of the Chola king Parakesarivarman or
Tribhuvanachakravartin Kulottungacholadeva III, 'who was
pleased to take Madurai (Madura), and the crowned head of
the Pandya,' in the nineteenth year. Says that the king was
present at the Rajarajantirumandapam to see the Ani festival
in the temple of Tiruvorriyur Udaiyar. The devadana village
Adanpakkam in Suratturnadu, a sub-division of Puliyurkottam or Kulottungasolavalanadu being reported by the chief
of the matha, the *stanattar*, the temple supervisor, manager,
chief accountant and tenants of the villages to be lying waste
for want of tenants, the king ordered that it might be leased
out to certain persons specified in the inscription.

369 of 1911 (Tamil) — On the same wall. Dated in the
reign of the Chola king Parakesarivarman or Tribhuvana
Chakravartin Rajarajadeva II. Records in his seventeenth
year a gift of 12 buffaloes for a lamp by Aryan
Tiruchchirambelamudaiyan Paduman or Kattiman of

Kasmirapura to the temple of Tiruvorriyur Udaiyar at Tiruvorriyur in Pularkottam, a sub-division of Vikramasolavalanadu in Jayangondasolamandalam. Mentions the king's queen Mukkokilanadigal.

370 of 1911 (Grantha and Tamil) — The same wall records in thirteenth year of king Tribhuvanachakravartin Rajarajadeva's gift of 32 cows and a bull for a lamp by a certain Tiruvendatacharanalayan, the headman of Nulappiyaru in Ambatturnadu.

371 of 1911(Grantha and Tamil) — On the same wall. A record of the ninth year of King Rajakaserivarman or Tribhuvanachakravartin Rajadhirajadeva II (1172-16). It records that the king was present on the occasion of Panguni Uttiram festival in the temple of Padambakka. Nayakadeva Chaturanana-Pandita, who owned a matha in the temple and Vagiswara-Panditha and expounded the Somasiddhanta (i.e. the doctrine of the Kapalika Saivas), the Koyil Nayaka, the Srikarya and others were also present to hear the purana of Aludaiyanambi. On hearing that the devadana village Vadugaperrumbakkam was lying waste (for want of tenants), the king ordered it to be leased out to a certain Amudangilavan Periyan Soman. The inscription is interrupted by a wall in the middle. (Vagiswara Pandita was different from Vakkanandamuni who, according to Tamil literary tradition, lived in the time of Kulottunga III and at whose instance the Venbappattiyal was composed by Gunavira Pandita. He was the author of the Gnanamrutam, on Pati, Pasu and Pasa.)

372 of 1911 (Tamil) — On a slab built into the floor, at the entrance into the same prakara. A damaged record of the 'Ganga Pallava' king Vijaya Kampavarman (son of Nandivarman III and brother of Nripatunga), dated in his nineteenth year. It registers a gift of land by Niranjanaguravar of Tiruvorriyur to the temple of Niranjadesvarattu Mahadeva

which he had constructed at that village. It is stated that the
assembly of Manali sold the land to Naranjanaguravar.
Mentions one of the signatories whose name was Peruntalaik-
kavadi Tiruvorriyuran.

98 of 1912 (Tamil) — The south wall of the central shrine
in the Adhipuriswara temple. Records in the third year of
the Chola king Tribhuvanachakravartin Rajadhirajadeva II's
gift of ninety sheep for a lamp to the temple of Tiruvorriyur
Udaiyar by Vallaikilan Madavan Padambakka. Nayakan
or Tiruchchirambala Muvendavelan, a native of
Kadarpakkam.

99 of 1912 (Tamil) — On the same wall. Dated in the reign
of the Chola king Tribhuvanachakravartin Rajarajadeva III.
Records in his twenty-seventh year Dhanus, ba. di. 2,
Wednesday, Punarpusam (Wednesday, 10th December, 1243),
gift of 32 cows, a bull and a lampstand by a native of Anangur
in Panaiyurnadu, a sub-division of Naduvunadu or
Rajarajavala Nadu. The donor was evidently residing at
Konrur Villipakkam, which was a sub-division of Ambatturnadu in the district of Pulalkottam alias Vikkiramasolavalanadu in Jayangondasolamandalam.

100 of 1912 (Tamil) — On the same wall. Dated in the
reign of the Chola king Tribhuvanachakravartin Rajadirajadeva
II. Records in the tenth year of his reign gift of 12 buffaloes
for a lamp by Kaliyan Tandai Tirunattaperumal or
Vikkiramasola Padavurnadalvan, to the same temple. He is
stated to have been the officer-in-charge of Tiruvellaikkaval
(the precincts) of the temple at Tiruvorriyur.

101 of 1912 (Tamil) — On the same wall. A record of
Chola king Tribhuvanachakravartin Rajadhirajadeva II, in his
fourth year, registering a gift of 32 cows for a perpetual lamp
by one of the servants of the temple doing the duty called
Kalumpidarum.

102 of 1912 (Tamil) — On the same wall. Dated in the reign of the Chola king Rajakesarivarman or Udaiyar Sri Rajadhirajadeva I. Records in his twenty-eighth year and 134th day a sale of land by certain members of the assembly of Manali or Singavishnuchaturvedimandalam, a devadana village of the temple of Tiruvorriyurudaiyar to the military officer (*Dandanayakam*) Parantakamarayan or Rajadhiraja-Ni'gargaraiyar, a resident of Sattimangalam in Innambarnadu, which was a sub-division of Rajendrasingavalanadu, a district of Solamandalam. (For the various meanings of Perundanam and Sirudanam see Ep. Rep.1913, p.97.)

103 of 1912 (Tamil) — On the same wall. A record of the Chola king Rajakesarivarman or Udaiyar Sri Rajadhirajadeva I. It records in his twenty-sixth year an enquiry into temple affairs by the officers (*adhikari*) Valavan Muvendavelar and Vikkiramasinga Muvendavelar, (Perundanam Dandanayakam) held in the mandapa of the temple called Mannaikondasolan. The inscription says that certain lands which had been lying waste were improved and cultivated at the instance of the officers. It incidentally mentions that 14,648 *kulis* (7 1/8 *velis*) had to pay tax (or temple share) at the rate of 28 *kalams* of paddy by Arumolitevan Marakkal. (total 199 kalams, 1 tu, 1 pa.) Again 10,752 kulis (5 velis and 2 1/2 mas) had to pay at the rate of 19 kalams a veli (Total 102 ka, 1 ku, 4 na.). Prices of articles are given.

104 of 1912 (Tamil) — On the same wall. A record of the Chola king Parakesarivarman or Udaiyar Sri Rajendra Choladeva I, (1012-43). Records in his 31st year gift of 150 *kasus* by Chaturanana Pandita of Tiruvorriyur for bathing the god Mahadeva of that place with clarified butter on the birthday festival of the king which fell on the *nakshatra* Tiruvadirai in the month of Margali. See No. 965 above for the later Chaturanana Pandita and No. 1050 for the earlier.

It is evident that Chaturanana is a general title rather than an individual name. Kamba, it may be noted, refers in one of his stray verses to the matha.

105 of 1912 (Tamil) — On the same wall. A damaged record of the Chola king Parakesarivarman or Udaiyar Sri Rajendra Choladeva I, dated in his thirty-second year.

106 of 1912 (Tamil) — On the west wall of the same shrine. A record of the Chola king Tribhuvanachakravartin Rajarajadeva III. Records in his thirteenth year, Karkataka 9th day, Makha and Dvitiya, corresponding to Wednesday, July 5, 1228 A.D., gift of ninety ewes, a ram and a lampstand by Sambuvarayan Alagasiyan, son of Sambuvarayan Pallavandar.

107 of 1912 (Tamil) — On the same wall. An unfinished record of the Chola king Tribhuvanachakravartin Rajadhirajadeva I, dated in his sixth year. Records gift of 32 cows for a lamp by a certain Periyanayan or Manikkavasagan, one of the devotees doing service in the temple of Tiruvorriyur Udaiyar.

108 of 1912 (Tamil) — On the same wall. A record of the Chola king Tribhuvanachakravartin Virarajendracholadeva (Kulottunga III). Records in his ninth year, Karkataka (which should be eighth year, Mesha) su. di. 13, Revati, corresponding to Friday, 19th April, 1186 A.D., gift of 300 cows, called Asangadagandan-surabhi for providing panchagavya to the temple of Tiruvorriyur Udaiya Nayanar, by Kulottunga Sola Paiyurnadalvan Valayalmalagiyan Orri Arasan.

109 of 1912 (Tamil) — On the same wall. A record of the Chola king Tribhuvanachakravartin Rajarajadeva III. Records in his eighth year, gift of money for offerings to the god Karanai Vitankadeva, on the day of Tiruvadirai in the month of Margali, by a native of Paluvur in Damarkottam, a sub-division of Jayangondasolamandalam. The money was

deposited with the inhabtants of Iganaiyur, a devadana village of the temple. (Mr. Krishna Sastri infers that the place might have been called Karanai after the well-known home of Lakulisa.)

110 of 1912 (Tamil) — On the same wall. A record of the Pandya king Jatavarman or Tribhuvanachakravartin Sundara Pandyadeva III (1276-90). Records in his thirteenth year Simha, ba. di. 3, Friday, Uttirattadi, corresponding to August 5, A.D. 1289, an agreement by which the residents of Pularkottam, granted the pon-vari collected both in the northern and southern divisions of Tiruvorriyur for maintaining the Vyakhyanamandapa (the hall where discussions were held) and conducting repairs in the temple. The inscription shows that provision was made for Vyakhyana or expoundation of doctrines.

111 of 1912 (Tamil) — On the same wall. A record of the Chola king Rajakesarivarman or Chakravartin Kulottunga Choladeva I. Records in his eighteenth year gift of 90 sheep for a lamp by Solansorudaiyal or Kadavan Mahadevi, queen of Chakravartin Kulottunga Choladeva to the temple of Tiruvorriyurudaiyar. (This queen has not been mentioned in any other inscriptions hitherto collected).

112 of 1912 (Tamil) — On the same wall. An unfinished record of the Chola king Rajakesarivarman or Tribhuvanachakravartin Kulottunga Choladeva I, dated in his thirty-seventh year. Records sale of land for conducting certain festivals in the temple, to the assembly of Manali or Singavishnuchaturvedimangalam by Pallikondan Ramadevanar or Irumadisola Muvendavelar, a native of Sirramur in Vendalai Velur Kurram, a subdivision of Rajendrasolavalanadu in Solamandalam.

113 of 1912 (Tamil) — On the same wall. A record of the Chola king Tribhuvanachakravartin Rajarajadeva III, providing

in his twenty-first year for a flower garland and offerings by Orri Arasan, son of Paiyurnadalvan Valaiyam Alagiyan, who is evidently identical with the donor mentioned above.

114 of 1912 (Tamil) — On the same wall. Dated in the reign of the Chola king Tribhuvanachakravartin Kulottunga Choladeva. Records in his eleventh year, gift of twelve buffaloes for a lamp and a lamp-stand shared like himself to Tiruvorriyurudaiyar by Tiruvarangamudaiyar or Danmaparipalan Rajadhiraja Malayarayan, son of Munaiyadarayan or Kulottungasola Malayarayan of Naduvilmalai Tirunedumperai in Perumurnadu, a sub-division of Manavilkottam. Records also the gift of twelve buffaloes for a lamp, a silver lampstand, and a silver bugle (kalam) to the goddess Aludaiya Nachchiyar. The lampstands were called Darmaparipalam after the donor.

115 of 1912 (Tamil) — On the same wall. Dated in the reign of the Chola king Tribhuvanachakravartin Rajarajadeva III. Records in his twenty-sixth year, Tula, twenty-third day, ba. di. 14, Asvati (Sunday, 20th October, 1241), a gift of thirty-two cows, a bull and a lampstand for two flats by a resident of a Velur which was a devadana village of the temple.

116 of 1912 (Tamil) — On the same wall. Belongs to the reign of the Chola king Tribhuvanachakravartin Rajarajadeva III. Records in his third year, gift of thirty-two cows for a lamp by one of the worshippers (*devakarmin*) of the temple, named Suryadevan, or Vyakaranadana Bhatta.

117 of 1912 (Tamil) — On the north wall of the same shrine. Dated in the reign of Tribhuvanachakravartin Vijaya Gandagopaladeva in his tenth year, Kanni, ba. di. 5 Pusam, (Saturday, 13th September, 1259.) Records gift of ninety ewes and two rams for a lamp, by Perumal Nachchi, senior queen of prince (pillaiyar) Panchanadivanan Nilagangaraiyar.

118 of 1912 (Tamil) — On the same wall. A record of the Chola king Rajakesarivarman or Tribhuvanachakravartin Kulottunga Choladeva I; records in his twenty-third year gift of ninety sheep for a lamp to the temple of Tiruvorriyurudaiyar by Seyyan Orrikondan, son of Orriseyyan or Solavallava Muvendavelan, a native of Ilanagar in Purangarambai Nadu, a district of Solamandalam.

119 of 1912 (Tamil) — On the same wall. Dated in the reign of the Chola king Rajakesarivarman or Chakravartin Kulottunga Choladeva I. Records in his thirtieth year gift of ninety sheep for a lamp by Muvamudala Jnanamurti Panditan or Madurantaka Brahmadhirajan of Vatsa gotra, a native of Nalur and the commandant of forces (senapati) of Chakravartin Kulottunga Choladeva. (The same Brahman military officer is mentioned in No. 121.)

120 of 1912 (Tamil) — On the same wall. Dated in the reign of Tribhuvanachakravartin Tribhuvanaviradeva who 'was pleased to perform to anointment of heroes and the anointment of victors ' (i.e. Kulottunga Chola III). Records in his twenty-sixth year, gift of the village Kulappakkam or Sivapadasekharanallur in Puliyurkottam or Kulottungasolavalanadu and of gold ornaments to the God Vyakaranadana Perumal and his consort at the request of a certain female mendicant called Tiruvorriyurammai. The king is here referred to as Ulaguyya Nayanar. (god Vyakaranadana Perumal is evidently so called because Siva is said to have produced the first fourteen aphorisms of Panini from his kettle-drum.)

121 of 1912 (Grantha) — On the same wall. A record of the Chola king Jayadhara (i.e., Kulottunga I), records in his thirtieth year, gift of a lamp to the god Siva at Adhipura by Jnanamurthi or Madhurantaka, perhaps identical with the military officer mentioned in No. 19 above. Published in Ep.

Ind. Vol. V, p.106, but here Jnanamurti is said to have been the father or preceptor of the donor.

122 of 1912 (Tamil) — On the same wall. Dated in the reign of the Chola king Tribhuvanachakravartin Rajarajadeva III. Records in his nineteenth year, Simha, su. di. 3, Uttirattadi, corresponding to Sunday, July 30, A.D. 1234, gift of five women and their descendants for husking paddy in the temple by Vayalurkilavan Tiruvegambam Udaiya Sendamaraikkannan or Senninallur in Perurnadu, a sub-division of Puliyurkottam or Kulottungasolavalanadu which was a district of Jayangondasolamandalam.

123 of 1912 (Tamil) — On the same wall. A record of the Chola king Rajakesarivarman or Tribhuvanachakravartin Rajarajadeva II. Records in his twenty-seventh year (A.D. 1172) gift of ninety-six cows for three lamps by Kulottunga-sola Mahipala, son of Arrur Nadalvan, a native of Eyilnurnilaiamur or Cholandrasinganallurpalli in Paiyurkottam, a sub-division of Vikkiramasolavalanadu in Jayangonda-solamandalam.

124 of 1912 (Tamil) — On the same wall. Dated in the reign of the Chola king Rajakesarivarman or Chakravartin Kulottunga Choladeva I. Records in his thirty-seventh year gift of a lamp and ninety sheep by a native of the Chola Kingdom named Araiyan Rajendrasolan or Rajasekharamuvendavelan.

125 of 1912 (Tamil) — On the same wall. An unfinished record of the Chola king Parakesarivarman or Tribhuvanachakravartin Ulaguyyavanda Perumal (i.e. Kulottunga III), dated in his third year. Refers to a certain Pugalvanaiyan of Karuvili in Milalaikurram in Pandinadu, who received from the king, while the latter was encamped at that place, the chiefship of Ponmaru in Kalavaynadu, a sub-division of Puliyurkottam in Jayangondasolamandalam,

which was a division of Tondaimandalam. (The inscription refers to Rajadhrohins at Ponmaru and the appointment of a man of the south so far in the north is significant.)

126 of 1912 (Grantha) — On the south base of the same shrine. Records that the vimana (i.e. the central shrine) was built by the architect Ravi or Vira Chola at the bidding of Chaturanana, the pupil of Niranjana Guravar, and under the auspices of Rajendra Chola I (1012-43), son of Rajaraja. The inscription is of a high technical value as many architectural terms are given. See Cg. 965 and 973 above for reference to Chaturanana Pandita.

127 of 1912 (Tamil) — On the same wall. Dated in the reign of the Chola king Udaiyar Sri Rajadhirajadeva I. Records in his third year sale of land (2,308 kulis) irrigational facilities and house sites for tenants; 120 kulis also sold by the residents of Veshsharupadi to the Brahman lady, Ariyavammai, wife of Prabhakara Bhatta of Merkalapura in Aryadesa (northern country), for the purpose of feeding the Maheswaras in Rajendrasolan which was evidently a matha built by her in the temple. See No. 132.

128 of 1912 (Tamil) — On the west base of the same shrine. A record of the Chola king Virarajendradeva I (1063-70). Records that some waste land of the temple (60 velis) in Singavishnuchaturvedimangalam was reclaimed by the order of the king and being named Virarajendravilagan after the king, its produce was utilized for services in the temple, including the recital of Manikkavasaga's Tiruvembavai, the Devaram Tiruppadiyams and maintenance of priests, dancing masters and girls.

129 of 1912 (Tamil) — On the same base. A record of the Chola king Rajakesarivarman or Udaiyar Sri Rajadhirajadeva I (1018-52). Records in his thirty-eighth year sale of land by the assembly of Kurattur in Ambatturnadu, a

sub-division of Pularkottam, for conducting the daily servies in the temple of Tiruvorriyurudaiyar Karanaivitankadevar. Tiruvallivayal is stated to have been a village in Tudamuninadu, a sub-division of Puliyurkottam. Typical document of sale.

130 of 1912 (Tamil) — On the same base. Dated in the reign of the Chola king Rajakesarivarman or Kulottunga Choladeva I. Registers in his seventh year and 290th day that Kulamular Eran Kuttanur or Rajaraja Muvendavelar, an officer (adhikari) of the king held an enquiry into temple affairs in the mandapa called Rajarajan (within the temple) and assigned some money for the services called Virarajendrantirupalliveluchchi,

131 of 1912 (Tamil) — On the west and south bases of the same shrine. A record of the Chola king Rajakesarivarman or Udaiyar Sri Rajendra Choladeva (Kulottunga Choladeva I). Records in his second year, gift of 12 velis of land purchased for 240 kasus by the military officer (*senapati*) Rajarajan Paranriparakshasanar or Virasola Ilangovelar, in order to conduct the service called Tiruchchandadal of the god Karanai Vitankadevar. Partly published in S.I.I., Vol. III, p.132. See No. 109 above. (The income from the 12 velis is said to be 576 kalams worth 144 kasus. The price of one veli = 20 kasus, i.e., 100 kulis cost 1 kasu. The measurement is by the 16-span-rod. Amongst the dues called antaraya and kudimai payable are mentioned and puppon panchavaram, velikkasu, nirvilai, vetti, muttaiyal, echchoru, and kurunnel).

132 of 1912 (Tamil) — On the same bases. A record of the Chola king Rajakesarivarman or Udaiyar Sri Rajadhirajadeva I. Records in his thirty-first year, a sale of land by the assembly of the brahmadeya villages of Sundarasolachaturvedimangalam and Vanavanmahadevichaturvedimangalam. It was purchased by Nagalavvaichchani

or Ariyammai, wife of Prabhakara Bhatta, a resident of Megalapuram in the Aryadesa and a devotee of the temple of Tiruvorriyurudaiya Mahadeva. The purchased land was given to the matha called Rajendrasolan which was built by that lady. Records also other sales of land to the same lady and for the same purpose, by the residents of Ennur, in Navalurnadu, which was a sub-division of Pularkottam and by the merchants (nagarattar) of Tiruvorriyur in the years thirty-one and twenty-seven of the same reign, respectively. See No. 127 above.

133 of 1912 (Tamil) — On the north base of the same shrine. A record of the Chola king Rajakesarivarman or Udaiyar Sri Rajendra Choladeva (Kulottunga Choladeva I). Records in his third year, sale of land by the residents of Ennur in Navalnadu, a sub-division of Pularkottam for midday services in the temple and for feeding a Brahmana learned in the Vedas and a Sivayogin, the money being paid by the oficer Adittan Taraparamporular or Madurantaka Muvendavelar, a native of Aridayamangalam in Mudichchonadu, which was a sub-division of Kalyanapurangondasola-valanadu (evidently named after Rajadhiraja I, 1018-52). (The income from the land is said to be 35 kalams per veli — a poor return. Three ways of irrigation are authorized, viz., by damming the river, by hand piccotas, and by baskets.)

134 of 1912 (Tamil) — On the same base. An unfinished record of the Vijayanagara king Virapratapadevamaharaya-Krishnadeva Maharaya, dated S.1448, Bhava (wrong) Karttika, sixth day, Thursday, ba. di.

135 of 1912 (Tamil) — On the same base. A record of the Chola king Rajakesarivarman or Udaiyar Sri Virarajendradeva. Records in his fourth year, sale of land by the residents of Elinulai, a village in Paiyyurkottam, a sub-division of Jayagondasolamandalam, for the Rajendrasola-

matham. The price money for the land was paid by
Tiruvarangadevan or Mummudisola Brahmamarayan, a
native of Viranarayanachaturvedimangalam which was a
taniyur in Rajendrasinghavalanadu of Solamandalam.

136 of 1912 (Tamil) — On the same base. A record of
the Chola king Rajakesarivarman or Udaiyar Sri
Virarajendradeva. Records in his second year, apportionment
of money paid by the weaver (*saliya*) merchants residing
in the quarter called Fayasingakulakalaperunderu in
Tiruvorriyur. This was for special services to be offered in
the temple on the day of Aslesha on which the king was born,
as settled by the officer Jayasingakulakala Vilupparaiyar
of Karugudi, in Kilarkurram, a sub-division of
Nittavinodavalanadu in Solamandalam. Jayasingakulakala
was an epithet of Virarajendra as he was the opponent of the
western Chalukyan king Jayasimha III.

137 of 1912 (Tamil) — On the same base, a record of
the Chola king Rajakesarivarman or Udaiyar Sri
Rajadhirajadeva I, (1018-53). Records in his twenty-eight
year, a gift of money for special offerings on the day following
the festival of Panguni Uttiram. The assembly of Kavanur or
Kamalanarayanachaturvedimangalam received the amount
(80 kasus) and agreed to pay as interest 75 kalams of paddy
every year for the expenses of that day. A good idea of temple
establishment and salaries of temple servants and prices is
given. (The Tiruttondattogai, the original nucleus of the
Periapurana, composed by Sundaramurti is referred to in the
inscription, as well as the images of the sixty-three saints.)

138 of 1912 (Tamil) — On a pillar of the verandah round
the same shrine. A record of the Chola king Parakesarivarman
or Udaiyar Sri Rajendra Choladeva I. Records in thirtieth year
gift of 90 sheep for a lamp by a Gangakondasolan or
Uttamasolamarayan of Tiruvarurkurram, a sub-division of

Kshtriasikhamanivalanadu, for the merit of a certain Ganavadi Idumban or Tannaimunivarpendirganda Viasaiyarayan who stabbed himself and died in order to relieve the distress of the donor. The record incidentally registers another gift of 90 sheep for a lamp by Nimbaladevi, wife of Indaladeva of Talaigrama in Viratadesa (Hangal in Dharwar). For another emigrant see N.A.672 and C.G. 1024, p.120 below. Also Mysore and Coorg pp. 186-8, Ep. Rep. 1908-9.

139 of 1912 (Tamil) — On the second pillar in the same place. A record of the Chola king Parakesarivarman or Udaiyar Sri Rajendra Choladeva I. Records in his twenty-ninth year gift of money deposited on interest in paddy with the inhabitants of Iganaiyur, for providing offerings every year on the festival of the first crop (*pudiyidu*), and made by Nakkan Kodai or Kanchipuranangai, a maid-servant (*magal*) of Tiruvegambanudaiya Mahadeva of the city (*Nagaram*) of Kanchipuram, in Eyirkottam, a sub-division of Jayangondasolamandalam.

140 of 1912 (Tamil) — On the third pillar in the same place. A record of the Chola Parakesarivarman or Udaiyar Sri Rajendra Choladeva I (1012-43). Records in his twenty-ninth year a gift of money (tulai-nirai pon and Madurantaka-devanmedai) for celebrating the festival of Margali Tiruvadirai and feeding the three Brahmans well versed in the Vedas. The money was borrowed on interest in paddy by the merchants (*nagarattar*) of Tiruvorriyur and by the residents of Manjiyankaranai, a village in Karigaipperurnadu, a sub-division of Pularkottam, the interest on paddy being 90 kalams. (The interest on one kalanju was 2 kalams of paddy per annum by the Rajakesarimerakkal; and the interest on one Madurantakadevanmadai was also 2 kalams. The latter, therefore, says Mr. Krishna Sastri, should have weighed one kalanju of gold.)

141 of 1912 (Tamil) — On the fourth pillar in the same place. A record of Parakesarivarman or Udaiyar Sri Rajendra Choladeva I. Records in twenty-ninth year a gift of money (Rajarajan kasu) for feeding a Brahman, by Kuttan Ganavadi, the military officer of Gangaikondan or Uttamasola Marayan. The money was received by the merchants of Tiruvorriyur, on interest, to be paid in paddy. Mentions also Ariyammai and her money gift. (The Rajarajan kasu, points out Mr. Krishna Sastri, should have been half of Madurantakadevamadai in weight and value as the interest on it was one-half of that.)

142 of 1912 (Tamil) — On the fifth pillar in the same place. A record of the Chola king Rajakesarivarman or Udaiyar Sri Rajadhirajadeva I. Records in his twenty-seventh year gift of money by the members of the assembly of Manali or Singavishnuchaturvedimangalam. (Was this derived from the Pallava king Simhavishnu?). The money was deposited on interest in paddy with the revenue accountant (*puravuvaritinaikalattu kanakkan*) of Siruvappedu, or *mummudi solanallur* for conducting the festival of Masi Magham.

143 of 1912 (Tamil) — On the sixth pillar in the same place. A record of the Chola king Parakesarivarman or Udaiyar Sri Rajendradeva. Records in his third year gift of 90 sheep for a lamp by Velala Madurantakam alias Tandanayakan Rajadhiraja Ilangovelan of Nadar, a village in Tiraimurnadu which was a sub-division of Uyyakondon-valanadu in Solamandalam.

144 of 1912 (Tamil) — On the seventh pillar in the same place. A record of the Chola king Rajakesarivarman or Udaiyar Sri Rajadhirajadeva I, dated in his twenty-seventh year. The inscription stops with the introduction of the king.

145 of 1912 (Tamil) — On the eighth pillar in the same place. A record of the Chola king Rajakesarivarman or

Kulottunga Choladeva I. Records in his tenth year a gift of milch cows for panchagavya and lamps, by Achchan Tiruchchirambala Mudaiyan or Gurukularajar of Ponparri in Milalaikurram, a district of Rajarajapandinadu.

146 of 1912 (Tamil) — On the ninth pillar in the same place. Dated in the reign of the Chola king Parakesarivarman or Udaiyar Sri Rajendra Choladeva I (1012-45). Records in his twenty-sixth year that the officer Rajendrasingha Muvendavelar enquired into temple affairs in the hall called Vakkanikkummandapa and fixed the details of services to be maintained from kurradandam and the excess paddy collected from the servants of the temple and the tenants of te devadana villages. (The articles to be purchased are enumerated and the prices given).

147 of 1912 (Tamil) — On the tenth pillar in the same place. A record of the Chola king Rajakesarivarman or Udaiyar Sri Rajadhirajadeva I. Records in his thirty-first year, a gift of 90 sheep for a perpetual lamp to the temple of Tiruvorriyurudaiya Mahadeva by Chaturan Chaturi, wife of Nagan Perangadan and a dancing girl (devaradiyal) of the temple. (Mr. Krishna Sastri surmises from this that regular marriage and conjugal life existed among this community in those days).

148 of 1912 (Tamil) — On the leventh pillar in the same place. A record of the Chola king Rajakesarivarman or Udaiyar Sri Rajadhirajadeva I. Records in his twenty-ninth year a gift of paddy for offerings by certain Peruman Madurantakan or Rajendrasola Vengannattaraiyan, for maintaining land which he purchased in Amur or Cholendrasinganallur in Paiyyurkottam. (The interest on 10 kalams of paddy for a year is 1 *kuruni* of pattettukuttal rice.)

149 of 1912 (Tamil) — On the twelfth pillar in the same place. A record of the Chola king Rajakesarivarman or Udaiyar Sri Vijiarajendradeva (Rajadhirajadeva 1). Records in

his thirty-third year gift of 92 sheep for a lamp by a certain
Sundarasola Pandya Vilupparayan who was a servant of the
temple (*panimagan*) and a resident of Kanchipura in
Eyilnadu, a sub-division of Eyirkottam.

150 of 1912 (Tamil) — On the thirteenth pillar in the same
place. A record of the Chola king Parakesarivarman or
Udaiyar Sri Rajendradeva (1050-62), dated in his sixth year.
Contains only the historical introduction beginning with
tirumaruviyasengol, etc., and the date.

151 of 1912 (Tamil) — On the fourteenth pillar in the same
place. A damaged record of the Chola king Rajakesarivarman
or Udaiyar Sri Rajadhirajadeva I, dated in his twenty-second
year. Records gift of money for providing a bundle of grass for
a cow every day, and for other services. The kasus invested for
interest of 4 1/4 kasus every year for feeding Brahmanas.

152 of 1912 (Tamil) — On the fifteenth pillar in the same
place. A damaged record of the Chola king Parakesarivarman
or Udaiyar Sri Rajendradeva (1050-62), dated in his eighth
year. Records a gift of 90 sheep for a lamp by a native of
Tirukkanaperur in Tirukkanaperurnadu, which was a sub-
division of Rajaraja Pandinadu.

153 of 1912 (Tamil) — On the sixteenth pillar in the same
place. A record of the Chola king Parakesarivarman or
Udaiyar Sri Rajendra Choladeva I. Records in his twenty-
sixth year a sale of land (24 1/2 pattis) by the residents of
the devadana village Iganaiyur to Sattan Iramadeviyar who
was called the *anukkaiyar* (maid servant?) of the king. The
purpose of the sale was to maintain twelve *devaradiyar* in the
temple to serve the goddess Gauri.

154 of 1912 (Tamil) — On the seventeenth pillar in the
same place. A record of the Chola king Rajakesarivarman or
Kulottunga Choladeva I. Records in his seventh year and two
hundred and ninetieth day, a sale of land by the residents of

Iganaiyur Siralan Gandaradittan or Irumudisola Vilupparayan of Korramangalam in Tirunarayurnadu, a sub-division of Kshatriyasikhamanivalanadu which was a district of Solamandalam for maintaining a shed for drinking water in the quarter called Sankarappadi or Rajarajapperunderu at Tiruvorriyur. (A tax called Kalavupattam is mentioned. It is surmised that it was imposed on the measures of grain in temple granaries. But this is doubtful.)

155 of 1912 (Tamil) — On the eighteenth pillar in the same place. Dated in the reign of Rajendra Choladeva I. Records in his thirtieth year sale of land (4,000 kulis) for maintaining a flower garden and supplying flowers to Nagalabaisani or Ariyavammai, wife of Prabhakara Bhatta of Merakalapuram in the Aryadesa. The land belonged to the villages of Adambakkam and Savanna in Suratturnadu, a sub-division of Puliyurkottam. (The lands purchased included house-sites for tenants and it was specified that the tenants were not to pay any kind of irai or kudimai such as vetti, amanji, kurunnel, etc. The measuring rod of 16 spans (*padinarusankol*) is mentioned. See 138 above).

156 of 1912 (Tamil) — On the nineteenth pillar in the same place. A record of the Chola king Parakesarivarman or Udaiyar Sri Rajendra Choladeva I. Records in his thirtieth year sale of land (2,000 kulis by padinarusankol for 8 Madhurantakamadais) by the assembly of Manalideva or Singavishnuchaturvedimangalam to a native of Parittikudi in Nenmalinadu, a sub-division of Arumolidevavalanadu, was a district of Solamandalam, for presenting it to the temple. So one Madurantakadevamadai was the cost of 250 kulis of land. The madai must have been issued, says Mr. Krishna Sastri, either by Rajendra Chola I or Uttamachola Madurantaka (970-85), the immediate predecessor of Rajaraja I. For the value of the madai see 140 and 141 above.

157 of 1912 (Tamil) — On the west wall of the same verandah. A record of the Chola king Parakesarivarman or Tribhuvanachakravartin Rajarajadeva II. Records in his sixth year gift of 32 cows for a lamp by a native of Munaippadainadu in Naduvilnadu.

158 of 1912 (Tamil) — On a slab built into the floor of the same verandah. Records in fourth year of the Ganga Pallava king Ko Vijiya Aparajitavarman gift of urkarchemmai gold for a lamp to the god Tiruvorriyur Mahadeva by Ammati or Kurumbakolai, a concubine (*bhogi*) of Vairameghan or Vanakovaraiyar, son of Perunangai. The amount (30 kalanjus) was placed in the hands of the assembly of Adambakkam, a hamlet of Tiruvorriyur, and the Amritagana committee, on interest at 3 *manjadi* per kalanju, every year. (Vairameghan had the title Vanakovariyan as he was probably in charge of the feudatory Bana kingdom. The inscription is of value in mentioning the rate of interest in the 9th century to be 3 manjadis on 1 kalanju (i.e., 20 manjadis) and so 15 per cent).

159 of 1912 (Grantha and Tamil) — On the second slab in the same place. Records in the eighth year of the Ganga-Pallava king Ko Vijiya Aparajitavarman Pottaraiyar, a gift of 60 kalanjus of urkkarchmmai gold for offerings and lamp by Paitangikandan, chief of Kattur in Vadagarai Innambarnadu, a district of Solanadu.

160 of 1912 (Grantha and Tamil) — On a third slab in the same place. A damaged record of the Chola king Madiraikonda Parakesarivarman· (Parantaka I), dated in his thirty-fourth year. Records gift of a lamp to the temple of Tiruvorriyur Mahadeva by Maran Paramesvaran or Sembiyan Soliyavarayan of Sirukulattur in Poyyurkurram, a sub-division of Tenkarainadu which was a district of Solanadu. (Refers to a military officer of the king who defeated Sitpuli, destroyed Nellore, and on his return from there made the

grant. See No. 236 below. The inscription is very important as proving Parantaka's conquest beyond Tondai).

161 of 1912 (Tamil) — On the fourth slab in the same place. A record of the Ganga Pallava king Ko Vijiya Aparajitavarman. Records in his fourth year a gift of gold (30 kalanjus) for a lamp to the same temple by Sappakan or Patradani who was concubine (bhogi?) of Virameghan or Vanakovariyar, son of Sami Akkan. Mentions the assembly of Adambakkam, a suburb of Tiruvoyyiyur and the Amritagana committee. A portion of the slab at the bottom is apparently cut off. (Mr. Krishna Sastri believes that this Sami Akkan is the same as Perunargai in No. 158 above. He further surmises that Virameghan was perhaps the son of Aparajita and was called Vanakovariyar as he was probably in charge of the Bana kingdom.)

162 of 1992 (Tamil) — On the fifth slab in the same place. A record of the Ganga Pallava king Ko Vijiya Nripatungavarman. Records in his eighteenth year gift of gold for offerings by Paliyappillai, one of the queens Videlvidugu-pallavariyar of Umbalanadu. A portion of the slab at the bottom is apparently cut off. See No. 332 of 1909 for the Chola feudatory of the same name.

163 of 1912 (Tamil) — On the sixth slab in the same place. A record of the Ganga Pallava king Ko Vijaya Aparajitavaram. Records in his seventh year a gift of gold (30 kalanjus) for a lamp by the queen Mahadevi Adigal to the temple of Tiruvorriyur Mahadeva. The assembly of Adambakkam, a suburb of Tiruvorriyur in Puliyurkottam, Amritagama committee, received the gold on interest.

164 of 1912 (Grantha and Tamil) — On the seventh slab in the same place. A damaged record of the Chola king Maduraikonda Parakesarivarman (Parantaka I), dated in his thirtieth year. Records a gift of gold for two lamps by

Kodandaranmar, eldest son the Chola king Parakesarivarman.
A portion of the gold seems to have been borrowed on interest
in the thirty-fifth year of the king, by the residents of
Vellivayill, a village in Pulalerikkilnadu. See 318 and 347 if
1904 at Kudimiyamalai and 203 of 193 at Tondamanadu near
Kalahasti.

165 of 1912 (Tamil) — On the eighth slab in the same
place. A damaged record of the Chola king Parakesarivarman,
probably Parantaka I, dated in his seventh year. Records gift
of gold for a lamp by Karanai Viluparaiyur Arivalan Puttan.
The assembly of Manali in charge of Tiruvorriyur received
the amount on interest.

166 of 1912 (Tamil) — On the ninth slab in the same place.
A damaged record of the Chola king Uttama Choladeva
Parakesarivarman (son of Gandaratiya, 970-86) dated in his
fifteenth year. Records gift of an image of Sribalideva, eight
bugles (*kala*) and 24 fly whisks with gold handles by the king.
The inscription refers to Senniyarippadai or the army which
was victorious at Senni. See 245 below.

167 of 1912 (Grantha and Tamil) — On the tenth slab in
the same place. Records in the twenty-seventh year of the
Chola king Maduraikonda Parakesarivarman, a gift of 90
sheep for a lamp by Devan Kesari or Kunjaramalla
Pallavariyan, a resident of Perumpanur, in Velarnadu, a sub-
division of Solanadu. The inscription shows that Parantaka
had the title Kunjaramalla.

168 of 1912 (Grantha and Tamil) — On the eleventh slab
in the same place. A damaged record of the Chola king
Maduraikonda Parakesarivarman (Parantaka I), dated in his
thirty-fifth year. Records gift of gold (50 kalanjus) for
feeding two *Mahavratis* everyday, by Iladaipperaraiyan or
Solasikhamani Pallavariyan. Solasikhamani was a title of
Parantaka I.

169 of 1912 (Grantha and Tamil) — A record of the Chola king Maduraikonda Parakesarivarman (Parantaka I). Records in his twenty-ninth year, a gift of gold for a lamp by Iravi Nili, daughter of Vijayaraghavadeva, the Chera king. The amount was apparently invested on a field at Tiruvorriyur which yielded the annual interet of 4 1/2 kalanjus. (The inscription shows the friendly relation of Parantaka with the Cheras.)

170 of 1912 (Grantha and Tamil) — On the same slab. Records in the thirtieth year of Maduraikonda Parakesarivarman gift of gold for a lamp by Arindigai-perumanar, son of Chola Perumanadigal, (i.e. Paranataka I) to the god Siva of Adhigrama.

171 of 1912 (Tamil) — On the thirteenth slab built into the floor of the same verandah. A much damaged record, the date and the name of the king are doubtful. Seems to record a gift of gold which was received on interest by the assembly of Adambakkam, a suburb of Tiruvorriyur, and the Amritagana committee.

172 of 1912 (Tamil) — On the fourteenth slab in the same place. A fragment record of the Chola king Rajarajakesarivarman (Rajaraja I), dated in his seventeenth year. Seems to record a gift of gold for feeding a Brahman.

173 of 1912 (Tamil) — On the fifteenth slab in the same place. A fragment of record of the Chola king Maduraikonda Parakesarivarman, dated in his twentieth year. Mentions the wife of Kerala Kurumban(?) or Parakesari Muvendavelar, of Valudivalmangalam in Tirukkannapperkurram I Munai-pandinadu.

174 of 1912 (Tamil) — On the sixteenth slab in the same place. Records in the reign of the Ganga Pallava king Ko Vijiya Kampavarman gift of twenty-seven kalanjus of gold for offerings by Pudi Arindigai, wife of Videlvidugu Ilangovelar of Kodumbalur in Konadu. The money was placed in the hands

of the residents of Vaikkatur (a suburb) of Tiruvorriyur, on interest at 3 manjadis per kalanju, per annum. (See 188 below.)

175 of 1912 (Tamil) — On the seventeenth slab in the same place. A damaged record of the Chola king Parakesarivarman (probably) Parantaka I, dated in his seventh year. Seems to record a sale of land which was situated in Iganaiyur, a village of Tiruvorriyur.

176 of 1912 (Tamil) — On the eighteenth slab in the same place. Records in the twenty-fourth year of the Chola king Parakesarivarman (probably) Parantaka I, gift of gold for a lamp by Sembiyan Muvendavelan or Sattan Ulagan, chief of Vandalanjeri in Tirunaraiyurnadu of Solanadu. The money was deposited for interest with the residents of Kulumanippakkam near Mangadu in Puliyurkottam.

177 of 1912 (Grantha and Tamil) — On the nineteenth slab in the same place. Dated in the reign of Rashtrakuta king Kannaradeva (Krishna III), 'who took Kachchi and Tanjai.' Records in his eighteenth year, gift of gold (30 kalanjus) for a lamp by Narasingayyan, son of Lakshmanaiyyan, a merchant in the camp (*kataka*) of the vallabha (Rashtrakuta) king. The merchant was a native of Manyakheta. The gold was deposited with the residents of Seruppedu (modern Chetput) in Tudarmuniyurnadu, a district of Puliyurkottam. The inscription is of interest in showing that peaceful men followed the Rashtrakuta army of invasion to the south thereby introducing the Kanarese people in that region.

178 of 1912 (Tamil) — On the same slab. Records in the nineteenth year of the Rashtrakuta king Kannaradeva, 'who took Kachchi and Tanjai' gift of ninety sheep for a lamp and one Ila lampstand by Tatpurushabhatara of Kalakkudi.

179 of 1912 (Tamil) — On the same slab. Records in the twenty-second year of the Rashtrakuta king Kannaradeva 'who took Kachchi and Tanjai', gift of gold for a lamp by the

mother of the Vallabha king Kannaradeva. The gold was deposited on permanent interest of 15 per cent. With the assembly of Kurattur or Parantakachaturvedimangalam in Ambatturerikilnadu, a sub-division of Pularkottam.

180 of 1912 (Tamil verse) — On the eighteenth slab built into the floor of the same verandah. Records in the twelfth year of the Ganga Pallava king Aparajita (the upper portion of the stone in missing) gift of land, by purchase, from the residents of Iganaimudur, for offerings to a shrine called Solammal Iswara in the temple at Orrimudur (Tiruvorriyur.) The donor's name is lost. (The relation between the Ganga Pallava line with the Chola is evidenced by the inscription.)

181 of 1912 (Grantha and Tamil) — On the twenty-first slab in the same place. A record of the Rashtrakuta king Kannaradeva (Krishna III). Records in his twentieth year, gift of money (100 nishkas of pure gold) by Chaturanana Pandita, the pupil of Niranjanaguru, for providing sacrifice in the temple at Tiruvorriyur. The Grantha portion gives an interesting account of the early career of Chaturanana. It says that he was a native of Kerala and a favourite of the Rashtrakuta king Vallabha, that he went over to the Chola country, became a friend of a Rajaditya and at his death in the hands of the Rashtrakuta king, blamed himself for not dying with him, became a sanyasin, being initiated by Niranjanaguru, and came to Tiruvorriyur. Mr. Krishna Sastri surmises that he was a spy. For the prevalence of certain Kerala customs in the temple see Ep. Rep. 1913.

182 of 1912 (Tamil) — On a slab built into the floor of the same shrine. Records in the twenty-ninth year of the Chola king Maduraikonda Parakesarivarman gift of gold for feeding a learned Brahmana by a native of Ettiyarkurichchi in Pandinadu, who had accepted service in the temple.

183 of 1912 (Tamil) — On a slab built into the floor of

the mandapa in front of the same shrine. Appears to record in Bhadudanya, an order of Muttambi Mudaliyar, who was the minister of Hijarat Davadu Khan, authorising a certain Ulli Venkatesa Settiyar to conduct the charities connected with the temple. (Daud Khan was Nawab of the Karnatik from 1703-10. Venkata Chetti was not improbably the merchant who rented Tiruvorriyur and four other villages granted by Daud Khan to the Company in 1708.) See *Vestiges of Madras*, II pp. 21-22.

184 of 1912 (Grantha and Tamil) — On a second slab in the same place. Records in the twenty-sixth year of the Chola king Madiraikonda Parakesarivarman gift of ninety sheep for a lamp and one Ila lampstand, by a native of Solanadu.

185 of 1912. — (Tamil). On a third slab in the same place. A much-damaged record. Seems to register a sale of land as bhattavritti by a certain Murtiperumanar.

186 of 1912 (Tamil) — On the fourth slab in the same place. Records in his twenty-first year gift of two Ila lampstands, 360 sheep for maintaining two perpetual lamps and a chauri, with a gold handle, by Muvenda Pallavariyan or Aditta Pidaran, son of Vira Narana Pallavaraiyan or Arunmoli, who was a native of Kugur in Vada Panangadu, a sub-division of Mikkuru in Solanadu.

187 of 1912 (Tamil) — On the same slab. A much-damaged record of the Chola king Maduraikonda Parakesarivarman (Parantaka I, 905-47) dated in his twenty-sixth year. Mentions a quarter of Tiruvorriyur called Surasulamanipperunderu. (Sulamani reminds one of the celebrated Jaina work of that name by Tolamolitteva.) It has been suggested that it was written in the reign of the Pandya king Jayanta, son of Maravarman Avanichulamani and grandson of Kadungon (about A.D. 620). *Tamil Studies* p.219.

188 of 1912 (Tamil) — On the fifth slab in the same place.

A damaged record of the Ganga Pallava king Ko Vijaya Kampavikramavarman dated in his ninth year. Records gift of gold for lamps by Kanjaram Amarnidi or Pallavadiraiyar, a native of Kanjanur, in Indalurnadu, which was a sub-division of Solanadu. See No.174. (Amarnidi was evidently named after the Saivite saint of that name for whose career see *Periyapurana*, 1905 edition, pp. 129-132).

189 of 1912 (Tamil) — On the sixth slab in the same place. A damaged record of the Ganga Pallava king Kampavarman dated in his sixth year. Records gift of gold for a lamp by Vemban Kunungan Amman of Irayanseri residing at Mayilappil (Mylapore). The amount was deposited for interest with the assembly of Manali which was a village of Tiruvorriyur.

190 of 1912 (Tamil) — On the same slab. Records in the sixth year of the Ganga Pallava king Ko Vijiya Aparajitavikrama-Pottaraiyar gift of gold for two lamps by the community of Maheswaras. The same assembly took possession of the amount.

191 of 1912 (Tamil) — On the south wall of the first prakara of the same temple. Registers in twenty-first year an order (olai) of Madurantaka Pottappichcholan.

192 of 1912 (Tamil) — On the same wall. Records in the fourth year of the Chola king Rajakesarivarman or Tribhuvanachakravartin Kullottunga Choladeva II sale of 8,593 3/4 kulis of land, by the assembly of Punnaivayil or Rajanarayanachaturvedimangalam in Vikkiramasolavalanadu, a district of Jayangondasolamandalam, to certain private individuals who gifted it to the temple of Udaiyar Tiruvorriyurar, for maintaining 28 perpetual lamps.

193 of 1912 (Tamil) — On the same wall. An unfinished historical introduction of the Chola king Parakesarivarman or Rajarajadeva II (1146-78) beginning with Pumaruviyapolilelum.

194 of 1912 (Tamil) — On the same wall. A record of the time of Sakalalokachakravartin Rajanarayanan Sambuvaraya. Seems to record a gift of land for offerings by a certain Alagaiyarayan Virrirunda Perumal Kulandaipillai to the temple of Tiruvorriyur-udaiya Nayanar.

195 of 1912 (Tamil) — On the same wall. Records that in the time of the Vijayanagara king Kampana Udaiyar II, son of Bokkana (Bukka I), in Sadharana, the temple authorities assembled in the Vyakaranadana hall under the leadership of the officer (adhikari) Tunaiyirundanambi Kongaraiyar and settled the order of precedence to be followed during services in the temple, by Ishabattaliyilar and Devaradiyar. See Ep. Rep. 1913, p.118, for very interesting details about the temple servants, their disputes for privileges and the decisions of the trustees and Nattars thereon.

196 of 1912 (Tamil) — On the west wall of the same prakara. Dated in the reign of the Vijayanagara king Ariyaraya (Harihara II). Seems to record in Dundubhi, Kanni, su. di. Paurnai, Uttirattadi, corresponding to Monday, 22nd September, 1382, a procedure similar to that mentioned in No. 195.

197 of 1912 (Tamil) — On the same wall. Records in the thirty-second year of the Chola king Tirbhuvanachakravartin Tirbhuvanaviradeva "who took Madurai (Madura), Ilam (Ceylon), Karuvur and the crowned head of the Pandya and who was pleased to perform the anointment of heroes and the anointment of victors" (Kulottunga III), sale of land to a certain Udaiyapillai or Pandarangan Vairagi of Madurantakachaturvedimangalam, by the assembly of Punnaivayil or Rajanarayanachaturvedimangalam in Pulal-nadu, a district of Pularkottam or Vikkiramasolavalanadu in Jayangondasolamandalam. The land was assigned to maintain a flower garden for the temple and to provide for offerings on certain festive occasions.

198 of 1912 (Tamil) — On the same wall. Records in the twenty-second year of the Chola king Tribhuvanachakravartin Rajarajadeva III an order of Madhurantaka Pottapicholan. Records also gift of Ularur or Sembiyan Karuppur in Kotturnadu, a sub-division of Puliyurkottam as a devadana village to the temple, by a certain Karuppular Perumandi Nayakkar.

199 of 1912 (Tamil) — On the same wall. Records in the seventh year of the Chola king Tribhuvanachakravartin Rajarajadeva III, an order of Vira Narasingha or Yadavarayan. The king declared that Tiruvorriyur and the other villages of the temple which had originally been rent-free (*irangal*) were to be taxed, the collections, however, being made payable into the treasury of the temple. They were, in other words, placed in the ningal list. The taxes enumerated are vetti, pudavaimudal, Tiraikkasu, asuvigalkasu, kudikasu, inavarikasu, karrtigaikasu, velichchinnam, vettikasus, siruppadikkaval. Kanikani fees, kurradandam, pattidandam, and fees on uvachchar, weavers, oil mongers, dyers, salt-pans etc. For Vira Narasimha Yadavaraya, see No. 227 below and Tirumalai inscriptions (Chittoor district).

200 of 1912 (Tamil) — On the same wall. Dated in the reign of the Chola king Rajakesarivarman or Chakravartin Kulottunga Choladeva I. Records in his forty-ninth year, a gift of a portion of Pavanambakkam near Araisur in Paiyyurkottom renamed Eluttarivarnallur, for feeding fifty devotees in Kullottungasolanmatha, situated within the temple of Tiruvorriyur Udaiyar. The order was issued at the instance of the king while he was in his palace at Gangaikondasolapuram.

201 of 1912 (Tamil) — On the same wall. A record of the Chola king Tribhuvanachakravartin Konerimaikondan (Kulottunga III.) Records in his thirty-eighth year and two

hundred and thirty-ninth day gift of 80 velis of land at Kulattur
or Kulottungasolan Kavanur detached from Punnaivayil or
Rajanarayanachaturvedimangalam by Durgaiyandi Nayakkan,
agent of Sittaraisan, for the maintenance of the Vyakaranadana
Vyakhyana mandapa built by himself in the temple of
Tiruvorriyur. The officer Vanadarayar and the tirumandiraolai,
Neriyudaichchola Muvendavelan, are also mentioned. The land
was free of tax (including Antarayappattam.)

202 of 1912 (Tamil) — On the same wall. A record of the
Chola king Tribhuvanachakravartin Tribhuvanaviradeva, "who
was pleased to perform the anointment of heroes and the
anointment of visitors" (Kulottunga III). Records in his thirty-
fifth year, Simha, su.di. 12, Uttirattadi, (Friday, 10th August,
1212) the circumstances under which the grant recorded in No.
201 was made. (The inscription refers to the levying of ponvari
on land at 1/4 madai per veli (without the usual exemption of
waste land) and to the compulsion of the assembly of
Punnavayal to bear the responsibility of collecting the whole.
As they would not, they were arrested and freed after the sale
of 80 velis for 200 kasus to clear the arrears. The inscription
also refers to the Vyakarana mandapa, its teachers and pupils.)

203 of 1912 (Tamil) — On the north wall of the same
prakara. A record of Sakalalokachakravartin Rajanarayanan
Sambuvarayar in his seventh year, Singa ba. di. 2, Thursday,
Punarpusam, that certain lands and house sites were
confiscated to the temple, the owners having misappropriated
the temple treasures buried underground which had escaped
the Mohammedans (Tulukkar) who had, before this, occupied
the country. The reference is the invasion of 1327. See Ind.
Antq. 1914, p.4.

204 of 1912 (Tamil) — On the same wall. Records in
Pingala an order of the temple trustees (tanattar) assigning the
quarter called Narppattannayirapperunderu for the exclusive

dwelling of sculptors and other artisans. See N.A. 715, S.A. 921 and Cg. 147.

205 of 1912 (Tamil) — On the same wall. Dated in the reign of the Vijayanagara king Ariyana Udaiyar (Harihara II). Records in Raudri, Kanni, su. di. 12, Tuesday (which should be Wednesday), Avittam, a gift of 1/2 karai of land in the village of Padiadumperumalnallur, to the temple of Tiruvorriyur-udaiya Nayanar for celebrating certain festivals and the Angarayan Matha by Angarayar Mudaliar and others of Pulal or Rajasundarinallur. The date corresponds to 12th September, 1380.

206 of 1912 (Grantha and Tamil) — On the same wall. A record of the Chola king Tribhuvanchakravartin Rajadhirajadeva II. Records in his ninth year, that gifts of cows made in the previous years but not engraved on stone, were now so recorded by the temple accountant Tiruvorriyurudaiyan Uraavakkinan (maitrikara in Sanskrit) at the instance of the mathapati Chaturanana Pandita. See No. 181 above.

207 of 1912 (Tamil) — On the same wall. Records in the twelfth year of Sakalalokachakravartin Rajanarayanan Sambuvarayar, Purattadi, first day, a gift of land, at Kaduvankottam with the order of Tikkama-Nayaka declaring the land tax-free, for offerings and festivals, by Vagisuradeva Mudaliyar of Kilaimatham, while he was on his death bed. The purchase of this land is stated to have been engraved on the stone wall of the Tirumulattanamudaiya Nayanar temple at Pulal. A portion of the land was also assigned to Alagaiya Tiruchchirambalamudaiyar who was to succeed Vagisa as the head of the matha. This Vagisa was, of course, different from the one mentioned in No. 371 of 1911 above.

208 of 1912 (Tamil) — On the same wall. An unfinished record of the Vijayanagara king Kampana Udaiyar II, dated S. 1290, Kilaka, Kumbha, su. di. 14, Asvati, corresponding

to Sunday, 11th February, 1369. Records that as the order of precedence in service to be followed by Ishabattaliyilar and Devaradiyar as settled in the fifth year of Rajanarayana Sambuvarayar by the Mudaliar of Melai matha in Perumbarrapuliyur, was not found to be satisfactory, Kamarasa Vittappa of Anaigundi inquired into temple affairs and instituted necessary changes. (Gives an example of the interference of central government in temple affairs.)

209 of 1912 (Tamil) — On the same wall. A record of the Chola king Tribhuvanachakravartin Konerimaikondan (i.e., Kulottunga III) in his twenty-seventh year and sixty-ninth day. Records gift of land for maintaining a special service called Tribhuvanaviransandi. The land (100 velis) was situated in Kulappakkam, also called Sivapadasekaranallur, a village in Puliyurkottam or Kulottungasolavalanadu and was granted rent-free on the Chitra Vishu day of the twenty-sixth year. The royal secretary (tirumandiraolai) was Minavan Muvendavelan. The document is signed by eight officers.

210 of 1912 (Tamil) — On the same wall. The Vijayanagara king Kampana Udaiyar records in Plavanga, Kambha, ba. di. 3, Wednesday (mistake), Attam, corresponding to Monday, 7th February, 1368, sale of a house to the temple of Tiruvorriyur-udaiya Nayanar at Tiruvorriyur, which was a ningal village.

211 of 1912 (Tamil) — On the same wall. The Chola king Tribhuvanachakravartin Rajarajadeva III records in his nineteenth year and forty-third day, Simha, su. di, an order on the occasion when he heard a temple Padiyilar sing in the Agamarga style in the Rajarajantirumandapam on the night of the eighth day of the Avani Tirunal. It was to detach sixty velis of land which had been purchased by a native of Velsharu, from Manali or Singavishnuchaturvedimangalam and to call it Uravakkinanallur as suggested by the temple trustees. See No. 142 above.

212 of 1912 (Tamil) — On the same wall. Rajanarayana Sambuvarayar refers in his fifth year to the settlement of the due order of precedence in temple service as among the Ishabattaliyilar, the Devaradaiyar, and the Padiyilar who had become either extinct or reduced after the former settlement during the office of Pottapparayar or Vanaraiyar in the reign of Perumal Sundara Pandyadeva (i.e., Jatavarman I, 1251-64) 'who took every country.' The inscription enumerates in detail their duties, see Ep. Rep. 1913, p.127-8.

213 of 1912 (Tamil) — On the same wall. Dated in the reign of the Vijayanagara king Sayana Udaiyar. Records in his seventh year, Vijaya, sale of land (2 karai) in the village Nayappakkam, also called Padiadumperumalnallur for maintaining certain festivals in the temple, by some residents of Pulal alias Rajasundarinallur (See also No.205 above). The God is called Mudaliyar-Padi-Aduvar.

214 of 1912 (Tamil) — On the same wall. A record of the Chola king Tribhuvanachakravartin Rajarajadeva III. Records in his fourth year, Dhanus, ba. di. Sodi and Ekadasi (Wednesday, 4th December, 1219), gift of 17 buffaloes and one lampstand of three flats by the chief of Parameswaramangalam or Solakulatilakachaturvedimangalam in Semburkottam, a district of Jayangondasolamandalam.

215 of 1912 (Tamil) — On the same wall. Registers a sale of two houses by the temple, to Mudaliyar Vagisuradeva of Kilai Matha at Tiruvarur. See No.207 above.

216 of 1912 (Tamil) — On the south wall of the Kali shrine inside the same temple. Records in the sixth year of Chola king Tribhuvanachakravartin Virarajendra Choladeva (Kulottunga III), a gift of money by Alagan Jnanasambandan, a native of Paluvur in Damarkottam, for the festival called Uttirayanasirappu in the temple. The money was deposited with three residents of Velsaru.

217 of 1912 (Tamil) — On the base of the stone pedestal of the Nataraja image in the Nataraja shrine of the same temple. Records that Virarajendran caused this pedestal to be built by Sivalokanadan of Tiruvenkadu.

218 of 1912 (Tamil) — On a slab built into the floor of the same shrine. A damaged record of the Chola king Rajaraja Rajakesarivarman, also called Rajarajadeva I dated in his nineteenth year. Seems to register sale of houses belonging to the temple.

219 of 1912 (Tamil) — On the east, the north, and the west bases of the same shrine. A record of the Chola king Parakesarivarman or Udaiyar Sri Adhirajendradeva. Records a sale of land in his third year, by the assembly of Sundarasolachaturvedimangalam in Pulalnadu, a district of Jayangondasolamandalam to the temple of Tiruvorriyur Udaiyar. Beginning and end built in.

210 of 1912 (Tamil) — On the same base. A record of the Chola king Rajakesarivarman or Udaiyar Sri Rajadhirajadeva I. Records in his twenty-eighth year sale of land for offerings in the temple of Karanai Vitankadeva at Tiruvorriyur, by the assemblies of Sundarasola-chaturvedimangalam and Vanavanmadevichaturvedi Mangalam. Beginning and end built in.

221 of 1912 (Tamil) — On the same base. A record of the Chola king Rajakesarivarman or Kulottunga Choladeva I. Records in his tenth year a gift of 30 kalams of paddy for offerings to the shrine of Kumaraswamideva, under orders from the officers Sundarasola Muvendavelar and Gurukalarayar. Beginning and end built in. [Some lands originally enjoyed by the Taliyilar are said to have been resumed and others given in stead.]

222 of 1912 (Tamil) — On the same base. Dated in the reign of the Chola king Rajakesarivarman alias Udaiyar Sri

Rajendra Choladeva (Kulottunga I). Records sale of land to the temple by the assemblies of the two villages mentioned in No.220 above. Beginning and end built in.

223 of 1912 (Tamil) — On the east wall of the mandapa in front of the same shrine. Records in Subhakrit, Panguni, twenty-ninth day, assignment of servants and a lamp to the temple of Tirruvorriyur Udaiyar Tambiranar, for the merit of Sadasivaraya, by Sarvarasa Kondamarasayya.

224 of 1912 (Tamil) — On the same wall. Dated in the reign of the Vijayanagara king Devaraya Maharaya II. Records in Virodhi, Adi, second day, a gift of paddy for offerings by a certain Alagiya Tiruchirrambalamudaiyan Nallanayanar of Pullur.

225 of 1912 (Tamil) — On the same wall. Dated in the reign of the Vijayanagara king Kumara Bukkana Udaiyar. Records in Kshaya, Kumba, su. di. 14, Friday, Pusam, gift of land by a dancing girl named Ainnuruttalaikkoli, for a special service which was to be named after her.

226 of 1912 (Tamil) — On the same wall. A record of the Vijayanagara king Virapratapa Devaraya Maharaya II. Records in Plavanga an order (rayasam) of the king to the effect that some lands which had originally been in the hands of the tenants and servants of the temple of Tirruvorriyur in Chandragirirajya and which had been taken away from them by a new system of lease introduced by the government, be redeemed and restored at the State cost; and that the taxes of Fodi, Mugamparvai, Angasalai, Sambadam, Viseshadayam, Arisi Kanam, Nallerudu, Narpasu, Vetti and Kattayam be henceforth collected by the Mahesvaras.

227 of 1912 (Tamil) — On the south base of the Subramanya shrine in the same temple. Records in the ninth year of the Chola king Tribhuvanachakravartin Rajarajadeva III, an order of Vira Narasimhadevan or Yadavarayan and the

gift of the village Periya Mullaivayil in Nayarunadu, a sub-
division of Pulalkottam, for offerings to the god Vira
Narasimhesvaramudaiya Nayanar, set up by him in the
verandah around the central shrine of the temple.

228 of 1912 (Tamil) — On the north base of the Gaurisvara
shrine in the same temple. Records in the fifth year of the Chola
king Rajakesarivarman or Udaiyar Sri Virarajendradeva I
(1063-70) sale of land to the temple of Tirruvorriyur Udaiya
Padambak Kanayakkar by the assemblies of Sundarasola-
chaturvedimangalam and Vanvanmadevichaturvedimangalam.
Another document which was drawn up in the sixth year of the
king is recorded in continuation. It consists also of a sale of
land by the assembly of Singavishnuchaturvedimangalam for
a garden (named Virarajendran Tirunandavan) founded by
Pasupati Tiruvarangadevan or Rajendra Muvendavelar of
Manakkaddi in Idayannadu, a sub-division of Virarajendra-
valanadu in Jayangondasolamandalam.

229 of 1912 (Tamil) — On the same base. Records in the
twenty-eighth year of Chakravartin Kulottunga Choladeva I,
sale of land to certain mendicants (tapasvi) of the temple,
by the assembly of Punnaivayil or Rajanayayana
Chaturvedimangalam. Beginning lost.

230 of 1912 (Tamil) — On the west base of the same
shrine. A record of the Chola king Rajakesarivarman or
Kulottunga Choladeva I, records in his tenth year, a gift of
90 sheep for a lamp by a native of Anangur in Panaiyurnadu,
a sub-division of Rajendrasolavalanadu.

231 of 1912 (Tamil) — On the south base of the same
shrine. Records a gift of a lamp by Chola king in his twelfth
year. End built in. Begins with the historical introduction
Tirumagal Jayamagal, etc.

232 of 1912 (Tamil) — On the same base. Records in the
fifth year of the Chola king Rajakesarivarman or Udaiyar Sri

Virarajendradeva I (1063-70) that this stone temple was constructed for Padambakkanayakkadeva by the chief mentioned in No. 228 above. The term Padambakka connects the place with the local tradition; but the government epigraphist points out that the present image of Gauliswara therein is not improbably that of Lakulisa himself.

233 of 1912 (Tamil verse) — On the same base. A record evidently in praise of Kulottunga Choladeva I.

234 of 1912 (Tamil) — On a pillar of the kitchen in the same temple. Records gift of gold (30 kalanjus) for a lamp to the temple of Tirruvorriyur Mahadeva. The amount was placed in the hands of the residents of Kandalur in Paiyyurkottam, a devadana village of Tiruvorriyur. Beginning lost.

235 of 1912 (Tamil) — On the second pillar of the same kitchen. A record of the Chola king Rajakesarivarman or Mummudi Choladeva Rajaraja I. Records in his third year, a gift of a gold necklace (pallitongal) called 'Rajarajan,' a shell-like cup of gold (Ottuvattil) called 'Mummudisolan' and a gold door for the mevasi, called 'Rajarajan,' by a certain Gunasilan of Mullikurumbu in Uraiyurkurram of the Chola country, for the merit of Adigal Niradi, chief of Urrukaddu, a village in Avurkurram of Sonadu, who was in charge of the temple affairs (srikarya) of the god Tiruvorriyur Alvar.

236 of 1912 (Grantha and Tamil) — On a broken pillar lying near the same. The Grantha portion mentions a military officer of Sirukalattur who was victorious at Nellore and was desirous of making a gift to the temple of Siva at Adhigrama. The Tamil portion refers to land which, not being tax-free before, was made tax-free in the thirty-eighth year of Chakravartin (Parantaka I) and given to same god; vide No. 160 above. Chitpuli was probably the E. Chalukyan Bhima II or some feudatory of his.

237 of 1912 (Tamil) — On a pillar lying near the shrine of the goddess in the same temple. Records gift of this door-

way called 'Ellandalaiyanna Perumal Tiruvaṣal,' for the merit
of Perumal Sundara Pandyadeva, by Enadi Merkudaiyan
Periyanayan or Pottappirayan. [The government epigraphist
identifies the king with Jatavarman Sundara Pandya I
(1251-64).]

238 of 1912 (Tamil) — On the gopura of the same temple,
right of entrance. Dated in the reign of Tribhuvanachakravartin
Vijayagandagopaladeva. Records in his fifteenth year, Makara,
su. di. sodi, (Monday, 2nd September, 1264), a gift of land for
feeding Mahesvaras in the Tirujnanasambhandamatha at
Tiruvorriyur, a village of Pularkottam or Vikkiramasolavalanadu in Jayangondasolamandalam by a merchant of
Tirunavalur, who purchased it from a certain Paduvurnadalvan
of Kattupakkam in Elumur Tudarmudi Nadu, a district of the
same kottam.

239 of 1912 (Tamil) — In the same place. A record of
Tribhuvanachakravartin Vijayagandagopaladeva in his third
year, Rishabha, su. di. 5, Anusham. Records gift of land at
Perungarai in Payyurkottam, to the matham of Nandikesvara
or Aryavratamkonda Mudaliar and his pupils, by a certain
Kidarattaraiyan.

240 of 1912 (Tamil) — In the same place. A damaged
record of the Vijayanagara king Savana Udaiyar I dated in his
ninth year (i.e. A D 1357). Mentions that some of the
agambadiyar, serving under the chief of Paduvur (viz.,
Kalingarayan, Sediyarayan, Adittan etc.) lived in the village
and served as *kaval* for a long time, neglected their duty for
reasons unexplained and caused much loss to the people and
so had to be punished.

241 of 1912 (Tamil) — On the same gopura, left of
entrance. Records in the second year, an order of Madurantaka
Pottapicholan. Remission of certain taxes payable by the
shepherds in consideration of five perpetual lamps maintained

by them in the temple of Tiruvorriyur Udaiya Nayanar. The document bears the signature of Manavijaya.

242 of 1912 (Tamil) — In the same place. A record of Tribhuvanachakravartin Sriranganadha Yadavarayar. Records in his sixteenth year Khara, Rishba, ba.di. 14, Tuesday, Urohani, a gift for a special service in the temple, called 'Kaliyurkilavansandi' by a resident of Serrupedu (Chetput) in Elumur Tudarmuninadu which was a sub-division of Pularkottam or Vikkiramasolavalanadu in Jayangondasola-mandalam, of land situated in Kaduvankottam or Aliyavradamkondavilagam, which was detached from Selaivasal in Pulalnadu and formed as a part of the western boundary of Tiruvorriyur.

243 of 1912 (Tamil) — In the same place. A record of Tribhuvanachakravartin Vijayagandagopaladeva in his twenty-first year, Simha, su.di. 5, Sodi, corresponding to Wednesday, 12th August, 1271. Gift of eight cows for a quarter lamp, by a resident of Tiruvorriyur.

244 of 1912 (Tamil) — In the same place. The Saluva king Narasingayadeva records in Chitrabanu Tai, 10, gift of the taxes sekkayam and magamai for maintaining a lamp and conducting repairs in the temple of Tiruvorriyur Udaiya Nayanar with the permission of Isura Nayakkar who was the agent of the king. (He was evidently the father of Narasa Nayaka).

245 of 1912 (Tamil) — On a pillar lying to the south of the tank in front of the same temple. The Chola king Uttamacholadeva (1070-86) , also called Parakesarivarman, records in his sixteenth year, a gift of 868 kalanjus of (tulai nirai) gold for a plate (kulit tattu) and of 40 kalanjus for offerings, to the temple of Tiruvorriyur Alvar, by Nandisaran or Parakesari Viluparayan of Elinur in Purangarambainadu, a district of Sonadu, who was the officer managing the temple affairs at the time. See 166 above.

246 of 1912 (Tamil) — On a pillar lying to the south of the same temple. A record of the Chola king Maduraikonda Rajakesarivarman (whom Mr. Krishna Sastri identifies with Gandaraditya.) Records in his fifth year, a gift of 90 sheep for a lamp by Kaduttalai Nagamayyan, son of Singamayyan of Kalesi. Perundaram who had accompanied Udaiyar Uttamasoladeva (Gandaraditya's son) to the temple of Tiruvorriyur Mahadeva.

104 of 1892 (Sanskrit) — East wall of the second prakara of the Adhipuriswara temple, right of entrance. A record of the Chola king Tammu Sidhi, dated 1129. The inscription gives the geneology of Tammu Siddhi's line and mentions Karikal Chola, Madhurantaka Pottapicholan etc. See Ep. Ind. VII, 148-52.

105 of 1892 (Sanskrit) — South wall of the first prakara of the Adhipuriswara temple. A record of the Chola king Rajendra, the son of Rajaraja.

106 of 1892 (Tamil) — West and south walls of the first prakara of the Adhipuriswara temple. A record of the Chola king Ko Rajakesarivarman or Rajendra Choladeva II (i.e., Kulottunga I) dated in his second year. A general grants 240 kasus which the temple authorities employ in purchasing land from 5 villages. (S.I.I. III, No.64, pp.132-4).

107 of 1892 (Tamil) — South wall of the first prakara of the Adhipuriswara temple. Records in the thirty-first year of the Chola king Ko Rajakesarivarman or Rajadhirajadeva a gift of land by Ariyammai who purchased the land from the Sabha.

108 of 1892 (Tamil) — West wall of the first prakara of the Adhipuriswara temple. A record of the Tribhuvanachakravartin Rajadhirajadeva dated in his sixth year.

109 of 1892 (Sanskrit) — North wall of the first prakara of the Adhipuriswara temple. A gift of lamp by one Madhurantaka in the thirtieth year of Jayadhara (i.e., Kulottunga Chola I). See

Ep. Ind. V. p.106. It is said to have been made for the merit of the 'illustrious Jnanamurti.'

110 of 1892 (Tamil) — North wall of the first prakara of the Adhipuriswara temple. A record of the Chola king Tribhuvanachakravartin Rajarajadeva, dated in his eleventh year. See Ep. Ind. VI, p.283.

399 of 1896 (Tamil) — On the south wall of the central shrine of the Adhipuriswara temple. A record of the Chola king Ko Parakesarivarman or Rajendra Choladeva I (1011-43) dated in his thirty-first year. Opens with the same historical introduction as the Tanjore inscription of the nineteenth year Chaturanana Pandita of Tirunarayana matha at Tiruvorriyur deposits 150 kasus in the temple treasury for Neyyadi during Margali Tiruvadirai. See S.I.I. II, No.20.

400 of 1896 (Tamil) — On the west wall of the same shrine. Records in the thirteenth year of the Pandya king Ko Jatavarman or Sundara Pandyadeva III (1276-90) a gift of land. See Ep. Ind. VI, 310-1, where Dr. Kielhorn points out that the exact date is Friday, 5th August, 1289.

401 of 1896 (Tamil) — On the same wall. A record of the Chola king Ko Rajakesarivarman or Kulottunga Choladeva dated in his seventh year. End built in.

402 of 1896 (Tamil) — On a stone built into the floor of the north wall of the first prakara of the same temple. The Chola king Ko Parakesarivarman records in his seventh year a gift of gold for a lamp.

403 of 1896 (Grantha and Tamil) — On the east wall of the second prakara of the same temple, left of entrance. A record of the Chola king Ko Rajakesarivarman or Rajadhirajadeva dated in his ninth year. Built in the middle.

404 of 1896 (Tamil) — On the same wall. A record of the Chola king Ko Parakesarivarman or Kulottunga Choladeva III 'who took Madurai and the crowned, head of the Pandya,'

dated in his nineteenth year. Built in the middle.

405 of 1896 (Grantha and Tamil) — On the north wall of the same prakara. Records in the ninth year of the Chola king Tribhuvanachakravartin Rajadhirajadeva (II?) a gift of cows for a lamp.

NOTES

1. Partha is another name for Arjuna and Sarathi means driver. As Krishna acted as charioteer to Arjuna during the great Mahabharata war he is named Parthasarathi. It was then that the world-known *Gita* was delivered. There is a very fine sculptural representation of this scene in the temple of Pushpagiri, in the Cuddapah district, which the Saivites call Madhya Kailasam being midway between Benares and Uttara or north Kailasa) and Chidambaram (Dakshina or south Kailasa) and the Vaishnavites, Tirumala Madhya Ahobilam, being midway between Tirupati and Ahobilam.

2. Balarama, according to some authorities, is considered to be one of the ten avatars of Vishnu. He possessed immense strength and was much occupied in agricultural labour. As a patron of the art of agriculture, his figure is always represented with a country plough as a symbol in one of his hands. So he is 'the bearer of the plough,' as his sculptures show him. There is a figure of his, along with those of Krishna and their sister Subhadra, in the famous temple of Jagannath Puri. Also in the temple of Tiruchchanur (Lower Tirupati is a shrine containing the images of Sri Krishna, Balarama, etc.

3. This image in a standing posture is said to represent the personified form of Adisesha.

4. This is the personified form of the chakra (discus) of Vishnu and in this he is represented in standing attitude.

5. The merit of tapas or penance is believed to be proportionate to its length and severity. Its power controls gods and men alike.

6. Brindavana is a famous place of pilgrimage in northern India.

It is situated at a distance of about 6 miles to the north of Mathura, with a Railway station of its own. The river Yamuna (Jamna) passes through it. The Yadavas (shepherds) when troubled by Kamsa, uncle of Sri Krishna, emigrated to this place. Here, in this river, Sri Krishna performed very many of his lilas (sports) with the gopis.

7. There are eight different kinds of marriage — (1) *brahma*, in which a girl of noble descent is married to one of the same order who is also a good Vedic scholar, after adorning the girl in the best jewels possible; (2) *daivam*, in which a girl adorned with the most fashionable and valuable jewels possible is married to a ritvika at the beginning of a yajna, or sacrifice, after worshipping him; (3) *arsham*, in which a girl is married to one after accepting from him the gift of a cow for the propagation of dharma; (4) *prajapatyam*, in which a girl is given to a person after telling him that they should jointly propagate dharma; (5) *rakshasa*, where the girl is carried off by force without the consent of the girl's party; (6) *gandharvam*, where clandestine marriage is done by mutual consent; (7) *asuram*, where money is paid for the girl for marriage; and (8) *pisacha*, where a person marries a girl who is not able to maintain her virtue on account of administering to herself soporific drugs. There is yet another kind of marriage called *atra*, where the parents marry the two people after noticing strong signs of love in both.

8. *Inscriptions of the Madras Presidency*, Government of Madras, 1919, Vol. II pp. 988-89.

9. There is a similar representation of this figure, where the goddess in the form of a peacock worships the linga, on the western side of the east gopura of Sri Mayuranathaswami temple at Mayavaram.

10. Siva is generally worshipped in the form of the linga (phallus) fixed in a circular or quadrangular receptacle on a high monolithic pedastal known as Yoni Panivattam or Avadaiyar.

11. He is one of the 63 devotees called Nayanars (Nayan in Tamil means chief). The sculptures of the 63 saints are to be found in the covered passage around the sanctum in all Siva temples.

They occupy a prominent position on account of their extreme
devotion, under the most trying circumstances as a means of
testing their devotion. This Brahman youth (Sambandar) was
born in Shiyali. When very young, his parents were bathing in
the tank within the temple leaving the baby on the bank. When
he wept for his mother's milk the goddess herself is said to have
descended and satisfied the need of the boy! Thereafter he had
the divine blessing and went round visiting various shrines and
singing songs in praise of the presiding god everywhere. While
worshipping the god in Tirukkolakka a pair of divine golden
Talam (cymbals) was put into his hands! His sculptures are
shown as holding these. By his songs he cured several incurable
diseases and also removed the poverty of the country! He
reconverted the Pandya king who adhered to Jainism. In one
place the female palm tree was converted into a male one! In
Mylapore he resuscitated the cremated bones of a Chetti girl!

12. He is one of the twelve Vaishnava saints called Alwars found
in most Vishnu temples. They were extreme in their devotion
and were deified. Peyalwar, Bhudattalwar and Poygaialwar hold
a special position of their own.

13. A well-polished stature of the saint Pattinattu Pillaiyar is placed
in the east gopuram (tower) of the temple at Tiruvidamaruthur,
near Kumbakonam, and he is said to have lived in the holy place
for a long time and performed many miracles there. He was
born to a Chetti merchant in Cauveripatam. He is supposed to
be an amsa of Kubera, the god of wealth. When Siva was taking
an aerial flight with his retinue inclusive of Kubera, when
nearing Tiruvendadu, Kubera desired to be born on earth, and
that in accordance with this wish this saint was born. He visited
various shrines and worked several miracles. At last in
Tiruvorriyur near Madras he quit this world, and there is a
temple in memory of this incident at the place.

14. Madras Epigraphical Department (Annual Reports published
by the Government of Madras), 1912-13, p.86.

15. *Inscriptions of the Madras Presidency*, Government of Madras,
1919, Vol.I, pp. 431 to 459.

Chapter 2

CONJEEVARAM

This place of pilgrimage, one of the seven holy cities of India, lies in north latitude 12°50', east longitude 79°46'. The sacred river Vegavati passes on the west of the town and the town is studded with temples dedicated both to Siva and Vishnu. On this account arose the proverb 'If you go to Conjeevaram you may eat without labour meaning thereby that there are plenty of Choultries'. It was the seat both of the Pallavas and Cholas. Jainas also occupied the town and traces of their architecture are still to be found within the suburb called Tirupparuttikunram.

Inscriptions in plenty are met with in most temples and these offer plenty of information for making out the history of ancient Hindu kings of various lines.

The Saptapuris, or the seven holy cities of India, are Conjeevaram, Ayodhya or Oudh, Mathura or Muttra, Maya or Haridwar, Kasi or Benares, Avantika and Dwaraka. Of these, three are sacred to Siva, and three to Vishnu; while Conjeevaram is pre-eminent, for it is sacred both to Siva and Vishnu. This last city, situated at a distance of about 45 miles on the southwest of Madras, is the best place for the close study of the antiquarian remains of southern India. Saivism, Vaishnavism, Buddhism, and Jainism have all had their influence here in turn and have left behind distinct traces of their existence in the architectural peculiarities of the place. At one time, the city is said to have possessed 108 Saiva temples and 18 Vishnu temples.

According to the epigraphical records now available, the country in which Conjeevaram is situated was originally named Tundapa Vishaya, the Tamil equivalent of which was Tondaimandalam, during the period of Tundapa Vishaya Pallava ascendancy; later on it was called Jayangondasola-mandalam, when the Chola kings acquired possession of the territory about the 11th century. According to the Chinese pilgrim, Hiuen Tsang, who visited India about the 7th century, Buddhism had a strong influence in this city at that time. He mentions several hundreds of *Sangharamas*, and a large number of priests of that time. This city, he says, was the capital of the Dravida country and about 6 miles in circumference, and the people were superior in bravery, learning, and piety, to all others he had met with in his travels all over India. The revival of Saivism by Sri Sankara, and of Vaishnavism under its able exponent Sri Ramanuja contributed in a large measure to the decline of Buddhism and Jainism.

It is mentioned in some of the Tamil works that the heart of the town was exclusively occupied by Brahmans. The houses of the agricultural and other classes, the temple of the Tiruvekha and the Royal Palace were all situated outside the town. Provisions for the training of the cavalry and infantry was made on the outskirts of the town. When a severe famine struck the country, the king on the advice of his counsellors, dug a large tank to the southwest of the city and laid out a large garden on its banks, affording relief to the sufferers.

SAIVA TEMPLES
SRI KAMAKSHI AMMAN TEMPLE

The temple of Kamakshi Amman is the most important. Here the goddess is depicted in the form of a *Yantra*. The city was built strictly according to the rules laid down in the Sastras. In the case of almost all Hindu temples the image of the goddess is always associated with *Chakra*, Yantra or *Peetha* (geometrical figures enclosing mystic letters) and the sculptural representations rest on Chakra which is embedded in the earth, and which accounts for the puja or worship being performed at the feet of the image. But in the Kamakshi Amman temple the Chakra is placed in front of the idol which is peculiar.

At one time when the influence of the deity began to decline, Sri Sankaracharya, (whose image too is worshipped in the temple even today), put up a peetham in front of the deity with the Ashtalakshmis cut on the cardinal points, and thus brought back thoroughly the power of the deity. To the northeast of the temple tank there is a Vishnu shrine. There is a small shrine of the goddess Annapurna (bestower of food in plenty) within the temple.

SRI EKAMBARANATHA TEMPLE

Ekambaranatha's temple is another important temple of Siva. On the walls of the temple of Ekambaranatha, there is a sculptural figure of the destruction of Kama (lust) by Siva. Karikkal Chola, who is said to have carried out many repairs to the temple, is also represented. The shrine has a mango tree and great sanctity is attached to it, on account of the fact that Siva appeared unto the goddess Parvati under this tree, when She prayed for him near the Vegavati river. In accordance with this legend there is a sculptural representation of the goddess embracing Siva in the temple of Saktimuttam at Pattisvaram,

near Kumbakonam. Tirukkurippuththonda[1] Nayanar's fame is
connected with this place.

One of the inscriptions in this temple furnishes the pedigree
of the Kakatiya rulers of Warangal. Another records that
Bhuvanekavira (Bhuvanaikavira) or Samarakolahala granted
both to this Ekambara and the neighbouring Kamakshi temple
two villages in Pandyamandalam (Pandya country), which
were called after him Samarakolahalanalur, Bhuvanekaviranallur
in Saka 1391. Coins issued by this king bear on the obverse
a kneeling figure of Garuda and on the reverse the Tamil legend
Bhuvanekaviran and Samarakolahalan.

In the temple of Kailasanatha there is a figure of
Ardhanariswara (the deity as a hermaphrodite). The feminine
aspect has a *veena* or violin in her hand, while the masculine
aspect of Siva, is seated on a bull. This model is peculiar to
this place.

The inscriptions here open with a benediction addressed
to Ganga and the mythical pedigree of the Pallavas, the
founder of the race of Pallavas. In the race of these Pallavas
was born Rajasimha who built this temple and called it after
his own name Rajasimha Pallaveswara or Rajasimheswara. In
front of the central shrine is a small shrine styled nowadays as
Naradeswara and there are inscriptions therein stating that
Mahendra, the son of Rajasimha and grandson of Lokaditya,
built this shrine which he called Mahendreswara after his own
name. An enumeration of 700 *birudas* of King Rajasimha are also
recorded. The date of the foundation of this temple is sometime
in 567 A.D. During the reign of Kulottunga Choladeva this
temple was closed, its landed property sold and its compound
and environs transferred to the temple of Anekatangavadam.

This temple is famous for the beauty of its sculptures. It
stands secluded to the west of the town and its plan is peculiar
in having a series of cells with sculptures within.

In the temple of Kachchapeswara Vishnu in the form of a kurma (tortoise) is shown worshipping Siva. The name Kachchipedu is given to the place in some inscriptions.

The sanctum walls of the Jvarahareswara are built in a semi-circular form, which is peculiar.

The Merrali (western temple) is in the Weavers' Quarters, also known as Pillayar Palayam, evidently so named after the boy saint Sambanda. The other shrines of Onakanteswar near the Sarvatirtham tank, Anegatangavadam, Airavateswara, Tirurkaraikadu spoken of as Nerikkaraikadu in the Periyapurana, one mile east of Conjeevaram, and Chitragupta[2] have traditions of their own.

VISHNU TEMPLES

The most important temples of Vishnu in this town are Varadaraja, Vaikuntaperumal, Pandavadutar, Vilakkoliperumal or Tiruttanka, Ashtabhuja and Ulagalandaperumal. These Vaishnava temples are in the western part of the town, and owing to their small number compared to that of the temples of Siva, the locality is called 'Little Conjeevaram' or 'Vishnu Conjeevaram.' The other locality is called 'Big Conjeevaram' or 'Siva Conjeevaram.'

The ancient name of the Pandavadutar temple was Tiruppadegam (Padagam of the Prabhandas). The inscriptions in this temple refer to the victories of Kulottunga Choladeva or Rajendra Choladeva at Sakkarakkottam and Vayiragaram. He is also said to have vanquished the king of Kuntala country and that he crowned himself as king of the country on the banks of the Kaveri, i.e., of the Chola country.

The last temple Ulagalanda Perumal is identified as the Uragam (Sanskrit Uraka) of the Prabhandam and therein is said to have stood the Karikala Terri hall, so called after the ancient Chola king Karikala. Though this hall does not exist now, inscriptions prove its existence in the olden days.

SRI VARADARAJA TEMPLE

The temple of Varadaraja is built on a hillock called Hastigiri Satyavratakshetra or Attiyur and Brahma is said to have performed a sacrifice here.

Vijayanagar king Achyuta Raya visited the Varadaraja Perumal (Arulala Perumal) temple at Conjeevaram with his queen and two sons on the day of the Mula asterism, which was a Sunday and the 12th tithi of the first half of the Solar month Karkata of the Nandana year, while the visit to the Kamakshi temple took place next year. This king also gave 17 villages to this temple, while the Kamakshi temple got only 8. The former got, in addition, silk cloths and a breast plate in which diamonds, lapis lazuli, saphires, rubies, emeralds, topaz and a large number of pearls were embedded. About two months after the date of the first grant, the king presented to this temple a conch, a discus, a pair of bands uplifted for protection and a Vaishnava forehead mark — all adorned with jewels. The conquest of Kalinga by King Vikrama Chola and the name of his queen Mukkokkilanadigal are also mentioned. It is said that King Ravivarma or Kulasekhara or Sangramadhira of Yadu race was born in Saka 1188, married to a Pandya princess, ascended the Kerala throne at the age of 33 years (i.e., Saka 1221), conquered Vira Pandya and got himself crowned in the bank of the Vegavati (Vaigai at Madurai) at the age of 46 (Saka 1234).

The ancient records of this place show that King Achyuta Raya of the Vijayanagar dynasty visited the temple and in commemoration of his visit he made large presents of pearls and a thousand cows. This important ceremony is called *Tulapurushadhana*[3] (weighing against pearls). It is also recorded that this city was visited by many ancient kings of India when this same meritorious ceremony also called

Tulabhara (weighing oneself against gold) and the gifts called Mahabhutaghata[4] were performed, and the wealth was subsequently endowed for the worship of the god or distributed among the deserving people. The 16 gifts prescribed for kings are mentioned in one of the inscriptions at Nagalapuram, Chingleput district, viz., Brahmandam, Visvakchakram, Gadam, Mahabhudam, Rathnadhenu, Saptambothi, Kalpavriksha, Kamadhenu, Svarnakshima, Hiranya-asva, Hiranya-ratha, Tulapurusha, Gosahasra, Hemagarbha, Panchalanga and Hemakumbha.[5]

[6]"According to the inscription on the slab in front of the Thayar shrine in the Varadarajaswami temple the Delhi emperor Aurangzeb fitted out an expedition about 1688 A.D. against the Mahrattas of the South. Conjeevaram, as well as several other important centres of South India, felt the shock of this iconoclastic invasion. The temple authorities of the three premier temples of that city thereupon apprehending desecration at the profane hands of the invaders, disguised the images of the temple gods as corpses and conveyed them secretly out of the town and found an asylum in the jungles of Udayarpalayam in the Trichinopoly district. But when the danger was past and Conjeevaram was considered safe, the local chieftain of Udayarpalayam, who was much enraptured at the image of the god refused to restore it to its original abode at Kanchi, with the result that at the special intercession of Attan Jiyar, his disciple Lala Todarmalla terrorised the chief with a strong contingent of troops at his back and safely brought back the image and reinstated it in the temple with great pomp and splendour in Saka 1632, (1710 A.D.). This incident is even today commemorated in an annual festival called the Udayarppelayam festival. A set of three statues, probably those of Todarmalla is left uncared for in a lamp room in the recess of the gopura called Tondaradippodi Vasal."

"On the southern wall there is another important and interesting record dated in Saka 1645 (1723 A.D.) referring to the starting of a water-supply project by digging an underground aqueduct from the Sarvatirtham tank to the tank within this temple which could catch up the spring water percolating from the river-bed near the village of Ambil."

SRI VAIKUNTHA PERUMAL TEMPLE

Various forms of Vishnu are depicted in sculpture in the temple of Vaikuntha Perumal. The famous Vaishnava saint Tirumangai Alwar has composed several verses in praise of the deity of this place. This is also the birthplace of another saint Poygai Alwar.

The important and interesting feature of this temple is that the central shrine has tiers of 3 shrines, one over the other, with figures of Vishnu in each shrine.

[7]"The four walls of the raised verandah, which runs round the central shrine of this temple, are covered with two rows of sculptures separated by a small belt, which was apparently intended for engraving notes explaining the sculptures. They are divided into a number of compartments each of which was evidently meant to denote a particular event in contemporary history. The original sculptures are considerably mutilated but the temple authorities have tried to repair them with brick and mortar. The explanatory notes have not been filled in completely, but are found only on a small portion of the south verandah and explain 13 compartments of the upper row of sculptures. The first of these notes refers to the death of Paramesvaravarman of the Pallava family which was descended from the god Brahma, and mentions the Mahamatras, the Ghatakayar, the Mulaprakriti and Hiranyavarma Maharaja. It is partially damaged but ends with the Tamil word idam or 'place.' The second compartment ends with the words enru sonna idam or 'the place where (he)

said that..... The fourth mentions Srimalla Ranamalla, Samgramamalla and Pallavamalla and ends with the words Paramesvaran nan povenenru toludu ninra idam. The place where Paramesvara stood in a worshipping (posture) saying "he would go." Subsequently, Hiranyavarma Maharaja and Dharani Konda Posar are mentioned; also the nagarathar (i.e., the citizen of Conjeevaram), the mulaprakriti and Muttarayar. Mention is also made of the coronation (abisheka) of some person, whose name cannot be made out.

After the death of Paramesvaravarman II, Nandivarman, son of Hiranyavarman, was chosen by his subjects. It may, therefore, be concluded that the sculptures were intended to represent the various events connected with the accession of Nandivarman, who might be the prince referred to in the notes as Pallavamalla. As the Vaikuntha Perumal temple was called Paramesvara Vinnagaram very probably after the Pallava king Paramesvaravarman II, it may be supposed that both the sculptures and the explanatory notes accompanying them were cut out soon after the temple itself was built."

SRI SANKARACHARYA MUTT

The math of Sri Sankaracharya, known as Kamakoti Pitha, was situated in Kanchipuram until 1686 A.D. During the earlier part of its history it was located in Vishnukanchi on the west of the temple of Hastisailanatha i.e., of the Varadarajaswami and at a later period a new math was erected in Siva Kanchi. Pratapa Simha, the Raja of Tanjore, invited the then Swami to Tanjore where a temple was constructed for the goddess Kamakshi. As Kumbakonam seemed to have better suited the inclinations of the Swami, King Sarfoji of Tanjore, in the Saka[8] year 1743, constructed the present math in Kumbakonam.

The Historical Sketches of Ancient Dekhan says:

"One of the most ancient cities of southern India, which

retains at the present day part at least of its past greatness, is Conjeevaram in the Chingleput district.[9]

Everyone knows that it is a chief centre of pilgrimage in the Dekhan resorted to by a large concourse of people of both the Vaishnava and Saiva creeds. Unlike Madurai, Uraiyur[10] and Cranganore[11] the capitals of the Pandya, the Chola and the Chera sovereigns, this city which was once the capital of the Pallavas abounds in structural monuments of early ages containing a very large number of lithic records from which it is possible to make out its history from the earliest times.[12]

If any city of southern India has a claim to our study on account of its antiquarian interest, Conjeevaram is pre-eminently one among them[13]. The time-honoured sculptural monuments enshrined in the city show to some extent the importance of the place; and there is not the least doubt that in its entrails lie hidden more interesting specimens of olden times awaiting the application of the explorer's spade to come into view. When the city rose into prominence, how many dynasties of kings ruled over it, what vicissitudes of life it witnessed and the degree of civilisation it reached in the past, are questions whose solution would interest any student of ancient history.

The place is variously called Kachchipedu, Kachchi, Kanchipuram and Kanchchi. The form Kachchipedu[14] of which Kachchi[15] is a contraction, occurs in early inscriptions and is perhaps the fullest and the most original. Both Kachchi and Kanchi find place in Tamil works composed in the middle of the 7th century A.D.[16] The popular form Kanchi[17] is an authorised change from Kachchi obtained by softening the hard consonant. Kanchi is a further change from Kanchi and is derived by the lengthening of the initial short consonant. These changes are supported by rules of Tamil grammar[18]. We may also note here the opinion of some that Kanchi is the

Sanskritised form of the name Kachchipedu[19]. Dr. Burnell gave out that the Sanskrit Kanchi is a mistranslation of the Dravidian Kanchi[20] Varahamihira locates Kanchi in the southern division[21] and Hiuen Tsang calls this Kin-chi-pulo and states that it was the capital of Ta-lo-pi-cha, i.e., Dravida, and that it was 30 li round[22].

Some of the early records omit to give the name of the district in which the town was situated. They mention only the larger division Tundaka Vishaya[23]. It may be noted that this term had several variants, viz., Tondira, Tundira, Tonda, Tondai, etc.[24] The Tamil equivalent of it is Tondaimandalam. Twenty-four districts called Kottam were comprised in this division[25] and Kanchipuram, was the principal town in one of them viz., Eyilkottam[26]. During the time of the Chola King Rajaraja I, i.e., at the beginning of the 11th century A.D., the name Tondaimandalam was changed into Jayangondasolamandalam after one of the surnames of that king and it was by this latter name the territory was known for several centuries i.e., until the Vijayanagar times.[27] But it may be said that though the original names of villages, districts and sub-divisions of a country underwent changes at different periods in the history of their existence and were known sometimes by two names and at other times exclusively by the new names, the original names survived to the very last while the intermediate ones died out completely.[28] We have an instance of this in the name Tondaimandalam and its later equivalent Jayangondacholamandalam.

References of this ancient city are not wanting. The facts connected with the place incline one to the belief that from the earliest times it was a stronghold of people of various religions. From the Chinese pilgrims Hiuen Tsang, we learn that as far back as the 5th century B.C. when Tathagata, i.e., Buddha was living in this world he frequented this country much; he preached the law here and converted men; and therefore, the king Asoka built stupas at all the sacred spots where these traces exist. Kanchipuram was the native place of Dharmapala Boddhisatva who assumed the robes of a recluse and attained a brilliant reputation.[29] To the south of the city, not a great way off, is a large Sangharama frequented by men of talent and learning and there is a stupa about 100 ft. high built by King Asoka.[30] At best we can only regard this account of the pilgrim as a record of what the people of Conjeevaram had to say in the 7th century A.D. concerning the origin of Buddhism in the place. But even as representing the belief or tradition of the 7th century, the reference is certainly valuable. The truth of the pilgrim's account cannot be assumed without subjecting it to scrutiny. We are not in a position to test the correctness of the first part of the statement which connects Buddha with Kanchi. As Buddhism does not appear to have made any real progress in the south during the lifetime of its founder, we are inclined to think that the statement is not grounded on solid fact. But it is not improbable that at the time of Asoka, Buddhist stupas came to be erected at Conjeevaram. Though the edicts of Asoka do not include the capital of Dravida among the places to which he sent missionaries, the Sinhalese chronicle Mahavansa gives a long list of countries to which the Buddhist apostles were sent by the Maurya Emperor.[31] Some of these countries are in the neighbourhood of Dravida. An inscription of Asoka has been discovered at Siddhapura in the Mysore state, the ancient Mahishamandala.[32] The countries of the Pandya, Chola and Keralaputra, and where Buddhism found votaries at the time of Asoka, are not far off from Conjeevaram. It will not be a wild conjecture, therefore, to suppose that some of the missionaries to these parts exercised their influence at Conjeevaram as well and were instrumental in building the monasteries and stupas referred to by Hiuen Tsang. That

Conjeevaram had in early days a large number of sangharamas and mendicants of high order, is also learnt from the Tamil work *Manimegalai* which states that at the time when the Chola capital Kaverippumpattinam was destroyed by the encroachment of the sea, the inhabitants of that place moved to Conjeevaram and changed their faith to Buddhism[33]. We are here informed that Ilankilli, the brother of the Chola king Todukalarkilli also built a big Buddhist monastery at Conjeevaram[34]. The book completely bears testimony to the pilgrim's words that there were some hundreds of sangharamas and 10,000 priests at the time of his visit i.e. in the middle of the 7th century A.D.[35]. These monuments of the Buddhists should have been constructed by the Pallavas, who ruled the country at the time the pilgrim visited the place and prior to it for several centuries. But it must be noted that the vestiges of Buddhist influence at Kanchi have all disappeared without a single exception. The religious revival[36] of Saivism[37] and Vaishnavism[38] is perhaps the chief cause of the disappearance of Buddhist and Jaina monuments of the place.

As the principal objects of interest in the city have already been stated to consist in its temples, even a meagre account of the place should not fail to mention at least the more important of them. The earliest Hindu temples of the place are those noticed in the Devaram and the Nalayiraprabhandam. Tirukkachchi Ekambam[39] and Nerikaraikkadu[40] are celebrated in the hymns of Jnanasambandha who lived in the middle of the 7th century A.D. Meerali[41] is mentioned by Jnanasambandha's contemporary, Appar Sundaramurti who could be assigned to the 8th century A.D. has sung in praise of Anekatangavadam[42] and Onkandanrali.[43] It may be said that the first three of these temples were in existence prior to the 7th century and that the last two attained notoriety in the interval between the time of Jnanasambandha and Sundaramurti. Of these, the

Ekambaranatha temple contains the celebrated earth linga, one of the five famous lingas of southern India.[44] The ancient name of the modern Ekambaranatha is Ekamban and this name seems to be connected with Kambai, i.e., the river Vegavati on whose banks the town is situated. In fact one of the stanzas in Jnanasambandha's hymns bears out this view. At present they trace the origin of the name Ekambaranatha to a single mango tree found in the temple. Onakandan means the lover of the constellation Sravana. Merrali should have been so-called on account of its position on the western side. The significance of the term Anekatangavadam is not apparent. Perhaps this temple was situated in a forest or garden frequented by a large concourse of people and was on that account called by that name. Besides the temples enumerated above, the Pallava king Rajasimha built a stone temple of Siva called Rajasimheswara and this is now known as Kailasanatha. An inscription found in it registers the fact that when Vikramaditya, the western Chalukya king, invaded the Pallava dominions, he renovated this temple. The shrine of Muktiswara, whose vicinity is now kept in a most deplorable state is another Pallava structure, as clearly evidenced by an inscription of Nandivaram dated in the 28th year of the king.[45] According to this record, the ancient name of the temple was Dharmamahadevivara. It should have been called after Dharmamhadevi, probably a Pallava queen. So far no epigraph refers to this lady. The sculptural representations on either side of the mendapa in front of the central shrine of this temple bear bold outlines and fineness of touch, though very much damaged.

Among the Vishnu temples of the place, fourteen are mentioned in the songs of Alvars, and Professor Hultzsch has identified the following six of them from a study of their inscriptions.[46] Tiruppadagam,[47] Tiruttanka,[48] Attabuyagaram,[49] Uragam,[50] Attiyur[51] and Parameswarinnagaram[52] are respectively the Pandava Perumal, Vilakkolli Perumal, Ashtabhuja, Ulaganada Perumal, Varadaraja and Vaikuntha Perumal temples of Conjeeveram. The remaining eight are Vellukkai[53] now called Mugundanayaka, Niragam[54] now known as Jagannatha Perumal, Nilatingaltundam,[55] Tiruvehka[56] also called Yadoktakari, Karagam i.e., the modern Karunakara Perumal, Karvanam, Kalvar, i.e., Tirukkalvanar, the Varaha Perumal and Pavalavannar. From an inscription in the Vaikuntha Perumal temple, we learn that its ancient name was Parameswara Vishnugriha and it is, therefore, evident that it was built by the Pallava king Paramameswara, the immediate predecessor of Nandivarman Pallavamalla, whose military achievements are recorded in the hymns of the saint Tirumangai Alvar.[57] The peculiar feature of this temple consists in its sculptures found on the four walls of the raised verandah running round the central shrine, all of which represent particular events in contemporary history of the time of Nandivarman Pallavamalla, as noted in the labels engraved below them.[58] The temple of Varadaraja is the biggest structure in Little Conjeevaram. It is said to be literally covered with inscriptions, the decipherment of which will surely reveal valuable information regarding the history of the place.

In the last quarter of the 8th century A.D. Kanchipuram was subjected to the influence of Sankaracharya, the powerful exponent of the Advaita philosophy. He is believed to have subdued the power of Kamakshi who in the form of Kali, is said to have been causing havoc at nights till his day. Sankara is said to have extracted a promise from the goddess that without his permission she would not stir out of the temple. There is an image of the reformer in the Kamakshi temple before which they halt the procession of the goddess whenever the latter is taken into the town in order that she may take permission. Whatever the truth of this may be, there is not much doubt as to Sankara's connection with Kanchi where he is said to have established his matha. That he was an ardent worshipper of Ramakotyambika is also fairly certain. It may be added that but for the importance attached to the town as a place of religious activity from very early times, even the little of his history that is now preserved would not have come down to us.

Tamil literature often describes the place as being situated on the bank of the river Kambai,[59] which is another name for Vegavati,[60] as being strongly fortified and resplendent with towering palaces,[61] as having high fort walls[62] which were surrounded by a deep moat[63] and as containing a number of weavers' families[64] and big streets fit for cars to run upon.[7"]

INSCRIPTIONS

The inscriptions recorded in the walls of the various temples have been copied by the Epigraphical Department during the years 1888, 1890, 1893, 1895, 1900, 1906, 1910, 1919 and 1921. Besides these there is also a copper plate in the Madras Museum belonging to the time of King Uttama Chola of the 10th century published in the South Indian Inscriptions Vol.III, part III, pages 267 to 279. It says:

"The inscriptions also supply some valuable information about the town Kachehipedu (i.e. modern Conjeevaram). Four quarters are referred to, viz., Kambutanpadi; Atimanappadi; Kanjagappadi and Erruvalichcheri which are mostly inhabited by weavers who were patronised by the king and consisted of two sections of pattasalins. The appointment of these pattasalins as the managers of the temple and the royal patronage extended them suggests the high social status which they must have been enjoying at this early period. Even now the name Pillaipalayam given to the weavers' quarters suggests the favourite position which these weavers occupied either with reference to the temple or to the king — the word pillai or Pillaiyar being frequently applied in this sense..........The Saiva quarters Ranajayappadi, Ekavirappadi and Vamanasankarappadi of Conjeevaram are also mentioned. Solaniyamam seems to have been still another such quarter of Conjeevaram in which the inhabitants were exempt from all taxes in consideration of their payment of fixed quantities of rice and oil to the temple of Uragam. In this connection it is also interesting to learn that this quarter of Solaniyamam was at first inhabited by a class of people known as Tolachcheviyar or Elakkaiyar. Tolachcheviyar literally means "those whose ears are not bored" and "Elkkaiyar" 'those whose bands would not accept gifts.' The first is, perhaps, the opposite of Karnapravritas mentioned in the Tanjore inscription and of Tollaikkadar, a term applied to the tribes of Maravan, Kallan, Sanan, etc. Two other cheris of Kachchipedu which we learn from the inscriptions were Tundunukkachcheri whose lands were watered by the two irrigation channels named respectively 'the high-level sluice' and 'the low-level sluice' and Virappadi. Whether these several quarters (padi or cheri in Tamil and vati or vataka in Sanskrit) were suburban villages adjoining Conjeevaram or the different quarters of that city cannot be ascertained. Conjeevaram must have also been the seat of the king whose palace is referred to therein. The temple of Uragam (known as Uraka in Sanskrit) at Kachchipedu is mentioned in the Nalayiraprabhandam and has been identified with the present Ulagalanda Perumal, some of whose inscriptions mention the temple by that name. The Karikkalaterri hall which formed an important portion of the temple must have been so called after the ancient Chola king Karikala. The present temple of Ulagalanda Perumal which is in a badly neglected condition shows that the surrounding hall, if at all contemporaneous with the central shrine, must have been renovated in a much later period and could not represent the old Karikkala-terri.

"Kolnirai Kuli and Kalavu Kuli which were assigned to the temple of Uragam are explained in the Sanskrit portion as "tolls on (articles) measured by weight (tula) and by capacity (*prastha*)." The city had a strong guild of merchants (Nagara, Nagarattar or Managarattom) who apparently represented the city council with a chief person (Managaramalvan) at their head. The guild was given full liberty to supervise the proper management of the temple business, to appoint the watchmen and clerks of the temple and to exempt these latter from payment of (municipal) taxes. An item of interesting information supplied by the record is that a Brahmana knowing the Vedas was appointed for worship in the temple of Uragam, only in case a person conversant with the Vaishnava system of temple-worship (*koyilnambu*) was not available. Vedic Brahmanas, as a rule, do not appear to have had anything to do with temple-worship from early times. The details of expenditure recorded in the grant on account of the several festivals were audited by the chief merchant and the annual supervision committee and all difficulties in way of the proper conduct of the charities were to be removed by the Vaishnava devotees of the temple, in the 18 Nadus.

"The geographical names that occur in the inscription, viz., Kuram, Ariyar Perumbakkam, Ulaiur and Olukkaipakkam, are all situated in the Chingleput district and are respectively identical with Kuram and Ariyaperumbakkam in the Conjeevaram Taluk and Olaiyur and Olukkarai in the Madurantakam Taluk. Sikkal, the native village of an officer Solamuvendavelan, is identical with Sikkil near Negapatam in the Tanjore district."

[66]"An inscription from Conjeevaram (No. 35 of 1921) dated in *Saka* 1378, Dhatu, corresponding to A.D. 1456-57, records the duties that had to be performed by Srikaranachchiyar in return for the 400 *kuli* of land granted to him. He had to sing daily hymns to god Karanisvaram Udaiya Nayanar, to provide a garland and to sing hymns, besides providing arecanuts when god Ekambaranatha halts at the entrance of the karanisvara temple under a special canopy. The reception (*mandapa padi*) of the god Ekambaranatha on important festival days at the entrance of the Karanisvara temple is continued even to this day."

"Another inscription from Conjeevaram (No. 29 of 1921) gives us an idea of the constitution of the *sannidhi* (facing the temple-street) of the Sonnavannamseyda Perumal temple. The surroundings of a temple are generally places much coveted by the orthodox people and they are, as a rule, occupied by those who have some connexion with the temple. It is recorded in this inscription that the *Sannidhi* street of Sonnavannamseyda Perumal was divided into 33 houses and that this block was named Sundaracharyapuram. The village Varanavasi was assigned to the temple, from the income of which midday offerings were to be provided to the god. These offerings had to be divided among the 33 houses. Another interesting feature of the inscription is that it gives the names of the owners of these 33 houses. The 1st, 3rd and 4th houses were occupied by Tatachaya Ayyan, the 14th house by Muppirali Narana Dikshitar Govindayyar and the 15th house was occupied by Pandipakkam Kumandur Anantayyar."

[67]"The history of Conjeevaram can hardly be attempted here. See *Antiquities* I, pp. 176-77, and bibliography given therein. For political, religious and literary history of the land it is unequalled in interest. The inscriptions of this place collected by Colonel Mackenzie have been enumerated and

summarised by Rev. Taylor in his *Rais Catal.* III, pp. 329-41, and number 140 (three. however, belonging to Sriperumbudur). I have not endeavoured to compare this list with the departmental list. The original Mack. MSS containing them (No. 845, old Nos. 50 C.M. 1019) is missing. Another list, made by Sir Walter Elliot, is given in *Antiquities* I, pp. 178-87, and contains 283 epigraphs. I have not thought it necessary to examine them as the departmental list is not yet complete and so a proper comparison is impossible at this stage.

1 of 1888 (Sanskrit) — Around Rajasimhesvara shrine in the Kailasanatha temple. A record of Rajasimha (Narasimhavaraman II) its builder. See *S.I.I.* I, No. 24, pp. 12-14.

2 of 1888 (Sanskrit) — Inside prakara of the Rajasimhesvara shrine in the Kailasanatha temple, first to third tiers. A record of Rajasimha; in Pallava characters. See *S.I.I.* Vol. I, No. 25, pp. 14-21. The record gives a string of titles of the king (Narasimhavarman II).

3 of 1888 (Sanskrit) — Inside prakara of Rajasimhesvara shrine in the Kailasanatha temple, fourth tier. A record of the same king. See *S.I.I.* Vol. I, No. 26, pp. 21-22.

4 of 1888 (Sanskrit) — Around Mahendravarmesvara shrine in the Kailasanatha temple. A record of Mahendra, Sanskrit verses.) Third niche to the right of front entrance. A record of Rangapataka (queen of Narasimha Vishnu) in Pallava characters. [Ibid, No. 29, pp. 23-24.]

7 of 1888 (Sanskrit) — Fifth niche to the right of front entrance. A record in Pallava characters of a queen. [Ibid, No. 30, p. 24.]

8 of 1888 (Kanarese) — On the back of a pillar in the mandapa in front of Rajasimhesvara shrine in the Kailasanatha temple in the same place. A record of the W. Chalukyan Vikramaditya II. Records that, after his conquest of Conjeevaram, Vikramaditya Satyasraya did not confiscate the

property of the Rajasimhesvara temple, but returned it. See *Ep. Ind,* III, pp. 359-60.

9 of 1888 (Tamil and Grantha) — Inside Rajasimhesvara shrine in the Kailasanatha temple. A record of Maduraikonda Ko Parakesarivarman. Seems to record an agreement of the people of two *seris* of Conjeevaram. *S.I.I.* I, No. 145, pp. 139-40.

10 of 1888 (Tamil and Grantha) — Inside Rajasimhesvara shrine in the Kailasanatha temple. A record of Ko Rajakesarivarman. Records an agreement made by the *Sabha* of some village to furnish daily one *ulakku* of oil for a lamp as interest for fifteen kalanjus of gold deposited with it. *S.I.I.* I, No. 147, pp. 140-41.

11 of 1888 (Tamil and Grantha) — Inside Rajasimhesvara shrine in the Kailasanatha temple. A fragment of record in Sanskrit. *Danarnavanripa* mentioned.

12 of 1888 (Tamil and Grantha) — Inside mahamandapa of Rajasimhesvara shrine in the Kailasanatha temple.

13 and 14 of 1888 (Sanskrit) — Inside mahamandapa of Rajasimhesvara shrine in the Kailasanatha temple. A fragment of record.

15 of 1888 (Sanskrit) — Inside mahamandapa of Rajasimhesvara shrine in the Kailasanatha temple. A fragmentary record, *Chola Trinetra* mentioned.

16 of 1888 (Tanuk and Grantha) — Inside mahamandapa of Rajasimhesvara shrine in the Kailasanatha temple. A record in the fifteenth year of Ko Parakesarivarman. Contains an agreement made by the inhabitants of some village to pay for a lamp (one ulakku per day and 7 *nalis* and I *uri* per mensem) as interest for a sum of money deposited with it by the temple authorities. *S.I.I.* I, No. 148, pp. 141-42.

17 of 1888 (Tamil and Grantha) — Inside mahamandapa of Rajasimhesvara shrine in the Kailasanatha temple. A record of Ko Parakesarivarman.

18 of 1888 (Tamil and Grantha) — Inside mahamandapa of Rajasimhesvara shrine in the Kailasanatha temple. A record in the twelth year of Koraja Rajakesarivarman I, saying that the Sabha of a village pledged itself to supply annually 140 kadies of paddy as interest for the sum of 33 kalanjus deposited with it, to the temple treasurers. The penalty for failure was a fine of 1/4 pon dail. S.I.I. I, No. 146, p. 140.

19 of 1888 (Sanskrit) — Inside mahamandapa of Rajasimhesvara shrine in the Kailasanatha temple. A fragmentary record.

20 of 1888 (Tamil and Grantha) — Inside mahamandapa of Rajasimhesvara shrine in the Kailasanatha temple. A record in the third year of Ko Rajakesarivarman. The villagers of Manalur pledge themselves to furnish oil for a lamp from the interest of 18 kalanjus, 3 manjadis and 1 *kunri* of gold deposited with them by the temple treasury. The interest was I ulakku of oil every day. S.I.I. I, No. 84, pp. 115-16.

21 of 1888 (Tamil and Grantha) — At the entrance into the mahamandapa of Rajasimhesvara shrine in the Kailasanatha temple. Fragment of a record.

22 of 1888 (Tamil and Grantha) — Round the base of the mandapa in front of Rajasimhesvara shrine in the Kailasanatha temple. A record in the fourth year of Ko Parakesarivarman. Records that the villagers of Kalladupur pledged themselves to furnish every year 90 *kadis* of paddy as interest for 20 kalanjus of gold deposited with them by Adidasa Chandesvara at Tiruvottur. S.I.I. I, No. 85, pp.1161-17.

23 and 24 of 1888 (Tamil and Grantha) — Pillars in the mandapa in front of Rajasimhesvara shrine. A record in the fifteenth year of Maduraikonda Ko Parakesarivarman (Parantaka I). Records that a certain Chandaparakramavira

gave 270 sheep for three lamps to the Rajasimhesvara shrine. S.I.I. I, Nos.82 and 83, pp.112-15.

Certain Mannadi families undertake to provide the daily ghee.

25 of 1888 (Tamil and Grantha) — Pillars in the mandapa in front of the Rajasimhesvara shrine in the Kailasanatha temple. A record in the twenty-sixth year of Tribhuvana-chakravartin Rajarajadeva. Records that some person pledged himself to supply daily one ulakku of ghee for five lamps. S.I.I. I, No.159, p.143.

26 of 1888 (Tamil and Grantha) — Pillars in the mandapa in front of Rajasimhesvara shrine in the Kailasanatha temple. A fragmentary record.

27 and 28 of 1888 (Tamil and Grantha) — On the pillars in the mandapa in front of Rajasimhesvara shrine in the Kailasanatha temple. Records of Kampana Udaiyar II in S. 1286 (expired), Visvavasu. The first records that in the time of Kulottunga Chola, the Rajasimhesvara temple had been closed, its landed property sold and its environs transferred to a neighbouring shrine, and that Koppanangal, the minister of Kampana, reopened the temple and restored its property. See S.I.I. I Nos.80, 86, pp. 117-18. The second one records that with the sanction of Koppanangal, the temple authorities sold some houses in the northern row of the Sannadhi street to certain Mudalis at the price of 150 *panas*. See S.I.I. I, No. 97, pp. 120-23.

29 of 1888 (Tamil and Grantha) — Pillars in the mandapa in front of the Rajasimhesvara shrine in the Kailasanatha temple. A record in Kilaka (S. 1291) of Vira Kampana Udaiyar. Records that, with the sanction of Koppanangal, the temple authorities gave a matha near the temple and some land to a certain Gangaiyar of Tirumudukunram (Vriddhachalam?) S.I.I. I, No. 88, pp. 123-25.

30 of 1888 (Tamil and Grantha) — Window of the same mandapa. No details.

31 of 1888 (Tamil and Grantha) — Northern wall of the same mandapa. No details.

32 of 1888 (Sanskrit) — Around the garbhagriha of the Vaikuntha Perumal temple. A fragmentary record.

33 of 1888 (Sanskrit and Tamil) — Around the garbhagriha of Vaikuntha Perumal temple. Fragment of a record.

34 of 1888 (Tamil and Grantha) — Around the garbhagriha of Vaikuntha Perumal temple. A record in the seventeenth year of some maharaja, whose name is lost. The inscription afterwards mentions Dantivarma Maharaja. [Paramesvaravarman II was the builder of this temple. See No. 237.]

35 of 1888 (Tamil and Grantha) — Around the garbhagriha of Vaikuntha-Perumal temple. A record in the forty-sixth year of Ko Rajakesarivarman or Chakravartin Kulottunga Choladeva I.

36 of 1888 (Tamil and Grantha) — Around the garbhagriha of Vaikuntha Perumal temple. A record in the forty-eighth year of Ko-Rajakesarivarman or Chakravartin Kulottunga Choladeva I.

37 of 1888 (Tamil and Grantha) — Inside verandah round the garbhagriha of Vaikuntha Perumal temple. Hiranyavarma Maharaja mentioned. For a description of the sculptures in this place and the light they throw on Pallava history see Ep. Rep., 1906, pp. 62-3. Venkayya believed that they represent the events which took place at the death of Paramesvaravarman II and the choice of Nandivarman Pallavamalla, the son of Hiranyavarman, as the king by the people.

38 of 1888 (Sanskrit) — First cave from north, south wall of the temple at Mamandur near the same place. All but illegible. See p. 381 and supplement to this district.

39 of 1888 (Tamil and Grantha) — Second cave from north, north wall. A record in the sixteenth year of Ko Rajaraja Rajakesarivarman I.

40 of 1888 (Tamil and Grantha) — Second cave from north, south wall. A record in the fifth year of Ko Parakesarivarman.

228 of 1910 (Tamil) On the south base of the Jvaraharesvara temple. Records in the twentieth year of Tribhuvanachakravartin Vijaya Gandagopaladeva gift of tax on looms to the temple of Suravattaramudaiya Nayanar in the city (nagaram) of Kanchipuram in Eyirkottam, a district of Jayangondasolamandalam, by the Pallava chief Tripurasar Nallasittarasan of Ambalur.

229 of 1910 (Tamil) — On the north base of the same temple. Dated in the fifth year of the Chola king Tribhuvana-chakravartin Vikrama Choladeva (1118-35). Records gift of land by Sundra Sola Velar, a native of Visharu (or Kulivallanallur) in Virpedunadu, a sub-division of Kaliyur-kottam which was a district of Jayangondasolamandalam, to the Suravattalamudaiya Nayanar. Sundarachola built a mandapam and the king inspected it.

230 of 1910 (Tamil) — On the same base. The Vijayanagara king Kampana Udaiyar II recods in Kilaka (i.e., S. 1291) gift of the privilege of supervision in the temple of Suravadinda Nayanar, to a certain Alagiyatiruchchirrambalamudaiyar, son of Bhuvanaikabahudevar.

11 of 1895 (Kanarese) — On a pillar in the Kailasanatha temple. A record of the western Chalukya king Vikramaditya II. Kielhorn's Southern List No. 43. Published in the *Epigraphia Indica*, Vol.III, page 359 f.

12 of 1895 (Tamil) — On a stone built into the verandah round the garbhagriha of the Ulagalanda Perumal temple in the same place. A record of the Pallava king Tellarrerinda

Nandipottaraiyar III, dated in his eighteenth year. Published by Mr. Venkayya in the Madras Christian College Magazine, Vol.III, page 98 ff.

1 of 1893 (Tamil) — South wall of the Smasanesvara shrine in the Ekambaranatha temple. A record of the Chola king Ko Rajakesarivarman alias Kulottunga Choladeva I, dated in his sixth year.

2 of 1893 (Tamil) — North wall of the second prakara of the same temple. A record of the Kakatiya king Ganapati, dated S. 1172 (expired).

3 of 1892 (Telugu) — North wall of the second prakara of the same temple. A record of the Vijayanagara king Sadasivadeva, dated S. 1472, Saumya.

4 of 1893 (Tamil) — West wall of the second prakara of the same temple. A record of the Chola king Tribhuvanachakravartin Rajarajadeva, dated in his fifteenth year.

5 (a) of 1893 (Tamil) — West wall of the second prakara of the same temple. A record of the Chola king Tribhuvanachakravartin Rajarajadeva, dated in his nineteenth year.

5 (b) of 1893 (Tamil) — West wall of the second prakara of the same temple. A record of the Chola king Ko Rajakesarivarman or Kulottunga Choladeva, dated in his second year.

6 of 1893 (Tamil) — West wall of the second prakara of the same temple. A record of the seventeenth year of the Chola king Tribhuvanchakravartin Rajarajadeva III. Mentions Ganda Gopala. See Ep. Ind., VI, where the date is pointed out be Tuesday, 18th January, 1233 A.D.

7 (a) of 1893 (Tamil) — West wall of the second prakara of the same temple. A record of the Chola king Ko Parakesarivarman or Rajadhirajadeva (?), dated in his second year.

7 (b) of 1893 (Tamil) — West wall of the second prakara of the same temple. A record of the Chola king Rajarajadeva, dated in his nineteenth year.

7 (c) of 1893 (Tamil) — West wall of the second prakara of the same temple. A record of the Chola king Tribhuvana-chakravartin Rajadhirajadeva (II?), dated in his eighth year.

8 of 1893 (Tamil) — West wall of the second prakara of the same temple. A record of the Chola king Rajarajadeva, dated in his second year.

9 of 1893 (Tamil) — South wall of the second prakara of the same temple. A record of the Chola king Ko Parakesarivarman or Rajarajadeva II, dated in his fifteenth year, corresponding to Thursday, 12th January, 1161 A.D. Ep. Ind, VIII, 3.

10 of 1893 (Tamil) — North wall of the second prakara of the same temple. A record of the Chola king Tribhuvanachakravartin Kulottunga Choladeva III, dated in his twenty-seventh year. Ep. Ind. VI, 251.

11 of 1893 (Tamil) — West wall of the second prakara of the same temple. A record of the Chola king Ko Rajakesarivarman or Kulottunga Choladeva, dated in his second year.

12 of 1893 (Tamil) — East wall of the Nataraja shrine in the same temple. A record of the Vijayanagara king Bukkaraya II, dated S. 1328 (expired), Vyaya.

13 of 1893 (Sanskrit fragment) — In the gopuram of the 1,000-pillared mandapa in the same temple.

14 of 1893 (Tamil) — West, south and east walls of the Muktisvara temple. A record of the Pallava king Nandivarman, dated in his twenty-eighth year.

15 of 1893 (Tamil) — North wall of the same temple. An incomplete record of the Chola king Ko Parakesarivarman alias Rajendra Choladeva I, dated in his eighteenth year.

16 of 1893 (Tamil) — North and west walls of the same temple. An obliterated record of the Vijayanagara king Tirumaladeva (A.D. 1566-77.)

17 of 1893 (Tamil) — North wall of the Pandava Perumal temple (the Tiruppadagam of the Nalayiraprabandha). A record of the Chola king Ko Rajakesarivarman or Kulottanga Choladeva I, dated in his fifth year. Records that a merchant provided the temple with a flower garden and purchased some land for the benefit of the gardeners from the village of Oriravirukkai. S.I.I., III, No.68 pp. 140-3. The cost of 2,000 kulis (tax-free) was 11 kalanjus equal in fineness to the Madhurantaka madai and the assembly could not levy in consequence Velikkasu, Nirailai, Silvari, Sorumattu, etc.

18 of 1893 (Tamil) — South wall of the same temple. A record of the Chola king Ko Rajakesarivarman or Kulottunga Choladeva I, dated in his thirty-ninth year. Records gift of two kalanjus and two manjadis by a merchant to the Pujaris who were to supply two nalis of curds daily. Ibid.; No. 74, pp. 163-4.

33 of 1893 (Tamil) — Base of the west wall of the rock in the Arulala Perumal temple. A record of the ninth year of the Chola king Ko Prakesarivarman or Vikrama Choladeva. Records the gift of 780 kalams of paddy the interest of which had to be used for worship during thirteen days of Jyeshtha, the alleged constellation of Budattalvar and Poygai Alvars, to be held every year. [The inscription is of great literary and religious value as it refers to the worship of the Alvars and the Iyarpa of the Nalayiraprabandha. It, however differs, in assigning a single star to both the Alvars, from the Guruparamparas. The inscription gives also the prices of the articles to be bought. See S.I.I. III, No. 80, p. 186-90.]

34 of 1893 (Sanskrit in Kanarese characters) — Base of the west wall of the rock in the Arulala Perumal temple

records in the reign of Chola Tikka ((son of Manma Siddhi), in S. 1157, a gift of cows by the minister Tripurantaka.

35 of 1893 (Sanskrit) — Base of the north wall of the same. A record of Tammu siddhi, dated S. 1127. Records the erection of portions of the temple. Informs that the king was crowned at the city of Nellore. Gives the genealogy of the line. See Ep. Rep., 1893, p. 5 and Ep. Ind. Vol. VII, 152-5.

36 of 1893 (Tamil) — Base of the north wall of the same. A record of the Chola king Tribhuvanachakravartin Kulottunga Choladeva, dated in his twenty-seventh year.

34 of 1893 (Tamil) —

37 of 1893 (Tamil) — Base of the east wall of the same. A record of the Gandagopala.

38 of 1893 (Tamil) — Left entrance to the Narasimha shrine in the same temple. A record of the Chola king Tribhuvanachakravartin Kulottunga Choladeva, dated in his sixteenth year.

39 of 1893 (Tamil) — Base of the verandah round the rock in the same temple, east. Tribhuvanachakravartin Gandagopaladeva mentions in his seventeenth year a feudatory, Nala Siddha of Kanchi.

40 of 1893 (Tamil) — South side of the same. A record of Tribhuvanachakravartin Konerinmaikondan. Refers to the coins of Kodandaraman and Koliyugaraman. For descriptions of these see *Madras Journal*, 1887-8.

41 of 1893 (Sanskrit and Tamil) — South side of the same. A record of Tribhuvanachakravartin Gandagopaladeva, dated in his twenty-second year. [The name Nilaganga appears in connection with this chief. He was the contemporary of Kulottunga III, who ascended the throne in 1177-8 as the inscriptions at Manimangalam (21 of 1896) and Madhurantakam (131 of 1896) show.]

42 of 1893 (Tamil) — South side of the same. A record of Tribhuvanachakravartin Konerinmaikondan, dated in his twenty-first year. Only beginning copied. See No. 40 above which it resembles in its numismatic interest.

43 of 1893 (Grantha and Tamil) — West side of the same. A record of the Kakatiya king Prataparudra, dated S. 1238, expired, Nala. See Ep. Ind., VII, 128-32, where Dr. Hultzsch edits the inscription. It says that Muppidi Nayaka, the general of Prataparudra, came to Kanchi, and installed a certain Manavira as Governor and granted the revenues of two villages to the Arulala Perumal temple, which amounted to 1002 Gandagopalamadai. The dates of the two grants were Friday, 11th June, 1316 A.D. and Wednesday, 16th June, 1316 A.D. The inscription is of interest as showing that Prataparudra (whose inscriptions are found as far as Jambukesvaram) was in possession of Kanchi soon after it had been in the hands of Ravivarman of Kerala. Dr. Hultzsch therefore believes that Muppidi Nayaka perhaps drove him away and installed Manavira, evidently a member of the later Cholas denoted by Gandagopala, Nallasiddhi, etc., as his feudatory. See Ep. Ind., VII, 128-132.

44 of 1893 (Tamil) — West wall of the second prakara of the same temple. A record of Tribhuvanachakravartin Gandagopaladeva.

45 of 1893 (Sanskrit) — West wall of the second prakara of the same temple.

46 of 1893 (Tamil) — North wall of the second prakara of the same temple. A record of Alluntikamaharaja Gandagopaladeva, dated in his seventh year.

47 of 1893 (Tamil) — North wall of the second prakara of the same temple. Mentions Tribhuvanachakravartin Gandagopaladeva and records a grant by Brahma Setti, a minister of Ganapati (Kakatiya, evidently).

48 of 1893 (Tamil) — North wall of the second prakara of the same temple. A record of the Chola king Tribhuvanachakravartin Rajadhirajadeva (II?) in his fourteenth year. Mentions a Ganga chief, Ahavamallarasan.

49 of 1893 (Tamil) — In the gopura near the Abhisheka mandapa in the same temple, left of entrance. A record of the Chola king Ko Rajakesarivarman alias Kulottunga Choladeva I, dated in his forty-third year.

50 of 1893 (Sanskrit and Tamil) — In the same gopura, right of entrance. Addressed to the Vedic scholar Sayana. Mentions his mother Srimayi, his father Mayana, his elder brother Madhava, his younger brother the poet Bhoganatha and his preceptor Srikantanatha. The inscription is thus of great value.

51 of 1893 (Sanskrit) — In the outermost gopura of the same temple, right of entrance. A record of the Chola king Champa, son of Vira Chola, dated S. 1236, presenting a new car to the temple. See Ep. Ind., III, 71-2. See No. 3 of 1890 at Tiruvallam in North Arcot district.

52 of 1893 (Sanskrit) — In the outermost gopura of the same temple, right of the entrance. A record of the Pandya king Sundara Pandya (Jatavarman) who ascended the throne in 1251A.D.

53 of 1893 (Sanskrit) — On the same gopura, left of entrance. Tikka (I?) boasts of victories over various kings. See No. 34.

54 of 1893 (Tamil) — West and north walls of the Smasanesvara shrine in the Ekambaranatha temple. A record of the Chola king Ko Rajakesarivarman or Rajadhirajadeva I, dated in his twenty-seventh year. Only historical introduction copied. One Maran Tevadigal deposits five kalanjus in temple treasury for offerings. The interest on this (at the rate of one ka two tu for each kalanjus) is eight ka. [The account of expenditure and prices given.]

22 of 1890 — South base of the Anekatangapadam temple. Records in the thirty-fourth year of Kulottunga I grant of two velis of land to the temple of Anaiyapadanga. The land granted was at Conjeevaram itself, north of the temple of Tirukkarrali Mahadeva. (i.e., Rajasimhesvara or Kailasanatha). Sec S.I.I. Vol. II, No.78, pp. 392-3.

23 of 1890 — North base of the same. Seems to be dated in Nala. Records that the authorities of the Anekatanga temple assigned 1,400 kulis of land to certain Kaikkolars connected with the temple.

24 of 1890 — West base of the same. A record of Kulottunga Choladeva I dated in his twentieth year, saying that he granted three velis of land at Tamar (i.e., Damal) or Nittavinodanallur in Tamurnadu, a sub-division of Tamar-kottam, to the Mahadeva of the Anekatangapadam temple. See S.I.I. Vol. II, No.77, pp. 390-2.

25 of 1890 — West and south walls of the Sabhanayaka shrine in the Ekambaranatha temple. A record of the Pandya king Bhuvanekavira or Samarakolahala, dated S. 1391 (expired), Virodhi. Records that he granted to the temples of Ekambaranatha and Kamakshi, two villages in the Pandya country named after himself. For his coins see Elliot's Coins of S. Ind., Plate III, No. 138, and Ep. Rep., 1890, p-2.

26 of 1890 (Sanskrit verse) — North wall of the second prakara of the same temple. A record of the Kakatiya king Ganapati, dated S. 1172, Saumya year. Mentions Rudradeva and Mahadeva also, and the gift of a village by his minister Samanta Bhoja. See Ind. Antq., XXI, 197 ff., where Dr. Hultzsch has published it.

27 of 1890 (Sanskrit verse) — North wall of the second prakara of the same temple. A record of Tribhuvanachakravartin Vijaya Gandagopaladeva, dated S. 1187, sixteenth rignal year. So he ascended the throne in S. 1172 (1250 A.D.). See also 35 and 36.

28 of 1890 — South wall of the Nayar mandapa in the Ekambaranatha temple. A record of Kampana Udaiyar, dated Ananda year.

29 of 1890 — Right of the entrance into the inner prakara of the Kamakshi temple. A record of the Vijayanagara king Harihara II, dated S. 1315 (expired), Srimukha year.

30 of 1890 — Left of the front entrance into the Ulagalanda Perumal temple. A record of Sakalalokachakravartin Rajanarayana Sambuvaraya, dated S. 1268 (expired), Vyaya, ninth rignal year. So he ascended the throne in S. 1259, (1337 A.D.).

31 of 1890 — Right of the entrance into the east wall of the second prakara of the Arulala Perumal temple. A record of Hariyana Udaiyar II, dated S. 1300 (expired), Krodhana year.

32 of 1890 — Left of the entrance into the same temple. A record of the Vira Hariyana Udaiyar II, dated S. 1300 (expired), Kalayukti year.

33 of 1890 — Right of the entrance into the Thayar Sannadhi at the same temple. A record of Vira Kampana Udaiyar, dated S. 1288 (expired), Prabhava year.

34 of 1890 (Sanskrit verse) — East wall of the so-called rock (malai) in the same temple. A record of the Kerala king Jayasimha and his son Ravivarman. The latter, also called Kulasekhar Sangramadhira, was born in S. 1188, and married a Pandya princess. At the age of 33 he ascended the throne of Kerala. He then conquered Vira Pandya and was crowned at Madura in his forty-sixth year (i.e., S. 1234). He was the ruler of Kupaka and Kollam. See Ep. Ind., IV, 145-8.

35 of 1890 — South wall of the rock in the same temple. A record of Tribhuvanachakravartin Vijaya Gandagopaladeva, dated S. 1187, sixteenth rignal year.

36 of 1890 — South wall of the rock in the same temple.

A record of Tribhuvanachakravartin Vijaya Gandagopaladeva, dated S. 1187, fifteenth rignal year.

37 of 1890 — Left of the entrance into the first prakara of the same temple. A record of the Vijayanagara king Mallikarjunadeva, dated S. 1387 (expired), Parthiva year.

38 of 1890 — East wall of the Abhisheka mandapa at the same temple. A record of Sakalabhuvanachakravartin Ko Perunjingadeva, dated S. 1182, expired eighteenth rignal year. So he ascended the throne in S. 1165, (1243 A.D.). He must have been the predecessor of Vijaya Gandagopaladeva referred to in Nos. 27, 35 and 36. The exact date of the present inscription, according to Kielhorn, is Sunday, 31st Oct., 1260 A.D. Ep. Ind., VII, p. 164.

39 of 1890 — South wall of the Abhisheka mandapa at the same temple. A record of the Vijayanagara king Virupakshadeva, dated S. 1392 (expired), Vikriti year.

49 of 1900 (Tamil) — On the south wall of the first prakara of the Kamakshi temple. A record of Achyuta Raya of Vijayanagar, dated S. 1456 (1534 A.D.), Vijaya. Refers to his conquest and records the grant of eight villages to the temple.

50 of 1900 — On the south wall of the second prakara of the Arulala Perumal temple. A record of Achyuta Raya of Vijayanagar, dated S. 1454 (1632 A.D.) (expired), Nandana. Refers to his conquests and records the gift of jewels and seventeen villages to the temple.

51 of 1900 — On the same place. A record of the same king in the same date. Records gift of a jewelled couch, discus, etc., to the king (A.D. 1050-62.)

416 of 1902 (Tamil) — On the north wall of the central shrine in the Tirukkalisvara temple at Veppangulam near Conjeevaram. Records a gift of land in the sixth year of Parakesarivarman Udaiyar Rajendradeva (A.D. 1050-62.)

417 of 1902 (Tamil) — On the south, west and north walls

of the same shrine. A record of the twenty-eighth year of Rajakesarivarman Udaiyar Rajadhirajadeva (I?).

418 of 1902 (Tamil) — On the same walls. A record of the third year of Parakesarivarman Adhirajendradeva. Partly built in.

419 of 1902 (Tamil) — In the same place. A record of the sixteenth year of Parakesarivarman Rajendra Choladeva (A.D. 1011-43) providing for a supply of paddy by a number of villages in payment of interest on the gold borrowed from the temple.

420 of 1902 (Tamil) — On the east wall of the same shrine. Records gift of 90 sheep for a lamp in the sixth year of Parakesarivarman Rajendra Choladeva (A.D. 1011-43).

1 of 1906 (Tamil) — On the south wall of Sakkesvara temple. Records a sale of land in the fifteenth year of the Chola king Parakesarivarman.

2 of 1906 — On a stone built into the floor at the entrance into the Smasanesvara shrine in the Ekambaranatha temple. Mutilated inscription of the first (fifth) year of Parakesarivarman or Uttama Choladeva.

3 of 1906 — On the same stone. Mutilated. Mentions queen Viranarani (yar). Date lost. By the same king.

4 of 1906 — On the big gopura in the same temple. Unfinished. Refers to Idangaivari. Dated in S. 1378, Dhatri, in the reign of the Vijayanagara king Vira Mallikarjunadeva Maharaya.

C.P. No. 146 of Mr. Sewell's List (and Madras Museum plate No. 8) (Tamil) — Records a document declaring the settlement of a dispute about some lands, between some men of the Mudaliar caste. It is dated in S. 1456 (1534 A.D.), Kaliyuga 4434, Nandana date inconsistent. See Tamil and Sanskrit Inscrns., pp. 154-6, where it has been edited.

A C.P. grant of Ko Parakesarivarman Uttama Choladeva in the sixteenth year of his reign, at the request of a minister of his confirming the contents of the stone inscriptions which refer to the dues to be paid to the temple of Vishnu at Kachchippedu. See Nos. 16, 18, 20, 22, for instance. For Uttama Chola's coins, see Elliot's *Coins of South India*, Nos. 151 and 154. For the description of the present plates see Ep. Rep., 1891, pp. 4-5

A C.P. dated S. 1646 (referred to by Taylor in his Rais. Catal., III, p. 340). Commemorates a gift of thirteen villages in free tenure, through Ramanujachariar.

Among the copper plates of Conjeevaram there are a number of forged ones. One of these (No. 6, Appendix A, Madr. Ep. Rep., 1910) is deposited in the Madras Museum and consists of a single plate. Mr. Krishna Sastri believes that it is "one of a series of forgeries compiled by the Idangai faction in its zeal to justify its preference over the Valangai, in matters social. The dates given, viz., S. 1098 and K. 4421, do not correspond. Nevertheless the story related of how the car procession of Kamakshi Amman at Conjeevaram was successfully managed by the Idangai Kammalans, in spite of the obstacles thrown in its way by their opponents of the Valangai section, and how in this matter the Kambalattans from Malabar helped the former by their ingenuity in exorcism, has its own interest to the ethnologist." (Madr. Ep. Rep. 1910, p. 11.)

Another forged grant of the same character dealing with the voluntary levying of a fee by the Anju Panchalattar (i.e., the five Kammalars) among themselves. This is also dated in S. 1098, K. 4421. (Ibid.)

343 of 1919 (Tamil) — On the east side of the rock, Arulala Perumal temple, Little Conjeevaram, Conjeevaram taluk, Chingleput district. Gift of 33 head of cattle for a perpetual lamp by a native of Malai mandalam to the temple of Arulala Perumal who was pleased to take his stand in

Tiruvattiyur. Mentions the liquid measure Ariyannavallannali.

344 of 1919 — On the same wall. Arulala Perumal temple, Little Conjeevaram, Conjeevaram taluk, Chingleput district. Gift of one-eighth perpetual lamp by Gollapundi Devi Nayakkan residing in Sirumanai in Pakkanadu to the same temple. The trustees of the temple took charge of the lamp.

345 of 1919 — On the same wall. Arulala Perumal temple, Little Conjeevaram, Conjeevaram taluk, Chingleput district. The first two lines are unfinished. Gift of 33 head of cattle for a perpetual lamp and a lampstand by Pittima Devikkamayana, one of the servants of Madurantaka Pottappichcholan Manumasiddharasan Tirukkalattidevan or Gandagopalan to the temple of the Perumal.

346 of 1919 — On the same wall. Arulala Perumal temple, Little Conjeevaram Conjeevaram taluk, Chingleput district. Gift of 135 goats and sheep for 1 1/2 perpetual lamps by Rama Raman of Muranottamangalam in Valluvanadu, a district of Malai Mandalam to the temple of Arulala-Perumal.

347 of 1919 (Grantha) — On the same wall. A Sanskrit verse in praise of Tatacharya, who celebrated 100 marriages every day!

348 of 1919 (Tamil) — On the same wall. Registers the names of the individulas and the number of lamps which each had to burn in the temple of Arulala Perumal at Tiruvattiyur in the city of Conjeevaram in Eyirkottam, a district of Jayangondasolamandalam.

349 of 1919 (Tamil) — On the same wall. Unfinished. Gift of 48 sheep for half-a-lamp to the temple of Alvar at Attiyur in Eyilkottam, a district of Jayangondasolamandalam by Machaladevi, daughter of Bhutteya Nayaka of Dorasamudra.

350 of 1919 (Tamil) — Assignment of certain taxes in Solamandalam for offerings and repairs in the same temple by Kadakkan or Nilagangaraiyan.

351 of 1919 (Tamil) — On the same wall. Gift of 12 buffaloes for a perpetual lamp to the temple of Arulala Perumal by Alvankon, son of Pandavadutan Valavaraiyakon of Pattur. Mentions the liquid measure Arumolinangainali.

352 of 1919 (Tamil) — On the same wall. Gift of 33 head of cattle for a perpetual lamp to the temple of Arulala Perumal by Kommanappangaru of Mottupalli.

353 of 1919 (Tamil) — On the same wall. Built in at the beginning. Gift of 44 cows for a perpetual lamp to the same temple by Chandrasetti of Mandagattali in Nellurnadu.

354 of 1919 (Grantha) — On the same wall. Records the construction of a Vimana by Tatacharya at Phanipatigiri (i.e., Tirupati).

355 of 1919 (Tamil) — On the same side. Gift of 32 cows and one bull for a perpetual lamp to the same temple by Paramesvaramangalamudaiyan Silambamindan Ambalakkuttan Sediyarayan of Paramesvaramangalam or Solakulatilaka Chaturvedimangalam in Semburkottam.

356 of 1919 (Tamil) — On the same side. Gift of 15 Nellurmadai coins for maintaining a perpetual lamp in the same temple by Sevakkal, sister-in-law of Annadadevan of Nellur.

357 of 1919 (Tamil) — On the same side. Gift of land in the village of Karanai for worship at the service called Gandagopalansandi, repairs etc. in the temple of Arulala Perumal at Tiruvattiyur in Kanchipuram in Eyirkottam, a district of Jayangondasolamandalam by Madurantaka Pottappichola Manumasiddharasan Tirukkalattidevan or Gandagopalan. The gift was made in the 18th year of Rajarajadeva.

358 of 1919 (Tamil) — On the same side. Gift of cows and bulls for 2 lamps to the same temple by Nulappiyarrulan Narayananambi Damodaran, one of his Kelivi Mudalis of Gandagopaladeva.

359 of 1919 (Tamil) — On the same side. Gift of cows and a lampstand for a perpetual lamp to the same temple by Maharajan Rajadevan, a feudatory of the king. The chief bears many birudas.

360 of 1919 (Tamil) — On the same side. Gift of 10 Bujabalanmadai for burning a lamp in the same temple by a native of Pulal in Poysalanadu.

361 of 1919 (Tamil) — On the same side. Gift of 33 head of cattle for a lamp by a native of Oralachcheri in Vellappanadu, a district of Malaimandalam.

362 of 1919 (Tamil) — On the same side. Gift of land in Kaveripakkam or Vikramacholachaturvedimangalam in Paduvurkottam for festivals, worship at the service called Gandagopalansandi and repairs, in the temple by Madurantaka Pottappichcholan Manumasiddharasan Tirukkalattidevan or Gandagopalan in the 16th year of Rajarajadeva.

363 of 1919 (Grantha) — Sanskrit verse in praise of Tatayadesika.

364 of 1919 (Tamil) — On the same side. Gift of a lamp by Tikki Nayakkan, brother of Padiyari Vayirappa Nayakan, the Mahapradhana of Madurantaka Pottappichcholan or Erasiddarasan of Nellurnadu.

365 of 1919 (Tamil) — Gift of 96 sheep and a ram for a lamp to the same temple by Arunagiri Perumal, one of the sons of Panchanadivana Nilagangaraiyar who is called pillayar (son).

366 of 1919 (Tamil) — On the same side. Gift of 33 head of cattle and a lampstand for a perpetual lamp to the same temple by Valliaya Dandanayaka, son of Dudappillai Dandanayaka of Aranaipuram, one of the Ministers of Hoysala Vira Somesvaradevarasa.

367 of 1919 (Tamil) — On the same side. Gift of 33 head of cattle and one lampstand for a lamp to the same temple

by Kami Nayakan, one of the mudalis of Madurantaka Pottappichola Tirukkalattideva Gandagopala. The latter is called Pillaiyar (son).

368 of 1919 (Tamil) — On the same side. Gift of 33 head of cattle for a lamp to the same temple by Vellappagada Kanrakodu, Gandan Iraman or Purushamanikka Setti.

369 of 1919 (Tamil) — On the same side. Gift of 11 cows for providing milk at the midnight service by Polalvi Dandanayakan, one of the ministers of Hoysala Vira Somesvaradevarasa.

370 of 1919 (Tamil) — On the same side. Gift of the village of Pulambakkam in Vadappanadu, a sub-division of Puttanurkottam, a district of Padaividurajya in Jayangondasolamandalam, for celebrating the festival in the month of Avani by Vyasa Tirtha (A Madhvaguru), disciple of Brahmanya Tirtha. Vyasa Tirtha seems to have got the village as a gift from Krishnaraya and the festival was instituted in his name. Vyasa Tirtha also made a gift of the serpent vehicle to be carried in procession on the 4th day of all festivals.

371 of 1919 (Tamil) — On the same side. Gift of the village of Arpakkam in Magaralnadu for conducting the daily expenses in the same temple. Gurukularayan, Nigarilisolappallavarayan and Nilagangarayan figure among the signatories.

372 of 1919 (Tamil) — Registers the total yield of paddy received from the lands of Arpakkam which was granted to the same temple. The land seem to have included those belonging to Kunrankilan Velan Atkondavilli which were separated from Arpakkam under the name Periya Perumal Vilagam in the 23rd year of Rajaraja.

373 of 1919 (Grantha and Tamil) — On the same side. Gift of three villages Kalappalanpattu, Tarkolappattu and Panrittangal in Damarkottam of Chandragiri rajya in Solingapuram circuit, by Parankusa Jiyar, a disciple of

Narayana Jiyar for meeting the expenses of 15 Ekadasi days.

374 of 1919 (Tamil) — On the same side. Incomplete. Gift of gold by the same individuala for meeting the expenses on the 9 Ekadasi days and on the Kausika Dvadasi days during the Chaturmasa (4 months) after hearing the Kausika Purana. The items of expenditure included the presentation of a cloth to Van Satagopa Jiyar who seems to have read the Kausika Purana.

375 of 1919 (Tamil) — On the same side. Gift of land for offerings to the god Per Arulailar by the king. The gift was registered in the name of Sripati Ayyan by the temple authorities.

376 of 1919 (Tamil) — On the same side. Gift of the village Tupaluruagrahara for certain festivals to be conducted in the temple.

377 of 1919 (Tamil) — On the same side. Records certain privileges in the temple given to Satyavijaya Tirtha, a Madhva guru of Uttaradimatha.

378 of 1919 (Tamil) — On the same side. Records a gift of 32 cows and one bull for a perpetual lamp and 2,000 kulis of land for rearing two flower gardens by Padiyra Vayirappa Nayaka, one of the Ministers of Madurantaka Pattappicholan or Erasidda-Arasan of Nellur for the merit of his mother Kamasaniyar.

379 of 1919 (Tamil) — On the same side. Registers a change of villages effected by Ettur Tirumali Kumara Tatacharya.

380 of 1919 (Tamil) — On the same side. Registers a gift of 5 villages by the temple authorities for conducting the festival in the month of Vaigasi for the merit of Achyutappa Nayaka, son of Adappam Sinna Savappa Nayaka.

381 of 1919 (Tamil) — On the same side. Gift of the villages of Putturapattu to Ettur Tirumal Kumara Tatacharya for conducting certain festivals in the month of Adi while the god was taken to the Yajnasala (within the temple) after performing the Argnishthoma sacrifice.

382 of 1919 (Tamil) — On the same side. Registers a gift of land for certain festivals in the 16-pillared mandapa situated in the Visva Panditta Toppu to Visva Panditta, son of Timma Panditta and grandson of Visva Panditta, agent of Ettur Tirumali Kumara Tatacharya for the merit of the latter.

383 of 1919 (Tamil) — On the same side. Records the sale of certain services and the celebration of certain festivals in the temple to Tiruvengadasirukkar or Sri Parankusa Tirupani Pillai of the temple at Tiruppullani in Pandi Mandala, by Ettur Tirumali Kumara Tatacharya and others of temple. There was another appointed but the order was cancelled subsequently in favour of the above individual by Venkatapatirasayyan (probably Venkata I).

384 of 1919 (Tamil) — On the same side. Gift of 14 villages by the king for the big special offering in the temple for the king's own merit.

385 of 1919 (Tamil) — On the south side of the rock. Gift of 10 Gandagopalanmadai for a lamp by a Pottidevaya Nayaka, one of the servants of pillayar (son) Gandagopala.

386 of 1919 (Tamil) — On the same wall. Gift of 25 madai for a lamp by a native of Kollam(?) in Melmandalam. Refers to the 2nd year of the Chola (?) king and gives 30 panam as equivalent to 4 madai.

387 of 1919 (Tamil) — On the same wall. Records an order of Madurantaka Pottappichcholan. Registers the exemption of taxes on the lands forming the flower garden of Arulanantha in Padaiyuru or Devapperumalnallur in Urrukattikottan. Rajagandagopalan figures as the signatory in the end.

388 of 1919 (Tamil) — On the south side of the same rock. Gift of cows for half-a-lamp by a lady residing in Vadaur to the temple of Arulala Perumal at Kanchipuram in Eyirkottam, a district of Jayangondasolamandalam.

389 of 1919 (Tamil) — On the same wall. Gift of land in

Sirilangovilagam in Ulagalanda Cholanallur, a hamlet of Rajendracholachaturvedimangalam for maintaining a matha.

390 of 1919 (Tamil) — On the same wall. Unfinished. Mentions Rajendracholachaturvedimangalam in Kaliyurkottam, a district of Jayangondasolamandalam.

391 of 1919 (Tamil) — On the same wall. Damaged. Seems to record a gift of land to the temple of Alagapperumal by Madurantaka Pottappichcholan or Manumasiddarasadeva in the 2nd year of Rajarajadeva.

392 of 1919 (Tamil) — On the same wall. Gift of a lamp to the temple of Arulala Perumal by a native of Palaiyur in Tumanadu in Malaimandalam.

393 of 1919 (Tamil) — On the same wall. Gift of a lamp to the same temple by a Nayaka of the Malaimandalam.

394 of 1919 (Tamil) — On the same wall. Gift of the village of Ukkal or Vikramabaranachaturvedimangalam for conducting the service called Gandagopalansandi festivals and repairs in the same temple by the chief mentioned in No. 362 above. The gift was made in the 16th year of Rajarajadeva.

395 of 1919 (Tamil) — On the same wall. Gift of the village of Padaipparu or Devapperumalnallur in Kaliyurkottam for conducting the service called Gandagopalansandi offerings and repairs by Madhurantaka Pottappichcholan Manumasiddharasan Tirukkalattidevan or Gandagopalan in the 17th year of Rajarajadeva.

396 of 1919 (Tamil) — On the same wall. Gift of a lamp by Iravi Irayiran, one of the merchants of Nellur residing in Muranottamangalam in Valluvanadu.

397 of 1919 (Tamil) — On the same wall. Gift of (the vilage of) Manjapalli by Mallappa Dandanayaka for offerings and a flower garden.

398 of 1919 (Grantha and Tamil) — On the same wall. Records the privileges given to Srivangacharya, son of

Vadibhikara Srinivasaguru of Srivatsagotra, in the temple of Devapperumal.

399 of 1919 (Tamil) — On the same wall. Gift of two lamps by a native of Muranottamangalam in Valluvanadu, a district of Malaimandalam.

400 of 1919 (Tamil) — On the same wall. Gift of 2 lamps by a servant of the temple of Arulala Perumal.

401 of 1919 (Tamil) — On the south side of the same rock. Records that Kampaya Dannayaka agreed to conduct certain festivities in the grove called Ninaittadumuditta Perumal Tiruttoppu instituted by Echchaya Dannayakkar while Vira Vallaladeva was camping at Kanchipuram.

402 of 1919 (Tamil) — On the same wall. Gift of land, free of taxes, in the village of Solamangalam or Rajasikhamanichaturvedimangalam for defraying the expenses of the Arulala Perumal temple.

403 of 1919 (Tamil) — On the same wall. Gift of land as devadana to the temple of Tiruvattiyur Alvar.

404 of 1919 (Tamil) — On the same wall. Gift of the village of Tirayalam in Elavurnadu, a sub-division of Eyil Nadu by Dandinagopa Jagadhobhaganda Gopaya Dandanayaka, son of Malla Dandanayaka, one of the feudatories of Vishnuvardhana Vira Narasingadeva.

405 of 1919 (Tamil) — On the same wall. Gift of lamp by Gundur Singaperumal or Abhinava Bhatta Bana of Velichcheri.

406 of 1919 (Tamil) — On the same wall. Begins with the historical introduction of Kulottunga Chola II and registers a sale of land for the maintenance of a matha in the temple of Arulala Perumal. The record bears an introductory remark that it registers a gift of land for feeding Sri Vaishnava Brahmanas who came to witness the festivals in the months of Masi and Vaigasi by Arpakkilan Sirilango or Valavan Muvendavelan.

407 of 1919 (Tamil) — On the same wall. Gift of 33 head

of cattle and two lampstands for a lamp by a native of Irunadikkudal Mallaippalli in Malaimandalam to the same temple.

408 of 1919 (Tamil) — On the same wall. Gift of 36 head of cattle and a lampstand for a lamp by Ammana Dandanayaka, the Minister of Hoysala Vishnuvardhana Vira Narasingadeva.

409 of 1919 (Tamil) — On the same wall. Gift of 33 head of cattle and a lampstand for a lamp by a native of Malaimandalam.

410 of 1919 (Tamil) — On the same wall. Gift of 33 head of cattle and a lampstand for a lamp by a native of Karayappalli.

411 of 1919 (Tamil) — On the same wall. Gift of land in (Van) Sadagopuram for burning camphor, for offerings and for Brahmanas by Appa Pillai. The land seems to have been handed over to him by Narasingaraya Maharaya.

412 of 1919 (Telugu) — Gift of silver vessels for offerings and bath.

413 of 1919 (Telugu) — On the same wall. Gift of a jewelled pendant by Rayasam Sripattayya.

414 of 1919 (Telugu) — On the south side of the same rock. Gift of 10 madai by Narapparasayya, agent of Rayasam Sripattayya for offerings on certain festival days.

415 of 1919 (Tamil) — On the same wall. Records the gift of the village of Pundi by Madurantaka Pottappichcholan Tirukkalattideva or Gandagopaladeva for offerings and worship to the god and for repairs to the temple of Kalamegha Perumal in Kandaravirapettai or Gandagopalachaturvediangalam in the district of Paduvurkottam in Jayangondasolamandalam in the 22nd year of Rajarajadeva.

416 of 1919 (Tamil) — On the same wall. Gift of two lampstands and 33 cows and one bull, by Tyagasamudrapattayar

Bhimarasar, one of the mudalis of Madurantakpottappichcholan Tirukkalattideva or Gandagopaladeva for a perpetual lamp.

417 of 1919 (Tamil) — On the same wall. Records the gift of houses and lands to 200 persons who serve the god and who are called Tribhuvanaviranpadiyilar.

418 of 1919 (Tamil) — On the same wall. Gift of money for the daily supply of two sacred threads (yanjopavita), champaka flowers and one lime fruit to Adhikaram Narapparasayyar for use in the temple, by Rayasam Ayyapparasayyar, son of Gottimukkil Tipparasar.

419 of 1919 (Tamil) — On the same wall. Records an order of Madurtankapottappichcholan and the gift, free of all taxes, of the village of Tukankudal in Nirvelurnadu in the district of Urrukkattukottam, for conducting the Arpisi festival and for rendering the service called Rajagandagopalansandi.

420 of 1919 (Tamil) — On the same wall. Damaged at the end. Records an order of Madurantakapottappichcholan. Gift of the village of Attuputtur, free of taxes, in Nirvelur Nadu in the district of Urrukkattukottam for conducting the Adi festival and for rendering the service called Rajagandagopalansandi.

421 of 1919 (Tamil) — On the same wall. Gift of land in the Brahmana village of Narranallur or Ramabhadrapuram for conducting the festivals Tiruvadhyanam Udaiyavansirappu and Ulagamunda Peruvayan Sirappu, in the month of Margali to Nallammangar, wife of Amman Appaiyyangar, son of Pattangi Periya Perumal by Visva Panditar, agent of Ettur Tirumalai Kumara Tatacharya, one of the managers of the Arulala Perumal temple.

422 of 1919 (Tamil) — On the same wall. Gift of money for offerings to be offered when the god is seated in the mandapa of the Hanuman temple in the Sannadhi street by

Kandadai Immadi Ramanuja Ayyangar for the merit of Periya Tirumalaiya Maharaya, who is also called Mahamandalesvara Chalukkaraja.

423 of 1919 (Tamil) — On the south wall of the same rock. In modern characters. Records that Govindacharya, son of Prativadibhayankara Rangacharya, is entitled to receive first tirtham, Arulappadu and other privileges in the temple.

424 of 1919 (Tamil) — On the same wall. In modern characters. Seems to record that Maharajarajasree Sitakunnirayar dug out a channel that connected the Sarvatirtha and the Anantasaras while Nawab Sadullakhan Bahadur was governing the Karnatic provinces.

425 of 1919 (Grantha and Tamil) — On the west wall of the same rock. In modern characters. Registers the grant of certain privileges in the temple of Arulala Perumal to a certain Konappachariyar.

426 of 1919 (Tamil) — On the same wall. Gift of land to the temple of Arulala Perumal by a native of Velurnadu.

427 of 1919 (Tamil) — On the same wall. Gift of land to the temple by a native of Panangudi in Valivalakurram, a sub-division of Arumolidevavalanadu, a district of Solamandalam.

428 of 1919 (Tamil) — On the same wall. Gift of 17 Gandagopalanmadai coins, then current, to the same temple, by Vallitunai Aparasar, son of Sindamarasar of Tyagasamudrappatti. The money was held in trust by the residents of Amur in Tenpaiyurkottam, a district of Jayangodasolamandalam.

429 of 1919 (Tamil) — On the same wall. Gift of 33 head of cattle for a lamp by a native of Malaiyamandalam.

430 of 1919 (Tamil verse) — On the same wall. Records the gift of gold, yajnopavita thread and ten perpetual lamps to god Vishnu of Attiyur by Kalingarkon.

431 of 1919 (Tamil) — On the same wall. Registers that

a lady Perarulalan Korri, daughter of Settalur Pemman of Kuttanur made a will that 100 kulis of land purchased by the sale of her jewels will belong to the temple after her demise.

432 of 1919 (Tamil) — On the same wall. Gift of the village of Uludamangalam, the northern hamlet of Madurantakachaturvedimangalam, for conducting the festivals in the months of Adi and Purattasi and the service called Gandagopalansandi and repairs by Madurantaka Pottappichola Manumasiddarasan in the 15th year of the reign of Rajarajadeva.

433 of 1919 (Tamil) — On the same wall. Gift of 96 sheep and a ram for a lamp by a native of Varagur or Alagiyasola-chaturvedimangalam, an independent village (taniyur) in Vadagarai Vesalippadi, a sub-division of Naduvunadu or Rajarajavalanadu.

434 of 1919 (Tamil) — On the south wall of the same rock. Gift of the village of Vayalaiyarrur including Puducheri, free of taxes, for conducting the festivals in the months of Adi and Purattasi and for rendering the service called Gandagopalansandi by Madhurantaka Pottappichchola Manumasiddarasan Tirukkalattidevan Gandagopalan in the 15th year of Rajarajadeva.

435 of 1919 (Tamil) — On the same wall. Gift of 43 head of cattle for a lamp to the same temple.

436 of 1919 (Tamil) — On the same wall. Begins with the historical introduction. Gift of 96 sheep for a lamp by a native of Sirramur in Vallanadu, a sub-division of Venkunrakottam.

437 of 1919 (Tamil) — On the same wall. Gift of 12 buffaloes for ½ lamp by a native of Nellur in Pattaiyanadu.

438 of 1919 (Tamil) — On the same wall. Gift of the village of Paluyur or Rajendrasolanallur, free of taxes, for conducting the festivals in the months of Adi and Purattasi

and for rendering the service called Gandagopalansandi by the individual mentioned in No. 434 above in the 18th year of Rajarajadeva.

439 of 1919 (Tamil) — On the same wall. Gift of money for offerings and for Dhanurmasa worship in the month of Margali by Vengadattar, mother of Munjai Ragava Panditar.

440 of 1919 (Tamil) — On the same wall. Incomplete. Begins with the words-the historical introduction of Vikramachola. Records a sale of land free of taxes, for offerings, in the villages of Avinasinallur separated from Peymambakkam and Vadamambakkam, the northern hamlets of Madurantaka-chadurvedimangalam.

441 of 1919 (Tamil) — On the same wall. Gift of 1,750 Nellurpudumadai coins for purchase of land for offerings by a merchant of Karayappalli in Malaimandalam.

442 of 1919 (Tamil) — On the same wall. Records an order of Madurantaka Pottappichchola declaring a gift of 13 velis of land stipulating that the land that can be converted into a flower garden should be so utilised, the remaining portion can be enjoyed free of taxes by the devotees in charge of the flower garden.

443 of 1919 (Tamil) — (Tamil.) On the same wall. Gift of the four villages, Nedungal, Karumbakkam, Mambakkam, and Sangaracharyapuram or Suruttil by Alagiyamanavala Jiyar, the kelvi of Periyakoil.

444 of 1919 (Grantha and Tamil) — On the west wall of the same rock. Records the gift of the village of Udaiyakamam in Antannudravishaya by Somaladevi Mahadevi for daily worship and offerings to the god. It also mentions Srimat Anantavarma Rahuttaraya who is stated to have belonged to the Ganga family and some of his birudas. He is stated to have camped at Abhinava Varanavasi (perhaps Conjeevaram.)

445 of 1919 (Tamil) — On the same wall. Records the gift of 128 cows and four bulls by Kalingesvara Aniyanga Bhimadeva Rahutta for four perpetual lamps in the temple.

446 of 1919 (Grantha and Tamil) — On the same wall. Gives the geneology of Gandagopala and records the gift of a number of villages for conducting the festivals in the months of Adi and Purattasi, the service called Gandagopalansandi and repairs by Madurantaka Pottappichcholan Manumasiddarasan Tirukkalattidevan or Gandagopalan.

447 of 1919 (Tamil) — On the same wall. Records a gift of land by Alagyamanavala Jiyar mentioned in No. 443 above for offerings. Mentions the shrine of Tondaradippodi Alvar and Pratapadevarajendrapuram or Etirajapuram.

448 of 1919 (Tamil) — On the same wall. Records a gift of land for offerings by the same individual. Mentions the shrines of Alagiyasingar and Tiruppanalvar.

449 of 1919 (Grantha and Tamil) — On the west and south walls of the same rock. Gift of gold for offering cakes during festival days by Satagopa [mman] Lakshmana [mman], a disciple of Satagopa Jiyar. It is stated at Urukkattu-kottam in which Kanchipuram was situated is said to have belonged to Chandragirirajya.

450 of 1919 (Tamil) — On the north wall of the same rock. Gift of a lamp by a Nayaka of the Malaimandalam.

451 of 1919 (Tamil) — On the same wall. Gift of a lamp and a lamp-stand to the same temple by Eraniyakka Manavalan of Karayapalli in Malaimandalam.

452 of 1919 (Tamil) — On the same wall. Gift of 32 cows and one bull for a lamp to the same temple by a native of Ainjurmullaippadi in Sengunranadu, a sub-division of Kalatturkottam, a district of Jayangondasolamandalam.

543 of 1919 (Tamil) — On the same wall. Gift of 15

Bhujabalan Annagakkaranmadai (coin) for a lamp by Posani [Pu] doli Reddi of Savukkanseruvu in Mundanadu, a sub-division of Nellurnadu.

454 of 1919 (Tamil) — On the north wall of the same rock. Gift of the villages of Amedinallur or Anavaratasundara-chaturvedimangalam and Akkaramerpakkam in Payyur-kottam for conducting the service called Gandagopalansandi and for celebrating festivals in the temple by Madurantaka Pottappichcholan Manumasiddarasan Tirukkalattideva or Gandagopala in the 18th year of Rajarajadeva. It is also stated at the end that in the 141st year of Perumal Sundara Pandyadeva, the village Akkaramerpakkam was exclusively assigned for the benefit of the Perumal.

455 of 1919 (Tamil) — On the same wall. Gift of 132 sheep for a lamp to the same temple by Siddappa Nayaka Surappa Nayaka of Vinnamalai in Pattainadu of Vimarasar Tantrapalar of Tyagasamudrapatti, one of the Mudalis of Gandagopaladeva.

456 of 1919 (Tamil) — On the same wall. Gift of 96 sheep for a lamp by Peddarasar, son of Madurantaka Pottappichcholan Nallasiddarasan to the same temple.

457 of 1919 (Tamil) — On the same wall. Gift of 71 sheep, 31 goats and one ram for a lamp by a native of Segattur in the Nellore district.

458 of 1919 (Tamil) — On the same wall. Gift of the village of Madaganmedu, a hamlet of Ukkal in Kaliyur-kottam, for conducting the service called Gandagopalansandi and for certain festivals in the temple by Madurantaka Pottappichcholan Manumasiddarasan Tirukkalattidevan or Gandagopala in the 18th year of Rajarajadeva.

459 of 1919 (Tamil) — On the same wall. Gift of 32 cows, one bull and a brass lampstand for burning a lamp in the same temple by a native of Urukkadu in Urukattukottam.

460 of 1919 (Tamil) — On the same wall. Gift of 32 cows, 1 bull, and a lampstand by Perumanadi Setti, son of Nakkampandai of the weaver caste in Mayilappur, for burning a lamp.

461 of 1919 (Tamil) — On the same wall. Gift of the village of Paiyinur or Rajakesarichaturvedimangalam in Amurkottam for conducting the service called Gandagopalan-sandi, for festivals and repairs by Madurantaka Pottappichcholan Manumasiddarasan Tirukkalattidevan or Gandagopala in the 17th year of Rajarajadeva.

462 of 1919 (Grantha) — On the same wall. Verse in praise of Tatayadesika.

463 of 1919 (Tamil) — On the same wall. Gift of the village of Mavandur including Erusevagachcheri in Erikilnadu, a sub-division of Kaliyurkottam, for conducting the service called Gandagopalansandi, for festivals and repairs by the chief mentioned in No.461 above in the 15th year of Rajarajadeva.

464 of 1919 (Tamil) — On the north wall of the same rock. Registers the gift of the village of Pudur including Vallaivayil, the northern hamlet of Madurantakachaturvedimangalam. The object of the grant and the donor are the same as in No. 463 above. The gift was made in the 15th year of Rajarajadeva.

465 of 1919 (Tamil) — On the same wall. Damaged at the end. Begins with the historical introduction. Gift of 96 sheep for a lamp by a private individual.

466 of 1919 (Tamil) — On the same wall. Gift of the village of Manimangalam or Gramasikhamanichaturvedimangalam in Puliyurkottam. The object of the grant and the donor are the same as in No. 362 above. Quotes the 16th year of Rajarajadeva.

467 of 1919 (Tamil) — On the same wall. Gift of the

village of Kundiyarrurtandalam in Kaliyurkottam. The object of the grant and the donor are the same as in No. 362 above. Quotes the 16th year of Rajarajadeva.

468 of 1919 (Tamil) — On the same wall. Gift of the village of Karanai in Kachchiyurnadu for offerings in the temple by a private individual.

469 of 1919 (Tamil) — On the same wall. Gift of the village of Tiruninravur or Virudarajabuyankarachaturvedimangalam in Pularkottam. The object of the grant and the name of the donor are the same as in No. 363 above. Quotes the 18th year of Rajarajadeva.

470 of 1919 (Tamil) — On the same wall. Gift of the village of Vayalai (ka?) vur in Eyilkottam. The object of the grant and the name of the donor are the same as in No.363 above. Quotes the 15th year of Rajarajadeva.

471 of 1919 (Tamil) — On the same wall. Damaged. Begins with the historical introduction. Seems to record a gift of land for bathing with 81 potfuls of water, the god Arulala Perumal who was pleased to take his stand at Tiruvattiyr in Eyilnadu, a sub-division of Eyilkottam, a district of Jayangondasolamandalam.

472 of 1919 (Tamil) — On the same wall. Records an agreement by the trustees of the temple to Kanappa Settiyar, son of Settiyar of the Vannikkagotra to provide certain sacred offerings to the god on particular occasions for an amount of 100 pon deposited by him in the temple treasury.

473 of 1919 (Grantha) — On the same wall. Records the construction by an individual (probably a king) referred to as Naralokavira, of the kitchen rooms, a mandapa and the prakara walls, the setting up of a recumbent image of Hari and the further gifts of a gold pinnacle to this new shrine, ten perpetual lamps and land for a flower garden.

474 of 1919 (Telugu) — On the same wall. The

introductory portion of the inscription mentions the king's conquests and the rest of the record registers a gift of five villages yielding an annual income of 1,500 varahas from sacred offerings to the god.

475 of 1919 (Grantha) — On the north wall of the same rock. Records that the worshipful Kamalanandana Tatayya constructed all the necessary vehicles (vahanas) for the god, that he covered the Kalyanakoti and Punyakoti vimanas with thick gold plates and that he dug a tank called Devarajarnava for the god's delight.

476 of 1919 (Tamil) — On the same wall. Gift of money for offerings on certain festival days.

477 of 1919 (Tamil) — On the same wall. Records the assignment of all the taxes accruing from all the villages, except fifty per cent of the local devadana lands in Salukkipparru in Venkunrakottam, to provide for the expenses amounting to 3,000 pon required for the services called Virakeralansandi and Narayanan Anantan or Sundara Pandya Kalingarayansandi and for feeding Brahmans. Iraniyamuttanadu in Pandimandalam and Tiruvandapuram are mentioned.

478 of 1919 (Grantha and Tamil) — On the same wall. Gives in Sanskrit verse the genealogy of the king and records in Tamil that for the merit of his father Narasa Nayaka Udaiyar and his mother Nagajiamman, he had the Punyakoti-vimana of the god, gilded with pure gold.

479 of 1919 (Tamil) — On the same wall. Registers an agreement given by the treasurers of the temple and the manager Ettur Tirumalai Kumara Tatacharya Ayyan to Toppur Tirumalai Nayaka, the *delevay* (military commander) under Mahamandalesvara Ramaraju Venkatapatideva Maharaja, to provide certain offerings and worship to the gods Perarulalar, Ashtabhujattemberuman, Sonnavannamseydaperumal, the goddesses Perundeviyar and Serakulavalli Nachchiyar and for

certain Alvars on certain festival days in return for 570 pon of gold which was the income derivable from the two villages, Ravuttanallur in Nagariyilsirmai in Padaividurajya, a subdivision of Jayangondasolamandalam or Tondaimandalam and Serukkupettuvur in Sengalunirpattusirmai in Chandragirirajya.

480 of 1919 (Grantha and Tamil) — On the same wall. The Sanskrit verse praises the king's munificence to poets and the Tamil verse describes his prowess.

481 of 1919 (Tamil) — On the base of the east verandah round the rock. Records that Narasayya of Solaippakkam, son of Virupaksha Danayaka of Puhattur, assigned the income of the village of Pallichiruppakkam to the temple authorities for conducting certain offerings to the god and also made provision for the supply of a portion of the prasada to his son Chitamaraja.

482 of 1919to the temple authorities — On the base of the east verandah round the rock. End much damaged. Records the gift, by purchase, of the village Kudaluragraharam by Surappa Nayaka, son of Pottu Nayaka of Kasyapa gotra, for the Padivettai and the Topputirunal festivals.

483 of 1919 (Tamil) — On the same base. Registers sale of one veli of land for 200 pon to Nayanar Tondaimanar of Chakrapaninallur, in Sevvirurnadu, a district of Pandimandalam, which was then presented by him to one Samantanarayanan for rearing a flower garden for the god. The measuring rod nadualakkumkol is mentioned.

484 of 1919 (Tamil) — On the same base. Records a gift of goldi by Chennayyangar, son of Timmayyangar of Pallipadu, for certain repairs to a ruined tank called Porramaraikkulam and for offerings to the god to be made in the adjoining garden, on four festival days. The above charities are stated to have been made for the merit of Raja Ramaraju Ayyan.

485 of 1919 (Tamil) — On the same base. Records

gift by purchase, by Madhusudanan Apatsahayan or Ramachandradeva (a resident of Seravanmadevi in Pandimandalam, of the village of Kambantangal or Apatsahayanallur in Salukkipparru, a sub-division of Anukkavurnadu in Venkunrakottam which was a district of Jayangondasolamandalam) to a matha, for rearing a flower garden and supplying three garlands to the god daily.

486 of 1919 (Tamil) — On the same base. Damaged. Seems to record a gift of money by (Tri) parikkon Tayandan or Viluppadarayan, a manradi of Tirunavalur in Tirumunaippadinadu, a district of Naduvinmandalam, for the daily supply of four tirutolla garlands to the god.

487 of 1919 (Tamil) — On the base of the south verandah round the same rock. Records the gift, free of taxes, of the village of Alattur in Uttaramelurparru, a sub-division of Irumbedunadu in Venkunrakottam by Ilaialvan Kalingarayan of Nettur, for offerings to the god every month on the asterism of Chitra in which he was born and for worship to the image of Tiruvali Alvar consecrated by him.

488 of 1919 (Tamil) — On the same base. Incomplete. Mentions only the name of the donor, viz., Terpoliyaninran Tamatandan or Soliyadaraiyan of Melaikkodumalur or Uttamapandyanallur in Vadatalai Sembiyanadu, a sub-division of Pandi-nadu.

489 of 1919 (Tamil) — On the same base. Records the gift as sarvamanya of the village of Tindurai in Amarurnadu, a sub-division of Pulalkottam by Madurantaka Pottapichcholan Rajagandagopala for offerings and worship, to the god during the service called Anaikattina Sankaranarayanansandi. Quotes the 8th year (presumably of Rajarajadeva).

490 of 1919 (Tamil) — On the base of the south verandah round the same rock. Ratification of the order contained in No. 489 above by the residents of Tindurai.

491 of 1919 (Tamil) — On the same base. Records the gift of 32 cows and 1 bull by Jnanamperran Villavarayan Tiruvekamba Udaiyan, a desavellala of Vaigavur in Urrukkattukottam for the supply of ghee for a perpetual lamp and of milk to the god.

492 of 1919 (Tamil) — On the same base. Records gift of cows by a private individual of Narayanapuram for a perpetual lamp for the god.

493 of 1919 (Tamil) — On the same base. Records the gift, by Ilaiyalvan Kalingarayar of Nettur, of the taxes of the villages of Sirukoli and Perunkoli in Uttaramelurparru, for the expenses connected with the offerings to the god Nayanar Emberumanar consecrated by him, for the repairs the temple, and bhashyavritti for expounding the Ramanujabhashya and the feeding of certain jiyars in the temple matha.

494 of 1919 (Tamil) — On the same base. Records the gift, by Mahabalivanarayar of the village of Kulottunga-vilagam in the eastern portion of Urrukkattukottam, free of taxes, for offerings, daily worship, lamp, garland and other things required for the god Pagaiyarmudisudumperumal set up by him in the temple.

495 of 1919 (Tamil) — On the same base. Registers an agreement by the temple trustees and the manager Alagiyamanavalajiyar to provide certain offerings to the god on certain days from the income of Vallattanjeri Perichchambakkam presented by Tiruvengalappar, son of Siruttirumalaiyangar of Talappakkam.

496 of 1919 (Tamil) — On the same base. Registers an agreement given by the temple authorities to Periyatirumalaiyangar, son of Annamaiyangar and Siruttirumalaiyangar, son of Periyatirumalaiyangar of Talapakkam for providing certain offerings to the god and for conducting certain festivals at specified scales of expenditure.

497 of 1919 (Grantha) — On the same base. One of the verses records the gift of the village Sardulapakam (Pulippakkam) in Tondaimandalam by Kodandaraghava for expenses connected with the daily worship of the god. Another is a benedictory verse in praise of the god and the third praises the king's prowess.

498 of 1919 (Grantha and Tamil) — On the same base. Incomplete. Records the gift made by Srimatu Kumara Danayaka, of Talayarimanya to the sattina Sri Vaishnavas of the temple, for the merit of Rayasam Ayyapparasayyan and Narasayyan of Salaippakkam.

499 of 1919 (Tamil) — On the same base. Built in. Gift of money for meeting the expenses on certain festival days. The grant was registered in the name of Porerru Nayinar, son of Uruppattur Tiruvengadaiyan by Periya Tirumalainambi Chakkarayar, agent of Ettur Tirumalai Kumara Tatacharya Ayyan, manager of the temple.

500 of 1919 (Tamil) — On the west verandah round the same rock. End built in. Records gift of cows by a private individual for a perpetual lamp to the god.

501 of 1919 (Tamil) — On the same verandah. Records gift of 32 cows and 1 bull by Grakki Perumandidevan, son of Kamarasar, for a perpetual lamp for the god.

502 of 1919 (Telugu) — On the same verandah. Records gift of the village of [Musuli] by Tamappa Nayadu, son of Chinnakrishna Nayadu of Pachada and grandson of Tamma Nayadu as Tiruvidaiyattam for the expenses connected with the worship, offerings to the god and for conducting a festival during the Rohini asterism every month.

503 of 1919 (Tamil) — On the same verandah. Records gift of 32 cows and 1 bull by Ramanakkan, a nayaka of Malai-mandalam for a perpetual lamp for the god.

504 of 1919 (Tamil) — On the same verandah. Gift of

money, accruing as income from a village, for offerings on festival days and for a flower garden. The amount was entrusted with Rangayadevasola Maharaja, son of Chalikyadeva Chola Maharaya.

505 of 1919 (Telugu) — On the same verandah. Seems to record a gift of land for offerings to god Varadarajasvamin on the Rohini festival day. Mentions Tammi Bhupati, son of Chinna Krishna.

506 of 1919 (Tamil) — On the north verandah round the same rock. Beginning built in. Mentions Tirumalainambi Ramanujaiyangar and Tirumalai Anantachari.

507 of 1919 (Tamil) — On the same verandah. Gift of money which accrued from the village Pambundi or Krishnapuram which was assigned by Mahamandalesvara Ramaraju Chinna Timmayadeva Maharaja to Mahamandalesvara Vallabhayadeva Maharaja who had to conduct the charities.

508 of 1919 (Tamil) — On the same verandah. Registers the orders of Nilagangaraiyan Tiruvekambamudaiyan making a gift, free of taxes, of the village of Vallavadaraiyancheri in Urrukkattukottam for offerings and worship, to the god and for the service called Kumaragopalansandi instituted by him.

509 of 1919 (Tamil) — On the same verandah. Gift of money by Perumal Dasar for making offerings to the god at the festival in the vasantantoppu in the month of Chittirai.

510 of 1919 (Kanarese) — On the same verandah. End built in. Seems to record the fact that Krishnaraya (name not mentioned) gilded the Punyakotivimana with fine gold for the merit of himself, his father Narasananayaka Vodeya and his mother Nagaladevi.

511 of 1919 (Sanskrit in Grantha) — On the north verandah round the same rock. The same verses are re-engraved above this inscription in Kanarese, Nagari and Telugu characters respectively. Records that King

Achyutaraya, son of Narasa, performed the Muktatulabhara ceremony for himself and his queen Varadambikadevi at Kanchi and that his son China Venkatadri gave munificent gifts to Brahmans.

512 of 1919 (Tamil) — On the same verandah. Built in at the beginning. Records gift by Ramanujapanditar Ayyan of 50 panam of gold, which was to be invested on land and the income therefrom utilized for providing certain offerings to the god on certain specified ocasions.

513 of 1919 (Sanskrit in Kanarese) — On the base of the east, south and west verandahs round the same rock. Same as No. 478 above.

514 of 1919 (Tamil) — Left of entrance into the Narasimhasvamin shrine in the same temple. Records gift of one lampstand and cows by Kettamaladeviyar, one of the wives of pillayar Gandagopalar for a perpetual lamp to the god.

515 of 1919 (Tamil) — In the same place. Beginning built in. Seems to record gift of 96 sheep by a manradi of Pallapuram in Puliyurkottam for a perpetual lamp. Tirunarayanam is mentioned as a liquid measure.

516 of 1919 (Tamil) — In the same place. Beginning and end built in. Begins with the historical introduction. Seems to record gift of 197 1/2 kalanjus of gold of 9 5/8 marru fineness tested by the temple touchstone (koyilkal) for a bathing vessel (sahasradhara) for the god Srirangasayi or Vikramasola (vinnagar perumal) in the temple by Kanjaran Vasishtan Kumarasvami of Tenkanjaru in Tiruvindalurnadu.

517 of 1919 (Tamil) — On the right wall, inside the same shrine. Records gift of land in the meltundam of Tirukkattukottam, free of taxes, for the expenses of the service called Kulottungasolansandi and for offerings to the god. Vanduvaravatavirruirundan Palavarayan of Mutturukurram in Pandimandalam figures as a signatory.

518 of 1919 (Tamil) — On the same wall. Incomplete. Fragment.

519 of 1919 (Tamil) — On the same wall. Begins with a historical introduction. The inscription is highly damaged and is incomplete. Records the gift of an ear ornament and of sheep for a perpetual lamp to the god Tiruvattiyur Alvar by Setti Rajamanikkattar or Nulambamadeviyar, the daughter of Ayyan Settiyar, the headman of Kolavaimang in Arumolidevavalanadu. Her full name is given Jayangondasola Viranulambamadeviyar.

520 of 1919 (Tamil) — On the left wall, inside the same shrine. Begins with the historical introduction. Gift of land and a salt pan in Taiyur or Rajakesarinallur in Kumilinadu in Amurkottam.

521 of 1919 (Tamil) — On the left wall, inside the same shrine. Seems to ratify the grant recorded in No. 520 above.

522 of 1919 (Tamil) — On the left wall of the gopura in front of the same shrine. Damaged. Begins with a historical introduction. Sale of land by the assembly to the temple for offerings and worship.

523 of 1919 (Tamil) — On the right of entrance into the first prakara. Records the gift of the village of Melaivilagam in Vadakarai Manavilkottam for supplying a garland to the temple and for a flower garden by one of the servants of Sayana Udaiyar.

524 of 1919 (Tamil) — On the left of entrance into the same prakara. Gift of 300 kulis of land in Tenkarai Tiruchcholai for a flower garden.

525 of 1919 (Tamil) — On the east wall of the second prakara. Registers the gift of the village Meykavanur in Puliyurkottam in Tiruttanisirmai for daily offerings.

526 of 1919 (Tamil) — On the same wall. Gift of land for a flower garden to the temple by Saluva Timmaraja, son of

Saluva Vijayadeva Maharaja who was a feudatory of the king.

527 of 1919 (Telugu) — On the same wall. Gift of the village of Vadakanipakkam for offerings to the god by Gopinayaningaru, the agent of Ramaraju Chinna Timmayadeva Maharaya for the merit of the latter.

528 of 1919 (Tamil) — On the same wall. Records gift of money by Mattili Varadaraja, son of Mattili Somaraju Potturaja for providing daily offerings, to the god and for special offerings on his natal-star day. Mattili Varadaraja bears a number of birudas.

529 of 1919 (Tamil) — On the same wall. Gift of money for offerings. The money was deposited for interest with Madabusi Ugrani Rayar.

530 of 1919 (Tamil) — On the same wall. Registers that Vallabhayadeva Maharaya, son of Somavamsadhisvara Sriman Mahamandalesvara Ramarajuraya Varadaraja of Atreyagotra, made a gift of a garden for the merit of his mother Krishnamma, and left it in the possession of Uttandarayar to be utilized as a flower garden and for conducting the garden festival and leased out permanently to Narasayya, son of Samkirtana Ramanujayya, the village of Sittananjeri in the Poliyursirmai, the income from which was to be utilized for conducting the topputirumal festivals of the god.

531 of 1919 (Tamil) — On the east wall of the second prakara. Records the gift of the village of Paruttiputtur in Tiruttanisirmai for offerings by Tirumalainambi Chakrarayar, the agent of Acharya Ayyan of Ettur, Tirumalai, Kumbakonam and Tirumalirunjolai. The gift was inscribed in the name of Aramudalvar, grandson of Kidambi Srinivasa Ayyangar and others.

532 of 1919 (Telugu) — On the same wall. Same as No. 530 above.

533 of 1919 (Telugu) — On the same wall. Same as No. 474 above.

534 of 1919 (Tamil) — On the same wall. Records the assignment, on interest of the income of certain villages to Rayasam Venkatadri, son of Mosalimadugu Timmaraja, for providing offerings to the god.

535 of 1919 (Tamil) — On the same wall. Records the assignment of the income of certain villages to Ramaraja, son of Mahamandalesvara Chikkaraja of Araviti (?) for conducting the annual festivals of the god and for providing certain offerings and cakes.

536 of 1919 (Tamil) — On the same wall. Gift of certain lands for providing cakes to the god.

537 of 1919 (Tamil) — On the south wall of the same prakara. Gift of cows and a lampstand by Mayyur Ramannadevan, a member of the Nayakanmar of Malai-mandalam for a perpetual lamp in the temple.

538 of 1919 (Tamil) — On the same wall. Gift of cows for a perpetual lamp to the temple by Srikumaran, a member of the Nayakanmar of Malaimandalam.

539 of 1919 (Tamil) — On the same wall. Gift of 32 cows and a bull by Tiruvattiyurkorri of Tiruvayppadi for a perpetual lamp in the temple.

540 of 1919 (Telugu) — On the same wall. Records the repair of prakara walls in the Varadaraja temple at Kanchi, by the son of Doddayacharya.

541 of 1919 (Kanarese) — On the same wall. Same as No. 50 of 1900.

542 of 1919 (Telugu) — On the same wall. Same as No. 541 above.

543 of 1919 (Tamil) — On the south wall of the second prakara. Assignment of the income of 17 villages to the temple for providing special offerings at the instance of the king when he visited the temple and weighed himself against pearl in company with his wife Varadadevi Amman and Kumara Venkatadri Udayar and made a gift of 1,000 cows.

544 of 1919 (Tamil) — On the same wall. Records that in the year Virodhi, on the day of Karttikabahula panchami, on the occasion of his coronation, king Achyutaraya directed Saluva Nayaka to assign villages to the temples of Varadaraja and Ekambaranatha equally, neither more nor less. But as Saluva Nayaka gave more to Ekambaranatha. On hearing this, Achyutaraya equalised the number of villages by redistribution.

545 of 1919 (Telugu) — On the same wall. Same as No. 544 above.

546 of 1919 (Kanarese) — On the same wall. Registers gift of villages and lands to the temple of Varadarajasvamin on the occasion of the tulabhara ceremony of the king.

547 of 1919 (Kanarese) — On the same wall. Registers grant of certain villages to Varadarajasvamin and Ekambaranatha equally on the occasion of the coronation of the king.

548 of 1919 (Nagari) — On the same wall. Same as No. 547 above.

549 of 1919 (Kanarese in Nagari) — On the same wall. Same as No. 541 above.

550 of 1919 (Tamil) — On the same wall. Assignment of certain lands granted for providing offerings during the time of Krishnaraya by Vadamalai Annan and Viramaraja. These lands were now made over to Nagaraja, son of Siddaraja of Somavamsa.

551 of 1919 (Tamil) — On the west wall of the same prakara. Gift of 115 sheep for a lamp by a native of Karum(bu)r.

552 of 1919 (Tamil) — On the same wall. Gift of 33 head of cattle for a lamp by a native of Puliyur in Puliyurkottam.

553 of 1919 (Tamil) — On the same wall. Records a gift of 4 cows for 1/8 lamp.

554 of 1919 (Tamil) — On the same wall. Gift of 32 cows

and a bull for a lamp and of 120 kasus for conducting worship and offerings at the service called Dhanmaparipalan-sandi and for feeding five devotees in the temple by Tiruvarangamudaiyan or Rajadhiraja Malaiyarayan or Danmaparipalan, son of Munaiyadaraiyan or Kulottungasola Malaiyarayan, one of the Malai Mudalis residing in Tirunedumbirai in Perumurnadu, a sub-division of Manavir-kottam.

555 of 1919 (Tamil) — On the west wall of the second prakara. Gift of 33 head of cattle for a lamp by Kondu Nagadevaraja or Gopa(la) Perumal of Nattapadinadu.

556 of 1919 (Tamil) — On the same wall. Registers an order of Madurantaka Pottappichcholan stating that the assembly of the people of Jayangondasolamandalam remitted six kalam of paddy per veli of land granted as devadanam, tiruvidaiyattam, pallichchandam, agaraparru, madapparru, jivitaparru, padaiparru, and vanniyaparu.

557 of 1919 (Tamil) — On the same wall. Gift of 17 3/4 veli of land in Periyananjeri or Virasimhachaturvedimangalam, a hamlet of Ukkal in Kaliyurkottam, a district of Jayangonda-solamadalam, by Periya Perumal or Perumaldasan to 58 Brahmans for reciting the Vaishnava hymn tirumoli.

558 of 1919 (Tamil) — On the same wall. Gift of 16 buffaloes for 1/2 lamp by a native of Urrukkadu or Rajarajachaturvedimangalam in Avurkurram, a sub-division of Nittavinodavalanadu.

559 of 1919 (Tamil) — On the same wall. Gift of 32 cows, a bull and a lampstand for burning a perpetual lamp in the temple by a native of Vendattur in Sengattunadu, a sub-division of Sengattukottam, a district of Jayangondasolamandalam.

560 of 1919 (Tamil) — On the same wall. Gift of 99 head of cattle for 3 perpetual lamps by the individual mentioned in No. 557 above.

561 of 1919 (Tamil) — On the same wall. Gift of 80 pon for offering cakes on the festival days in the months of Ani, Purattasi, Masi and Vaigasi, out of the 9 pon and 6 panam accruing as interest every year at 1 panam per cent. During one of the festivals the god had to be taken to the temple of Sonnavannamseyda Perumal on two days and cakes were offered.

562 of 1919 (Tamil) — On the same wall. Gift of land by Allalagamundan, Viragamundan, Srirangagamundan and Gavundaiyan, the Pradhani mudalis of Idainadu in Poysala-rajya, for supplying cardamom to the temple.

563 of 1919 (Tamil) — On the same wall. Gift of 11 buffaloes for a perpetual lamp by Tondaimandala Gurukularayan, a native of Velichcheri or Silasikhamani-chaturvedimangalam in Puliyurkottam.

564 of 1919 (Tamil) — On the same wall. Unfinished. Records the gift of the village of Sirupuliyur in Ukkalparru by Kattari Saluvan.

565 of 1919 (Tamil) — On the same wall. Records a gift of land by purchase for providing offerings to the god by a native of Melmandalam.

566 of 1919 (Tamil) — On the west wall of the second prakara. Records a gift of land in Perunagar in Perunagarnadu, a sub-division of Venkunrakottam, a district of Jayangonda-solamandalam by Viraperumal Edirilisola Sambuvarayan Alappirandanayan or Rajaraja Sambuvarayan, grandson of Sengeni Viragaran Ammsiappan for offerings and worship at the service called Alappirandansandi following the service called Gandagopalansandi. The donor made a gift of land in Panangattuppundi, a hamlet of Ukkal for the supply of flower garlands to the god.

567 of 1919 (Tamil) — On the same wall. Gift of certain privileges in the temple to Venkatadri, son of Dharmayya of Krottapalli.

568 of 1919 (Tamil) — On the same wall. Gift of land in the villages of Perumbudur with its hamlets Melaipattu, Kottuppakkam, Panchalipattu, Payvaniyapattu, Kusapattu and Kachchipattu for conducting the service Rahuttarayansandi called after the donor Nalla Siddarasa, who bears various birudas and who is stated to have been born of the Pallava family and of Bharadvaja gotra.

569 of 1919 (Telugu) — On the same wall. Same as No. 498 above.

570 of 1919 (Tamil) — On the same wall. Built in at the beginning. Records the gift of 32 cows and 1 bull by one of the handmaids of Gandagopaladeva, for a perpetual lamp in the temple.

571 of 1919 (Tamil) — On the north wall of the same prakara. Gift of land in Eriyagaram, a hamlet of Kuttanur or Rajadhirajachaturvedimangalam, by a native of the latter village for maintaining a flower garden for supplying sacred garlands.

572 of 1919 (Tamil) — On the same wall. Seems to record that, while the king, seated with his consorts under the canopy called Ariyannavallan on the throne of Viravallala in the Abhishekamandapa, was listening to the songs of Sadagopan, he directed that a house for dwelling together with certain privileges may be given to a certain Karambichettu Narasinga-bhattan who appears to have been an approved devotee of god.

573 of 1919 (Tamil) — On the same wall. Records the assignment of all taxes levied on the village of Murukkambakkam belonging to the temple to a servant (name lost) of Saluva Mangu Maharaja made on an occasion similar to the one mentioned in No.572 above.

574 of 1919 (Tamil) — On the same wall. Records that the god invested the title of Brahmatantra Svatantra Jiyan on Vaishnavadasa and directed that a matha should be established

for him with the lands necessary for its maintenance, that the
books procured by him should be left with him and that towards
the propagation of Ramanujadarsana by him and his disciples
after him, all disciples of Ramanuja and other devotees of the
god should take him in their community. The occasion for the
grant is the same as that mentioned in No. 572 above.

575 of 1919 (Tamil) — On the north wall of the
second prakara. Gift of the village of Tirumukkudal in
Salaipakkamsirmai in Kalatturkottam, a hamlet detached
from Madurantakam, for offerings by Salakkaraja Periya
Tirumalaiyadeva Maharaja, one of the feudatories of the king.

576 of 1919 (Tamil) — On the same wall. Records that
the king directed that, out of 1200 pon assigned by him, in
the year Vikriti, for offerings to the temple, 150 pon should
be transferred in the name of Govindayyangar, son of his
preceptor Urupputtur Nallan Chakravarti Sirrayyangar, who
was to receive 1/8th of the offerings as such.

577 of 1919 (Tamil) — On the same wall. Gift of 120 pon
for offerings to the temple of Raghunatha in Vegavati. The
money was deposited on interest with Ramabhatta, son of
Bhutanatha Chittibhatlu.

578 of 1919 (Tamil) — On the same wall. Stones missing
and mutilated. Seems to record a gift similar to that contained
in No. 572 above to a certain Vindukan.

579 of 1919 (Tamil) — On the same wall. Gift of 100
panam for celebrating the day of Sriyajanti festival on which
Sri Krishna was born. In making provision for worship and
offerings, it was particularly noted that the image of Krishna
should be represented as child drinking milk, placing the conch
at the mouth. The gift was engraved on stone in the name of
Vada Tiruvengadajiyar, the koil kelvi, who was the disciple of
Paravastu Nayinar Ayyangar at the instance of Kandadai
Ramanuja Ayyangar, one of the managers of the temple.

580 of 1919 (Tamil) — On the same wall. Gift of land for offerings by Tiruppadiraja for the merit of this father Mahamandalesvara Saluva Chinnayadeva Maharaja of the lunar race and gift of a garden for the merit of his daughter Akkamma.

581 of 1919 (Tamil) — On the same wall. Built in at the beginning. Gift of the village of Uttirasolal in Damalkottam by Tiruvengada Annan, son of Bhattadi(p)iran of Srivillipputtur.

582 of 1919 (Tamil) — On the same wall. Beginning built in. Gift of the village of Sittananjeri by Ramabhatta, son of Bhutanatha Chittabhatlu for making offerings to the god Vegavati Raghunathan.

583 of 1919 (Tamil) — On the same wall. Records that Narayana Settiyar, son of Periyanagu Settiyar of the Nedunkumara gotra, gave 530 gold coins to the god, the interest from which was ordered to be utilised for sacred offerings on certain festival days. Mentions also a temple and a matha dedicated to Tirukkachinambi, the Vaishnava devotee.

584 of 1919 (Tamil) — On the north wall of the second prakara. Records that the king, soon after his coronation in the year Virodhi, directed that the gift of villages made to the temple of Varadarajadeva and Ekambaranatha should be of equal value and ordered Saluva Nayaka to attend to it. But the latter gave more to Ekambaranatha than to Varadaraja and that, on hearing this, Achyuta went to Conjeevaram in person and effected the equalization between the two temples by casting lots.

585 of 1919 (Tamil) — On the same wall. Similar to No. 572 above. The recipient herein is Pottarasan, the minister (pradhani) of Saluva Mangu Maharaja. In addition, he was also given the right of levying taxes at 2 panam on storeyed houses and 1 panam on houses with inside verandahs.

586 of 1919 (Tamil) — On the same wall. Gift of the

village of Chedirayankuppam of Urattiparu in Nallurnadu, a sub-division of Venkunrakottam in Padaividurajyam for offerings and for conducting festivals by (Ettur) Tirumalai Kumara Tatacharya.

587 of 1919 (Tamil) — On the same wall. Gift of the villages of Alambakkam, Anambadi in Kurumbarainadu, a sub-division of Kalatturkottam in Padaividurajyam for offerings by the donor mentioned in No. 586 above. The gift was engraved in the name of Rangappayyangar, son of Annavayyangar, grandson of Pattangi Nayinar Ayyan.

588 of 1919 (Tamil) — On the same wall. Gift of the village of Telatteru in Idaivasalsirmai for conducting certain festivals. The record was engraved in the name of the Acharya of Tirumalai, Kumbakonam and Tiruma(rbar)pirunjolai (Tirumalirunjolai), Who had to meet the expenses out of the interest accruing on the money-income of the village.

589 of 1919 (Grantha and Tamil) — On the base of the south wall of the Anantalvar shrine in the same prakara. Records that Siyaganga of the Ganga dynasty built the Anantalvar shrine with stone. It refers to Cholendrasimha as his father and gives him the birudas Kuvalalapuraparamesvara, Gangakulotbhava and Siraimittaperumal.

590 of 1919 (Tamil) — Inside the Karumanikkavarada shrine in the same prakara. Records that the king set up in the temple, the image of Vikramachola Vinnagar Alvar and for its daily worship, made a gift of land, as devadana, in the village of Vilvalam, which was renamed Akalankanallur, in Kaliyurnadu, a sub-division of Kaliyurkottam.

591 of 1919 (Tamil) — On the base of the south wall of the same shrine. Gift of the village of Merpakkam near Anjur in Sengalunirpattusirmai which belonged to Dalavay Timmaraja, the agent of Mahamandalesvara Ramaraja Vithalaraja Chinna Timmaraja Pappu Timmayadeva Maharaja. The village was handed over to Dalavay Timmaraja

on lease for providing offerings to Arulala Perumal.

592 of 1919 (Tamil) — On the base of the north wall of same shrine. Records the assignment of the village of Iraiyur, the income from which, amounting to 120 pon, was ordered to be utilised for sacred offerings, garlands and butter for the god by Dalavay Koppu Nayakar, the agent of Mahamandalesvara Ramaraja Timmaraja Chinnatimmayadeva, for the merit of his master.

593 of 1919 (Tamil) — On the east wall of the Abhisheka mandapa in the same temple. Records the gift of 30 cows and a bull for a perpetual lamp in the temple of Sri Ramachandra Perumal in Visiranadu in Vadamandalam by the managers of the Arulala Perumal temple at Conjeevaram.

594 of 1919 (Tamil) — On the same wall. Gift of 33 head of cattle and a lampstand for a perpetual lamp by Nulappiyarrulan Narayananmbi Damodaran, one of the kelvi mudalis of Gandagopaladeva.

595 of 1919 (Tamil) — On the same wall. Records the building of the mandapa by Ilambilakattu Nayakar.

596 of 1919 (Tamil) — On the same wall. Gift of 33 head of cattle for a perpetual lamp by a native of Muranottamangalam in Valluvanadu in Malaimandalam.

597 of 1919 (Tamil) — On the same wall. Gift of 33 head of cattle and one lampstand for a perpetual lamp by Kandan Eranambi residing in the city of Kulamukku in Malai mandalam.

598 of 1919 (Tamil) — On the same wall. Gift of 33 head of cattle and a lampstand for a perpetual lamp by Iyyakkan Ayyanambi, a native of Karayappalli in Malaimandalam.

599 of 1919 (Tamil) — On the same wall. Incomplete. Gift of 100 panam for offering cakes during certain festivals.

600 of 1919 (Tamil) — On the same wall. Gift of money for offerings by a native of Kadavarayanpattu.

601 of 1919 (Tamil) — On the same wall. Gift·of 3,000 panam for offering cakes. The money was deposited with a native of Narasingarayapuram.

602 of 1919 (Grantha and Tamil) — On the south wall of the same mandapa. Built in at the beginning and incomplete. Mentions that king Somesvara was descended from the family of the Yadus and that Devika born of the Chalukya family was his chief queen.

603 of 1919 (Tamil) — On the same wall. Gift of 33 head of cattle and a lampstand for a perpetual lamp by a native of Rajarajapuram, a sub-division of Venkunrakottam.

604 of 1919 (Tamil) — On the same wall. Enumerates the localities to which the (image of the) god may resort to after it was carried in procession on the elephant, horse and garuda vehicles respectively and after the car festival.

605 of 1919 (Tamil) — On the same wall. Gift of 33 cattle for a perpetual lamp, in the shrine of (Periyapirattiyar) the senior consort of Arulala Perumal, by a native of Tirumunaippadinadu in Naduvilmandalam.

606 of 1919 (Tamil) — On the same wall. Gift of 4 cows for one-eighth lamp by a native of Sural in Vellnadu.

607 of 1919 (Tamil) — On the same wall. Refers to an order of Madurantaka Pottappichcholan according to which taxes were levied on all oil merchants in Mammudi-cholapperunderuvu in Conjeevaram. Baudhapalli is mentioned as one of the places exempted from this tax. Stones with the insignia of Gandagopala are meant to mark his jurisdiction.

608 of 1919 (Tamil) — On the same wall. Gift of 97 cows and one bull for three perpetual lamps by Kon Kattaiyan, a minister of Ganapatideva.

609 of 1919 (Tamil) — On the same wall. Refers to the order of Madurantaka Pottappichcholan. Records a grant similar to that mentioned in No. 607 above. The tax was

levied herein on merchants, Saliya weavers and other people residing in the streets of Arumolidevapperunderuvu, Rajarajapperunderuvu, Nigarllisolapperunderuvu or Gandagopalapperunderuvu and Kuraivaniyapperunderuvu.

610 of 1919 (Tamil) — On the same wall. Gift of cows and sheep for a perpetual lamp by a servant of Gandagopala.

611 of 1919 (Tamil) — On the same wall. Gift of 33 head of cattle for a perpetual lamp by Mallaya Dandanayaka, son of Appaya Dandanayaka, brother (?) of the mahapradhani Dandinagopa.

612 of 1919 (Tamil) — On the same wall. Gift of 33 head of cattle for a perpetual lamp by Kesava Dandanayaka, son of the individual mentioned in No. 611 above.

613 of 1919 (Tamil) — On the same wall. Incomplete. Mentions a king, with Saluva Birudas, whose name is lost.

614 of 1919 (Tamil) — On the same wall. Gift of 250 panam for offering cakes on Ekadasi days after the return of the god from procession. The money was deposited on interest with the manradis of Tiruvattiyur.

615 of 1919 (Tamil) — On the same wall. Gift of 33 head of cattle for perpetual lamp by Goppaya Dandanayaka, younger brother of Mallaya Dandanayaka, son of Appaya Dandanayaka.

616 of 1919 (Tamil) — On the same wall. Gift of a flower garden, by purchase, by Madayya Dandanayaka for supplying flowers and garlands.

617 of 1919 (Tamil) — On the same wall. Gift of 33 head of cattle for a prepetual lamp by mahapradhani Dandinagopa Madaya Dandanayaka.

618 of 1919 (Tamil) — On the same wall. Beginning built in. Gift of land and cows by Taluvakkulaindan Vanadaraya of Perungurumbur for garlands, sacred offerings and perpetual lamp to the god. The cows were left with Garudanmelalagiyar

of the Nambi caste and the possession of the land was given to Uttaravedialagiyar for rearing a flower garden.

619 of 1919 (Tamil) — On the west wall of the same mandapa. Gift of 33 head of cattle for a perpetual lamp by a native of Nellore.

620 of 1919 (Tamil) — On the same wall. Gift of 40 cows and one bull for a perpetual lamp and for offering milk to the god by Ammaiappan Kannudaipperumal or Vikrama Chola Sambuvarayan.

621 of 1919 (Tamil) — On the same wall. Gift of the village of Kukkulam, a sub-division of Vada Payirkottam, a district of Jayangondasolamandaam for worship and offerings to the god Alagar at Tirumalirunjolai in Pandimandalam by Madurantaka Pottappichcholan Manumasiddarasan Tirukkalattidevan or Gandagopalan, at the service (sandi) named after him.

622 of 1919 (Tamil) — On the same wall. Gift of the village of Valluvappakkam in Urrukkattukottam, a district of Jayangondasolamandalam for the maintenance of Tiruvaliparappinankuttam who had to recite *sindu* (ode) in the temple of Arulala Perumal by the individual mentioned in No. 621 above.

623 of 1919 (Tamil) — On the same wall. Unfinished. Registers that the cows and sheep belonging to the temple may freely graze on certain lands in a large number of villages in Tondaimandalam whose names are enumerated and that no tax will be levied on them by the owners.

624 of 1919 (Tamil prose and verse) — On the same wall. Damaged. Seems to record a gift of lamp and appears to refer to the king as belonging to the Pallava family.

625 of 1919 (Tamil) — On the same wall. Much damaged. Quotes the order of Madurantaka Pottappichcholan and records the assignment of certain taxes.

626 of 1919 (Tamil) — On the same wall. Gift of land in the village of Alagiyasolanallur for daily worship by Ammai Appan Pandinadu-kondan.

627 of 1919 (Tamil) — On the north wall of the same mandapa. Registers the gift of the two villages Ka(lanjanu)r and Aiyyankulattur in Kaliyurkottam by Madurantaka Pottappichcholan Manumasiddarasan Tirukkalattideva Gandagopalan in the 19th year of Rajarajadeva.

628 of 1919 (Tamil) — On the same wall. Records gift of land in the village of Kaliyurkottam for a flower garden by the individual mentioned in No. 627 above and refers to the 19th year of Rajarajadeva.

629 of 1919 (Tamil) — On the same wall. Gift of land in Kaliyur for forming an agaram, to the bhattas of the temple of Gandagopala Vinnagar Emberuman at Kaliyur in the 24th year of Rajarajadeva. Refers to the order of Madurantaka Pottappichcholan.

630 of 1919 (Tamil) — On the same wall. Records the order of Madurantaka Pottappichcholan, fixing the share of the produce which the occupiers of the arecanut and betel gardens belonging to the temple had to set apart and granting certain special privileges to be enjoyed by the owners on the lands.

631 of 1919 (Tamil) — On the east wall of the gopura in front of the Abhisheka mandapa. Incomplete. Begins with the introduction.

632 of 1919 (Tamil) — On the right wall of the same goura. Begins with a historical introduction. Gift of money for offerings at the early morning service by Vangamulaiyur Udaiyan Araiyan Mummudisolan or Anukkappallavaraivan of Manninadu, a sub-division of Virudarajabhayankara-valanadu, a district of Solamandalam.

633 of 1919 (Grantha and Tamil) — On the left wall of the same gopura. Incomplete. The record ends with the date.

634 of 1919 (Grantha and Tamil) — On the same wall.
Records that Vasantaraya, son of Anapota Nayaka and brother
of Singa Nayaka made a gift of the four dvarapala images
Chanda and Prachanda at the second and third gopuras
respectively and the two pinnacles of gold for the car.

635 of 1919 (Tamil) — On the same wall. The
commencement of each line is very much damaged. Begins
with the historical introduction. Registers a sale of land, free
of taxes, by the people of Vaidavur in Urrukkadunadu, a sub-
division of Urrukkadukottam, a district of Jayangondasolamandalam to the Mahamuni of Periyakoil who was
feeding the Brahmans versed in the sacred lore at
Arikesuvanmatha situated on the north bank of the sacred tank
(Tiruppoigai), of Arulala Perumal.

636 of 1919 (Tamil) — On the wall to the right of entrance
into the Thayar shrine in the same temple. Built in. Records
the assignment of certain taxes from the village of Nallalam
in Vayalamurparru. A certain Goppanan figures as the
signatory.

637 of 1919 (Tamil) — On the same wall. Remission of
taxes for supplying sacred garlands to Periyapirrattiyar, on
certain lands in Pandinadu or Devapperumalnallur in
Kaliyurkottam which was given for flower garden, by
Siddarasa.

638 of 1919 (Tamil) — On the same wall. Built in at the
beginning. Records a gift of money by Narasadeviyar, wife
of Kommaraja Periya Timmaraja Udaiyar for daily offerings
to the god.

639 of 1919 (Sanskrit verse in Telugu) — On a stone
placed in front of the Thayar shrine, to the right of entrance.
Records that in compliance with the order of Srinivasa or
Attan Tiruvengana Ramanuja Jiyar, his pupil the chieftain
Raja Sri Lala Todaramalla brought back the image of

Varadaraja and his consorts from Udaiyarpalayam and set them up in the temple at Conjeevaram.

640 of 1919 (Tamil) — On the wall to the left of entrance into the same shrine. Records a gift of land to the god, by purchase, in Devaperumalnallur, a padapparra in Urrukkattukottam, by Tirukkalatti Udaiyar, the headman (kilavan) of Ambalvaymanallur in Pulal Nadu, a sub-division of Pulalkottam or Vikramasolavalanadu, a district of Jayangondasolamandalam, for the purpose of rearing a flower garden.

641 of 1919 (Tamil) — On the same wall. Built in. States that while Krishnadeva Maharaya was camping at Kanchi, he granted two villages for the floating festival of god Ekambaranatha and that he constructed two small cars for the Vinayaka in that temple and for Krishna in the Perumal temple. It also specifies the routes which the Siva and Vishnu temple cars should take on respective festival days.

642 of 1919 (Tamil) — On the wall above the steps leading to the same shrine, right of entrance. Registers that Tunai-irundam Nambi Kongarayan assigned certain individuals as *tirunandavilakkukudi* to the temple and exempted them from taxes, for burning two perpetual lamps in the shrines of Nachchiyar Perarulalar and Perundeviyar in the lampstands presented to the temple by the king.

643 of 1919 (Tamil) — On the same wall. Seems to record a gift of gold for a perpetual lamp. Attipparru, a sub-division of Padaividurajya is mentioned.

644 of 1919 (Telugu) — On the same wall. Records that Venkamma and Janaki, the wives of the headman of Alampalli, the son of Venkatapati Tirumalarao, paid a visit to the temple.

645 of 1919 (Tamil) — In the mandapa in front of the same shrine, left of entrance. Built in. Records gift of 54 panam of

gold for burning a twilight lamp to the god Varantarumperumal. The donee's name is obliterated.

646 of 1919 (Tamil) — On the north wall of the same shrine. Built in at the beginning and incomplete. Registers an agreement by the temple trustees given to Kandadal Ramanuja Ayyangar, the agent of the charis of the Ramanujakutamatham in the Sannadhi street, that for 2,600 chakram gold coins deposited in the temple treasury, certain specified festivals, processions and offerings to Perarulalar and Mahalakshmi will be conducted. A supplementary charity of Narapparasayan, the agent of Rayasam Ayyapparasayan for some other festivals and offerings is also mentioned.

647 of 1919 (Sanskrit in Grantha) — On the west wall of the same shrine. Same as No. 347 above.

648 of 1919 (Tamil) — On the west and south walls of the same shrine. Records that Virupakshadanayaka, the son of Gangadhara of the Asrayana-gotra, and a Vasalmahapradhani of Narasingaraya Maharaya, made a present of money for the reconsecration (?) ceremony of the images of Nachchiyar Perarulalar and Perundeviyar in the temple.He also formed a new town called Virupakshadanayapapuram. Having dug an irrigation canal in the temple lands and planted groves all around, he ordered that from the produce of these lands certain offerings were to be made to these images and that a fourth of these offerings should be given to the Ramanujakuta matha.

649 of 1919 (Grantha and Tamil verse) — On the south wall of the same shrine. States that Tatacharya repaired and regilded the Punyakotivimana, which was originally erected by Krishnaraya and which had become dilapidated, and that he also erected the Kalyanakotivimna and also had it gilded with gold.

650 of 1919 (Grantha) — On the same wall. Refers to the

same events as in No. 649 above, and gives the details of the date on which these consecrations took place.

651 of 1919 (Sanskrit verse in Grantha) — On the north, west and south walls of the same shrine. A set of twenty verses in praise of god Hanuman consecrated in the temple on the bank of Tatasamudram, a tank dug by and named after Tatacharya. The verses are re-engraved on the east and north walls of the rock, and also on the outer-most gopura, right of entrance.

652 of 1919 (Tamil) — On the western base of the hundred-pillared mandapa in the second prakara of the same temple. Damaged. Seems to record a gift of land for certain festivals and offerings.

653 of 1919 (Tamil) — On the west wall of the third prakara, right of entrance. Registers a gift of land, by purchase, in Agaram Navettekulattur and Agaram Devaraya-maharayapuram or Poigaippakkam by Paradaya Alagiyasingar, son of Mudumbai Appilai Annayyangar of Tirunarayanapuram and of the Srivatsa gotra, for offering sweets to the god on the birthdays of certain Alvars and Acharyapurushas and on certain other festival days.

654 of 1919 (Tamil) — On the same wall. Built in at the beginning. Gift of 3,500 kulis of land, houses and house sites, by Allumtirukkalattideva, Maharaya Gandagopaladeva for the construction of the temple and its prakara walls and for growing a flower garden adjoining it.

655 of 1919 (Tamil) — On the same wall. Registers an agreement between the temple treasurers and the temple agent Ramanujaya Tiruppanipillai on the one hand and the tenants of the temple lands on the other to the effect that as the areca, coconut and mango trees growing on these lands had withered on account of drought, fresh trees should be planted. The share in the produce which the tenant should

reserve for himself being was refixed on an improved basis.

656 of 1919 (Sanskrit verse in Grantha) — On the same wall, left of entrance. Records that Ramaraya ordered the repair of the stone steps of the tank called Anantasaras and made some gifts to the Ekambaranatha and Varadaraja temples. Gives the genealogy of the earlier members of the Karnata dynasty. The composer of the verses is one Obhala Dikshita of Krishnapuram.

657 of 1919 (Tamil) — On the south wall of the third prakara, opposite the Udaiyavar sannidhi. Registers a gift of land in Kuvalaivedu by Rayasam Timmakkan for certain festivals and for singing the Tiruppallandu hymns of Periyalvar, a function which was being conducted by Kandadai Annavaiyangar.

658 of 1919 (Tamil) — On the wall of a dilapidated mandapa next to the Manavalar sannidhi. Records that two pieces of land, which belonged to the temple in Padaipparru or Teperumalnallur and which remained uncultivated on account of its non-irrigable high level, were purchased as Ulavukkani by the treasury of Tirumelisaialvar, reclaimed and brought under cultivation and that these lands were leased out for 200 panams of gold per year by the temple.

659 of 1919 (Tamil) — On the left wall of the stable mandapa. Records a gift of land, purchased for 170 panams of gold, for offerings to the god on particular festival days by Vengayar Kalastinatha of Paramesvaramangalam, the tiruppenivasal kanakku in the temple.

660 of 1919 (Tamil) — On the right wall of the same mandapa. Records gift of land purchased for 50 panams of gold by Kamaiyan, son of Uttamerurudaiyan Amarapadikattar Nallappar, Periya Erappan Chinna Erappan and Angandai for offering sweets to the god, on five particular festival days in different months.

661 of 1919 (Tamil) — On the wall of the outermost gopura, right of entrance. End much damaged. Records the gift of 32 cows and a bull for maintaining a perpetual lamp in the temple by Obhaladeva Maharaja. A large number of high-sounding birudas are mentioned of Pulaiyar Podukkam Aubaladeva Maharaja who appears to be the father of the donor of the gift.

662 of 1919 (Tamil) — On the same wall. Records the assignment, free of taxes, of Uttamacholanallur or Kolipakkam, a village in Brahmadesapparru in Virpedunadu, in the sub-division of Kaliyurkottam, by Konappa, son of Muddappar, for worship and daily offerings to the god. Arumbagandan and Bashaikkatappuvarayaragandan are mentioned as birudas of Muddappar.

663 of 1919 (Tamil verse) — On the wall of the outermost gopura, left of entrance. Contains two laudatory verses in praise of one Ramanujayya of Tiruppulani, who is stated to have undertaken some extensive repairs to the temple at Conjeevaram and to have attained great fame and beatitude.

664 of 1919 (Tamil verse) — On the same wall, right of entrance. Records that king Krishnaraya covered the Punnyakotivimana of the god with gold plate.

665 of 1919 (Tamil) — On the same wall, left of entrance. In modern characters.

666 of 1919 (Tamil) — On the east base of the same gopura, left of entrance. States that Raghavan and Chellaperumal, the agents of Tirumalai Nayaka, made, arrangements with certain individuals of Dusi and Tenneri of the Vayalaikkavurparru on the occasion of Sankramapunyakala, for burning lamps before the god.

667 of 1919 (Tamil) — On the same base, right of entrance. Registers an agreement by Ayiamman and Isvarappan to burn a lamp before the god, for the merit of the king.

668 of 1919 (Tamil) — On the west base of the same gopura, left of entrance. Records the employment of certain individuals in Padaividu, under the charge of Karpurajiyar as Tiruvilakkukudi, by Egappa Nayaka Tirumalai Nayaka for burning lamps before the god.

1 of 1921 (Tamil) — On the north wall of the central shrine in the Punyakotisvara temple. Registers the appointment of Alagiya Tiruchirrambalam Udaiyar, son of Bhuvaneka Bahudevar, as the temple supervisor (palamudal kankani) and the gift of a house to him in virtue of that office, by the trustees of the temple of Punyatirthamudaiya Nayanar at Conjeevaram, a city in Urrukkattukottam, a district of Jayangondasolamandalam.

2 of 1921 (Tamil) — On the base of the north and west walls of the same shrine. Damaged. Records the agreement reached by four private individuals with Villavarayar, the agent of Mudaliyar Semmasettiyar, to burn four perpetual lamps in the temple of Punyatirthamudaiya Nayanar of Kanchipuram, a city in Kaliyurkottam, a district of Jayangondasolamandalam, for 72 Nellore Gandagopalanpudumadai received by him.

3 of 1921 (Tamil) — On the base of the north wall of the same shrine. In modern characters. Registers the leasing of certain temple lands in the village of Sattiyappantangal by a private individual named Namasivayan, a member of the Tantari community in Ayyangulattur.

4 of 1921 (Tamil) — On the base of the south wall of the same shrine. Built in the middle. Records that the village of Tangi in Urrukkattukottam was renamed Tribhuvanaviranallur and that 108 velis of land, at the instance of a certain Solakon, was granted as a tax-free gift for the expenses of the same temple.

5 of 1921 (Tamil) — On the south wall of the mandapa in front of the same shrine. Built in by a pial. Seems to refer to

some gift made by a merchant in Arumolidevapperunderuvu of Kanchipuram, a city in Eyirkottam to the god Kshetrapala-pillaiyar in the temple of Udaiyar Punyatirthamudaiya Nayanar at Kanchipuram, a city in Kaliyurkottam.

6 of 1921 (Tamil) — On the north wall of the central shrine, Ashtabhujam Perumal temple in the same village. Records the tax-free gift of 1,000 kulis of land as devadana and of 3,600 kulis by sale for 47 kalanjus, by the residents of Kanchipuram in Eyirkottam, a district of Jayangondasolamandalam, for conducting worship in the temple of Tiruashtabhujagrihattu Mahavishnu, for providing offerings to the god and for burning a perpetual lamp in the temple.

7 of 1921 (Tamil) — On the same wall. Much damaged. Records that some temple lands in Amaramangalam in Tepparayanpattu were taken over by the residents of that place and that from the income of some other lands which were given in exchange in Narranallur through Etirajayangar, certain offerings were provided for the god Tiruashtabhujattemberuman.

8 of 1921 (Tamil) — On the south wall of the same shrine. Begins with the introduction. Records gift and sale of certain lands by the assembly of Sri Rajasundarichaturvedimangalam, a brahmadeya village in Virpedunadu, a sub-division of Kaliyurkottam, a district of Jayangondasolamandalam, for the kitchen expenses of the temple of Tiruashtabhujagrihattu-ninraruliya Paramasvamin in Kanchipuram, a city of Eyirkottam.

9 of 1921 (Tamil) — On the same wall. Written in continuation of the above and belongs to the same king. Records a further tax-free gift of land by the assembly of Rajendracholachaturvedimangalam, an independent village in Kaliyurkottam to the same temple for kitchen purpposes and stipulates that after two years from the date of the gift,

a tax of not more than half a kasu per veli of land was to be collected on these lands.

10 of 1921 (Tamil) — On the base of the same wall. Records an assurance given by the temple officials including Tirappani Singarayyangar, the agent of Ettur Tirumalai Kumaratata Chariyar to Nallammangar, wife of Appayyangar, son of Periyaperumal of Addangi to provide certain offerings to the god on certain occasions from the income of some land given by her in Narranallur or Sri Ramabhadrapuram, a village in Arrukkattukottam in Chandragirirajya.

11 of 1921 (Tamil) — On the base of the north wall of the central shrine in the Tiruttangavilakkoliperumal temple in the same village. Registers the gift by the residents of Vilakkottu of certain lands in that village to the temples of Tiruttangavilakkoli Perumal and Alariyar of Tirruvelirukkai in the proportion of two to one, in obedience to the order of Madurantakapottappichcholan. Mentions the 7th year, Vaikasi month, probably of Rajaraja III. The name Manavijadeva is engraved at the end.

12 of 1921 (Tamil) — On the base of the south and east walls of the same shrine. Records gift of the village of Ilaippakkam, a village in Vadavurnadu, a sub-division of Venkunrakottam for the repairs, to the temples of Tiruttangavilakkoli Perumal and Alariyar, which were being supervised in the name of the king by Srirangaraya of Ilangudi in Pandimandalam and for making offerings to the gods in the temples.

13 of 1921 (Sanskrit in Grantha) — On the wall to the left of entrance into the temple. A verse stating that Alagiyamanavala Jiyar built certain prakaras and mandapas in the temple of Dipaprakasa (i.e., Vilakkoliperumal.)

14 of 1921 (Tamil) — On the base of the north wall of the Alagiyasinga Perumal temple in the same village. Records

that an amount of 12 pons was given every year to
Satagopayyangar of Tirunarayanapuram from the proceeds of
the village of Nallapillaiperral and that he had to provide for
certain offerings in the name of Tatacharya to the god Alari-
emberuman of Kachchattirukkai in Kanchipuram.

15 of 1921 (Tamil) — On the north wall of the mandapa
in front of the central shrine in the Phanamanisvara temple
in the same village. Begins with the introduction of Rajendra
Chola I. Damaged at the end of each line. Records gift of land
for offerings and worship to the temples of Tiruppadamadam
Udaiyar and Tirukkaronam.

16 of 1921 (Tamil) — On the base of the same wall.
Damaged. Seems to record gift of gold from the interest
from which a lamp was to be burnt in the temple of
Tiruppadamadam Udaiyar in the evening.

17 of 1921 (Tamil) — On the base of the same wall.
Records gift of 50 kalanjus of gold by the queen Danmaponnar
or Trailokyamahadeviyar and that 200 kadi of paddy was to be
supplied to the temple, as interest on this amount, at the rate
of 4 kadi per kalanju. The money was deposited with the
residents of Tiraiyamangalam.

18 of 1921 (Tamil) — On the base of the east wall of the
same mandapa. Damaged. Records gift of 50 kalanjus of
gold by the same queen. The residents of Pannaippuram were
required to supply 100 kadi of paddy to the temple as interest.

19 of 1921 (Tamil) — On the same base. Records gift of
30 kalanjus of gold by the same queen for burning a perpetual
lamp in the temple of Tiruppadamadam Udaiyar by the
residents of Pondur.

20 of 1921 (Tamil) — On the same base. Much damaged.

21 of 1921 (Tamil) — On the north wall of the central
shrine in the Yathoktakarin temple in the same village.
Registers the sale of the lands in Kannamangalam, a village

in Eyil Nadu, a sub-division of Eyilkottam, to the temple of Anantanarayana Paramasvami of Kachchippedu, who was pleased to lie as an anicut to Tiruvehka (river Vegavati), by certain private individuals of the same village for the sum of 367 kalanjus of gold.

22 of 1921 (Tamil) — On the base of the east wall of the same shrine. Records gift of certain houses in the Sannidhi street to Cheranaivenrasolakumara and Manangattar Amudaduvan who had to provide for certain offerings to the god and for burning a lamp in the temple of Anantanarayanasvamin in Kanchipuram.

23 of 1921 (Tamil) — On the south wall of the same shrine. Records sale by certain merchants of Kanchipuram, of one tuni of land as a tax-free devadana for 127 kalanjus of gold, to the temple of Tiruvekka Anaikkidandaru-linaparamasvamin at Kanchipuram.

24 of 1921 (Tamil) — On the same wall. Records gift by Alkonda Chediraya of a village in Karitaduttur or Hastinivaranachaturvedimangalam in Virpedunadu, a sub-division of Kaliyurkottam, a district of Jayangondasola-mandalam, to 32 Brahmans of the village.

25 of 1921 (Tamil) — On the same wall. Records that the hamlet of Salaimangalm Kuppanjer or Sundaracharyapuram in the sima of Kuttambakkami in Konadinadu, a sub-division of Sengattukottam, a district of Jayangondasolamandalam was obtained as gift from the king by Kulasekharan Tirumalainambi in the presence of Ettur Tirumalai Kumaratatacharya and that the lands in it were distributed among certain Sri Vaishnavas living near the temple of Sonnavannamseyda Perumal.

26 of 1921 (Tamil) — On the south wall of the second prakara of the same temple. Records that the Mandalam, son of Srirangaraja of Nadatur in Kannantangal, founded a village on the banks of the tank dug by him to the west of the temple

of Sonnavannamseyda Perumal. He also built a mandapa of the temple, erected a shed for drinking water and also gave a gift of 25 panams of gold for offerings and lamp to the god Hanumantadeva set up by him.

27 of 1921 (Tamil) — On the south wall of the second prakara of the same temple. States that the king while seated in the Janakimandapa granted to Sri Parakalanambi the name of Karunakaradasan with certain honours, privileges and a dwelling house.

28 of 1921 (Sanskrit in Grantha) — On the wall of the gopura, left of entrance. A verse in praise of Tatayadesika.

29 of 1921 (Tamil) — On the same wall. Incomplete. Records the gift by Ettur Tirumalai Kumaratatacharya, the son of Ayyavayyangar of the Satamarshanagotra and the Apastamba sutra and of the family of Periyatirumalainambi, of house sites to certain Brahmans who formed a colony named Sundaracharyapuram near the temple and of the village of Varanavasi for the mid-day offerings to the god Sonnavannamseyda Perumal.

30 of 1921 (Tamil) — On the same wall. Incomplete. Records the gift to Ettur Tirumalai Kumaratatacharya, son of Ayyavayyangar, of the village of Puliyur for providing daily offerings and conducting worship and certain festivals to the god Sonnavannamseyda Perumal of the tempple at Kanchipuram, a city in Virpedunadu, a sub-division of Urrukkattukottam in Chandragirirajya, in Jayangondasola-mandalam.

31 of 1921 (Tamil) — On the same wall. Records gift of money by sale of land by the temple trustees headed by Alagiyasingar, agent of Kumaratatacharya to Tirumalirunjolai Ayyangar, son of Tatacharya Ayyavayyangar of Ettur Tirumalai and Kumbakonam, for providing sweets and making offerings to the god and for conducting certain festivities on certain days.

32 of 1921 (Tamil) — On the same wall, right of entrance. Records gift of certain house sites by the individuals mentioned in No.31 above to Tatacharya, son of Ayyavayyangar.

33 of 1921 (Tamil) — In the recess of the gopura, left of entrance. Incomplete. Records gift of land to the temple for the expenses of conducting the summer festival of the god.

34 of 1921 (Tamil) — In the same recess, right of entrance. Built in. Records gift of certain lands for conducting the floating festival of the god.

35 of 1921 (Tamil) — On the base of the west wall of the central shrine in the Sri Karanisvara temple in Sengalunirodai street at Big Conjeevaram. Records gift, as a tax-free sarvamanya, of 400 kulis of land in Butampaninelvay to Sri Karanachchiyar, a devotee, for singing hymns daily in the temple and for supplying a garland to the god Sri Karanisvaraudaiya Nayanar.

36 of 1921 (Tamil) — On the base of the north wall of the same shrine. Records that the village of Bhutampaninelvay in Nirvelurnadu, a sub-division of Urrukkattukottam, was given to the charge of Nelvayiludaiyan Ethinayan Sundarasola (Mu)vendavelan of Nelvayil, in (Pu)rangarambainadu on behalf of the temple of Sri Karanisvaramudaiya Mahadeva in Arumolidevapperunderuvu of Kanchipuram.

37 of 1921 (Tamil) — On the base of the west wall of the central shrine in the Pandava Perumal temple in the same village. Records gift of 32 cows by Niranindan or Sedirayan of Taiyur in Panangudi, a village of Rajaraja-valanadu, a district of Solamandalam, for a perpetual lamp to the god ˙Tiruppadagattalvar.

38 of 1921 (Tamil) — On the north wall of the central shrine in the Ulaagalanda Perumal temple in the same village. Records gift of 300 kulis of land in Alagiyapallava-chaturvedimangalam by three Brahmans residing in Panganur,

a hamlet of Kalattur or Vikramsimhachaturvedimangalam in Damarkottam to the temple of Tiruvuragattuninrarulina-paramasvamin in Kanchipuram for the expenses on sankramana day.

39 of 1921 (Tamil) — On the same wall. Records that during his visit to the temple with his two consorts Tribhuvanamudaiyal and Solakulavalli, the king made a gift of land for offerings and worship in the temple. These lands belonged to the temple but were possessed by the weavers. They did not cultivate them and the king resumed the lands and made a gift of them to the temple again.

40 of 1921 (Tamil) — On the same wall. Records gift of 15 palanguligaipanams by a merchant living in the Rajarajapperunderuvu in the city of Kanchipuram for burning a twilight lamp in the temple of Tiruvuragattuninrarulina-paramasvamin.

41 of 1921 (Tamil) — On the east wall of the same shrine. Records the remission of certain taxes on the charities made previously to the temple for a perpetual lamp.

42 of 1921 (Tamil) — On the same wall. Grants permission to certain unspecified individuals to enact street-plays in Kanchipuram and Tondaimandalam.

43 of 1921 (Tamil) — On the south wall of the same shrine. Gift of 2 1/2 madai of gold by a private individual of Tiruvayumiyur in Puliyurkottam for burning a twilight lamp in the same temple.

44 of 1921 (Tamil) — On the same wall. Gift of 2 madai of gold by the headman of Mappudam in Siruvanpedu in Payyurkottam for burning a twilight lamp in the temple.

45 of 1921 (Tamil) — On the same wall. Begins with the introduction. Records that, at the request of his queen Tribhuvanamudaiyal, the king made a tax-free gift of the village of Sirrichchambakkam, a brahmadeya of

Nirvelurnadu, a sub-division of Urrukkattukottam. Having renamed it as Kampadevinallur after the queen, he ordered that the proceeds therefrom be utilized for certain festivals and offerings to the god on the asterisms of Pushya and Svati.

46 of 1921 (Tamil) — On the base of the south wall of the same shrine. Records that a weaver of Ravikulamanikka-perunderuvu in Kanchipuram reclaimed to cultivation certain lands belonging to Tiruvuragattemberuman and dug a small irrigation tank for 200 kasus and allowed the produce from the land to be utilized for making offerings to the god.

47 of 1921 (Tamil) — On the base of the south wall of the same shrine. Records the agreement reached by the 48,000 residents of Kanchipuram to supervise the conduct of all the daily services, worship and offerings and also to do the same during the special festivals in the temple of Tiruvuragattalvar as established by old custom.

48 of 1921 (Tamil) — On the wall of the gopura, left of entrance. Records gift of land and house sites, by purchase, by Perungarunaialan Tiruvengadamudaiyan Kalingarayan as varyavritti to a Brahman for supplying water and maintaining a watershed near the road-side well in Sevvanmedu or Naharisvarachaturvedimangalam, a village in Virpedunadu, a sub-division of Kaliyurkottam, a district of Jayangondasola-mandalam.

49 of 1921 (Grantha and Tamil) — In the same gopura, right of entrance. Records a further gift, by purchase, by the same individual as in No. 48 above for the same watershed and for rearing a grove around it.

50 of 1921 (Tamil) — On the same place. Records sale of certain temple land by Putalai Lingappayyar, the agent of Polepalli Venkana Panditar, the Diwan of the temple of Tiruvuragam Ulagalanda Perumal to Seshadri Ayyangar of Madaipusu, for 340 panams.

51 of 1921 (Tamil) — On the base of the east wall of the Mahakalisvara temple near Kamakshiaman temple in the same village. Registers the agreement reached by certain temple Brahmans to measure out ghee for the perpetual lamps instituted by Kannudaip Perumal Sambuvaraya, Vachchamadeviyar (the wife of Chalamattigandan Nallasiddarasan) and Tikkammaideviyar, (the wife of Pillaiyar Nallasiddarasar) in the temple of Tirukalisvaramudaiya Nayanar in return for certain cows and buffaloes received from them.

52 of 1921 (Tamil) — On the north wall of the central shrine in the Tiruvirattanesvara temple in the same village. Records the appointment of Alagiyatiruchchirrambalamudaiyar, son of Bhuvaneka Bahudevar, to supervise the services and expenses in the temples of Tiruvirattanamudaiya Nayanar, Muttikodutta Nayanar, and Sri Karanisvaramudaiya Nayanar in Kanchipuram.

53 of 1921 (Tamil) — On the west wall of the same shrine. Records that three individuals made a gift of 120 panams from the interest of which, offerings were to be provided to the god Tiruvirattanamudaiya Tambiranar during nights for the merit of their mother Purriyar.

54 of 1921 (Tamil) — On the same wall. Records gift of gold and a lampstand by a weaver, for burning two twilight lamps in the temple.

55 of 1921 (Tamil) — On the same wall. Records gift of 32 cows by Chedirayan of Panangudi in Rajarajavalanadu, a district of Solamandalam for a perpetual lamp in the temple. The donee belonged to the community known as Sambuvarayarkanmi.

56 of 1921 (Tamil) — On the same wall. Built in. Records the gift of a lampstand and certain bell-metal utensils by a dancing girl of the temple, called Sivanaimuludumudaiyal.

57 of 1921 (Tamil) — On the south wall inside the the

same temple. Built in at the beginning. Seems to record gift of 3 kasus by a certain Muruganallurudaiyan of Puliyurnadu in Solamandalam for a twilight lamp in the temple.

58 of 1921 (Tamil) — On the south wall of the mandapa in front of the central shrine in Kachchisvara temple in the same village. Begins with the introduction. Records sale of tax-free land by the residents of Kalikainallur in Urrukkattunadu to Arayan Parudimanikkam, the headman of Arubamkkam in Manayilnadu in a sub-division of Manaiyilkottam for supplying a potful of water for the sacred bath of the god Aludaiyar Tirukkachchalaiudaiyar of Kanchipuram, a city in Eyilkottam, a district of Jayangondasolamandalam.

59 of 1921 (Tamil) — On the same wall. Records gift of 32 cows by Niranindan or Sedirayan of Urandaiyur, a village of Panangudi in Kulottungasolavalanadu, a subdivision of Solamandalam, for a perpetual lamp in the temple of Tirukkachchalaiudaiyar.

60 of 1921 (Tamil) — On the same wall. Records gift of two lampstands by a dancing girl of the temple and of 12 kasus by her, her sister and her daughter collectively, for burning three twilight lamps in them.

61 of 1921 (Tamil) — On the same wall. Records gift of 4 kasus by Malaialvan Aludaiyan of Sirukkalattur in Kalattur-nadu, a sub-division of Puliyurkottam, for burning a twilight lamp in the temple.

62 of 1921 (Tamil) — On the east wall of the same mandapa. Records gift of 8 kasus by Adavallan Tirthan for burning two twilight lamps in the temple.

63 of 1921 (Tamil) — On the same wall. Records gift of money, cows and buffaloes by Kakkunayakan of Tiruppalural or Gangeyarayan, the headman of Sirumattur in Maganurnadu, a sub-division of Sengattukottam, for a perpetual lamp in the temple.

64 of 1921 (Tamil) — On the same wall. Records gift of 32 cows and one bull by a woman of Sirudavur in Amurnadu, a sub-division of Sengattukottam, for a perpetual lamp in the temple.

65 of 1921 (Tamil) — On the same wall. Records gift of 4 kasus by Ambalamkoyilkondan Vallalagandan, the headman of Alaikkonrai in Tkkattunadu, a sub-division of Tkkattukottam for a twilight lamp in the temple.

66 of 1921 (Tamil) — On the same wall. Records gift of gold by a dancing girl of Seyyur or Virarajendrasolanallur in Palaraiyurnadu, a sub-division of Semburkottam, for a twilight lamp in the temple.

67 of 1921 (Tamil) — On the same wall. Records gift of 90 sheep by Ammaiyappakkon, a member of the community called Sambuvarayakanmis of Varakur or Alagiyasola-chaturvedimangalam, an independent village of Vesalippadi on the northern bank in Rajarajavalanadu, a sub-division of Naduvilnadu, for burning a perpetual lamp in the temple.

68 of 1921 (Tamil) — On the north wall of the same mandapa. Begins with the introduction. States that, in response to a petition made by Pavalakkundinanadudaiyan of Pundi to the king, while he was seated in a hall at Perumbarrapuliyur, the king issued an order to his secretaries to grant the village of Puduppakkam in Pusal, a sub-division of Kaliyurkottam as a tax-free devadana to the temple of Tirukkachchalaiudaiyar.

69 of 1921 (Tamil) — On the same wall. Begins with the introduction. States that the individual mentioned in No. 68 above, availed a gift of five velis of land from the king, to feed twenty-five Brahmans in addition to the ten Brahmans who were already being fed from a previous endowment of his.

70 of 1921 (Tamil) — On the same wall. Records that a majority of the temple lands in Kalikainallur (a devadana

village), mortgaged to Ariyan Kariya Perumal, was now redeemed by Manaiyaliparamesvara Nayakar, a nayaka of Malaimandalam for 317 panams. The temple trustees agreed to utilise the produce from this land, both in paddy and money, partly for the morning offerings to the god Tirukkachchalaiudaiya Nayanar and partly for maintaining a watershed for the merit of the donee.

71 of 1921 (Tamil) — On the same wall. Engraved in continuation of the above. States that in addition to the charities to be provided as mentioned in No. 70 above, a service called Paramesvaransandi was also instituted by the donee from the income of the same lands.

72 of 1921 (Telugu) — On a slab in the flooring of the mandapa in front of the central shrine. Damaged. Mentions Gopalarajayya, the grandson of Rangaparajayya of the Atreyagotra and of the house of Araviti and also the Gangaikondanmandapa at Kanchipuram.

73 of 1921 (Tamil) — On the east wall of the Durga shrine in the same temple. Begins with the introduction. Records gift of gold by Nigarili Lokamadevi, a servant of the queen Mukkokkilanadigal, and by a temple dancing girl called Perri Ponnambalam for two perpetual lamps to be burnt in the shrine of the goddess Ainjanjandi Durgaiyar.

74 of 1921 (Tamil) — On the base of the same wall. Gift of 95 sheep by a private individual of Alisavur in Alisavurnadu, a sub-division of Kaliyurkottam, to the temple of Anjanjandi Durgabhattarakki.

75 of 1921 (Tamil) — On the base of the same wall. Records a gift 90 sheep, probably in the same reign as No. 74 above, by Sadayan Attiyuran, a soldier under Udaiyar Padaimutta Vikkiramabharanavira, for a perpetual lamp. The residents of Mulli in Pulivalanadu, a sub-division of Kaliyur-kottam, undertook to maintain the charity.

76 of 1921 (Tamil) — On the base of the east and north walls of the same shrine. Records sale of land by the merchants of Kanchipuram for offerings and worship to the god Ganapatiyar Kanchipuraalagar situated in the northern side of the temple called Anjanjandiambalam Rajendrasolan.

77 of 1921 (Tamil) — On the base of the north and west walls of the same shrine. Damaged. Begins with the introduction. Records a gift of gold by a private individual of Magaral in Eyirkottam for offerings and worship to the goddess Durgaiyar during the pushya day in the month of Arpisi every year.

78 of 1921 (Tamil) — On the base of the north and west walls of the same shrine. Begins with the introduction. Records gift of 60 kalanjus of gold by the residents of Sirunanraiyur, a devadana situated in Ambinadu in Eyilkottam, for burning four perpetual lamps in the name of the king, in the temple of Anjanjandi Durgaiyar of Kanchipuram.

79 of 1921 (Tamil) — On the base of the west wall of the same shrine. Records gift of 900 sheep by the king for 10 perpetual lamps to be burnt in the temple in his name and states that Vidivitankan or Villavamuvandavelan of Uttaram in Arvalakurram, the adhikarin of the king distributed them among certain individuals who had to supply the required ghee. The 900 sheep were acquired when Sippulinadu and Pagainadu were conquered.

80 of 1921 (Tamil) — On the base of the west wall of the same shrine. Incomplete. Probably a partial copy of No. 79 above.

81 of 1921 (Sanskrit in Grantha) — On a pillar in the mandapa in front of the same shrine. Contains six verses from the Surya Sataka of Mayura in praise of the Sun god.

82 of 1921 (Pallava Grantha) — On a pillar, in a ruined

mandapa near the 1000 pillared mandapa, in the third prakara in the Ekambaranatha temple in the same village. Mentions some of the birudas of Mahendravarman I, such as Kuchatrana, Chitrkarapuli, Drudhabhakti, Vamkambu, etc.

83 of 1921 (English) — On the outer eastern wall of the third prakara of the same temple. States that 30 yards of the prakara wall were repaired by Collector Hodgson.

84 of 1921 (Tamil) — On the base of the south wall of the Sokanathesyara temple near the eastern gopura of the Kamakshi temple in the same village. Records gift of land purchased from the merchants of Kanchipuram, by Achcham Senachan, belonging to the community called Muttavalperra-Kaikkolar for making offerings to the god Karikalappillaiyar, in the temple of Terkirundanakkar in the western block of Kadumbidugu in Kanchipuram and gift of 3 kasus for a twiight lamp in that temple.

85 of 1921 (Tamil) — On the north wall of the central shrine in the Sarvatirthesvara temple in the same village. Begins with the introduction. The inscription has been chiselled away after the introduction. The god is called Sarvatirthamudaiya Mahadevar.

86 of 1921 (Tamil) — On the base of the west wall of the central shrine in the Tirumerralli in Pillaipalayam in the same village. Records gift of 2 velis of land inclusive of all taxes, in the village of Nundavensudarvilagam (a devadana in Eyilkottam) to the temple of Udaiyar Tirumerraliudaiya Nayanar.

87 of 1921 (Tamil) — On the east wall of the mandapa in front of the same shrine. Records that a private individual made a gift of some paddy and a plate, for making offerings to the god once daily and for burning a twilight lamp in the temple.

88 of 1921 (Tamil) — On the same wall. Records that a

tax of 5 1/2 panams per loom was collected from the weavers of the street and that offerings and worship to the god and lamps in the temple were ordered to be provided therefrom by Kondamarasayya, for the merit of Tirumalayadeva Maharaya.

89 of 1921 (Tamil) — On a slab in the flooring at the entrance into the temple. A fragment. Mentions a certain Muttarayan who petitioned for some charities to the temple of Tirumerrali and a certain matha attached to it.

90 of 1921 (Sanskrit in Nagari) — On a slab in the flooring in the same place. Damaged.

91 of 1921 (Tamil) — On the south wall of the Cholesvara temple in the same village. Fragment and built-in. Mentions the name of the god as Karikala Cholisvaramudaiya Nayanar and seems to record remission of certain taxes to the temple.

TIRUPPARUTTIKUNRAM

This famous place of Jaina archaeological interest is a village a few miles away from Little Conjeevaram, and it contains the ruins of Buddhist and Jaina temples. The Jaina temple here is dedicated to Vardhamana and contains a number of Chola and Vijayanagara inscriptions. Amongst the latter, there are two of Irugappa, the son of Dandanatha (general) Vaichaya. Irugappa was the son of Chaicha or Chaichapa, who built the Jaina temple at Vijayanagara.

INSCRIPTIONS

40 of 1890 — North wall of the store room in the Jaina temple. A record of Rajarajadeva dated in his twentieth year.

41 of 1890 (Tamil and Grantha) — Base of the same wall. A record of Irugappa, son of Dandanatha Vaichaya, dated Dundubhi year (S. 1305.) Records that Irugappa made a grant to the temple, for the benefit of Bukkaraja II, the son of

Harihara II. Dr. Hultsch points out that the chief is the same as the Iruga, son of Chaicha, who built the Jaina temple at Vijayanagara in S. 1307. See S.I.I. II, p. 156. For the present epigraph see Ep. Ind. VII, 115-6. According to Dr. Kielhorn the details of the date do not work out correctly. See Ep. Ind. VI, p. 329.

42 of 1890 (Grantha) — On the roof of the mandapa in front of the shrine in the same temple. A record in Prabhava year (1387-8.) Records that the mandapa was built by the same General Irugappa at the instance of his preceptor Pushpasena. See Ep. Ind. VII, p. 116.

43 of 1890 — On the base of the verandah in front of the same shrine. A record of Tribhuvanachakravartin Kulottunga Choladeva dated in his twenty-first year.

44 of 1890 — West wall of the Santimandapa in the same temple. A record of Rajarajadeva dated in his eighteenth year.

45 of 1890 — Right of the entrance into the same temple. A record of Vijayanagara king Krishnadeva dated in S. 1440 (expired), Bahudhanya year.

188 of 1901 (Tamil) — On the base of the verandah in front of the Jaina temple of Trailokyanatha. A record of the Vijayanagara king Krishnaraya. It records in Dhatri, gift of a village, by the king to the temple.

189 of 1901 (Tamil verse) — On a stone built into the platform in the same temple.

NOTE

1. Tirukkurippuththonda Nayanar was a washerman in Conjeevaram. He was much interested in getting the clothes of Saiva *bhakthas* washed. To test his devotion the presiding god of the place Sri Ekambaranata, in the disguise of an aged

Brahman, made him wash his torn rag just before the onset of evening. At the same time he made the day cloudy to disable this Nayanar in keeping to time. On observing the approach of the evening, this washerman began to dash his head at the stone instead of disappointing the devotee, when the god appeared in his true form and gave him salvation!

2. This is the only temple as yet known in South India specially dedicated to this god. The sculpture in the sanctum also, is similar to the metal figure in the temple as illustrated, bearing the *cadjan* book (of palmyra leaves) in one hand, and in the other the iron stile, on account of the fact that he records the good and bad actions of human beings on earth. On death, in the court of Yama, presided over by ten judges, this faithful chief accountant of the god of death, is supposed to read out the good and the bad actions of each, so that in accordance therewith, judgement may be given, apportioning heaven or hell. Special worship to him is made on the CHITRAPOURNAMI day i.e., the full-moon day in the month of Sithari (April-May) when the asterism *Chittra* prevails.

3. For an excellent note on *Tulapurushadhana* see Archaeological Survey of India Report, for the year 1912-13, p. 142 f.

4. I.e. the great pot containing the five elements. This is one of the sixteen great gifts which are prescribed for the wealthy classes and kings by the Hindu Sastras; in the *Matsya Purana* and in *Hemadri Danakhanda*, see *Epigraphia Indica* Vol. I, p. 368, footnote 58.

5. This is numbered as 621 of 1904 in Madras Epigraphical Department (*Annual Reports* published by the Government of Madras.)

6. Madras Epigraphical Department (*Annual Reports* published by the Government of Madras), 1920-21, pp. 104 & 105.

7. Madras Epigraphical Department (*Annual Reports* published by the Government of Madras), 1905-06, para 2.

8. *Saka* is the era named after King Salivahana and it is reckoned from A.D. 78. The word Salivahana has arisen from Satavahanas. A line of kings of this dynasty is said to have ruled in northwest

Mysore under the general name Satakarni and consequently the Mysore state has been spoken of in A.D. 1717 as in the Salivahana country. The territory of these Satavahanas extended over the whole of the Dekhan, and Satakarni is called 'the lord of Dakshinapatha.' Their chief capital appears to have been Dhanakataka in the east (Dharanikota) on the river Krishna now identified with Amaravati in Guntur district, and their chief city in the west was Paithan on the river Godavari (Rice, *Mysore and Coorg from the Inscriptions* 1909 Edition.)

The Saka era is called the Salivahana era or an era rounded by Salivahana. When it began to be attributed to him it is difficult to determine precisely. All the copper plate grants up to the eleventh century speak of the era as Sakanripakala, i.e., the era of the Saka king, or Sakakala, i.e., the era of the Saka, and in an inscription at Badami, it is stated to be the era beginning from 'the coronation of the Saka king.' Subsequently, the simple expression 'Sake, in the year of the Saka,' was used: and therefore Sake or 'in the Saka.' ;The word Saka thus came to be understood as equivalent to an era generally, the original sense being forgotten. And since the era had to be connected with some great king it was associated with the name of Salivahana, and thus we now use the expression Salivahana Saka, which etymologically can have no sense and is made up of the names of two Royal families. The current legend makes Salivahana, the son of a Brahman girl, who was a sojourner at Paithan and lived with her two brothers in the house of a potter. On one occasion she went to the Godavari to bathe, when Sesha, the king of serpents, becoming enamoured with her, transformed himself into a man and embraced her! In due course she gave birth to Salivahana, who was brought up in the house of the potter. After sometime, King Vikramaditya of Ujjayini, to whom a certain deity had revealed that he was destined to die at the hands of the son of a girl of two years, set about his *Vetala* or king of ghosts to find out if there was such a child anywhere. The *Vetala* saw Salivahana playing with his girlish mother and informed Vikramaditya. Thereupon he invaded Paithan with a large army, but Salivahana infused life into clay figures of horses, elephants and men, by means of a charm communicated to him by his father, the king of serpants. He encountered Vikramaditya and defeated him!

There are also several literary traditions connected with the name of Satavahana or Salivahana. A work of the name of *Brihatkatha* written in that form of the Prakrit which is called the Paisachi or the language of goblins is mentioned by Dandin in his work the *Kavyadarsa*. Somadeva, the author of the *Kathasaritsagara* and Kshemendra, the author of another *Brihatkatha*, profess to have derived their stories from this Paisachi Brihatkatha. The stories comprised in this, are said to have been communicated to Gunadhya, who for sometime had been minister to Satavahana, by a ghost named Kanabhuti. They were written in blood and arranged in seven books. Gunadhya offered them to King Satavahana, but he refused to receive such a ghastly work written in blood and in the language of goblins, whereupon Gunadhya burnt six of them. After sometime, King Satavahana having been informed of the charming nature of those stories went to Gunadhya and asked for them. But the last or the seventh book alone remained, and this the king obtained from his pupils with his permission.

It is narrated in the *Kathasaritsagara* that once while bathing with his wives in a tank in a pleasure-garden, Satavahana threw water at one of them. As she was tired, she told the king not to sprinkle water on her, using the words *modakaih paritadaya mam*. The king not understanding that the first word was composed of two words, *ma*='do not' and *udakaih*='with waters,' but taking it to be one word meaning 'pieces of sweetmeat,' ordered for sweetmeat and began to throw pieces at the queen! Thereupon she laughed and told the king that he did not know the phonetic rules of Sanskrit and that what she meant was to tell him not to sprinkle her with water. There was no occasion for the sweetmeat at the place, and this ought to have led the king to the true sense; but he was not. Thereupon the king was ashamed of his own ignorance while his queen was so learned and became disconsolate! [B.G. Vol. I, part II, pp. 169, 170).

9. Conjeevaram is 43 miles southwest of Madras and 20 miles west-north-west of Chingleput (Sewell's *List of Antiquities,* Vol. I, p. 146) with which it is connected by the South Indian Railway.

10. The Cholas had several capitals at different periods of their rule and Uraiyur is one among them. The inscriptions found in this village do not take us to a period earlier than the 11th century A.D. The place is said to have been destroyed by a shower of stand. The other capitals are Kaverippumpattinam now known as Kaveripattinam in the Shiyali taluk, Tanjore, Gangaikondasolapuram.

11. This is Tiruvanjaikalam, 10 miles east of Ponnani in the Cochin state. There is a Siva temple in this village.

12. No less than 283 inscriptions have been collected by Sir Walter Elliot from Conjeevaram. Mr. Sewell, who notices them, remarks that they do not exhaust the number of epigraphs in the place. (*Lists of Antiquities* Vol. I, pp. 178 to 187).

13. Buddhism, Jainism, Saivism, and Vaishnavism, each in its turn had powerful hold on the city and have left unmistakable marks of their influence.

14. *South Indian Inscriptions,* Vol. I, pp. 113, 114, 117, 139, 141, and 143.

15. Inscriptions of the Rashtrakuta king Krishna III state that he took Kachchi and Tanjai. Sir Walter Elliot figures a coin which bears the legend Kachchivalangumperuman. Kulottunga Chola III claims to have captured Kachchi in one of his inscriptions at Tirukoilur (No.2 of the Madras Epigraphical collection, for 1905. Also see, *Ep. Ind.* Vol. III, pp. 284-5).

16. See the hymns of Tirunavukkarasu Nayanar, and Jnanasambandha on the temples of Conjeevaram.

17. The temple of Tirrukkamakottam (Kamakotyambika) is popularly called Kanchi Kamakshi.

18. For these changes see *Nannul Punariyal.*

19. *Bombay Gazetteer,* Vol. I, Part II, pp. 315, Note 3.

20. *South Indian Palaeography,* IX, Note 2.

21. *Ind. Ant.* Vol. XII, pp. 171 and 180.

22. Beal's *Si-yu-ki*, Vol. II, pp. 228.
23. *South Ind. Inscrs.*, Vol. I, pp. 146.
24. Bombay Gazetteer, Vol. I, Part II, p. 318, where Dr. Fleet gives references to the places where these forms occur.
25. The Tamil work Tondamandalasadakam states that Tondamandalam was divided into 24 Kottams. Mr. Kanakasabai Pillai, in his Tamils 1800 years ago, names these districts as follows:

(1) Pulakottam, (2) Ikkattukottam, (3) Manavirkottam, (4) Sengattukottam, (5) Paiyurkottam, (6) Eyilkottam, (7) Damalkottam, (8) Urukattukottam, (9) Kalatturkottam, (10) Semburkottam, (11) Amburkottam, (12) Venkunrakottam, (13) Palakunrakottam, (14) Ilangadukottam (15) Kaliyurkottam, (16) Chemkarai, (17) Paduvurkottam, (18) Kadikur, (19) Sendirukkai (20) Kunravattanakottam, (21) Vengadakottam, (22) Velurkottam, (23) Sethoor and (24) Puliyurkottam. Here is an interesting question of ancient geography for study. Except for a few of these kottams, the rest are all mentioned in inscriptions. Each of them appears to have had a number of sub-divisions called nadu under it. Ambatturnadu and Pulalnadu were in Pulalkottam. The fact that Tiruvorriyur was situated in Pulalnadu and Pulalnadu was in Pulalkottam. The fact that Tiruvorriyur was situated in Pulalnadu were some of the divisions in Sengattukottam. Paiyurkottam, also known as Paiyur Ilangottam, had in it Tekkurnadu in which the modern village of Satyavedu (Ponneri taluk) was situated. The city of Kanchi was Eyilkottam. The modern villages of Damal and Urrukadu in the Cingleput district, ought to have been chief places in ancient times in the divisions which bear their names. Vallanadu was a sub-division in Damalkottam, while Velimanadu, Kunranadu, and Damanurnadu were some of the territorial divisions included in Urukkattukottam. The country round Tirukkallukunram was comprised in Kalatturkottam which had in it Paidavurnadu, Kalatturnadu and Sengunranadu. From the inscriptions of Parameswaramangalam we know that it was a village in Semburkottam. And from other records we learn that Amurnadu,

Kumilinadu and Padavurnadu were in Amurkottam and that
Mangalurnadu and Vaittya-nadu were in Kunravattanakottam.
Vengadakottam must be the country near the Tirupati hill. Madras
and its suburban villages were situated in Puliyurkottam. Among
the sub-divisions of this district are mentioned Kotturnadu,
Nedungunranadu, Mangadunadu and Suratturnadu.

26. South Ind. Inscrs., Vol. I, p.125.

27. Inscriptions earlier than the time of Rajaraja I, mention the
territorial division Tondaimandalam and it is only in the latter
part of the reign of Rajaraja I, that the other name Jayangondasolamandalam came to be applied to it.

28. When the Cholas had permanently conquered or annexed the
dominions of other kings, they appear to have given, in addition
to the original name of villages, districits and sub-divisions, new
designations called after their own names and surnames or those
of their ancestors. This innovation was first started during the
times of the Pallavas. The renaming of places was not necessarily
effected after a conquest or an annexation, though that was
certainly one of the many occasions when it seems to have been
done. There was a general tendency among the Chola kings to
change the existing names of all places situated within their
territory and call them after the names of Chola kings. This was,
perhaps, done to mark out the places by their very names as
belonging to the Cholas. Some of the later members of the family
further altered the new names and thus we have several surnames
for a single place. A proper study of these names alongside,
affords a clue to find out the surnames of Chola kings. The
survival of the original names and complete effacement of the
intermediate ones, may be accounted for by the fact that it is the
former that find place in literature, in perference to the latter.

29. Beel's Si Yu Ki. Vol. II, p. 229.

30. *Ibid.* p. 230.

31. Wijesinha's translation, p. 116 f. See also the author's paper on
the origin and decline of Buddhism and Jainism in Southern
India in *Ind. Ant.* Vol. XL.

32. References in ancient Tamil literature to *Erumaiyur,* show that

it is iden.ical with the present Mysore state. Erumaiyur is an exact rendering of Mahishamandala. The *thera* Majhantika was deputed to Kasmira and Gandara, the thera Mahadeva to Mahishamandala, the thera Rakkita to Vanavasi, the thera Yona-Dhammarikita to Aparantaka, the thera Maha-Dhammarakkita to Mahratta, the thera Maharakkita to the Yona country, the thera majjhina to the Himavanta, the two theras Soma and Uttara to Suvannabhumi and the thera Maha Mahinda together with Moggali's disciples to Lanka.

33. See Canto 28.

34. Annual Report of the Director-General of Archaeology in India for 1906-7, p. 220.

35. Beal's *Buddhist Record of the Western World*, Vol. II, p. 229.

36. *Vide* the Origin and Decline of Buddhism and Jainism in Southern India, *Ind. Ant.* Vol. XL.

37. Of the sixty-three Saiva devotees mentioned by Sundaramurti-Nayanar, six belong to Tondaimandalam. These are Sakkiya-Nayanar of Sangaramangai, Sivanesar and Vayilar of Mayilai, i.e. Mylapore, Thirukkuripputtondar of Kanchi, Murukka-Nayanar and Kaliyar of Tiruvorriyur. Sekkilar the author of the *Periyapurana* was also a native of Tondai Mandalam. Thirty-two Siva temples of the country are celebrated in the *Devaram*.

38. Kanchi was the native place of Poygaialvar. Budattalvar born at Kadalamallai, i.e., Mavalivaram, one of the principal towns of the Pallavas, Peyalvar whose birthplace was Tirumayilai, Tirumalisai, who is connected with the city of the same name and Tirumangai have referred to the temples at Kanchi. The first three of these are considered the earliest of the Vaishnava saints and the works of the last two are noted for sweetness of melody and high thoughts. Tondai Mandalam contains 22 places sacred to Vaishnavas.

39. This is the well-known Ekambaranatha temple situated in Big Conjeevaram.

40. It is now known as Tirukkaleswara and is near Veppangulam, one mile to the east of Conjeevaram. Later Chola inscriptions found on the walls of it, call the temple by the Tirukkaraikkadu.

41. This temple is in the weavers' street and contains four comparatively modern inscriptions.

42. This temple is situated quite close to the Kailasanatha and is called its inscriptions Anaiyapadangavudaiya Nayanar (S.I.I. Vol. I, p. 117).

43. This is identical with the Onakanteswara temple, near the Sarvatirtham tank.

44. The other four are *Ap.* water linga at Jambukeswaram, Fire linga at Tiruvannamalai, *Vayu* linga at Kalahasti and *Akasa* linga at Chidambaram.

45. No. 14 of 1893 in the Annual Report on Epigraphy.

46. *Annual Report on Epigraphy* for 1893, p. 5.

47. Tirumalisai Alvar refers to this temple in his Tiruchchandaviruttam (stanzas 63 and 64) and Saint Tirumangai in one of the stanzas of his hymn on Tirunariyur and in the 127th couplet of his *Periyatirumadal.* It is also mentioned by Budattalvar in the second *Tiruvandadi* (v 94) and Peyalvar in the third *Tiruvandadi* (v.30).

48. This temple is referred to by Tirumangai Alvar in two stanzas is' one of which Vikakkoli also occurs.

49. Both Tirumangai and Peyalvar mention Auabuyagaram. In the last verse of the former's hymn on this temple, it is stated that the god was worshipped by Vayiramegan, the king of the Tondaiyur, i.e., a Pallava. Mr. Venkayya has shown that this king must be identical with Dantivarman, son of Pallavalmala.

50. Tirumalisai states that Vishnu assumes here a standing posture.

51. Budattalvar refers to Attigiri in verse 96 of the second *Tiruvandadi.*

52. Tirumangai contributes, in priase of the temple, ten stanzas wherein he describes the military achievements of N. Pallavamalla.

53. Velukkai is referred to by Peyalwar in the third *Tiruvandadi,* (vv. 26, 34 and 62) and by Tirumangai in his *Periyatirumadal* (127th couplet): In the last of these references the temple is said to be situated in the high-walled Kanchi.

54. These six temples are mentioned by Tirumangai Alvar.

55. These six temples are mentioned by Tirumangai Alvar.

56. Tirumalisai, Tirumangai, Peyalvar and Poygai refer to the temple of Tiruvehka. The god is said to be lying down.

57. The defeat of the Pandya and several of the battles fought by Pallavamalla are here referred to. The saint was a contemporary of Nandivarman, Pallavamalla and his son Dantivarman, who had the surname *Vayiramegan.*

58. *Annual Report on Epigraphy* for 1906, pp. 62 and 63. The mention of Muttaraiyan in one of the labels shows that he played some part in the civil war perhaps taking the side of Pallavlamalla.

59. *Ponmalaram Kambaikkaraiy Ekambamudaiyannai* occurs in one of the hymns of Ekambam.

60. See Winslow under Kambai.

61. Jnanasambandha has *Vimamar Nedumadanongi Vilangiya Kachchi Tannul* and Tirumalisai *Madanedu Kachchi.*

62. In one of the poems of Tirumangai we get *Kollar Madilsul Kachchinagar.*

63. *Alkidangus ul vayalum madil pulgiyi alag amarum nen marugir kali kachchi* (Jnanasambandha).

64. *Sedar ser kali Kachchi* (Jnansambandha).

65. *Terur nedu vidi chchelun Kachchi* (Jnanasambandha).

66. *Madras Epigraphical Department* (Annual Reports published by the Government of Madras), 1920-21.

67. *Inscriptions of the Madras Presidency*, Government of Madras, 1919, Vol. I, pp. 354 to 365.

Chapter 3

TIRUKKALUKKUNRAM
OR "THE HILL OF THE KITES"

The sacred place, also known as Pakshitirtham, nine miles southeast of Chingleput, derives its name from two kites that are said to worship the presiding deity here. The Puranic version connected with the kites is that two sages, who had sinned, were cursed by God and transformed into kites! These kites are said to worship God in this place every day in order to obtain salvation. They visit the temple on the hill every midday when they are fed. En route they are said to make a similar halt on the rock known as Mahadevamalai, about 8 miles to the east of Gudiyattam, North Arcot district.

The place is also known as Vedagiri (Veda = Scripture and giri = hill); for it is said that the Vedas[1] worshipped God in this place. Another legend is that Indra[2], the guardian of the east, worshipped the deity here; and once in 12 years he visits this holy shrine in the form of a thunderbolt.

Great sanctity is attached to the hill which is about 500 feet in height, and a walk around it is not only considered sacred but is also supposed to cure physical ailments.

The Madras Epigraphical Department in their annual report for the year 1908-09, pages 73, 76 & 77 writes:

"The central shrine of the Vedagiriswarar temple on the summit of the hill is built of three huge blocks of stone which form its inner walls. On these walls are cut many figures which the temple priests explained to me as follows:

1. On the west wall. Siva and Parvati in the centre with Balasubrahmanya seated between them. Brahma is on the south and Vishnu is on the north side of the central group. Below, near the feet of Siva, is Markandeya.

2. On the north wall, Yogadakshinamurti and near him the two Rishis supposed to have been the accursed birds that are now held to be regular visitors to the hill.

3. On the south wall, Nandikeswara and Chandikeswara with a weapon in hand.

It is not unlikely that this Vedagiriswarar shrine, which is apparently very ancient, is identical with the Mulasthana temple referred to in the early Tamil records of the Bhaktavatsaleswara temple and in the Orukal mandapa inscription of Narasimhavarman I. It may also be the case that the neglected in the cell at Orukal mandapa represents the original Mulasthana. In any case the Mulasthana temple to which Skandavishya made a grant was the earliest temple in the Tamil country and was situated somewhere at Tirukkalukkunram.

The monolithic cave called Orukal mandapa on the Vedagiriswarar hill at Tirukkalukkunram, lies to the east of the hill, some 50 steps down the descending side of the pradakshana, to its right. Being cut into the boulder at a level about 9 feet from its foot, the cave is reached by very narrow flights of steps from the northern and southern sides, which meet the cave at its front side. There are two verandahs in the cave, an upper and a lower one, the latter being only a few inches below the former. Each of these two verandahs is supported by four massive pillars, of which the two middle ones are free. These latter, where they are rectangular, measure roughly 2 feet by 1 foot 11 inches. The middle portions of the pillars are octagonal though the facets are not always of equal breadth. In the lower verandah are two graceful lifesize statues which are decorated with ornaments round the neck, wrists and shoulders and which have a girdle and an undergarment on. In the upper verandah there exists only one cell in the centre and in it there is a huge Linga on a pedestal. The cell is at a higher level than the verandah and is approached by two steps. On either side of the entrance into the cell is the image of a dvarapala. Standing figures of Brahma and Vishnu flank the central cell and are placed against the back wall of the cave not in a line with the Linga inside the cell but some feet in front of it. The following measurement will show that the central cell is cut deeper than the rest of the cave and was perhaps meant to be the sanctuary:

Breadth of cave: 21 feet 6 1/2 inches.

Depth of the back wall of the cell: 26 feet 2 inches.

Depth to the entrance of the cell: 17 feet 4 inches.

Depth to the figures of Brahma and Vishnu: 18 feet 6 inches.

Height of the cave: 8 feet 5 1/2 inches.

The importance of the central cell is also indicated by its being fashioned into a fine-looking mandapa with a basement rising in tiers and supporting short pillars over which the beams and the rounded caves seem to rest.

Thus the monolithic cave on the hill at Tirukkalukkunram appears to have been meant as a place of worship for the three gods of the Hindu Trinity — Brahma, Vishnu and Siva. It is, however, now neglected and no ceremonial worship is conducted in it. Nevertheless, pilgrims bow before the uncared-for Linga which is believed represent the Siva who, according to the sthalapurana, cursed the two Rishis dwelling on the hill to become kites. These sacred Rishi-birds are still held to visit the hill regularly at about midday and receive the morsels of cooked rice and ghee from the hands of a priest known as Pakshipandaram. The pillars and walls of both the verandahs in the cave bear the signature of a large number of Dutch visitors in Roman characters. The Dutch writer Havart in his *Open Ondergang van Coromandel*, published in 1693, says that he and the other Dutchmen visited the hill on the 3rd of January, 1681, and saw two sacred birds feeding around midday. It might be noted here that an old Tamil, inscription found on one of the pillars, suggests that the cave must have come into existence in the time of the Pallava king Vatapikonda-Narasingappottaraja (i.e., Narasimhavarman I) about the end of the 7th century A.D.

Mahendravarman's son was Narasimhavarman I or Narasimhavishnu, the famous conqueror of Vatapi i.e., Badami, in the Bijapur district of the Bombay Presidency. On a rock at Badami is a mutilated inscription which testifies to his actual capture of the town and gives for him the biruda Mahamalla from which the name Mavallavaram (correctly Mahamallapuram) of the modern Seven Pagodas is derived. This conquest of Vatapi secured for Narasimhavarman I the Tamil title Valotapikonda. An inscription on the west wall of the strong room in the Bhaktavatsaleswara temple at Tirukkalukkunram records the interesting fact of a second renewal by Rajakesarivarman Aditya I of a grant, originally made to the temple of Mulasthana by the Pallava king Skandasishya and renewed by Vatapikonda Narasingappottaraiyar identical with the Pallava king Narasimhavarman I who captured Vatapis. The fine tall figures of Brahma and Vishnu in the upper verandah and those of the others in the lower, with their figures pointing towards the central shrine, are features peculiar enough to distinguish the Orukal mandapa from the plain monolythic caves of Mahendravarman I at Vallam and Pallavaram. Besides, the figures bear such close resemblance to those in the Dharmarajaratha at Mahabalipuram that it looks very likely that the Orukal mandapa on the hill at Tirukkalukkunram was excavated in the time of Vitapikonda Narasimhavarman I, in whose time the rathas at Mahabalipuram are supposed to have been commenced."

On the northern wall of the central shrine on the summit of the hill there is a figure of Somaskanda,[3] in the south there are the images of Brahma and Vishnu, while at the feet of the God is represented the sage Markandeya. On the north side of the outer wall of the temple, there is the figure of Yoga Dakshinamurti.[4]

The place is also considered holy on account of its having been the ground of penance by Nandi, Siva's bull. On one occasion Nandi is reported to have disobeyed the divine dictate of Siva, and prevented Garuda, the divine eagle of Vishnu) from entering the presence of God. As a consequence Nandi obtained a curse, which was wiped out by his penance. Siva is also said to have appeared before the famous Tamil saint Manikkavachakar,[5] in the form of Dakshinamurti, at this place.

Near the temple on the hill there is an Orukal mandapa or monolithic hall. The Dutch visitors, who appear to have gone to the place in A.D. 1861 and witnessed the feeding of the kites on the 3rd June, have engraved their signatures on the rock. There is a beautiful tank at the foot of the hill, which is known as Sankhatirtha on account of the conch shells found therein. Occasionally, the Valamburi Sankha[6] i.e., right-turned conch (Turbinella pyrum), which is considered very sacred, is also found in this tank.

According to the inscriptions the place was named Ulagalandasolapuram and the deity was at one time perhaps known as Mulasthanesvara; the victory of the Chola king Kulottunga over the Pandyas is also recorded. One Suryadeva of Puvinur Village is said to have erected the steps for ascending the hill and also the shrine of Vinayaka in the southern wall of Vedagiriswara temple. The copper-plate Sasanam in the Madras Museum says that Vijayaranga Chokkanatha Nayaka constructed a matha in this place and also made provision of funds for its upkeep on the 21st November, 1717.

King Kulottunga I drove away Vikkalan (Vikramaditya VI) from Nangili in the Kolar district, by way of Manalur to the river Tungabhadra, and that he conquered the Gangamandalam and Singanam. Having thus secured his frontier in the north, he turned against the Pandyas and subdued the south-westren portion of the peninsula as far as the Gulf of Mannar, the Podyil mountain in the district of Tinnevelly, Cape Comorin, Kottaru, the Sahya or the Western Ghats and Kudamalainadu or the Malabar. There is reference also to an endowment for the maintenance of a matha or mutt of Naminandiadigal, one of the 63 devotees of Siva. Chola king Rajakesarivarman in the 27th year of his reign, renewed a grant which had been made by Skandasishya and confirmed by Narasimhavarman, both of whom are soken *purva rajakkal* (former kings) Madirakonda Parakesarivarman in his 13th year is said to have covered, with gold; the hall at Chidambaram called in a Sanskrit 'Vyaghragrahara' and in Tamil 'Puliyur.'

PURANIC IMPORTANCE

It is the belief of the Hindus that the devas or celestial beings often take birth as mortals in this mundane world of ours, somtimes to undergo punishment for the commissions or omissions in the celestial region, and, at other times, to benefit humanity.

Once upon a time, an attendant of Lord Siva, named Tundeera over the kingdom of Tundeera, which subsequently came to be known as Tondanadu, the country ruled over by a king who wore a garland made of Athonda flowers. In that country arose a famous religious city, which subsequently came to be known by different appellations such as Vedagiri, Pakshithirtham, Tirukkalukkunram and Rudrakoti. It is now an important place of pilgrimage for the Hindus in the Chingleput district, Tirukkalukkunram is named in Sanskrit as 'Pakshithirtham' and in the Tamil 'Tevaram' as Kalukkunram or 'the hill of the kites.'

The origin of the name 'Vedagiri' is very interesting. The four Vedas of the Hindus are compared to the parts of a mountain. The Rig Veda is said to be the root; the Yajur Veda the middle; the Sama Veda the beautiful and attractive mountain-top and the Atharva Veda the peak at the top. The four Vedas wered at one time intact, but the many divisions were made in it by Brahma, Bharadwaja and others. Gayatri Mantra, the potent incantation of the Hindus, was obtained from it by the sage Bharadwaja. Many other sages gleaned many other potent incantations from the Vedas. The Vedas resented their divisions and desired to remain intact having combined their six Angams or parts into one. With this object in view, they approached Lord Siva, one of the Hindu Trinity, who lived in his abode on Mount Kailash. Having made representations to him, they awaited his advice.

After a while, Lord Siva directed the Vedas to go to the earth and remain at Vedagiri as six hills — one hill representing one Angam of the Vedas, promising them that he would himself become a dweller at their tops in the form of a lingam or phallic symbol forever accepting and enjoying their worship. He also added that the people on earth fail to recognise and worship even Him, on account of the influence of Maya or ignorance, and yet for the sake of the Vedas, he would be shining at their tops as a beacon of wisdom for the ignorant. Having said this, he dismissed the Vedas from his presence. As directed by Lord Siva, the five Angams or divisions of the Vedas took up their abode in a city of the king Tundeera, and the city itself came to be known as Vedagiri meaning 'the place where the Vedas remain as hills.' Siva also came to reside on the tops of these hills. Hence this place became an important religious centre, thronged by many millions of pilgrims and others.

The importance of the place has been substantiate by a large number of interesting religious myths.

Siva is described as a beggar collecting alms in a human skull, riding on a bull, and wandering over forests and cremation grounds, though one of the mighty murtis (a form of god) of the Hindus. On one occasion Vishnu paid a visit to him on Mount Kailash having arrived there on his vehicle Garuda, the Brahmani kite, or the king of birds. Nandi, Siva's bull and vehicle was guarding the Mount Kailash. While Siva and Vishnu were conversing inside, an altercation ensued between Nandi and Garuda in which the latter spoke disparagingly of Siva calling him a beggar and so on. Blazing with anger at the disrespect shown towards his noble master Siva, Nandi heaved a breath of anger, of such a force, that Garuda swung backward and forward with every expiration and inspiration of Nandi. Unable to bear the pain caused by this swing, Garuda cried to his master Vishnu for help, who thereupon obtained permission from Siva to direct Nandi to leave Garuda in peace.

When Vishnu communicated Siva's pleasure that Garuda should be left in peace, Nandi's calmness of mind had not returned and he even then blazed with anger. Personal slight, he would not mind much. But a slight shown to his noble master, he would not tolerate and let go unpunished. "Garuda must foreit his life" said Nandi in reply to Vishnu's representations. Vishnu once more went back to Siva and repeated his request. Siva sent for Nandi and commanded him to let Garuda go in peace. Even now, Nandi had not regained his calmness of mind. He was still angry, so he expressed his reluctance to excuse Garuda, Siva's blasphemer; whereupon Siva rebuked him and said that wise never allow themselves to be carried away by anger. His anger having cooled down Nandi felt the force of Siva's rebuke. He felt sorry not only for his having given way to anger but also for having disobeyed his master's order in the beginning. He desired to wipe off the sin of having disobeyed his lord by undergoing suitable punishment. When Siva heard of his Nandi's resolve to be absolved from the sin of disobedience he said that the earth was the fittest place to undergo punishment for sin committed as well as for learning about virtue and vice. Nandi was now placed between the horns of a dilemma. He knew that an order from his master was very rare and most difficult to get. Fool that he was he lost sight of this fact and unnecessarily became a sinner, having disobeyed his commands. Fain would he go to the earth dwell there to wipe off the sin, but he was too reluctant to leave Siva's presence — a position unattainable even by the greatest of the Devas. Tossed between two such conflicting feelings, he at last made up his mind and prayed to Siva to tell him a place where he can do penance to obtain freedom from sin in as short a time as possible. Siva understood Nandi's conflicting feelings, took pity on him and selected for him a place called Rudrakoti, a favourite haunt of his for the purpose. Nandi thereupon retired to this place chosen for him by Siva and was performing penance there. One day, while roaming around, he found a tank filled with cool and crystal water covered over with beautiful golden lilies and blue, white and red lotuses. After having bathed in that tank, he gathered the flowers and worshipped Siva with great devotion and fervour. He then began the performance of a very severe penance with deep concentration. Siva wanted to test his devotee's mental strength. He sent for Indra and directed him to send a celestial nymph to wean his attention away and thus thwart him in his attempts at getting liberation from the bondage of sin. Indra found himself in a dilemma. He was afraid of Siva's anger if he disobeyed his orders. Knowing as he did of what Garuda had suffered by provoking Nandi's wrath he did not have the courage to make an attempt at spoiling his penance as suggested by Siva. He did not know what to do. He at last came to the decision that obedience to Siva's commands was the best thing to do under the circumstances. So he directed the celestial nymph Tilottama to carry out the orders of Lord Siva. In the guise of a beautiful cow, she approached Nandi who was in a deep trance of devotion and penance and tried to rouse his passions by licking him and by gently rubbing her body against him. For a long time Nandi remained undisturbed by her caresses. At last, disturbed by her actions, he grew angry and cursed her, saying "Do thou wander in the forests even as a cow whose form you have assumed to disturb my penance."

Tilottama in great alarm begged Nandi to forgive her saying that she was merely an instrument of Indra whose orders she could not disobey. Nandi thereupon took pity on her and said that she would regain her original form when killed in a hunt near Vedagiri by King Devaguru of the solar dynasty who would rule over Mahabalipuram sometime during the Kali age. Tilottama wandered in the forest in the form of a cow, eating grass and drinking water for a very long time, and at last regained her original celestial form of a nymph as predicted by Nandi, in the beginning of the Kali age.

Nandi thereupon continued his penance undisturbed for a long time. At last Siva was leased with his penance and appeared before him with all his attendants and asked him to make a wish. Nandi asked that even the greatest sinner on earth should be washed of all his sins, if he but came to that place and worshipped Siva, and his prayer was accordingly granted to him.

The origin of the names Pakshithirtham and Tirukkalukkunram are also very interesting. The word Pakshithirtham means 'water made holy by the birds' and the word Tirukkalukkunram means 'the hill of the beautiful vulture.' The names have originated from a myth which is as follows:

Once upon a time there were two brothers. The elder was devoted to Siva and the younger to his consort Sakti. On one occasion the two brothers began quarrelling over the question of superiority of their respective deities. The elder said that Siva was superior to Sakti while the younger persisted that without Sakti, Siva was a non-entity. Siva interfered and said that Siva and Sakti were equal and consequently the question of superiority of one over the other did not arise. Even then the brothers were not be satisfied, and continued their quarrel. Siva in anger at their persistence in a silly quarrel caused them to become vultures! The brothers were filled with grief and begged and prayed to Siva to forgive them. Siva rebuked and said that they would regain their form at the end of the Dwapara age. They did regain their original form under the name of Puda and Vritha and performed severe penance invoking the presence of Siva who appeared before them and promised them Mukti — liberation from the wheel of birth and death — after sometime. The brothers wanted Mukti immediately and persisted in their demands. This made Siva angry and he caused them to become vultures once more and live in the world till the end of the Kali age. They were accordingly born as vultures and remained with Sage Kasyapa in the beginning of the Kali age. They are named Sambu and Adi and worship Siva daily. Arrangements are made to feed them daily and the birds are supposed to visit other sacred places also such as Kasi (Benares) Chidambaram Tiruvarur-original form and attain Mukti at the end of the Kali age.

The reason for the name Rudrakoti is in brief as follows:

Hindus believe that there are seven oceans in the universe namely the ocean of salt water. The second ocean is filled with the juice of sugar cane, the third with honey, the fourth with ghee, the fifth with curd, the sixth with milk and the seventh with pure water.

On one occasion the Devas desired to churn the ocean of milk and obtain nectar from it. They wanted a churn and selected the mountain Mandhara for the purpose. When it was removed a deep cavity was left, out of which came hosts and hosts of Asuras of the nether world, and fought with the Devas.

The Devas complained to Lord Siva who thereupon directed his ganas, hosts of attendants called Rudras, to fight against and destroy the Asuras. They said that the action would be sinful, since the Asuras, though giving trouble to the world now, had formerly acquired great merit having performed severe penance, and that it had been ordained that the killing of those endowed with the merit of penance was a sin. Siva said in reply that the sins resulting from actions helping the Devas were no sins at all and could be wiped out easily by worshipping him at Vedagiri. The Rudrakotis thereupon fell upon the Asuras and destroyed them to the intense joy of the Devas. Unable to bear the burden of the sin of having destroyed the Asuras, the Rudrakotis went to Vedagiri and worshipped Siva there and got purified of their sins. From this incident, the place came to be honoured with the name of Rudrakoti meaning 'Place worshipped by hosts of Rudras' or Siva's attendants.

Once a great fight ensued between the Devas and the Asuras. The Asuras were sheltered by Sage Bhrigu's wife. Vishnu, one of the Hindu Trinity, representing the cause of the Devas, wanted the lady to deliver up the Asuras for punishment. This she stoutly refused to do and Vishnu in great wrath caused the destruction of the lady and the forest she lived in, by fire. Bhrigu, the husband of the deceased lady, thereupon cursed Vishnu that he too would be separated from his wife in future and suffer the misery of the bereavement. This curse took effect when Vishnu was born as Rama, prince of Ayodhya and his wife Sita was carried off by Ravana, king of Lanka while he was living as an exile from his kingdom in the forest of Dandaka.

Vishnu is said to have worshipped Siva at Vedagiri to be absolved from the sin of having destroyed the wife of the sage Bhrigu.

The celestial king Indra is said to have been absolved from the sin of having offended Siva by worshipping him at Devagiri. Once he took up the cause of a celestial damsel whose golden ball was forcibly taken away by a Gandharva. He accused Siva and Parvati of the deed without knowing who they were, since the ball was lying near them. In order to wipe off his sin Indra worshipped Vedagiriswarar as advised by the celestial guru (preceptor) Brihaspati.

According to another myth the eight Vasus of the Hindus were cursed by the divine cow Kamadhenu to live a life of one hundred years of misery in the mortal world for the sin of having attempted to milk her to satisfy the wife of one of them. They were eventually taken by the sage Narada to the sage Markanda; who directed them to worship Siva on the Vedagiri hills in order to be absolved from their sin.

Thus it is seen that the place is considered to be most sacred by the Hindus and thousands of pilgrims throng the place every year not only to wipe off their sins, but also to have a look at the two vultures boldly approaching and eating from the hands of a man. The food left over by these vultures is considered very precious and is freely distributed among those who want it.

VISIT OF THE DUTCH

Several Dutch gentlemen have visited this hill and their signatures are seen over the pillars of the mandapa on the hill. The following signatures relating to them are detailed in the report of the Madras Government Epigraphist for the year 1908-09:

"L. Hemsinck
De. E. Hr. Ant. Pavilioen
Johs. H.(u) yemn
(d) Ha. (r) t
Johs. Paviln
A. (D) Klerck
L. Hemsinck De Jonge
Pieter Kemsinck
H. Helene (H) emsing
Heussen
Amerentia Hemsinck
Joannes Blockhevins
Martinus Pit
Marten P (i) t
Jacomina Baffart
Wilhenuna Dinker

Johanna Duicker
D (e). (E). W.C. Hartsink
De. Wit
J. Corbisier
Wm. Groenege (u) s
Laurens Pit D' (i) onge
Helene Dinker

The signatures in Roman characters engraved on the pillars of the Orukal mandapa on the Tirukkalukkunram hill bear dates below them, ranging between. A.D. 1664 and 1687. Of these De E (Edele) Hr (Heer) Ant. (Anthoni) Pavilioen (i.e., the Honourable Mr. Anthony Pavilioen) whose name is inscribed on the east face of the second pillar in the upper verandah of the cave, was evidently from the title "Edelle" which was given only to the governors of the Coromandal Coast or to members of their Council, a personage of high position.) Some interesting details about him are given in Valentyn's *Ond en Nieum Oost Indien*. He was the chief at Masulipatam in A.D. 1658 and the Commander (Chief) at Jaffna in A.D. 1661. He appears to have continued in this latter position till 1st September, 1665, when he was appointed governor of Coromandal and held that high position at Pulicat for 13 years from 10th October, 1665 to 1676. He was made an extraordinary member of the Batavia Council in A.D. 1668 and an ordinary member in 1676. His Excellency perhaps visited Sadras in 1670 and on his way paid a visit to the hill at Tirukkalukkunram from Tirupolur which was along the inland route from Sadraspatam to Pulicat. Tirupolur, which is stated by Valentyn to contain a 'beautiful heathen temple' must be the modern Tirupporur, about 7 miles north-east of Tirukkalukkunram. A memoir drawn up by Anthony Pavilioen on the eve of his departure from Jaffnapatam has been printed at the end of the book entitled *Memoirs and Instructions of Dutch Governors, Commanders, etc.*, published by the Ceylon Government. Johs. (i.e. Jodannes) Pavilioen (5) is probably to be identified with the son of the Honourable Anthony Pavilioen and he is the second in the factory at Negapatam from 1672 to 1673.

Laurens Pit D'Jonge (Lawrence Pit, Junior) was another of the Governors of the coast from 1687 to 1698. He was born in India and perhaps visited Sadras in the Company of Laurens Pit Senior (Governor of the coast from 1652 to 1663) while he was yet young and took a pleasure trip to the Tirukkalukkunram hill. Before becoming governor he was the Chief of Masulipatam from 1685 to 1687 and in that capacity went in 1686 on an embassy to Golconda. He took Pondicherry from the French and signed the articles of capitulation in 1693.

De E (dele) W.C. Hartsink, whose signature is on the east face of the first pillar in the lower verandah, must be identified with Willem Carel Hartsink who was born in Japan on 12th July, 1638, and was the chief merchant and President at Pulicat from 1679 to 1681. Hartsink was the second at Draksharamam in the Godavari district from 1660 to 1663 and the Chief of the Golconda factory from 1663 to 1677. In 1668, however, he appears as the second at Masulipatam. He occupied the position of the Chief at Masulipatam from 1677 till 1679 when he was appointed the chief merchant and, pending the appointment of a Governor, President at Pulicat. He returned to Masulipatam in 1681, retired from service in 1685 and died in Holland on 22nd May, 1689. A few lines below the signature of this gentleman, a passage in Tamil registers, respect paid (evidently to the god Siva in the cave) by a certain Virakuvan of Palavakkattu, which is perhaps, a variant of Palaverkkadu, the old name of Pulicat. Virakuvan (i.e., Vira Ragavan) may have been a follower, of the Hon'ble W.C. Hartsink from Pulicat.

Martinus Pit has probably to be identified with another son of the elder Pit. In 1674 he signed the articles of capitulation by the French at St. Thome. He was born at Pulicat and served for many years on the coast. Before 1675 he was the chief merchant of Devanampatam and from 1575 to 1677 he appears to have been the chief merchant at Pulicat and second-in-council. Perhaps in this latter capacity he went in 1675 to Batavia with a letter from Anthony Pavilion, Governor of the Coromandel coast, and on 12th July, 1676, returned in charge of three ships from Batavia. In 1677 he appears to have been called again to Batavia in consequence of a misunderstanding which he had with the then Governor of the Coromandel and was at Batavia on the 11th November, 1677. He was still in Batavia in 1678 and there he attended the funeral of the Governor-General on the 7th January, 1678. On the 3rd October in the same year he was appointed Visitateur-General (Accountant-General). His career henceforward appears to have been in Batavia where he stayed as an ordinary member of council from 1683 to 1690.

L. Hemsinck was the under-merchant and Chief at Sadraspatam from A.D. 1666 to 1686. His appointment was made on 28th May, 1666. The wife of Lambert Hemsinck was Amarentia Hemsinck nee Blockhovius whose tomb at Sadras is described on page 198 of Mr. Cotton's *Tombs*.

These signatures here signify the visit to this hill of many Dutch people among whom were governors and chiefs of settlements. The summit of the hill commanding from its height a fine view of the plain below, right up to the sea-shore at Mahabalipuram, must have attracted the attention of the Dutch factors who frequently travelled between Pulicat and Sadras by way of Tirupporur. There is an illustration of the hill in "Havart" who himself visited it on 3rd January, 1681.

INSCRIPTIONS

The inscriptions here have been copied during the year 1894, 1910 and 1911 by the Madras Epigraphical Department.

"This is the celebrated Pakshitirtha, mentioned in the Devaram and known in Chola times as Ulagalandasolapuram in Kalatturnadu in Kalatturkottam. See Antiquities I, 191 and Ind. Antq. X. 198.

167 of 1894 (Tamil) — On the wall of the strong room of the Vedagirisvarar temple. A record of the Chola king Ko Rajakesarivarman (a predecessor of Parantaka I,) dated in his twenty-seventh year, renewing a grant made by the Pallava kings Skandasishya and Vatapikonda Narasimhavarman (See Madras Christian College magazine for October 1890, and Ep. Ind. III, 277-80). Mr. Venkayya identifies Narasimha with Narasimhavarman I, the contemporary of Jnanasambandha and Siruttonda.

168 of 1894 (Tamil) — On the same wall. A record of the Chola king Madirakonda Ko Parakesarivarman (i.e., Parantaka I) in his thirteenth year. Records gift of a lamp by Nedumal Sattan Sennipperayan of Karaikkattur and his mother in Amurkottam. See Ep. Ind. III, 280-1.

169 of 1894 (Tamil) — On the same wall. A record of the Rashtrakuta king Kannaradeva (Krishna III), dated in his seventeenth year. Published by Mr. Venkayya in the Madras Christian College magazine for April 1892, and Ep. Ind. III, pp. 282-6. Records gift of lamp by a native of Karai.

170 of 1894 (Tamil) — On the same wall. A record of the Rashtrakuta king Kannaradeva, dated in his nineteenth year. Records that a Sattan of Karai built a hall in the shrine and provided for water, fire, etc, besides one patti of land which he had purchased from Isana Siva or Nakkadi Bhatta. The money was deposited with the local sabha.

171 of 1894 (Tamil) — On the same wall. A record of the Chola king Ko Parakesarivarman or Rajendra Choladeva 1, (1012-43) in his sixteenth year. Gift of a lamp.

172 of 1894 (Tamil) — On the same wall. Records in the twenty-sixth year of the Chola king Ko Rajakesarivarman or Rajadhi Rajadeva gift of land. (The king was very probably Rajadhiraja I who ruled from 1018 to 1052.)

173 of 1894 (Tamil) — On the same wall. Records in the fifth year of the Chola king Ko Parakesarivarman or Rajendradeva (1052-63) a gift of land.

174 of 1894 (Tamil) — On the same wall. Records in the fourteenth year of the Chola king Rajakesarivarman or Kulottunga Choladeva (1070-1118) gift of 90 cows for a lamp. See. S.I.I. III, No. 69, pp. 143-8.

175 of 1894 (Tamil) — On the same wall. Records in the seventh year of the Chola king Ko Rajakesarivarman or Vira Rajendradeva I? (1063-70) gift of a lamp.

176 of 1894 (Tamil) — On the same wall. Records in the third year of the Chola king Vikrama Choladeva (1118-35) gift of a lamp.

177 of 1894 (Tamil) — On the east wall of the second prakara of the same temple, right of entrance. A damaged record of the Vira Devaraya Udaiyar dated Vikriti.

178 of 1894 (Tamil) — On the same wall. Records in the third year of Raja Narayana Samburaya (i.e., 1340 A.D.) gift of a lamp.

179 of 1894 (Tamil) — On the south wall of the prakara. A record of the Chola king Ko Rajakesarivarman or Kulottunga Choladeva I, dated in his forty-second year Records that an inhabitant of Rajarajapuram made over 10 kasus to temple authorities who purchased some land with this, for maintaining a matha of Naminandi Adaigal and one of the 63 devotees of Siva. S.I.I. III, No. 75, pp. 164-8,

also Ins. S. Dts., p. 169, No. 6 and Ind. Antq. Vol. XXI, p. 281-ff.

180 of 1894 (Tamil) — On the same wall. Records in the twenty-third year of the Chola king Ko Rajakesarivarman or Kulottunga Choladeva a copy of a former copper plate recording the boundaries of Tirukkalukkunram. This inscription is given in Ins. S. Dts. p. 170, No. 8, but the year is given as 33.

181 of 1894 (Tamil) — On the same wall. Ko Perunjingadeva records in his twenty-first year, gift of a lamp. See Ep. Ind. VII, 165. The date corresponded, according to Kielhorn, to Saturday, 10th February, 1274 A.D.

182 of 1894 (Tamil) — On the same wall. A record of Tribhuvanaviradeva, i.e., Kulottunga III (1178-1216) in his thirty-seventh year, relating to gift of a lamp.

183 of 1894 (Tamil) — On the west wall of the same prakara. An incomplete record of the Chola king Ko Parakesarivarman or Rajadhirajadeva (II?), dated in his ninth year. Records gift of lamp.

184 of 1894 (Tamil) — On the west wall of the same prakara. An incomplete record of the Chola king Ko Parakesarivarman or Rajadhirajadeva (II?), dated in his ninth year. Records gift of a lamp.

184 of 1894 (Tamil) — On the same wall. Gift of land by Konerimaikondan in his thirty-fourth year, for repairs of the temple.

185 of 1894 (Tamil) — On the inside of the east wall of third prakara of the same temple, right of entrance. A damaged record of Kampama Udaiyar (II?), son of Vira (Bukka I?) dated Ananda. This is evidently Inscription No. 22, in Ins. S. Dts. p. 174, No. 22. It says that the property of the deity worth 750 panams, stolen by a man was restored at his own expense.

186 of 1894 (Tamil) — On the west wall of the Tripurasundari shrine in the same temple. Records gift of a lamp in the ninth year of the Pandya king Ko Jatavarman or Sundara Pandyadeva, I (1251-64). See Ep. Ind. VI, 307, where Kielhorn points out that the exact date is Sunday, 15th June, 1259 A.D. See Ins. S.Dts., p 173, No. 19, where the reignal year is misread as I.

187 of 1894 (Tamil) — On the same wall. Records in the ninth year of the Pandya king Ko Jatavarman or Sundara Pandyadeva (1251-64) gift of gold. Ind. Antq. XXI, 343. (See the Srirangam and Tiruppukkuli inscriptions, Ind. Antq. XXII, p. 221 and Ep. Ind. VI, p. 307, where Kielhorn gives the date as Tuesday, 29th April, 1259). See also Ins. S.Dts., p. 173, No. 20.

188 of 1894 (Tamil) — On both sides of the entrance into the second prakara of the same temple. Records in the ninth year of the Pandya king Sundara Pandyadeva the setting up of a linga by a chief of Adigai and gift of 67 1/2 panams. See Ins. 8. Dis. p. 174, No. 21, where this inscription is given.

189 of 1894 (Tamil) — On the south wall of the Bhaktavatsaleswara temple on the hill. A much-damaged record of the Pandya king Sundara Pandya.

57 of 1909 (Tamil) — On the north wall of the kitchen in the Bhaktavatsaleswarar temple, left of entrance. The Vijayanagara king Virapratapa Bukkaraya II records in S. 1328, Vyaya, a gift of land for repairs and for the festival called Bukkarayansandi (named after the king), to the temple of Tirukkalukkunramudaiya Nayanar. See Ins. S. Dts., p. 171 of No. 10.

58 of 1909 (Tamil) — In the same place. Dated in the reign of the Vijayanagara king Pratapa Bukkaraya II. Records in S. 328, Vyaya, a gift of land to the temple of Tirumalai Aludaiya Nayanar, by the people of Ayinavellipparu. See Ins. S. Dts., p. 171, No. 11, where this inscription is given.

59 of 1909 (Tamil) — In the same place. A damaged record of the Pandya king Jatavarman or Tribhuvanachakravartin Vira Pandyadeva, dated in his 13th year. Records gift of a village for the festival called Kalingarayansandi to the same temple by the inhabitants of Kalatturparru. Tirukkalukunram was a village in Kalatturkottam in Jayangondasolamandalam. Mentions Kappalur Ulagalandasolanallur in Mutturukkuram in Pandimandalam. (The king came to the throne in 1253 and so the year of the inscription was 1266 A.D. I have traced this inscription in the Mack MSS.) See Ins. S.Dts., p. 172, No. 13.

60 of 1909 (Tamil) — In the same place. A damaged record of the Vijayanagara king Virapratapa Devaraya, dated in S. 1320, Paridhavi. (This inscription is given in the Mack MSS. It is said to record the grant of Vangalappakam to Tirukkalukkunram Nayanar.) See Ins. S.Dts., p.171, No.12.

61 of 1909 (Tamil) — On the same wall, right of entrance. Records in the tenth year of Sakalalokachakravartin Rajanarayana Sambuvaraya (i.e. 1347 A.D.) gift of land, by purchase, to the temple of Tirukkalukkunramudaiya Nayanar. Mentions Pudupattinam or Solamarttandanallur in Mondurnadu, a sub-division of Amurkottam, a district of Jayangondasolamandalam. See Ins. S. Dts., p. 172, No. 16. It says that the village was worth 350 panams.

62 of 1909 (Tamil) — In the same place. Records in the seventh year of the Pandya king Maravarman or Tribhuvanachakravartin Vikrama Pandyadeva gift of cows for a lamp for the shrine of Shanmukhapillaiyar by a native of Vanavanadevichaturvedimangalam in Amurkottam. (Is this king identical with that Maravarman Vikrama Pandya who ascended the throne in 1282, and who was victorious over Viraganda Gopala and Ganapati of the Kakatiya dynasty?)

63 of 1909 (Tamil) — In the same place. Records in the reign of the Vijayanagara king Vira Vijaya Bhupatiraya

(Bukka III) in the Vijaya, gift of taxes for a festival by Nagesvaramudaiyan Villavarayan, who was the agent of the king. See Ins. S. Dts., p. 172, No. 14.

64 of 1909 (Tamil) — In the same place. Records, in the reign of the Vijayanagara king Bhupatiraya, in S. 1330, a gift of 32 cows for a lamp by a native of Nerkulam, at the rate of 1/4 measure of ghee daily for a lamp. See. Ins. S. Dts., p. 172, No. 15 also. [Bhupati was son of Bukka II].

65 of 1909 (Tamil) — At the top of the second pillar from the right in the upper verandah of the Orukal mandapa, on the hill. A damaged record. Mentions Kalatturkottam, Mulatanattu Perumanadigal and Vatapikonda Narasingapottarasa (i.e. Narasimhavarman I, the conqueror of Vatapi).

66 to 73 of 1909 (English) — On the eight pillars of the upper and lower verandah in the same mandapa. Records in seventeenth century A.D. signatures of Dutch officers.

74 of 1909 (English) — On the walls of the same mandapa. Records in the seventeenth century A.D. Signatures of Dutch officers.

75 of 1909 (English) — At the entrance into one of the temple kitchens of the same hill. Records signatures of Dutch officers of the nineteenth century.

329 (a) to (m) of 1911 (Roman characters) — On the wall at the entrance into the birds' kitchen, on the hill. The following names (read tentatively) are engraved:

(a) A.D. Kiegr I-m i-d 1666; (b) C.J. Keys, Price, ... Gyfford; (c) ... H. C. Rabel, 89 Alack, L Gray ... Anne; (d) H. Dubon 1749; (e) .... vkerck; (f) T. Campic.... (g) D.V.A.S.; (h) J.A. Van Braam Nederld Commiss XX Febry MDCCCXIII, C-40 IS. Peelman; (i) N.D. Jong Heere 1749; (j) 85. T. Poughion, 35; (k) P.E. Van Hogendrop A. Vandenbroek; (See Cotton's Tombs, p. 187, No. 1006). A.M.E.L. Brachi-1793, M. Dormx, Wed. L Alag. .... C.W.

Cantervisscher 179. ....; (1) W. Van Somesan....; P. St. Paul C.J. Keveseeg, 1750 C.P. Keller; (m) Lucas, L. Hemsinck. ... 8-m 13-d 1662. The last was either the chief at Sadraspatam from A.D. 1666 to 1686 or an engineer of that name who died in 1661, See Ep. Rep. 1912, 92 for details.)

330 of 1911 (Roman characters) — On the wall of the temple kitchen of the same hill. Perhaps damaged at the right end. Registers the names: W. Silves H. Stee... 5

331 of 1911 (Roman characters) — On the west wall of a ruined mandapa in the north main street of the same village. "Geo: Dawson lived in thsi Choy Fm. 18th October to 9th December, 1769." Dawson was a Madras civilian, entered the company's service in 1751. Member of Madras Council, 1768, Chief of Cuddalore, 1769. Returned to England, 1776. See Ep. Rep. 1912, p. 92.

On the south wall of the gate in the temple of Bhaktavatsalasvami. Records that one Tondamana Rayan purchased the village Echencaurana for 250 golden panams and granted it to the god in Vibhava. Ins. ced. Dts., p. 151, No. 1.

In the same place. Records that one Narayanadeva and another gave in the reign of Virupanna Udaiyar, the village of Vampattu (1) for 1360 panams. Ibid., No. 2.

On the south wall of the gate of Bhaktavatsala temple. Records that in the same reign in Vibhava, 53 velis of land in a village were sold for 1,560 panams, Ibid., No. 3.

In the same place. Records that Vira Kampana Udaiyar levied a tax of 70 panams per annum on the local weavers, to be paid to the deity. Ibid., No. 4.

In the same place. Records that in the reign of Vira Bukkana Udaiyar, in Nala, certain allowances were made to the deity. Ibid., No. 5.

On the southern surrounding wall. Records that Tillaimuvayiranambi and his brother Ramabhatta purchased four patakam of land for 100 kasus and granted it to the god Tirukkalukkunra Nayanar in the twenty-fifth year of Kulottunga Choladeva. Ibid., No. 7.

In the same place in the same wall. Records that in the same year in the reign of the same king, one Kanakaraya granted 90 sheep for ghee at the rate of 1/4 measure daily. Ins. ced. Dts., p. 158, No. 9.

On the eastern wall of the gate of the kitchen in the Bhaktavatsala shrine. Records in the shrine of Devaraya the sale of 3 3/4 karai of land at Kottappakkam for 820 panams and its endowment to the deity. Ibid., p. 173, No. 17.

On the north prakara wall. Records that Tiruvenkattu Udaiyan granted 550 kulis of land to the deity in twenty-first year of Tribhuvanaviradeva (Kulottunga III). Ibid., p. 173, No. 18.

On a stone in the tank of Sankhatirtham. Records that Kulottunga Choladeva granted in his third year 32 velis of land in the village of Kulottungacholanellore. Ibid., p. 875, No. 23.

In the prakara of the pagoda on the top of the hill. Records that a certain chief erected the mandapam in front of the Vedagiriswami temple. Ibid. p. 175, No. 24.

On the south wall of the inner temple. Records the presentation of a jewel to the god by a private person. Ibid., p. 176, No. 25.

On a step leading to of the Vinayaka temple in the southen wall of Vedagirisvarar temple. Records that one Suryadeva of Puvinur village erected the steps to ascend the hill and the pagoda of Vinayaka. Ibid., p. 176, No. 26.

On the western wall of the mandapam of the Amman shrine. Records the gift of the village of Amaranputtur for the Avani festival by the inhabitants of a village to god Adichandresvara. Ibid., p. 177, No. 27.

RUDRANKOIL

At a distance of a few furlongs stands the village of Rudrankoil, where Siva is said to have fought with several Asuras or demons and gained a victory over them. There is now an ancient Siva temple at the spot.

NOTES

1. The Vedas are said to have worshipped god at certain other shrines in the Tanjore district, such as Vedaranyam, Tiruvalandur and Tiruppunavasal near Shiyali. God is said to have expounded the truth of the Vedas to the sages at Tiruvottur, near Conjeevaram, and to the goddess at Uttirakosamangai, near Ramnad. Tradition also says that god himself, disguised as a brahmacharin (bachelor), chanted the Vedas in Tiruturutti near Mayavaram.

2. Indra, god of the east, the storm and the elements, is one of the eight guardians of the cardinal points: he has the white elephant Airavata for his mount and carries the *Rohitam* or the iris as an invincible bow. The others are: Agni, God of fire, the guardian of the southeast, lightning in the air and as fire on earth. Yama, God of death, rides on a buffalo, carries a club and guards the south. It is considered inauspicious to sit facing the south on sacred occasions. Nirithi, the guardian of the south-west, rides on a demon and is personified as brandishing a sword. Varuna, God of rain, who is the guardian of the west, rides on Makara, a sea-monster and carries a trident. Vayu, God of wind and the guardian of the northwest, drives an antelope. Kubera, God of wealth, is in the north and carries a mace and rides on horse. Esana of the northeast rides on a bull.

3. This aspect of Siva is prevalent in most temples, on processional occasions. Here Siva and Parvati are seated with young Skanda standing between them.

4. Siva in the aspect of a spiritual teacher taught to the world Yoga, music and other sciences and arts through four sages named Sanaka, Sanandana, Sanatana, and Sanatkumara. He is also called Yoga Dakshinamurthi, Jnana Dakshinamurthi, Vina Dakshinamurthi and Vyakyana Dakshinamurthi and any one of these sculptures is to be found on the southern wall of all Siva temples and they are considered very auspicious.

5. The four (*Nalvar*) viz., Sundarar, Sambandhar, Manikkavachakar and Appar hold a prominent position among the Saiva saints. Manikkavachakar is specially worshipped in Avadayarkoil.

6. The goddess at one time doubted the omnipotence of the god who cursed her to be born on earth as the daughter of Daksha. She appeared in the form of a conch on a lotus flower in the river Jamna (Kalindi which rises in the mountain Kalinda) near Prayag or Gaya. Great sanctity is then attached to the conch, and its possession is supposed to bring wealth.

7. This figure is from the temple of Avur near Kumbakonam.

Chapter 4

MAHABALIPURAM[1]
OR "THE SEVEN PAGODAS."

This place of great architectural importance, known also as Mallapuram or Mamallapuram, Mavalipuram and Mahamalaipuram lying in 12° 37 "north latitude and 80° 14" east longitude, is situated at a distance of about 35 miles to the south of Madras and about 20 miles on the south-east of Chingleput. It is also known as the 'Seven Pagodas', name a probably given by the European sailors on account of the seven pinnacles of the Hindu temples. The rock-cut sculptures here are traced to the earliest known examples of the Dravidian style of architecture of southern India and these consist of *rathas*, caves and bas-reliefs. From early Tamil writings it is known that about the 11th century there existed many palatial buildings about this place which are all now probably submerged under the sea. The Stalasayana temple is now washed by the sea and is in consequence called the shore temple. The Vaishnava work *Nalayiraprabandha* mentions this temple as the Talasayana (Stalasayana) of Kadal Mallai (aea rock), the old name of Mahabalipuram. With the exception of the shore temple all the other existing monolithic buildings are hewn out of the rocks which rise abruptly above the surrounding sandy plain. The Vaishnava saint Tirumangai

Alvar mentions that the god Siva was living here with Vishnu and so we find the shrines of both these gods standing close to each other in this temple.

The Varaha, or the boar incarnation of Vishnu, is of special importance in this place, and this deity is seen standing with his right foot resting on Adisesha[2] (god of snakes) and the goddess of earth resting on his right thigh. The scene represents the god rescuing the goddess of earth from the Rakshasas or demons who stole her and hid her in the sea. Adisesha, on whose expanded hood Mother Earth is said to rest, is seen gradually emerging out of the sea. Opposite to this representation in the Varaha rock-cut temple we find the various scenes of the Vamana Trivikrama incarnation.

In the other caves, natural and artificial, we find beautiful sculptural representations of the various Puranic scenes. In one cave the goddess Mahishasuramardini[3] with several attendants is represented as engaged in destroying Rakshasas. The sculptures are all beautiful and lifelike. In the Samanyalakshmi[4] panel two huge elephants are shown as pouring water over the goddess. Most of these sculptures here attest to the art of sculpture having been carried to perfection by the ancient Hindus.

The famous Vaishnava saint Bhudattalvar is said to have been incarnated at this place and on that account also it has an importance of its own.

From inscriptions it is gathered that this place together with Saluvankuppam closeby, formed one large city and that the place was ruled by the kings of the Pallava dynasty. The place also appears to have been a flourishing centre of trade, having business with distant foreign countries. Several varieties of coins have been discovered in the ruins which substantiates the view that the town was a business centre, where people of different countries met together for this purpose.

In the Arjuna's penance which is sculptured on the rock for nearly 100 feet in length and 50 feet in height, Arjuna[5] (one of the five Pandava brothers of *Mahabharata*) is seen standing on one leg quite emaciated with uplifted arms and in a penitent attitude. Next to him is the figure of Siva holding the Pasupatastra. In another place, on the same rock, is shown the scene of King Bali holding his darbar, attended by warriors, Rajas and several wild animals. This representation is Patala Loka[6] (the nether world) whither he was sent down by the Vamana Trivikrama avatar (the dwarf incarnation of Vishnu) to rule over the place. In the middle of the same rock is shown Vasuki (Lord of serpents) in the aspect of a dragon under a canopy. The other figures are of his daughter Ulupi seated below, and of a penitent.

In the Krishna mandapa there is the sculpture of Sri Krishna supporting the hill with his left hand to protect cattle against the fury of Indra, the god of rain. Close to him the cattle are being tended and milked. On the right side there is an affrighted bull, with its head slightly turned and its forefoot extended. This lila or sport of Sri Krishna is popularly known as Govardhana Uddhara[7].

PURANIC IMPORTANCE

The following translation of the *Stalapurana* appears in the Annual Report of the Madras Archaeological Department, for the year 1901-02:

"Stalapuranam. — Origin of Gnanappiran or Vishnu in his boar-incarnation, and as Stalasayana Perumal, in the temple at Mallavaram, for whose worship the shrine is supposed to have been built.

The account of the origin of these gods, and the erection

of the temple in their honour, comprises eight chapters in the *Brahmandapuranam* as related by Brahma, the Creator to the sage Narada.

A sacred and pious Brahman, by the name of Pundarika, worshipped the feet of god with lotus flowers everyday. He visited all the temples in the world (probably meant for India) one after another, and worshipped the gods there with these flowers. Once he happened to visit the temples on the east coast of Carnatic and went to a place called Tiruvidaventhi. There he worshipped the god in his boar incarnation seated with his wife Lakshmi on his left lap. From there he passed through some extensive forests on the south and saw omens which indicated or augured good luck. He inferred from these that he might become subject to the mercy of the Creator and obtain beatitude; and so he continued his travels piously meditating upon god. He came to a verdant garden, with a number of pools and water tanks, around which had grown flowering plants, fruit and sandalwood trees and others emitting a pleasant aroma.

In this garden, he saw a sacred Brahman, named Vishnusarma who, with twelve *namams* marked, seated devotedly meditating on god. Pundarika Rishi prostrated himself before him and received his blessing and hospitality. Thence he proceeded a short distance towards the south, where he saw a pool covered with beautiful lotus flowers, the dust or pollen of which was collected in the air, in the form of clouds, and shining as the rays of the rising sun. He approached the pool and found the flowers, large and full, with 1,000 petals each. Being pleased with the beauty and fragrance of the flowers, he leapt with joy at having been so fortunate as to behold such a scene. He decided to gather them all and use them for worshipping god. God was pleased at his devotion and true love, and in order to spare him of any more

wanderings on his pilgrimage, thought of appearing before
him. The Rishi then heard a heavenly command that he should
worship god in his lying posture in the sea of milk (while god
thought of how the Rishi was to overcome the difficulty of
coming across the seas, and decided that he would go himself
to the place where the Rishi was).

When Pundarika Rishi heard the voice from Heaven, he
was pleased that he had found the lotus flowers, commended
even by the deities in the sky, and collected all of them
without leaving even one. While he was so engaged, he saw
a large crocodile, whose tongue having been cut, floating
senseless in the water. The Rishi cast at it a look full of mercy
and kindness, at which the crocodile recovered from its
swoon, and musing on its past life addressed the Rishi thus:
"O Rishi! O my Guru, the effect of your merciful look has
nullified a curse placed upon me." Surprised at these words,
the Rishi asked the crocodile to mention the cause of the
curse, to which the latter replied: "O Brahma Rishi! I was,
before this transformation, a Maharaja in Mallavaram ruling
all my subjects with great mercy and kindness. My son is still
there engaged in worshipping our god Vishnu in his boar
incarnation in that town." Pundarika Rishi interrupted the
crocodile, and asked as to the locality of Mallavaram, the time
when Vishnu first incarnated himself in avatar and to which
of his devoted votaries did god thus present himself.

The crocodile answered "Mallavaram is situated at a
distance of a *kros* south of the pool near whihc they are
conversing. The town is populated with virtuous men; it is full
of riches, and is not inferior to the heaven of Indra in its
comforts, and that it is two *yojanas* in length and half a yojana
in breadth. The population consists of Srivaishnava Brahmans
who are well versed in the *Sastras,* by Rishis performing
austere penances, by heroic warriors fully equipped with

chaturangabala and righteous men and members of the royal family who are all devoted followers of Vishnu. It is a seaport where precious articles are imported for sale from other coastal towns. I, Haripriyan, was a ruler in Mallavaram. Now, Sadananda, my son, is its king, known in public as the righteous Malleswara. He devotedly worships Vishnu in his boar incarnation Bhuvaraha Perumal three times a day according to *Sastric* rules. I will now answer your last question as to the story of the origin of Bhuvaraha Perumal as handed down to me by my ancestors."

"O Pundarika Rishi! In the days of yore, one of my ancestors, a king named Harisekharachakravarti, reputed to be righteous, honest, strong and a devotee of Vishnu, ruled the kingdom. He with his mother would regularly, in the noon, visit Tiruvidaventhi, a place of Varaha Kshetram (boar incarnation) at a distance of a yojana towards the north and worship the god there. He would then walk that distance back again to his place, there pay all due homage to about 4,000 Brahmans and feed them sumptuously. After they had been fed, he would take his own food. Vishnu, Bhuvaraha Perumal, the closest observer of the actions of his votaries, pleased with his faith in him, thought of going himself to the king and saving him the trouble of travelling such a long distance. So he transformed himself into a very old and infirm Srivaishnava Brahman and his consort into a girl, whom he held by his right hand. Supporting himself with a staff in his left hand, he walked down with tottering feet to the place of Harisekhara Maharaja. The king and his mother were pleased to see such a reverential old sage entering their palace, and bestowed on him due hospitality. The king then prepared himself to attend to his daily routine. At this stage the venerable old man told the king that since he was very old and both he and his young companion were tired and famished, the king should give them food first so that they might not succumb to their privations. The king offered his consolation and begged permission to first go on his daily journey for the worship of Bhuvarahasvami; and assured them that on his return their wants would be supplied. The pious Brahmin replied, the girl being young and having travelled a long distance, was unable longer to endure the pangs of hunger, and he too being infirm with age, would not tolerate any more delay. The king was greatly moved by their request. He meditated upon God Bhuvarahasvami, and thought of sage the old as representing his god, and the young girl his consort. He took them to his palace and made them sit on a golden throne set with precious gems. He then served them with delicious food with various kinds of preparations in golden vessels. When this was done, the king meditated on his deity, prostrated before his guest. On rising therefrom, requested him to his astonishment, he saw god and his consort in accept the food in front of him. His face gleamed with joy and he ejaculated 'what grace god has conferred on me, his humble servant.' To behold him is impossible even for the great yogis and rishis. It is certainly god's mercy and love towards his devotees that has prompted him to enter this humble place without even his vehicle, garuda, and his followers, and receive the humble hospitality which has been shown to him. Overjoyed at the god's presence, he prostrated himself again and again offering praises and worship to the deity.

When this incident took place thousands of Brahmins waiting outside for food, felt as if they had been already sumptuously fed, although they had eaten nothing. They felt surprised and informed the king of the strange phenomenon. When they reached the place, they saw the god in his boar incarnation and his consort seated on a stately throne studded with precious stones in a magnificent mandapa. Elated at this sight, they praised him and repeated verses from the Vedas. They then prayed god to be ever present there in that guise to enable all his devotees to witness him in that glorious state. God granted their request. He said, a vehicle will arrive for him and his goddess at Hastagiri, about five yojanas from this place, during the horse-sacrifice to be offered by Brahma; and so he said he would sit facing west. This is the origin of Bhuvarahasvami in Mallavaram.'

The crocodile proceeded with his story — 'Harisekhara Maharaja worshipped the god for a long period of time, and his son and descendants did likewise. O Rishi! my father Harinandana Maharaja continued ruling the kingdom for 25,000 years and then conferred on me the sovereignty, when I was 300 years old. He then performed a severe penance, and attained salvation as Raja Rishi. Thereafter, I ruled the kingdom very righteously, making large gifts, and performing many sacrifices with due regard to all the principles of morality. On a certain day, during my reign, it so happened that a Brahmin worshipper of Vishnu begged me to give him a daily quantity of rice. Being myself vain of the large gifts and charities I was then making, I was careless in complying with, and slighted his request. At this, the Brahmin with his curse transformed me into a crocodile. The Srivaishnavas in my kingdom and myself prayed him for deliverance from the curse. He replied, as a crocodile I shall have an opportunity of receiving a merciful look from a devoted worshipper of Vishnu and shall hold conversation with him when I shall be released from the curse. It is then that I was transformed into a crocodile, and got into this pond. In this accursed state I spent 32,000 years of my life, and swallowed many living creatures. Even now, I approached you and mistook your feet for a lotus creeper and bit it, and in so doing cut my tongue which brought me into a swoon, and consequently I floated on the water. Blessed now with your merciful look, I crave permission that I may leave off this guise and attain salvation.' The rishi granted him his request and Haripriya Maharaja regained his human form, and attained salvation.

The rishi collected all the lotus flowers in the pond, tied a garland with some of them, and then placed the whole on his head. He then decided to go the sea of milk. He proceeded a little towards the east, but was disheartened at the sight of the great sea confronting him. He went on soliloquising 'what shall I do? How shall I reach the sea of milk? Unless the sea water is wholly dried up or evaporated, it is impossible for me to go.' With these thoughts he ran excitedly along the shore not knowing what to do. He finally decided that he would remove the water with his hands. So he raised an embankment by the sea side, to prevent the water running back into the sea, and facing west, started removing the water with his hands and continued to do this for a year. He thought of the flowers so long kept on the shore without being used for the worship for which he had intended them and became disheartened. He then thought that he must put his sole trust upon god, and that it was he alone who should fulfil his desires. With this idea, he offered prayers to god, solely entrusting himself to the mercy of the omnipotent, omnicient, all-pervading and protector of all beings. Then the great god, responding to his devotee's call, transformed himself into an aged man, and came from the sea of milk to the place where Pundarika rishi stood. The rishi turned, and saw the old Brahmin with a smiling countenance, and thought that he was laughing at him. The old man nevertheless approached, supporting himself with a stick and enquired about his welfare in kind terms. The object of god in coming to the rishi in this guise was to console and help him in his undertaking. The god asked the reason of his being in a state of desperation, and also why the sea appeared as if some water had been taken therefrom and why the garland of lotus flowers lay on the shore. The rishi pointed out the uselessness of his questioning him any further, old and infirm as he was. Neither could he help him nor allay the anguish under which he was labouring. He asked him to return from whence he had come. The old man however, insisted on having an answer. The rishi narrated the whole story to the old man and lamented that the sea seemed to be a great obstacle and his flowers would fade away without having been used for worship. In order to test his faith still further, the old man tried to persuade him that he could never achieve his purpose as it was impossible to empty the sea. Instead of losing his life in this vain effort he might easily worship god in any other place. The rishi was sorry at this remonstrance, and insisted that he would not relent even though he might lose his life in the attempt. The god being pleased with his firm faith, wished not to trouble him any more, and proposed giving him an opportunity to accomplish his aim. He told the rishi that as he was very old and had walked a long distance, he felt much fatigued and hungry. He asked the rishi to bring him some water and food, and that in the meanwhile, he himself would undertake his task. Saying this he tied a cloth around his waist, got down into the sea and in a few attempts, he soon removed a great volume of water and the sea itself also voluntarily receded to the distance of a kros. Pundarika rishi was surprised at the result and begged permission to go and bring food and drink. His request was granted. The rishi repaired immediately to the adjacent town of Mallavaram, entered a sacred Brahmin's house and begged some rice and other food from him. When he returned he was amazed to see the receding sea with god Vishnu himself engaged in emptying the waters from the sea.

Vishnu who usually lies on his bed of a coiled and hooded snake now laid himself down on the raised mound of earth near the shore, so that salvation might thereby be gained by his devotee. He took the lotus flowers preserved by the rishi for his worship, which remained unfaded under his influence, and being pleased with their beauty and fragrance, thought them fit for his consort, though he would have been pleased to wear them himself. So the rishi picked up the garland at once, and put it around the neck of the god who expressed much pleasure thereat. The god now reclined on his right arm, and as if indicating that he would give salvation to those who sought shelter under his feet, stretched his left hand towards them. His eyes were full of mercy, bent on protecting the people who sought his refuge. In order that the rishi might worship his feet with the lotus flowers, he stretched them out and lay facing the east. Pundarika rishi saw god lying in the manner described, and his eyes were full of tears of joy at the sight. The god who used to lie on the sea of milk was now lying before him. The rishi was much elated at god's mercy in allowing him the privilege of witnessing and worshipping him. Overjoyed at the manner of his salvation, attained by only a few, he prostrated himself before him repeatedly, meditating that he had achieved what was difficult even for great rishis. He then picked up the loose lotus flowers and worshipped god's feet with them and adorned his head. God ordered the rishi to make any request which he chose and which he said he would grant. The rishi requested him to be ever present in that locality in the manner he was pleased now to apppear to him, and give salvation to all those whoever sought his refuge, and worshipped him in the manner he did. God was pleased with the request made by the rishi, and granting it said, that he found the place a pleasing one, and that he would remain there, and ordered his consort and all attendants to be with him. The celestials were so elated with the generosity of the god, that the Gandharvas sang, apsaras danced, and Kinnaras played music. The other deities such as Brahma, Indra and others arrived there, and prostrated themselves before god. The deities said that the place in which he had chosen was superior to all others, even heaven itself, inasmuch as it is the spot where he gave salvation to one of his true worshippers, and for whose sake he incarnated himself. The deities also expressed their desire to remain there with him. The god, however, ordered Brahma to return to his sphere, to attend to his work of creation. Indra's request of coming here once in a year, and worshipping him was granted. Meanwhile, Sadananda, the king of Mallavaram, and his having heard of this, hastened to the spot, and worshipped god. Some repeated verses from the Vedas and others same songs in praise of him and shed tears of joy in gratitude for the boon conferred upon them by their god. God desired that he should be known thereafter as Sthalasayana Perumal in honour of his having taken earth as his bed for the sake of giving salvation to Pundarika Rishi, his devoted votary. Then Pundarika Rishi and all the people assembled there, praised god and repeated verses in his new name. The people said they would honour his disciples as those of their household gods and pay them due respect, any one violating this being doomed to hell. They said they believed that worshippers of the deity were everything, and that it was for the sake of Pundarika Rishi that he took an avatar. They then addressed Pundarika Rishi and said that his faith in god was marvellous inasmuch as it was superior to all those entertained by Saraka Rishi, Sananda Rishi, Sanatkumara Rishi and others. They prostrated themselves before him and requested him to tell them how god presented himself at their locality. Pundarika Rishi repeated the whole account and narrated how the crocodile Haripriyan in the pool had obtained salvation. On hearing this, his son Sadananda, the king of Mallavaram, bowed himself before the Rishi, and held his feet in gratitude for having been the means of his father's salvation. The rishi advised him to bathe in the Pundarika tirtha, the pool in which he collected so many lotus flowers and saw the crocodile and which had become very important and sacred owing to the presence of Sthalasayana Perumal close by, and perform rites, and to give alms to the poor. Such gifts, he said, at that spot would have beneficial effects in many ways. In honour of god's presence there, and his having given him salvation, he requested that he might make large gifts of fertile lands to several Srivaishnava Brahmans, and that his kingdom may ever after be known as *Harisaulabbhyaprakasakam.* He asked that all those worshipping Sthalasayana Perumal here may obtain beatitude. Sadananda obeyed all the commands of Pundarika Rishi. The god being pleased with the king for his obeying the commands of his faithful devotee readily blessed him and allowed him to make a wish. The king requested him to be ever present in his kingdom in the glory he had exhibited to him and his subjects. God consented to do so. Pundarika Rishi ordered the king to erect a temple with gopuram for god and make the necessary arrangements for the conduct of worship, all of which he obeyed. The celestials present there worshipped god and were absolved of their sins. Once a year a grand *utsavam* is conducted here on the day of Visaka, in the month of Chittirai. In proof of the several virtues which will be conferred on anybody visiting Mallavaram, an instance is quoted, in which a sacred Brahmin had failed in the performance of his karmas and had committed several sins, eaten flesh, drunk intoxicating liquors, and the like against the tenets of his faith. In the course of his journeys he visited Mallavaram. In consequence of his visit to this holy place, he was delivered of the effects of all his sins, and was relieved by god's angels from the torments to which he was being subjected by Yama's servants. The sinner was carried to heaven in a vehicle.

Several virtues are also attributed to the Pundarika *tirtham* near Mallavaram, and a superiority ascribed to it over the Ganges and other sacred rivers, in support of which several instances are quoted.

Having heard of the virtues of this locality, the sage Agastya came here, bathed in the pool and went to the temple to pray. He first prostrated himself at the entrance to the Gopuram, then before the Dvarapalakas and entered the temple. He again bowed successively before the *Balipitam, Dvajastambham* and the tower of the innermost shrine. He then walked around the prakaram of the Garbhagriham, went into the shrine, and prostrated himself before the god. Agastya's worship was so pleasing to the deity that he was ordered to remain in the *Asvathasramam* to the north of the Pundarika tirtham and perform his worship daily. It is said that at first, Pundarika Rishi worshipped Stalasayana Perumal for a period of 1,000 years, then Sadananda, the Maharaja of Mallavaram's son Gopta, for another 1,000 years. Both obtained salvation. Then Garuda worshipped there for many years, and was amply rewarded, as was also another Karkathar who did so. God would seem to have said that as he came there solely for the purpose of giving salvation to his devotee Pundarika Rishi, and to the one he promised to remain there, he would further grant salvation to all who came and worshipped him there.

Several virtues are also ascribed to the readers and hearers of this account."

During the days of King Namuchi, one of Bali's[8] successors, two celestial nymphs from heaven are said to have visited this city, when they became enamoured of this king. They took him for a visit to their celestial region, and on his return he is said to have beautified the city on lines similar to that which he saw in heaven. Indra got displeased at a mortal king imitating him, and is therefore said to have caused the clouds to encroach upon the city in the form of rain and bring about its destruction.

The Panchapandava Rathas or the five chariots lie on the south of the village. The northernmost, named Draupadi Ratha, covers a square plinth of 11 feet, and is nearly 18 feet in height. The image of Draupadi inside is like that of the goddess Lakshmi. The monolithic elephant and lion on the west and the Nandi on the east are objects of admiration to the visitors. A pillared gallery runs all round the Vimana or tower of Bhima Ratha.

"The son of Bali was Banasura, who is represented as a giant with a thousand hands. Aniruddha[9], the son of Krishna, came to his court in disguise, and seduced his daughter. This caused a war, in the course of which Aniruddha was taken prisoner, and brought to Mahabalipura[10]; Krishna came in person from his capital Dwaraka, and laid seige to the place. Siva guarded the gates, and fought for Banasura, who worshipped him with his thousand hands; but Krishna found means to overthrow Siva, and having taken the city, cut off all Banasura's hands, except two, with which he obliged him to do him homage. He continued in subjection to Krishna till his death. For a long period following this episode there is no mention anywhere of this place, till a prince named Malecheron[11], restored the kingdom to great splendour, and enlarged and beautified the capital. But in his time the calamity is said to have happened which completely destroyed the city.

In an excursion made by Malecheron one day, he came to a garden in the environs of the city, where two celestial nymphs had come down to bathe in a fountain. The prince became enamoured with one of them, and she and her sister-ymph started to have frequent meetings in that garden. On one of those occasions, they brought with them a male inhabitant of the heavenly regions to whom they introduced the prince; and between him and Malecheron a friendship ensued; the male agreed, at the raja's earnest request, to carry him in disguise to see the court of the divine Indra, a favour never before granted to any mortal. The prince returned from there with new ideas of splendour and magnificence, which he immediately adopted in regulating his court, and his retinue, and in beautifying his seat of government. By this means Mahabalipura soon became celebrated beyond all the cities of the earth; its magnificence spread at the court of Indra. This made them jealous and they sent orders to the god of the sea to let loose his billows, and overflow a place which impiously pretended to vie in splendour with their celestial mansions. This command was obeyed, and the city was at once overflowed by that furious element, and has ever since never been able to rear its head."

LITERARY EVIDENCE.

In the odes composed in praise of the god at the Chola capital, Uraiyur, it has been mentioned that the god here has been worshipped by three of the kings at Mallai, and this has been the seat of some of the Chola kings. Further the Chola king Suraguru is said to have ruled with Mallai for his capital, which had a number of storeyed buildings. He was a strong-minded king who had repaired the temple at Tirukkalukkunram and was also otherwise known as Sutharerajan.

Mention is made in an ancient Tamil literature that in Amur, close by, the Pallavas were overcome by Porvaikopperunarkilli, son of the Chola king at Urayur

Thithan. As the Pallavas ruled over Tondamandalam, they were also called Tondamans. The Pallava king Karunakaran who was commander-in-chief to the Chola king Iyyatharan, proceeded against the Kalinga king, as the tribute of the Chola king had not been paid. He fought against and subjugated the kingdom to the Cholas. In exchange he got Tondamandalam for himself, and had therein the three chief places of Kancheepuram, Mylapur, and Mallai. He was also called Karunakarathondaman.

The principal deity of the place is mentioned in old Tamil works as being in the village of "Kakalmallai" which necessarily means an important seaport. Mention is also made that this Vishnu deity is in conjunction with Siva and consequently we may assume that the temple concerned is the Shore temple. From other works it is evident that during 1170-1117 A.D., i.e., the time of Sekkilar, there were many palacial buildings in this village, and as such, the submersion of all existing traces of them must have occurred after this period.

Certain poets of Methilapatti in the Ramnad District profix their names with the Mallai, and this leads to the inference that the people, consequent on the havoc made by inroads of the sea during the eleventh century, may have gone and settled there.

SCULPTURES

The most interesting of the sculptures is the one depicting Arjuna's penance, which has been described in detail in various works dealing with the place. The following description, which appears in Carr's *Seven Pagodas,* gives full account of the importance relating to this piece of sculpture that first attracts the notice of all the visitors to the station:

"In this group of sculptures, the principal figure, that of Arjuna, is not the largest. He is seen on the left of the fissure in the posture of penance; his arms are raised above his head and his right leg is lifted up. He is supposed to stand on the great toe of his left foot. His arms and right leg appear withered, but his left leg is of the natural size. His chest and ribs are prominent, but the stomach and abdomen sunken; the whole figure represents emaciation from long fasting. Besides this figure there is a multitude of others both of men and animals; and among the latter two well-proportioned elephants as large as life. The largest of them measures 17 feet from the proboscis to the tail, and 14 feet in height. The smaller has a height of 10 feet, and a length of 11. Under the belly of the larger elephant there is a small one, with the heads and trunks of two others, while the head of a fourth is seen between his proboscis and forefeet. These figures of elephants are cut on the rock in the right on a level with the ground. On the rock to the left, near the fissure, and below the figure of Arjuna, is a neat little temple[12], with a niche and a figure[13] in it. Just within the fissure itself is a figure like that of the mermaid, but in the native language it has a name purporting half-woman and half-snake[14]. Scattered over the face of both rocks there are many representations of men, ascetics, monkeys, lions, tigers, antelopes, birds, satyrs and monstrous animals which would puzzle a naturalist of the present age to nomenclate[15]. The entire sculpture is executed with considerable spirit, and occupies a space of about 2,400 square feet.

The story of the penance of Arjuna may be told as follows:

The five sons of Panduraja lost their dominions in play with their cousin Duryodhana; who, however, played unfairly, and won through guile and wicked stratagem[5]. The consequence was that they and their followers were banished for twelve years, and were doomed to wander in jungles, wilds and solitudes. During this period the elder brother took counsel with the others, how they might repossess themselves of their patrimony after the term of banishment had expired;

Kanchipuram.

The Kanchipuram temple at dusk.

The Mahabalipuram shore temple.

Tiruvannamalai.

The Chidambaram temple with its exquisite golden dome.

Gangaikondacholapuram.

The Tanjore temple.

The Rock temple at Tiruchmapalli.

The Tanjore temple.

The Meenakshi temple.

The hall of thousand pillars.

The Madurai temple.

The Rameshwaram temple.

Halebid.

Belur.

Belur.

and in order to attain this it appeared desirable to gain the mantra *Pasupatastra*[17]. This mantra, or incantation, was so effective, that if it was uttered while in the act of shooting an arrow, the arrow became inevitably destructive, and possessed the power of producing or generating other weapons, which not only scattered death on all sides, but were able to caused the destruction of the whole world.[18] This mantra could be obtained only from the god Iswara (a name of Siva) and Arjuna, as he was distinguished among his brethern for his prudence, fortitude and valour, and was employed to procure it[19]

The hero of this story had to travel far to the north of the Himalaya mountains to perform austere and rigid penance in order to propitiate the god and obtain His favour, and as a preparatory measure he was instructed in all requisite mantras and mystic ceremonies. On reaching the appointed place he found a delightful retreat; a grove or forest abounding with streams and fruits and flowers with whatever could regale the senses or charm the eye. Not only was the earth most bountiful, but the air was filled with the strains of celestial melody. In this place Arjuna commenced and carried on his austerities by meditation, by prayer and by ceremonial purification.

During the first month he ate but once in four days, during the second month but once in seven days, during the third month only once in fourteen days, and during the fourth month he did not eat at all, but completed his penance by standing on the tip of his great toe, the other leg being lifted from the ground, and his hands raised above his head.[20] It is this that the sculptor has selected for illustration in the curious work. The figure of Arjuna is exhibited in a posture agreeing exactly with the story, the relation of which, however, it seems necessary to continue a little further, in order to explain the accessories, the figures of men and animals, with which the whole face of the rock is covered.

The nearest rishis (hermits or ascetics, who by austerities and meditation may attain riches, power, supernatural arms, or beatitude), seeing the intense devotion of Arjuna, went and reported it to the god Isvara, who was highly gratified. To test the constancy and courage of the hero, the deity assumed the form of a wild hunter.[21] One of his accompanying attendants was transformed into a wild boar[22]. Arjuna preparing to shoot it was interrupted by the unknown deity, who forbade him to strike his game. Arjuna notwithstanding let fly a shaft and so did the disguised hunter, and the boar fell lifeless. This occasioned an altercation, which brought on a personal combat; and when Arjuna had expended all his arrows on his opponent without effect, he tore up rocks and mountains to hurl at him, but they too fell harmless at his feet. This so enraged our hero, that he attacked his foe with his hand. Such was the daring audacity of this act that the heaven was filled with surprise, and the beasts of the forest, and the inhabitants of the etherial regions alike flocked to witness the contest. It was finally terminated by the God's revealing himself and bestowing on his votary the boon of *Pasupatastra*[23] he wished for.

This congregating of the inhabitants of the skies and of the forest of men and brutes makes probable the supposition that it is the second point or period of the story that has been selected by the artist for exemplification, as instanced by the particular postures and variety of the figures seen in this curious carving."

GOVARDHANA UDDHARA

Wilson in his translation of *Vishnu Purana,* one of the great eighteen puranas of India, narrating the circumstances under which this sport was performed by Lord Sri Krishna, writes:

Krishna, repairing to Vraja, found all the cow-herds busily engaged in preparing for a sacrifice to be offered to Indra, and going to the elders, he asked them, what festival of Indra it was in which they took so much pleasure. Nanda replied to this question, and said, "Indra is the sovereign of the clouds and of the waters; sent by him, the former bestows moisture upon the earth, which springs the grain, by which we and all embodied beings subsist. With water we please the gods, these cows bear calves, yield milk, and are happy and well-nourished. So when the clouds are seen distented with rain, the earth is neither barren of corn, nor bare of verdure, nor is man distressed by hunger. Indra, the giver of water, having drank the milk of earth by the solar ray, sheds it again upon the earth for the sustenance of all the world. On this account all sovereign princes offer sacrifices to Indra at the end of the rains, and so also we and other people.

"When Krishna heard this speech from Nanda replied: "We, father, are neither cultivators of the soil, nor dealers in merchandise. We are sojourners in forests and cows are our divinities. There are four branches of knowledge, logical, scriptural, practical and political. Here let me describe what practical science is. The knowledge of agriculture, commerce, and tending of cattle constitutes practical science. Agriculture provides subsistence to farmers; buying and selling, to traders. Rearing of cattle gives us support. Thus the knowledge of means of support is three-fold. The object that is cultivated by any one should be to him as his chief divinity; that should be venerated and worshipped, as it is his benefactor. He who worships the deity of another, and divests from him the reward that is his due, obtains not a prosperous station either in this world or in the next. Where the land ceases to be cultivated there are bounds assigned, beyond which commences the forest; the forests are bounded by the hills, and so far do our limits extend. We are not shut in with doors, nor confined within walls; we have neither fields nor houses; we wander about happily wherever we list, travelling in our waggons. The spirits of these mountains, it is said, walk the woods in different forms. If they should be displeased with those who inhabit the forests, then, transformed to lions and beasts of prey they will kill the offenders. We then are bound to worship the mountains, to offer sacrifices to cattle. What have we to do with Indra? Cattle and mountains are our gods. Brahmans offer worship with prayers; cultivators of the earth adore their land marks; but we who tend our herds in the forests and mountains should worship them and our kin. Let prayer and offerings then be addressed to the mountain Govardhana, and kill a victim in due form. Let the whole station collect their milk without delay, and feed with it the Brahmans and all who may desire to partake of it. When the oblations have been presented, and the Brahmans have been fed, let the Gopas circumambulate the cow, decorated with garlands of autumnal flowers. If the cowherds will attend to these suggestions, they will secure the favour of the mountain, of the cattle, and also mine."

"When Nanda and other Gopas heard these words of Krishna, their faces beamed, and they said that he had spoken well. 'You have judged rightly, child,' exclaimed they and added 'we will do exactly as you have proposed, and offer adoration to the mountain.' Accordingly the inhabitants of Vraja worshipped the mountain, presenting to it curds and milk and fish; and they fed hundreds and thousands of Brahmans and many other guests, who came to the ceremony. When they had made their offerings, they circumambulated the cows and the bulls that bellowed as loud as roaring clouds. Upon the summit of Govardhana, Krishna presented himself, saying, 'I am the mountain,' and partook of much food

presented by the Gopis, whilst in his own form as Krishna
he ascended the hill along with the cowherds, and worshipped
his other self. Having promised them many blessings, the
mountain-person of Krishna, vanished; and the ceremony
being completed, the cowherds returned to their station.

Indra, being thus deprived of his offerings, was
exceedingly angry, and thus addressed a cohort of his
attendant clouds called Samvarttaka: 'Ho, clouds,' he said,
'hear my words, and without delay execute what I command.
The insensate cowherd Nanda, assisted by his fellows, has
withheld the usual offerings to us, relying upon the protection
of Krishna. Now, therefore, afflict the cattle that are their
sustenance, and whence their occupation is derived, with rain
and win. Mounted upon my elephant as vast as a mountain
peak, I will give you aid in strengthening the tempest.' When
Indra ceased, the clouds, obedient to his commands, came
down in a fearful storm of rain and wind to destroy the cattle.
In an instant the earth, the points of the horizon, and the sky,
were all blended into one by the heavy and incessant shower.
The clouds roared aloud, as if in terror of the lightning's
scourge, and poured down uninterrupted torrents. The whole
earth was enveloped in impenetrable darkness by the thick
clouds; and above, below, and on every side, the world was
water. The cattle, pelted by the storm, shrunk into the smallest
size, or gave up their breath. Some covered their calves with
their flanks, and some beheld their young ones carried away
by the flood. The calves, trembling in the wind, looked
piteously at their mothers, or implored in low moans, as it
were, the succour of Krishna. Hari, beholding all Gokula
agitated with alarm, reflected, 'This is the work of the
Mahendra, in resentment of the prevention of his sacrifice,
and it is incumbent on we to defend this station of herdsmen.
I will lift up this spacious mountain from its stony base, and

hold it up, as a large umbrella, over the cow-pens.' Having thus determined, Krishna immediately plucked up the mountain Govardhana, and held it aloft with one hand in sport, saying to the herdsmen, 'Lo the mountain is so high; enter beneath it quickly, and it will shelter you from the storm: here you will be secure and at your ease, defended from the wind: enter without delay and fear not that the mountain will fall.' Upon this all the people, with their herds, and their waggons and goods, and the Gopis, distressed by the rain, repaired to the shelter of the mountain, which Krishna held steadily over their heads. Krishna was contemplated by the dwellers of Vraja with joy and wonder; and, as their eyes opened wide with astonishment and pleasure, the Gopas and Gopis, sang his praise. For seven days and nights did the vast clouds sent by Indra rain upon the Gokula of Nanda to destroy its inhabitants, but they were protected by the elevation of the mountain; and the slayer of Bala, Indra, being foiled in his purpose, commanded the clouds to cease. The threats of Indra having been fruitless, and the heavens clear, all Gokula came forth from its shelter, and returned to its own people. Then Krishna restored the great mountain Govardhana to its original site."

INSCRIPTIONS[24]

The inscriptions over the Shore temple state that King Rajarajadeva built a jewel-like hall at Kandalur and conquered several countries. Kandalur is identified with Chidambaram where this king erected all kinds of towers, walls, mandapas and flights of steps. The temple also went by the name Jalasayana or Kshatriyasimha Pallava Iswaradeva. The latter name suggests the building of this temple by the Pallava king Kshatriyasimha. Those at Dharmaraja Ratha mention the birudas of the Pallava king Narasimha while those of the Ganesa temple and Darmaraja mandapa record that these two temples were built by King Atyantakama and were called after him as Atyantakama Pallavesvara griha.

The Madras Government epigraphist in his *Annual Report* for the year 1886-87 says:

"Atyantakama (about A.D. 550) was the founder of the so-called Ganesa temple, Dharmaraja mandapa and Ramanuja mandapa at Mamallapuram; another inscription of his is found in the third storey of the Dharmaraja Ratha . . . The inscriptions of the Dharmaraja Ratha at Mamallapuram, which as stated above, belong to a Pallava king Narasimha, have been assigned by Dr. Burnell to about the fifth century A.D. for palaeographical reasons. It only remains for me to remark that, according to one of the three Tamil inscriptions at the so-called Shore temple at Mamallapuram, this temple seems to have been founded by a Pallava king Kshatriya Simha, about whose age nothing is known."

For an excellent account of the local architectural works and a valuable bibliography on the same see *Antiquities* 1, 189-91. The place is well-known in Vaishnavite history as the birthplace of one of the three first *Alvars* and referred to both in the *Devaram* and *Nalayirprabhandham.*

"1 of 1887 — Inside shore temple. Records that in the ninth year of Vira Rajendrachola (1 or II?) the Mahasabha of Siridavur or Narasimhamangalam gave 2,000 kulis of land to the Lord of Tirukkadalmalli. See *S.I. Inscrns.* Vol. I, pp. 68-9.

2 of 1887 — On the south base of the shore temple. A record of the twenty-fifth year of Ko Rajakesarivarman Rajaraja I, giving very interesting details of a contract amongst the villagers for the division of land among them and the dues of the land cess. *S.I. Inscrns.* No.40, pp. 63-6.

3 of 1887 — On the north base of the shore temple. A record of the twenty-sixth year of Rajaraja I. Mentions the three shrines of Rajasimha Pallavesvaradeva, Kshatriyasimha

Pallavesvaradeva and Pallikondar. (Tirumangai Alvar refers to the existence side by side of Siva and Vishnu.)

4 of 1887 — Inside Gangaikonda mandapam. No details.

5 of 1887 — Front wall of the Varahasvami temple. No details.

54 of 1890 — On a rock-cut niche into the left of the Varahasvamin temple. A record of the Chola king Ko Parakesarivarman or Udaiyar Rajendradeva (1050-62), dated in his ninth year.

55 of 1890 — On a stone near the tank at Pavalakkaran sattram (*chavadi*). A record of the Vijayanagara king Achyutadeva, dated in S. 1457 expired, Manmatha. (Sir Walter Elliot has misinterpreted this inscription as that of Vikramadeva, dated S. 1157.)

310 of 1901 (Tamil) — On the east wall of the Gangaikonda mandapa. A record of the fourteenth year of Tribhuvanachakravartin Kulottungacholadeva. Mentions Amurnadu in Amurkottam in Jayankondacholamandalam.

512 to 528 of 1907 (Archaic script) — Inscriptions on the Dharamaraja Ratha. See *South Ind. Inscrns.* Vol. I, Nos. 1 to 17. They consist of a string of titles of the Pallava king Narasimhavarman II. See *Ep. Rep.* 1913, p. 89.

529 of 1907 — On the third storey of the same Ratha, west. The Ratha is called Atyantakama Pallaveswara griham (owing to his identification of Atyantakama with Paramesvaravarman I and Rajasimha with his predecessor. Hultzch believes that the son appropriated to himself the Dharmaraja Ratha which his father had excavated, but the excavator was probably Parameswara's son Narasimhavarman II and he was himself Atyantakama.

530 of 1907 — On a pillar of the rock-cut mandapa south-west of the 'Gopis' churn' in the same village. Consists of the biruda Vamanikusa.

531 of 1907 — In the Ganesa temple in the same village. The alphabet of this and the next is attributed by Burnell on palaeographical grounds to about A.D. 700. It differs from the alphabet of 58-74 in being extremely florid. See *South Ind. Ins.,* Vol. I, No. 18.

532 of 1907 — In the Dharmaraja mandapa in the same village. The inscription says that the Ganesa shrine and this mandapa were made by Atyantakama (Narasimhavarman II.) See *South Ind. Ins.,* Vol. I, No. 19.

533 of 1907 — In the Ramanuja mandapa in the same village. This inscription consists of the last verse of the above two inscriptions and seems to have been a third inscription of Atyantakama. See *South Ind. Ins.,* Vol. I, No. 20.

566 of 1912 (Pallava grantha) — On the plinths of two *balipithas* recently excavated in the courtyard of the Shore temple. A damaged record of the Pallava king Narasimhavarman II who had the titles of Rajasimha and Atyantakama. Registers four Sanskrit verses in praise of the king.

On a stone in the temple of Varahasvami. Records gift of land by the people of Chennapuram in the ninth year of ... Varma. *Ins. S. Dts.* p. 187, No. 13.

On a stone in the temple of Stalasayana Perumal temple. Records grant of 1,000 kulis to the God in the twentieth year of the reign of Ko Parakesarivarman. *Ins. S. Dts.* p. 187, No. 14.

On the north wall of the same temple. Records that Dalavay Tirumalanayaka granted the village of Kunnattur to Stalasayana Perumal in Bahudhanya, in the reign of Sri Rangaraya. Ibid. No. 15.

Below the above. Records grant of land in Chedirayanellore to the God and Sri Vaishnava Brahmans in the reign of Varma Rangaraja. Ibid. p. 188, No. 16.

On the south side of the temple. Records gift of 12 madas to the priests for a lamp by Adinarayana in the reign of Tribhuvanachakravartin. Ibid. p. 180, No. 17.

Below the above. Records that in the reign of "Soomukaharayan in Svabhanu, the people of Mahabalipuram and twelve other villages declared, the lands of Sthalasayana Perumal to be rent-free. Ibid. No. 18."

SADRAS

Sadras (Tamil Chaturangapattanam), one of the early settlements of the Dutch, lies at a distance of about 10 miles on the south of Mahabalipuram. The fort here is square in plan, was built of brick, flanked with bastions; most of which were destroyed in A.D. 1781. Only the ruins now remain. There is a cemetry[25] with carved tombstones.

NOTES

1. According to the *Annual Report* of the Madras Epigraphical Department for the year 1903-04, para 26, this place was so named after the Pallava king Narasimhavarman I, one of whose titles was *Mahamalla*, the great wrestler and who lived in the 7th century A.D.

2. Adisesha is the primal serpent forming by its many coils, a bed on which Vishnu rests; and with its many heads erect, and forked tongues projecting, it forms a canopy over Vishnu's head.

3. The Asuras that gave trouble to the men on earth were overcome both by Siva and Vishnu who became incarnate with the express object of destroying these vicious beings. One of the powerful Asuras went to the length of causing great trouble and he appeared in the form of a *mahisha* (*mahisha*, in Sanskrit, means buffalo). A goddess with eight hands

holding different weapons in each of them strode over the huffalo-headed Asura and put him down. This gave satisfaction to the devas and hence the goddess came to be known as Mahishasuramardini. This form is generally shown in one of the niches on the northern outer wall of the sanctum in Saiva shrines.

4. A description and figure of the form of the goddess appears on pages 187 & 188 of the South Indian Images of Gods and Goddesses.

5. The circumstances under which Arjuna obtained the weapon *Pasupatastra* are detailed in the chapter dealing with Bezwada.

6. One of the seven worlds of the Hindu tehology. The seven worlds are *Atala, Vitala, Sutala, Talatala, Rasatala, Mahatala and Patala.*

7. Govardhan Mountain lies at a distance of about 13 miles to the south of Mathura. Another version of this story is that at one time on the advice of Sri Krishna, the shepherds put a stop to the worship they annually made to Indra, the god of rain. Whereupon Indra directed the clouds to destroy the place with heavy rain. To save them Sri Krishna uplifted this mountain with one of his hands and protected them!! This was done to put down the pride of Indra. Then Indra submitted to Krishna and also took a lesson from this incident. Afterwards the usual annual worship was resumed. This festival to Indra is known as Bhogi-pandigai and it is observed on the last day of *Margali* (December-January), the previous day to Makara Sankaranti or the day on which the Sun enters the Capricorns.

8. Bana's [son Mahavali or Mahabali (Bali the Great)] descendants went by the name Banas and these had own connection with Mahabalipura or the sevan pagodas. Their flag displayed a black buck, and their crest was the bull. Many of their inscriptions are found at Tiruvallam, North Arcot District, known also as Vanapuram (Banapuram), situated in Perum-Banappadi, the great Bana country where they settled later on.

9. Anirudha was the grandson, not the son, of Krishna.

10. Sonitapura, according to the *Vishnu Purana,* Cp. Wilson's trans. Book V, Chap. 33.

11. The same as Mallesudu. Cp. Taylor.

12. At the south-east corner of this little fane, in a sitting and stooping posture, and entirely detached from the rock, is an admirable figure of an ascetic, miserably emaciated, which, though somewhat worn by exposure to the weather, bears evidence to the talent, skill, and anatomical knowledge of the artist. Said to be Drona (see note p. 31 *supra*), the figures, now headless, of whose pupils are in front, and somewhat below that of their preceptor.

13. Said to be Krishna.

14. Naga, the name of demi-gods inhabiting the lower regions, the upper part of whose bodies is human, and the lower part that of a serpent. There is the figure of a male Naga as well as that of a female, but the upper part of the body has fallen off and is lying in front of the rock.

15. On the north side of the crevice, at the foot of the rock, is the figure of a cat standing on its hind legs, with its fore-paws raised above its head in seeming imitation of Arjuna, performing penance — after eating part of Krishna's butter-ball — in order that the sea may dry up and she be thus able to devour all the fish. Near the cat are rats enjoying apparently temporary immunity from persecution.

16. See Wheeler's *History of India,* Vol. I, Chap. 7.

17. The *Pasupata* weapon, not mantra.

18. Cp. Muir's *Sanskrit Texts,* part IV, p. 196.

19. He went first to Indra by the advice of his grandfather Vyasa, and afterwards, at the suggestion of Indra, to the Himalaya, to obtain a sight of Mahadeva — Cp. Monier William's *Indian Epic Poetry,* pp. 103-104, and Muir's *Sanskrit Texts,* part IV, p. 194-ff.

20. See the passage from the Mahabharata given in the Appendix.

21. Kirata.

22. A Danava (demon) in the form of a boar was about to attack Arjuna.

23. The story is related in the Vanaparva of the Mahabarata, Cp. Muir's *Sanskrit Texts*, part IV, pp. 194-196. The combat between Arjuna and Siva, disguised as a Kirata, is the subject of the poem *Kiratarjuniya*, by Bharavi.
24. *Inscriptions of the Madras Presidency*, Government of Madras, 1919, Vol. I, pp. 327 to 329.
25. This is illustrated in Mr. Rea's *Monumental Remains of the Dutch East India Company* published by the Government of Madras.

Chapter 5

GINGEE

This ancient fortified city, closely connected in popular tradition with Desing Raja, its renowned chief, possesses palatial buildings of great architectural value, and is situated 20 miles away to the west of Tindivanam in the South Arcot district. The Tamil name of the place is Senji. The fort of Gingee is one of the few ancient places of historic interest which has been preserved in all its ancient glory. It appears to have been the seat of government of a former Vijayanagar kingdom. The Muhammadans conquered the place in 1564 A.D. and drove away the Hindu kings. A terrible famine in 1661 compelled evacuation of the place by the Muhammadans. Its later history, and its occupation by the French and the English, in close succession, may be found in any work on the history of South India.

FORTRESSES

The fortress consists of three strongly fortified hills in close proximity to each other, Rajagiri in the middle is the most important, and the two others Krishnagiri and the northernmost Chandrayandrug, where the execution of criminals is said to have been done, are of less importance. Besides these three, there are four others of minor importance, and all the seven lay within the fort walls extending over a circumference of 10 miles. The main citadel is on the Rajagiri and at the foot of it is the inner fort in which is the famous Kalyana Mahal. The building is modelled after the Vijayanagar style. It consists of a square court surrounded by rooms for ladies. In the middle of one side is a square tower with eight storeys. It is 80 feet high, and ends in the form of a pyramid. A clay water pipe has been laid out to the 6th storey, from a tank 60 yards away from the fort on the top of the hill closeby. The pipe is carried under the walls of the fort to the back of the harem and thence to the roof of the *mahal.* The Raja's bathing stone measures 15 square feet and is 5 inches in thickness and the prisoner's cell, 20 feet deep, is cut out of a single boulder.

The fort of Rajagiri contains the temple of Ranganatha, the audience hall, the treasury, etc. The structures here are said to be similar to those at Krishnagiri. The Raja is said to have lived during the *Sukla Paksha* (the bright fortnight before the full moon) in Rajagiri, and during the *Krishna Paksha* (the dark days) in Krishnagiri. Hence these hills are so called.

In the temple of Venugopalasvami[1] within the inner fort, the various aspects of Sri Krishna are depicted very skilfully. The depiction of the prison house on the upper door of the Pondicherry gate and the work at the bastion, form fine specimens of the ancient art. Over the walls of the Venkataramana temple are found splendid carvings of the incidents of the *Ramayana* and the ten incarnations of Vishnu. The high carved pillars planted round the statue of Dupleix at Pondicherry are said to have been removed from this temple. The temple of Pattabhiramasvami has also many fine carvings.

PURANIC VERSION

The original founder of this fort and the shrine of Visvanatha in it, according to the puranic account, was Surasarma, the king of Benares. After abdicating his throne in favour of his brother, he visited the holy places in the south. When he came to this part of the country he dreamt of having been asked to settle down here. He then built a temple here, after which a son was born to him, whom he called Visvanathan. The latter, after ruling the country for 43 years, left the kingdom in the hands of his son Thandan who improved and expanded it. Raja Desing is said to be the 22nd in descent.

It cannot be precisely ascertained when the city was formed, but tradition says that it was built by Tupakkal Krishnappa Naick. He was a native of Conjeevaram and kept a flower garden dedicated to Varadaraja Perumal, the celebrated god of that place. In order to test Krishnappa Naick's piety, god Varadaraja assumed the shape of a boar and began the destruction of the flower garden. All attempts by the gardeners to catch the animal proved futile, and Krishnappa himself went in chase of the animal. But Krishnappa also failed in his attempt to kill it after several days' pursuit. And Varadaraja having been confirmed in his devotee's piety, resolved to show himself *in propria persona* to Naick.

The miraculous boar approached a rock near Singavaram, 3 miles to the south-west of Gingee fort, bored himself a cave in the rock and appeared unto Krishnappa Naick, in his natural form. Krishnappa Naick, who was bewildered at this strange phenomenon, invoked the blessing of the deity. The god then directed Naick to build a temple at Singavaram and to obtain funds for the construction of the temple from an ascetic. The ascetic instead of helping the Naick tried to kill him by throwing him in a boiling caldron. Krishnappa Naick suspected the foul intention of the ascetic, and threw the man into the caldron instead. The dead body of the ascetic was converted into gold, with which the temple was built! This was the origin of the lofty structures that are seen today at Gingee and

Singavaram. It is also said that the golden carcass was hidden in a secret place and that it exists even today, though the place cannot be identified by any one. The Indian sunflower plant in the sacred park, is said to have been planted by the mystic boar.

STORY OF DESING RAJA

The romance connected with Gingee and Desing, one of its most illustrious chiefs, is most interesting. The Gingee chiefs were vassals to the Emperor of Delhi, and their tribute fell in arrears. The Emperor sent one of his generals, Tyrop Singh, to collect the arrears, who after defeating the chief, became the Raja. The Emperor had a steed called *Bara Hazari* or 'the Twelve thousander' and as it was a very restive animal, no one could dare to ride the animal. All the chiefs, including Tyrop Singh failed in their attempts to ride the animal and in the end they were all imprisoned. Tyrop Singh's son, the hero of the romance, who displayed great valour and courage undertook to ride the animal, in spite of his mother's dissuasion. Young Desing would not relent, he appeared before the Emperor and rode the animal. No sooner had he mounted the animal than it began to carry him aloft in the air, which caused much annoyance to the young rider, who then prayed to his patron deity Ranganatha. Ranganatha appeared unto Desing and caused the horse (which was his creation) to obey him. Desing then appeared before the Emperor and demanded the release of his father Tyrop Singh. Desing, with honours heaped on him by the Emperor, returned to Gingee with his father and the magic horse. Desing was also made the supreme Raja of Gingee, and the Emperor waived all claims for tribute from the chiefs from that date. The Nawab of Arcot who heard of the honour bestowed upon Desing, grew jealous of him, and put forward a claim for the annual tribute. Desing repudiated this and informed him that Gingee had been made an independant principality by the Emperor of Delhi. The Nawab disbelieved this, and commanded Desing to produce the *Sannad* (title), which he unfortunately had failed to get from the Emperor. The Nawab put forward the claim for a second time. This put out Desing and he sent a message to the Nawab saying that if he insisted on the payment of the tribute, he must receive it at the point of the sword. The Nawab became enraged and invaded Gingee. Even when the opposing armies reached the gate of Gingee, Desing was performing his *puja* (worship) and he never thought of the pressing emergency. When his uncle suggested to him to make peace with the Nawab, Desing became indignant, and made preparations for fighting the enemy. He embarked on this expedition much against the wish of all. The first battle was fought near Pudupet, 4 miles away from Gingee and just as the point when victory was being declared in favour of Desing, some unknown man shot him dead. The dead body was then taken to the palace, where Desing's wife received it with all honours, and she also in the end performed *sati*,[2] much against the will of the Nawab who deeply regretted his error. Desing's steed also was killed, and his friend Muhammad Khan. The tombs of the famous Desing Raja and his wife, who became a sati, are to the west of Chettikulam, near the Kalyana mandapa in the fort. The Nawab of Arcot admiring the conjugal fidelity of the Rani (queen) founded the town of Ranipet near Arcot in the North Arcot district in her memory.

The family deity of Desing was the idol Ranganatha at Singavaram through whose blessings he obtained the favour of the Emperor of Delhi and founded the independant principality of Gingee. The exploits of Desing are sung in an Indian ballad.

Manual of the North Arcot District, 1894, page 433 says:

"Ranipet is 2 miles to the west of Walajapet, and upon the left bank of the Palar, just opposite to the town of Arcot.... The town was built, about the year 1771, by Sadatulla Khan in honour of the youthful widow of Desing Raja of Gingee, who performed sati upon her husband's death. There is a favourite Telugu ballad which describes how Desing Raja refused to pay tribute to the Nawab, and, girt with a magic sword, sallied out to meet him in battle near Gingee. He at first defeated the Muhammadan troops, but the powers of his weapon were to last only for a short time, and when the Nawab resumed fighting, Desing, in spite of the utmost gallantry, was overcome and slain. Out of respect for his valour and his wife's devotion, the Nawab founded a new village near to Arcot, and named it Ranipet.

About a mile east of Ranipet is a remarkable tope extending along the Palar for a distance of about 3 miles. It is known as the Naulakh Bagh, since it is supposed to contain nine lakhs of trees, chiefly mango, orange, coconut and other fruit trees. On the site of the Naulakh Bagh there formerly stood two of the six forest temples of the Rishis, erected by a Chola King in days when all the country was under forest (whence the name *aru kadu,* six forests). These two shrines were raised in honour of Gautama Rishi and Visvamitra Rishi. The Muhammadans utterly destroyed the former, and left but little of the latter, when the tope was laid out. The other four temples are at Punkadu (the flower forest) near the Palar anicut, Veppur (the village of neem trees), Visharam and Vannivedu. The seventh temple, in honour of Atreya Maharishi, was subsequently constructed at Kudimallur or Gudumallur on the river."

Manual of the South Arcot District, 1878, page 420 says:

"We close our accounts of Gingee with the story of the *genius loci* Desing Raja. His real name Was Tej Singh, and he was the son of Sarup Singh, a Rajput governor of Gingee, who affected independence. He was killed in a fight near Gingee with Sadatullah Khan, the Mogul Nawab of Arcot, in 1721. The story of his fate forms the subject of a ballad which is still sung, it is said, in the neighbourhood of Gingee and runs as follows:

While the Gingee country was held as a fief of Bijapur, one of the Naick chiefs of Gingee refused to pay the customary tribute. After capturing Bijapur the Emperor Aurangzeb sent Sarup Singh to collect tribue from Gingee tribute and to reduce the Naick to obedience. This he did, and was made Raja of Gingee. At this time the Emperor possessed a wonderful horse which none of his chieftains could ride or master. All who tried failed and were imprisoned, and this included Sarup Singh. Meanwhile, his son Desing Raja had developed into a youth of extraordinary valour, and was summoned to court to ride the Emperor's horse. He did so, and the horse soared into the air with him. In mid-air the Singavaramswami appeared to him, and, encouraging him, ordered the horse, which was of his own creation to be ever obedient to Desing Raja. On the horse alighting once more on *terra firma,* the Emperor gave it to Desing Raja, released his father and absolved him from the obligation of paying tribute. On the death of his father, Desing Raja became ruler of Gingee, but the Nawab of Arcot, jealous of his independence, preferred a claim to tribute which was indignantly rejected; whereupon the Nawab at once invaded his territory. Desing Raja made no preparations to resist him, but when the Nawab's army was quite close to Gingee he sallied out to fight in spite of the remonstrances to his friends. His parting from his wife is pathetically told in the ballad. A curtain separated them at the interview and a braceletted arm stretched from beneath it gave him the parting *pan supari* and a girlish voice of his bride bade him do his devoir gallantly. He then asked a blessing on his sword for two hours from his tutelary deity, the Singavaramswami, and set out to fight the Nawab, assisted by a Mussalman friend named

Mahabat Khan. The battle was fought about four miles from Gingee, the Nawab's army was routed, and Desing set out to return to the fort. By this time the virtue of the blessing on the sword had gone away, and word being brought that the Nawab, whom he imagined was killed, was alive, he returned and again attacked him. The Nawab rode on an elephant, and Desing's horse, while rearing up, had its forelegs cut off by a swordsman. Desing continued the fight on foot, but was at length overpowered and killed. His wife committed *sattee,* and the Nawab out of respect for her, on his return to Arcot, built a town which he called Ranipet after her.

Desing Raja's body was burnt, it is said, in a small mandapam (still standing, though in ruins) in the Chettikulam tank. A stone with an inscription recording the fate is also said to have long existed, but it is not now to be found."

INSCRIPTIONS[3]

The inscriptions in Gingee and Singavaram have been copied by the Madras Epigraphical Department during the years 1904 and 1905.

[4]A genealogy of the family of Chenji (i.e., Gingee) chiefs is furnished in an inscription dated Saka 1593 (A.D. 1670-71) belonging to Varadappa-Nayaka of this family. The list of kings begin with the 25th generation prior to this chief. A certain Sirigiri Nayaka (i.e., Srigiri Nayaka) who belonged to the (12th generation prior to Varadappa Nayaka of the inscription) is stated to have migrated from Maninagapura (Manikpur) in the Aryavarta (Northern India) to Vijayanagara, evidently the capital of the Vijayanagara empire. The migration of this family in the time of Pedda Krishnappa Nayaka from Vijayanagara to Chenji five generations before Varadappa Nayaka must have happened about the middle of the 16th century.

"This fine hill fortress was the seat of an important province in the Vijayanagara period as is plain from a grant of Harihara II dated in 1645 A.D. when it fell into the hands of Bijapur. Thirty years later it fell into the hands of Shivaji but was captured by the Mughals in 1698 after a celebrated siege of seven years. Its place as capital of the province was taken by Arcot; but thanks to its location and its strength; it figured largely in the Carnatic wars, being taken by the French in 1750 and by the English in 1761. The whole history is ably and succinctly summarised in the *South Arcot Gazetter,* Garstin's *Manual* etc. The descriptions of the three fortified hills of the place and of the antiquities therein are ample and show the historic significance of the place. A fine account of Gingee under the Vijayanagara and later rulers is contained in one of the *Mack* MSS., the *Karnataka Rajas' Savistara Charitra,* a summary of which is given in Taylor's *Rain, Catal.,* Vol. III. I have given ample reference to the Nayak rulers of the place and their activities in my *History of the Nayak Kingdom* (*Ind. Antq.*1915). As for the history of the place under the Mahrattas, Mughals and the Nawabs we have got ample materials of which the interesting ballad of Desing Raja deserves mention. See Duff's *History of the Mahrattas,* Orme's *Monumental History Madras Journal* XVI, 348 f, etc. It is curious that the inscriptions of such an important place are so small in number. The department has discovered thus far two and these are:

57 of 1905 (Persian) — On a slab built into the threshold of the main gate of the fort of Gingee. Records in Hijra 1125 that the fort was captured by Sadatullah Khan, A.D. 1712-13. See *S.A. Gazr.,* p. 362.

240 of 1904 (Tamil) — On the south wall of the central shrine in the Venkataramsvamin temple at Gingee. A record of the Vijayanagara king Virapratapa Vira Sadasivadeva Maharaya in S. 1472, *Sadharana.* Records gift of land by the

king. The inscription also records a gift by Surappa Nayakar for the merit of Sadasivadeva, and another gift by Adappattu Mallappa Nayakar for festival.

No. 70 of Mr. Sewell's List (Tamil) — Records a document drawn up by Vala (Bala) Venkatapati Nayakan, son (or descendant) of Vala Krishnappa Nayakan, Raja of Senji, (Jinji, Ginji), in S. 1386 (1464 A.D.) *Kaliyuga* 4565, *Parthiva,* adjudicating on a religious dispute. The name of Rama Deva Maha Raya is mentioned as paramount sovereign.

224 of 1904 (Tamil) — On the east wall of the central shrine in the Ranganatha temple, Singavaram. A damaged record.

225 of 1904 (Tamil) — On the east base of the mandapa is front of the same shrine. A record in the thirtieth year of the Chola king Rajakesarivarman or Tribhuvanachakravartin Kulottunga Choladeva (unidentified). Records gift of thirty-two cows for a lamp.

226 of 1904 (Tamil) — On the same base. A record of the Pandya king Maravarman. Tribhuvanachakravartin Vira Pandyadeva, the date of which is lost. Beginning built in. [Was he the same as the successor of Vikrama Pandya?]

227 of 1904 (Tamil) — On the east base of the mandapa in front of the central shrine in the same temple. A record in the seventh year of the Chola king Parakesarivarman or Udaiyar Rajendradeva (1050-63?). Records a gift of a lamp by a chief in atonement for having stabbed a military officer. See *S.A. Gazr.,* pp. 393, 570, 580, 594.

228 of 1904 (Tamil) — On the left of the flight of steps leading up to the same shrine. A record in the fourth year of the Pallava king Sakalabhuvanachakravartin Avanialappirandan Kopperunjingadeva. Records gift of thirty cows for a lamp. see *Conjeevaram Inscriptions, Ep. Ind.,* Vol. VII, p. 165.

229 of 1904 (Tamil) — On the east wall of the central shrine in the ruined Adivaraha Perumal temple in the same village.

A record of the Vijayanagara king Pratapa Devaraya Maharaya (whom Venkayya considers to be the younger brother of Devaraya II) in Paridhavin. Records that a certain private individual and his family were made over to the temple of Panri Alvar to look after the lamps. See No. 665 of 1904 at Tirumullaivayil in Chingleput district for the same chief.

230 of 1904 (Tamil) — On the same wall. A record of the Vijayanagara king Pratapa Devaraya Maharaya in Krodhin. Records a gift similar to that in No. 229. See *S.A. Gazr.,* p. 380.

231 of 1904 (Tamil) — On the south base of the same shrine. A record in the thirtieth year of the Pandya king Maravarman Tribhuvanachakravartin Kulasekharadeva I (1268-1308). Records gift of land. See *Ep. Ind.,* Vol. VIII, p. 277, where it is pointed out that the date corresponded to Wednesday, 31st July, 1297.

232 of 1904 (Tamil) — On the same base. A record of the Vijayanagara king Mallikarjuna-Maharaya, son of Devaraya Maharaya II 'who had witnessed the elephant hunt,' in S. 1378, Dhatri. Records a gift similar to that of No. 380.

233 of 1904 (Tamil) — On the west base of the same shrine. A record in Kilaka. Records a gift similar to that of No. 380 above.

234 of 1904 (Tamil) — On the north base of the same shrine. A record of the Vijayanagara king Kumara Viruppanna Udaiyar (i.e., Virupaksha 1, son of Harihara II) in Kshaya (S. 1309). Records a gift similar to that of No. 229. [The name Kumara has been added to distinguish him from his namesake, the son of Bukka I, who seems to have had nothing to do with the Tamil country.] Virupaksha, according to the Alampundi grant (*Ep.Ind.,* Vol. III, p. 224 ff.) and the Sanskrit drama *Narayanavilasa,* conquered the Tondira, Chola and Pandya countries. See *S.A. Gazr.,* p. 336.

235 of 1904 (Tamil) — On the same base. A damaged record of the Vijayanagara king Sadasivadeva Maharaya in S. 1483, Durmati. The king bears Saluva birudas.

236 of 1904 (Telugu) — On the Ellukkuttaipparai in the same village. A private record in Kalayukta.

237 of 1904 (Tamil) — On two boulders at the foot of the hill in the same village. Records the foundation of a village called Srikaranapperunjeri at the request of an agent of Nilagangaraiyan Annavanattadigal for providing offerings and for burning lamps in the temple of the Alvar at Panvikunru.

238 of 1904 (Tamil) — On a rock in the Tirunatharkunru near the same village. Records the *nisidika* of Ilaiyappadarar who fasted for 30 days. The reference is to the Jaina habit of religious suicide.

239 of 1904 (Archaic Vatteluttu) — On the same rock. Records the nisidika of Chandranandi Acharya who fasted for 57 days."

NOTES

1. This is one of the forms of Sri Krishna in which he is playing the flute. The various other forms are : The baby Krishna; crawling Krishna; *Navaneeta* Krishna (Krishna eating butter) *Kaliyamardana* (Krishna standing on the serpent Kaliya); Parthasarathi Krishna (Krishna acting as charioteer to Partha or Arjuna) and Krishna with his consort Rukmini.

2. SATI was a custom among the Hindus in which a widow immolated herself on the funeral pyre of her husband to show her conjugal fidelity. This custom was put down by the British Government.

    Sir Monier Williams says, 'Indeed, Hindu wives are generally perfect patterns of conjugal fidelity; nor can it be doubted that in these delightful portraits of the *pativrata* or devoted wife, we have true representations of the purity and simplicity of Hindu domestic manners in early times.'

Count Bjornstjerna in his *Theogony of the Hindus* writes: "Among other remarkable particulars in this poem is the pure light in which it sets the noble character and high-minded devotion of the women of India."

3. *Inscriptions of the Madras Presidency*, Government of Madras, 1919, Vol. I, pp. 171, 172, 174 and 175.

4. Report of the Madras Epigraphical Department for the year 1917-18, p. 173.

Chapter 6

TIRUVANNAMALAI

This town, which is a station on the Villupuram-Katpadi line of the Southern Railway, is famous for its worship of the fire Linga, installed there. It lies in north latitude 13° 15' and east longitude 70° 07' at a height of about 3000 feet. The hill by the side of the temple is said to represent Siva, and it draws a large number of worshippers annually. The temple at the foot of the hill is one of the largest in South India and is famous penance Parvati performed to obtain the *Vamabhaga*[1] or the left half of Siva's body. Near the temple is a tank called the Mulaippal Tirtham or tank containing mother's milk.

According to meftedogy there arose a conflict once between Vishnu and Brahma over the question of superiority. In the course of the heated controversy there ascended a huge flame, which is said to have been no other than Siva appearing to convince them that there was yet one superior to them. At that time Brahma took the form of a swan and flew up above to discover the top of the flame, and Vishnu became a *Varaha* or boar and tore the earth with his powerful tusk and tried to discover the base of the flame. This scene, called the Lingothbhava[2] in the science of Hindu Iconology, is generally represented on the outer western wall of all the sanctums in Saiva shrines.

SAINT ARUNAGIRINATHAR

The famous saint Arunagirinathar, the author of the songs called *Tirupugal*, is said to have lived here. There is a representation of him as well as of his patron deity Subrahmanya beautifully sculptured on the east of the hill.

BUILDINGS MENTIONED IN INSCRIPTIONS

The famous gopura or gate tower consists of 11 storeys. From the inscriptions at this place and the Sanskrit work *Sahitya Ratnakara* it is seen that the hill here was called Sonasaila *and* Sonachala, 'the red mountain' and that the construction of the tower was started by King Krishna Deva Raya of Vijayanagar about the year 1516 A.D. It appears to have been completed by King Sevappa Nayak of Tanjore. Besides this gopura, King Krishna Deva also constructed a thousand-pillared mandapa and dug a tank near it. These inscriptions relating to him also mention the *Tulabharadhana*,[3] or weighing against gold that the king performed at the temple of Amaravathi in the district of Guntur to commemorate his victory in the east. Another inscription mentions the rules regarding the sale of house sites in the temple streets of Tiruvannamalai. It is also said that King Rajanarayana Sambhuvarayar constructed a gopura in the Arunachaleswara temple at Tiruvannamalai. It was here that Vamadeva, whose patron was Sambhuvaraya, wrote the original and commentary of *Firnoddhara Dasaka*, a work relating to repairs to temples. Rajanarayana's reign is said to have started from A.D. 1336-1337.

HISTORICAL REFERENCE

Between 1753 and 1991 the place was besieged several times. The French occupied it in 1757 and the British in 1760.

INSCRIPTIONS[4]

The inscriptions here have been copied during the year 1902 by the Madras Epigraphical Department.

469 of 1902 (Tamil) — On the south wall of the central shrine in the Arunachalesvara temple. A record of the Chola king Parakesarivarman, who took the head of the Vira Pandya, the date of which is doubtful. Records gift of 96 sheep for a lamp (the king referred to is probably Parantaka II Uttama Chola "the destroyer of Vira Pandya").

470 of 1902 (Tamil) — On the same wall. A record in the third year of the Chola king Parakesarivarman. Records gift of gold for a lamp by the Chera queen Kilanadigal.

471 of 1902 (Tamil) — On the same wall. A record in the third year of the Chola king Parakesarivarman, who took the head of Vira-Pandya. Records gift of 90 sheep for a lamp.

472 of 1902 (Tamil) — On the same wall. A record of the Chola king Parakesarivarman, the date of which is doubtful. Records gift of 90 sheep for a lamp.

473 of 1902 (Tamil) — On the same wall. A record in the fourth year of the Chola king Parakesarivarman. Records gift of 90 sheep for a lamp.

474 of 1902 (Tamil) — On the same wall. A damaged record of the Chola king Parakesarivarman, the date of which is lost.

475 of 1902 (Tamil) — On the same wall. A record of the Rashtrakuta king Kannaradeva (Krishna III), the date of which is doubtful. Records gift of 20 cows.

476 of 1902 (Tamil) — On the west wall of the same shrine. A record in the fifteenth year of the Chola king Madiraikonda Parakesarivarman (Parantaka I). Records gift of 90 sheep for a lamp.

477 of 1902 (Tamil) — On the south wall of the first prakara of the same temple. A record in the nineteenth year of the Chola king Parakesarivarman or Udaiyar Rajendra Choladeva I (1012-43). Records gift of land for offerings by a servant of the king.

478 of 1902 (Tamil) — On the same wall. A record in the eighteenth year of the Chola king Parakesarivarman or Udaiyar Rajendra Choladeva I (1012-43). The inscription opens with the usual historical introduction of Rajendra Choladeva I. Records sale of land.

479 of 1902 (Tamil) — On the same wall. A record in the twenty-seventh year of the Chola king Parakesarivarman or Udaiyar Rajendra Choladeva I (1012-43). Records gift of land.

480 of 1902 (Tamil verse) — On the west wall of the same prakara. A record of the Pallava king Nassankamala Sakalabhuvanachakravartin Kopperunjingadeva, the protector of Mallai (Mavalivaram). Records gift of ornaments by the king and the erection of buildings by his son. [The latter claims to have driven the *Telungar* to the north to perish. Mr. Venkayya thinks it might refer to his fighting against the Kakatiyas who, during the time of Ganapati, took possession of Conjeevaram. (*Ind. Antq.*, Vol. XXI, p. 197.) Mr. Venkayya believed that the victor was one of the princes who took advantage of the subsequent weakness of the Kakatiyas, and was able to go as far as Draksharamam itself. In his view, the Kopperunjingas of Conjeevaram, Draksharamam and Tirupurantakam were identical.]

481 of 1902 (Tamil) — On the west wall of the same prakara. A record in the seventh year of the Pandya king Maravarman or Tribhuvanachakravartin Kulasekharadeva. Records gift of 54 cows.

482 of 1902 (Tamil) — On the west wall of the same prakara. A record in the sixteenth year of the

Pandya king Konerimaikondan Tribhuvanachakravartin Kulasekharadeva. Records gift of 32 cows and 1 bull by Sriranganathar *or* Malavachakravartin of Varanavasi. (Sriranganatha was probably a member of the Yadavaraya line.)

483 of 1902 (Tamil) — On the west wall of the same prakara. A record of the Vijayanagara king Vira Virupanna Udaiyar II (Virupaksha I), son of Hariyappa Udaiyar (Harihara II) in S. 1311, Sukla. Records gift of land.

484 of 1902 (Tamil and Grantha) — On the west wall of the same prakara. A record in the twentieth year of the Pandya king Maravarman or Tribhuvanachakravartin Kulasekharadeva (I?). Records gift of 73 cows and 25 calves by Parakrama Pandyadeva.

485 of 1902 (Tamil) — On the north wall of the same prakara. A record in the sixteenth year of the Chola king Tribhuvanachakravartin Rajarajadeva III (1216-48), corresponding to Saturday, 22nd May, 1232. Records gift of land to an image set up by Meykandadevan of Tiruvennai-nallur. *Ep. Ind.,* Vol. VIII, p. 268. (The inscription gives a clue to the date of Meykanda, the disciple of Paranjoti Muni and the author of *Sivagnanabodham,* the chief Bible of Saiva Siddhanta philosophy. It is thus very important in the history of Tamil literature.)

486 of 1902 (Tamil) — On the same wall. A record in twenty-sixth year of the Chola king Tribhuvanachakravartin Kulottunga Choladeva. Records rules regarding the sale of house sites in the temple street.

487 of 1902 (Tamil) — On the north wall of the first prakara of the Arunachalesvara temple. A record in the thirty-sixth year of the Pallava king Sakalabhuvanachakravartion Kopperunjingadeva (contemporary of Rajaraja III). Records gift of 32 cows and one bull by Kakku Nayakadeva, son of

Madhusudanadeva, who was younger brother of Vijaya Gandagopaladeva.

488 (a) of 1902 (Tamil) — On the same wall. A record in the thirty-first year of the Chola king Tribhuvanachakravartin Rajarajadeva (III?) (1216-48). Records gift of vessels and ornaments by the queen of Sadumperumal.

488 (b) of 1902 (Tamil) — On the same wall. A record in the ninth year of the Pallava king Sakalabhuvanachakravartin Kopperunjingadeva. Records gift of silver vessels by the same queen.

489 of 1902 (Tamil) — On the same wall. A record in the thirty-first year of the Pallava king Alagia Siyan Sakalabhuvanachakravartion Kopperunjingadeva. Records gift of land. From the fact that Maharaja Simha of Tripurantakam (Kurnool District) had the same birudas as Perunjinga, and both had the title of *Siya,* Venkayya infers that both are identical. See 197, 198 and 202 of 1905 at Tripurantakam.

490 of 1902 (Tamil) — On the same wall. A record in the twenty-seventh year of the Chola king Tribhuvanachakravartin Rajarajadeva (III?). Records gift of land by Rajarajadevan Vanakovaraiyan for the merit of Ponparippina Perumal.

491 of 1902 (Tamil) — On the same wall. A record in the thirty-second year of the Chola king Tribhuvanachakravartin Rajarajadeva III, corresponding to Friday, February 7th, A.D. 1248. Records gift of 32 cows and 1 bull for a lamp. See *Ep. Ind.,* Vol. VIII, p. 6.

492 of 1902 (Tamil) — On the same wall. A record in the thirty-second year of the Chola king Rajakesarivarman or Udaiyar Rajadhirajadeva. Records gift of gold. [Evidently Rajadhiraja I (1018-52) is intended, as he alone ruled for more than 32 years].

493 of 1902 (Tamil) — On the same wall. A record in the twentieth year of the Chola king Tribhuvanachakravartin

Rajarajadeva (III?). Records that a number of people joined together to reclaim certain land which had been neglected.

494 of 1902 (Tamil) — On the same wall. A record in the eighteenth year of the Chola king Tribhuvanachakravartin Rajarajadeva III, corresponding to Sunday, 13th November, 1233. Records gift of 120 sheep by the daughter of an officer of Yadavarayar. *Ep. Ind.,* Vol. VIII, p. 269.

495 of 1902 (Tamil) — On the same wall. A record in the thirtieth year of the Chola king Tribhuvanachakravartin Rajarajadeva (III?). Records gift of land, 32 cows and 1 bull by Tirukkalattidevan.

496 of 1902 (Tamil) — On the same wall. A record in the fifth year of the Chola king Tribhuvanachakravartin Rajarajadeva (III?). Records that two persons pledged themselves not to leave the service of prince Pirudi Gangar.

497 of 1902 (Tamil and Grantha) — On the same wall. A record in the twenty-fourth year of the Chola king Tribhuvanachakravartin Rajarajadeva (III?). Records gift of land by Rajagambhira Chediyarayan of Kiliyur.

498 of 1902 (Tamil and Grantha) — On the same wall. A record in the fifth year (1250-51) of the Chola king Tribhuvanachakravartin Rajendra Choladeva III. Records gift of land by Simhana Dandanatha for the merit of his uncle Kampayya.

499 of 1902 (Tamil) — On the same wall. A record of the Hoysala king Pratapachakravartin Vira Vallaladeva III in S. 1262, Vikrama. Records gift of land by Vallappadannayakar.

500 of 1902 (Tamil) — On the same wall. A record in the fifth year of the Pallava king Sakalabhuvanachakravartin Kopperunjingadeva. Records gift of land by the king.

501 of 1902 (Tamil) — On the same wall. A record of the Chola king Tribhuvanachakravartin Rajarajadeva (III?), the

date of which is doubtful. Records gift of 32 cows and 1 bull for a lamp.

502 of 1902 (Tamil) — On the same wall. A record in the twenty-fifth year or the Chola king Tribhuvanachakravartin Rajarajadeva III. Records gift of 32 cows and 1 bull for a lamp.

503 of 1902 (Tamil) — On the same wall. A record in the thirty-second year of the Chola king Tribhuvanachakravartin Rajarajadeva III, corresponding to Wednesday, April 22, A.D. 1248. Records gift of land by Umai Alvar, queen of Ilakkumadevar. *Ep. Ind.,* Vol. VIII, p. 6.

504 of 1902 (Tamil) — On the same wall. A record in the thirtieth year of the Chola king Tribhuvanachakravartin Rajarajadeva III. Records gift of 50 cows by Venavudaiyan, the younger brother of Solakon, an officer of Kopperunjingan. Compare *Ep. Ind.,* Vol. III, p. 272, where it is pointed out that the date corresponded to Sunday, December 17, A.D. 1245.

505 of 1902 (Tamil) — On the same wall. A record in the second year of the Pallava king Sakalabhuvanachakravartin Kopperunjingadeva. Records gift of 96 cows and 3 bulls for three lamps by Nila Gangaraiyan.

506 of 1902 (Tamil) — On the same wall. A record in the twenty-sixth year of the Chola king Tribhuvanachakravartin Rajarajadeva (III?). Records gift of land by Tikkanai Perumal.

507 of 1902 (Tamil verse) — On the same wall. Praises Vanadivakaran Ponparappinan or Magadai Perumal.

508 of 1902 (Tamil) — On the same wall. A record in he fifteenth year of the Pallava king Sakalabhuvanachakravartin Kopperunjingadeva. Records gift of a golden spoon and cup by the queen of Sadum Perumal.

509 of 1902 (Grantha and Tamil) — On the same wall. A record of the Hoysala king Pratapachakravartin Vira

Vallaladeva III in S. 1262. Records gift of a lamp by Vallappadannayakkar.

510 of 1902 (Tamil) — On the same wall. An incomplete record in the thirtieth year of the Chola king Tribhuvanachakravartin Rajarajadeva III. Records gift of a lamp by Umai Alwar, the queen of Ilakumadevar.

511 of 1902 (Tamil) — On the same wall. A record in the thirty-first year of the Chola king Tribhuvanachakravartin Rajarajadeva. Records gift of 32 cows and 1 bull for a lamp by the queen of Katti Arasar.

512 of 1902 (Tamil) — On the same wall. A record in the ninth year of the Pallava king Alagiya Siyan Sakalabhuvanachakravartin Kopperunjingadeva. Records an order of Kopperunjingadevan.

513 of 1902 (Tamil) — On the same wall. A record in the fourth year of the Pallava king Sakalabhuvanachakravartin Kopperunjingadeva. Records gift of a necklace by Kopperunjingadeva.

514 of 1902 (Tamil) — On the same wall. A record of the Pallava king Kopperunjingadeva, the date of which is doubtful. Records gift of 48 cows and 2 bulls for one-and-a-half lamp by Kuttaduvan or Chediyarayan. See Nos. 434 and 444.

515 of 1902 (Tamil) — On the same wall. A record in the eighteenth year on the Chola king Tribhuvanachakravartin Rajarajadeva (III?). Records gift of money.

516 of 1902 (Tamil) — On the same wall. A record in the twenty-seventh yer of the Chola king Tribhuvanachakravartin Kulottunga Choladeva III, who took Madura, Ceylon, Karuvur and the crowned head of the Pandya. Records that several chiefs promised allegiance to the king and to Chedirayadeva, apparently the Prime Minister, and not to act against their interests or orders.

517 of 1902 (Tamil) — On the south wall of the Subrahmanya shrine in the same temple. An incomplete record in the twenty-seventh year of the Pallava king Sakalabhuvanachakravartin Kopperunjingadeva. Records gift of land. Mentions Nila Gangaraiyar.

518 of 1902 (Tamil) — On the same wall. A record in the twenty-seventh year of the Pallava king Alagiya Siyan Sakalabhuvanachakravartin Kopperunjingadeva. Records that Nangai Alvar, queen of Nila Gangaraiyar, granted land to an image which she had set up in the temple.

519 of 1902 (Tamil) — On the south wall of the Ekambaranathar shrine in the same temple. A record in the thirteenth year of the Pallava king Sakalabhuvanachakravartin Kopperunjingadeva. Records gift of cows for lamps.

520 of 1902 (Tamil) — On the same wall. A record in the fourth year of the Chola king Tribhuvanachakravartin Vijayarajendra Choladeva. Records gift of land by Rajadhiraja Karkatamarayan.

521 of 1902 (Tamil) — On the same wall. A record in the twelfth year of the Pallava king Sakalabhuvanachakravartin Kopperunjingadeva. Records gift of 32 cows and 1 bull for a lamp by a merchant.

522 of 1902 (Tamil) — On the west wall of the same shrine. A record in the eleventh year, Chitrabhanu, of the Chola king Tribhuvanavira Choladeva. Records gift of land by a queen. (Dr. Kielhorn points out that the king referred to here is not Kulottunga Chola III as the date does not agree; that the only date between 1000 and 1500 A.D. which is equal to the date of the epigraph is Friday, 23rd August, 1342, and that we have therefore to infer that there was a king named Tribhuvanavirachola who began to rule sometime between August 31, 1331 and August 23, 1332.) See *Ep. Ind.,* Vol. VIII, p. 7-8.

523 of 1902 (Tamil) — On the south and west walls of the same shrine. A record of the Vijayanagara king Vira Sadasivadeva Maharaya in S. 1470, Kilaka. Records gift of land. Mentions Rajanarayanapuram or Arkadu (the modern Arcot).

524 of 1902 (Tamil) — On the south wall of the same shrine. A record in the twenty-sixth year of the Chola king Tribhuvanachakravartin Kulottunga Choladeva. Records gift of 16 cows for half a lamp.

525 of 1902 (Tamil) — On the south wall of the Chidambaresvara shrine in the Arunachalesvara temple. A record in the fourth year of the Chola king Tribhuvanachakravartin Rajadhirajadeva (I?). Records that 52 cows and 1 bull were given for one-and-a-half lamp by a private person (Nagan Kailayan) in order to atone for having accidentally killed another Solan-devan when aiming an arrow at antelope. (The expiation of grievous harm was always made in Chola times in this manner. See N.A. 700 below.)

526 of 1902 (Tamil) — On the same wall. A damaged record in the second year of the Chola king Tribhuvanachakravartin Kulottunga Choladeva. Records gift of gold and land.

527 of 1902 (Tamil) — On the same wall. A record in the fourth year of the Chola king Tribhuvanachakravartin Rajadhirajadeva. Records gift of 32 cows and 1 bull for a lamp.

528 of 1902 (Tamil) — On the west wall of the same shrine. A damaged record of the Chola king Tribhuvanachakravartin Virarajendra Choladeva, the date of which is lost. Records gift of a lamp. (Virarajendra was the title of the king who ruled from 1063 to 1070 and Kulottnnga III. Very probably it is the latter that is referred to here.)

529 of 1902 (Tamil) — On the same wall. A record in the seventh year of the Chola king Tribhuvanachakravartin

Rajadhirajadeva. Records gift of 32 cows and 1 bull for lamp.

530 of 1902 (Tamil) — On the *Kili gopura* in the same temple, right of entrance. A record in the twenty-first year of the Pallava king Kopperunjingadeva. Records gift of 32 cows and 1 bull for a lamp.

531 of 1902 (Tamil) — In the same place. A record in the thirteenth year of the Chola king Tribhuvanachakravartin Kulottunga Choladeva. Records gift of an ornament by Virasekhara Kadavarayan.

532 of 1902 (Tamil) — In the same place. A record in the twenty-first year of the Chola king Kulottunga Choladeva III. Records gift of 96 cows and 3 bulls for 3 lamps by Rajarajadevan Ponparappinan or Vanakovaraiyan of Arakalur.

533 of 1902 (Tamil prose and verse) — In the same place. A record in the twenty-first year of the Chola king Kulottunga Choladeva. Records gift of land by the same person.

534 of 1902 (Tamil) — In the same place. A record in the twenty-fifth year of the Chola king Tribhuvanachakravartin Kulottunga Choladeva III. Records gift of land for a lamp by an officer of Rajagambhira Chediyarayar.

535 of 1902 (Tamil) — In the same place. A record in the fourteenth year of the Chola king Tribhuvanachakravartin Kulottunga Choladeva. Records gift of ornaments by Kulottunga Chola Malayakularayan. (The last mentioned chief was evidently Chediyaraya).

536 of 1902 (Tamil) — In the same place. A record in the tenth year of the Chola king Tribhuvanachakravartin Kulottunga Choladeva. Records gift of Malaiyanur in Tagadanadu by Rajarajadevan or Adiyaman of Tagadur (Dharmapuri) in Ganganadu. Mr. Venkayya identifies the Chola king with Kulottunga III as he asserts "we know from

other inscriptions that the son of that Rajaraja was a vassal of the same Chola king."

537 of 1902 (Tamil) — In the same place. A record in the eighteenth year of the Chola king Tribhuvanachakravartin Kulottunga Choladeva. Records gift of land.

538 of 1902 (Tamil) — In the same place. A record in the twenty-seventh year of the Chola king Tribhuvanachakravartin Kulottunga Choladeva III (1178-1216), who took Madura, Ceylon and the crowned head of the Pandya. Records gift of land by Malaiyan Narasimhavarman or Karikala Chola Adaiyurnadalvan.

539 (a) of 1902 (Tamil) — In the same place. A record in the twenty-eighth year of the Chola king Kulottunga Choladeva (III?). Records gift of land by Malaiyan Venaivenran or Karikala Chola Adaiyurnadalvan.

539 (b) of 1902 (Tamil) — In the same place. A record in the twenty-seventh year of the Chola king Kulottunga Choladeva (III?). Records gift of two villages by Nila Gangan Kariya Perumal.

540 of 1902 (Tamil) — In the same place. A record in the fourteenth year of the Chola king Tribhuvanachakravartin Kulottunga Choladeva. Records gift of 64 cows and 2 bulls for two lamps.

541 of 1902 (Tamil) — In the same place. A record in the eighteenth year of the Chola king Tribhuvanachakravartin Kulottunga Choladeva. Records gift of 32 cows and 1 bull for a lamp by a chief of Tagadur.

542 of 1902 (Grantha) — In the same place. Records the building of the gopura by the minister Bhaskara. We have no evidence to say whether this person was Bhaskara Raya, the author of the *Vaidika Nigantu,* and *Bhavanopanishad Prayogavidhi* or Bhaskara, the author of the *Siddantakaumudivilasa.* His name also reminds us of Bhaskara

Irugappa Dandanatha who complied the *Nanartharatnamala* and of the author of the *Samarajagana Prayoga*. See Dr. Hultsch's *Rep. Sans. MSS.*, Vol. III.

543 of 1902 (Tamil verse) — On the Kili gopura in the Arunachaleswara temple, right of entrance. Mentions Magadan Vanarpiran.

544 of 1902 (Grantha) — In the same place. Alludes to the gilding of the temple by Bana chief.

545 of 1902 (Tamil) — In the same place. Records gift of taxes.

546 of 1902 (Tamil) — On the same gopura, left of entrance. A record in the thirteenth year of the Chola king Tribhuvanachakravartin Kulottunga Choladeva (III?). Records gift of land by a chief of Pangalanadu named Piridivi Gangan Vanniya Madevan.

547 of 1902 (Tamil) — In the same place. A record in the twentieth year of the Chola king Tribhuvanachakravartin Kulottunga Choladeva. Records gift of money by a guild of merchants.

548 of 1902 (Tamil) — In the same place. A record in the twenty-ninth year of Chola king Tribhuvanachakravartin Kulottunga Choladeva. Records gift of land by Sediran Vanarayan.

549 of 1902 (Tamil) — In the same place. A record in the thirtieth year of the Chola king Tribhuvanachakravartin Kulottunga Choladeva. Records gift of 2 cows for a lamp.

550 of 1902 (Tamil) — In the same place. A record in the fifth year of the Chola king Tribhuvanachakravartin Kulottunga Choladeva. Records that certain merchants vowed to supply a flag at each of the three annual festivals.

551 of 1902 (Tamil) — In the same place. A record in the nineteenth year of the Chola king Tribhuvanachakravartin Rajarajadeva. Records gift of 32

cows and 1 bull for a lamp by Edirili Chola Sambuvarayan. See No. 509.

552 of 1902 (Tamil) — In the same place. A record in the second year of the Chola king Virarajendra Choladeva (I or II?). Records repairs to a tank.

553 of 1902 (Tamil) — In the same place. A record in the thirteenth year of the Chola king Tribhuvanachakravartin Kulottunga Choladeva. Records gift of 32 cows and 1 bull for a lamp by Vikrama Chola Sambuvarayan. See No. 507.

554 of 1902 (Tamil verse) — In the same place. Praises Ponparappinan or Magadai Perumal. See Nos. 462, 487 and 513.

555 of 1902 (Tamil) — In the same place. A record in the twenty-seventh year of the Chola king Tribhuvanachakravartin Kulottunga Choladeva. Records gift of 32 cows and 1 bull for a lamp.

556 of 1902 (Tamil) — In the same place. A record in the thirty-second year of the Chola king Tribhuvanachakravartin Kulottunga Choladeva. Records gift of land.

557 of 1902 (Tamil) — In the same place. A record in the thirty-fifth year of the Chola king Tribhuvanaviradeva (Kulottunga III). Records the guilding of the central shrine and the gift of three villages by Rajarajadevan Ponparappinan or Vanakovaraiyan of Arkalur. The date correspond to Sunday, 2nd June, A.D. 1213. See No. 487 above and *Ep. Ind.,* Vol. VIII, p. 4.

558 of 1902 (Tamil) — In the same place. A record in the twenty-seventh year of the Chola king Tribhuvanachakravartin Kulottunga Choladeva III, who took Madura, Ceylon and the crowned head of the Pandya. Records gift of land by Cholendrasimha Prithivi Gangan.

559 of 1902 (Tamil) — In the same place. A record in the twenty-seventh year of the Chola king Tribhuvanachakravartin

Kulottunga Choladeva. States the purposes for which the proceeds of certain taxes had to be utilised.

560 of 1902 (Tamil) — In the same place. A record in the twenty-fourth year of the Chola king Tribhuvanachakravartin Kulottunga Choladeva. Records that the temple authorities assigned certain land to two persons in recognition of benefits conferred on the temple.

561 of 1902 (Tamil) — In the same place. A record in the twenty-ninth year of the Chola king Tribhuvanachakravartin Rajarajadeva. Records gift of 24 sheep for a quarter lamp.

562 of 1902 (Tamil) — On the Vallala gopura in the Arunachalesvara temple, right of entrance. A record of the Vijayanagara king Ariyanna Udaiyar (Harihara II) in S. 1299, Pingala. Records gift of paddy and money for the maintenance of the watchman at the Vira Vallala gate. See Mr. Sewell's local list No. 2 (*Antiquities,* Vol. I, p. 207.)

563 of 1902 (Tamil) — In the same place. A damaged record of the Vijayanagara king Krishnadeva Maharaya in S. 1433, Pramoduta. Records gift of land. (This is apparently Mr. Sewell's local list No. 12 where it is said to record an exchange of land between some private parties.)

564 of 1902 (Tamil) — In the same place. A record of the Vijayanagara king Vira Vijayabhupatiraya Udaiyar, son of Vira Devaraya I, in S. 1340, Vilambin. Orders that the Idangai and the Valangai castes of Tiruvannamalai should enjoy the same privileges. See Sewell's local list No. 8 in his *Antiquities,* Vol. I, p. 207.

565 of 1902 (Tamil) — In the same place. A record of the Vijayanagara king Vira Viruppanna Udayar II (Virupaksha I), son of Ariyappa Udaiyar (Harihara II) in S. 1310, Vibhava. Records remission of taxes to the temple.

566 of 1902 (Tamil) — In the same place. A damaged record of the Vijayanagara king Virapratapa Devaraya

Maharaya, the date of which is lost. See Mr. Sewells local
list No. 7.

567 of 1902 (Tamil) — In the same place. A record of the
Vijayanagara king Sadasivadeva Maharaya in S. 1489,
Prabhava. Records remission of certain taxes in the villages
belonging to the temple by order of Achyutappa Nayaka.
(This is evidently No. 9 of Mr. Sewell's local list, which is
however doubtful.)

568 of 1902 (Tamil and Grantha) — In the same place.
A record of the Vijayanagara king Vira Vijayabhupatiraya
Udaiyar, son of Vira Devaraya Maharaya I in S. 1325, Vijaya.
Records gift of 32 cows and 1 bull for a lamp by Annadata
Udaiyar, son of the minister Savundappa Udaiyar.

569 of 1902 (Tamil and Kanarese) — In the same gopura,
left of entrance. A record of the Vijayanagara king Devaraya
Maharaya II in S. 1359, Pingala. Records gift of land.

570 of 1902 (Tamil) — In the same place. A record of the
Vijayanagara king Vira Mallikarjunaraya, son of Devaraya II
in S. 1375, Srimukha. Records gift of land.

571 of 1902 (Tamil) — In the same place. A record in the
twenty-second year of the Pandya king Tribhuvanachakravartin
Sri Vallabhadeva. Records remission of taxes.

572 of 1902 (Tamil) — On the west wall of the second
prakara of the same temple, right of entrance. A record of the
Vijayanagara king Viruppanna Udaiyar II (Virupaksha I,) son
of Hariyanna Udaiyar (Harihara II) in S. 1310, Vibhava.
Records that the king's cousin Jammana Udaiyar (son of
Kampana II and grandson of Bukka II) granted land to
provide for the five persons who had to recite the Veda for
the merit of his deceased father Kampana Udaiyar II. (In. S.
Ind. Incrns., Vol. I, No. 72. Jammana is misread as Ommana.
In *Mack. MSS.* (*Ins. S. Dts.*, p. 123, No. 2) the Saka date is
given as 1312).

573 of 1902 (Tamil) — On the gopura in the west wall of the third prakara of the same temple, right of entrance. A record of the Vijayanagara king Jammana Udaiyar, son of Kampana Udaiyar II, son of Vira Bokkana Udaiyar I, in S. 1296 Ananda. Refers to the same grant. See note to the previous inscription.

574 of 1902 (Tamil) — On a slab set up in front of 1000-pillared mandapa in the same temple. A record on the Vijayanagara king Krishnadeva Maharaya in S. 1436, Dhatu. Refers to the King's conquests of Udayagiri, Rauttaraya, Mahapatra, Addanki, Vinukonda, Bellamkonda, Kondavidu, etc., the capture and pardon of Virabhadrayya, the son of Prataparudra of Orissa, Naraharideva, son of Kumara Hammirappatra, Mallu Khan of Rachur etc. To commemorate this he built the Amareswara temple at Dharanikota. The inscription records that at Tiruvannamalai he built the thousand-pillared mandapa, the tank near the same, the gopura of eleven storeys, etc. (See the Amaravati and Sendamangalam inscriptions. See also *Ins. S. Dts.,* p. 122, No. 1 and *Antiquities,* p. 106, No. 2 in the local list.)

On certain copper pots for camphor lamp. Records that Venkatapati Raya "the Prime Minister of Mysore *Samasthanam"* gave in S. 1668, Akshya, a pot (4Ç *bharas* in weight) to God Arunachaleswara. *Ins. S. Dts.,* p. 23, No. 3.

A C.P. in the *'Pareyand" matham.* Records that in the reign of Krishnadeva Maharaya, a certain Aravalutha Modalian and the inhabitants of the 56 Nadus erected a matham for the Tambiran of "aleyarum conda," besides the *Vimana* of the Amman temple, and gave the village of Melapalayur (?) as a free gift to the temple for the maintenance of the Tambirans, besides an allowance of 6 *Panams* in marriage, rice and cloth. See *MSS. Dts.,* p. 123, No. 5.

NOTES

1. There is a sculpture of the goddess in union with the *Linga* in the temple of Pattisvaram near Kumbakonam.

2. This incident is said to have taken place on the night of the fourteenth day of dark fortnight in Magha (January-February) which is known as Sivaratri, when Siva is worshipped. When Brahma and Vishnu desired to worship Siva, He is said to have appeared in the form of a bright light on the day of Karttikai; generally the full-moon day of the month of Kartika (November-December) when the asterism Kritika will prevail. This accounts for the importance of the Karttikai festival in Tiruvanumalai.

3. A sculptural representation of Tulabharadhana is seen over the ceiling of a mandapam on the north of the Mahamakam Tank in Kumbakonam.

4. *Inscriptions of the Madras Presidency*, Government of Madras, 1919, Vol. I, pp. 84 to 96.

Chapter 7

CHIDAMBARAM

Chidambaram, which is also known as Koyil (the Temple), Tillai, Pundarikapuram, Vyagrapuram, Sirrambalam, Puliyur and Chitrakuta, lies between the river Vellar (Svetanadi according to the Puranas) on the north, the Bay of Bengal on the east, the Coleroon on the south, and Viranam tank on the west. The temple in this place is considered one of the most important in Southern India and devotees from all parts of the country visit the place all the year round. The idol of Nataraja (Siva in his dancing aspect) is unvirlad only on specified occasions of worship. Behind the veil is revealed mere space, out of which the blissful Nataraja is said to have emerged.

Chidambaram is famous for the simplicity of its objects of worship, which consist of *Akasa* (ethereal space) and *Rahasya* or a *Chakra* on the wall to the rear of the idol. In the *Chit Sabha,* or hall within the temple, Isvara is said to have danced while blessing the two great devotees — Patanjali and Vyaghrapada. The five steps leading to the hall are covered with silver plates and signify the five sacred letters of the *Panchakshara Mantara.*

The Chit Sabha of the temple is located within it in the position of the heart in a human body, the man lying with his head to the south. The hall serves the position of the sanctum in other temples. The temple is longer from north to south, unlike the generality of temples which measure longer from east to west.

PURANIC VERSION

In ancient days Simhavarma of north India happened to halt at this place when he was on a pilgrimage to south India. At that period this place was covered by a forest. While bathing in the tank within the temple he found that he had been changed into a person bearing a golden appearance. Since then, he was known as *Hiranyavarma* or gold-armoured! Tradition says that the gold recovered from the well near the Chit Sabha was utilised for the roof of the temple. The palaces of the ancient Hindu kings are said to have stood on the east of the town and even now there is a suburb called Korravankudi (*Korravan* in Tamil means king), the site of the present railway station.

ARCHITECTURAL WORKS

[1]The temples at Chidambaram are the oldest in the south of India, and portions of them are gem of Dravidian art.....

The roof (of the temple of Parvati) is supported by bracketing shafts tied with transverse parlins till a space of only 9 feet is left to the spanned. The outer enclosure in which this temple stands is very elaborate, with two storeys of pillars.

There is also a tiny shrine (*Nritta Sabha*), of which Mr. Fergussoh says: "The oldest thing now existing here is a little shrine in the innermost enclosure. A porch of 56 pillars about 8 feet high, and most delicately carved, resting on a stylobate, ornamented with dancing figures, more graceful and more elegantly executed than any others of their class, so far as I know, in Southern India. At the sides are wheels and horses, the whole being intended to represent a car."

There are four courts in Chidambaram temple. The third contains the famous Thousand-Pillared Hall, 350' by 260', from which a good view of the minor shrines is obtained. The second has a shrine of Siva and other deities. The Nritta Sabha has fine sculptural representation in its base. Inside, there is *Kanaka Sabha* or the dancing hall of Nataraja, covered with a golden roof. The fine architectural carvings, which attract the eye, are on the niches of the four main outer gopuras. These contribute in a great measure to the greatness of the temple. The holy Sivaganga tank, 175' long and 100' wide, situated within the temple, has an attractive colonnade around it. The Subrahmanya Shrine, popularly known as Pandyanar Subrahmanya Temple, so called probably after Pandya Kings, has many beautiful carvings. Many Puranic legends are represented on the roof of the Sivakami Amman Shrine; while on the south-west of the temple there is the shrine of a huge Ganesa (elephant-god).

Situated within the innermost prakara of the temple itself on the south-east is the shrine of Govindaraja Perumal (Vishnu), who is also said to have witnessed the dance of Siva.

The gopura or tower on the northern entrance to the temple was built by Krishna Devaraya of Vijayanagar in commemoration of his victory over the king of Orissa. The towers facing the east and the west contain beautiful representations of the 108 different postures of the art of dancing mentioned in the *Bharata Natya Sastra* — the standard authority on the subject. The gopura at the southern entrance was constructed by a Pallava prince called Perunjingadeva.

Besides the metal figures of the sages Vyaghrapada[2] (tiger-footed), and Patanjali[3] (snake-bodied), sculptures of those who danced with god Nataraja are also to be found in the eastern gopura of the temple at Chidambaram. There is also a beautiful representation of Siva as Chandesanugrahamurti where the devotee Chandesa holds an axe between his folded arms. A fine carving of Tripurantaka is also to be found. The most interesting piece of the sculptural carving is that of Siva as warrior. It is said that Siva, desirous of overcoming the powerful Tripurasura, came out in battle carray with the earth for chariot, the sun and the moon for its wheels, drawn by four horses composed of the Vedas, the Upanishads for the reins, Mount Meru for his bow, the ocean for his quiver and god Vishnu for his arrow. There is also seen the sculptural representation of *Surya* or the Sun with three faces of Brahma, Vishnu and Siva seated on a chariot drawn by seven horses and driven by Aruna, his charioteer. But this does not seem to be correct; for in another chapter on the Navagraha sculpture in Gangaikondasolapuram, Saturn is seen to drive the horses.

There are also beautiful figures of the *Ashtadikpalas* or the eight deities of the cardinal points, each having been assigned a separate place in the temple.

Tirunilakanda Nayanar,[4] one of the 63 Tamil saints and a potter by birth, is said to have lived here enjoying the favour of the God. There also lived many Hindu saints Manikkavachaka, Sambhanda, and Nanda in this city. It is also said that Manikkavachaka defeated the Buddhist scholars in a controversy when they came here with the avowed object of questioning the sanctity of the shrine and to overthrow the worship of the deity.

Nanda,[5] also one of the 63 Saiva devotees, was a Pariah[6] by birth. By his great devotion to God he converted several of his fellowmen to a highly spiritual individuals. Admiring his devotion, in Tirupangur near Vaithisvarankoil, Siva directed his sacred bull Nandi to move aside in order to enable Nanda to have a sight of the Linga in the central shrine!! Even today we find that the stone bull in this place is moved from the place where it ought to have been. Nanda, who is said to have been blessed by God for his devotion, is enshrined here.

PERIYAPURANA OR THE LIVES OF THE GREAT SAIVA DEVOTEES

Periyapurana (*Periyar* meaning eminent in the spiritual sense, and *purana* meaning story) records the lives of the 63 great Saiva devotees together with those of 9 classes of different *bhaktas* (devotees) whose sculptures surround the sanctum of all Siva temples. In the raised platform around the verandah on the inside of the first court wall, the devotees, who were raised to prominence by their deeds, stand in miniature sculptures. They are worshipped daily, in particular on the days when they are supposed to have left their physical body. About the qualifications of such eminent men, the great Tamil poet Tiruvalluvar in his famous *Kural* records:

"Behold the men who have renounced sense enjoyments and live a life of discipline: the scriptures exalt their glory above any other good.

Behold the men who have weighed this life with the next and have renounced; the earth is made radiant by their greatness.

Behold the man whose firm will controlls his five senses even as the goading hook controlls the elephant: he is a seed fit for the fields of heaven.

Behold the man who appreciates at their true value the sensations of touch, taste, sight, sound and smell (who knows that they are translent and at the same time misleading, and who therefore endeavours to transcend them); he will command the world.

The scriptures of the world proclaim the greatness of the name of the mighty world."

Though the five parts that pertain to all other Puranas —
Panchalakshnam[7] — are wanting in this work, it has assumed
prominence even amongst ancient works, on account of the
men, whose lives are narrated therein. "Puranas are elaborate
commentaries of the sacred Vedas and these explain the
philosophical details through easy stories. They are intended
for the exclusive benefit and elevation of the lower orders of
society that do not possess the requisite intellectual capacities
to catch the true import of the Vedas. Unlike the other
Puranas, the Periyapurana alone records the lives of historical
personages who have contributed to enrich Saivism during the
recent period, as will be seen later from the inscriptions
recorded in temples dating from the 19th century onwards.
This work in consequence has become a standard work in
Tamil literature and it ranks amongst those to be religiously
read daily like the Ramayana. Again, this work is said to have
obtained the grace of Nataraja, the presiding deity of the
temple at Chidambaram, which amongst the Saiva temples is
known as 'The Temple' and has earned the epithet 'Arutpa'
in consequence hereof."

Of the 63 Nayanmars, Chandesa is declared the head, and
even the temple accounts of Saiva gods were used to be
written in his name. It was Chandesa that did not care even
for his father in his zealous worship of the God. So the God
crowned[8] him and gave him a place near him. All the used-
up garlands are thrown over him and he is held in much
esteem in all Siva temples. Worshippers are in consequence
enjoined to take leave of him, without which the visit to the
temple is supposed to be incomplete and unfructifying. In due
reverence to him, all worshippers clap their hands, thus
proving their visit to the temple and soliciting his patronage.

There are numerous grants recorded in temples, examined
hitherto by the Madras Epigraphical Department, testifying

to the fact that all sale transactions relating to the temples were conducted in the name of this head devotee Adichandesa — and not in the names of the trustees as is done these days.

Sankaracharya has praised some of the devotees in several of his works, thus showing that they are important personages who helped spread Saivism.

The mythical origin of Periyapurana is contained in the great "Sivarahasya" 9th Canto, wherein Siva is said to have revealed to his consort Parvati the future birth of 63 devotees who would be immortalized in the world. In accordance with this divine dictate, Sundaramurthi, one of the 63 devotees of the Periyapurana, was born in this world and he spent the major part of his life in the sacred Tiruvarur (Tanjore District). Then there arose an occasion for him to compose in 11 stanzas, the lives of these saints. This is said to have been done at the command of the presiding God of that place and it went by the name of "Tiruttondaththogai" or "the number of the devotees" which formed the nucleus for the great Periyapurana. Completing his stay in this mundane world, Sundarar entered the region of Siva at Mount Kailas, which was witnessed by sage Upamanyu, and he in his turn proclaimed the lives of Sundara and the other of the 63 to his followers. This work is entitled *Upamanyu Bhaktavilasam*. Sage Agastya has also narrated this story in one of his works called *Agastya Bhaktavilasam*. Its importance being great, a Telugu translation of it was produced by one Palkuriki Soma, a great Virasaiva author of the 13th century in his work entitled *Basava Purana*. In due course, Vinayaka the patron deity of the place, revealed the mysteries of this Tiruttondaththogai to the boy devotee Nambiandar Nambi of Tirunaraujur. He also informed of the existence of that work in palm leaf in a room on the northwest of the Sabha wherein god Nataraja at Chidambaram dances blissfully for ever. With the Chola king Rajaraja Abhayakulasekhara or Kulottunga I who had his capital at Tiruvarur, Nambiandar proceeded to Chidambaram, took out the book from the room and arranged them as revealed to him by his Vinayaka, in a work entitled *Deveram*. He also composed *Andadi* which is about the lives of the Saiva devotees.

On the north wall of the mandapa in front of the Aksheswara temple at Achcharapakkam is an inscription which mentions the image of Kulottunga I designated as Rajakesari Varman or Tribhuvanachakravartin Kulottunga Choladeva that was set up in this temple during the fifth year of the king (107475 A.D.). This inscription has been numbered as 247 of 1901 in the Annual Report of the Madras Epigraphical Department. Later on King Anapaya Chola, who has been identified with Kulottunga II by the Madras Epigraphical Department, had for his prime minister Arunmolithevar of Kunrattur (Saidapet Taluk of Chingleput district) belonging to the then Tondaimandalam. He went by the popular name of Sekkilar, as he belonged to that sect of the Vellala[9] caste. The king also conferred on him the title of "Uttamacholapallaya" and "Tondarserparavuvar." He had for his patron deity the God at Tirunageswaram near Kumbakonam and on this account constructed a temple in his native village by that name. Regretting the regard paid by the king to a Jaina work *Feevakachintamani* and the consequent evil effect upon the people to lean towards that religion, and in accordance with the proverb "As is the king so are the people", Sekkilar attempted to narrate the importance of Tiruthondaththogai and Anthathi which narrate the merits of Saivism. The king took a fancy to the great work and directed him to compose it in an easier style and in an enlarged form. Accordingly the prime minister left Tiruvarur, the capital, and went to Chidambaram. With the grace of God Nataraja he composed the Periyapurana, or Thirutondarpuranam in the thousand-pillared hall within the temple. He commenced the work on a Chaitra month Arudra asterism day and completed it on the same day next year. The king proceeded to the place and in the midst of a great assembly of the learned received the grand work. Sekkilar spent his remaining days in Chidambaram. A small shrine in his honour now exists on the northern bank of a tank which goes by the name of Gyanavapi. In addition to these, 3 unpublished copies of the work entitled *Sivabhakta Mahatmya,* which describes the lives of these 63 Nayanmars and explains the way in which they gained salvation, are available in Oriental Manuscripts Library at Madras.

There are references to these saints in the inscriptions of the temples at Tanjore, Tiruvarur (Tanjore district) and Tiruvorriyur[10] (belonging to Chingleput district near Madras) and several other places. Though sculptures of these great men are seen in almost all Siva temples, and metal figures also exist in the temples at Avanasi (Coimbatore district), Kalahasti, and Mylapore within the city of Madras, it is only in the great temple at Darasuram near Kumbakonam (Tanjore district) that their lives are delineated in full in bas-relief over the outer sanctum wall of the central shrine. On the south wall of the Andavar shrine in the Siddharatneswara temple at Uttattur (Trichinopoly district) is a record dated the 24th year of Chola king Kulottunga relating to the gift for maintaining worship to the images of Saiva Saints (Nayanmars) in the shrine of Togumamani Nayanar at Uttattur.

On the first niche of the west enclosure of the great Brihadiswara temple in Tanjore, is an inscription describing some of the Nayanmars, such as Nambi Aruranar (Sundaramurti), Nangai Paravaiyar, Tirunavukkaraiyar,

Tirugnana Sambandanadigal and a number of ornaments which had been given to these images. Again on two pillars of the west enclosure of this temple is another record relating to the 3rd year of the reign of Rajendra Choladeva (10th century) recording the setting up of a copper image of Miladudaiyar who has been identified with Meypporul Nayanar of the Periyapurana, in the South Indian Inscriptions, Vol. II, page 167. Another on the base of the west enclosure refers to images of Siruthonda Nambi, his wife Thiruvenkattu Nangai and their son Siraladevar.

The Tyagarajaswami temple at Tiruvarur contains an inscription[11] of the Chola king Anapaya whose name as such occurs in each of the two Sanskrit verses at the end of the inscription, while in the introductory passage the king is called Rajakesarivarman or Tribhuvanachakravartin Sri Kulottunga Choladeva II (1133 to 1148). In the 7th year of his reign he made gifts to the Nayanars Aludaiya Nambi (Sundaramurti), Paravai Nachiyar his wife, Aludaiya Pillayar (Tirugnanasambandar) and Tirunavukkarasudevar. The translation, as recorded in the *South Indian Inscriptions,* Vol.II, Part II, page 154, reads as follows:

"King Anapaya whose head glitters when placed at the feet of the Lord of the Golden Hall, gave land, gold, brass, silver and other excellent treasures to the blessed Brahmapuris (Tirugnanasambandar), Vaghadipati (Thirunavukkaraiyar) and Svasvarmimitra (Sundaramurti) at the shrine of the blessed Lord of Arur.

"I, Anapaya, the bee at the lotus feet of Natesa at the Golden Hall, in the excellent Vyaghragrahara (Chidambaram), bow my head at the lotus feet of (future) princes, who are disposed to protect the charitable gifts made at Lakshmialaya (Tiruvarur) by other kings. The mother of Aludaiya Nambi was Isaignaniyar.

The mother of the Saint (Sundaramurti) called Gnani, was born at this (town of) Kamalapura, in the family of Gnanasivacharya, in the Saiva (doctrine) and in the Gautama Gotra."

Another inscription of this temple dated in the 5th year of Parakesarivarman or Tribhuvanachakravartin Sri Vikrama Choladeva (12th century) gives reference to the legend of the calf which was accidentally run over by the chariot of the son of the Chola King, Manu. This finds a place in the introduction of the Periya Purana and it is also one of the 364 *leelas* (sports) which Sri Tyagaraja, the presiding deity here, is said to have performed in this holy city. Sculptural representation[12] of the scenes relating to the dead calf, its mother cow ringing the bell in front of the palace, and the Chola King's son Veedividangan or Sundara Chola being trodden under the wheels of a car are all very vividly shown in front of the eastern gopura of the temple here.

The Annual Report of the Madras Epigraphical Department for the year 1908-09, page 103, says:

"The revival of the Saiva religion and the consequent disappearance of the Jaina and Buddhist influence in southern India is known to have commenced about the beginning of the 7th century A.D., when the famous Saiva saints Appar, Tirugnanasambandar and Siruthonda Nayanar flourished. How these saints advanced the cause of Saivism, by miracles or other means, is learnt from the stories related in the Periyapuranam. That they must have been very great men, even so great as to be deified by the people, is evident from the fact of their images being set up and worshipped in almost every Siva temple of the South. Tamil records are not wanting, in which provision is made for the recital of the Tiruppadiyam, Tirumurai or the Tevaram hymns composed by two of the above mentioned saints in praise of the Saiva shrines visited by them. An equally great saint and poet was Manikkavasagar, also called Tiruvadavur Nayanar, whose famous work Tiruvasagam has been edited by the Rev. G.U. Pope. The time during which Manikkavasagar flourished was about the middle of the 9th century. We do not know of any epigraphic evidence earlier than the records of Rajaraja I, where the recital of the sacred Saiva hymns of the Tevaram are referred to for the first time as being instituted by him. Rajendra Chola I appears to have supported the cause of Saivism by going a step further than his father and setting up the images of some of the famous Saiva saints in the temple of Rajarajeswara at Tanjavur."

The following short notes of the inscriptions relating to some of the devotees are from the volumes of *Inscriptions of the Madras Presidency* issued by the Government of Madras in 1919:

KOCHENGANNAN

On the west wall of the second prakara of the great temple at Jambukeswaram at Trichinopoly, is a record (No. 25 of 1891) of the Pandya king Ko Maravarman or Kulasekharadeva, dated in his 10th year (5th January, 1278 A.D.), referring to a street called after the presiding God here, who transformed a spider into this king, as narrated in the Periyapurana!! This is also dealt with in the *Epigraphia Indica*, Vol. VI, page 39.

MEYPPORUL NAYANAR

Inside the west prakara of the great temple, Tanjore (7th and 8th pillars) is a record (No. 100 of 1888) of the 3rd year of Ko Parakesarivarman or Rajendra Choladeva I, regarding the setting up of the image of Miladudaiyar, who is popularly known as Meypporul Nayanar.

SIRUTTONDA

On the west wall of the Ganapatiswara temple, Tiruchengattangudi at Tanjore, is a record (No. 56 of 1913) of Chola king Rajakesarivarman Rajarajadeva I, in his 3rd year, making gifts of 1 and for the burning of 2 lamps to the shrine of Siraladeva, son of Siruttonda, who was sacrificed to Siva, in the form of Bhairava. He appeared as a guest of Siruttonda. Again in the 19th year of this king (No. 57 of 1913) he made gifts of land for feeding the devotees attending the festival of Sittirai Tiruvadirai when the image of Siraladeva was taken in procession to the mandapa of Siruttonda; also (No. 59 and No. 63 of 1913) on the west base of the mandapa in front of the Ganapatiswara shrine is the inscription mentioning Rajarajadeva III in his 3rd year, made gift of land to the shrine of Siruttonda. No. 66 of 1913, on the north wall of the mandapa in front of Ganapatiswara temple, contains the record of Kulottunga III, in his 8th year and 330th day, relating to the purchase of land for laying out a road to carry the procession of Sirala from the mandapa of Siruttonda to the village of Tirumarugal and the worship of Sirala (No. 67 of 1913). No. 69 of 1913 on the north base of the mandapa in front of Ganapatiswara is a record relating to Rajarajadeva III providing offerings in the mandapa called Tirumuttuvaneri during the festival of Sittirai Barani when the God Uttarapata gave salvation to Siruttonda. No. 77 of 1913 of Rajendra III (A.D. 1245-67) on the 2nd gopura, left of entrance, provides for the Barani festival of Sittirai and Arpasi months. Another record in the same place (No. 76 of 1913) of the Pandya king Parakrama provides for the repairs to the Sirala Siruttonda mandapa.

NAMINANDI ADIGAL

On the south wall of the 2nd prakara of Vedagiriswara temple, Tirukkalukkunram, is a record (No. 179 of 1894) of Kulottunga

I, dated in his 42nd year, relating to the maintenance of a matha to this devotee.

TIRUNAVUKKARASU OR APPAR

On the south wall of the mandapa in front of Sivankureswara temple, Tirthanagiri (Cuddalore taluk), is a record (No. 121 of 1904) of the Pandya king Vira Pandya, in his 9th year for the celebration of 12 festivals commencing with that of Appar or Tirunavukkarasu.

A detached stone built into the south wall of the mandapa in front of the Anjanakshiamman shrine within the temple of Kachchapeswara, Tikukkachchur (Chingleput taluk), (No. 316 of 1909) contains a fragmentary record of Kulottunga III referring to the setting up of an image of Appar.

The epigraph on the north wall of the central shrine in Dandiswara temple, Velachcheri (Chingleput district), (No. 303 of 1911) records in the 25th year of Kulottunga III gift of land in this village to the matha of Tirunavukkarasu at Tiruvanmiyur.

NARASINGAR

On the south wall of the central shrine of Trivikrama temple, Tirukkoyilur (South Arcot district), is a record (No. 120 of 1900) relating to architect Sembangudaiyan Narayana Aditya or Solasundara Muvendavelan having rebuilt the central shrine for the merit of Narasingavanmar who was the Lord of Miladu.

KANNAPPAR

On the east wall of mandapa in front of the Kripanathaswami shrine in the temple of Tiruppanangadu (Cheyyar taluk; North Arcot district), is a record (No. 247 of 1906) which mentions the name of some hunters who claimed to belong to the family of Tirukkannappar.

The inscription on the north wall of the mandapa in front of the central shrine of Kapardiswara at Tiruvalanjuli (Tanjore district), (No. 628 of 1902) records gifts of land to Tirukkannappadevar.

SUNDARAR

On the east wall of the 2nd prakara of the Vyaghrapadeswara temple, Siddhalingamadam (Tirukkoyilur taluk, South Arcot district), is a record (No. 418 of 1909) of the Pandya king Jatavarman or Sundara Pandya (A.D. 1270-1302) providing for the offerings in the shrine of Aludaiya Pillayar.

On the east wall of the 2nd prakara in the Adhipuriswara temple, Tiruvothiyur (Chingleput district), is a record (No. 371 of 1911) of Rajadhiraja II (1172-86) relating to his hearing the purana of Aludaiya Nambi on a Panguni Uttiram day and another (No. 114 of 1912) on the west wall of the central shrine of the same temple recording a gift of 12 buffaloes for a lamp, a silver lampstand, and a silver kalam (bugle) for the goddess Aludaiya Nachiyar in the 11th year of Kulottunga.

On the west wall of Avanasiswara temple, Avanasi, (Coimbatore district), is a record (No. 181 of 1909) of the 31st year of Sundara Pandya making gifts to the shrine of Sundara Nayanar, on the tank-bund at Pukkuliyr (Avanasi.)

SAMBANDAR

On the gopura of the Adhipuriswara temple, Tiruvothiyur (Chingleput district), right of entrance, is a record (No. 238 of 1912) of Vijayagandagopaladeva, in his 15th year (2nd Sept., 1264) for feeding in the Tirugnanasambhandar matha at this place.

ADI CHANDESWARA

In the Choleswara temple, Vellattukottai (Vellutercota,

Tiruvallur taluk, Chingleput district), is a record of the Hoysala king Ramanatha's 8th year, when the oil-mongers of Vallam undertook to supply oil daily for a lamp to Adichandeswara.

Inside east gopura on the second pillar of Brihadeswara temple, Tanjore, is a record (No. 33 of 1888) which describes the copper images made by Rajarajadeva I, to represent scenes from the life of Chandeswara and the Lord of his heart.

KUNGILIYAKKALAYA NAYANAR

On the north wall of the first prakara of the Arunajateswara temple at Tiruppanandal (Tanjore district), is an inscription (No. 40 of 1914) which records gift of land for offerings to the images of Tirukkadavur Kungiliyakkalaya Nayanar, who is said to have turned the face of the deity to its normal position from which it had previously been diverted by the Lord's desire to save Tataki's shame, and other Saiva devotees in the temple at Tiruppanandal.

TIRUMULAR

The epigraph on the north wall of the central shrine of Manatunaiisar of Valivalam (Negapatam taluk, Tanjore district), (No. 116 of 1911) records sale of land to the matha of this saint, whose tradition is connected with Tiruvaduturai, by the priests of the temple.

MANAKKANJARAN

On the gopura of Nityeswara temple at Srimushnam, (South Arcot district), above the figure of Saint Manakkanjaran, is an inscription (No. 255 of 1916) which states that this holy personage recited the Tiruppadiyam of this temple and quitted his life there.

INSCRIPTIONS[13]

The inscriptions recorded in the walls of the temple here have been copied by the Madras Epigraphical Department during the years 1888, 1892, 1902, 1913 and 1918.

The Madras Government Epigraphist in his *Annual Report* for the year 1888 remarks:

"Special interest attaches to three inscriptions, which mention three Chola princesses, viz., Kundavai, Ammangai and Madurantaki. The first of these princes is called Rajarajan Kundavi, the younger sister of Kulottunga Choladeva (or Rajendra Choladeva) and may be identified with Kundava, the daughter of Rajaraja and younger sister of Rajendra Chola, who married the eastern Chalukya king Vimaladitya (Saka 937 to 944). The second of the princesses 'Ammangai, the daughter of Kulottunnga Choladeva' is probably identical with Ammangadevi, the daughter of Rajendra Chola, who married Chalukya king Rajaraja I (Saka 944 to 895). The third of the princesses 'Madurantaki, the younger sister of our Lord (Kulottunga Choladeva)' seems to be distinct from the Madurantaki, who was the daughter of Rajendradeva and the wife of Kulottunga Choladeva I (Saka 985 to 1034)."

Epigraphical records show that the Chola king Parantaka or Vira Chola, who reigned between 907 and 951 A.D., renovated the hall, making several additions of his own and endowing large grants for conducting the festivals of the temple. His successors also contributed much to the improvement of the roof of the dancing hall.

In the east wall of the 1st prakara is an inscription which eulogises the victories of Kulottunga Chola over the Pandyas, burning the fort of Korgara durga (Korgara), the defeating of the Keralas and the placing of a pillar of victory on the Sahyadri mountain (the western ghats). It is also said that this illustrious kings' fame was sung by the tender women of the Parsis or Persians, who were the representatives of the most distant nations which were known to him. The daughter of Rajaraja and younger sister of Kulottunga-Chola Kundavai Alvar presented the god with a golden vessel and covered the shrine with gold. The precious stone given to Chola king Rajendra by the king of Kamboja was inserted into the hall of the God.

Kulottunga III (1178-1216 A.D.) is said to have built the Mukha mandapa of Sabhapati and the gopura of the shrine of the goddess Girindraja and the enclosing verandah (prakara harmya) and the king has been described as an unequalled devotee (ekabakta) of Sri Nataraja.

According to the copper plate inscriptions available in the Madras Museum, Muthu Vijaya Rangappa Kalakala Tola Wodaiyar gave on the 30th June, 1784, a portion of land in the village of Sendorai to the Sabhanayaka temple for the regular performance of Uchchikalapuja or the mid-day worship.

The inscriptions here have been copied by the Madras Epigraphical Department during the years 1888, 1892, 1902, 1913 and 1918.

A connected account of Chidambaram based on the inscriptions of its temples is given in *Madras Ep*. Re. 1914, p. 88. It is remarkable that while the history of the place goes to the age of the Prabhandas and the Devaram, i.e., the Pallava times, no records even of the early Cholas are to be found in its walls, the earliest being those or Rajendra Chola I and Kulottunga I. The records of Vikrama Chola then follow and give details of his holy works and the works of his predecessor. The local inscriptions are given in Mackenzie's list in *Ins. S. Dts.*, p. 162-7, in various and scattered notices in *Rais. Catal.* Vol. III and in the original Mack. MSS. Owing to the enormous difficulty involved in comparing these and the unprofitable nature of such an examination and comparison, I have not attempted it fully. I have given therefore the departmental list alone, and identifications of six of the sixteen inscriptions in *Ins. S. Dts.* For a full account of the local history antiquities, etc. See *S.A. Gazr.*, p. 965-74.

115 of 1888 — Outside the first prakara in the east. Two Sanskrit verses which praise the victories of Kulottunga Chola I, over the five Pandyas and the Keralas, and which record that he burnt the fort of Kottara (near Cape Comorin) and put up a pillar of victory on a peak of the Sahyadri mountains. See *S. Ind. Inscrns.*, Vol. I, p. 168 f. and *P. Ind.*, Vol. V, p. 103-4. "The king's fame is said to be sung even on the further shore of the ocean by the young women of the Persians (Parsi)".

116 of 1888 — On the mandapa in front of the east entrance into the first prakara. Sanskrit fragment.

117 of 1888 — Outside first prakara in the north. Dated in the forty-sixth year of Kulottunga Choladeva, mentions Madurantaki, "the younger sister of our Lord." Srirambalam, here also called Puliyur, became Chidambaram in Sanskrit, and a different interpretation came to be given to the latter which meant "the space of chit." The other names of the place Puliyur, Perumbararrapuliyur and Tillai are mentioned both in the Prabhandas and Devaram. Chidambaram had as many as 14 hamlets as its inscriptions show.

118 of 1888 — Outside first prakara in the north. A record of Ko Rajakesarivarman or Udaiyar Rajendra Choladeva I, twenty-fourth year. This is the earliest record in the temple. (This provides also for the recital of Tiruttondathogai on Masi Magha day.)

119 of 1888 — Outside first prakara in the north. The inscription records several gifts to the god (Aludaiyar) of Chidambaram (Tillai of Tiruchchirrambalam) by Rajarajan

Kundavi, the daughter of the Chalukya king Rajaraja I (A.D. 1022-63) and younger sister of Tribhuvanachakravartin Kulottunga Choladeva I. Further it records that Rajendra Choladeva II (Kulottunga I) put up in the wall of a hall in front of the temple a stone, which he had received from the King of Kamboja. A portion of the inscription was published in *Ind. Antq.* Vol. XXIII, p. 298 and *Ep. Ind.* Vol. IV, p. 70. It is dated in forty-fourth year of Jayadhara. Kielhorn calculates the details of the date to be Friday, 13th March, A.D. 1114, also see *Ep. Ind.* Vol. V, p. 105-6.

120 of 1888 — Outside first prakara in the west. Long defaced inscription in Sanskrit verse.

121 of 1888 — Inside second prakara in the west, left of entrance. A record of Ko Parakesarivarman or Tribhuvanachakravartin. The inscription which is much worn, mentions Ammangai, the daughter of Kulottunga Choladeva.

122 of 1888 — Inside second prakara in the west, right of entrance. A record of Ko Parakesarivarman or Tribhuvanachakravartin Vira Rajendradeva, in his fifth year.

123 of 1888 — East gopura. A record of Vikrama Pandya.

124 of 1888 — West gopura. A record of Ko Maravarman Tribhuvanachakravartin Kulasekaradeva, in his twenty-eighth year. (Most probably the king was Kulasekara I who ruled from 1268-1308).

170 of 1892 (Tamil verse) — Right of entrance to the east gopura of the Nataraja temple. A record of the Pandya king.

171 of 1892 (Tamil verse) — Right of entrance to the east gopura of the Nataraja temple. A record of the Pandya king Sundara-pandya (Jatavarman who ascended the throne in 1251).

172 of 1892 (Tamil verse) — Right of entrance to the east gopura of the Nataraja temple. A record of the Pandya king Sundara Pandya.

173 of 1892 (Tamil verse) — Right of entrance to the east gopura of the Nataraja temple. A record in modern characters.

174 of 1892 — Left of entrance to the north gopura of the same temple. A record of the Vijayanagara king Krishnadeva (1509-30). Records the building of the gopura.

175 of 1892 — Left of entrance to the north gopura of the same temple. A record of the Vijayanagara king Krishnadeva (1509-30).

176 of 1892 (Tamil) — Right of west entrance to the second prakara of the same temple. A record of the Tondaiman. Opens with the usual Sanskrit birudas of Sundara Pandya (1251-64) whose vassal the donor appears to have been.

177 of 1892 (Sanskrit verse) — Right of west entrance to the second prakara of the same temple. A record of the Pandya king Sundara Pandya (1251-64).

178 of 1892 (Sanskrit verse) — South wall of the second prakara of the same temple. A record of the Pandya king Sundara Pandya (1251-64).

183 of 1892 (Sanskrit and Tamil) — West wall of the second prakara of the same temple. A record of the Pandya king Sundara Pandya (1251-64).

184 of 1892 (Sanskrit verse) — Right of west entrance to the second prakara of the same temple. A record of the Pandya king Sundara Pandya (Jatavarman 1251-64.)

455 of 1902 (Tamil) — On the west wall of the second prakara of the Nataraja temple. A record inn the thirty-sixth year of the Pallava king Avaniyalappirandan Sakalabhuvanachakravartin Kopperunjingadeva. Records gift of land. He was the contemporary of Rajaraja III (1216-48), who made himself master of an extensive part of Chola dominions and ruled from 1243 to 1280. See S.A. 124, etc. for details.

456 of 1902 (Tamil) — On the same wall. A record in the thirty-sixth year of the Pallava king Sakalabhuvanachakravartin Kopperunjingadeva. Records an order of Venadudiyan, referring to a gift of land.

457 of 1902 (Tamil) — On the same wall. A record in the ninth year (and eighty-eighth day) of the Chola king Kulottunga Chola III. Published in *South Ind. Inscr.* Vol. III, No. 86, pp. 210-3. Records a grant of land to temple by a certain Keralarajan, for a flower garden. The inscription gives very minute fractions of velis and land measures and is thus of value to the historian of land tenure and revenue.

458 of 1902 (Tamil) — On the same wall. A record in the eleventh year (and one hundred and eighteenth day) of the Chola king Kulottunga Chola III. (Published in Ibid No. 87, pp. 213-17. Records the king's sanction of a grant of land to the temple by a certain Valuvarayan for the maintenance of a flower garden.)

459 of 1902 (Tamil) — On the same wall. A record in the fifth year of the Pallava king Sakalabhuvanachakravartin Kopperunjingadeva. Records an order of Solakon of Aragur or Perumal Pillai, one of the King's chief officers. He was the brother of Venadudiyan referred to in S.A. 32.

460 of 1902 (Tamil) — On the same wall. A record in the eighth year of the Pallava king Sakalabhuvanachakravartin Kopperunjingadeva. Records an order of Solakon. See S.A. 329 for details about Kopperunjingadeva. [In Ins. S. Dts. (Mack. MSS) p. 163, No. 5, an inscription of this chief in this year granting 1½ velis etc., to the goddess and houses for worshippers, is given but it is doubtful whether it is the same].

461 of 1902 (Tamil) — On the west wall of the second prakara of the Nataraja temple. A record in the thirty-fourth

year of the Pallava king Sakalabhuvanachakravartin Kopperunjingadeva. Records an order of Venadudiyan, brother of Solakon.

462 of 1902 (Tamil) — On the north wall of the same prakara. A record in the third year of the Pallava king Sakalabhuvanachakravartin Kopperunjingadeva. Records gift of land. Compare Ep. Ind. Vol. III, page 166.

463 of 1902 (Tamil) — On the same wall. A record in the fifth year of the Pallava king Sakalabhuvanachakravartin Kopperunjingadeva. Records an order of Solakon.

464 of 1902 (Tamil) — On the same wall. A record in the fifth year of the Pallava king Sakalabhuvanachakravartin Kopperunjingadeva. Records an order of Solakon.

465 of 1902 (Tamil) — On the same wall. A record in the third year of the Pallava king Sakalabhuvanachakravartin Kopperunjingadeva. Records an order of Salokan.

466 of 1902 (Tamil) — On the same wall. A record in the third year of the Pallava king Sakalabhuvanachakravartin Kopperunjingadeva. Records an order of Solakon.

467 of 1902 (Tamil) — On the same wall. A record in the sixteenth year of the Palava king Sakalabhuvanachakravartin Kopperunjingadeva. Records an order of Solakon.

468 of 1902 (Tamil) — On the same wall. A record in the sixteenth year of the Pallava king Sakalabhuvanachakravartin Kopperunjingadeva. Records an order of Solakon.

390 of 1903 (Tamil) — On the east wall of the central shrine in the Tillayamman temple. A record in the third year of the Pallava king Sakalabhuvanachakravartin Kopperunjingadeva. Records gift of land.

391 of 1903 (Tamil) — On the same wall. A record in the third year of the Pallava king Sakalabhuvanachakravartin Kopperunjingadeva. Records sale of land.

392 of 1903 (Tamil) — On the south wall of the same

shrine. Records in the third year sale of land. The king's name is not mentioned.

393 of 1903 (Tamil) — On the north wall of the same shrine. A record in the third year of the Pallava king Sakalabhuvanachakravartin Kopperunjingadeva. Records sale of land.

394 of 1903 (Tamil) — On the north base of the mandapa in front of the same shrine. A record in the fifth year of the Pallava king Sakalabhuvanachakravartin Kopperunjingadeva. Records sale of land.

395 of 1903 (Tamil) — On the south wall of the same mandapa. Records in the third year of the sale of land. The king's name is not mentioned.

396 of 1903 (Tamil) — On the same wall. The king's name is not mentioned. Provides in the fourteenth year of the supply of saffron and other goods required for the temple of Tillavanamudaiya Paramesuri.

397 of 1903 (Tamil) — On the same wall. A record of the Pallava king Sakalabhuvanachakravartin Kopperunjingadeva, the date of which is doubtful. Records sale of land.

398 of 1903 (Tamil) — On the north wall of the same mandapa. A record in the fifth year of the Pallava king Sakalabhuvanachakravartin Kopperunjingadeva. Records sale of land.

399 of 1903 (Tamil) — On the same wall. A record in the third year of the Pallava king Sakalabhuvanachakravartin Kopperunjingadeva. Records sale of land.

400 of 1903 (Tamil) — On the south and east walls of the Bhairava shrine in the same temple. A record of the Pallava king Sakalabhuvanachakravartin Kopperunjingadeva, the date of which is doubtful. Records an order of Solakon.

401 of 1903 (Tamil) — On the north wall of the same shrine. A record in the eighth year (A.D. 1250) of the Pallava

king Sakalabhuvanachakravartin Kopperunjingadeva. Mentions the temple of Varanavasi Madevar, and records a sale of land to Solakonar for building a temple of Pidariyar.

260 of 1913 (Tamil) — On the south wall of the Bhimeswara temple at Singaratoppu near the same place. A record in the sixth year, Karkataka, first day of the Chola king Tribhuvanachakravartin Virarajendradeva (Kulottunga III, 1178-1216). Records gift of land at the hamlet of Manalur for two lamps to the temple of Tirukkalanjedi Mahadeva at Perumbarrapuliyur, a taniyur in Rajadhirajavalanadu.

261 of 1913 (Tamil) — On the same wall. A record in the eleventh year, Mesha, fifth day of the Pallava king Sakalabhuvanachakravartin Kopperunjingadeva. Records sale of nine mas of land, for 5,000 kasus to the temple of Nayanar Tirukkalanjedi Udaiyar at Pannangudichcheri or Paramesarinallur, a hamlet of Perumbalapuliyur. The land sold was a field of the western hamlet of Ilanangur or Sundarasolapandyanallur which was situated in Gangaikondasolaperilamainadu and the sale was witnessed by the assembly of the village. (It is not improbable that Sundarasolapandyanallur owed its name to the son of Rajendrachola I.)

262 of 1913 (Tamil) — On the north wall of the same temple. A record in the second year and one hundred and twenty-fifth day of the Chola king Parakesarivarman or Tribhuvanachakravartin Kulottunga Choladeva III (1178-86). Registers an order of the king, that from this date, the assessed lands (tarram-perra-nilam) standing in the name of the Subrahmaniyapillayar shrine in the Arumoliswara temple of this village be included with those of the latter, that the lands declared to be superior to eighth class be assessed as per those of the eighth class (ettam tarram) and that those below the eighth class be allowed to continue as

before and that the site of the temple Tiruttondathogai
Isvaram Udaiyar, its enclosures, premises and the sacred
tank, till now included in the account of assessed lands, be
removed from that register. The order was executed by the
"land survey" committee (milam alavupadi pperumakkal) of
the village assembly of Perumbarrappuliyur. Full details of
the lands (extent, boundaries, etc.) this dealt with are
recorded. (The inscription is of great value in the history of
land revenue assessment. Similar land survey and
assessments were made in the time of Rajaraja I and
Kulottunga I. See No. 109 below.)

263 of 1913 (Tamil) — On the same wall. A record in the
second year, and one hundred and twenty-first day of the
Chola king Tribhuvanachakravartin Rajadhirajadeva or
Karikala Choladeva. Refers to the order registered in No. 262
(S.A. 54) and states that it was issued by Villavarayan at the
request of Vaidumbarayan. The document is signed by ten
officers of the king of whom the Tirumandira Olainayaka was
Narayana Muvendavelan. As these officers occur in the
inscriptions of Kulottunga Chola III, the government
epigraphist surmises that Rajadhiraja Karikala was his
another name.

264 of 1913 (Tamil) — On the same wall. A record in the
seventeenth year, Kanni, twenty-first day of the Chola king
Tribhuvanachakravartin Kulottunga Choladeva III (1178-
1216), 'who took Madurai (Madura) and was pleased to take
the crowned head of the Pandya.' Records gift of interest on
1,100 kasus for maintaining a lamp and a lampstand. It is
stipulated that the grant is to be renewed at the end of every
five years, after it is produced after each period before the
assembly and the *sthanattar*.

265 of 1913 (Tamil) — On the same wall. A damaged
record on the Chola king Tribhuvanachakravartin Kulottnga

Choladeva III (1178-1216) 'who was pleased to take Madurai (Madura), Ilam (Ceylon) and the crowned head of the Pandya,' in his twentieth year and one hundred and twenty-first day. Seems to record a gift of lamp.

266 of 1913 (Tamil) — On the east wall of the first prakara of the Nataraja temple, right of entrance. A record in the seventeenth year and two hundred and seventy-second day of the Chola king Tribhuvanachakravartin Rajarajadeva. Records gift of land belonging to the village of Pandur or Kulottungasolan Vallam in Rajadhirajavalanadu for maintaining the feeding house named Arapperunjeleisolal at Perumbarrappuliyur in the west street called Mudittalaigonda Perumal Tiruvidhi.

267 of 1913 (Tamil) — In the same place. A record in the fourth year and two hundred and fiftieth day of the Chola king Tribhuvanachakravartin Rajarajadeva. Records gift of land for the offering called tiruppavadai on the day of Pushya in the month of Tai to the god Aludaiyar. The inscription was ordered to be engraved on the Kulottungasolantirumaligai by the Tirumandiravolai Rajanarayana Muvendavelan.

268 of 1913 (Tamil) — On the same wall, left of entrance. A record in the third year and ninety-fifth day of the Chola king Parakesarivarman or Tribhuvanachakravartin Vikrama Choladeva (1118-35). Records gift of land by a native of Tiraimur in Tiraimurnadu which was a district of Uyyakondar-valanadu at Manarkudikattalai, a hamlet of Jayangondasolachaturvedimangalam in Merkalnadu, a sub-division of Virudarajabhayankaravalanadu, for a flower garden. Also records another gift of land in Pannanangudichcheri or Parakesarinallur which was a hamlet of Perumbarappuliyur with four tenants (kudi) for maintaining the garden and for providing the mantrapushpa in the temple of Tiruchchirrambalam Udaiyar.

269 of 1913 (Tamil) — In the same place. A record in the eighth year and fifty-seventh day of the Pandya king Maravarman Tribhuvanachakravartin Vira Pandyadeva. Registers that under the orders of Vikrama Pandya Gangeyarayan some land was set apart for building a quarter to be inhabited exclusively by the weavers (soliya saliyar) and named Teriyavaraninraperumalpuram, on condition that these weavers supplied four pieces new cloth (every year) to the goddess Sivakamasundari on the day of the Tiruppudiyidu festival and five other small pieces cloth for the shrines of Tirugnanasambandan. See S.A. 71 below, for the identity of the king. The Saliyars are described in Mr. Thurston's *Castes and Tribes*, Vol. VI, p. 276-9.

270 of 1913 (Tamil) — In the same place. A record in the fifth year and two hundred and seventieth day of the Pandya king Maravarman Tribhuvanachakravartin Vikrama Pandyadeva. Built in at the beginning. Registers that, under orders of Gangeyarayan, land was granted for supplying garlands on the occasion of the service called Rajakkalnayan-sandi after the king, and on the day of a festival called Rajakalnayanperiyatirumal. See S.A. 71 below.

271 of 1913 (Tamil) — In the same place. A record of the Vijayanagara king Mahamandaleswara Srirangaraya VI in S. 1565, Svabhanu, Panguni 7, Panchami, Friday and Revati, which Mr. Swamikannu Pillai calculated to be 2nd February, A.D. 1644. (The real month, however, he says, must be Masi and not Panguni.) Records that the king repaired the big mandapa in front of the Tillai Govindarajaswamin shrine in Tiru Chitrakudam, the gopura of the shrine, the vimanas of the goddess Pundarikavallinachchiyar and Sudikkodutta-nachchiyar and the mandapa in front of Tiruvali-Alwan. He is also stated to have made rent-free the five villages Adur, Karunguli, Kuriyamangalam, Marudantanallur and Udaiyur

in which the Sri Vaishnavas were permanently living. (See Ind. S. Dts., p. 162, No. 2. For the history of the Govindaraja shrine see note to the next inscription. Here it may be noted that the members of the last Vijayanagar dynasty were staunch. Vaishnavites had the Tatacharyas for their gurus.)

272 of 1913 (Tamil) — On the south wall of the same prakara. A record of the Vijayanagara king Achutaya Maharaya in S. 1461, Vishnu (wrong) Mithuna, su. di, 14, Sadhyayoga, Saturday, Anuradha, which corresponded according to Mr. Swamikannu Pillai, to May 31, A.D. 1539. The king ordered that the image of Tillai Govindaraja Perumal at Perumbalapuliyur in Valudalambattuusavadi, a sub-division of Vennaiyurnadu in Rajadhirajavalanadu, might be set up according to the ritual of Vaikhanasa Sutra, and granted 500 pons which was the income from four villages for the upkeep of daily worship. The Govindaraja shrine has held an eventful history. That it existed in the Pallava period is proved by the fact that the Alwars Kulasekharan and Tirumagai Mannan refer to it. The next reference is by Manikkavasaga who must be assigned to the middle of the ninth century. See his *Tiruchchirrambalakovai*, Stanza 86. Coming to the Chola times we find from the Kulottunga Cholanulla, the Rajarajanulla and the Takkayagapparani the Kulottunga II, a bigotted Saivite, threw the image of Govindaraja into the sea. The Vaishnavite Guruparamparas on the contrary, say that in the time of Ramanuja, the Chitrakuta at Chidambaram was 'destroyed,' the image of Govindaraja was removed by the Vaishnavas to Tirupati, and that Ramanuja formally solemnized the consecration ceremony. See *Vadag Gurup.* 1913, p. 86. It is difficult to say whether the Tamil literary works mentioned above and the Guruparampara refer to the same incident. According to tradition, Ramanuja lived till 1137 and Kullottunga II ruled

as sole monarch from 1135 to 1146 and jointly with his predecessor Vikrama Chola from 1123 to 1135. If the vandalism of Kulottunga II followed his sole assumption of power, then the removal of the Vishnu shrine at Chidambaram and the consecration of the new shrine at Lower Tirupati should have been about 1135-6. The next literary reference to the fortunes of the shrine is in the time of Vedanta Desika. The Guruparampara says that he took advantage of an internal commotion in Chidambaram to make Goppanaraya of Gingee to re-establish the image about 1370. See *Vadag Gurup*. 1913, p. 154. The Prapannamritam, on the other hand, attributes this honour to Mahacharya or Doddacharya of Sholingur and of Rama Raya of "Chandragiri," whom it wrongly supposes to be a king and successor of Krishnadeva Raya. The present inscription would support the version of the Prapanamruita if Rama Raya is taken to be a mistake for Achyuta Raya. If not, we should have to support that after Achyuta Raya there was another Saivite attempt to remove the idol and a final restoration of it by Mahacharya and late in the sixteenth century. See Ins. S. Dts. p. 162, No. 1.

273 of 1913 (Tamil) — On the same wall. A record in the thirty-second year and one hundred and sixtieth day of the Chola king Tribhuvanachakravartin Tribhuvanaviradeva (1178-1216) "who, having taken Madurai (Madura), Ilam (Ceylon), Karuvur and the crowned head of the Pandya was pleased to perform the anointment of the heroes and the anointment of victors". Records that a gift of land for a flower garden called Ponambalakuttan, in the village of Koyilpundi, a hamlet of Perumbarappuliyur, was made to the temple of Aludaiyar by a certain Ponnambalakuttan or Nandipanman. He also provided for its upkeep by another gift of another piece of land made at Serundimangalam, which was a hamlet of Tyagavallichaturvedimangalam in Merkanadu. These

transactions and gifts were engraved on the walls of the
temple by the order of the king's officers at the request of
Nandipanman.

274 of 1913 (Tamil) — On the same wall. A record in the
fifteenth year and three-hundred and sixty-third day of the
Pandya king Jatavarman or Tribhuvanachakravartin Sundara
Padyadeva. Records an order of Villavarayan and other
officers of the king that the maintenance of the worship and
offerings in the temple of Devargal Nayanar was to be met
from certain grants of land made to that temple. (The chief
Vilavarayan occurs in S.A. 55 in the reign of Kolottunga III,
1178-1216. As the Sundara Pandya referred to is probably the
first of that name who ruled from 1251 to 1264, it is probable
that the Villavarayan of this epigraph is a son or successor of
his namesake in the other.)

275 of 1913 (Tamil) — On the same wall. An incomplete
record in the fourteenth year and one hundred and twenty-
fourth day of the Pandya king Jatavarman or Tribhuvanachakravartin Sundara Pandyadeva. Registers another order of
Villavarayan with reference to certain grants of land
providing flower garlands to the god and goddess. One of
these was situated in Vikramasolanallur (also called
Akkanpallipadai) near Perumbarappuliyur and was granted
by Svamidevar. Still another grant of land, in the hamlet of
Kolam or Solakeraladevanallur, was made for providing
offerings on the occasion when the images were taken on
procession to the sea.

276 of 1913 (Tamil) — On the same wall. A record in the
sixth year and three hundred and fifty-fifth day of the Pandya
king Maravarman or Tribhuvanachakravartin Vikrama
Pandyadeva. Registers an order of Vangattarayan to the temple
authorities to engrave on the walls of Vikramasolan Tirumaligai
the gift of lands in Pallipadai or Vikramasolanallur,

Erukkattanjeri or Jayangondasolanallur and Manalur or Jayangondasolanallur, for the flower garden Ulagamiludumaiyal Tirunadavanam which was so named after the queen. (The Pandyan king referred to came to the throne in A.D. 1282. He boasts of his conquests over the Cholas, Viragandagopala and Ganapati of the Kakataiya dynasty. See S.A. 342 and S.A. 157.)

277 of 1913 (Tamil) — On the same wall. A record in the thirteenth year of the Pandya king Tribhuvanachakravartin Konerimaikondan Sundara Pandyadeva (1? 1251-64). Registers the founding of an agrahara named Vikrama Pandya-chaturvedimangalam on the western side of Perumbarappuliyur and its presentation to 108 learned Brahmans. For the maintenance of these and of other village accessories (gramaparikara) the village Rajasikhamaninallur or Puliyangudi on the western bank of Ponneri was acquired and granted, being divided into 147 ¾ shares (pangu). The process of the foundation of a new village is typically illustrated here. For details see *Ep. Rep.* 1914, p. 92.

278 of 1913 (Tamil) — On the same wall. A record in the fifth year and 31st day of Tribhuvanachakravartin Konermaikondan. Records gift of 116 velis of land of Adur or Jnanathanallur to 108 Brahmans, to the god Ulagamududaiyapillayar, the matha etc. of Uagumududaiya-chaturvedimangalam, a hamlet on the western side of Perumba-rappuliyur. The recipients had no tax to pay, but to measure out 4 kalams on each veli of land to the temple of Tillainayaka as the donees of Vikrama Pandyachaturvedimangalam did. (See note to the above).

279 of 1913 (Tamil) — On the same wall. A record in the fourth year and 192nd day of the Pandya king Maravarman Tribhuvanachakravartin Vira Pandyadeva. Registers an order of Pallavarayan to the temple authorities to engrave on the

walls of the Kulottungasolantirumaligai, a gift of land for
offerings to the shrine of Alagiya Tiruchchirrambalamudaiyar
built by a Brahman at the hamlet of Karrangudi or
Pavitramanikanallur. Mr. Krishna Sastri suggests that this
king was the successor of Maravarman Vikrama Pandya (like
whom he had the title Rajakkal Tambiran) and identical with
that Vira Pandya who was the enemy of the Kerala king
Ravivarman Kulasekara. (See S.A. 61, 87, 112, 120, and 178.)

280 of 1913 (Tamil) — On the north wall of the same
prakara. A record in the fourteenth year and 107th day of
the Chola king Tribhuvanachakravartin Rajarajadeva
(probably Rajaraja III, 1216-48). Records gift of land at
Tiruniruchcholamangalam by a certain king Kalingarayan
for supplying 500 jackfruits, 5,000 mangoes and 5,000
plantains to the temple of Aludaiya Nayanar. The assembly
of that village agreed to make that land rent-free by charging
the taxes due on it to the village. The Tirumandiravolai was
Neriyudaichchola Muvendavelan. (See *Ins. S. Dts.* (Mack.
MSS.) p. 164, No. 8).

281 of 1913 (Tamil) — On the same wall. A record in
the tenth year and 235th day of the Chola king
Tribhuvanachakravartin Rajarajadeva. Built in at the end.
Records gift of land by two private individuals for a flower
garden. Provision was also made for the servants who looked
after the garden. (The Chola king, we may presume, was
Rajaraja III, 1216-48.)

282 of 1913 (Tamil) — On the same wall. Records in the
third year that under orders of Tondaiman, a land was
presented at Midinikkudi or Danavinodanallur for a flower
garden and made tax-free and the same was engraved on the
walls of Vikramasolantirumaligai.

283 of 1913 (Tamil) — On the same wall. A record in
the third year and 15th day of the Chola king

Tribhuvanachakravartin Rajarajadeva (III? 1216-48). Records gift of land at Vallam in Vennaiyurnadu, a sub-division of Rajadhirajavalanadu, for supplying a garland of 130 red lotuses every day. The document registering this grant was engraved under orders of Tondaiman, the Tirumandiravolai being Minavan Muvendavelan.

284 of 1913 (Tamil) — On the same wall. A record in the thirty-ninth year and 224th day of the Chola king Tribhuvanachakravartin Tribhuvanaviradeva (1178-1216) "who having taken Madurai (Madura), Ilam (Ceylon), Karuvur and the crowned head of the Pandya was pleased to perform the anointment of heroes and the anointment of victors." Registers an order for three officers of the king viz., Tondaiman, Tiruvaiyarudaiyan and Madhurantaka Brahma Marayan, that lands granted by certain Lankesvaran of Kiliyur for providing 206 red lotuses to the temple and for maintaining the people that grew them, was to be engraved on the walls of Vikramasolan Tirumaligai. The Tirumandiravolai is stated to be Neriyudaichchola Muvendavelan. Still another gift of land by the same person made for a flower garden in the "thirty-fourth year and fifty-second day" of the king was also engraved, the old document having "become worn out."

285 of 1913 (Tamil) — On the same wall. A record in the seventeenth year and 197th day of the Chola king Tribhuvanachakravartin Rajarajadeva (III? 1216-48). Records gift of garden land at Koyilpundi, a hamlet of Perumbalapuliyur, for providing garlands to the shrines of the god and the goddess by a certain Vanadhirajan. The order of the grant was as usual engraved on the walls of the temple.

286 of 1913 (Tamil) — On the same wall. A record in the fifth year and 353rd day of the Pandya king Maravarman

300

South Indian Shrines

Tribhuvanachakravartin Kulasekharadeva I (1268-1308).
Built in at the end. Records an order of Chediyarayan, to
engrave on the temple walls a gift of land for providing
offerings in a shrine situated in one of the streets of
Perumbarappuliyur. (The Chediyarayan of this inscription
could not bave been the same as the Pillai Perumal
Chediyarayan who figures in the life of Kamba.)

287 of 1913 (Tamil) — On the same wall. Registers in the
seventh year and 225th day of the king an order of Tondaiman
that an arrangement regarding a certain land made in order
to provide flowers, coconuts etc. be engraved on the wall of
Vikramasolantirumaligai.

288 of 1913 (Tamil) — On the same wall. A record in the
ninth year and 200th day of the Pandya king Sundara
Pandyadeva, "who was pleased to take all countries." Records
gift of land and order of Villavadaraiyan approving of certain
arrangements about specified temple's lands made by the
assembly (mula-parushaiyar) of Perumbarappuliyur. (The
king referred to was evidently Jatavarman Sundara Pandya I,
1251-64).

289 of 1913 (Tamil) — On the same wall. A record in the
seventh year and 252nd day of the Pandya king Sundara
Pandyadeva, "who was pleased to take all countries" (1251-
64). The first ten lines are engraved over another inscription
of Vikrama Choladeva, beginning with the historical
introduction.Mentions order of Tondaiman to the temple
authorities remitting certain taxes on lands which had been
originally granted for the maintenance of the servants of a
flower garden belonging to the temple. The reason for the
remission was that the said lands, being close to the sea, had
become filled up with sand and overgrown with weeds.
Mentions Virarakshasa Velaikkarar. (For an explanation of the
Velir see Abhidanachintamani, p. 933).

290 of 1913 (Tamil) — On the same wall. A record in the forty-seventh year of the Chola king Tribhuvanachakravartin Kulottunga Choladeva I. This is stated to be a copy of an inscription originally engraved on the opposite side shrine (Edir Ambalam). Records gift of land by purchase for supplying garlands of red lotuses to the temple.

291 of 1913 (Tamil) — On the same wall. An unfinished record in the forty-sixth year, Simha, 22nd tedi, of the Chola king Tribhuvanachakravartin Kulottunga Choladeva. This is evidently also a copy. Refers to the purchase of a devadana land by a private individual. (22½ nilas for 10 kalanjus).

292 of 1913 (Tamil) — On the same wall. Registers an order of Villavarayan and four other officers assigning the income in paddy from certain lands originally granted for the upkeep of a flower garden, for the maintenance of the servants of the temple and of the flower garden.

293 of 1913 (Tamil) — (Tamil) On the same wall. A record in the eleventh year and fifty-sixth day of the Pandya king Jatavarman or Tribhuvanachakravartin Sundara Pandyadeva (I? 1251-64). An order of the same officer remitting assesments on certain lands granted to the temple for a flower garden. The transactions were engraved on the Vikramasolan Tirumaligai.

294 of 1913 (Tamil) — On the same wall. Registers that certain lands granted by Gangeyarayan were made tax-free and exempted from duties. The car procession was to be maintained and the temple was to receive 100 kasus as kudimai assesment and 6 kalams of paddy as virabhoga on each veli of land.

295 of 1913 (Tamil) — On the same wall. A record in the fourth year and eighteenth day of the Pandya king Maravarman Tribhuvanachakravartin Vikrama Pandyadeva (1282?). Records an order of Kulasekharan Solakon

exempting duties and assessments on lands presented by a certain Chediyarayan for maintaining 36 persons employed in a watershed in the mandapa known as Anaiyerrukudam, south of the seven-storeyed gopura, 54 persons who prepared offerings for the god, 32 learned Brahmans, another 54 persons who prepared offerings at Shiali (the shrine of goddess) and lastly the temple supervisors. (See S.A. 71.)

296 of 1913 (Tamil) — On the north wall of the second prakara of the same temple. A record in the sixth year of the Pallava king Sakalabhuvanachakravartin Avaniyalappirandan or Kopperunjingadeva. Registers an order of Solakon that certain arrangements made by the temple authorities and the village assembly regarding the gift of a flower garden and the maintenance of its servants, may be engraved on the temple.

297 of 1913 (Tamil) — On the same wall. A damaged record in the eighth year of the Pandya king Jatavarman or Tribhuvanachakravartin Sundara Pandyadeva (1? 1251-64). Records an order of Kalappalarayar to register, as tirunamattukkani, certain lands granted for conducting festivals and providing offerings in the temple of Tiruchchirrambala Makali which was founded on the south side of the road by which the god was taken in procession for the sea-bath, and to engrave the same on stone.

298 of 1913 (Tamil) — On the same wall. A record in the thirty-fourth year and forty-fifth day of the Chola king Tribhuvanachakravartin Tribhuvanaviradeva III (1178-1216), "who being pleased to take Madurai (Madura), Karuvur, Ilam (Ceylon), and the crowned head of the Pandya, was pleased to perform the anointment of heroes and the anointment of victors." Registers that at the request of the chiefs Pottappicholan and Karanai Villupperiyan, the original documents pertaining to a gift of land which was made to the

temple for a flower garden, were preserved in the treasury of the temple and engraved on its walls.

299 of 1913 (Tamil) — On the same wall. A damaged record in the second year and fourteenth day of the Chola king Tribhuvanachakravartin Rajarajadeva (III?). Records gift of land for providing flower garlands to the temple. The grant was ordered to be engraved on the temple walls and the original documents deposited in the temple treasury. The Royal Secretary (tirumandiraolai) was Rajendrasinga-Muven-davelan.

300 of 1913 (Tamil) — On the same wall. A record in the second year and fourteenth day of the Chola king Tribhuvanachakravartin Rajarajadeva (III?). Records gift of lands for a flower garden and its servants by the donor mentioned in No. 91 above.

301 of 1913 (Tamil) — On the same wall. A record in the thirty-sixth year and one hundredth day of the king. A number of lands which had been granted for a flower garden and were partly utilised by the servants of the garden were included at the donor's request in the tirunamattukkani lands of the temple and the fact engraved on the temple walls. The tirumandiraolai was Neriyudaichchola Muvendavelan.

302 of 1913 (Tamil) — On the same wall. A record in the twelfth year of the Pallava king Sakalabhuvanachakravartin Avaniyalappirandan or Kopperunjingadeva. Registers an order of Perumal Pillai or Solakon and mentions the gift of land for a flower gorden.

303 of 1913 (Tamil) — On the same wall. A record in the third year and the fifty-seventh day of the Chola king Tribhuvanachakravartin Rajarajadeva. Mentions the gift of land for a flower garden by Umaiyalvi, daughter of Vijayanulamban, chief of Nulambapadi or Nigarilisolamandalam. She had purchased the land from different people.

304 of 1913 (Tamil) — On the same wall. A record in the seventh yer of the Pallava king Sakalabhuvanachakravartin Avanaiyalappirandan or Kopperunjingadeva. Registers an order of Solakon recording gift of land for a flower garden by a dancing girl.

305 of 1913 (Tamil) — On the same wall. A record in the seventh year of the Pallava king Sakalabhuvanachakravartin Avaniyalappirandan or Kopperunjingadeva. Registers an order of Solakon that eight sandi oblations like those offered at the shrine of Mulasthanam Udaiyar in (the temple of) Tiruchchirrambalam be also offered at the shrine of Dakshinamurti and that the gift of land made for providing five of these eight sandis, be made tax-free.

306 of 1913 (Tamil) — On the same wall. A record in the ninth year and eighty-fifth day of the Chola king Tribhuvanachakravartin (Rajarajadeva). Registers an order of the king's officers passed at the request of Gangeyarayan that certain lands granted to the temple for supplying flowers and maintaining the servants of the flower gardens, were to be made free of kudimai; that the documents pertaining to the lands in question were to be deposited in the temple treasury (tirukkaiotti?) and that the transaction was to be engraved on the walls of the temple.

307 of 1913 (Tamil) — On the same wall. A record in the seventeenth year of the Pallava king Sakalabhuvanachakravartin Kopperunjingadeva. Registers an order of Solakon that a gift of land was made for additional offerings in the shrine of Dakshinamurtideva (referred to in No. 305 above), and that this land was made a rent-free tirunamtatukkani under the command of the king.

308 of 1913 (Tamil) — On the same wall. A record in the eighth year of the Pallava king Sakalabhuvanachakravartin Avaniyalappirandan or Kopperunjingadeva. Registers an

order of Solakon that the Saliya merchants (nagara) were to be provided with land for building their houses on condition that they would supply the necessary cloths for the parisattam of the god and the goddess.

309 of 1913 (Tamil) — On the same wall. A record in the twelfth year and one hundred and twenty-fifth day; and Kumbha, eighth day (in the middle of the record) of the Chola king Tribhuvanachakravartin Kulottunga Choladeva III (1178-1216), "who was pleased to take Madurai (Madura) and the crowned head of the Pandya." Registers that a certain Edirilisolan or Irungolan founded a temple called Vikramasolisvaramudaiyar at Parakesarinallur, a hamlet of Perumbarappuliyur, after acquiring the required land from various people and having provided for houses of Brahmans and temple servants. The king ordered the assessment on this land to be deducted from the revenue of the village, to be entered in the temple accounts with the original documents preserved in the temple and the whole transaction engraved on the walls of the temple.

310 of 1913 (Tamil) — On the same wall. A Record in the twenty-first year and sixth day of the Chola king Tribhuvanachakravartin Kulottunga Choladeva III (1178-1216), "who was pleased to take Madurai (Madura) and the crowned head of the Pandya." Registers that a land was granted for a flower garden and another for maintaining its four servants. It was ordered that these lands might be included with other temple lands and that the excess (madakku) in measurement be deducted from the village accounts. The tirumandiraolai was Minavan Muvendavelan.

311 of 1913 (Tamil) — On the same wall. A record in the sixteenth year and two hundred and twenty-fourth day of the Chola king Tribhuvanachakravartin Kulottunga Choladeva III (1178-1216), "who was pleased to take Madurai (Madura)

and the crowned head of the Pandya." Records gift of land for a flower garden and its servants. Again the excess of land discovered by comparison with existing village accounts was granted to the temple and the village accountants (varikkuruseyvar) were ordered to correct their figures. The servants of the garden were exempted from certain services usual to nibandakarar. The tirumandiraolai was Rajanarayana Muvendavelan.

312 of 1913 (Tamil) — On the same wall. A record in the tenth year Simha, ninth day of the Pallava king Sakalabhuvanachakravartin Avaniyalappirandan or Kopperunjingadeva. Registers an order of Perumal Pillai or Solakon made for the welfare of the king. Records an exchange of land and refers incidentally to the temple (Srikoil) of the pidari called Tiruchchirrambala Makali on the south side of the street Vikkiramasolanterkuttiruvidi by which the god was taken on procession to the sea. See S.A. 32.

313 of 1913 (Tamil) — On the same wall. A record in the thirty-fourth year and fifty-second day of teh Chola king Tribhuvanachakravartin Tribhuvanaviradeva Kulottunga III (1178-1216), "who having pleased to take Madurai (Madura), Karuvur, Ilam (Ceylon) and the crowned head of the Pandya was pleased to perform the anointment of heroes and the anointment of victors." Records gift of land for a flower garden. It was ordered that the four servants of the garden must supply iruvachchi, malligai, and nandyavattai flowers to the temple regularly; when these failed other flowers had to be supplied.

314 of 1913 (Tamil) — On the same wall. A record in the thirty-ninth year of the Chola king Tribhuvanachakravartin Tribhuvanaviradeva (1178-1216), "who having been pleased to take Madurai (Madura), Karuvur, Ilam (Ceylon) and the crowned head of the Pandya was pleased to perform the anointment of heroes and the anointment of victors." Records

gift of land for a flower garden to supply flowers to the temple of the goddess. Refers to a transaction which happened in the thirty-third year of the king.

315 of 1913 (Tamil) — On the same wall. A record in the second year and sixty-ninth day of the Chola king Tribhuvanachakravartin Rajarajadeva (III? 1216-48). Registers that an additional land was granted by a certain Kundan or Lankesvara of Arasur for the maintenance of a flower garden which had been already granted by himself for supplying 700 red lotuses to the temple every day. The ten servants and a nayaka who cultivated the garden were permitted to utilise the land given to them as a kani. The transaction was engraved on the temple walls.

316 of 1913 (Tamil) — On the same wall. A record in the tenth year and three hundred and sixtieth day of the Chola king Tribhuvanachakravartin Rajarajadeva (III ? 1216-48). Registers that a flower garden had been founded for the benefit of the temple by a certain Karrupparudaiyan or Rajadhirajapallavarayan at the hamlet of Koilpundi called Kshatriyasikhamaninallur. It mentions that land in three different villages had been granted for the maintenance of the gardeners who had to water the flower plants, pick flowers and supply them to the temple, and that these lands were now included with other temple lands under orders of the King's officers, the transaction being engraved on temple walls and the original documents deposited in the temple treasury.

317 of 1913 (Tamil) — On the same wall. A record in the third year and twenty-fourth day of the Chola king Tribhuvanachakravartin Rajarajadeva. Records gift of land for growing red lotuses and for providing food (korru) and cloth-money to the gardeners who grew them. Refers to the land survey made in the sixteenth year of Sungandavirtta Kulottungasoladeva I (1070-1118) and to the twenty-fifth

year of Periyadevar Tribhuvanaviradeva Kulottunga III (1178-86). See No. 262 above.

318 of 1913 (Tamil) — On the same wall. A record in the ninth year of the Pallava king Sakalabhuvanachakravartin Avanialappirandan or Kopperunjingadeva. Registers an order of Perumal Pillai or Solakon, that certain gifts of land for the maintenance of gardeners, be recorded on the temple walls. See No. 312 above.

319 of 1913 (Tamil) — On the same wall. A record in the nineteenth year of the Pallava king Sakalabhuvanachakravartin Avaniyalappirandan or Kopperunjingadeva. Solakon ordered that a gift of land for a grove of trees be made a rent-free devadana and so registered on the temple walls.

320 of 1913 (Tamil) — On the same wall. A record in the ninth year and one hundred and sixty-sixth day of the Pandya king Maravarman Tribhuvanachakravartin Vira Pandyadeva. Registers an order of Vira Pandyadeva Vanadhirayan that a gift of one tiruvolai together with a piece of land for the maintenance of the latter made by a certain Dipattaraiyan at Solakulavallinallur, may be deducted from the accounts of Solakulavallinallur and added to the devadana lands of the temple and that the transaction may be engraved on the temple wall. See S.A. 71.

321 of 1913 (Tamil) — On a pillar of the western entrance into the second prakara of the same temple. This pillar of the entrance was presented by Perumal Pillai or Solakonar, one of the chiefs of Avaniyalappirandan Kopperunjingadeva, for the merit of his master. (Mr. Krishna Sastri points out that, according to an inscription at Tripurantaka Kurnool district, a certain king Maharaja Sinha built the eastern gopuram of this temple aad decorated the four sides of it with booty acquired from the four quarters and that this king was evidently Kopperunjingadeva.)

322 of 1913 (Tamil) — On the second pillar in the same entrance. Records in S. 1422 Rudri, Avani, fifteenth day, that Tirumalaikolundar, the agent of Narasa Nayaka, while he was in charge of the temple, enforced that ten cake-offerings and betel leaves, which must be distributed among certain specified individuals for the merit of Narasa Nayaka, were not to be withheld from them and used otherwise. (For the highly interesting figures in the western gopura which are illustrative and descriptive of the dancing art in this age, see *Ep. Rep.* 1914, pp. 82-3. Mr. Krishna Sastri quotes from the Bharatiya Natya Sastra to show how scientific these representations are).

323 of 1913 (Tamil) — At the southern entrance into the first prakara of the temple on the left side. A record of the Vijayanagara king Virapratapa Virakrishnayadeva Maharaya in S. 1432, Paramoduta, Makara, ba. di. Amavasya, Monday, Puradam (December 10, A.D. 1510). Records gift of three villages with an income 1400 rekai (gadyana) for the machapuja in the temple of Alagiya Tiruchchirrambalamudaiya Tambiranar (included in Arasurkilparru, sub-division of Vennaiyurnadu in Rajadhirajavalanadu which was itself a district on the northern bank (of the Coleroon), included in the province of Bhuvanekapattana) and for the maintenance of a feeding house, by a certain sirmai Appa Pillai.

324 of 1913 (Tamil) — On the door post of a new entrance cut close to the east gopura of the same temple. Seems as No. 321 of (S.A. 113) above. The pillar evidently belonged to a different part of the temple and has been put at this entrance by the Nattukottai Chettis.

325 of 1913 (Tamil) — On the gopura at the main entrance into the Sivakamiamman shrine in the same temple. Same as S.A. 113.

326 of 1913 (Tamil) — On the east wall of the Mahishasuramardhani shrine in the same temple. A record in

the twelfth year of Pallava king Sakalabhuvanachakravartin Avaniyalappirandan or Kopperunjingadeva. Registers an order of Solakon that a gift of land made for a flower garden to the shrine of Andabharanadeva be engraved on the wall of the shrine and the original documents connected herewith, be preserved in the temple treasury.

327 of 1913 (Tamil) — On the same wall. A record in the tenth year of the Pallava king Sakalabhuvanachakravartin Avaniyalappirandan or Kopperunjingadeva. Registers on order of Solakon that a gift of land made for a flower garden to the shrine of Andabhananadeva be engraved on the wall of the shrine and the original documents connected therewith, be preserved in the temple treasury.

328 of 1913 (Tamil) — On the base of the Nandi mandapa opposite to the eastern gopura of the same temple. A record of the Pandya king Maravarman Tribhuvanachakravartin Vira Pandyadeva, the date of which is lost. Consists of a number of mutilated and unconnected pieces. Refers to an arrangement (vyavastha) made by the temple managers. See S.A. 71 for the identification of the king.

329 of 1913 (Tamil) — On the base of the Nand mandapa opposite to the southern gopura of the same temple. Consists of six verses of which five refers to a battle fought evidently at Chidambaram by a certain Munaiyan Vallaiyan Adittan, chief of Panaiseyyar, on behalf of the Pandya (Minavan) against the Chola (Valavan). The author of the poetry was Tayanalla Perumal Munaiyadarayan alias Bhuvanekavira Tondaiman.

330 of 1913 (Tamil) — On the base of a small shrine in the western prakara of the same temple. An incomplete record in the sixth year, Simha, 26th day, of the Pandya king Jatavarman or Tribhuvanachakravartin Sundara Pandyadeva (I? 1251-64). Contains some detailed account of land measurement.

331 of 1913 (Tamil) — On a slab built into the floor in front of the Ganapati shrine in the same temple. An unfinished record in manmatha, Dhanus. Refers to a gift by purchase of some godowns, by a certain Nagama Nayaka. (Was the father of Visvanatha Naik, the founder of the Naik dynasty of Madura?)

332 of 1913 (Tamil verse) — On the east gopura of the same temple, right of entrance. Consists of two verses, the first of which refers to a conquest of the Pandya king over the Chola, the latter being driven into the forest. The second mention Kadavarkon and his army melting away before the Pandya king Sundarattol. (Mr. Krishna Sastri identifies Kadavarkon with Kopperunjingadeva and the Pandya with Jatavarman Sundara Pandya I).

333 of 1913 (Tamil verse) — In the same place. A record of the Vijayanagara king Krishnaraya in S. 1443, Vrisha, Karttika. (Details not enough for calculation). Records that a certain Mangarasan granted the village of Chidambaranathapuram to the temple.

334 of 1913 (Tamil) — In the same place. A record of the Vijayanagara king Virapratapa Venkatadeva Maharaya I in S. 1500, Parthiva (wrong) Simha, su. di 10, Monday, Subhayoga, Svati. Records gift of four villages to the temple of Chidambaresvara and Sivakamasundara Ammai to provide oblations and sacred bath in early mornings, for the merit of Vaiyappa, Krishnappa Kondama Nayaka. An irregular date. Most probably June 24, A.D. 1577 is intended. See *Ep. Rep.* 1914, p. 69. See S.A. 131 for another endowment by the same chief.

335 of 1913 (Tamil) — In the same place. A record of the Vijayanagara king Venkatadeva Maharaya I in S. 1510, Sarvadari, Margali, twenty-second day. Records gift of 300 pon for providing 20 (rice) offerings to the god

Chidambaresvara and distributing the same among begging devotees. It is stated that this amount was till then being set apart by the temple for the ilakkai and korru of the king and his followers (rajagaram). "Date can be calculated but not verified."

336 of 1913 (Tamil) — In the same place. Contains three verses, the first of which refers to a battle fought on the banks of the Vallaru in which a certain Bhuvanekaraviran was victorious. (The last refers to Maravarman Vikrama Pandya, who came to the throne in 1283.)

337 of 1913 (Tamil verse) — In the same place. One verse describing the anger of Vikrama Pandya. (See note to the above inscription.)

338 of 1913 (Tamil verse) — In the same place. One verse in praise of Sundara Pandya (Jatavarman I) and his weighing himself against gold. See S.A. 124, 132, 153 etc. See *Ep. Ind.* III p. ii, where his covering the vimana of the Ranganatha temple with gold is referred to.

339 of 1913 (Tamil) — In the same place. A record of the Vijayanagara king Venkatadeva Maharaya I in S. 1510, Sarvadhari, Tai, twenty-second day. Registers that Vaiyappa Krishnappa Kondama Nayaka ordered that the 30 (rice) offerings for which he had provided 50,000 kalams of paddy in the district of Viranarayanachchirmai, be distributed among Saiva mendicants (tiruottunayanar). "Date can be calculated but not verified." See S.A. 126.

340 of 1913 (Tamil verse) — In the same place. Glorifies the prowess of Sundara Maran (Sundara Pandya) who annihillated the forces of the Telingas that surrounded him and drove the Bana chief into the forest. (The king was evidently Sundara Pandya I, Jatavarman, whose inscriptions have the introduction Anaittulahumkondaruliya who ruled from 1251 to 1264.)

341 of 1913 (Tamil) — In the same place. Mentions Solakulavalli and appears to make provisions for singing the pamalai (hymns) of the Nayanar (Saiva saints) in the temple of Tirumulattanamudaiyan. Also mentions the village of Kalumalam. A record in (date doubtful) Ani, Svati.

342 of 1913 (Tamil) — In the same place, left of entrance. Registers that Suppammal, mother of Ayyalammal, who was the wife of Pachchaiyappa Mudaliyar of Kanchipuram, repaired this eastern gopura and founded a Brahman settlement (Agrahara.)

343 of 1913 (Grantha) — In niches on the inner walls of the same gopura. These are labels engraved below images representing women in various dancing postures. The inscriptions are in Sanskrit. For a discussion of these postures as given in the Bharata Natya Sastra and Illustrations, see *Madr. Ep. Rep.* 1914, pp. 74-83.

344 of 1913 (Tamil) — On the south gopura of the same temple; right of entrance. A record of the Saluva king Virapratapa Timmaraya in S. 1425, Rudhirodgarin, Simha, su. di. 14, Sravana, Monday (which should be Sunday). Records that a certain Mondukoli Ramanayakkar Mallanayakar gave the village of Karikkudi, the western hamlet of Perumbarappuliyur, for a double garland and offerings to be offered every day. The king receives the usual Vijayanagara titles. The date corresponded to 6th August, A.D. 1503.

345 of 1913 (Tamil verse) — In the same place. A much damaged record mentions Porpuliyur.

346 of 1913 (Tamil) — In the same place. A record of the Vijayanagara king Venkatadeva Maharaya (Venkata I, 1586-1613) in S. 1510, Sarvadharin, Margali, 22nd day. Same as No. 335 (S.A. 127) above.

347 of 1913 (Tamil) — In the same place. A record of the Vijaynagara king Venkatadeva Maharaya (Venkata I, 1586-

1614) in S. 1510, Sarvadharin, Tai, 22nd day. Same as No. 339 (S.A. 131) above.

348 of 1913 (Tamil) — In the same place. A record of the Vijayanagara king Srirangadeva Maharaya II in S. 1503, Vrisha, Kumbha, su. Di. 84, Thursday (which should be Tuesday), Sravishtha (Dhanishta). Records gift of seven villages and of income from pepper trade called milagutaragu, for oblations and festivals in the shrines of the god and goddess, by Vaiyappa Krishnappa Kondama Nayaka. See S.A. 126, and S.A. 131. (I have traced this inscription to *Ins. S. Dts.*, p. 163, No. 4, but here the name of the king is given as Venkatadeva).

349 of 1913 (Tamil) — In the same place. A record of the Vijayanagara king Venkatadeva Maharaya (Venkata I, 1586-1614) in S. 1510, Sarvadharin, Tai, 22nd day. Records that the provision made by the chief for twenty offerings to be distributed among the Saiva mendicants (paradesi) in the temple, was placed under the supervision of Namassivaya Udaiyar, the "Superintendent of all services (kattalai)". (The name Namassivaya reminds the Tamil literary student of the Guru Namassivaya, the disciple of Guhai Namassivaya who devoted himself, at the instance of his teacher, to holy work at Chidambaram, who composed the Paramarahasyamalai, the Chidambaravenba etc. who ultimately died at Tirupperundurai.) See N.A. 614.

350 of 1913 (Tamil) — In the same place. A record in the fourth year and sixty-seventh day of the Pandya king Maravarman Tribhuvanachakravartin Virakerala or Kulasekharadeva. Registers an order of Sediyarayan exempting certain lands granted for a flower garden by a native of Pallikodu in Malaimandalam from paying kadamai and Kudimai and declaring that these lands might enjoy the privileges of irrigation by channels, percolation and baling.

The king was identical with Ravivarman Kulasekhara, the Kerala conqueror. See *Ep. Ind.* vol. IV, p. 145, Ibid. Vol. VIII, p. 8. His father Jayasimha had the title Virakerala. *Ep. Ind.* Vol. IV, p. 293.

351 of 1913 (Tamil) — On the same gopura; left of entrance. A record in the fourth year and one hundred and twenty-third day of the Pandya king Maravarman or Tribhuvanachakravartin Vira Pandyadeva. Registers an order of Sediyarayan that the gift of garden lands made by a certain Villavadaraiyan together with lands provided for the maintenance of eighteen servants of the garden and of the water-shed within it, may be engraved on temple walls. See S.A. 71.

352 of 1913 (Tamil) — On a slab set up near the same gopura. A damaged record in S. 1520, Vilambin, Adi, first day. Provides for some specified repairs to the temple made for the merit of Muttu Krishnappa Nayaka, son of Vaiyappa Krishnappa Kondama Nayaka. Also mentions a mandapa on the bank of Kollidavaru, built by the same donor. See S.A. 126 and 131.

353 of 1913 (Tamil) — On the west gopura of the same temple; right of entrance. A record in praise of the Pandya king (Minavan) Vikrama Pandya (Maravarman) most probably.

354 of 1913 (Tamil) — In the same place. Three verses describing the glory of King Sundara Pandya who conquered the kings of Venadu (Travancore), those of the north (the Telingas) and those of the Kongu country and killed Gandagopala. (The king is of course Jatavarman Sundara Pandya I, 1251-54. See S.A. 153).

355 of 1913 (Tamil) — In the same place. A record of the Vijayanagara king Venkatadeva Maharaya (Venkata I, 1586-1614) in S. 1510, Sarvadharin, Margali, 22nd day. Same as No. 335 (S.A. 127 above).

356 of 1913 (Tamil) — In the same place. A record of the Cochin king Rama Varma Maharaja, of the family of Seraman Perumal Nayanar, in S. 1498, Dhatri, Margali, 12th day. The king is stated to have been born under the asterism Visakha. Provides for 33 taligai (offerings) to be offered to Anandatandava Perumal Nayanar and distributed among Brahmans, Mahesvaras and the temple cooks. (The king referred to was the king of Cochin, one of the successors of Godai Varma who came to the throne in 1561 and ruled for an unknown period).

357 of 1913 (Tamil verse) — In the same place. In praise of the Pandya king. Mentions Kudal (Madura).

358 of 1913 (Grantha and Tamil) — In the same place. A record of the Vijayanagara king Virabhupathiraya. Registers that 64 cows were granted for maintaining perpetual lamps in the presence of Nrittanatha, by the ministers Chaundarasa and Adittarasa. (The government epigraphist points out that if this Chaundarasa is the same as the Vedic scholar Chaundapacharya, Virabhupathi should be identified with the Bukka II in whose time that scholar flourished. *Ep. Rep.* 1909, p. 115.)

359 of 1913 (Tamil) — In the same place. A record of the Vijayanagara king Virapratapa Srirangadeva Maharaya II in S. 1503, Vrisha, Kumbha, su. di. 14, Thursday (should be Tuesday) Sravishtha (Danishta). Same as No. 348 (S.A. 140 above).

360 of 1913 (Tamil) — In the same place. Records in S. 1517, Dunmukhi, Chaitra, full-moon, Chitra, lunar eclipse gift of a village surnamed Purappettai, for meeting the expenses of one day during the Appisi Puram[14] festivities, in honour of the goddess.

361 of 1913 (Tamil verse) — In the same place. The record contains three verses and refers to the fight between Sundara

Pandya (evidently Jatavarman S.P.) and the Telungas at Mudugur in which the dead bodies were strewn up to the banks of the Peraru. See. S.A. 146 which directly refers to the battle.

362 of 1913 (Tamil) — In the same place. A record of the Vijayanagara king Venkatadeva Maharaya I (1586-1614) in S. 1510, Sarvadharin, Tai, 22nd day. Same as No. 349 above.

363 of 1913 (Tamil verse) — In the same place. Consists of two verses. There is apparently a reference to Sundara Pandya's weighing himself against gold and using it for covering the temple. See S.A. No. 130 above.

364 of 1913 (Tamil verse) — On the same gopura; left of entrance. A damaged record. Two of the verses are in praise of the Pandya king Maran.

365 of 1913 (Tamil verse) — In the same place. Three verses extolling Vikrama Pandya. The first says that he conquered the king of Venadu (Travancore) at Podiyil. In the second he is addressed as Bhuvanekavira and Korkai Kavala and is stated to have been the enemy of Ganapati. The third advises king Vikrama Pandya not to go to the north; for there is a foe — a woman ruling with a man's name! (The last refers to the celebrated Queen Rudramma of the Kakatiya dynasty. See S.A. 68, S.A. 342, etc., for further facts about Vikrama Pandya).

366 of 1913 (Tamil) — In the same place. A record in the twenty-ninth year of the Pandya king Maravarman Tribhuvanachakravartin Kulasekharadeva I (1268-1308). Built in at the bottom. Registers an order of Kalingarayan. Provides for offering to the God Kulottungasola Vinayaka Pillayar who is enshrined on the south side of the seven-storeyed gopura of Rajakkaltambirantirumaligai. Refers to Ellandalaiyana Perumalsandi. (Ellandalaiyana is the epithet of Jatavarman Sundara Pandya I, 1251-64.)

367 of 1913 (Tamil) — In the same place. A record of the Vijayanagara king Venkatadeva Maharaya I (1586-1614) in S. 1510, Sarvadharin, Tai, 22nd day. Same as No. 339 above.

368 of 1913 (Grantha) — In niches on the inner walls of the same gopura. Registers the names of the various dances in Sanskrit, as in No. 343 (S.A. 135).

369 of 1913 (Tamil) — On a slab set up near the same gopura. A record of the Vijayanagara king Venkatadeva Maharaya I in S. 1515, Vijia, Adi, 1st day, Saturday, Jyeshtha (30th June, 1593). Registers that for the merit of Vaiyappa Krishnappa Kondama Nayaka, the districts Devamandalasirmai, Viranarayanachchirmai, Terkunadu, Vadakkunadu, the five villages grouped under Asuvur and all others that had been enjoyed by the temple of Chidambaresvara from early times, were made tax-free and that a fresh provision was made for a daily offering of 750 taligai. This was called kondama nayakan kattalai. (I have traced this inscription to Ins. S. Dts., Mack. MSS., p. 167, No. 15).

370 of 1913 (Tamil) — On the north gopura of the same temple, right of entrance. A record of the Vijayanagara king Venkatadeva Maharaya I in S. 1510, Sarvadharin, Tai, 22nd day. Same as No. 339 above (S.A. 131).

371 of 1913 (Tamil) — In the same place. Registers that Virapratapa Krishnadeva Maharaya (1509-1530) after having started on a campaign against Simhadri Pottunuru planted a pillar of victory there and returning thence, he paid a visit to Ponnambalam (Chidambaram), worshipped the god and built the northern gopura of the temple. See S.A. 233.

372 of 1913 (Tamil) — On the same gopura left of entrance. A record of the Vijayanagra king Venkatadeva Maharaya I (1586-1614) in S. 1510, Sarvadharin, Margali, 22nd day. Same as No. 335 above (S.A. 127).

373 of 1913 (Tamil) — In the same place. A record of the Vijayanagara king Venkatadeva Maharaya I in S. 1510, Sarvadharin, Tai, 22nd day. Same as 349 above (S.A. 141).

374 of 1913 (Tamil verse) — In the same place. Registers that three gopuras were the gifts of kings who wore a crown. This (the northern gopura) was built by the God himself. The poet evidently means to say that this is the best of the four. We know from S.A. 163 that Krishnaraya built it.

375 of 1913 (Tamil) — On a slab set up near the same gopura. A record of the Vijayanagara king Venkatadeva Maharaya in S. 1515, Vijia, Adi, first day, Saturday, Jyeshtha (30th June, 1593). Same as No. 369 above (S.A. 161).

376 of 1913 (Tamil) — On the north wall of the Karpaga Vinayaka temple, at the western gopura of the same temple. A record of the Vijayanagara king Virapratapa Devaraya Maharaya II in S. 1349, Plavanga, Mina, su. di. 5, Sunday, Rohini (March 21, A.D. 1428). One stone is missing in the middle. Registers that the king ordered certain irregularities in temples and temple lands to be set right. A very interesting record which gives a clue to the beneficent rules of Devaraya. The inscription says that the king's officers unjustly collected Kanikkai, Arasuperu, Karanakkarjodi, Viseshadayam and other taxes from certain villages which were owned by temples and the people of which were tenants (by mortgage, purchase etc.) of these temples; that the villagers in consequence deserted; that worship in consequence ceased in the temples; and that the king issued an edict of freedom and restoration. See *Ep. Rep.* 1914, p. 97, and also *Ep. Rep.* 1908, p. 250.

1 of 1915 (Tamil) — On the north tier of the central shrine in the Govindaraja Perumal temple at Chidambaram. An unfinished record of the Vijayanagara king Achutadeva Maharaya (1530-42) in S. 1460, Vilambi, Panguni, 14th day,

Monday, Paurnima, Uttara Palguni. Records the reconsecration of Govindarajswamin at Chitrakuta by Achyutaraya. An irregular date. See *Ep. Rep.* 1915, p. 81. See 63 and 64.

545 of 1918 (Tamil) — On nine fragmentary stones from the east wall of the first prakara, Nataraja temple, Chidambaram. One of the fragments mentions the name of the king Tirubhuvanachakravartin Kulottunga Choladeva, two others contain part of the historical introduction of Kulottunga I, and the rest provide for offerings in the temple.

546 of 1918 (Tamil) — On the same wall. Of Pandya king Jatavarman. Registers a gift of land as jivita to a number of persons who had to look after garden called Sundarapandiyantiruththoppu and the street called Sundarapandiyantengutiruvethi.

547 of 1918 (Tamil) — On the same wall. A record of Pandya king Kulasekaradeva's 28th year and 190th day. Registers an order of Kalingarayan granting lands for the maintenance of certain flower-gardens, one of which was called Ayyanangakarantirunandavanam.

548 of 1918 (Tamil) — On the same wall, left and right sides. A record of Chola king Rajarajadeva's 10th year and 122nd day. Mentions gift of land for supplying pomegranates and offerings to the gods and goddesses in the temple.

549 of 1918 (Tamil) — On the right side of the same wall. A record of Pandya king Vikaramapandyadeva in the 7th year. Registers an order of Vengattarayan regarding gift of land for supplying plaintain fruits.

550 of 1918 (Tamil) — On six fragments built into the platform forming steps in front of the entrance. One of the fragments bears the regnal year 48. The others refer to gifts of lands.

551 of 1918 (Tamil) — On two other fragments collected from the same place. One of the fragments refers to the 8th

year of king Vikramacholadeva (12th century) and mentions Nangur in Nangurnadu and another contains a portion of the historical introduction of Raja Raja I (A.D. 985 to 1013).

TIRUVETKALAM

The temple of Tiruvetkalam, which is situated one mile to the east of Chidambaram, appears to have been at one time very important. It is said that Arjuna received his bow from Siva in this place and there are metal figures in this shrine depicting this incident.

TIRUNARAIYUR

The temple at Tirunaraiyur, a minor shrine nine miles away from Chidambaram, is famous for its Vinayaka (elephant god), who is said to have consumed the offerings of a youth called Nambiyandan, who subsequently became a great devotee! It is this Nambiyandan[15] who is said to have arranged the "Devaram" songs.

On account of the all-importance of the place amongst the Saiva shrines it is held in very high esteem. There are 274 such places in the whole of India which have been eulogised by Nayanmars or apostles whose lives are recorded in the Tamil work Periyapurana.

THE 274 SAIVA HOLY PLACES (*Padalpetha Sthalams.*)

1. Chidambaram. — Known as Koyil or "The Temple," it is the chief centre for the dancing Siva or Nataraja. It is here that the Almighty is worshipped in ether form. The room wherefrom the famous Tamil work Devaram hymns were taken out is preserved at the north-west corner of the second prakara of the temple. The Periyapurana was composed and read out in the thousand-pillared hall within this temple.

2. TIRUVETKALAM — Two miles east of Chidambaram. It is said that Arjuna had his Pasupatastra weapon at the hands of Siva here. There are metal figures of this form in the temple.

3. SIVAPURI (Nelvayil) — Three miles south-east of Chidambaram. The temple here is in a much-neglected condition.

4. TIRUKKAZHIPPALAI — Close to Sivapuri and seven miles south-east of Chidambaram. The temple is said to have stood in the village now known as Karaimedu and that in a flood of the river Coleroon there it was removed to this place.

5. ACHCHAPURAM (Nallurpperumanam) — Three miles east of Coleroon Railway Station. It has relevance with Saint Sambandar whose spirit is said to have merged into the linga of the temple here!!

6. KOYILADIPPALAYAM (Tirumayendrappalayam) — Four miles north-east of Achchapuram. Mayendra worshipped the Lord here.

7. TIRUMULLAVAYIL (South) — Eight miles east of Shiyali Railway Station. The Goddess had her initiation in the hands of the Lord here.

8. ANNAPPANPETTAI (Kalikkamur) — Three miles south-west of Tirumullavayil. Sage Parasara worshipped the Lord here.

9. SAYAVANAM (Saykkadu) — Nine miles south-east of Shiyali Railway Station. Upamanya worshipped the Lord here. This is one of the six places akin of Benares; the other five being Vedaranyam, Tiruvadi, Mayavaram, Tiruvadaimaruthur and Srivangiyam.

10. PALLAVANICHARAM — Close to Sayavanam, a Pallava king is said to have obtained salvation here.

11. TIRUVENKADU — Seven miles south-east of Shiyali Railway Station. The Agoramurti here is a powerful deity.

12. TIRUKATTUPPALLI (East) — One mile west of Tiruvenkadu. The Devas worshipped the Lord here.

13. TIRUKKURUKAVUR (Tirukkadavur) — Four miles east of Shiyali. This is connected with Saint Sundarar. The water of the well in front of the temple is said to turn white on Tai Amavasya day!!

14. SHIYALI — This is the birthplace of Saint Sambandar to whom is dedicated a separate shrine within the temple.

15. TIRUTTALAMUDAIYARKOIL (Tirukkolakka) — Close by Shiyali. Here Saint Sambandar had a golden cymbol appearing in his hand miraculously!!!

16. VAITHISWARANKOIL — The God is named physician-God. Tonsure ceremonies are performed here.

17. TIRUKKANNARKOIL (Kurumanakkudi) — Three miles from Vaithiswarankoil. Vishnu in Vamna (dwarf) form worshipped the God here as also Indra to get rid of a certain sin.

18. KEEZHUR (Tirukkadaimudi) — Six miles north-east of Anathandavapuram Railway Station. Brahma worshipped the Lord here.

19. TIRUNINRIYUR — Two miles north-east of Anathandavapuram Railway Station. Lakshmi worshipped the Lord here.

20. TIRUPUNGUR — Two miles west of Vaithiswarankoil Railway Station. This is connected with the Pariah devotee Nanda.

21. NEDUR — One mile south-west of Anathandavapuram Railway Station. Goddess Kali worshipped the Lord here. This is also connected with Saint Munaigaduvar.

22. PONNUR (Tiruanniyur) — Four miles south-west of Anathandavapuram Railway Station. Varuna worshipped the Lord here.

23. VELVIKKUDI — Three miles north-east of Kutthalam Railway Station. This place is important for the marriage scene of Siva.

24. TIRUMANANJERI (Edirkolpadi) — Two miles north of Velvikkudi. This is connected also with the marriage scene of Siva.

25. TIRUMANANJERI (East) — Close to Tirumananjeri. Manmatha worshipped the Lord here.

26. KURUKKAI — Four miles north-west of Ponnur. Manmatha was burnt to ashes here.

27. TALAIGNAYAR (Karuppareyalur) — Three miles north-west of Tirupungur. Indra worshipped the Lord here.

28. KURAKUKKA — One mile north of Talaignayar. Hanuman worshipped the Lord here.

29. VALAAPPUTHTHUR (Valoleppurrur) — Two miles west of Tirupungur. It is connected with Arjuna. A crab worshipped the Lord here.

30. ELUPPAIPPATTU (Mannippadikkarai) — One mile west of Valaappuththur. Here Siva swallowed the poison.

31. OMAMPULIYUR — Two miles north-west of Eluppaippattu. This is connected with the hunter's story of Sivaratri Festival.

32. KANATTUMULLUR — Three miles east of Omampuliyur. Sage Patanjali worshipped the Lord here.

33. TIRUNARAIYUR — Ten miles south-west of Chidambaram. It was here that the Vinayaka revealed the hidden Devaram songs to the world!!

34. KADAMBUR (West) — Four miles north-west of Omampuliyur. Indra prayed here for getting Amrita (nectar).

35. PANDANALLUR — Eight miles north-east of Tiruvidamaruthur Railway Station. The holy cow worshipped the Lord here.

36. KANJANUR — Six miles north-east of Tiruvidamaruthur Railway Station. This the birthplace of Haridattasivacharya whose figure is in the temple. This is also connected with Kamsa.

37. TIRUKKODIKAVAL — Two miles east of Tiruvidamaruthur Railway Station. Several sages worshipped the God here.

38. TIRUMANGALAKUDI — Three miles north of Aduthurai Railway Station. A dead body was brought to life by the Goddess here!!

39. TIRUPPANANDAL — Seven miles north of Aduthurai Railway Station. This is connected with Kungiliyakkalaya Nayanar whose figure is in the temple.

40. TIRUVAPPADI — Two miles west of Tiruppanandal. This is connected with Saint Chandesa.

41. TIRUCHENGALUR — Close to Tiruvappadi. This is connected with Saint Chandesa and God Subrahmanya.

42. TIRUNTUTEVANGUDI — Four miles north-west of Tiruvidamaruthur Railway Station. A crab worshipped the god here.

43. TIRUVISALUR — One mile south of Tiruntutevangudi. A dead body while being brought over to this sacred place was brought to life!!

44. KOTTAIYUR — Three miles north-west of Kumbakonam Railway Station. Sage Herandar, whose figure is in the temple, worshipped the Lord here.

45. INNAMBUR — Two miles north-west of Kottaiyur. Iravata worshipped the Lord here and the vimana is peculiar.

46. TIRUPPURAMBIYAM — Two miles north-west of

Innambur. The Dakshinamurthi is important here.

47. VIJIAMANGAI — Close to Tiruppurambiyam. Arjuna worshipped the Lord here.

48. TIRUVAIGAVUR — One mile west of Vijiamangai. This is connected with Sivaratri festival.

49. KURANGADUTHURAI (North) — Fourth mile north-west of Ayyampet Railway Station. Vali worshipped the Lord here.

50. TIRUPPAZHANAM — Three miles west of Kurangaduthurai. This is connected with Saint Appar and Appudi Adigal.

51. TIRUVADI — Seven miles north of Tanjore Railway Station. The river Kaveri is said to shine in full splendour at this place. Samudraraja (King of Oceans) worshipped her here. There is a shrine dedicated to Atkondar, the deity who appeared to save a devotee from the clutches of Yama.

52. TILLASTANAM (Tiruneittanam) — One mile west of Tiruvadi. Sarasvati worshipped the Lord here.

53. PERUMBULIYUR — Two miles north-west of Tiruvadi. Vyaghrapada worshipped the Lord here.

54. TIRUMAZHAPADI — Two miles north-west of Perumbuliyur. This is the scene of Nandi's marriage. The river Coleroon takes a northerly course here.

55. PAZHUVUR — Ten miles north-east of Tiruvadi. Parasurama worshipped the Lord here.

56. TIRUKKANUR — Seven miles north of Budalur Railway Station. Siva here appeared in the form of fire.

57. ANBIL (Anbilalanturai) — Twelve miles north of Budalur. Sage Vagisa worshipped the Lord here.

58. TIRUMANDURAI — Thirteen miles north-east of Trichinopoly Railway Station. The Maruts and Sage Kanvar worshipped the Lord here.

59. TIRUPPARTURAI — Four miles north of Tiruverumbur

Railway Station. When Markandeya was worshipping the Lord here, milk appeared in plenty.

60. TIRUVANAIKKA — Four miles north of Trichinopoly Railway Station. Also known as Jambukeswaram. Noted for the worship of water element!!

61. TIRUPPAINJILI — Twelve miles north-east of Trichinopoly Railway Station. This is connected with Saint Appar.

62. TIRUVASI — Three miles north-west of Tiruvanaikka. The Nataraja figure here is found to have matted hairs and the asura stands close by.

63. TIRUVINGANATHAMALAI — Five miles north-west of Kulittalai Railway Station. Sage Agastya worshipped the Lord here.

64. RATHNAGIRI (Vatpokki) — Seven miles south of Kulittalai. The lord here made gems appear before a Chola king!!

65. KADAMBARCOIL — Two miles north-west of Kulittalai. Sage Kanvar worshipped the Lord here.

66. TIRUPPARAITURAI — Two miles north-west of Ezumanur Railway Station. Saptarishis (seven sages) worshipped the Lord here.

67. UYYAKONDAN (Karkkudi) — Five miles north-west of Trichinopoly Railway Station. A king of Ceylon was blessed by the Lord here.

68. URAIYUR (Tirumukkichuram) — Two miles west of Trichinopoly. The linga appears in five colours in the course of each day!!

69. TRICHINOPOLY — The Lord appeared in the form of a midwife to help a forlorn woman in confinement!!

70. TIRUVERUMBUR — Devas in the form of ants worshipped the Lord here!!

71. TIRUNATTANGULAM (Nedunkalam) — Eight miles south-east of Tiruverumbur. Chola king Vangiyan had his blessings here.

72. TIRUKKATUPALLI (West) — Five miles north of Budalur Railway Station. Chola king Parantaka's queen was blessed here.

73. TIRUVALAMPOZHIL — Ten miles north-west of Tanjore Railway Station. Vasus worshipped the Lord here.

74. TIRUPPUNTHURUTTI — Eight miles north-east of Tanjore. Sage Kasyapa worshipped the Lord here.

75. KANDIYUR — Six miles north of Tanjore. Figures of Brahma and Sarasvati are available in the temple here.

76. SORRUTHURAI — Four miles north-east of Kandiyur. The sun's rays fall on the linga on certain days of the year!!

77. TIRUVEDIKUDI — Two miles east of Kandiyur. Vedas worshipped the Lord here.

78. TITTAI — Gautama worshipped the Lord here.

79. PASUPATICOVIL (Tiruppullamangai or Alanturai) — The Lord here is said to have swallowed the poison.

80. CHAKRAPPALLI — One mile west of Iyampet Railway Station. The Sapatamatas worshipped the Lord here.

81. TIRUKKALAVUR — Four miles south of Papanasam Railway Station. The Goddess here is in the form of a mortal who helped a woman in confinement!!

82. TIRUPPALAITHURAI — Two miles north-east of Papanasam Railway Station. The Lord here overcame a lion!!

83. NALLUR — Two miles south of Sundaraperumalcoil Railway Station. The colour of the linga changes five times in the course of the day!!

84. AVUR — Eight miles south-east of Papanasam Railway Station. The holy cow worshipped the Lord here.

85. SAKTIMUTTAM — Two miles south-west of Darsuram Railway Station. The sculpture of the Goddess embracing the linga is located here.

86. PATTISWARAM — Close to Saktimuttam. There is an old painting of Sri Rama, who worshipped the deity in the temple here.

87. PAZHAYARAI — Close to Pattiswaram. Chandra worshipped the Lord here.

88. TIRUVALANJULI — One mile east of Sundaraperumalkoil Railway Station. Sage Herandar, whose figure is available here, worshipped the Lord here. The Vinayaka here is very important.

89. KUMBAKONAM — The famous Mahamaga tank is located here. The linga is made up of pot pieces.

90. NAGESWARA — (A temple in Kumbakonam). Sun's rays fall on the linga on certain days!!

91. KASI-VISVANATHA — (A temple in Kumbakonam). Sculptures of the nine river maidens are found in this temple.

92. TIRUNAGESWARAM — The Nagaraja, king of serpants, worshipped the Lord here.

93. TIRUVIDAMARUTHUR — The Lord here removed the ghost that haunted a Pandya king!! Taipushya festival is important here.

94. ADUTHURAI (Ten Kurangaduthurai) — Sugriva and Hanuman worshipped the Lord here.

95. TENNALKUDI (Tirunelakudi) — Two miles south of Aduthurai, Varuna worshipped the Lord here.

96. VAIGAL (Vaiganmadakkoil) — Four miles south of Aduthurai. Chola king Kochengan was blessed here.

97. KONERIRAJAPURAM (Tirunallam) — Five miles south-east of Aduthurai. The Nataraja here is very big and attractive.

98. TIRUKKOZHAMBAM — Three miles south-east of Narasingampet Railway Station. A devotee who was troubled by Indra was saved by the Lord here.

99. TIRUVADUTHURAL — Two miles south-east of Narasingampet Railway Station. This is connected with Tirumula Nayanar whose figure is found in this temple.

100. KUTTALAM (Tirutturutti) — The Lord here revealed the truth of the Vedas.

101. TERAZHUNDUR (Tiruvazhuntur) — Three miles south-east of Kuttalam. Dikpalakas worshipped the Lord here.

102. MAYAVARAM (Mayiladuthurai) — The Goddess in a pen-hen form worshipped the Lord here. The Ganges is said to visit the Kaveri here through an under-current on the Aippasi new-moon day.

103. VILANAGAR — Four miles east of Mayavaram. A devotee who was carried away by flood was saved by the Lord here.

104. PARASALUR (Tiruppariyalur) — Two miles south-east of Vilanagar. Figures of Daksha and Virabhadra are found here.

105. SEMPONARKOVIL — Seven miles east of No. 102. Rathi prayed to the Lord here.

106. PUNJAI (Tirunanipalli) — Two miles north-east of Semponarkovil. This is the birth place of Saint Sambandar's mother.

107. PERUMPALLAM (Tiruvalampuram) — Eleven miles from Punjai. Vishnu worshipped the Lord and obtained Sankha (conch).

108. TALAICHENGADU — One mile south-west of Perumpallam. This is also connected with the worship of Vishnu.

109. AKKUR — Eleven miles east of Mayavaram. This is connected with Sirappuli Nayanar.

110. TIRUKKADAYUR — Thirteen miles south-east of Mayavaram. Here the Lord came out of his linga and kicked Yama to save Markandeya!!! There is a figure representing this scene.

111. MAYANAM — One mile south-east of Tirukkadayur. Brahma worshipped the Lord here.

112. TIRUVETTAKUDI — Four miles east of Poraiyar Railway Station. The Lord here appeared in Virata (hunter) form.

113. KOYIRPATTU (Tiruttelicheri) — One mile north-west of Porayar Railway Station. The sun's rays fall on the linga on certain days of the year!!!

114. DHARMAPURAM — One mile west of Karaikal Railway Station. Yama worshipped the Lord here.

115. TIRUNALLAR — Nala had the evil effects of Sani (Saturn) removed here. The shrine to Saturn is important.

116. KOTTARAM (Tirukkottaru) — Two miles north-east of Ambattur Railway Station. This is connected with Elayankudimara Nayanar.

117. AMBAR — Two miles east of Poontottam Railway Station. This is connected with Somasimara Nayanar.

118. AMBARMAKALAM — Close to Kottaram. Kali worshipped the Lord here.

119. TIRUMEYACHUR — One mile west of Peralam Railway Station. Surya (Sun) worshipped the Lord here seated on an elephant with Parvati.

120. ELANKOIL — This shrine is within Tirumeyachur, where Kali worshipped the Lord.

121. TILATAIPPADI (Koyirpattu) — One mile west of Poontottam Railway Station. The sun's rays fall on the linga on certain days of the year!!

122. TIRUPPAMPURAM — Three miles west of Poontottam Railway Station. Figure of Nagaraja (serpent god) is found here.

123. SIRUKUDI — Five miles south-west of Peralam Railway Station. The celestials worshipped the Lord here.

124. TIRUVIZHIMAZHALAI — Five miles west of Peralam Railway Station. Vishnu worshipped the Lord here with his eye when flowers failed to please!!

125. ANNUR (Tiruvanniyur) — Two miles north-west of Tiruvizhimazhalai. Agni (god of fire) worshipped the Lord here.

126. KARUVILI — Two miles south-west of Annur. Indra and Devas worshipped the Lord here.

127. TIRUPPANDURAI (Penuperunturai) — Eleven miles south-east of Kumbakonam Railway Station. God Subrahmanya was blessed here.

128. NARAIYUR — Two miles west of Tiruppandurai. Siddhas worshipped the Lord here.

129. ALAGARPUTTUR (Arisikaraipputtur) — Two miles north-west of Naraiyur. This is connected with Pugazhthunai Nayanar.

130. SIVAPURI — Three miles south-east of Kumbakonam Railway Station. Vishnu in his boar form worshipped the Lord here.

131. SAKKOTAI (Tirukkalayanallur) — Two miles south of Kumbakonam Railway Station. This was saved in a deluge.

132. MARUDANDANALLUR (Tirukkarukkudi) — One mile south of Sakkotai. King Sarguna was blessed here.

133. SRIVANJIYAM — Seven miles west of Nannilam Railway Station. Vishnu worshipped the Lord here. There is a shrine dedicated to Yama.

134. NANNILAM — Surya (Sun) worshipped the Lord here.

135. TIRUKKONDISWARAM. — Two miles west of Nannilam. The holy Cow worshipped the Lord here.

136. TIRUPPANAIYUR — One mile south-east of Nannilam. Sage Parasara worshipped the Lord here.

137. VIRKUDI — Four miles north-east of Vettar Railway Station. Jalandara was overcome by the Lord whose figure has Chakra (discus) on hand.

138. TIRUPPUGALUR. — Four miles east of Nannilam. There is a sculpture of God in the form of a tiger swallowing Saint Appar.

139. VARTHAMANICHURAM — This shrine is within Tiruppugalur. This is connected with Muruga Nayanar.

140. RAMANATICHCHURAM — One mile south of Tiruppugalur. Sri Rama worshipped the Lord here.

141. PAYATTANGUDI (Tiruppayarrur) — Three miles east of Virkudi. Sage Bhairava worshipped the Lord here.

142. TIRUCHCHENGATTANGUDI — Seven miles south-east of Nannilam. This is connected with Siruttondar whose figure is available in the temple. Vinayaka overcame Gajamukasura here.

143. TIRUMARUGAL — Two miles north-east of Tiruchchengattangudi. A girl that died from snake poison was revived!!

144. SEYYATAMANGAI (Sattamangai) — One mile north-east of Tirumarugal. This is connected with Saint Tiruneelanakka Nayanar whose figure is available in the temple.

145. NEGAPATAM — This is connected with Adipatta Nayanar.

146. SIKKAL — Vasishta worshipped the Lord here.

147. KIZHVELUR — Agastya worshipped the Lord here. Figures of Kubera and Indra are available here.

148. TEVUR — Three miles south of Kizhvelur. Devas worshipped the Lord here.

149. ARIKKARIYANPALLI (Palliyenmukkudal) — Two miles south-east of Vettar Railway Station. Sri Rama worshipped the Lord here.

150. TIRUVARUR — Lakshmi worshipped the Lord here. This was once a Chola Capital. God Tyagaraja is important here.

151. ARANERI — This shrine is within Tiruvarur. This is connected with Naminandi Adigal Nayanar.

152. TULANAYANARCOVIL — This is in the East Main Street in Tiruvarur. Durvasa's figure is found here.

153. VILAMAR — Two miles north-west of Tiruvarur. Figures of Patanjali and Vyaghrapada can be seen here.

154. KARAYAPURAM (Karaviram) — Five miles north-west of Kulittalai Railway Station. Gautama worshipped the Lord here.

155. KATTUR IYYAMPET (Peruvelur) — Two miles north-west of Karayapuram. This is also connected with Gautama.

156. TALAIALANGADU — Two miles west of Araneri. Kappilar worshipped the Lord here.

157. KUDAVASAL — Eight miles north of Koradacheri Railway Station. Garuda worshipped the Lord here.

158. UDAIYARCOIL (Tiruchchendurai) — Four miles north-east of Kudavasal. Daumeya worshipped the Lord here.

159. NALUR MAYANAM — Three miles north-east of Kudavasal. Apatsthambar worshipped the Lord here.

160. ANDARKOIL (Kaduvoikkaraippattur) — Four miles west of Seyyatamangai. Kasyapa worshipped the Lord here.

161. ALANGUDI (Erumpulai) — Four miles north of Nidamangalam Railway Station. Visvamitra worshipped the Lord here.

162. HARDIDHWARAMANGALAM (Arataipperumpali) — Eight miles north-east of Saliyamangalam Railway Station. The Lord here overcame Vishnu is his boar form.

163. AVALIVANALLUR — Seven miles north-east of Four Form. The Lord here in the form of a mortal gave evidence to save a devotee!! Sculpture representing this scene is available.

164. PARITHIYAPPARCOVIL (Paritineyamam) — Nine miles south-east of Tanjore Railway Station. Surya (sun) worshipped the Lord here.

165. KOVILVENNI (Tiruvenni) — The linga is of a peculiar shape as though composed of a bundle of sticks!!

166. POOVANUR — Three miles south of Nidamangalam Railway Station. Sage Sagar worshipped the Lord here.

167. PAMANI (Patalichuram) — Two miles north of Mannargudi Railway Station. Dananjeya worshipped the Lord here.

168. TIRUKKALAR — Nine miles south-west of Tiruthuraipundi Railway Station. Durvasa's figure can be seen in the temple here.

169. SIRRAMBUR (Tiruchchirremam) — Four miles north-west of Ponneri Railway Station. The Vedas worshipped the Lord here.

170. KOILUR — Two miles north of Mutupet Railway Station. Sri Rama had his initiation here.

171. IDUMBAVANAM — Ten miles south-west of Tirutturaipundi Railway Station. Idumban worshipped the Lord here.

172. KARPAKANARKOIL (Kadikkulam) — One mile east of Idumbavanam. The Vinayaka here won a mango fruit in a betting!!

173. TANDALAICHERI — Two miles north of Tirutturaipundi Railway Station. This is connected with Arivattaya Nayanar.

174. KOTTUR — Ten miles south of Mannargudi Railway Station. Devas worshipped the Lord here.

175. TIRUVANDUTHURAI (Tiruvendurai) — Six miles east of Mannargudi Railway Station. Bringi worshipped the Lord here.

176. TIRUKALAMBUR (Triukkollambudur) — Six miles north-east of Nidamangalam Railway Station. This is connected with Sambandar.

177. OGAI (Pereyil) — Three miles south-west of Tirunattiyattangudi Railway Station. Agni (god of fire) worshipped the Lord here.

178. KOLLIKKADU — Four miles west of Ponneri Railway Station. Agni and Saturn worshipped the Lord here.

179. TIRUTHENGOOR — Two miles south-west of Tirunellikka Railway Station. Navagrahas (nine planets) worshipped the Lord here.

180. TIRUNELLIKKA — The rays of the sun falls on the linga on certain days of the year!!

181. TIRUNATTIYATTANGUDI — This is connected with Kotpulinayanar whose figure is found in the temple.

182. TIRUKKARAIVASAL (Tirukkarayil) — Three miles south-east of Tirunattiyattangudi. Indra worshipped the Lord here. King Muchukunda installed the Tyagaraja here.

183. KANRAPPUR — Six miles east of Tirunattiyattangudi. The Lord appeared from a wooden peg!!

184. VALIVALAM — Two miles south of Kanrappur. Surya worshipped the Lord,here.

185. KAICHINAM — Two miles east of Tirunellikka. Indra worshipped the Lord here.

186. TIRUKKUVALAI (Tirukkolili) — Five miles east of Kaichinam. Figures of Bhima and Bakasura are found here.

187. TIRUVAIMUR — Three miles south-east of Tirukkuvalai. Surya worshipped the Lord here. King Muchukunda installed the Tyagaraja here.

188. VEDARANNIAM (Maraikkadu) — Vedas, Visvamitra and Sri Rama worshipped the Lord here.

189. AGATTYAMPALLI — Three miles south of Vedaranniam. Agastya's figure can be seen here.

190. KULAGARCOIL (Kodi) — Seven miles south of Agattyampalli. The linga here arose out of Amirta (nectar).

191. TRINCOMALEE — Indra worshipped the Lord in this place in Sri Lanka.

192. MATOTTAM (Tirukkethechuram) — This place in Sri Lanka is now in ruins. Brigu worshipped the Lord here.

193. MADURA (Alavoi) — The Goddess ruled the country here. The Lord here performed 64 miracles.

194. TIRUVAPUDIYARCOIL (Tiruvappanur) — In Madura, on the north bank of the river Vaigai.

195. TIRUPPARANKUNRAM — Subramanya married Devasenai here.

196. TIRUVEDAGAM — Three miles south-west of Solavandan Railway Station. This is connected with Saint Manikkavachakar and Kulachcherai Nayanar.

197. PIRANMALAI (Tirukkodunkunram) — Sixteen miles north-east of Ammayanayakanur Railway Station. Sage Mahodara worshipped the Lord here.

198. TIRUPPUTTUR — Fifteen miles south-east of Piranmalai. Lakshmi worshipped the Lord here.

199. TIRUPPUNAVAVAYAL — Twenty-one miles south-east of Arantangi Railway Station. Vedas worshipped the Lord here.

200. RAMESWARAM — The linga here was installed by Sri Rama himself. Here is Setu, where bath is of special importance.

201. TIRUVADANAI — Twelve miles south of Tiruppunavavayal. Brigu worshipped the Lord here.

202. KALAYARCOIL — Twenty-one miles west of Tiruvadanai. Iravata worshipped the Lord here.

203. TRIPUVANAM — God Sundaresa worked out a miracle here.

204. TIRUCHCHUZHIYAL — Fifteen miles south of Tripuvanam. Satananda worshipped the Lord here.

205. KUTTALAM — Three miles west of Tenkasi Railway Station. Agastya worshipped the Lord here.

206. TINNEVELLY — The God here appeared under a cluster of bamboo trees!!

207. TIRUVANJAIKKALAM — Four miles west of Irujalakkadai Railway Station. Parasurama worshipped the Lord here.

208. AVINASI (Tiruppukkuzhi) — Eleven miles north-west of Tiruppur Railway Station. This is connected with Sundarar.

209. TIRUMURUGANPUNDI — Eight miles north-west of Tiruppur Railway Station. Subrahmanya worshipped the Lord here. Once in 12 years water comes out of a rock here!!

210. BHAVANI — Nine miles north-west of Erode Railway Station. This is the confluence of Bhavani and Kaveri. Parasara worshipped the Lord here.

211. TIRUCHCHENGODE — Five miles east of Sankaridrug Railway Station. The deity is Arthanari (half-man half-woman).

212. VENJAMANKUDAL — Twelve miles south of Karur Railway Station. King Venjan had his capital here.

213. KODUMUDI — There are shrines to the Trinity here.

214. KARUR — This is connected with Pugalsolar and Eripatt Nayanar.

215. ARATTURAI — Twenty-four miles north-west of Chidambaram. This is connected with Sambandar.

216. PENNAKADAM (Tirukkadanthainagar) — Four miles north-east of Aratturai. This is connected with Kalikamba Nayanar.

217. KUDALAI-ARRUR — Sixteen miles west of Chidambaram Railway Station. This is connected with Sundarar.

218. RAJENDRAPATTANAM (Erukkattampuliyur) — Twenty-six miles west of Chidambaram Railway Station. This is connected with Tirunelakanda Perumbana Nayanar.

219. TIRTHANAGIRI (Tiruththinainagar) — Five miles south-west of Alambakkam Railway Station. A pariah devotee was blessed here!!

220. TYAGAVALLI (Tiruchchopuram) — Two miles east of Alambakkam Railway Station. Agastya worshipped the Lord here.

221. TIRUVADIGAI — Two miles east of Panruti Railway Station. The Lord here destroyed the Tripuras.

222. TIRUNAMANALLUR (Tirunavalur) — Twelve miles west of Panruti Railway Station. Birth place of Saint Sundarar. Sukra (Venus) worshipped the Lord here.

223. VRIDDACHALAM (Tirumutukunram) — Thirty-five miles south-west of Cuddalore Railway Station. This was founded prior to the mountains.

224. NEIVENNAI (Nelvennai) — Nineteen miles south-west of Mambazhapattu Railway Station. The four great Sanaka sages worshipped the Lord here.

225. TIRUKKOILUR — Andakasura was overcome here.

226. ARAIKANDANALLUR (Nelvennai) — Close to Tirukkoilur. Pandavas once resided over here.

227. IDAIYARU — Nine miles south-west of Mambazhapattu Railway Station. Suga worshipped the Lord here.

228. TIRUVENNAINALLUR — Six miles south of Mambazhapattu Railway Station. This is connected with Sundarar.

229. TIRUTHTHALUR (Tiruththuraiyur) — Two miles west of Virinjipakkam Railway Station. This is connected with Sundarar.

230. ANDARCOIL (Vadukur) — Two miles west of Chinnababusamudram Railway Station. Bhairava worshipped the Lord here.

231. TIRUMANIKULI — Five miles west of Cuddalore Railway Station. Vamana Vishnu worshipped the Lord here.

232. TIRUPPAPULIYUR — Vyaghrapada worshipped the Lord here.

233. KIRAMAM (Tirumundichchuram) — Three miles east of Tiruvennainallur. Brahma worshipped the Lord here.

234. PANAYAPURAM (Panankattur) — Two miles north-east of Mundiyampakkam Railway Station. The famous king Sipi worshipped the Lord here. The sun's rays fall on the linga on certain days of the year!!

235. TIRUVAMATTUR — Four miles north-west of Villupuram Railway Station. The divine Cow and Sri Rama worshipped the Lord here.

236. TIRUVANNAMALAI — This is important for fire worship the observance of Karttigai festival.

237. CONJEEVARAM — The Ekambara temple is important for earth worship.

238. CONJEEVARAM — Merrali in Conjeevaram. Vishnu

worshipped the Lord here and it is also connected with Sambandar.

239. CONJEEVARAM — Onakantantali in Conjeevaram. Two Asuras worshipped the Lord here.

240. CONJEEVARAM — Anegatangapadam. Vinayaka worshipped the Lord here.

241. CONJEEVARAM — Tirukkaliswarancoil in Conjeevaram. Budha (Mercury) worshipped the Lord here.

242. KURANGANIMUTTAM — Six miles south of Conjeevaram. Vali worshipped the Lord here.

243. MAGARAL — Ten miles south of Conjeevaram. Indra worshipped the Lord here.

244. TIRUVOTTUR. — Eighteen miles west of Conjeevaram. The Vedas were revealed by the Lord here. There is a stone Palmyra here!!

245. TIRUPANANKADU (Panankattur) — Nine miles south-west of Conjeevaram. Agastya worshipped the Lord here.

246. TIRUVALAM — The Navagrahas (nine planets) worshipped the Lord here.

247. TIRUMARPERU — Three miles south-west of Palur Railway Station. Vishnu worshipped the Lord here with one of his eyes.

248. TAKKOLAM (Tiruooral) — Water perpetually oozes out of the Nandi here!!

249. ELAMPAYAMKOTTUR. — Two miles south-west of Takkolam. Devakannies worshipped the Lord here.

250 KUVAM (Tiruvirkolam) — Five miles south-west of Kadambattur Railway Station. The Lord started from here to overcome the Tripuras. The colour of the linga changes predicting rain and war!!

251. TIRUVALANGADU — This is connected with Saiva Saintess Karaikkal Ammai and god Nataraja.

252. TIRUPPASUR — Five miles norths-west of Trivellore Railway Station. The Lord made a serpent dance at this place!! The Moon was blessed here.

253. TIRUVULAMBUTUR (Tiruvenpakkam) — Seven miles north of Trivellore Railway Station. This place is connected with Saint Sundarar.

254. TIRUKKALLAM — Twelve miles south-west of Ponneri Railway Station. Brigu worshipped the Lord here.

255. KALAHASTI — This is famous for Vayu worship and is connected with Kannappar.

256. TIRUVORRIYUR — A railway station near Madras connected with Saint Pattinattupillayar.

257. PADI (Tiruvalidayam) — Two miles south-west of Villivakkam Railway Station. Brihaspati (Jupiter) worshipped the Lord hre.

258. TIRUMULLAIVAYIL (North) — Five miles north-east of Avadi Railway Station. Subrahmanya worshipped the Lord here. There are two old Erukku (Calotropis gigantea) Pillars in this temple.

259. TIRUVERKADU — Four miles south-east of Avadi Railway Station. This is connected with Murka Nayanar.

260. MYLAPORE — Within the city of Madras. Goddess in pea-hen form worshipped the Lord here. This is also connected with Vayilar Nayanar.

261. TIRUVANMIYUR — Four miles south-east of Mylapore. Valmiki worshipped the Lord here.

262. ALAKKOIL — Two miles north-west of Singaperumalcoil Railway Station. Vishnu in tortoise form worshipped the Lord here.

263. TIRUVIDAICHURAM — Five miles east of Chingleput Railway Station. Sanatkumara worshipped the Lord here.

264. TIRRUKKALIKUNDRAM — Nine miles south-east of Chingleput Railway Station. Vedas worshipped the Lord here.

265. ACHARAPAKKAM — Kanwar and Gautama worshipped the Lord here.

266. TIRUVAKKARAI — Thirteen miles west of Pondicherry. The linga here has faces carved on it.

267. OLINDIYAPATTU (Tiruvarasili) — Seven miles north-east of Pondicherry. Vamadeva worshipped the Lord here.

268. IRUMBAIMAKALAM — Five miles north-east of Pondicherry Railway Station. Makalar worshipped the Lord here.

269. GOKARNAM — In the erstwhile Bombay Presidency. Vinayaka installed the linga here which was given to Ravana by Parameswara.

270. SRISAILAM — Sixty-four miles north-east of Nandyal Railway Station. Nandi and Brigu worshipped the Lord here.

271. INDRANILAPARVATAM — Probably located in the Himalayas.

272. GOWRIKUNDAM — In Northern India. Surya and Chandra worshipped the Lord here.

273. KEDARAM — On the Himalayas. Bringi worshipped the Lord here.

274. MOUNT KAILAS — On the Himalayas. Important for the worship of Rudra.

NOTES

1. Murray's *Hand Book for Travellers* in India 1919, pp. 579 and 580.

2. The tiger-footed sage Vyaghrapada is said by legend to have been bent upon procuring flowers in large quantities for the worship of Siva in the temple at Chidambaram. Because of his zeal to collect all the available flowers at the earliest, he was blessed with the feet of the tiger in order that he might quickly ascend the tree and pluck the flowers!! As the result of a severe penance, he was favoured with the witnessing of the dancing of Nataraja in Chidambaram.

3. The serpent-bodied Patanjali is no other than the incarnation of Adisesha. He was born to Anusuya, wife of sage Atri. As a consequence of his having fallen from heaven into the folded hands of Anusuya while she was praying for a son, he was named Patanjali. (*Pat* means fall; and *Anjali*, folded hands). He had this incarnation to witness the dancing of Nataraja in Chidambaram. The deity in the temple of Ananteswara on the west of Chidambaram town is the one that was personally worshipped by this sage.

4. Tirunilakanda Nayanar —Born in a potter's family at Chidambaram he used to pay his daily visits to Nataraja to obtain his blessing. While returning from the temple one day he happened to pass a dancing girl's house, at which his wife became annoyed. Although there was not even the slightest fault on the part of the Nayanar, his wife though living with him was not in real matrimonial relations with him. Because his wife dragged God's name into this and used the plural form instead of the singular, he not only had any matrimonial relations with his wife but also failed to have any such relationship with any other woman nor even thought of it. This is indeed an impossibility with the average man. Thus they grew old when Nataraja had to intervene and to prove to them the real state of affairs. Disguised as an aged Brahman the God handed a bit

of pottery to the couple and demanded it after some time. To their surprise it was found to be lost. As they were unable to return the object, God made them swear after bathing in a tank, which resulted in the removal of the misunderstanding that existed in the mind of the wife. Soon after they got out of the bath, they were transformed into a youthful couple!!! The tank in consequence was named afterwards as Ilamainayanar tank (*Ilamai* in Tamil meaning youth). In commemoration of this incident the tank and shrine still exist to the west of Nataraja temple at Chidambaram.

5. Nanda or Tirunalaippovar was born amongst the Pariahs of the village of Adanur in the district of Tanjore. By his staunch devotion of Siva he was raised to the rank of Nayanar. He respected his caste rules to reach an extent that he did not dare approach the sanctum but stood behind the flag staff in the temple at Tiruppangur near Vaithisvarankoil. The bull in front of the Linga in the sanctum was hiding it. Iswara was so pleased at this devotion that he caused the bull to move!! Even now we see the bull in this temple a little away from the position it should occupy. Then he sought the permission of his master; a Brahman gentleman of his village, to permit him to go to Chidambaram. The permission was not easily granted and the visit was put off day after day. So he got the name Tirumalaippovar, meaning "the person to go tomorrow." After all he did proceed to the holy Chidambaram, and there, after passing through the fire to purify himself, joined the ranks of the faithful devotees of Siva.

6. An outcaste of the lowest and the most despised class who is not permitted even to approach people of the higher classes.

7. *Pancha lakshanam* or "that which has five characteristic topics" relating to:
   • Primary creation or cosmogony.
   • Secondary creation or the destruction and renovation of the worlds, including chronology.
   • Genealogy of Gods and patriarchs.
   • Reigns of Manus or periods called *Manvantaras;*

- Mythological history, or such particulars as have been preserved of the princes of the solar and lunar races, and of their descendants to modern times.

8. This aspect of Siva goes by the name of Chandesanugrahamurti and a sculptural representation of this form exists in the outer wall of the great temple at Gangaikondasolapuram in the district of Trichinopoly.

9. *Vellala* is from the Tamil word *Vellalan* which is derived from *Vellanmai* (*Vellam* = water and *Anmai* = management) meaning cultivation, tillage. They were the lords of the flood and thus the cultivators of the soil. The mythological origin relating to this class of men is that when the inhabitants of the world were rude and ignorant of agriculture, a severe drought fell upon the land, and the people prayed to Bhudevi, the goddess of earth, for aid. She pitied them and produced from her body a man carrying a plough, who showed them how to till the soil and support themselves. His offsprings are the Vellalas, who aspire to belong to the Vaisya caste. *Castes and Tribes of South India,"* Vol. VII, pp. 361, 362.

10. The mention of the word *Tiruthondaththogai* is made and the festival to be held in honour of these 63 devotees is recorded in inscription No. 137 of 1912. [No.241 of 1904 in the records of the Madras Epigraphical Department.] On the west base of the ruined Iswara temple at Kunimedu, South Arcot District, is an inscription dated Saka 1455 during the reign of the Vijayanagara king Achyutaraya, which mentions certain gifts of taxes for the performance of festivals and says that those that observe the faithful performance of the same will be considered similar in merit to the 63 Nayanmars. This clearly proves what respect and admiration the Nayanmars commanded even in those days.

11. This is numbered as 269 in the *Annual Report of the Madras Epigraphical Department* for the year 1901.

12. This is illustrated in Plate X, Fig.3 and Plate XI of the *Annual Report of the Arcaheological Department, Madras*, for the year 1911-12.

13. *Inscriptions of the Madras Presidiency*, Government of Madras, 1919, Vol. I, pp. 354 to 365.
14. The Puram festival is observed generally in *Adi* at other places.
15. Nambiyandar, while young, was directed by his father, a priest of the temple at Tirunaraiyur, to offer food to Pollappillaiyar daily during his absence from the station for a few days. The boy accordingly, after getting the deity bathed with sacred waters, placed the daily offerings before the God thinking that like mortals He would consume the food. When to his disappointment he found the food untouched. He thought it was due to some fault on his part and fearing his father's commands began to bang his head against the wall; when the God to satisfy the boy actually ate the food!! As then his school time was over, fearing punishment at the hands of his teacher for late attendance, he begged of this Vinayaka to give him the day's school lessons. This too he had at the hands of the Almighty!!

On this information reaching the ears of the then Chola king Abhayakula at Tiruvarur he hastened to the place and attempted through this boy-devotee to get the sacred *Devaram* and Saiva Saints' life brought into the world and these Nambiyandar were blessed within the temple at Chidambaram.

Chapter 8

VAITHISVARANKOIL

This religious centre is on the southern railway between Chidambaram and Mayavaram. The presiding deity is Vaidyanatha after whom the place takes its name. The God is so-called because He is supposed to have acted as a physician to cure the wounds of the Ganas or attendants of Subrahmanya who overcame Surapadma and other Asuras or demons. The temple is within a short distance from the railway station. Great sanctity is attached to the sthala vriksha or the local margosa tree (Melia azadirachta) which possesses remarkable medicinal properties.

The temple faces the west and the western gopura or tower, several yards away from the central shrine, is so constructed that the rays of the sun pass through the gopura entrance and fall upon the linga at a particular part of the year for a few days!! The water of the temple tank is considered sacred, and lumps of jaggery are thrown into the tank as a votive offering for the cure of boils and other skin diseases. The tank has also a dome-shaped mandapa in its middle.

There is a fine metal figure of Gangavisarjanar[1] in this temple. It is said that Angaraka (Mars), Surya (Sun), Vedas, Sampati, and Fatayu (a mythological kite) worshipped the God here and a sculptural representation of this is enshrined on the eastern courtyard of the temple.

GOD SUBRAHMANYA

Subrahmanya here goes by the name of Muthukumara and the metal figure of this deity is very beautiful. When Parvati, the consort of Siva, desired the six-faced Skanda to assume one face, he so appeared before her, and as she was very much pleased, she presented him with a vel (an arrow) to slay the demons who caused troubles to rishis (sages) and men.

TONSURE CEREMONY

The tonsure ceremony of getting children shaved for the first time to promote the proper growth of their body is done in here. This practice is in practice in most of the holy places in India where the tutelary God is supposed to possess the attribute of curing men's ailments. A similar attribute is given to Viraraghavaperumal in Trivellore near Madras, Tirupati and several other important religious centres.

INSCRIPTIONS

The inscriptions here have been copied by the Madras Ephigraphical Department during the year 1918.

"419 of 1918 (Tamil) — On the steps in front of the Subrahmanya shrine in the Vaidhyanathaswami temple at Vaithiswarankoil. Records that shutter of the sluice at Sattainadapuram measured 35 inches in length and 8 inches in breadth.

420 of 1918 (Tamil) — Right of entrance into the Tirukkulam in the same temple. Records that the tank, Nachchiyar shrine and its mandapa, were completely renovated when Kaderayar was governing the Sigali Sirmai,

and during the management of the Vaidyanathaswami temple by Muthukumaraswamitambiran, a disciple of Sivagnanadesika Sambandar of the Dhamapuram Mutt.

421 of 1918 (Tamil) — In the same place on the left side. States that the wall of the second prakara, the tirumalaigaipatti, the courtyard of the Amman shrine and the Tattisurrimandapa were repaired and completed in the month Avani of the year Saka 1689, corresponding to Kali 4868 and Sarvasidhi.

422 of 1918 — On a slab built into the floor near the accountant's seat in the same temple. Registers a deed granted to Sankarabaragiri Rengopanditar by Ambalavanatambiran, the agent of the temple of Vaidyanathaswamin.

423 of 1918 (Tamil) — On the east gopura (inside) of the same temple. Registers the gift of taxes accruing from (Ma)nippallam in Tiruvalipparu."

TIRUVENKADU

Tiruvenkadu, also known as Svetaranya, a few miles away from Vaithisvarankoil, has a legend of its own. Aghoramurti[2], the furious aspect of god Siva, is the principal deity in the temple here.

MYTHOLOGY

Tradition says that at one time Marutvasura, son of Jalandhara a demon, troubled the devas to such an extent that they lived in disguise in this sacred place. When they appealed to Siva to save them from the asura, he sent his bull to overcome Marutvasura, who, after a fierce fight, was thrown into the sea. The asura then obtained Siva's sula (trident) by praying for it. He again appeared before the bull and the latter saw his lord's sula in the hands of his opponent and so he dared not attack him. Thereafter the asura wounded the bull and cut off its horns and tail. A sculpture of the bull thus mutilated is found even now!! When Siva heard of the wounds inflicted on His bull, He created himself as Aghora to overcome the asura. Aghora in his fury defeated the asura and crushed him to death.

Tiruvenkattu Nangai, the wife of the Saiva saint Siruttonda, owes her name to this village.

Inscriptions recorded on the temple walls relate to gift of gold bowl and string of rubies by the queens of Chola king Rajaraja in the nineteenth and twentieth years of his reign. A record of king Vikrama Pandya refers to the fight and victory over the Kakatiya king Ganapati.

INSCRIPTIONS[3]

The inscriptions here have been copied by the Madras Epigraphical Department during the years 1896 and 1918.

Known in the Periyapurana as the place of Siruttonda's wife. The epigraphs of the village belong to the Chola and Pandya periods. The inscription 122 which refers to the Kakatiya Ganapati is particularly noteworthy.

"110 of 1896 (Grantha) — On the south wall of the Svataranyesvara shrine. A record in the thirty-ninth year of the Chola king Kulottunga Chola I. Records gift of lamp. See *Ep. Ind.* Vol. V, p. 104, where Dr. Hultzch edits the inscription.

111 of 1896 (Tamil) — On the same wall. A record in the twentieth year of the Chola king Ko-Rajakesarivaram or Rajarajadeva 1. Records gift of a golden bowl by a queen of Rajarajadeva.

112 of 1896 (Tamil) — On the same wall. A record in the nineteenth year of the Chola king Ko Rajaraja Rajakesarivarman or Rajarajadeva I. Records gift of a string of rubies by another queen of his.

113 of 1896 (Tamil) — On the west wall of the same shrine. A record in the second year of the Chola king Ko

Parakesarivarman or Vira Rajendradeva. Records gift of several villages. (As the king was a Parakesari we have to infer that Vira Rajendra II (Kulottunga Chola III) was intended).

114 of 1896 (Tamil) — On the north wall of the same shrine. A record in the twenty-ninth year of the Chola king Ko Rajakesarivarman or Rajadhirajadeva I. Records gift of land. The king should be the first of that name, as the second did not rule for such a long period.

115 of 1896 (Tamil) — On the same wall. A record in the twenty-seventh year of the Chola king Ko Rajakesarivarman or Rajarajadeva I.

116 of 1896 (Tamil) — On the same wall. A record in the twenty-seventh year of the Chola king Ko Rajakesarivarman or Rajarajadeva I. Records gift of a lamp.

117 of 1896 (Tamil) — On the same wall. A record in the twenty-eighth year of the Chola king Ko Rajakesarivarman or Rajarajadeva I. Records gift of a lamp by the mother of a queen.

118 of 1896 (Tamil) — On the north wall of the second prakara of the same temple. A record in the eighth year of the Chola king Ko Parakesarivarman or Kulottunga Choladeva (III?). Records gift of a lamp.

119 of 1896 (Tamil) — On the same wall. A record in the twenty-second year of the Chola king Tribhuvanachakravartin Rajarajadeva. Records a sale of land to the temple.

120 of 1896 (Tamil) — On the same wall. A record in the fifth year of the Pandya king Ko Maravarman or Vikrama Pandya. Records gift of a lamp. (The king was not probably the same as one who ascended the throne in A.D. 1282, and who had the titles of "the Sun to the darkness of the Kerala race" and "the conqueror of Viragandagopala and Ganapati").

121 of 1896 (Tamil) — On the west wall of the same prakara, right of entrance. A record in the fifth year of the

Chola king Ko Parakesarivarmán or Vikrama Choladeva (1118-35). Records gift of land.

122 of 1896 (Tamil and Grantha) — On the same wall left of entrance. A record in the seventh year of the Pandya king Vikrama Pandyadeva. Records gift of land. The inscription refers to a victory over the Kakatiya king Ganapati. See No. 120 for the identity of the king.

442 of 1918 (Tamil) — On the north wall of the central shrine in the same temple. Built in at the beginning and middle. Records gift of 30 kasus for a lamp by queen Vanavan Mahadeviyar or Tribhuvana Mahadeviyar.

443 of 1918 (Tamil) — On the same wall. Registers a gift of gold to the temple of Sri Tiruvenkadadeva at Nangur in Vadakarainangurnadu.

444 of 1918 (Tamil) — On the same wall. Mentions the images made and jewels and vessels presented by Parantakan Mahadeviyar or Sembiyan Mahadeviyar, the daughter of Malavarayar, the mother of Uttama Chola and queen of Gandaraditya, in the fourth and sixth years of Uttama Chola. It was in the fourth year of the reign of Rajakesarivarman, in the third and tenth years of Parakesarivarman and in the second year of Gandaradityadeva or Mummudi Choladeva.

445 of 1918 (Tamil) — On the same wall. Seems to record a gift of money by a native of Kunram in (Venni) Kurram, for the requirements of the temple.

446 of 1918 (Tamil) — On the same wall. Records gift of money for two lamps to the temple of Tiruvenkadudaiyar by Araiyan Nambanangai, the mother of queen Trailokya Mudaiyar.

447 of 1918 (Tamil) — On the same wall. Records gift of gold for a lamp to the same temple by Nakkan Lokachintamaniyar, the mother of queen Villavan

Mahadeviyar. Nangurnadu is stated to be a sub-division of Vadagarai Rajendrasimhavalanadu.

448 of 1918 (Tamil) — On the same wall. Records gift of sheep for lamps to the same temple by Rajaraja's queen Vanavanmadeviyar or Tribhuvanamadeviyar, the mother of Rajendra Chola.

449 of 1918 (Tamil) — On the same wall. Records gift of gold as offerings to the image of Adavallar in the temple of Tiruvenkadudaiyar at Nangur in Nangurnadu, a sub-division of Rajendrasinghavalanadu, by Kuttan Viraniyar, a queen of the king.

450 of 1918 (Tamil) — On the north, west and south walls of the same shrine. Records that Amalan Seyyavayar set up the image of Pichchadevar, gave lands for its requirements, presented gold and silver ornaments, opened a charity house, and provided for its maintenance. The same person is said to have obtained lands for the temple from the king's father, 'who was pleased to take Purvadesam, Gangai and Kidaram'.

451 of 1918 (Tamil) — On the north, west and south walls of the same shrine. Records gift of gold and silver ornaments to the image of Pichchadevar by the donor mentioned in No. 450 above.

452 of 1918 (Tamil) — On the west and south walls of the same shrine. Recorods gift of taxes on certain villages for monthly festivals and offerings, to the temple of Tiruvenkadudiyar at Nangur in Nargurnadu, a sub-division of Rajadhiraja-valanadu, to be conducted on the birthday asterism Aslesha, of the king. The reignal year "2 + 1" is repeated as "second year and the 234th day" in the body of the inscription.

453 of 1918 (Tamil) — On the same wall. Records gift of gold to the same temple for worship, offerings, festivals and feeding.

454 of 1918 (Tamil) — On the south wall of the same shrine. Registers a gift of gold for Sengalunir tiruvasigai (an aureola of red lilies) and gold flowers to the temple of Tiruvenkadudeva, by the servants (mulaparivara and mulaparivaravitteru) of the king.

455 of 1918 (Tamil) — On the same wall. Records gift of money by the officers of the king for festivals in the month of Margali.

456 of 1918 (Tamil) — On the same wall. Records gift of money for offerings and jewels to the image of Vrishabavahanadeva set up in the same temple by Kolakkavan.

457 of 1918 (Tamil) — On the same wall. Records the setting up of a copper image of the goddess Vrishabavahanadeva, by certain persons belonging to the Rajaraja jananatha terinja parivara.

458 of 1918 (Tamil) — On the same wall. Records gift of sheep for a lamp to the temple of Trivenkadudaiyar.

459 of 1918 (Tamil) — Records gift of money for offerings, bathing, feeding etc. to the Tiruvengadudeva, by a cavalier of the king's troop who was a native of Attuppallinayaman.

460 of 1918 (Tamil) — On the same wall. Seems to register a gift of gold by Udaiyapirattiyar Tribhuvana Mahadeviyar, the mother of the king.

461 of 1918 (Tamil) — On the same wall. Records gift of sheep for a lamp.

462 of 1918 (Tamil) — On the same wall. Records gift of sheep for a lamp.

463 of 1918 (Tamil) — On the same wall. Records gift of sheep for a lamp to the temple of Tiruvengadudeva by a servant of the queen.

464 of 1918 (Tamil) — Records gift of money for incense

etc. by Queen Nakkan Parakkamandal or Panchavan Madeviyar.

465 of 1918 (Tamil) — On the pillar near the north wall of the same shrine. Records gift of land for offerings to the temple of Tiruvenkattuperumal, by a native of Kodungolur in Malainadu. Mentions the gosalai.

466 of 1918 (Tamil) — On the same pillar. Records gift of sheep for a lamp.

467 of 1918 (Tamil) — On the north wall of the mandapa in front of the same shrine. Records gift of land for offerings in connection with service instituted by a certain Vanadarayar in the temple of Tiruvenkadudaiyar.

468 of 1918 (Tamil) — On the same wall. Records a sale of land by the assembly of Kaliyugakannachaturvedimangalam in Adiyamangainadu, a sub-division of Rajadhirajavalanadu to the same temple. The assembly met in the hall called Rajadhirajachatussalai in the same village.

469 of 1918 (Tamil) — On the same wall. Contains only a portion of the historical introduction of the king and the names of the signatories.

470 of 1918 (Tamil) — On the west wall of the same mandapa. Records gift of land for offerings, flower-gardens etc. to the image of Devarganayakadeva in the temple at Tiruvenkadu by the assembly of Kaliyugakannachaturvedimangalam in Adiyamangainadu.

471 of 1918 (Tamil) — On the same wall. Fixes the amount of taxes that must be realised from certain temple lands.

472 of 1918 (Grantha and Sanskrit) — On the same wall.

473 of 1918 (Tamil) — On the east wall of the same mandapa. Records gift of land by purchase in Perundottam or Kaliyugakannachaturvedimangalam in Adiyamnagainadu, a sub-division of Rajadhirajavalanadu, for a matha established

in the street called Vikramasolantiruvidi. The king was seated
on the steps in the south side of the pavilion called Vikrama-
solantirumandapa in the temple of Tiruvenkadudaiyar in
Nangurnadu, a sub-division of Rajadhirajavalanadu. Refers to
the 44th year of the king's father Kulottunga Choladeva.

474 of 1918 (Tamil) — On the west wall of the
Dakshinamurthi shrine in the same temple. Registers a
sarvamanya grant for expenses connected with the service
called Nagarasansandi instituted by a certain Manunidikandan
Akalankan Nagarasar.

475 of 1918 (Grantha) — Registers the gift of a perpetual
lamp to Svetaranyesvara by a Brahman named Vyasa.

476 of 1918 (Tamil) — On the north wall of the
Chandrasekara shrine in the same temple. Records that the
village of Triuvembalanallur once granted to the temple of
Tiruvenkadudaiya Nayanar was in ruins and that Mallarasa,
son of Annamarasa, rehabitated it under the name
Virupparayanpattinam and set apart the monthly income from
it to the temple.

477 of 1918 (Tamil) — On the north wall of the Ganesa
shrine in the same temple. Records gift of money for a lamp
to the shrine of Periyapillayar by a native of Ilansu(r) in
Velanadu, a sub-division of Kulottungasolavalanadu.

478 of 1918 (Tamil) — On the west wall of the same
shrine. Records gift of land by purchase for offerings to the
same shrine by a native of Ulaguyyakkondasolachaturvedi-
mangalam.

479 of 1918 (Tamil) — On the east inner gopura of the
same temple, right of entrance. Registers a gift of gold by a
native of Nangur.

480 of 1918 — In the same place. Seems to register the
gift of the village of Virasolanallur in Rajadhirajavalanadu for
the service of Adaiyavalanandansandi instituted in the temple

at Tiruvenkadu. Mentions Vijaya Gandagopala, the younger brother of Malavarayar.

481 of 1918 (Tamil) — On the same place. Records gift of land in Tiruvenkadu, for service, festivals, etc., instituted in the name of the king in the same temple.

482 of 1918 (Tamil) — In the same place. Registers a gift of 25 kalanjus of gold for a lamp to the temple of Tiruvenkadudeva, by Sadurayan Uttamasiliyar, wife of Vannaduduiyar.

483 of 1918 (Tamil) — In the same place. Registers a similar gift of 25 kalanjus of gold for a lamp.

484 of 1918 (Tamil) — In the same place. Records gift of 90 sheep for a lamp to the same temple by a lady called Aruran Ambalattadigal.

485 of 1918 (Tamil) — In the same place. Seems to register gift of a lamp.

486 of 1918 (Tamil) — In the same place. Registers a gift of land for a lamp to the same temple by a queen of Uttama Chola.

487 of 1918 (Tamil) — On the same gopura, left side. Records gift of land in Viranarayananallur and other places for the service of Manangattansandi instituted in the temple of Tiruvenkadudaiyar, by Pichchan Malavarayar.

488 of 1918 (Tamil) — In the same place. Registers a gift of two velis of land and certain taxes, for conducting the service of Valattuvalvittansandi instituted in the same temple by Tondaimanar after his own name.

489 of 1918 (Tamil) — In the same place. Records gift of land for drummers.

490 of 1918 (Tamil) — In the same place. Records gift of 30 kalanjus of gold for offerings to the temple of Tiruvenkadudeva, by a merchant of Adirayamangalyapura in Merkanadu.

491 of 1918 (Tamil) — In the same place. Records gift of land by purchase for offerings to the temple of Tiruvenkadudeva, by a member of the community of Parthivasegaratterinja Kaikkolar.

492 of 1918 (Tamil) — On the outer east gopura of the same temple, right of entrance. States that the entrance was called Vikkirama Pandyantiruvasal.

493 of 1918 (Sanskrit in Grantha and Tamil) — In the same place. Records the assignment of certain revenues to the temple of Svetaranyanatha by the king.

494 of 1918 (Tamil) — On the west inner gopura in the same temple, right of entrance. Seems to register a gift of land.

495 of 1918 (Tamil) — On the same gopura on the left side. Seems to register gift of gold ornaments by a Kaikkolan. Below this is engraved a portion of an inscription which relates to the reclaiming of a certain temple land and the fresh assignment of it on a higher rate of rent.

496 of 1918 (Sanskrit in Grantha) — In the same place. Records gift of sheep for four lamps to the temple at Svetavana.

497 of 1918 (Tamil) — Seems to provide for the maintenance of a flower garden to the temple of Tiruvenkadudeva.

498 of 1918 (Tamil) — In the same place. Records gift of land for conducting service instituted in the temple by Kulasekhara Tondaimanar.

499 of 1918 (Tamil) — In the same place. Seems to register a gift of sheep for a lamp.

500 of 1918 (Tamil) — On the outer west gopura in the same temple, right side. Records gift of land for a lamp.

501 of 1918 (Sanskrit in Grantha) — On the same gopura, left side. Records that Setu, Vadavur, Chidambaram, Gokarnam, Pampapuri, Svetaranyam, Vatatavi, Sonadri,

Kanchi, Srigiri, Kalahasli, Nagari, Kedari, Varanasi, and Kailasa are mukti sthalas.

502 of 1918 (Tamil) — On the north wall of the first prakara of the same temple. Registers gift of money by several individuals for bringing under cultivation certain temple lands which had been lying waste, the donees agreeing to meet certain items of expenses such as burning lamps, reciting Vedas during the processions of the god Devaganayan and feeding Apurvins in the temple of Tiruvenkadudaiyar in Nangurnadu, a sub-division of Rajadhirajavalanadu and also to pay the taxes on the lands.

503 of 1918 (Tamil) — On the same wall. Records gift of land by purchase in Tirunalalvayil for lamps to the same temple by a native of Vagur or Alagiyasolachaturvedimangalam which was a taniyur in Vadagaraivesalippadi, a sub-division of Naduvilnadu or Rajarajavalanadu.

504 of 1918 (Tamil) — On the same wall. Registers a gift of land by purchase at Tiruppanangadu for lamps to the same temple for the merit of Tiruvenkattunachiyar, daughter of Araiyan Udaiyancheydan or Solakonar, the headman of Mattur and wife of Tayilunallaperumal or Ilangovelar of Sendamangalam in Rajendrasolavalanadu.

505 of 1918 (Tamil) — On the same wall. Registers a gift of land by purchase for lamps to the same temple by a native of Kunrattur in Kunratturnadu, a sub-division of Puliyurkottam or Kulottungasolavalanadu, which was a district of Jayangodasalomandalam.

506 of 1918 (Tamil) — On the west wall of the same prakara. Records the assignment to the same temple of income in kind and money from certain lands which were previously owned by three persons who had proved traitors and therefore dispossessed of their holdings. Mentions the royal secretary Neriyudaichchola Muvendavelan.

507 of 1918 (Tamil) — On the same wall. Records gift of land in Rajarajanallur, a hamlet of Talachchangadu which was a brahmadeya in the eastern division of Jayangondasolavalanadu for offerings, festivals, processions etc., to the same temple.

508 of 1918 (Tamil) — On the same wall. Records remission of taxes by the assembly of Irukkaiyur, a brahmadeya in Nangurnadu, a sub-division of Rajadhiraja-valanadu on certain lands which were given for a flower garden to the temple of Tiruchchirrambalamudaiyar at Perumbalappuliyur. The inscription was ordered to be engraved in the temple of Tiruvenkadudaiyar.

509 of 1918 (Tamil) — On the same wall. The inscription stops with the details of the date.

510 of 1918 (Tamil) — On the same wall. Records gift of land and house sites to certain Brahmans for reciting the Vedas, for making a flower garden and for providing offerings to the temple of Virapandisvaramudaiya Nayanar built in the name of the king by certain Vaidya Chakravarti. The goddess is called Veyanatoli Nachchiyar.

511 of 1918 (Tamil) — On the same wall. Records gift of land for offerings in connection with the service of Kaliyugaramanasandi instituted in the temple in the name of the king and for the bathing of the god and the Nayanmars at the mouth of the river (Kaveri).

512 of 1918 (Tamil) — On the same wall. Registers a gift of land by purchase by a native of Kulottungasola-chaturvedimangalam in Purangarambainadu, a sub-division of Rajendrasolavalanadu for lamps to the temple of Tiruvenkadudaiyar.

513 of 1918 (Tamil) — On the same wall. Seems to register the gift of the village of Abhimuktisuramangalam made at the instance of the king's officer Pallavarayar to the

same temple. Mentions the royal secretary Neriyudaichchola Muvendavelan.

514 of 1918 (Tamil) — On the same wall. Records that up to the thirty-second year of the king (Srivallabha) commencing from the time when Kopperunjingadeva was fighting against the Kannadiyas who were building fortress on the north bank of the river Kaveri, festivals of the temple were not conducted and that they were now ordered to be resumed. A certain Tondaimanar is stated to be an officer of this king and Sundara Pandyadeva.

515 of 1918 (Tamil) — On the east wall of the same prakara. Records gift of land under the name Kulottungasolan Pasali, in Tiruvalinadu for lamps to the same temple by a native of Pasali in Pasalinadu, a sub-division of Manavilkottam which was a district of Jayangondasolamandalam.

516 of 1918 (Tamil) — On the same wall. Seems to register a gift of land for lamps, to the same temple.

517 of 1918 (Tamil) — On the same wall. Records gift of land for a lamp to the same temple by a Brahmin lady of Vijayarajendrachaturvedimangalam.

518 of 1918 (Tamil) — On the same wall. Records gift of land by purchase for a lamp to the temple of Tiruvenkadudaiyar in Rajadhirajavalanadu by a native of Poruvanur in Pattinakurram, a sub-division of Geyamanikkavalanadu. Refers to a breach in the Kaveri at Tirupattur and the consequent silting up of the surrounding fields.

519 of 1918 (Tamil) — On the same wall. Records gift of land by purchase to the same temple for lamps by a native of Kunrattur in Kunratturnadu, a sub-division of Puliyurkottam or Kulottungasolavalanadu which was a district of Jayangondasolamandalam. As the land was lying

fallow for many years, the donor paid money for bringing it under cultivation.

520 of 1918 (Tamil) — On the same wall. Records gift of land by purchase in Nelvayil, by a native of Alampakkam, in Puliyurkottam or Kulottungasolavalanadu which was a district of Jayangondasolamandalam for lands to the temple of Tiruvenkadudaiyar. The donor also gave money for reclaiming the land.

521 of 1918 (Tamil) — On the west wall of the first prakara of the shrine of the goddess Brahmavidhe. Records that the walls of the shrine of the goddess Periyanayaki-amman were constructed by Dandayuda Pandaram.

NOTES

1. When Bhagiratha prayed for the flow of the celestial river Ganges into this world to give salvation to his deceased uncles, the god Siva to satisfy him received the Ganges in His matted hair. The goddess Parvati resented this idea of His thus having given prominence to another lady by receiving her in the head — a more elevated situation — and to satisfy her, He embraced the Goddess and entreated her, promising to lower the River Goddess from that elevated situation.

2. In this terrific form of the god Siva, there are two tusks, one on each side. The worship of this form is supposed to give victory and riches and also destroy even the worst sins, like *Brahamahatya* or Brahmanicide. Special worship is made to Him on the *Chadurdasi*, i.e., the fourteenth day of the dark fortnight in the month of Panguni (March-April) and hence that day is known as Agora Chadurdasi.

3. *Inscriptions of the Madras Presidency*, Government of Madras, 1919, Vol. II, pp. 1383 and 1384.

Chapter 9

MAYAVARAM

This sacred place is on the southern railway. The place is so called because the goddess Parvati[1] manifested herself in the form of a Mayura (Pea-hen) and worshipped Siva, and this is represented on the west of the eastern gopura (tower). Besides this, other fine sculptures are also found in the niches on the outside of the central shrine of the temple of Mayuranatha. Of these one is an Alinganamurti[2].

A bath in the river Kaveri at this place during the month of Tula (October-November) is said to be very holy.

"Bathing in the sacred waters of the Kaveri not only expiates all sins but also confers on the bather every sacrificial bliss, every desire and moksha (salvation) in the end. Waters in the fourteen worlds join the Kaveri in the month of Tula for the expiation of sins. It is impossible even for Adisesha (Hydra) to describe the sublimity of Tula-Kaveri. The greatest sinner will become a heavenly habitant by bathing for three days in the Kaveri in the month of Tula. From its source in the Sahya mountains till it joins the sea, the Kaveri is spotted on both sides by Siva and Vishnu shrines. There are many asramas (hermitages) of sages as well. The sacredness of Tula-Kaveri is indescribable by any except Brahma, Vishnu and Siva in in the three worlds. As the waves of the Kaveri

are a number of rivulets, its beds a number of tanks, its sands
a habitat for angels, bathing in it would give us the same *phala*
or result as bathing in innumerable sacred streams. The sacred
streams that join the Kaveri in the month of Tula are as
innumerable as the cosmic atoms, the stars in the heavens, the
showers of rain and rankest seeds. A drop in the Kaveri can
be regarded as a stream in itself. As the person that bathes
in the sacred waters of the Kaveri in the month of Tula is not
only relieved of all sins but sits at the feet of the Almighty.

On both sides of the Kaveri the river is flooded with
images of Siva as cosmic manifester. The pools formed on
the banks of the Kaveri are sacred streams in themselves, and
the sand and stones angelic hosts. The Kaveri which rises in
the Sahya mountains is therefore the best of all rivers. Many
a sacred stream joins it in the Tula month. It rids us of the
five greatest sins and gives us the fruit of the asvamedha
(horse-sacrifice). The angels, the pitris, the great sages and
others extol the sacredness of the Kaveri in this month. Who
bathes in the sacred waters for three days, is rid of all his sins
and reaches the threshold of Vaikunta (Paradise). He will be
worshipped in the Brahmaloka. Any small gift given to a good
person in a good time leads to great results. Any gift therefore
of rice and water in the Tula month multiplies a million-fold,
and a Vedic text says that any oblation offered to the pitris
in the shape of rice, Sraddha, or water with sesamee seed lasts
as long as the world. Brahma and other gods, the seven
mothers, the Apsaric hosts, Sarasvati, Lakshmi, Gouri,
Indrani, Rohni and other feminine angels make it a point to
bathe daily in the waters of the Kaveri at this time. Long ago
Brahma created the Kaveri, the best of sacred streams, to
bestow on mankind food and final beatitude. The men and
women born on its sacred banks are privileged with
multitudinous pleasures. Even the animals, birds, trees,

worms and all the creatures get moksha as soon as its fine
soft cold breeze falls on them. What doubt is there, therefore,
for people who bathe in it with bhakti to get moksha? Is it
possible for Sesha, who is able to narrate anything in detail
for a thousand years, to tell about its sacredness? I shall relate
to you briefly about it.

Is it possible for any other than the thousand-mouthed
Sesha to talk of the importance of education, the sacredness
of Tulasi and the Ganges, the fasting on Ekadasi day, the
worship of the idol of Siva by Tulasi? Listen attentively to
all that I tell you about the sacredness of the Kaveri.

The Ganges rising from the feet of Vishnu is regarded the
most sacred among rivers, the Tulasi amongst flowers, the
Ekadasi day amongst vratas, the five great sacrifices amongst
yajnas, Madhava amongst gods, the Omkara amongst sounds,
the Gayatri amongst mantras, the Sama amongst the Vedas,
Sankara amongst the Rudras, Arunthathi amongst Brahman
wives, Rama amongst womankind, the moon amongst the
planets, the sun amongst radiant objects, sacrifice of the mind
amongst sacrifices, charity amongst friends, japa amongst
tapas, married life amongst asramas, the Brahman amongst
castes, the Brahmastra amongst Astikas, Sriranga amongst
sacred placed, Ramasetu amongst the purifiers, the
Purushasukta amongst the Suktas, Kamadhenu (the angelic
cow) amongst cows, Krita Yuga amongst the Yugas, so is the
Kaveri amongst sacred streams. Chanting the name of
Ganges, visiting Dhanushkoti, listening to Ramayana
meditating on the Kaveri or lead to mukti.

Human life is the result of good deeds in many a thousand
prior incarnation. And by good deeds done in millions of
previous human existences a man becomes *dwija* or twice-
born. A person who does not bathe in the Kaveri is a fool.
The man who constantly bathes in the Kaveri in the Tula

month need not be troubled with other vratas. By bathing once in the Kaveri he becomes as Narayana. There are expiations for any shortcomings in other vratas. A *thushmin* bath, even without a mantra, or any rule, rids one of all sins committed in seven former births. If the same is done observing all the rules, the parents for seven generations attain moksha and the bather reaches Hari. Rising in Brahma muhurta in the early morn, meditating on Hari, chanting the name of Kaveri, worshipping Ranganatha, telling the Aghamarshana Sukta, wearing a clean white cloth and dabbing sacred ashes on the forehead and while performing the daily ablutions, one should hear the story patiently, after worshipping the Brahman well-versed in narrating the Purana.

The people should all assemble at a particular spot, greet the best of Brahmans and as a mark of respect offer him new clothes and jewels. A good Brahman is a subduer of the senses, a patient man, well-versed in the Vedas and Vedangas, is fondly bent on hearing the Vedanta and an observer of the Dharma Sastras. He is well conversant with the Puranas, one extremely diligent and always treads the path of virtue. They should consider him to be no other than the great Vyasa, and with hands uplifted should prostrate before him and inform him of their desire to hear the Kaveri Mahatmya.

The bath in the Kaveri must be taken observing certain rules otherwise it is utterly useless. If one is unable to maintain a discipline, one may take a thushmin bath. A bath taken in the proper way leads to the attainment of svarga (heaven). Anointing the head with oil, sleeping during day time beetle-chewing, friendship with the vicious, sleeping on a mat, using forbidden vegetables, receiving of gifts, taking meals in a stranger's house, going on a journey — all these are forbidden. So is consuming Kushmanda, Embylic myrabolam, Bengal gram, pulse drumstick, cucumber, etc., or eating in a plate, stale food, fried food, remnants of food eaten by boys, cold rice, food not consecrated to the gods, food filled with hair, sraddha remnants, Sudra remnants. As moksha cannot be attained except by hard and often painful application of the physique, these rules must be observed. There is hardly any doubt that the person who bathes in the Kaveri without all desire or the enjoyment of previously enjoyed objects, obtains mukti.

This mundane existence of ours is a mere bubble. Yama is always pouncing on this jeeva of ours lying in our body. Morning and evening are devourers of time. We must seek for the attainment of moksha while the senses, are intact and while the body is easily pliable. I tell you over and over again not to waste the day. While sacred streams are available, in the pleasant winter season, one must give up the devil-like sleep, rise very early in the morning and bathe in the waters of the Kaveri. I raise my right hand and hammer my thoughts into you. The Kaveri, which would rid you of all sins, flows on forever. Its waters, therefore, are capable of yielding excellent results unattainable otherwise.

Those that bathe in its waters will be purged of all sin and would attain riches of all sorts. Those who commit matricide, patricide, cow-killing, abortion, adultery with a guru's wife and other similar horrible deeds, those who do not study the Vedas, or do not pursue a time-honoured correct custom, would be adorned in the Brahmaloka by bathing but once in the sacred waters of the Kaveri. So can drunkards, eaters of food not consecrated to the deity or used by guests, non-performers of agnihotra, aupasana, vaisvadeva and other similar sacrificial rites, and other doers of various sorts of sinful deeds. Those who cannot bathe in its icy-cold waters, can do so at least by warming it. And those who cannot do even that must at least hear the *Tula Kaveri Mahatmya*. He who cannot do even that must amply remunerate the reader. If poor, he must with a good heart extol the reader and make others reward him. As women, Sudras, boys, and lower orders have no Vedic rites, they must rise very early in the morning and must do a thushmin bath. Those who offer libations to the devas, rishis and pitris with sesamum seeds and rice after bathing at dawn, will be blessed with long life. Suras, Naras, Uragas, Yakshas, Kimpurushas, Rudras, Adityas, Maruts and others would be well-pleased with him. Everyone must hear the *Kaveri Mahatmya*, after prostrating to Surya, the Sun god, the witness of all the worlds. He would became Vachaspati, at whose house a manuscript of the Mahatmya is kept and worshipped. If a Mahatmya kosa is reserved for a man (Brahman) of letters, he would be rid of all sin and would attain Vaikuntha.

I shall narrate the charities that can be offered in the month. Whoever with a good heart offers libations to men, devas, rishis and pitris and feeds Brahmans with food of the season, will be adored in Brahmaloka. Whoever in the month of Tula lights lamps of ghee or oil before Hari or Hara will go to Suryaloka and thence come back to the world as a *jnani*. Whoever offers a cloth to a poor Brahman will be blessed with long life and prosperity, and finally attain Chandraloka. Whoever, while bathing in the Kaveri in the month of Tula, bestows on a poverty-stricken, wayfaring intelligent Brahman with a large family, a gift of a plot of ground or a house, will enjoy all sorts of terrestrial comforts and then the comforts of Brahmaloka, and then come back to earth as a king. Whoever gives money or grain to the poor will become the friend of Kubera, and will be blessed with long life. He who gives money in the month of Tula, will have plenty of children, though he be barren at present. Whoever gives a pair of oxen to a poor Brahman agriculturist, will enjoy all the

pleasures of Goloka, and will regenerate on earth as king.
Whoever gives a cow with a calf, will be blessed with
children, will become great, will be rid of the three sorts of
loans, will reach the world of pitris and his family will live
long. A donor of a buffalo has no reason to fear untimely death
and his family will live for hundred years. A giver of grain
to a poor Brahman, will live in peace and plenty and be
blessed with offspring. He would then live with an excellent
woman for the period of fourteen Indras, and then become a
landowner. Kali will not live in the house of a man who offers
rice to a poor man. Rambha's (an angelic woman) breasts will
be sucked by the man who gives Rambhaphala (plantain-
fruits) as charity; and her lips by the bestower of cocoanuts
and pan-supari. The giver of camphor, sandal, musk and other
scents to a Brahman, will enjoy the company of apsaras in
svarga and then regenerate on earth as lord paramount. The
bestower of cow's milk, cow's ghee, cow's curd will have
cattle and children in plenty, and will be blessed with long
life. The offerer of myrabolam powder will become a
metaphysician and an excellent theist. Whoever in the month
of Tula gives sesamum to a Brahman as an oblation to the
pitris, will attain the same position as one who performs
Sraddha at Gaya. He who gives to a poor family-man a cot,
a soft cushion, a mat, a pillow, etc. will enjoy the sweet soft
embrace of a lovely woman. An umbrella-giver will live in
a storeyed house. Whoever offers lotuses and other flowers
of the season for the adoration of Vishnu with bhakti will
enjoy all the pleasures of this life, live for a length of time
in Brahmaloka, and thence return to earth as a wealthy Vishnu
disciple with plenty of children. The giver of a pair of
yagnopavitas (sacerdotal threads) will regenerate ten times as
a Vedic seer. Whoever offers deer's skin (Maunji) to a
bachelor will be rid of disease of any sort, and will become

a great intellectual; and one who gives cotton for the preparation of the sacerdotal thread will not be attached with leprosy. He who gives the best Tulasi to a disciple of Vishnu will live in the best possible way in all the worlds, and eventually become a Sarvabhauma. The giver of sacrificial sticks (palasa) will become an intelligent performer of sacrifices. Whoever feeds sumptuously with various sorts of vegetables, fruits, sweet-scented viands, will undoubtedly attain god-head. The gift of Bengal gram, honey, oil, pepper and other pungeants, jaggery, sugar, ghee etc., as far as practicable, will lead not only to heaven, but will make him a resident of the other happy worlds in succession. In days of yore an unchaste Brahman woman rode sublime upon the wings of ecstasy, and saw the living throne by bathing in the sacred waters of the Kaveri. The three million and a half of tirthas, with the Ganges in front, commingle with the Kaveri in the month of Tula by Kesava's orders. Whoever maintains the bath in the Ganges as a strict religious observance for hundred years, it is only he who would be able to bathe in the Kaveri in the month of Tula.

The world-purifying Ganges once went to Brahma and wept bitterly and asked how best she would be rid of the sins which have been transferred from her bathers. Brahma informed that the best solution to the question would be by bathing in the waters of the Kaveri.

Sins for seven generations will be removed by bathing in the Kaveri. A bath in the month of Tula will feed the body and purify the soul. Is there any one better than Sesha to extoll the glories of Kaveri?

On the borders of the Vrishabha mountains and on the banks of Kritamala river was the beautiful city of Mathura inhabitat with charioteers, elephant drivers, cavalry and infantry, hemmed in on all sides with lofty parapets. There

were storeyed houses of Brahmans, Kshatriyas, Vaisyas and
Sudras, with ramparts, towers, porticos, shops, busy centres
and bowers. In the city there livied a Brahman, Vedarasi by
name, deeply learned in the Vedas and Vedengas. A subduer
of Indrias (senses), and the friend of everybody, he was far
above the agitation of both the extremes — cold and heat,
wealth and woe, profit and loss, victory and defeat —
unenvious, a Vishnu devotee, a yogi an ideal host, a bather
at the early moon, an observer of the five sacrifices and the
foremost among the wise. He had a pure chaste wife,
Chandrakanta by name, with the face resembling the moon,
breasts like the frontal lobes of fattened elephants, the body
of a golden hue, the pace of the fattened elephant and red lips.
Bedecked with pearl necklace, diamond ornaments, she kept
the body smeared all over with sweet-scented sandal paste.
This lady, intent on attaining eternal bliss, was doing the
greatest amount of good service to her dearly-cherished lord.
Close by was Vidyavati, a Brahman woman, who slew her
husband. She was the most abject, fickle-minded and spoiler
of feminine chastity. This prostitute, intent on schooling the
lady in her ways of life, approached her, and said: 'My dear
Chandrakanta, my mother, lotus-eyed, I am your best friend.
If you have any secrets, you can freely communicate them to
me. Does your husband obey your orders? The beauty of
feminine life is ephemeral. Do you enjoy sexual happiness
independently? If not, I shall put you in the way of your doing
so?' The lady, hearing the poisoned horrible words of the
woman, was overcome by shame and said, 'How dare you talk
such trash before me with an evil heart? If I do not reply to
you, you will ruin me by spreading all sorts of rumours
against me.' Thinking thus, and fearing the consequences, she
replied, 'The best period for copulation is from the fifth day
after menstruation till the sixteenth, and my husband, well

versed in Srutis and Smritis, will cohabit with me during these twelve days, exclusive of the days unenjoined by law. We are enjoying temporal felicity as ordained by the Sastras, and are paving the way for celestial bliss. The wise say that if conception is formed on a good day of copulation, the son that will issue forth from such an act, will be intelligent, live long, and be rich; while those born at other times will be short-lived and sickly, and will be a source of woe to the parents. The following days are excluded for copulation: the 6th, 8th, 11th, 12th, 14th, new moon, full moon, the passage of the sun into the various signs of the Zodiac, the annual ceremony (Sraddha) days for parents, the star of birth, star by name Sravana: vrata period, morning, twilights etc. During the above mentioned period, the person that shaves, copulates, anoints or cleans his teeth though he be well-versed in all the four Vedas, will assuredly become an outcaste. Thus have I briefly told you the ordinances enjoined for a grihasta (a family man).' To which Vidyavati, intent on bringing Chandrakanta to her own level, replied, 'O madchap, you have spoiled all your happiness. Hear my word, therefore. As this sickly coil is dear to all animate existences, why do you waste your flush of womanhood? Why not enjoy sexual happiness? In old age the constitution will be shattered by disordered breasts, and abstinence will bring on its attendant evils — premature old age and disease. You are practically unaware of the humbug of your husband. He is keeping himself engaged with the maid-servant from morning to night, you are too simple, unhypocritical and pure-hearted, whereas your husband is a firebrand and pretends to be a good man externally. I heard too well of his misdeeds from an intimate prostitute friend of mine. I have told you all this as I am a sharer in all your joys and sorrows.' After hearing the sinful words of Vidyavati, Chandrakanta said, 'A husband is a god to woman, be he a mischievous, hot tempered, sickly, vile, and fellow. Apart from the adoration of the husband, there are no observances or free-will offerings of any sort or kind enjoined by the Vedas. To those women who aspire after svarga, a husband is the greatest of gods. The woman who abuses her lord will be born a dog.' The vile wretch of a Vidyavati, determined on outraging the chastity of Chandrakanta, replied, 'O mad fool! Have not Urvasi, Menaka, Rambha, Gritachi, Punjikasthala and other angelic women acted by the greatest of Rishis, and but for all that remained happy? The wise, considering the ephemerality of this mortal coil, enjoy happiness, terrestrial and celestial. All must covet felicity. Who has seen heaven or hell? Whatever we actually enjoy is heaven. I am aware of the truth of happiness and misery. Independence is happiness. I became independent and rid myself of all fear by murdering my husband. The free man is the happiest being. He alone is filled with tapas. He alone is fortunate. Is there any happiness for a servile wretch?' With illustrations like these which would abuse the mind and make it as fickle as possible, with thoughts which would lead one to hell in no time, Chandrakanta set at naught all hereditary acharas and remained a prostitute in private for a month, owing to the strange irony of fate, feminine fickleness, mental unrest and being overcome by the finely-pointed darts of Cupid. Then her Lord found out by her conduct in life, foul tongue etc., that she was immoral, ejected her out of the house, was wonder-struck at what happened even to his wife, made gifts of cattle, money, grain, houses, etc. to the deserving, was sore dismayed for illicit intercourse with a prostitute wife, and, as an expiation for the sin committed, went and reached the banks of the Kaveri."

INSCRIPTIONS[4]

Famous in Saivite tradition as the place where the Siva transformed his wife Parvati into a mayura (peahen) for disobedience and then restored her.

300 of 1911 (Tamil) — On the south wall of the first prakara of the Mayuranathaswami temple. A damaged and incomplete record in the fourteenth year of the Chola king Rajakesarivarman or Tribhuvanachakravartin Rajadhirajadeva II "who took Madurai (Madura) and Ilam (Ceylon)." Given the latter portion of the historical introduction beginning with Kadalsulnda. For the legend in connection with the Mayuranathaswami temple see *Tanj. Gazar.*, Vol. I, p. 231.

301 of 1911 (Tamil) — On the three faces of a pillar set up in the street in front of the same temple. A damaged record in the tenth year of the Pandya king Jatavarman Tribhuvanachakravartin Sundara-Pandyadeva. It is not known which of the three Pandyas of this name is referred to.

371 of 1907 (Tamil) — On the south wall of the first prakara of the same temple. A record in the twenty-sixth year of the Chola king Tribhuvanachakravartin Sri Rajadhirajadeva III. Records gift of money.

372 of 1907 (Tamil) — In one of the shrines in the northern side of the same temple. A record in the fourteenth year of the Chola king Tribhuvanachakravartin Sri Rajarajadeva III. Records gift of land to the shrine of the Goddess called Tiruppalliarai Nachiyar in the temple of Tirumayiladuturai Udaiyar. See *Ep. Ind.* Vol. X, p.134, where it is pointed out that the date corresponded to Sunday, October 7, A.D. 1229.

373 of 1907 (Tamil) — On a stone built into the floor in front of the central shrine in the same temple. A fragmentary record.

374 of 1907 (Tamil) — On the north wall of the mandapa in front of the central shrine in the Panchanadesvara temple in the same village. A damaged record in the thirty-first year of the king. Seems to record a gift of land.

375 of 1907 (Tamil) — On the same wall. A record in the thirty-second year of the Tribhuvanachakravartin Konerinmaikondan linked with the above. The temple is described as in No. 377 below.

376 of 1907 (Tamil) — On the same wall. A record in the nineteenth year of the king, whose name is not mentioned. Mentions the Vikrama Solan Madam and Kulottunga Solanallur or Kulottunga Solan Kurralam. Refers to the twenty-first year of Udaiyar Singandavirttarulinga Kulottunga Soladeva I (1070-1118).

377 of 1907 (Tamil) — On the same wall. A record in the nineteenth year of the king. Records gift of land to the image of Tiruvayarudaiyar set up at Kulottungasolanallur or Kulottunga Solankurralam, in Tiruvalundurnadu, a sub-division of Jayangondacholavalanadu. Refers also to the twenty-first year of Sungandavirtarulina Kulottunga Soladevar I (1070-1118).

378 of 1907 (Tamil) — On the north wall of the mandapa in front of the central shrine in the Panchanadesvara shrine. A record in the thirtieth year of Tribhuvanachakravartin Konerinmaikondan. Records gift of land.

379 of 1907 (Tamil) — On the same wall. A record in the thirtieth year of the king whose name is not mentioned. Records gift of land. Refers to the twenty-first year of Udaiyar Sungandavirttarulina Kulottunga Soladevar I (1070-1118).

380 of 1907 (Tamil) — On the same wall. A record in the twenty-fifth year of the Chola king Tribhuvanachakravartin Sri Kulottunga Choladeva III, "who was pleased to take Madurai (Madura), Ilam (Ceylon), Karuvur and the crowned

head of the Pandya." Records gift of land to the temple of Udaiyar Tiruvayarudaiyar at Kulottungasolankurralam in Tiruvalundur-nadu, a sub-division of Jayangondachola-valanadu. See *Ep. Ind.,* Vol. X, p.130. Date same as that of the next epigraph.

881 of 1907 (Tamil) — On the east wall of the same mandapa. A record in the twenty-fifth year (Makara, Purva 14, Monday) of the Chola King Tribhuvanachakravartin Sri Kulototunga Choladeva III, "who was pleased to take Madurai (Madura), Ilam (Ceylon), Karuvur and the crowned head of the Pandyan." Records gift of paddy. Mentions Sivapadasekharachaturvedimangalam. See *Ep. Ind.,* Vol. X, p.130, where it is pointed out that the date corresponded to Monday, December 30, A.D. 1202 (but the "tithi" 14 ought to be 15).

382 of 1907 (Tamil) — On the same wall. A record in the thirty-third year of the Chola king Tribhuvanachakravartin Tribhuvanaviradeva Kulottunga III (1178-1216), "who was pleased to take Madurai (Madura), Ilam (Ceylon), Karuvur and the crowned head of the Pandya and was pleased to perform the anointment of heroes and the anointment of victors." Records gift of land by the sabha of Nallur Padukkudi.

383 of 1907 (Tamil) — On the same wall. A record in the twenty-fifth year of the Chola king Tribhuvanachakravartin Sri Kulototunga Choladeva III, "who was pleased to take Madurai (Madura), Ilam (Ceylon), Karuvur and the crowned head of the Pandya." Records gift of land. See *Ep. Ind.,* Vol.X, p.131 and No. 621, above.

384 of 1907 (Tamil) — On the same wall. A record of the Chola king Tribhuvanachakravartin Sri Kulottunga Choladeva III, "who was pleased to take Madurai (Madura), Ilam (Ceylon) and the crowned head of the Pandya," the date of which is damaged. Records gift of land.

385 of 1907 (Tamil) — On the south wall of the same mandapa. A record in the nineteenth year of the Chola king Tribhuvanachakravartin Sri Kulottunga Choladeva III "who took Madurai (Madura), Ilam (Ceylon) and was pleased to take the crowned head of the Pandya." Records sale of land.

TIRUVALUNDUR

Tiruvalundur or Enthaiur, called after the worship of Vishnu by the moon, is a small Vaishnava shrine on the north of the Kaveri. (*Entlm* in Tamil means the moon).

VAZHUVUR

Vazhuvur, another important shrine, is five miles away to the south-west of Mayavaram. Siva is represented here in the form of Viratteswara (Fig. 53). The story runs that the sages in ancient days, doubting the supremacy of god Siva, created an elephant to test their doubt. Siva took the form of Gajasamharamurti (slayer of the elephant) killed the animal, and wore its skin as a garment. The elephant, which is said to have come out from the temple tank, is installed between the conventional bull and the central shrine. Though Parvati got frightened at the new aspect of Siva, she took her stand close by Him, with the baby Skanda in her arms. Metallic figures of this aspect of Bikshadana[5] and Mohini[6] (temptress) connected with the story are installed in the temple.

INSCRIPTIONS[7]

The inscriptions available in this temple have been copied in the year 1912 by the Madras Epigraphical Department.

418 of 1922 (Tamil) — On the south wall of the central shrine in the Viratteswara temple. A party damaged record in the eleventh year of the Chola king Parakesarivarman or Tribhuvanachakravartin Rajarajadeva II. Records gift of

money for lamps to the temple of Virattanam Udaiyar at Valugur (Tiruvalundurnadu, which was a district of Jayangondasolavalanadu). Quotes the sixth year of Periyadevar of Vikrama Choladeva. (The Government Epigraphist surmises that Periyadevar may be taken to denote that Vikrama Chola was the father of Rajaraja II.)

419 of 1912 (Tamil) — On the south base of the same shrine. A record of the Chola king Rajarajadeva II in his fifteenth year Tula, ba, di. 10, Tuesday, Ayilyam (Tuesday, 27th September, 1169). Registers gift of money (100 kasus) with lands for two lamps and two lamp-stands, one of which was given by a native of Sirrarkadu in Arkattukurram of Pandyakulasanivalanadu, for the merit of Kundavai.

420 of 1912 (Tamil) — On the south wall of the mandapa in front of the same shrine. A record in the third year of the Chola king Parakesarivarman or Tribhuvanachakravartin Virarajendradeva (Kulottunga III). Built in the middle. Records gift of land by purchase for offerings in the image of Vadayur Nayanar set up in the temple of Tiruvirattanam Udaiyar by a native of Mulangudi in Velanadu, a sub-division of Kulottungasolavalanadu. Records also gift of money for other articles required for worship. See note to the next eipgraph.

421 of 1912 (Tamil) — On the same wall. A record of the Chola king Tribhuvanachakravartin Rajarajadeva II in his fifth year Karkataka su di. 13, Saturday (1st July, 1167). Built in the middle. Records gift of money by the same individual for getting the Tiruvembavai recited before the image of Vadavuradi Nayanar in the temple on Margali Tiruvadirai festival and for also maintaining the festival of Panguni. Tiruvadavurar was the celebrated Manikkavasaga, the contemporary of Varaguna Pandya in the ninth century and the author of the Tiruvembavai.

422 of 1912 (Tamil) — On the same wall. A record of the Vijiayanagara king Vira Bokkana Odaiyar (Bukka II, 1399-1406) in S. 1324, Chitrabhanu. Records that certain lands (Parru) which had been submerged and lying waste for some years on account of flood in the Kaveri were brought under cultivation, being granted favourable concessions in the payment of assessment. The lands belonged to Valavur in Tiruvalundurnadu, a sub-division of Elumuriparru. See *Ep. Rep.,* 193, pp.118-9, for a full summary of the concessions given. The record is very interesting as it illustrates the fiscal policy of the age.

423 of 1912 (Tamil) — On the same wall. A record in the thirty-third year of the Chola king Parakesarivarman or Tribhuvanachakravartin Tribhuvanaviradeva (1178-1216) "who being pleased to take Madurai (Madura), Ilam (Ceylon), Karuvur and the crowned heads of the Pandya, was pleased to perform the anointment of heroes and the anointment of victors." Built in at the end. Records gift of money by a Brahmana lady to the shrine of Tiruchchattimurram Udaiyar consecrated by her in the twenty-ninth year of the king in the temple of Tiru Virattanam Udaiyar at Valugur, a brahmadeya in Tiruvalundurnadu, a sub-division of Jayangondasolavalanadu.

424 of 1912 (Tamil) — On the west wall of the same mandapa. A record of the Vijayanagara king Pratapadevaraya Maharaya II in S. 1356, Pramadin, Mithuna, ... 5. Built in at the end. Seems to refer to certain additions made to the temple from the year Sobhakrit when apparently, a tank and an irrigation channel were constructed.

425 of 1912 (Tamil) — On the same wall. A record of the Chola king Tribhuvanachakravartin Rajendra Choladeva III in his 2nd year Dhanus, su. di. 4 Monday, Tiruvonam. Built in the middle. Records gift of money for a lamp. Begins with an unusual historical introduction Pumaruviya tirumadandai (the

usual introduction being Bhumiyum tiruvum). The money was received by the temple authorities and a land assigned for the amount. The king is said to have established the six systems of religion which was obeyed by all kings including the Seralas.

426 of 1912 (Tamil) — On the north wall of the same mandapa. A record of the Pandya king Jatavarman Tribhuvanachakravartin Sundara-Pandyadeva III in his fifth (sixth) year, Makara su. di., Wednesday, Sodi, corresponding to 30th December, 1276. Registers that a tenant of the temple having absconded without paying his dues, the amount was recovered from a man who had stood surety for him, by selling his land.

427 of 1912 (Tamil) — On the same wall. A record of the Chola king Parakesarivarman or Tribhuvanachakravartin Kulottunga Choladeva III in his second year Rishabha, su. di., 5th Thursday, Tiruvonam, corresponding to the 15th May, 1180. Records gift of money by a lamp to the same temple by a native of Modappakkam in Suratturnadu, a sub-division of Puliyurkottam or Kulottungasolavalanadu in Jayangodasolamandalam.

428 of 1912 (Tamil) — On the same wall. A record of the Chola king Rajakesarivarman or Tribhuvanachakravartin Rajadhirajadeva II in the fifteenth year, Simha, ba. di. 8, Thursday, Rohini, corresponding to 18th August, 1177. Records gift of money for purchasing land to maintain a lamp in the temple of Tiruvirattanam Udaiyar at Valugur, by a native of Tiyangudi in Tiruvarukurram, a sub-division of Geyamanikkavalanadu. The land was situated at Kirangudi, a hamlet of Virarajendrachaturvedimangalam which was a Brahmadeya in Tiruvalandurnadu. Mentions the sixteenth year of Rajaraja II.

429 of 1912 (Tamil) — On the north verandah of the first prakara of the same temple. A record in the fifth year of the

Chola king Rajakesarivarman or Tribhuvanachakravartin
Virarajendradeva (Kulottunga Chola III). Registers the
construction of the shrine of the Goddess in the north-
west corner of the north verandah by Ekavachakan
Ulagukanviduttaperumal or Vanakovaraiyar, chief of
Tondanadu in Mudigondasolavalanadu. Also records gift of
money in the eighth year of the king for purchasing land and
maintaining worship in the same shrine.

430 of 1912 (Tamil) — On either side of the entrance into
the main gopura of the same temple. Records in Subhanu the
construction of the gopura and the prakara wall by
Alagapperumal-Pillai, son of Gangeyar Ganapathinayanar
Pillai of Nallalvur in Irungolappandinadu.

431 of 1912 (Tamil) — On the four sides of the same
gopura. Records the gift of Bhikshatanamurti, the main
gopura, the prakara wall, by the same Alagapperumal
Pillai.

432 of 1912 (Tamil) — On a slab set up in a grove in
the same village. Records in Durmukha gift of land
(mukkalvattam, nattam and tidal) in Valavarayakuppam the
residents of that village including Tamba-Pillai.

TIRUKKADAYUR

Tirukkadayur, another Saiva religious centre, is about 12
miles to the south-east of Mayavaram. The deity of the temple
is known as Amritakadesvara, who was at one time
worshipped by Durga (fighting form of Goddess), Vasuki
(Serpent chief), Saptakanyaka[8] (the celestial nymphs).

PURANIC VERSION

The special importance of this place lies in the tradition, that
Siva came out of his linga to save Markandeya, a boy-sage,
from the hands of death. This is illustrated in a pretty metallic

figure, on the Dhvajastambha (flag staff) in front of the central shrine.

The Siva devotee Kungiliyakkalayanayanar[9] and Karinayanar[10] spent the greater part of their lives in the service of the deity here.

INSCRIPTIONS[11]

The inscriptions here have been copied by the Madras Epigraphical Department during the year 1906.

The temple is well-known as the place where Siva killed the god of death at the instance of the devotee, Markandeya. In literary history this place is important as the birth-place of Abhirama Bhatta, the author of *Abhirami Andadi* (Abhidhana Chintamani, p.45.) There is no epigraph concerning him.

15 of 1906 (Tamil) — On the north wall of the central shrine in the Amritaghatesvara temple. A damaged record in the second year of the Chola king Tribhuvanachakravartin Vikramacholadeva (1118-35).

16 of 1906 (Tamil) — On the same wall. A damaged record in the foroty-eighth year of the Chola king Rajakesarivarman or Tribhuvanachakravartin Kulottunga Choladeva I.

17 of 1906 (Tamil) — On the east wall of the same shrine. A partly damaged record in the forty-fourth year of the Chola king Rajakesarivarman or Tribhuvanachakravartin Kulottunga Choladeva I. Records gift of a lamp and a lamp-stand. The temple is called Udaiyar Sri Kalakaladeva at Tirukkadayur. Another much damaged inscription of Kulottunga is also found on the same wall.

18 of 1906 (Tamil) — On the south wall of the same shrine. An incomplete record of the Chola king Rajakesarivarman or Tribhuvanachakravartin Kulottunga Choladeva, the date of which is lost. Records gift of lamp.

19 of 1906 (Tamil) — On the same wall. A very much damaged record of the Chola king Rajakesarivarman or Tribhuvanachakravartin Kulottunga Choladeva, the date of which is lost.

20 of 1906 (Tamil) — On the north base of the same shrine. A record in the fifteenth year of the Chola king Parakesarivarman or Udaiyar Sri Rajendra Choladeva I (1011-43). Records an agreement of the sabha of Padeviya Tirukkadavur in Ambarnadu, a district of Uyyakondarvalanadu.

21 of 1906 (Tamil) — On the east base of the same shrine. A record in the twenty-third year of the Chola king Rajaraja Rajakesarivarman or Sri Rajarajadeva I (985-1013). The inscription seems to be unfinished and ends abruptly with the word Mummudi Solan. Records sale of land for a lamp.

22 of 1906 (Tamil) — On the same base. A record in the fourteenth year of the Chola king Rajarajakesarivarman (985-1013). Records gift of land. Mentions the conquest of Salai, Gangapadi, Nulambapadi, Kadigaivali and Vengainadu. The temple is called Sri Kalakaladeva at Padaieviya Tirukkadavur in Ambarnadu.

23 of 1906 (Tamil) — On the same base. A damaged record in the fifteenth year of the Chola king Rajaraja Rajakesarivarman I (985-1013). Mentions that the sabha of Kadavur gave certain land as kani to a person for doing certain services in the temple. Mentions the conquest of Kandalur Salai, Vengainadu. Refers to the shrine called Tiruvirattanattu Perumanadigal.

24 of 1906 (Tamil) — On the same base. An incomplete record in the thirteenth year of the Chola king Parakesarivarman or Udaiyar Sri Rajendra Choladeva (1011-43). Mentions Nallur in Nallurnadu, a district of Nittavinodavalanadu. The conquests extended up to the Ganga.

25 of 1906 (Tamil) — On the south base of the same shrine. A damaged record in the twenty-sixth year of the Chola king Rajakesarivarman or Tribhuvanachakravartin Kulottunga Choladeva. Registers an agreement of the assembly of Upadaeviya Tirukkadavur in Ambarnadu, a district of Rajanarayanavalanadu. Mentions Kungiliyak Kalaya Nayanar.

26 of 1906 (Tamil) — On the same base. A slightly damaged and incomplete record of the Chola king Rajarajakesarivarman (985-1013) in his sixteenth year, Mithuna, Panchami, Thursday, Revati. Records sale of land.

27 of 1906 (Tamil) — On the same base. An incomplete record in the sixteenth year of the Chola king Rajarajakesarivarman (Rajaraja I), Purattasi, Monday, Punarvasu. Records sale of land. The village is called Padaieviya Tirukkadavur in Ambarnadu. See *Ep. Ind.*, Vol. IX, p.208, where it is shown that the date corresponded to Monday, the 23rd September, A.D. 1000.

28 of 1906 (Tamil) — On the north wall of the mandapa in front of the same shrine. A mutilated record of the Pandya king Maravarman or Tribhuvanachakravartin Kulasekaradeva I (1268-1308), "who was pleased to take every country," the date or which is lost. Quotes the thirteenth year of the reign of Perumal Sundra Pandyadeva (evidently the eldest son and murderer of Kulasekhara.)

29 of 1906 (Tamil) — On the south wall of the same mandap. A mutilated record in the seventh year of the Chola king Parakesarivarman or Tribhuvanachakravartin Vikrama Choladeva (1118-35.) Records gift of money for a lamp.

30 of 1906 (Tamil) — On the same wall. An incomplete record in the sixth year (Vrischika, Margasirsha, Wednesday) of the Chola king Parakesarivarman or Tribhuvanachakravartin Vikrama Choladeva (1118-35.) See *Ep. Ind.*, Vol. IX, p.209,

where the date is calculated to be Wednesday, November 7, A.D. 1123.

31 of 1906 (Tamil) — On the west wall of the same mandapa. A record in the fifth year of the Chola king Tribhuvanachakravartin Rajarajadeva. The shrine is called Udaiyar Sri Kalakaladeva, at Tirukkadavur in Akkurnadu, a district of Jayangordacholavalanadu.

32 of 1906 (Tamil) — On the south wall of the first prakara of the same temple. A record in the eighteenth year of the Chola king Tribhuvanachakravartin Rajarajadeva. Registers the lamps granted to the temple and the lands reclaimed at Manarkunru in Erukkattachcheri for their maintenance. One of the donors is Vedavanamudaiyan Ammaiyappan of Palaiyanur in Melmalai Palaiyanurnadu.

33 of 1906 (Tamil) — On the same wall. A record in the twenty-firsit year of the Chola king Tribhuvanachakravartin Rajarajadeva. Mentions a document referring to the village dated in the thirteenth year of Periyadevar (Kulottunga III) and quoted the twentieth year of the king. (As Kulotunga III is referred to, Rajaraja mentioned here should be the third of his name.)

34 of 1906 (Tamil) — On the same wall. A record in the second year of the Chola king Tribhuvanachakravartin Virarajendra Choladeva. Records gift of land for lamps to the temple of Udaiyur Sri Kalakaladeva at Tirukkadavur in Akkurnadu, a district of Jayangondacholavalanadu. (Is Virarajendra II, or Kulottunga III, intended?)

35 of 1906 (Tamil) — On the same wall. A record of the Chola king Tribhuvanachakravartin Rajadhirajadeva, the date of which is lost. Records gift of land for a lamp by a native of Emapperur in Emapperurnadu (a sub-division) of Naudubilanadu or Rajarajavalanadu. Another lamp was given by a native of Nadar in Pamburanadu, a district of Uyyakondarvalanadu (sic).

36 of 1906 (Tamil) — On the same wall. A record in the twelfth year of the Chola king Tribhuvanachakravartin Rajadhirajadeva II, "who was pleased to take Madurai and Ilam (Ceylon)." Records gift of land for a lamp by a native of Pudalur in Pudalurvattam, a districit of Pandikulasani-valanadu.

37 of 1906 (Tamil) — On the same wall. A record in the ninth year of the Chola king Tribhuvanachakravartin Kulottunga Choladeva III, "who was pleased to take Madurai." Records gift of land for a lamp by a native of Mullangudi in Nallarurnadu, a district of Virudarajabhayankaravalanadu.

38 of 1906 (Tamil) — On the same wall. A record in the ninth year of the Chola king Tribhuvanachakravartin Kulottunga Choladeva III (1186-1216), "who was pleased to take Madurai." Records gift of land at Manalkunru in Erukkattuchcheri by a native of Perunallur in Kilvengainadu, a district of Rajarajavalanadu.

39 of 1906 (Tamil) — On the same wall. A record in the fourth year of the Chola king Tribhuvanachakravartin Kulottunga Choladeva. Records gift of land in the same locality by Sekkilan Ammaiappan Parantakadevanm or Karikala Chola Pallavaraiyan of Kunratturnadu, a district of Puliyurkottam or Kulottunga Cholavalanadu. (The inscription is very important as it refers to Sekkilar of Kunrattur who, according to Tamil literary tradition, was the contemporary of Kulottunga II, and author of the *Periyapurana*. The poet was rewarded, it is said, by the king with the whole of Tondaimandalam, but as Sekkilar turned an ascetic, the king appointed his brother Pallavaraya as minister.)

40 of 1906 (Tamil) — On the same wall. A record in the seventeenth year of the Chola king Tribhuvanachakravartin Kulottunga Choladeva III (1178-1216), "who took Madurai and was pleased to take the crowned head of the Pandya."

Records that a certain Svamidevar cancelled an order of the king appointing two Saiva Acharya and put in two others who possessed hereditary rights to the office. Mentions the shrine of Kalakaladeva Kuttadundevar, Kulototunga-Cholisvaramudaiyar and Vikrama Cholisvaramudaiyar in the temple of Tiruvirattanamudaiyar.

41 of 1906 (Tamil) — On the same wall. A record in the fourteenth year of the Chola king Parakesarivarman or Tribhuvanachakravartin Rajarajadeva. Records gift of land. (The king may be Rajaraja II, but the historical introduction is different.)

42 of 1906 (Tamil) — On the same wall. A record in the sixteenth year of the Chola king Parakesarivarman or Tribhuvanachakravartin Kulottunga Choladeva III, "who took Madurai and was pleased to take the crowned head of the Pandya." Records gift of land to the image of Rajaraja Iswara set up by Araiyan Rajarajadevar or Vanadharayar.

43 of 1906 (Tamil) — On the same wall. A record in the sixteenth year Mesha, Purva 8, Thursday, Pushya, of the Chola king Parakesarivarman or Tribhuvanachakravartin Kulottunga Choladeva III, "who was pleased to take Madurai and the crowned head of the Pandya." Records gift of land to the image of Rajaraja Iswara by the sabha Ulppadameviya Tirukkadavur in Ambarnadu, a sub-division of Akkurnadu, a district of Jayangondasolavalanadu. See *Ep. Ind.,* Vol. IX, p.213, where it is shown that the date corresponded to 31st March, A.D. 1194. Virapandya is said to have taken refuge with his relations in Kollam.

44 of 1906 (Tamil) — On the base of the verandah enclosing the central shrine in the same temple on the south. Records gift of land in the village of Velanmanai in Kanattur-nadu to the temple of Kalakaledeva at Olugammangalam.

45 of 1906 (Tamil) — On the same base. A record in the

thirty-fourth year of the Pandya king Jatavarman Tribhuvanachakravartin Virapandyadeva. Records gift of land. Mentions the forty-first year of the king's predecessor and the shrine of Vikrama Cholichuramudaiyar. (Is this the king who ascended the throne in A.D. 1253?).

46 of 1906 (Tamil) — On the same base. A record in the thirty-fourth year of the Pandya king Maravarman Tribhuvanachakravartin Kulasekharadeva (I? 1268-1308). Records gift of land for forty lamps for the merit of Ulagudaiya Perumal. The country is said to have been in a state of confusion for a long time and the inhabitants to be suffering distress evidently in consequence of the king's making over a portion of his dominions to his younger brothers. The king resumed the lands and the people returned.

47 of 1906 (Tamil verse) — On the third gopura of the same temple. A record in Vishaya (Vrisha?) of the Vijayanagara king Krishnaraya. A certain Brahman named Apatsahaya of Tirukkadavur repaired the temple. He is said to have taken part in the war against Rachchur!! "The epigraph gives thus an example of a Brahman's military career." For an account of Raichur siege see *Forg. Emp.*, pp.136-54.

48 of 1906 (Tamil) — On the same gopura. Records that a native of the Pandya country presented the simhasana in the room of the god Kalakaladeva.

49 of 1906 (Tamil) — On the same gopura. A damaged record. Mentions Kadavarkon.

50 of 1906 (Tamil verse) — On the same gopura. Composed by Kalakala, king of Ceylon.

51 of 1906 (Tamil) — On the same gopura. A damaged record of the Pandya king Perumal Sundara Pandya, the date of which is lost.

52 of 1906 (Tamil) — On the north wall of the Sundaresvara shrine in the same temple. A record in the tenth year of the Chola king Tribhuvanachakravartin Rajarajadeva. Records gift of land.

NOTES

1. Parvati, at one time, offended Siva and a result was transformed to a pea-hen. When she repented for this imprudent action on her part, Siva was pleased to reduce the period of punishment. She wandered on earth worshipping the God. The important places where she worshipped god Siva, in that form, are Mylapore and this place. It is here that she as Abhaiyambal got rid of the pea-hen form and joined Siva. Hence it is that the deity here is known as Mayuranathar (*mayura* means, as already explained, a pea-hen).

2. In this *Alinganamurti,* Siva is seen embracing the Goddess. Here He is a *santamurti, i.e.,* of a pacific disposition. This form is one of those relating to Chandrasekhara, who is also named Pradoshamurti. It is this Chandrasekhara image that is taken out in procession on occasions of *pradosha* or the evening twilight of each fortnight on Chaturdasi (fourteenth day). This is a very pleasant representation of Siva with a smiling countenance.

3. This forms part of *Agneya-Purana* and a regular translation of the first few chapters appear in the *Indian Antiquary* of September 1901, November 1902 and March 1904, from which this has been extracted.

4. *Inscriptions of the Madras Presidency*, Government of Madras, 1919, Vol. II, pp. 1306 to 1308.

5 & 6. When the sages of the Darukavana forest began to show disrespect to the Almighty and indulge in talks that mere exertion alone could grant Moksha or heaven, Siva assumed a lovely naked form and went out as a wandering begger and engaged himself with the wives of the sages; when Vishnu in

the form of Mohini approached the sages. Then the sages were convinced of the superiority of the Almighty. This is commonly known as the begging form and the speciality of this form is that there is no Devi figure close to that of Bikshadana.

7. *Inscriptions of the Madras Presidency*, Government of Madras, 1919, Vol. II, pp. 1315 to 132.

8. These are the *saktis* (the feminine elements in gods) or counterparts of seven important gods that went out with god Siva when he started to overcome the giant Andhakasura, who gave immense trouble to Devas and others. They drank the blood that emanated from the body of this Asura and thus helped Siva in destroying him. Though these are worshipped in most temples, the Selliyamman shrine at Alambakkam in the district of Trichinopoly, is important for the special worship of these maidens. The Madras Epigraphical Department in their *Annual Report* for 1909-10, page 85 says:

"A place not mentioned in the *Devaram* but which was nevertheless one of great antiquity is the modern Alambakkam. Its early name was Dantivarmamangalam. This surname of Alambakkam was apparently current till the end of the reign of Rajaraja I after which the place appears to have received the surname Madurantaka Chadurvedimangalam. The Saptamatrika temple referred to in a record of the 25th year of an unspecified Rajakesarivarman, is interesting enough inasmuch as it supplies to us the earliest mention of a temple dedicated to 'the seven mothers' in Epigraphical records. The Saptamatrikas are enumerated in the Sanskrit lexicon *Amarakosa* to be (1) Brahmi, (2) Mahesvari, (3) Kaumari, (4) Vaishnavi, (5) Varahi, (6) Indrani, and (7) Chamunde. This temple of 'the seven mothers' at Alambakkam must be identical with the modern Selliamman temple, on the walls of which the record quoted above is engraved and in which, I am informed, most of these figures still exist . . . . Thus it becomes clear that the temple Alambakkam, its tanks and suburbs, date from very early times and are of much interest as being attributable to a period prior to the 10th century A.D. The place where these Saptamatrikas worshipped Siva is, in the seven shrines near the village of Chakrapalli, close by Ayyampet, on the South Indian Railway in the Madras-Danushkodi line.

9. Kungliyakklayanayanar. In a Brahman family at Tirukkadayur this Nayanar was born. He was then named Kalayar. As he was always in the habit of burning incense in the presence of the local deity in the temple he was called Kungiliya Kalayan (*Kungiliyam* in Tamil means Benzoin). In course of time he became so poor that one day when his wife gave him her marriage *tali* (the sacred ornament worn by a married woman on her neck which she is not permitted to remove until the death of her husband), to purchase the bare necessities of life, he purchased Benzoin and burnt it before the God. On his return home he found his house filled with riches!

One day on learning that the chief linga in the central shrine of Tiruppanandal near Gangaikondasolapuram was out of its position and that in spite of the best efforts of the Chola king to put it in position with the help of the palace elephants, it did not move, the Nayanar proceeded thither and attempted by his devotion to set the linga in position, and did it, which very much pleased the king and other spectators. There is a metal figure of the Nayanar in this temple.

10. Karinayanar was born in Tirukkadayur. He was a great Tamil scholar. The presents he obtained for his valuable works were utilised for repairs to temples.

11. *Inscriptions of the Madras Presidency*, Government of Madras, 1919, Vol. II, pp. 1308 to 1313.

Chapter 10

GANGAIKONDASOLAPURAM

This is one of the most famous places in southern India. It was at one time the capital of the Chola dynasty.

PURANIC VERSION

According to the puranic history of the place Rajendra Chola built and dedicated the city to Siva, as a monument to commemorate the conquest of the kingdoms lying on the banks of the Ganges. It is also stated that the victorious Rajendra directed the vanquished chiefs to carry water from the Ganges to the lion-faced well, Singakkinaru, dug out in the north-east corner of the shrine. This city seems to have been in ancient days one of the flourising centres of trade and was the capital of the Chola kingdom. The inscriptions in the temple and the Tamil poem *Kalingattupparani* depict the exploits of King Kulottunga I, grandson of Rajendra Chola, the founder of the shrine.

The legend connected with the idol in the central shrine is that Siva gave a linga to Banasura, a demon, who seems to have installed it here. Later a pious Chola king wanted to hold communion with the God. When the temple priest was approached on the matter he promised to help the king if he should build a temple. At the completion of the temple the God appeared unto the king and answered his prayer. The priest, who was a witness to this scene, is said to have been struck dumb, in order to prevent him from proclaiming the news to the world.

EPIGRAPHICAL IMPORTANCE

[1]Rajendra Chola I succeded to the throne in A.D. 1012. His conquests were even more extensive and wide than those of his father and comprised the regions beyond Kalinga, viz., Kosala, Vangala and the banks of the Ganges. Gangaikonda Chola was one of the birudas adopted by the king in consequence of these conquests. The Tiruvalangadu[2] plates distinctly state that he got the conquered chiefs of the north to carry the sacred water of the Ganges to be poured into a tank called 'a pillar of victory' which he constructed at Gangaikondasolapuram, a town which was founded by him and which served as the Chola capital for a sufficiently long time. Mudigonda Chola was a surname of Rajendra Chola I and this he must have deservedly assumed ; for, in his historical introduction he is stated to have taken the crown (mudi) of the king of Ilam (Ceylon) with that of his queen, the crown of Sundara, the crown of the king of Kerala and the crown which Parasurama had deposited in Santimattivu (identified with the Kerala country). Gangaikondasolapuram, which was founded by him must have also borne the name Mudigondasolapuram. In later times this city was occupied by the Pandya king Maravarman Sundara Pandya who boasts of having performed the anointment of heroes and victors there.

At present we have very few traces of the ancient greatness of the place, besides the ruins of the palace at a short distance to the south-west of the local shrine of Brihadesvara.

The plan of the building appears to have been similar to that of the Tanjore temple having the same architecitural peculiarity of possessing a lofty stone erection over the sanctum, unlike most of the other edifices, which have the largest gopura at the main entrance. The crown over the tower is said to have been formed of a single block of stone, and placed in its present position by means of an inclined plane laid out from the village of Paranam, which is a few miles off. There are still slight traces of stone bastions of ancient days.

In the interior of the temple a monolithic representation of the Navagrahas (the 9 planets) is installed in the shape of a chariot with a lotus flower at the top. Surya occupies the topmost place in the chariot, and Saturn is the driver. The other planets occupy places on the sides. There is also a fine sculpture of Mahishasura-Mardini, the Goddess in the aspect of the slayer of the buffalo demon.

The sculptures over the outer walls of the temple are of fine workmanship. The story of Chandesa, a devotee of Siva, is depicted in a most appreciative manner in a niche in the northern wall, and it is called Chandesanugrahamurti.[3]

ARCHAEOLOGICAL INFORMATION[4]

"The temple is enclosed in a single courtyard. It is one of the most important of the temples erected by the Cholas in the 11th century. Though not as large as the great temple at Tanjore, it is of similar plan and design and of a slightly earlier date. It has the same unique architectural feature of a lofty stone tower over the shrine. In this respect these two examples are distinguished from the majority of south Indian temples which are architecturally defective in having the most lofty structures over the gateways. As with Tanjore, the crowning member of the tower the Sikara is formed of a single block of stone, said to have been placed in position by means of an inclined plane laid from the village of Paranam situated some miles to the westward in the Udayarpalayam Zamindari. Around the tower are numbers of archaic sculptures and inscriptions. In front of the shrine is an immense Nandi cut out of a block of stone. In the courtyard is a large round well entered by an underground passage with a large figure of a Yali at the entrance. The water of the Ganges is traditionally stateted to have flowed into the well, hence the name of the place. Another derivation is that the place was named after the Chola who ruled here. The temple had at one time been fortified by bastions at the four corners of the courtyard but the walls have been demolished.

About a mile to the south-west are a number of mounds. These are said to mark the site of the palace of the Chola king who built the temple and who also had his residence here. Traces of surrounding moat are at places visible. The mounds extend over several acres, and are too extensive for those of a palace only; they must also have included a town The greatest of the mounds probably hides the ruins of the palace. It covers over an acre of ground, but traces of the building buried under it extend beyond this area. It is about 10 feet in height. The foundations of the walls are about 6 feet below the present surface of the surrounding ground. The walls are 4 feet in thickness and built of large bricks similar to those found in Buddhist types.

INSCRIPTIONS[5]

The inscriptions here have been copied by the Madras Epigraphical Department during the years 1892 and 1908.

For notices of this historic place see *Moor's District Manual*, p.342, *Ind. Antq.,* Vol. IX, p.117; F.A.S.B. 1880, Pt. I, *Mr. Sewell's Antiquities*, Vol. I, p.264 and *Trichinopoly*

Gazar., Vol. I, based on Elliott's collections. Mr. Sewell gives twenty inscriptions in this place, but of these Nos. 3, 4, 5, 6, 7, 8, 11 and 14 are very vague and cannot be identified with any in the following list:

75 of 1892 (Tamil) (No. 17 of Elliott's lists) — East wall of the second prakara of the Brihadesvara temple. A record of the Pandya king Ko-Maravarman Kulasekharadeva II (1314-21) in his fourth year. See *Ep. Ind.,* Vol. VI., p.313, where Dr. Kielhorn discusses the date and points and that Saturday, Uttarashada, Purvapaksha, Chaturdasi, Karkataka, corresponded to 23rd July, A.D. 1317.

76 of 1892 (Tamil) — South wall of the second prakara of the Brihadesvara temple. A record of the Pandya king Konerinmaikondan Vikrama Pandyadeva in his sixth year. This is No. 15 of Elliott's lists (*Antiquities,* Vol. I, p.265.)

77 of 1892 (Tamil) — South wall of the second prakara of the Brihadesvara temple. A record of the Pandya king Konerimmaikondan Sundara Pandyadeva, in his second year. (No. 18 of Elliott's lists.)

78 of 1892 (Telugu) (No. 16 of Elliott's lists) — South wall of the second prakara of the Brihadesvara temple. A record of the Pandya king Ko Maravarman Kulasekharadeva II, in his fifth year. See *Ep. Ind.,* Vol. VI, p.313, where Dr. Keilhorn calculates that the date (Monday, Pusya, Purvapaksha, Trayodasi, Simha) corresponded to Monday, 5th March, A.D. 1319.

79 of 1892 (Tamil) (No. 9 of Elliott's lists) — West wall of the second prakara of the Brihadesavara temple's second tier. A record in S. 1385, expired, Subhanu.

80 of 1892 (Tamil) (No. 10 of Elliott's lists) — West wall of the second prakara of the Brihadesavara temple's first tier. A record of Chola king Kulottunga Choladeva (I?) in his forty-ninth year. Beginning of each line lost.

398 *South Indian Shrines*

81 of 1892 (Tamil) (No. 13 of Elliott's lists) — West wall of the second prakara of the same temple, second tier. Records in Subhanud, gift by Tiruvengadamudaiyan ; S.I.I., Vol. I, p.78.

82 of 1892 (Tamil) — North and west walls of the second prakara of the same temple. A considerably mutilated record of the Chola king Ko Rajakesaraivarman or Vira Rajendradeva in his fifth (twenty-third?) year two hundred and seventy-fourth-day. (This seems to correspond to Nos. 1 and 2 in Elliott's lists. It records a grant by sixty-eighth chiefs and refers to the king's conquests of the Vengi country.)

83 of 1892 (Tamil) (No. 19 Elliott's lists) — Right of the entrance to the north wall of the second prakara of the Brihadesvara temple. A record of the Vijayanagara king Virupakshraya (son of Mallikarjuna) in 1405 expired, Sobhakrit.

29 of 1908 (Tamil and Grantha) — On the west wall of the central shrine in the Brihadesvara temple. A unfinished record of the Chola king Rajakesarivarman or Tribhuvanachakravartin Sri Kulottunga Choladeva (I?) in his forty-first year. After the date is the Sanskrit passage Akunthotkantha. (This is perhaps No. 20 of Mr. Elliott's List given in the *Antiquities*, Vol. I, p.265. But the date given there is fortieth year.)

30 of 1908 (Tamil) — On the same wall. A much damaged record in S. 1384, expired, Chitrabhanu of the Vijayanagar king. Mentions Devaraya once and Mallikarjunaraya twice.

31 of 1908 (Tamil) — On the south wall of the same shrine. A record of the Pandya king Tribhuvanachakravartin, the date of which is lost. The inscription probably belongs to the reign of Sundara Pandya. But the name Perumal Parakrama Pandya occurs in a damaged line above the inscription.

32 of 1908 (Tamil) — On the north wall of the mandapa in front of the same shrine. A record of the Chola king Kulottunga III. Fragment containing a portion of the historical introduction of the king.

33 of 1908 (Tamil) — On the south wall of the same mandapa. A record of Tribhuvanachakravartin Konerinmaikondan, the date of which is lost. Registers an order of the king relating to the emoluments of a temple servant.

34 of 1908 (Tamil) — On the east wall of the same mandapa. A record of Tribhuvanachakravartin, the date of which is lost. End of each line is mutilated.

NOTES

1. *Annual Report* of the Madras Epigraphical Department for the year 1908-09, pages 92 & 93.
2. For a complete text and translation of this copper plate, see pages 383 to 459 of the *South Indian Inscriptions,* Vol. III, Part III published by the Government of Madras in 1920.
3. In the Chola country on the banks of the river Manniyar in the village of Seygnalur there was born in the *Gotra* of the sage Kasyapa, Vicharasarma. While going to school he saw a cow, which has been considered divine by the Hindus at all times, ill-treated and in consequence of took upon himself the duty of grazing the cows of the whole village. The cows began to give plenty of milk and with the whole quantity drawn from them, he bathed a linga, which he had set up with sand in the village close by, on the other side of the river, by name Tiruvappadi. As by so doing the cows yielded only a lesser quantity in their houses, the villagers recognised this and complained to the father of the boy, who on going to the spot got provoked and kicked the sand-made linga. The boy could

not put up with this atrocity and so cut off the father's leg with the axe in his hand. Seeing the devotion of this youth, Isvara at once appeared with his consort and gave him his full grace by making him the steward of Kailasa and naming the Chandesa. Siva also crowned him with the garland worn by him, as is shown in the sculptural representation here. Siva also then ordered that all the offerings and clothes of Him, should be set aside for this devotee. Chandesa is always depicted with the axe on the right shoulder with which he is said to have cut off the leg of his father.

4. Report of the Archaeological Survey Department for May 1891.
5. *Inscriptions of the Madras Presidency*, Government of Madras, 1919, Vol. III, pp. 1607 to 1609.

Chapter 11

TIRUVIDAIMARUDUR

This religious centre lies on the South Indian Railway between Mayavaram and Kumbakonam. It is also called Madhyarjunam from its being situated betwteen Mallikarjuna or Srisaila in the district of Kurnool and Sputarjuna or Tiruppudaimarudur in the south near Ambasamudram in the Tinnevelly district. The Kaveri passes through this town and Idaimarudu, (*Idai* meaning 'the middle' in Tamil corresponds to *madhya* in Sanskrit). The principal deity of the place in the temple is Mahalinga or the great linga, so named on account of His all importance and the annual festival of Taipushyam in December-January is of much local importance.

Asuamedhapradakshinam or a perambulation of the temple courtyard here is considered not only healthy but also supposed to provide the benefits of having gone round the whole of sacred India. People suffering from mental affliction visit this place for healing.

At one time Siva is said to have ordered his son Ganapathi to worship him here. So the deity is called Agya Ganapathi (*Agya* is Tamil means command), and this legend dates probably from the Buddhist period.

STORY OF SOLA BRAHMAHATTI

One of the inner gopura on the eastern side contains the sculpture of the Sola Brahmahatti. The local tradition connected with it is that an evil spirit possessed a Chola king immediately he happened to kill a Brahman. Ever since, the king was greatly afflicted as the evil spirit did inot leave him. With a view to get rid of it the king is said to have undertaken a number of charitable acts such as building temples, pilgrimages to centres of worship, etc. It was usual with the Brahmahatti to temporarily dispossess the suffering king on his entering the sacred precincts of a temple and await his return to continue its torments. At this place of great religious importance he was shorn of the evil as on reaching Tribhuvanam, a mile on the west, he did not feel its effect.

Hence King Varaguna Pandya of Madura, who is said to have been haunted by the ghost of a Brahman that was accidently killed by him while on a hunt, was exorcised of the ghost by a visit to the place. The sculptural representation of the ghost can be seen on the gopura at the second entrance.

SAINT PATTINATTUPPILLAIYAR

The famous Tamil saint Pattinattu Pillaiyar[1] lived here for some time with Bathruhari and a well-polished sculptural representation of the saint is placed on the right side of the outer eastern gopura.

EPIGRAPHICAL IMPORTANCE

The inscriptions over the temple walls record the revenue survey and settlement made in the 38th year of the reign of Kulottunga I, with other additions made in the various departments of the temple. Instructions regarding dances, the re-arrangement of streets and the procession of the deity on the occasions of festivals are also recorded.

Another engraving on the south wall of the second prakara relates to a Brahman of the place named Tiruchchirrambala Bhattar who joined the army of Vittaladeva Maharaja in Saka 1466 (A.D. 1544-45) while he was going on an expedition against 'Tiruvadi' to fight on his side from "Anantasayanam (Travancore) in the south to Mudugal in the north". Even while thus engaged in a military expedition this Brahman did not forget his native place and the presiding deity therein. He represented to his master that the villages Avanam and Sirradi belonging to the temple had passed into other hands. The matter was enquired into and the villages besides being restored to the temple, demarcation stones containing the seal of the god Marudappar were ordered to be planted in the said two villages.

Another inscription mentions that in the 4th year of King Parakesarivairman the trustees and other officers of the temple assembled in the theatre hall of the temple and made up an account of the gifts of gold made for maintaining lamps in that temple. It also mentions that the stones which bore the original inscriptions regarding those gifts were placed in underground cellars and when the temple was renovated, true copies of them were made of them. From these copies the documents were re-incised in the stone walls of the renovated temple. The holding of dramatic performances in the temple hall was in vogue in those days. There was a provision made by this king for the dance called Ariyakkuttu a regular dramatic performance in which dancing and singing holds a prominent place.

INSCRIPTIONS[2]

The inscriptions that stood on the walls of the temple here have been copied during the years 1895 and 1907 by the Madras Epigraphical Department.

Known as Madhyarjunam among the orthodox, this place prominent in Saivite legendary lore, is epigraphically very rich. For details of legends, festivals etc., see *Tanj. Gazr.*, Vol. I, p.223. From 1798 onward it has been the residence of the descendants of Amir Singh of Tanjore. The Devaram mentions it as Idaimarudu. In Chola time it was in Tiraimur-nadu in Uyyakonda Chola valanadu. The local epigraphs contain large number of Rajakesarivarmans who are mostly unidentifiable.

193 of 1907 (Tamil) — On the north wall of the central shrine in the Mahalingasvamin temple. A record in the tenth year of the Chola king Parakesarivarman. Records gift of money for a lamp. The money was entrusted to the assembly of Tirunilakudi in Tiraimurnadu.

194 of 1907 (Tamil) — On the same wall. A record in the fourteenth year of the Chola king Parakesarivarman. Records a sale of land.

195 of 1907 (Tamil) — On the same wall. A record in the thirty-eighth year of the Chola king Madiraikonda Parakesarivarman (Parantaka I). Mentions Irumudisola Pallavaraiyar and refers to the Palangavirinirodukal.

196 of 1907 (Tamil) — On the smae wall. A record of the Chola king Parakesarivarman, the date of which is damaged. Records purchase of land with the gold granted for a lamp by Pillayar Uttamasiliyar. Mentions Mahendramangalam and Nattuvaykkal. (Uttamasili was the son of Parantaka I, 905-47).

197 of 1907 (Tamil) — On the same wall. A record

in the tenth year of the Chola king Rajakesarivarman (Rajaraja I) "who destroyed the ships at Kandalur". Records gift of gold flower by a certain Hridayasiva of Tirupputtur.

198 of 1907 (Tamil) — On the same wall. A record in the fourth year of the Chola king Parakesarivarman. Records gift of gold hand set (hasta) with precious stones.

199 of 1907 (Tamil) — On the same wall. A record in the fourth year of the Chola king Parakesariviarman. Refers to the inscriptions registering money end owments for lamps to the temple and states that all the stones bearing them were used up when the central shrine was built of stone. Accordingly copies were made of these records, one of which belonged to the reign of the Kadupattigal Nandipottaraiyar. This king had endowed a lamp called Kumaramattanda. Kadupattigal Nandipottaraiyar was evidently the Pallava king Nandivarman III who must have had the title Kumaramarttanda.

200 of 1907 (Tamil) — On the same wall. A record in the third year of the Chola king Parakesarivarman or Sri Rajendra Choladeva I. Records gift of forty-five sheep for a lamp to burn at night at the gate called Ekanayakam Tiruvasal.

201 of 1907 (Tamil) — On the same wall. A record in the twentieth year of the Chola king Madiraikonda Parakesarivarman (Parantaka I). Records gift of gold for the green gram offering.

202 of 1907 (Tamil) — On the same wall. An incomplete record in the third year of the Chola king Rajakesarivarman.

203 of 1907 (Tamil) — On the same wall. A record in the thirty-seventh year of the Chola king Madiraikonda Parakesarivarman (Parantaka I). Records gift of hundred sheep for a lamp by the Manradi Kolli Pugalan.

204 of 1907 (Tamil) — On the same wall. A record in the thirty-seventh year of the Chola king Madiraikonda

Parakesarivarman (905-47). Records gift of ninety sheep for a lamp.

205 of 1907 (Tamil) — On the same wall. A record in the thirty-seventh year of the Chola king Madiraikonda Parakesarivarman (905-47). Records gift of eighty-seven sheep for a lamp.

206 of 1907 (Tamil) — On the north wall of the central shrine in the Mahalingasvamin temple. A record in the thirity-seventh year of the Chola king Madiraikonda Parakesarivarman (905-47). Records gift of ninety sheep for a lamp.

207 of 1907 (Tamil) — On the same wall. A record in the thirty-seventh year of the Chola king Madiraikonda Parakesarivarman (905-47). Mentions a certain Kavaramolimadevan or Tondaradippodi. (Tondaradippodi reminds one of the Vaishnava Alvar; but there is nothing to show that the saint is referred to here.)

208 of 1997 (Tamil) — On the same wall. A damaged record in the sixteenth year of the Chola king Parakesarivarman.

209 of 1907 (Tamil) — On the same wall. A damaged record in the twelfth year of the Chola king Parakesarivarman.

210 of 1907 (Tamil) — On the same wall. A record in the ninth year of the Chola king Parakesarivaran. Over this is another damaged inscription.

211 of 1907 (Tamil) — On the same wall. A much damaged record.

212 of 1907 (Tamil) — Mentions Inganattu Pallavaraiyan and the image of Tiruvidaimarudiladalvidangadevar which he set up. In the body of the inscription the sabha of Tiraimur is said to consist of 300 men and 400 citizens.

213 of 1907 (Tamil) — On the same wall. A partly damaged record in the fourth year of the Chola king Parakesarivarman. Records gift of lamps.

214 of 1907 (Tamil) — On the same wall. A record in the fourth year of the Chola king Parakesarivarman, "who took the head of the Pandya". The temple is called Tiruvidaimarudil Alvar Koil. Mentions Sirringanudaiyan Kovil Mayilai or Parantaka Muvendavelan. (Was the King Parantaka II, Uttamachola?)

215 of 1907 (Tamil) — On the same wall. A record in the sixth year of the Chola king Rajakesarivarman. Records that the Chola queen Vanavanmadevi came to worship the God.

216 of 1907 (Tamil) — On the same wall. A record in the seventeenth year of the Chola king Rajakesarivarman. Records the laying out of a jasmine flower garden.

217 of 1907 (Tamil) — On the north and west walls of the same shrine. A damaged record in the fourteenth year of the Chola king Parakesarivarman.

218 of 1907 (Tamil) — On the north and west walls of the same shrine. A record in the ninth year of the Chola king whose name is damaged. Records gift of land.

219 of 1907 (Tamil) — On the north, west and south walls of the same shrine. A record in the sixth year of the Chola king Parakesarivarman. Records public sale of land. Mentions Inganattu Pallavaraiyar and Sirringanudaiyan Koyil Mayilai or Madhurantaka Muvendavelan. See Nos. 241 above and 255 below.

220 of 1907 (Tamil) — On the north, west and south walls of the same shrine. A record in the twentieth year of Chola Parakesarivarman or Udaiyar Sri Rajendra Choladeva I. Built in at both ends and mutilated in the middle.

221 of 1907 (Tamil) — On the north, west and south walls of the same shrine. A record in the fourteenth year of the Chola king Parakesarivarman.

222 of 1907 (Tamil) — On the west wall of the same

shrine. A damaged record in the thirty-seventh year of the Chola king Madiraikonda Parakesarivarman (Parantaka I). Seems to record a gift of land for celebrating the Tiruvadirai, Sadiayam and Amavasai festivals.

223 of 1907 (Tamil) — On the same wall. A much damaged record of the Chola king Madiraikonda Parakesarivarman. Seems to record a gift of land.

224 of 1907 (Tamil) — On the same wall. A much damaged record in the twenty-seventh year of the king, whose name is lost. Seems to record a gift of lamps.

225 of 1907 (Tamil) — On the west wall of the central shrine in the Mahalingasvamin temple. A damaged record in the fourteenth year of the Chola king Parakesarivarman. Seems to record a gift of gold for a lamp.

226 of 1907 (Tamil) — On the same wall. A mutilated record of the Chola king Parakesarivarman or Rajendradeva I. Only the beginning of the historical introduction is reserved.

227 of 1907 (Tamil) — On the same wall. A record in the twenty-seventh year of the Chola king Madiraikonda Parakesarivarman (905-47). Records gift of land. Mentions Kumaramattandapuram.

228 of 1907 (Tamil) — On the same wall. A record in the fourteenth year of the Chola king Parakesarivarman. Mentions Sirringanudaiyan Pattan Kannan or Inganattu Pallavaraiyan.

229 of 1907 (Tamil) — On the same wall. Records in the fourteenth year gift of a gold bowl (mandai) by a native of Tanjavur (Tanjore).

230 of 1907 (Tamil) — On the same wall. A record in the eleventh year of the Chola king Parakesarivarman. Mentions Vennattu Varambusaludaiyan Sandirachchan Satturugandan.

231 of 1907 (Tamil) — On the same wall. A record in the

eleventh year of the Chola king Parakesarivarman. Mentions the same person.

232 of 1907 (Tamil) — On the same wall. A mutilated record in the tenth year of the king whose name is lost.

233 of 1907 (Tamil) — On the same wall. A fragment of record of the Chola king. Registers the grant of one veli of land to a person who had to sing dosi songs.

234 of 1907 (Tamil) — On the same wall. A record in the seventh year of the Chola king Parakesarivarman. Refers to the building of a temple ; also to the thirtieth year of Madiraikonda Parakesarivarman (905-47).

235 of 1907 (Tamil) — On the south wall of the same shrine. A damaged record in the thirty-first year of the Chola king Madiraikonda Parakesarivarman (905-47). Mentions Nalangilinallurkurram. Seems to provide for feeding two Brahmans.

236 of 1907 (Tamil) — On the same wall. A damaged record in the fourteenth year of the Chola king Parakesarivarman. Records gift of sixty-two cows.

237 of 1907 (Tamil) — On the same wall. A damaged record in the fourth year of the Chola king Parakesarivarman. Records gift of money for a lamp.

238 of 1907 (Tamil) — On the same wall. A record in the sixteenth year of the Chola king Madiraikonda Parakesarivarman (905-47). Records gift by a native of Irumbedu Magalurnadu, a sub-division of Sengattukottam in Tondainadu.

239 of 1907 (Tamil) — On the same wall. A record in the second year of the Chola king Rajakesarivarman. Records gift of eight Ilakkasus to the shrine of Purana Ganapati on the southern side of the Mulasthana at Tiruvidaimurudil by a native of Emanallur, a brahmadeya in Vadagaraimanninadu.

240 of 1907 (Tamil) — On the same wall. A damaged record in the thirty-seventh year of the Chola king Madiraikonda Parakesarivarman (905-47).

241 of 1907 (Tamil) — On the same wall. A record in the twenty-ninth year of the Chola king Madiraikonda Parakesarivarman (905-47). Records gift of a sheep for a lamp.

242 of 1907 (Tamil) — On the same wall. A record in the third year of the Chola king Rajakesarivarman. Provides for the supply of the tender coconuts to the God.

243 of 1907 (Tamil) — On the same wall. Mentions Tongamangalamudaiyan, one of the Mutta Pirantakaanukkar.

244 of 1907 (Tamil) — On the same wall. A record in the second year of the Chola king Parakesarivarman. Mentions the Singalantakaterinda Kaikkolar.

245 of 1907 (Tamil) — On the south wall of the central shrine in the Mahalingasvamin temple. A record in the seventeenth year of the Chola king Madiraikonda Parakesarivarman (905-47). Records gift of paddy by the inhabitants of Tiruvilainadu.

246 of 1907 (Tamil) — On the same wall. A record of the Chola king Madiraikonda Parakesarivarman (905-47), the date of which is lost. Records gift of ninety-one sheep. Mentions the Taipusam festival.

247 of 1907 (Tamil) — On the same wall. A record in the third year of the Chola king Parakesarivarman. Records gift of a silver kalasam by a native of Tulakkilimangalam in Pandinadu.

248 of 1907 (Tamil) — On the same wall. A damaged record in the twelfth-year of the Chola king Madiraikonda Parakesarivarman (905-47). Records gift of a lamp. Mentions the festival of Taipusam.

249 of 1907 (Tamil) — On the same wall. A damaged record of the Chola king Parakesarivarman, "who took the

head of the Pandya," the date of which is lost. Records a gift of land for maintaining the champaka flower garden laid out by Tiruvenkattu Pichchan. (The king referred to might be Parantaka II Sundara Chola.)

250 of 1907 (Tamil) — On the same wall. A damaged record in the thirty-sixth year of the Chola king Madiraikonda Parakesarivarman (905-47). Records gift of gold vessels.

251 of 1907 (Tamil) — On the same wall. A damaged record in the thirty-fourth year of the Chola king Madiraikonda Parakesarivarman (905-47).

252 of 1907 (Tamil) — On the same wall. A record in the thirty-eighth year of the Chola king Madiraikonda Parakesarivarman (905-47). Records gift of a lamp for the merit of Arinjiyaipirattiyar. She was the daughter of Arikulakesari, the son of Parantaka I (905-47.)

253 of 1907 (Tamil) — On the same wall. A record in the second year of the Chola king Parakesarivarman. Refers to the putting up of a window, the door, the doorpost and the steps in front of the big mandapa by the regiment called Kaikkola Perumbadai. The mandapa was called Tigai Ayirattannurruvar.

254 of 1907 (Tamil) — On the same wall. A record of the Chola king Rajaraja Rajakesarivarman I (985-1013), "who destroyed the ships at Salai," in his tenth year and two hundred and seventy-eighth day. Records gift of a gold image of Umasahitar by the queen Panchavanmahadevi.

255 of 1907 (Tamil) — On the same wall. A damaged record in the fifth year of the Chola king Parakesarivarman, "who took the head of the Pandya." (Was the king intended Parantaka II Sundara Chola ?)

256 of 1907 (Tamil) — On the same wall. An unfinished record in the fourth year of the Chola king Parakesarivarman, "who defeated Vira Pandya and took his head." See note to the above.

257 of 1907 (Tamil) — On the same wall. A record in the sixth year of the Chola king Konerinmaikondan. Records a gift in favour of Sirukulatturudayan Araiyan Parantakan or Sembiyan Soliyavaraiyan. The sixth year of Parakesarivarman is quoted in the body of the inscription.

258 of 1907 (Tamil) — On the same wall. A record in the thirtieth year of the Chola king Madiraikonda Parakesarivarman (905-47). Registers an endowment in favour of the drummers (uvachagal). Refers to the agent of the Chola king Kongu. (See the Tiruchengodu inscriptions for Parantaka's conquests in Kongu).

259 of 1907 (Tamil) — On the same wall. A record in the twenty-fourth year of the Chola king Madiraikonda Parakesarivarman (905-47). Records gift of ninety sheep for a lamp by a native of Anaimangalam in Pattinakkurram.

260 of 1907 (Tamil) — On the same wall. A record in the ninth year of othe Chola king Rajakesarivarman. Refers to the laying out of a sirusenbaga flower-garden by Tiruvenkattu Pichchan.

261 of 1907 (Tamil) — On the south wall of the central shrine in the Mahalingasvamin temple. A record in the nineteenth year of the Chola king Madirakonda Parakesarivarman (905-47). Records gift of gold for a lamp. Mentions the Nampirattiyar Kokkilan Adigal.

262 of 1907 (Tamil) — On the same wall. A record in the eighteenth year of the Chola king Madiraikonda Parakesarivarman (905-47). Records gift of gold for a lamp by a merchant of Kumaramattandapuram in Tenkarai-Tiraimurnadu.

263 of 1907 (Tamil) — On the same wall. Beginning of inscription is much damaged. Records gift of two lamps.

264 of 1907 (Tamil) — On the same wall. A record in the thirty-second year of the Chola king Rajakesarivarman or

Udaiyar Sri Rajadhirajadeva I (1018-52). Registers an endowment of 2 velis and 2 mas in favour of Ariyan Tiruvidaimarududaiyan or Mummudi Sola Nittaperaiyan and his troupe. The grant proper begins with the word "ko no-inmai kondan". The record says that a daily allowance of 2 tuni of paddy and annual allowance of 240 kalams should be given to the padavyam-vasippar.

265 of 1907 (Tamil) — On the same wall. A record of the Chola king Uttama Chola or Parakesarivarman in Kaliyuga 4083 and in his thirteenth year. Mentions Kanjanur or Simhavishnu Chaturvedimangalam, brahmadeya in Vadagarainallurnadu. (The inscription is of unique value in giving the Kali and reignal years together and distinctly proves that Parakesarivarman Madhurantaka Uttamachola came to the throne in A.D. 969-70).

266 of 1907 (Tamil) — On the same wall. A record in the thirteenth year of the Chola king Madairaikonda Parakesarivarman (905-47). Records gift of ninety sheep for a lamp by a native of Kattivaiyal in Mutturrukurram, a district of Pandinadu.

267 of 1907 (Tamil) — On the same wall. Mentions Tirutturutti Nalli Srikanthar and Sivacharanasekharan. Close to this is a sculpture representing a linga, a worshipper, an attendant and a lampstand.

268 of 1907 (Tamil) — On the east wall of the same shrine. A damaged record of the Chola king Parakesarivarman, the date of which is doubtful. Records gift of sheep for two lamps.

269 of 1907 (Tamil) — On the same wall. A damaged record of the Chola king Madiraikonda Parakesarivarman (905-47), the date of which is lost.

270 of 1907 (Tamil) — On the same wall. Damaged in the beginning. Mentions Kudamukki (Kumbakonam).

271 of 1907 (Tamil) — On the west wall of the mandapa

in front of the shrine. A record of the Vijayanagara king Virapratapa Achyutadeva Maharaya (1530-42) in S. 1456, expired Jaya. Records gift of a village for the merit of Vasavannayaka.

272 of 1907 (Tamil) — On the south base of the same mandapa. A record in the seventh year of the Chola king Parakesarivarman or Tribhuvanachakravartin Sri Vikrama Cholaldeva (1118-35). Records gift of the village of Vannakudi or Tyagasamudrachaturvedimangalam. Refers to a revenue settlement in the thirty-eighth year of Kulottunga I.

273 of 1907 (Tamil) — On the south base of the mandapa in front of the central shrine in the same temple. A record in the seventh year of the Chola king Parakesarivarman or Tribhuvanachakravartin Sri Vikrama Choladeva (1118-35). Connected with the above epigraph. Mentions Vannakudi or Tyagasamudrachaturvedimangalam, a brahmadeya in Tiraimurnadu, a sub-division of Uyyakondarvalanadu. Refers to the revenue survey of the country and to the revenue settlement in the thirty-eighth year of Kulottunga I.

274 of 1907 (Tamil) — On the same base. A mutilated record of the Chola king Parakesarivarman or Tribhuvanachakravartin Sri Vikrama Choladeva (1118-135), the date of which is lost. The ninth year of the king is referred to on one of the stones. Seems to record a gift of lamps.

275 of 1907 (Tamil) — On the north base of the same mandapa. A record in the ninth year of the Chola king Parakesarivarman or Tribhuvanachakravartin Sri Vikrama Choladeva (1118-35). Refers to the shrine of Vikrama Sola Isvaramudaiyar in the temple at Tiruvidaimarudur and records the grant of the village of Madhurantakanallur or Arindavan-

sattamangalam under the name of Vikramasolanallur. Mentions the revenue survey and settlement made in the thirty-eighth year of Kulottunga I.

276 of 1907 (Tamil) — On the same base. A record in the tenth year of the Chola king Parakesarivarman or Tribhuvanachakravartin Sri Vikrama Choladeva (1118-35.) Records gift of the village of Nalladi in Tirunaraiyurnadu, a sub-division of Kulottunga Solavalanadu. Queen Tribhuvanamulududaiyal is mentioned. The king was seated on the conch called Solankon.

277 of 1907 (Tamil) — On a stone built into the floor of the same mandapa. A fragment of record of the Chola king Parakesarivarman or Rajendra Choladeva I (1012-43), the date of which is lost. Contains a portion of the historical introduction of the king.

278 of 1907 (Tamil) — On a pillar of the same mandapa. A record in the ninth year of the Chola king Rajaraja Rajakesarivarman (985-1013). Records gift of ornaments (irrattaimana, tali etc., weighing nine kalanjus of gold) to the Goddess of Umabhattaraki by the Nambirattyar Sri Panchavanmadeviyar.

279 of 1907 (Tamil) — On the east wall of the first prakara of the same temple, right of entrance. A record in the forty-first year of the Chola king Tribhuvanachakravartin Sri Kulottunga Choladeva I (1070-1118). Provides for the supply of bathing water-pot to the temple. The donor was a native of Gangaikondasolapuram.

280 of 1907 (Tamil) — In the same placle. A record in the third year of the Chola king Tribhuvanachakravartin Sri Vikrama Choladeva (1118-35). Records gift of money for supplying periodically an earthern pot of Sembangudi in Tiruvindalurnadu, a sub-division of Rajadhirajavalanadu.

281 of 1907 (Tamil) — On the east wall of the first prakara

of the same temple, right of entrance. A record in the forty-first year of the Chola king Tribhuvanachakravartin Sri Kulottunga Choladeva I. Records gift of money for a lamp by a native of Gangaikondasolapuram.

282 of 1907 (Tamil) — In the same place. A record in the seventh year of the Chola king Tribhuvanachakravartin Sri Vikrama Choladeva (1118-35). Records gift of money for a lamp and for a bathing water-pot by a native of Suttamali-chaturvedimangalam, a brahmadeya in Purangarambainadu, a sub-division of Rajendra Cholavalandu.

283 of 1907 (Tamil) — In the same place, left of entrance. A record in the fifth year of the Chola king Tribhuvanachakravartin Sri Vikrama Choladeva (1118-35). Records gift of money for a lamp and of a lamp-stand by a native of Tiraimur in Vilainadu, a sub-division of Rajanarayanavalanadu.

284 of 1907 (Tamil) — In the same place. A record in the seventh year of the Chola king Tribhuvanachakravartin Sri Vikrama Choladeva (1118-35). Records gift of money for a lamp and for a bathing water-pot by a native of the village.

285 of 1907 (Tamil) — In the same place. A record in the tenth year of the Chola king Parakesarivarman or Tribhuvanachakravartin Sri Vikrama Choladeva (1118-35). Records gift of money for a lamp by a certain Andapillayandar.

286 of 1907 (Tamil) — In the same place. A record in the fifth year of the Chola king Parakesarivarman or Udaiyar Sri Vikrama Choladeva. Records gift of land for offerings to the image of Manikkakuttar in the same temple at Tiruvidaimarudur and money for a bathing water-pot.

287 of 1908 (Tamil) — In the same place. A record in the

fourth year of the Chola king Parakesarivarman or Tribhuvanachakravartin Sri Vikrama Choladeva (1118-35). Recordos gift of land at the village site.

288 of 1907 (Tamil) — In the same place. A record in the sixteenth year of the Chola king Parakesarivarman or Tribhuvanachakravartin Sri Kulottunga Choladeva III, "who was pleased to take Madurai (Madura) and the crowned head of the Pandya." Registers an order of the king altering the procession of the God during festivals and arranging the streets of Tiruvidaimarudur.

289 of 1907 (Tamil) — In the same place. A mutilated record in the twenty-eighth year of the Chola king Tribhuvanachakravartin Sri Kulottunga Choladeva III, "who took Madura, Kuruvur and Ilam (Ceylon) and who was pleased to take the crowned head of the Pandya." Records gift to the image of Aludaiya Pillaiyar set up by Vanadhirajan of the village of Kulottungasolanpundi or Vikramasolansuralur in Tiruvalundurnadu, a sub-division of Jayangondachola-valanadu. Refers to the revenue survey in the sixteenth year of Sungandavirtta Kulottunga Choladeva I.

290 of 1907 (Tamil) — In the same place. A record in the third year of the Chola king Tribhuvanachakravartin Sri Vikrama Choladeva (1118-35). Records gift of money for a bathing water-pot.

291 of 1907 (Tamil) — In the same place. A mutilated record (on Wednesday, Pushya Makara Purvapaksha Panchami) of the twenty-seventh year of the Chola king Tribhuvanachakravartin Sri Rajarajadeva III. Records sale of land. (See *Ep. Ind.,* Vol. X, p.135, where Mr. R. Sewell points out that the fifth thithi is a mistake for the fifteenth and then equates the date to Wednesday, 7th January, A.D. 1243.)

292 of 1907 (Tamil) — On the south wall of the same prakara. A record in the fourth year of the Chola king Vikrama

Choladeva (1118-35). Records gift of money for a bathing water-pot by a native of Sattamangalam in Innambanadu, a sub-division of Viridurajabhayankaravalanadu.

293 of 1907 (Tamil) — On the south wall of the first prakara of the Mahalingasvami temple. A record in the fourth year of the Chola king Vikrama Choladeva (1118-35). Records gift of money for bathing water-pot by a native of Gangaikondasolapuram.

294 of 1907 (Tamil) — On the same wall. A record in the sixth year of the Chola king Vikrama Choladeva (1118-35). Records gift of money for four lamps by another native of Gangaikondasolapuram.

295 of 1907 (Tamil) — On the same wall. A record in the fourth year of the Chola king Vikrama Choladeva (1118-35). Records gift of money for a bathing water-pot and for a lamp by the Vellalanganda Avaiyampukkan or Adalaiyurnattu Pallavaraiyan of Serrur in Rajarajapandinadu.

296 of 1907 (Tamil) — On the same wall. A damaged record in the fourth year of the Chola king Vikrama Choladeva (1118-35). Records gift of money.

297 of 1907 (Tamil) — On the same wall. A record in the fourth year of the Chola king Vikrama Choladeva (1118-35). Records gift of money for two lamps by a native of Uttamasilichaturvedimangalam in Pandikulasanivalanadu.

298 of 1907 (Tamil) — On the same wall. A record in the seventh year of the Chola king Tribhuvanachakravartin Sri Vikrama Choladeva (1118-35). Records gift of a cow for a lamp by a woman of Mulanallur in Tiraimurnadu.

299 of 1907 (Tamil) — On the same wall. A record in the seventh year of the Chola king Tribhuvanachakravartin Sri Vikrama Choladeva (1118-35). Records gift of a cow for a lamp by a dancing girl (*devar adiyal*).

300 of 1907 (Tamil) — On the same wall. A record in the twenty-seventh year of the Chola king Rajakesarivarman or Chakravartin Sri Kulottunga Choladeva (I?). Records gift of sixty sheep for a lamp and of a lamp-stand.

301 of 1907 (Tamil) — On the same wall. A record in the fourth year of the Chola king Parakesarivarman or Tribhuvanachakravartin Sri Vikrama Choladeva (1118-35). Records gift of land to the image of Kulottunga Cholisvaramudaiya Mahadeva set up by Svamidevar Srikanthasiva at Mangalakkudi, a hamlet of Solamattanda-chaturvedimangalama in Manninadu, a sub-division of Virudarajabhayamkaravalanadu for the merit of Udaiyar Sri Kulottunga Choladeva I. (In his list of Sans. MSS. in the Tiruvidaimarudur library Dr. Hultzsch mentions a Srikantha Sivacharya who wrote the Vedantic work *Brahmamimamsa Bhashya* and a Srikantha, a tantric writer who belonged to the Kashmir school and composed the *Ratnatraya Pariksha* about the close of the eleventh century. The present epigraph probably refers to the former. See also Prof. Rangacharya's Des. Cat. Sans. MSS., Vol. X, No. 5092, p.3874-6. The famous Appayya Dikshita has written a commentary on Srikantha's Bhashya. See Ibid., p.3876-7. Srikanta's son was Somesvara or Isvara Siva who wrote the *Siddharta Ratnakara*. This Isvara Siva was the guru of Kulottunga III (1178-1216) and consecrated the temple while he built at Tribhuvanam. The Government Epigraphist surmises that this Isvara Siva might be the same as Isana Siva, the author of the *Siddhantasara*, but different from this namesake of the Amarda matha who wrote the *Krinakranadyotika*.

302 of 1907 (Tamil) — On the same wall. A record in the third year of the Chola king Parakesarivarman or Tribhuvanachakravartin Sri Vikrama Choladeva (1118-35.) Records gift of land to the same image set up in the same

village, here said to be the eastern hamlet of Solamattanda-chaturvediimangalam in Manninadu, a sub-division of Virudarajabhayankaravalanadu.

303 of 1907 (Tamil) — On the south wall of the first prakara of the same temple. A record in the eighth year of the Chola king Rajakesarivarman or Tribhuvanachakravartin Sri Kulottunga Choladeva (II?). Records sale of land to a native of Tandantottam by the sabha of Kulottunga-solamangalama detached from Keralantaka-chaturvedimangalam, a brahmadeya in Vennadu, a sub-division of Uyyakondarvalanadu. Refers to the fourth year of Sri Vikrama Choladeva (1118-35).

304 or 1907 (Tamil) — On the same wall. A record in the twenty-sixth year of the Chola king Rajakesarivarman alias Chakravartin Sri Kulottunga Choladeva I. Records gift of 180 sheep for three lamps by the Nambirattiyar Siraman Arumolinangaiyar or Elulagumudaiyar.

305 of 1907 (Tamil) — On the same wall. A record in the thirteenth year of Tribhuvanachakravartin Konerinmaikondan. Refers to the revenue survey in the sixteenth year of Sungandavirta Kulottunga Choladeva I.

306 of 1907 (Tamil) — On the same wall. A record in the thirteenth year of the Chola king Tribhuvanachakravartin Sri Kulottunga Choladeva III, "who took Madura and was pleased to take the crowned head of the Pandya." Records an addition made to the dancing masters of the temple. The new incumbent had to dance with gestures.

307 of 1907 (Tamil) — On the same wall. A record in the twenty-second year of Tribhuvanachakravartin Konerinmaikondan. Records gift of land to the shrine of the Pidari Yogirunda Paramesvari in the fourth prakara of the temple.

308 of 1907 (Tamil) — On the same wall. An unfinished

record in the ninth year of the Chola king Kulottunga Choladeva. Mentions Panan Irumudi Solan Piran or Asainjalapperayan.

309 of 1907 (Tamil) — On the west wall of the same prakara. A record in the twenty-first year of the Tribhuvanachakravartin Konerinmaikondan. Records gift of land. Mentions Irumarabunduya Perumal Chaturvedimangalam in Uyyakondarvalanadu and refers to land which had been granted tax-free for the worship of Aludaiya Pillaiyar and Aludaiya Nambi (Saint Sundaramurti.)

310 of 1907 (Tamil) — On the second eastern gopura of the same temple, right of entrance. A damaged record in the seventh year of the Chola king Tribhuvanachakravartin Sri Rajarajadeva (III?). A few syllables of each line were inaccessible at the end. Mentions Tribhuvanavira-chaturvedimangalam.

311 of 1907 (Tamil) — On the same gopura left of entrance. A record in the third year of the Pandya king Maravarman Tribhuvanachakravartin Kulasekharadeva. Seems to record a gift of land for temple repairs. (It is doubtful whether the king is the first or second of that name (1268-1308) or (1314-21.)

312 of 1907 (Tamil) — On the third eastern gopura of the same temple, right of entrance. A much damaged record.

313 of 1907 (Grantha and Tamil) — On the same gopura, left of entrance. A damaged record in the third year of the Pandya king Vikrama Pandya. Seems to record a gift of land for celebrating a festival called Vikrama Pandyan Sandi.

130 of 1895 (Tamil) — On the east wall of the second prakara of the Mahalingasvamin temple, right of entrance. A record in the fifth year of the Chola king Ko Parakesarivarman or Vikrama Choladeva (1118-35). Records gift of land and money.

131 of 1895 (Tamil) — In the same place. A record in the seventh year of the Chola king Tribhuvanachakravartin Vikrama Choladeva (1118-35). Records gift of money for two lamps.

132 of 1895 (Tamil) — In the same place. A record in the twenty-sixth year and one hundred and seventy-second day of the Chola king Ko Rajakesarivarman or Kulottunga Choladeva I. Records gift of 120 sheep for two lamps. Mentions the four queens of the king. See S.I.I., Vo. III, No. 72, pp.156-9. The priests and the local assembly were trustees and undertook to supply one uri of ghee per day by the Ekanayaka measure.

133 of 1895 (Tamil) — On the same wall, left of entrance. A record in the forty-ninth year of the Chola king Tribhuvanachakravartin Kulottunga Choladeva I. Records gift of money for a pot.

134 of 1895 (Tamil) — In the same place. A record in the forty-ninth year of the Chola king Tribhuvanachakravartin Kulottunga Choladeva I. Records gift of money for a lamp.

135 of 1895 (Tamil) — In the same place. A record in the eighteenth year of Sakalabhuvanachakravartin Ko Perunjingadeva. Records gift of land. See *Ep. Ind.,* Vol. VII, p.165 where Dr. Kielhorn calculates the exact date to be Friday, 30th July, A.D.1249.

136 of 1895 (Tamil) — On the south wall of the same prakara. A record in the sixth year of the Chola king Vikrama Choladeva (1118-35). Records gift of money for a lamp.

137 of 1895 (Tamil) — In the same place. A record in the sixth year of the Chola king Vikrama Choladeva (1118-35). Records gift of money for a lamp by an inhabitant of Conjeevaram.

138 of 1895 (Tamil) — In the same place. A record in the fourth year of the Chola king Ko Parakesarivarman or

Vikrama Choladeva (1118-35). Refers to the twenty-fifth year of Kulottunga Choladeva I.

139 of 1895 (Tamil) — In the same place. A record in the seventh year of the Chola king Ko Parakesarivarman or Vikrama Choladeva (1118-35).

140 of 1895 (Tamil) — In the same place. A record of the Vijayanagara king Sadasivadeva Maharaya in S. 1466, expired, Krodhin. Records gift of two villages by Ramaraju Vittaladeva Maharaja. (He was the conqueror of southern India in 1545 and was then Viceroy for about a decade.)

141 of 1895 (Tamil) — In the same place. A record in the ninth year of the Chola king Ko Rajakesarivarman or Kulottunga Choladeva (I?). Records gift of land.

142 of 1895 (Tamil) — In the same place. A record in the twelfth year of the Chola king Tribhuvanachakravartin Kulottunga Choladeva III, "who took Madurai and cut off the crowned head of the Pandya." Records allotment of shares.

143 of 1895 (Tamil) — In the same place. A record in the second year of the Chola king Tribhuvanachakravartin Rajarajadeva. Records gift of land.

144 of 1895 (Tamil) — In the same place. A record in the eighteenth year of Tribhuvanachakravartin Konerinmaikondan. Records gift of land.

145 of 1895 (Tamil) — On the south wall of the mandapa in front of the shrine in the same temple. A record in the fourth year of the Chola king Ko Parakesarivarman. Records gift of money for a lamp.

146 of 1895 (Tamil) — On the same wall. A record of the Chola king Madiraikonda Ko Parakesarivarman (905-47), the date of which is doubtful. Records gift of gold.

147 of 1895 (Tamil) — On the south wall of the shrine in the same temple. A record in the thirty-seventh year of the

Chola king Madiraikonda Ko Parakesarivarman (Parantaka I, 905-47). Records gift of land for a lamp.

148 of 1895 (Tamil) — On the same wall. An incomplete record in the sixteenth year of the Chola king Ko Rajakesarivarman.

149 of 1895 (Tamil) — On the west wall of the same shrine. A record in the thirty-fifth year of the Chola king Madiraikonda Ko Parakesarivarman (Parantaka I, 905-47). Records gift of land.

150 of 1895 (Tamil) — On the same wall. A record in the eleventh year of the Chola king Ko Parakesarivarman. Records gift of utensils.

151 of 1895 (Tamil) — On the same wall. A record in the third year of the Chola king Ko Parakesarivarman. Records gift of lamp.

152 of 1895 (Tamil) — On the north wall of the same shrine. A record in the third year of the Chola king Ko Rajakesarivarman. Records gift of paddy.

153 of 1895 (Tamil) — On the same wall. A record of the Chola king Ko Rajakesarivarman, the date of which is lost. Records gift of land.

154 of 1895 (Tamil) — On the same wall. A record in the fourth year of the Chola king Ko Parakesarivarman "who cut off the head of the Pandya". Records gift of land. (The King referred to was evidently Parantaka II, Sundara Chola).

155 of 1895 (Tamil) — On the same wall. A record in the thirty-fourth year of the Chola king Madiraikonda Ko Parakesarivarman (905-47). Records gift of a lamp.

156 of 1895 (Tamil) — On the same wall. A record in the tenth year of the Chola king Ko Rajakesarivarman. Records gift of gold for a lamp.

157 of 1895 (Tamil) — On the same wall. A record in the thirty-seventh year of the Chola king Madiraikonda Ko Parakesarivarman (905-47). Records gift of land.

158 of 1895 (Tamil) — On the pillar in the mandapa surrounding the shrine in the same temple. A record in the fourteenth year of the Chola king Ko Rajakesarivarman. Records gift of land.

159 of 1895 (Tamil) — On another pillar in the same place. A record in the sixteenth year of the Chola king Ko Rajaraja Rajakesarivarman I (985-1013). Records gift of land.

SURYANARKOIL

The image of the Sun is regularly worshipped in Suryanarkoil which is two miles away from Tiruvidaimarudur, and so far, this is the only place where a temple has been dedicated to Sun. Brihaspati is depicted in front of the Sun in the sanctum. The other planets[3] also find a place here in separate shrines around the courtyard, and a horse depicted in front of the Sun is said to be the Vahana or vehicle of the deity.

The inscriptions of the temple go to show that it was known as Kulottoungachola Mattandalayam. It is also believed that king Kulottunga I, who built this temple, had some intimate relationship the Gahadavala Kings of Kanouj who were also Sun worshippers.

According to the Madras Ephigraphical[4] Department "Kulottunga I appears to have built a shrine of Surya in his own dominions. The temple of Suryanarkoil is perhaps the only one in the Tamil country where the Sun god is regularly worshipped as the presiding deity of a temple. The central shrine faces the west and is dedicated to the Sun-Brihaspati is given a place in front of the central shrine. The garbhagriha and the mukha mandapa of the temple are built of stone. The shrines of the remaining seven of the navagrahas viz., Rahu, Sukra, Ketu, Chandra, Angaraka, Budha and Sani are constructed of bricks around the central building. Two inscriptions of Kulottunga I are engraved in the base of the mukha mandapa. In one of them the temple is called Kulottungachola Mattandalalaiyam which shows that it was probably built during the reign of Kulottunga and that it was already dedicated to the Sun god.

[5]"Another important inscription in this year's (1920-21) collection is No. 81 of Appendix C which consists of the first six verses of the Suryasataka of Mayurakavi engraved in characters of about the early part of 11th century A. D. on a pillar in the mandapa in front of the Durga shrine in the Kachchisvara temple at Conjeevaram. In all probability, it was a votive pillar erected by somebody in honour of the Sun god (Suryadeva), one of the *Panchasandhi* deities (*Ainjandideva* as the group is called in Tamil), who is installed in small shrine in the compound of the same temple. The inscription under reference does not however contain any endorsement giving historical information as to when, by whom and under what circumstances, the inscription was incised on this pillar. There might have been more pillars of this type which might have contained other verses of the same sataka but they are not existent now and the presence of this pillar in the Durga shrine has to be accounted for by its probable displacement during temple repairs in later days — probably in the time of Kulottunga I, when the central shrine of the Kachchisvara temple seems to have undergone through overhauling (No. 68 of Appendix C).

Mayurakavi was a court-poet, who flourished in the court of Harsha in the first half of the 7th century A.D. and is reputed to have been the father-in-law of Banabhatta; while in the *Prabhanda Chintamani*, the relationship is mentioned as that of a brother-in-law (sister's husband) — (vide *Suryastakam* in the *Kavyamala* Series of Bombay). His only work is the *Suryastakam*, which is also popularly known by

the name of *Mayurasatkam*. The verses are written in the
Sragdhara metre and their literary merit coupled with the
miraculous results which are alleged to have attended their
composition, have secured for them great popularity among
the orthodox. The author appears to have been suffering
from blindness and to have been cured of his troublesome
disease by composing these verses in praise of god Surya,
so that even today these verses are used for purposes of
parayanam (devout recitation)!! This is therefore another
instance of purely literary matter engraved on stone ; and
this adds one more to the number of similar stray examples
which have been hitherto met with elsewhere in this
Presidency, viz., the music inscription at Kudimiyamalai
(*Ep. Ind.,* Vol. XII No. 28), the Bharatanatya verses at
Chidambaram (pages 74 to 81 of the *Annual Report on
Epigraphy* for 1913-14), the Devaram inscription at
Tiruvidavayal (No. 8 of 1918) and the Hanumadvimsati at
Conjeevaram (No. 651 of 1919)."

TRIBHUVANAM

Tribhuvanam is a village near Tiruvidaimarudur in the district
of Tanjore between Triuvidaimarudur and Kumbakonam. The
deity in the temple is named Kampahareswara as he is said
to have removed the Kampa (quaking) of a certain king who
was haunted by an evil spirit consequent on the sin committed
by him in killing a Brahman accidentally.

There is a shrine to Sarabha god wherein the metal image
enshrined is very attractive. In front of the shrine are two
dvarapalas of high architectural workmanship.

ARCHITECTURE

The architecture of the temple is similar to those found in
Tanjore, Gangaikondasolapuram, and Darasuram near

Kumbakonam. The Vimana (tower) over the sanctum in all these four places are unique in being very high unlike the majority of cases where the Vimana over the garbhagriham, will be short and unimposing.

EPIGRAPHICAL IMPORTANCE

An inscription, which records the building operations of Kulottunga Choladeva, is engraved on the south wall of the central shrine in the Kampahareswara temple at Tribhuvanam. Copies of the same are also recorded in the outer gopura of the said temple. The alphabet used therein both in the original over the sanctum wall as well as in the copies over the gopuram is Grantha and the language Sanskrit. It consists of four lines of writing, the whole having been in an excellent state of preservation till 1907 when it was copied by the Madras Epigraphical Department and numbered as 190 of 1907, except for parts of three letters only where the stone has been chiselled. It opens with the usual "Swasti Sri" which when translated means "Hai Prosperity" in accordance with the Hindu custom of commencing all such auspicious writings. The first two lines bear testimony to the king's victories while the last two lines detail his building operations. Out of the wealth obtained by his conquest of the northern countries he appears to have built the temple at Darasuram and Tribhuvanam on the model put up by his predecessors in Gangaikondasolapuram and Tanjore. At the same time he has also renovated the temple at Chidambaram, Madura, Tiruvidaimarudur and Tiruvarur.

Though the inscription is not dated we are in a position to settle the time of Kulottunga III by an inscription in the Ranganayaka temple at Nellore; according to which he commenced reigning in A.D. 1178. For a period of at least

39 years he reigned, as an inscription in the Nataraja temple at Chidambaram is dated in the 39th year of his reign. In the historical introduction of many inscriptions he goes by various names such as Triobhuvanachakravartin, Tribhuvanaviradeva, Parakesarivarman, Virarajendradeva II, Konerimaikondan, Rajathirajakarikalacholadeva, Ulagayya Nayanar, Ulagudayya Nayanar. Another on the north Prakara wall at Sayavanam, designates him as Periyadevar and he seems to have been the last of the Chola kings who was powerful. He held a durbar in a mandapa within the temple at Tiruvoriyur near Madras on a certain festival day.

INSCRIPTIONS[6]

The Government Epigraphist surmises that the village was founded by Kulottunga Chola III who had the title Tribhuvanaviradeva.

159 of 1911 (Tamil) — On the south base of the Ranganatha Perumal temple. A damaged record in the tenth year of the Pandya king Jatavarman Tribhuvanachakravartin Parakrama Pandyadeva. Registers a contract between the residents of "the city" of Tribhuvanavirapura and those of Kulamangala-nadu who owned the *urkaval* of that village. (The *urkaval* men take an oath not to be unjust or injure the people in any way and they receive, in return for their duty, a *selai* (cloth) on each marriage among the Kallarmakkal. They were to demand no selai on other marriages than the first).

160 of 1911 (Tamil) — On the north and west bases of the same temple. A mutilated record in the tenth year of the Pandya king Jatavarman Tribhuvanachakravartin Parakrama Pandyadeva. Refers to a contract similar to that registered in the above epigraph and mentions the chief

Udaiyar Kulasekharadeva or Kupakaraya in whose presence Sennaiperumal or Kulottungasolavaraiyan, agreed to the contract. (Is the king referred to the same as Jatavarman Parakrama who ascended the throne in 1334?)

189 of 1907 (Grantha) — On the south wall of the central shrine in the Kampaharesvara temple. A damaged record. Mentions Arya Sri Somanatha.

190 of 1907 (Grantha) — On the same wall. A record of the Chola king Sri Kulottunga Choladeva III. Registers the building operations of the king.

191 of 1907 (Grantha) — At the entrance into the outer gopura of the same temple on the right side. A record of the Chola king Tribhuvanavira. (This is a duplicate copy of the above epigraph.)

192 of 1907 (Grantha) — On the same gopura, left side. A record of the Chola king Sri Kulottunga Chola. (This is also a duplicate copy of No. 79.)

NOTES

1. A short life-sketch of this saint appears on page 43 footnote.
2. *Inscriptions of the Madras Presidency*, Government of Madras, 1919, Vol. II, pp.1265 to 1280.
3. The *Navagrahas* (nine planets) are worshipped with a view to acquire peace, prosperity, wealth and longevity in this world, or to bring down good showers of rain in the country. They are believed to influence the destinies of human beings. There are circular, quadrilateral, triangular, arrow-shaped, rectangular, pentagonal, bow-shaped, winnow-shaped, and flag-shaped seats prescribed for each of them. If with special care people should worship the planets hostile to them, they bless them with good.

4. Vide the *Annual Report* for 1907-1908.
5. *Madras Epigraphical Department* (Annual Reports published by the Government of Madras), 1920-21.
6. *Inscriptions of the Madras Presidency*, Government of Madras, 1919, Vol. II, pp.1245 to 1246.

Chapter 12

KUMBAKONAM

This ancient city on the river Kaveri, formerly called Kudamukku, with a number of Vishnu and Siva temples, is a railway station on the Madras-Danushkodi line. The town, lying in north latitude 0°57' and east longitude 79°25' at a height of 85 feet in a low level tract between two rivers — the Kaveri in the north and the Arasalar in the south — extending about two miles in length from north to south and one mile in breadth from east to west, derives its name from its presiding deity Kumbesvara whose temple has an immense local celebrity. The central linga is said to be composed of fragments of a pot installed in a box. There are several explanations of the origin of the name Kumbesvara.

This is the only place where the great Mahamagha festival occurring once in twelve years anud celebrated in February, takes place and which has temples dedicated to the Trimurtis — Brahma, Vishnu and Siva.

ANTIQUITY

The ruins of an ancient structure in a suburban village called Solamaligai or the palace of the Cholas indicate that Kumbakonam was the capital of the Chola kings. It is also said that king Srimara Pandya, who lived about the ninth century, defeated the armies of the Cholas and the Gangas here.

MAHAMAGHA FESTIVAL

The Mahamagha festival which comes off once in twelve years, when Jupiter passes the constellation of Simha or Leo, draws pilgrims from all parts of the country, and a bath in the Mahamagha tank on that day is considered very sacred. The tank is situated in the heart of the town and covers an area of twenty acres. There are sixteen mandapas along the banks and they are dedicated to various deities. It is believed that deities of the nine sacred rivers meet together on the Mahamagha day at Kumbakonam. Their sculptural representations are seen in the temple of Visvanadha. In the mandapa on the northern bank one sees a sculptural representation of Tulapurushadana (a ceremony of weighing oneself against gold), observed on the occasions of the equinox, the solstice, the commencement of an era (Yuga)[1] and its termination, eclipses and Sankaranti, (Pongal), etc. This ceremony is performed near sacred tanks, holy rivers or similar places. The amount of gold weighed against the person observing the ceremony is distributed amongst deserving men.

It is a strong belief held by Hindus in common with all other religions that after every Yuga (cosmic cycle) the whole world is immersed in a great deluge through the unmitigated wrath of Siva as a just punishment for sins committed by human beings on the earth. Since the last deluge the world has been reconstructed for the current Kaliyuga (Iron age) through the personal importunity of Brahma, the Creator. Siva declared that after the destruction of the world a pot full of Amritha (nectar) would move on till at last it would settle in a certain holy spot. Thus the divine pot reached Kumbakonam, when Siva in the form of Kirata (hunter) hit an arrow at the pot which broke, and from which were scattered many fragments — which accounts for so many temples in Kumbakonam, such as Kumbeswara, Nageswara, Someswara, Adi Visveswara (also known as Komata Visvanatha or Malathivaneswara), Abimukeswara, Goutameswara, Banapuriswara, Visvanatha, Varahar, Lakshminarayana, Sarangapani, Chakrapani and Varadaraja temples. The town itself is named after this incident, viz., the breaking of the holy pot. There are also 18 other important centres within a redius of ten miles and they are Tiruvidaimarudur, Tribhuvanam, Ammachatram, Tirunageswaram, Ayyavadi, Sivapuri, Sakkottai, Kottayur, Banadurai, Maruthanthanallur, Pattiswaram, Sakthimutham, Darasuram, Tiruvalanjuli, Swamimalai, Innambur, Karuppur and Tiruppirambiyam.

Astronomically the planet Jupiter passes over Leo on the Great Mahamagham festival day, when it is said to exercise certain powers over the waters of the tank and saturate it with mineral properties. On the same occasion a lake in Kotihar (Kashmir State) gets its full supply of water though it continues to remain dry for the remaining 11 years!!

Since the last deluge the world has been reconstructed by Brahma, the Creator, in honour of whom there is a temple in Kumbakonam specifically dedicated. It lies to the left of the Mahamagha tank in what is now called Pattunoolkara (silk-weaver) Street though he is cursed to be without a temple and as such no temple exists anywhere for this deity. At the entreaty of Brahma to give him a more detailed account about the Mahamagham tank, it was said by lord Siva that the sins of mortality were washed away after a bath there. It was suggested to the river nymphs that all of them should go to the tank in the month of Masi (February-March) when the asterism Makha (Leonis) holds sway and that God by his presence on that occasion would wash them of their sins. Even today may be seen on the right side of this tank a shrine containing the "9 Virgins Statues", viz., the Ganges, the Yamuna (Jamna), the Saraswathi, the Narmada, the Godavari, the Kaveri, the Mahanadi, the Payoshni (Palar) and the Sarayu; and these are supposed to bathe in the tank during the Mahamagham festival which occurs once in 12 years. This shrine of the nine Virgins is within the temple of Visvanatha facing the south on the north bank of the tank. Brahma thereafter also prayed to Siva for the grant of further boons to mortal beings created by him should they have the benefit of a bath in the tank on the occasion to which Siva replied not only He would be present in the tank but also Mahavishnu, Devas (celestials) and all the river nymphs would go in advance to occupy the centre of the tank. This is one of the beliefs of the Hindus.

Many stories of Puranic greatness and historical importance[2] are in record to show the importance of a bath in the tank on the occasion. A woman by name Kanigai of Sowrashtra country (Bombay Presidency) who was suffering from an incurable ailment, King Hehaya who was issueless in spite of his just administration, Prince Sutharma who lived on the banks of Tampraparni river (Tinnevelly District) who as the result of some curse lost his children, King Veerasarma of Kalinga country who had a deformed issue, Gyanavan of Konkana Desa who could not successfully perform a tortoise sacrifice were relieved of their ailments and troubles by visiting this tank and bathing therein. Men with chronic disease, like leprosy, elephantiasis, etc., get cured after a bath provided they have a firm belief, for in these days of advanced civilisation when science works out miracles, all belief flies before the devil of athesim!! Yet to those who have some belief in heaven, who think and feel that there is something higher than human beings that rules the destiny, they are sure to have the relief prayed for. There is a belief that the holy Ganga and other nymphs stretch out their lovely hands with healing powers, and this, King Achyutha Nayak of Tanjore is said to have actually witnessed in the presence of his prime minister Govinda Dikshitar to whom the construction of the 16 shrines on the sides of the tank is attributed. It is due to all this that the tank is held in great esteem from time immemorial which accounts for the multitudious masses that rush in for the occasion.

The importance of this festival bears also ample archaeological and epigraphical evidence. Archaeologically, it will be seen on the ceiling of the mandapam on the northern bank opposite to what is known as "Gangathirtham", that there is a sculptural representation of Tulapurushadhava (gift of weighing oneself against gold). The great prime minister of Nayak kings of Tanjore, Govinda Dikshithar, is said to have utilised the wealth thus obtained from the observance of this ceremony by the then nayak King in repairing this tank and also constructing the 16 shrines that are now seen on the sides of this tank. Epigraphically the famous Vijayanagara King Krishna Devaraya is said to have witnessed a Mahamagham festival during this time. At the entrance into the north gopura of the temple at Nagalapuram (Chingleput district) is a record of this king dated Saka 1445 referring to the visit the king paid to that village on his way to Kumbamonam to attend this festival. That the same King Krishna Devaraya made gifts to a temple on this holy occasion is proved by another inscription found on the northern wall of the mandapa in front of the central shrine at Kuthalam (Tanjore District).

NAGESVARA TEMPLE

The temple of Nagesvara contains a separate shrine for the Sun, who is said to have worshipped Siva in this place, and to this day the rays of the sun are seen to fall on the central linga on certain days of the year. There is also a sculptural representation of Uchchishta Ganapati[3] (the polluted Elephant-God) in this temple.

An inscription which is dated in the third year of Parakesarivarman (Aditya Karikala II), refers to a gift to one of the famous commentaries on the *Purva Mimamsa Sutras* which founded a new school of philosophy called Prabhakara Mata after its expounder the great Prabhakara who in point of time was contemporaneous with Bhattakumarila being one of his direct pupils and must, consequently, have flourished about the beginning of the 8th century. The Telugu work *Sakalurthasagara* also mentions of this Prabhakara. This temple goes by the name of Tirukkilkottam.

SARANGAPANI TEMPLE

The Vaishnava deity Sarangapani[4], an incarnation of Vishnu, appeared to a sage called Hema Rishi, who performed penance. The central shrine of the temple is in the form of a chariot drawn by horses and elephants with openings on either side, showing the descent of god Sarangapani from heaven in this chariot. The hermitage of the sage is said to have been on the bank of the temple tank named Pottamarai.

SRI RAMASWAMI TEMPLE

The Ramaswami temple, which lies in the west of Kumbakonam, is believed to have been constructed in the 16th century by Reghunatha Naik, king of Tanjore. The popular tradition of the construction of this temple is that the king discovered the idols of Rama and Sita and other deities in a tank at Darasuram, a village nearby and installed them in the temple close to the Sarangapani shrine. Sri Rama is represented in his coronation robes. The Mahamandapa in front of the temple has several fine sculptures — Vamana Tiruvikrama, Vishnu with his consorts Sridevi and Bhudevi, and of the marriage of Parvati.

In the Chakrapani temple, Vishnu appears in the form of a discus or chakra to put down the pride of Surya (the Sun), who subsequently became His devotee in the temple of Nageswara.

SRI SANKARACHARYA MATHA

Kumbakonam is also the seat of the Sankaracharya[5] matha, which was at one time in Conjeevaram. The seat was transferred to this place during the reign of Maharaja Pratap Singh of Tanjore.

Akkanna and Madanna were two brothers born of a very poor family in Golconda. They both entered service as shroffs in A.D. 1666 on a very poor pay. The former is said to have been cunning and a little roguish while the latter, known also as Suryaprakasa Rao, was highly intelligent. They in course of time rose to the status of a noble, which elevated Madanna to the office of a minister and thus the virtual ruler of the kingdom. He was well versed in several languages and was in close to the Dutch with whom he came in contact.

According to a copper-plate grant preserved in the matha here these eminent ministers gave certain villages to the matha by way of gift.

Ramdoss, the faithfull devotee of Sri Rama, whose adventures are sung in the form of a ballad, who held the office of a chief revenue officer under the Golconda chief, and was imprisoned and saved miraculously at the end is inferred to have been the nephew of these gentlemen!!

Later on in 1685 the Mugal king Aurangazeb plundered their house by entering Golconda and had them dragged along the streets in the presence of the people. The head of Akkanna was trampled under the foot of an elephant and Madanna was also liked and sent to Aurangazeb on the 29th of October, 1685. Thus ended the lives of these eminent men.

Another record of these two Brahman officers of the Golconda King Abdul Hassan, the last of the Kootbshahi line, is dated Saka 1602 (A.D. 1680) mentions Madanna Pandita, as he is called therein, as the chief officer of the king of Bhagnagara, which has been identified to be the ancient name of Hyderabad (Deccan). King Mahammad Kolly Kootb Shah (1581-86) is said to have built in 1581 a magnificent city called Bhaugnuggur (Hyderabad) 8 miles from Golconda, after his favourite mistress Bhagmutty, a public singer of whom he was greatly enamoured. This name Bhaugnuggur often assumes the form Bhagyanagara (the city of wealth on the analogy of the second name Vidyanagara which means the city learning of Vijayanagara, the capital of the Vijayanagar empire.

The copper-plate grant referred to in the report of the Madras Epigraphical Department for the year 1917-18 states that, while Lingoji Pandita was governing the Karnataka kingdom from Penukondapattana as a subordinate of Akkanna Pandita, the younger brother of Madanna Pandita, the chief officer of the king of Bhaugnuggur, gave some land in that village. It mentions also the gift of rates on pack-bullocks, shops, looms and marriages to Kumarayya by the "samayins" of Ayyavali etc., assembled in the temple mandapa of that place for daily offerings and lamps to the god Nanjundesvara.

The comprehensive character of the communal assembly is a prominent feature. The Ayyavale merchants, the Vaisyas of the 102 "gotras," the representatives of the chief Saiva "mathas," the "sampradayikas" (caste leaders), the members of the 18 sects, the "yajamanas," gavadas and karanams of the Lepakshi-stala at which the gift was made, the Pattanasvami sampradayika, the representatives of the 4 (chief) Reddi families, who were landowners (bhumi prabhus) and the members of the 18 professional classes of the early 17th century are represented.

INSCRIPTIONS[6]

The inscriptions in the temples here have been copied during the years 1908, 1911 & 1915 by the Madras Epigraphical Department.

The antiquity of Kumbakonam is well-recognized, its god Sarangapani or Aravamuda have been worshipped in the Prabhandas in the eighth century, but no epigraphical evidences are available to show its antiquity. It has twelve Saivite and four Vaishnavite shrines, besides a Brahma temple. The temples are comparatively modern (being the works of the Naik kings) in outer parts, but ancient, going back to the Chola period at least in inner parts. The Nagesvara shrine is famous for the adoration of its deity by the sun and the Chakrapani shrine for the statue of a Tanjore king holding a lamp for the God. The Sankaracharya matha is one of the most important historical institutions.

13 of 1908 (Tamil) — On the west wall of the shrine of the Goddess in the Nagesvara temple. A record in the eighth year of the Pandya king Maranjadaiyan. Records gift of 138 cows for milk and 100 kasu for two lamps by the king to the temples of Tirukkilakkotattu Bhatara at Tirukkudamukku. (The exact identity of Maranjadaiyan is not knwon.) Tirukkudandai Kilkottam is famous in Saivite tradition as the place where the Sun worshipped Siva and got back the splendour which he had lost owing to Visvakarma's curse!

14 of 1908 (Tamil) — On the north wall of the Suryanarayana shrine in the Nagesvara temple. A record of the Chola king Rajakesarin Udaiyar Sri Vijayarajendradeva (Rajadhiraja I) in his thirty-sixith year, Makha, Apara, Wednesday, Ayiliam. Records sale of land for 498 kalanju and lands made rent free. (See *Ep. Ind.,* Vol. X, p.121, where Mr. R. Sewell points out that the date corrresponds to December 29, A.D. 1053).

15 of 1908 (Tamil) — On the east wall of the same shrine. An unfinished record in the eighth year of the Chola king Parakesarivarman or Sri Rajendra Choladeva I. Seems to provide for offerings to the shrine of Chandrasekharadeva.

223 of 1908 (Tamil) — On the north wall of the central shrine in the Nagesvara temple. A record in the sixth year of the Chola king Sarivarman. Built in at the beginning. Records gift of 96 sheep for a lamp to the temple of Tirukkilkottattu Paramasvami at Tirukkudamukku in Vadagarai Pamburnadu, by Ingala Madevan Kodai Maran, a native of Ingalnadu.

224 of 1911(Tamil) — On the same wall. A record in the second year of the Chola king Parakesarivarman. Records sale of land to a certain Kadan Achchan for 25 kalanju which he had deposited in the same temple, for maintaining a prepetual lamp. (Mr. Krishna Sastri surmises that the king referred to might be Aditya Karikala II.)

225 of 1911(Tamil) — On the same wall. A record in the fifith year of the Chola king Parakesarivarman (Aditya II ?) "who took the head of the Pandya." Records sale of land by the assembly of Tirukkudamukku, a devadana in Vadagarai-pamburnadu, to the palace woman (pendatti) Periyan Tribhuvanasundari (a resident) of Palaiyavelam at Tanjavur in Tanjavurkurram, for 85 kalanju of gold which she had deposited, for feeding a Sivayogin in the temple of Tirukkikottattu Paramasvami. The land given by Kadan

Achchan (see the above epigraph) formed one of the boundaries of this land.

226 of 1911(Tamil) — On the same wall. A record in the fourth year of the Chola king Parakesarivarman (Aditya II?) "who took the head of the Pandya". Records gift of ninety sheep for a lamp to the temple of Tirukkilkottattu Paramesvara by Pendatti Devayan Pulakkan or Avanisikhamani (a resident) of Kilaivelam (quarter) at Tanjavur, called after Udaiyapirattiyar Kilanadigal, the mother of Anaimerrunjinar (Rajaditya who was killed by Bhutuga II while seated in his elephant and whose mother was Kokkilanadigal, the queen of Parantaka I. See Leyden Grant in Tam, and Sam. Ins., p. 204 ff; the Atakur inscription as interpreted by R. Narasimhachar in F.R. A.S., April 1909; and Mys. Arch. Rep. 1911, p.38).

227 of 1911(Tamil) — On the same wall. A record in the third year of the Chola king Rajakesarivarman. Records sale of land by the assembly of Tirukkudamukkil, to Arayan Kalangamalai, a Vellala of Tanjavur, for feeding a Sivayogin in the temple of Tirukkilkottattu Paramasavami.

228 of 1911(Tamil) — On the same wall. A record in the third year of the Chola king Rajakesarivarman (Gandaraditya?). Records gift of ninety sheep for a lamp by Kumaran Tuduvan, one of the Kaikkolas of Virasolatterinja Kaikkolar and a resident of Tanjavur. (Vira Chola was a surname of Parantaka I and the Kaikkolars evidently got the title from him. For similar epithets see Taj. 1397 and 1398.)

229 of 1911 (Tamil) — On the same wall. A damaged record in the eighth year of the Chola king Parakesarivarman. Records gift of ninety-six sheep for a lamp. Mr. Swamikannu Pillai calculates the date to Thursday, the 30th January, A.D.979, and so the king must have been Madhurantaka Uttama Chola who came to the throne in A.D.969-70.

230 of 1911 (Tamil) — On the same wall. A record in the third year of the Chola king Parakesarivarman (Aditya II?) "who took the head of the Pandya." Records sale of land by the assembly of Srikudandai to Koilmayilai or Parantaka Muvendavelan of Sirringan in Inganadu, for feeding twenty apurvins versed in the Vedas and five Sivayogins in the temple (srikoil) of Tirukkilkottattu Perumal. (Kudandai is the name of Kumbakonam by which orthodox Vaishnavites even now call it.)

231 of 1911 (Tamil) — On the same wall. A record in the fourth year of the Chola king Parakesarivarman, "who took the head of the Pandya." Records gift of land by the same person fer feeding fifty Brahmans.

232 of 1911 (Tamil) — On the same wall. A record in the twenty-seventh year of the Chola king Madiraikonda Parakesarivarman (Parantaka I). Built in at the end. An inscription to the left of this on the same wall has its beginning built in and records a gift of land for feeding a Sivayogin and maintaining a lamp in the temple of Tirukkilkottaoottu Perumanadigal.

233 of 1911 (Tamil) — On the same wall. A record in the third year of the Chola king Parakesarivarman, "who took the head of the Pandya." Records sale of land to Koyilmayilai or Parantaka Muvendavelan by the assembly of Tirukkudamukku which he presented as a bhattavritti to those who expounded Prabhakaram in the temple. (Mr. Krishna Sastri identifies the Chola king with Aditya Karikala II, but it seems that Parantaka II is more probable. Prabhakara Matha is one of the famous school of Mimamsa, founded by Prabhakara, a contemporary of Kumarila in the eighth century.)

234 of 1911 (Tamil) — On the same wall. A record in the eighth year of the Chola king Parakesarivarman. Records gift of ninety-six sheep for a lamp. Mentions Sri Uttamasola

Nambirattiyar. (Evidently refers to Madhurantaka Uttamacholadeva.)

235 of 1911 (Tamil) — On the west wall of the same shrine. A record in the fortieth year of the Chola king Parakesarivarman (Parantaka I, 906-47) "who took Madurai (Madura) and Ilam (Ceylon)." Records gift of ninety sheep for a lamp.

236 of 1911 (Tamil) — On the same wall. A damaged record in the fifth year of the Chola king Rajakesarivarman. Quotes the third year . . . kesarivarman and seems to record a gift of seventy Ilakkasu for offerings. (Ilakkasu—the coin of Ceylon.)

237 of 1911 (Tamil) — On the same wall. A much damaged record of the Chola king Parakesarivarman, the date of which is doubtful. Recorods gift of eighty kalanjus of gold for feeding Brahmans.

238 of 1911 (Tamil) — On the same wall. A much damaged record of the Chola king Madiraikonda Parakesarivarman (906-47), the date of which is lost. Records gift of ninety-six sheep for a lamp to the temple of Tirukkilkottattu Mahadeva, by a certain Kari Villupparaiyan.

239 of 1911 (Tamil) — On the same wall. A much damaged record of the Chola king Rajakesarivarman, the date of which is lost. Records gift of ninety-six sheep for a lamp.

240 of 1911 (Tamil) — On the same wall. A much damaged record in the thirteenth year of the Chola king Parakesarivarman. Records gift of land by Viranarayan Iyar, daughter of . . . and queen (nambirattiyar) of Sri Uttamasolar, for providing garlands of flowers to the temple of Tirukkilkottattu Perumal. (According to Mr. Swamikannu Pillai the date corresponds to Friday, the 9th June, A.D. 982 and so the king referred to is Madhurantaka Uttamachola, whose date of accession was A.D. 969-70.)

241 of 1911 (Tamil) — On the same wall. Records gift of gold for lamps by two private individuals.

242 of 1911 (Tamil) — On the west and south walls of the same shrine. A record in the second year of the Chola king Parakesarivarman. Records gift of ninety sheep for a lamp by a Kaikkolan named Devan Rajadittan.

243 of 1911 (Tamil) — On the same walls. A record in the fifth year of the Chola king Parakesarivarman. Records gift of sheep for lamps.

244 of 1911 (Tamil) — On the same walls. A record in the fifth year of the Chola king Parakesarivarman. Records gift of ninety-seven sheep for a lamp by a certain Devan Nakkan.

245 of 1911 (Tamil) — On the same walls. A much damaged record in the fourth year of the Chola king Parakesarivarman. Records sale of land by the assembly of Tirukkudamukku for maintaining a lamp in the temple of Tirukkilkototattu Paramasvamin in the name of Kari Kolamban, a Kaikkolan. (According to Mr. Swamikannu Pillai the date corresponded to Thursday, the 22nd April, A.D. 975, and so the king referred to is evidently Madhurantaka Uttamachola whose accession was in A.D. 969-70.)

246 of 1911 (Grantha and Tamil) — On the same walls. A record in the twenty-eighth year of the Chola king Parakesarivarman. Records gift of money for a lamp by Tanavadi Arangan or Panchavan, a native of Karuvur in Milalaikurram, to the temple of Tirukkilkottattu Bhattaraka.

247 of 1911 (Tamil) — On the south wall of the same shrine. An incomplete record in the fourth year of the Chola king Parakesarivarman. Records gift of land for feeding a Brahman by a merchant of Nandipuram.

248 of 1911 (Tamil) — On the same wall. A record in the third year of the Chola king Parakesarivarman. Records gift

of 25 kalanjus of gold for a lamp, by Puvan Kannan of Nedumpuraiyur in Malainadu.

249 of 1911 (Tamil) — On the same wall. A record of the Chola king Madiraikonda Parakesarivarman (Parantaka I), the date of which is lost. Built in at the end and damaged. Records sale of land by the assembly of Tirukkudamukku for feeding two persons in the temple of Tirukkilkottattu Perumanadigal. Mentions Ayirattali in Kilarkurram, a sub-division of Tenkarainadu.

250 of 1911 (Tamil) — On the same wall. A record in the thirty-eighth year of the Chola king Madiraikonda Parakesarivarman. Records gift of ninety-six sheep for a lamp by a certain Mainjan Kavaiyan, a native of Aiyyaru in Tirunaraiyurnadu.

251 of 1911 (Tamil) — On the same wall. A record in the fifteenth year of the Chola king Rajakesarivarman. Records gift of a lamp by Kalayan Manikkam, to the temple of Tirukkilkottattu Perumanadigal.

252 of 1911 (Tamil) — On the same wall. A record in the fifteenth year of the Chola king Rajakesarivarman. Records gift of a lamp by Kalayan Manikkam, to the temple of Tirukkilkottattu Perumanadigal.

253 of 1911 (Tamil) — On the same wall. A damaged record in the fortieth year of the Chola king Parakesarivarman (905-47), who took Madurai (Madura) and Ilam (Ceylon). Records gift of land for providing a lamp and burning incense (sidari) in the temple of Tirukkilkottattu Purumandigal and for maintaining two lamps in the shrine of Suryadevar.

254 of 1911 (Tamil) — On the same wall. A damaged record of the Chola king Madiraikonda Parakesarivarman (906-47), the date of which is lost. Records gift of 105 pieces of gold (tulaipon) by Villavan Peraraiyan or Sidupuyam Pandan, a native of Kavalur which was a devadhana of

Ayirattali in Kilarkurram, a sub-division of Tenkarainadu, for conducting festivals in the same temple.

255 of 1911 (Tamil) — On the same wall. A damaged record in the third year of the Chola king Rajakesarivarman (Gandaraditya). Records sale of land in Arisalur by the assembly of Tirukkudamukku to the temple of Tirukkilkottattu Paramasvami, for 500 kalanjus of gold, in order to pay a part of 3,000 kalanjus levied upon them as an impost (dandam) by Madiraikonda Udaiyar (Parantaka I) in his thirty-eighth year. Mentions the army of the Pandya (Pandipadai) and the temple of Jalasayana. (*Ep. Rep.*, 1907, p.73, Venkayya describes the three invasions of Parantaka I against the Pandya, in the last of which he conquered Ilam also. Inscriptions show that this took place in his thirty-seventh year. The present inscription corroborates it. The Pandipadayar has been interpreted to be the army which conquered the Pandya country.)

256 of 1911 (Tamil) — On the same wall. A much damaged record in the sixth year of the Chola king Parakesarivarman or Rajendra Choladeva I. Records gift of land for providing offerings to the image of Selvappiran in the Srivimana (central shrine) of the temple of Tirukkilkottam Udaiyar, by the assembly of Tirukkudamukku in Pamburnadu, a sub-division of Uyyakondaivalanadu.

257 of 1911 (Tamil) — On the north wall of the mandapa in front of the same shrine. A record in the twenty-second year of the Chola king Tribhuvanachakravartin Rajarajedava. Records gift of land by a Brahman lady, for organising certain festivals in the shrine of Madandaipaga Nayanar, situated in the temple of Tirukkilkottam Udaiyar at Tirukkudamukkil in Pamburnadu, a sub-division of Uyyakondarvalanadu. (This inscription is evidently the same as Ins. S. Dts., p.195, No.10. But the donors are named as Narayana Ambalattan and "Pramanavooyavundan.")

258 of 1911 (Tamil) — On the same wall. A record in the twentieth year (Chitra, Mina, firsit lunar fortnight) of the Chola king Rajakesarivarman or Tribhuvanachakravartin Rajarajadeva. Begins with a new historical introduction. Records gift of land for repairs and jewels to the same shrine by a certain Kuttadum Tirugnanasambhandar Madandaipagan. A gift of land by Kuttadum Tirugnanasambhandar Manikkavasagan, to the shrine of Kuttadum Tirugnanasambhandesvaram Udaiyar built by himself in the temple of Tirukkilkottoam Udaiyar, is recorded below the above. (Mr. Swamikannu Pillai calculates the year of the inscription to be 1235-36, and so the king should have been Rajaraja III (1216-48). I have traced this inscription in the Mack. Lists to Ins. S. Dts., p.195, No.II).

259 of 1911 (Tamil) — On the same wall. A record of Mahamandalesvara Pattukattari Konerideva Maharaja, "lord of Kanchipura, the best of towns," in S.1412, Sadharana. Registers that Timmanan (surnamed) Madandapaga Kongarayan, son of Sediraya Manikkam, was granted food, house and land by the authorities managing the temple of Madandaipaga Nayanar at Tirukkudamukku, a brahmadeya in Pamburattunadu, a sub-division of Uyyakondarsolavalanadu, for the services rendered by him to the temple. (Mr. Krishna Sastri believes that the king might be the same as he who is referred to in the Koyilolugu as the successor of Saluva Tirumal Raja in the Government of the Trichinopoly country who was an anti-Vaishnavite. This inscription is given in Ins. S. Dts., p.194, No.8 also.)

260 of 1911 (Tamil) — On the same wall. An unfinished record in the thirty-fifth year of the Chola king Tribhuvanachakravartin Tribhuvanaviradeva (Kulottunga III) "who being pleased to take Madurai (Madura), Ilam (Ceylon), Karuvur and the crowned head of the Pandya, was pleased to

perform the anointment of victors and heroes." Records that a certain Alvar Tiruppurambiyam Udaiyan or Sembiyan Pallavaraiyan of Velur had set up an image called Tiruppurambiyam Udaiyar in the eastern enclosure of the temple of Tirukkilkottam Udaiyur and presented 17,000 kasus for offerings and lamps to that image and for a makara torana to Tirukkilkottam Udaiyar. (This inscription is given in Ins. S. Dts., p.194, No.9.)

C.P. No.4 of 1915 — A Telugu record of the Penugonda king Virapratapa Venkatadeva Maharaja, dated S. 1630, Vikriti, Kartigai, su. di. 15, Monday, Rohini. Records grant of land by the Madura Naik king Vijia Ranga Chokkanatha for the maintenance of worship, feeding of Brahmans, etc., in the Sankaracharya matha at Jambukesvaram. For a full account of Vijia Ranga Chokkanatha, see *Ind. Antq.,* August and September 1917.

C.P. No. 5 of 1915 — Records an agreement in the reign of Srirangadeva Maharaya in St. 1663, Dundubhi, Tai 15, which the servants of Vijia Ragunatha Raya Tondaiman had with one Bhavani Venkatakrishnaiya of Conjeevaram regarding the fee (?) due to him from them.

C.P. No. 6 of 1915 — A Telugu record in S. 1608, Prabhava, Vaisakha, su. di. 15, Saturday, lunar eclipse. Registers that Mahadevendra Sarasvati, pupil of Chandrasekhara Sarasvati, of the Sankaracharya Sarada matha at Kanchi, gave to one Ramasastrulu of the Hoysana Kannadi sect land in the village of Melpaka, an annuity of two varahas in the matha, and certain collections in the Jaghir of Chingleput given to the matha by Akkanna and Madanna of Golconda. (These were the celebrated ministers of Abdulla Kutb Shah and Abdul Hassan of Golconda.) For a brief account of them as based on the Dutch journalist Havart, see *Ep. Rep.,* 1915, p.118. Mahadevendra Sarasvati was apparently the Acharya who presided over the matha from 1703 to 1746 and in whose time the matha was removed from Conjeevaram first to Udaiyarpalaiyam and then, at the instance of Prataba Singh of Tanjore and of his minister Dabhir Pant, to Kumbakonam.

C.P. No. 7 of 1915 — A record of Krishnadeva Raya in S. 1450, Virodhin, Vaisakha, Paurnami, in Sanskrit. Registers the gift of the village of Udayambakkam in Chingleput Sima, Kalatturkottam to Sadasiva Sarasvati, a disciple of Chandrasekhara Sarasvati. (In a list of Sankaracharyas of Kamakotipitha of Conjeevaram, later on removed to Kumbakonam, published by the talented scholar T.S. Narayana Sastri, I find that the fifty-fifth Acharya was called Chandrachudendra and that he presided over the matha from 1506-1512 and that fifty-sixth was Sadasivendra, who was in charge of the matha from 1512-1538. These are the two Acharyas apparently referred to in this epigraph.)

C.P. No. 8 of 1915 — Registers a grant by Krishnadeva Raya in S. 1444, Svabhanu, Margasirsha su. di. 12 of the village of Podavuru or Krishnarayapuram in Sengad Kurram, Nirvalurnadu in Chandragiri Rajya to Chandrachuda Sarasvati of Conjeevaram, disciple of Mahadeva Sarasvati. See the above epigraph.

TIRUVISALUR

Tiruvisalur, the ancient Vembarur or Solamarthanda-chaturvedimangalam, is a few miles to the north of Kumbakonam and here there are several valuable inscriptions of devotees inclusive of those relating to the Tulabharadana of king Rajaraja and the Hemagarbha or the ceremony of passing one-self through a golden cow, by his queen Lokamah Devi.

There is the sculpture of the king and queen as worshipping the linga in the mandapa within the temple. According to the inscriptions recorded therein the architect that constructed this mandapa, is one Anantasivan, whose figure is shown on the front wall of a shrine in the southern enclosure. He is shown as worshipping a linga with puja materials before him. The linga is decorated with lotus flowers and garlands and the puja materials consist of gandi, rudraksha, pela, flowers and a sankha (conch).

INSCRIPTIONS[7]

One of the 63 North Kaveri Saivite centres renowned as the place where a devotee who died of fear the king was revived by God's grace!! It was sung by Tirugnana sambhanda, and known in ancient times as Vembarrur or Cholamartanda-chaturvedimangalam.

1 of 1907 (Tamil) — On the south wall of the central shrine in the Sivayoganathasvamin temple. A record in the fourth year of the Chola king Parakesarivarman or Sri Rajendra Choladeva (1011-43). Records gift of a gold fillet to the temple of Tiruvisalur-Mahadevar at Vembarrur or Solamartandachaturvedimangalam, a brahmadeya in Manni-nadu, a sub-division of Vadagarai Rajendrasimhavalanadu.

2 of 1907 (Tamil) — On the same wall. A record in the tenth year of the Chola king Rajarajakesarivarman I (985-1013) "who destroyed the ships at Kandalur Salai." Records gift of money for a lamp.

3 of 1907 (Tamil) — On the same wall. A record in the tenth year of the Chola king Rajarajakesarivarman (Rajaraja I, 985-1013) "who destroyed the ships at Kandalur Salai." Records gift of money for a lamp to the temple of Tiruvisalur Perumal at Avani Narayanachaturvedimangalam, a devadana, and a brahmadeya.

4 of 1907 (Tamil) — On the same wall. A record in the second year of the Chola king Parakesarivarman. Records gift of 96 sheep for a lamp.

5 of 1907 (Tamil) — On the same wall. A record in the third year of the Chola king Rajakesarivarman. The date is expressed in words. But above the akshara "mu" of munravadu the numeral 20 seems to be inserted. If this is part of the date, it would be the twenty-third year of the king's reign.

6 of 1907 (Tamil) — On the same wall. A record in the third year of the Chola king Parakesarivarman. Makes provision for bathing the God.

7 of 1907 (Tamil) — On the same wall. A record in the fourth year of the Chola king Parakesarivarman. Built in at the end. Records gift of 180 sheep for two lamps.

8 of 1907 (Tamil) — On the same wall. A record of the Chola king Parakesarivarman. Built in at the end. Records gift of a lamp.

9 of 1907 (Tamil) — On the same wall. A record in the sixth year of the Chola king Parakesarivarman. Records gift of gold by Sembiyan Karaikkadudaiyan or Anniyaradigal.

10 of 1907 (Tamil) — On the same wall. A record in the third year of the Chola king Parakesarivarman. Records gift of a lamp to the temple of Tiruvisalur Perumal in Amani Narayanachaturvedimangalam, a devadana and a brahmadeya in the country on the northern bank (vadagarai) of the river Cauvery.

11 of 1907 (Tamil) — On the same wall. A partially damaged record in the fourteenth year of the Chola king Tribhuvanachakravartin Vikrama Choladeva (1118-35). Makes provision for bathing the God and for sacred garlands.

12 of 1907 (Tamil) — On the same wall. A record in the sixteenth year of the Chola king Madiraikonda Parakesarivarman (Parantaka I). Records gift of 180 sheep for two lamps.

13 of 1907 (Tamil) — On the same wall. An incomplete record in the ninth year of the reign of Chola king

Rajakesarivarman. Records sale of land to a relative of Karugavurkilavan Marudanpattan or Solavelan, son of Sembiyan Karaikkadudaiyan.

14 of 1907 (Tamil) — On the same wall. A record in the eighteenth year of the region of Chola king Parakesarivarman or Tribhuvanachakravartin Kulottunga Choladeva III, who was pleaseld to take Madura and the crowned head of the Pandya. Records sale of land. The village is called Vembarrur or Edirilisolachaturvedimangalam. See *Ep. Ind.,* Vol. IX, p.214 where Dr. Kielhorn, after pointing out certain irriegularities in the date, fixes it as Saturday, 3rd December, 1196.

15 of 1907 (Tamil) — On the same wall. A record in the third year of the Chola king Parakesarivarman or Rajendra Choladeva I (1011-43). Records a gift of gold in order to provide *sidari* for the incense.

16 of 1907 (Tamil) — On the same wall. An incomplete record in the third year of the Chola king Parakesarivarman. Records a gift of land.

17 of 1907 (Tamil) — On the same wall. A record in the thirty-second year of the Pandya king Varaguna Maharaja. Partly covered by a wall. (If he happens to be the same person who ascended the throne in A.D. 862, it has to be inferred that he ruled at least till A.D. 894.)

18 of 1907 (Tamil) — On the same wall. A record in the fourth year of the Chola king Parakesarivarman. Records a gift of hundred sheep for a lamp by Nakkan Arinjigai or Parantaka Pallavaraiyan.

19 of 1907 (Tamil) — On the west wall of the same shrine. A record of the Chola king Rajarajakesarivarman (Rajaraja I) in his fifth year, Mula, Dhanus. Records a gift of gold by a queen of Rajarajadeva. See *Ep. Ind.,* Vol. IX, p.207, where Dr. Kielhorn points out that the date corresponded to Sunday, 1st December, A.D. 989.

20 of 1907 (Tamil) — On the same wall. An incomplete record in the twenty-eighth year of the Chola king Maduraikonda Parakesarivarman (905-47). Records a gift by a native of Kulittandilai in Kurumburnadu.

21 of 1907 (Tamil) — On the same wall. A record of the Chola king Parakesarivarman, the date of which is doubtful. The date is expressed by the symbol for nine followed by that for ten. Records gift of a lamp.

22 of 1907 (Tamil) — On the same wall. A damaged record in the twenty-seventh year of the Chola king Maduraikonda Parakesarivarman (A.D. 905-47).

23 of 1907 (Tamil) — On the same wall. A record in the forty-first year of the Chola king Parakesarivarman (A.D. 905-47), who took Madirai and Ilam (Ceylon). Records a gift of gold for a lamp.

24 of 1907 (Tamil) — On the same wall. A damaged record in the sixteenth year of the Chola king Maduraikonda Parakesarivarman (A.D. 905-47).

25 of 1907 (Tamil) — On the north wall of the same shrine. A record in the tenth year of the Chola king Parakesarivarman. Records gift of ninety sheep for a lamp.

26 of 1907 (Tamil) — On the same wall. A record in the tenth year of the Chola king Parakesarivarman. Records gift of ninety sheep for a lamp.

27 of 1907 (Tamil) — On the same wall. A record in the fifteenth year of the Chola king Maduraikonda Parakesarivarman (A.D. 905-47). Records a gift of ninety-three sheep for a lamp.

28 of 1907 (Tamil) — On the same wall. A record of the Chola king Parakesarivarman or Kandaradittan Sri Madhurantakar (i.e., Madhurantaka, son of Gandaraditya). Records gift of ornaments by the king's mother. The king was probably Uttamachola.

29 of 1907 (Tamil) — On the same wall. A record in the third year of the Chola king Maduraikonda Parakesarivarman (A.D. 905-47). Built in at the beginning. Recorods a gift of sheep for a lamp.

30 of 1907 (Tamil) — On the same wall. A record in the tenth year of the Chola king Parakesarivarman. Built in at the beginning. Records a gift of ninety-three sheep for a lamp.

31 of 1907 (Grantha and Tamil) — On the same wall. A record in the twenty-second year of the Chola king Maduraikonda Parakesarivarman (A.D. 905-47). Records a gift of ninety-six sheep for a lamp.

32 of 1907 (Tamil) — On the same wall. An unfinished record in the fifth year of the Chola king Parakesarivarman.

33 of 1907 (Tamil) — On the same wall. A damaged record of the Chola king Maduraikonda Parakesarivarman, the date of which is lost. Records a gift of ninety sheep for a lamp.

34 of 1907 (Tamil) — On the same wall. An incomplete record in the fourth year of the Chola king Rajakesarivarman.

35 of 1907 (Tamil) — On the same wall. A record in the twenty-seventh year of the Chola king Maduraikonda Parakesarivarman (A.D. 905-47). Makes provision for the supply of bathing water from the Kaveri for the god. The temple is called Tiruvisalur Madevabhattarakar at Avani-narayanachaturvedimangalam or Vembarrur, a devadana and brahmadeya on the northern bank (vadagari) of the river Kaveri.

36 of 1907 (Tamil) — On the same wall. A record in the tenth year of the Chola king Parakesarivarman. Records a gift of ninety-six sheep for a lamp.

37 of 1907 (Tamil) — On the same wall. A record in the twelfth year of the Chola king Rajakesarivarman. Records a gift of ninety-six sheep for a lamp by a native of the Pandya country.

38 of 1907 (Tamil) — On the same wall. A record in the eighteenth year of the Chola king Madiraikonda Parakesarivarman (A.D. 905-47). Records gift of ninety sheep for a lamp.

39 of 1907 (Tamil) — On the same wall. A damaged and incomplete record of the Chola king Maduraikonda Parakesarivarman (905-47).

40 of 1907 (Grantha and Tamil) — On the same wall. A record in the fifth year of the Chola king Sundara Chola. Built in at the beginning.

41 of 1907 (Tamil) — On the south wall of the mandapa in front of the same shrine. A record in the tenth year of the Chola king Rajarajakesarivarman, 'who destroyed the ships at Kandalur Salai' (A.D. 985-1013). Records a gift of money for feeding two Brahmanas for incense and for lamps.

42 of 1908 (Tamil) — On the same wall. A record in the twenty-ninth year of the Chola king Rajarajakesarivarman or Sri Rajarajadeva I. The village is called Vembarrur or Solamattandachaturvedimangalam, a brahmadeya in Manninadu, a sub-division of Rajendrasimhavalanadu. Refers to the performance of tulabhara by the king and of *hemagarbha* by his queen Dantisakti Vitankiyar or Lokamahadeviyar in the temple at Tiruvisalur.

43 of 1907 (Tamil) — On the west wall of the same mandapa. A record in the twenty-fourth year of the Chola king Rajarajakesarivarman or Sri Rajarajadeva I (A.D. 985-1013). Records a gift of land for offerings at the shrine of Pichchadeva.

44 of 1907 (Tamil) — On the same wall. A record in the twenty-fourth year of the Chola king Rajarajakesarivarman or Sri Rajarajadeva I. Records a gift of land for offerings at the shrine of Pichchadeva. Refers to a revenue survey made some time prior to the date of the inscription.

45 of 1907 (Tamil) — On the north wall of the same mandapa. An incomplete record in the third year of the Chola king Parakesarivarman or Sir Rajendra Choladeva (A.D. 1011-43). Records a gift of land for lamps.

46 of 1907 (Tamil) — On the same wall. A record in the third year of the Chola king Parakesarivarman or Sri Rajendra Choladeva (A.D. 1011-43). Records a gift of ornaments by the queen of the Pandya king Srivalluvar (Srivallabhadeva).

47 of 1907 (Tamil) — On the same wall. Refers to the foundation of a matha on the northern bank of the fresh water tank in the temple of Tiruvisalurudaiya Mahadevar at Solamattandachaturvedimangalam in Manninadu, a subdivision of Virudarajabhayankaravalanadu.

48 of 1907 (Tamil) — On the same wall. An incomplete record in the thirtieth year of the Konerinmaikondan. The royal order was issued from Kanchipuram.

49 of 1907 (Tamil) — On the same wall. A record in the fifth year of the Chola king Kulkottunga Choladeva. Records a gift of land.

50 of 1907 (Tamil) — On the north wall of the shrine in the southern side of the same temple. Close to the inscription is a piece of suclpture which seems to represent a person called Anantasivan who built the mandapa.

51 of 1907 (Tamil) — On the same wall. A record in the fifth year of the Chola king Parakesarivarman, 'who took the head of the Pandya.' Records a gift of gold for a lamp. The temple is called Tiruvisalur Perumanadigal at Amaninarayanachaturvedimangalam, a devadana and brahmadeya in the country on the northern bank (vadagari) of the river Kaveri. The Government Epigraphist suggests that the king may be Aditya Karikala, son of Parantaka II or Sundarachola Parakesarivarman, who took the head of the Vira Pandya. See S.I.I., Vol. III, p.21.

52 of 1907 (Tamil) — On the inner gopura of the same temple, right of entrance. Records that the gopura as well as the enclosing verandah were built by Vikrama Chola (A.D. 1118-35).

314 of 1907 (Tamil) — On the north wall of the central shrine in the Sivayoganathasvamin temple. A record in the second year of the Chola king Rajakesarivarman. Records a gift of ninety sheep for a lamp by a native of Pennagadam in Tanjavurkurram.

315 of 1907 (Tamil) — On the north wall of the central shrine in the same temple. A record in the twenty-third year of the Chola king Maduraikonda Parakesarivarman (A.D. 905-47). Records a gift of 190 sheep for two lamps.

316 of 1907 (Tamil) — On the same wall. A record in the twenty-third year of the Chola king Maduraikonda Parakesarivarman (A.D. 905-47). Records a gift of 90 sheep for a lamp.

317 of 1907 (Tamil) — On the same wall. A record in the second year of the Chola king Rajakesarivarman. Records gift of land for feeding a Brahmana learned in the Vedas, by Pirantakan Irungolar or Siriyavelar of Kodumbalur. (The Kodumbalur chiefs belonged to the Kadava tribe and had Irukkuvel or Ilangovel for their family name. See *Ep. Rep.*, 1908, pp.87-9, for history of Kodumbalur and its chiefs).

318 of 1907 (Tamil) — On the same wall. An unfinished record in the fifth year of the Chola king Parakesarivarman.

319 of 1907 (Tamil) — On the same wall. A record of the Chola king Maduraikonda Parakesarivarman (A.D. 905-47), the date of which is illegible. Records a gift of 90 sheep for a lamp by a relative of Kalikesarin, the son of Karaikkadudaiyar.

320 of 1907 (Tamil) — On the same wall. A record in the fourth year of the Chola king Rajakesarivarman. Records a

gift of land by Pirantakan Irungolan or Siriyavelar. See No.317.

321 of 1907 (Tamil) — On the same wall. A record in the thirty-seventh year of the Chola king Maduraikonda Parakesarivarman (A.D. 905-47). Records a gift of 45 sheep for a lamp.

322 of 1907 (Tamil) — On the same wall. A record in the sixth year of the Chola king Rajakesarivarman. Records a gift of a lamp.

323 of 1907 (Tamil) — On the same wall. A damaged record in the sixth year of the Chola king Rajakesarivarman. Records a gift of a lamp.

324 of 1907 (Tamil) — On the same wall. An unfinished record in the fifth year of the Chola king Parakesarivarman. Seems to record the gift of a lamp.

325 of 1907 (Tamil) — On the same wall. A damaged record in the third year of the Chola king Rajakesarivarman. Records a gift of land by the queen of Uttama Choladeva, who seems to have been the daughter of Miladudaiyar.

326 of 1907 (Tamil) — On the same wall. An unfinished record of the Chola king Rajakesarivarman, the date of which is lost.

327 of 1907 (Tamil) — On the same wall. An unfinished record in the third year of the Chola king Rajakesarivarman. Close to this is an inscription which mentions the mother of Sri Uttama Choladeva.

328 of 1907 (Tamil) — (Tamil.) On the west wall of the same shrine. A much damaged record in the forty-first year of the Chola king Parakesarivarman (A.D. 905-47), 'who took Madurai and Ilam (Ceylon).'

329 of 1907 (Tamil) — On the same wall. A record of the Chcola king Maduraikonda Parakesarivarman (A.D. 905-47), the date of which is damaged. Records gift of a lamp by a

native of Mahendramangalam, a brahmadeya in Tenkarai Tiraimurnadu.

330 of 1907 (Tamil) — On the north and west walls of the same shrine. A record in the twenty-fourth year of the Chola king Maduraikonda Parakesarivarman. Records sale of land by two natives of Velimanallur in Urrukkattukottam, a sub-division of Tondainadu.

331 of 1907 (Tamil) — On the south wall of the same shrine. A damaged record in the ninth year of the Chola king Parakesarivarman. Built in at the end. Records gift of 90 sheep for a lamp.

332 of 1907 (Tamil) — On the same wall. A record of the Chola king Rajakesarivarman or Rajadhiraja I. Built in at the end. Contains a portion of the historical introduction of the king.

333 of 1907 (Tamil) — On the same wall. A damaged record in the seventeenth year of the Chola king Rajakesarivarman. Records a gift of 300 sheep for three lamps.

334 of 1907 (Tamil) — On the same wall. A record in the thirtieth year of the Chola king Maduraikonda Parakesarivarman (A.D. 905-47). Records gift of 90 sheep for a lamp.

335 of 1907 (Tamil) — On the same wall. A damaged record in the twelfth year of the Chola king Rajakesarivarman.

336 of 1907 (Tamil) — On the same wall. A record in the twenty-sixth year of the Chola king Maduraikonda Parakesarivarman (A.D. 905-47). Built in at the end. Records gift of 90 sheep for a lamp.

337 of 1907 (Tamil) — On the same wall. A record of the Chola king Parakesarivarman. Built in at the end. Records gift of sheep.

338 of 1907 (Tamil) — On the south wall of the mandapa in front of the central shrine in the Sivayoganathasvamin

temple. A damaged record in the second year of the Chola
king Parakesarivarman or Rajendra Choladeva I (A.D. 1011-
43). Records gift of lamps.

339 of 1907 (Tamil) — On the same wall. A record in
the third year of the Chola king Parakesarivarman or Sri
Rajendra Choladeva I (A.D. 1011-43). Records gift of
lamps.

340 of 1907 (Tamil) — On the same wall. A damaged
record in the third year of the Chola king Parakesarivarman
or Sri Rajendra Choladeva I (1011-43). Records gift of a silver
pot (*kalasa*) by a queen.

341 of 1907 (Tamil) — On the same wall. A record in the
third year of the Chola king Parakesarivarman or Sri Rajendra
Choladeva I (A.D. 1011-43.) Built in at the end. Refers to the
building of the Tiruchchurralaiyam and the gopura. The
temple is called Tiruvisalur Mahadevar at Vembarrur or
Srisolamattandachaturvedimangalam, a brahmadeya in
Manninadu, a district of Vadagari Rajendrasimhavalanadu.
The valangai caste is mentioned.

342 of 1907 (Tamil) — On the same wall. A damaged
record in the sixth year of the Chola king Rajakesarivarman
I (A.D. 985-1013.) Mentions as individual belonging to the
Udaiyar Kodandaramatanichchevagam. Records gift of nine
mas of land.

343 of 1907 (Tamil) — On the same wall. A record in the
fifth year of the Chola king Sri Kulottungatanichchevagam.
Records gift of nine mas of land.

344 of 1907 (Tamil) — On the same wall. A record of the
Chola king Parakesarivarman or Sri Rajendra Choladeva I
(A.D. 1011-43), the date of which is damaged. Records gift
of 28 kasus for a lamp.

345 of 1907 (Tamil) — On the west and south wall of the
same mandapa. An incomplete record of the Chola king

Rajakesarivarman or Udaiyar Sri Rajadhirajadeva I in his thirty-third year and sixty-fifth day.

346 of 1907 (Tamil) — On the west wall of the same mandapa. A record in the ninth year of the Chola king Parakesarivarman or Rajendra Choladeva (A.D. 1011-43). Records gift of twenty-five kasus for a lamp to the image of Umasahitar, entitled Andanayagar, by a native of Rajaraja-mandalam, i.e., Pandya country.

347 of 1907 (Tamil) — On the same wall. A damaged record in the twenty-ninth year of the Chola king Parakesarivarman or Udaiyar Sri Rajendra Choladeva I (A.D. 1011-43). Seems to record a gift of land for a lamp. Refers to the revenue survey of the country, probably in the reign of Rajaraja I.

348 of 1907 (Tamil) — On the north wall of the same mandapa. A record in the third year of the Chola king Parakesarivarman or Sri Rajendra Choladeva I (A.D. 1011-43). Records gift of land for a lamp by Nakkan Sembiyan Madaviyar, queen of Rajendra Choladeva.

349 of 1907 (Tamil) — On the same wall. A record in the fifth year of the Chola king Parakaserivarman or Sri Rajendra Choladeva I (A.D. 1011-43). Built in at the top and middle. Provides for feeding Brahmanas. Refers to a revenue survey and mentions Uruttiran Arumoli or Pirudimahadeviyar, the queen of Sri Rajarajadeva I. See No. 21 of 1897 at Tanjore.

350 of 1907 (Tamil) — On the same wall. A record in the fourth year of the Chola king Parakesarivarman or Sri Rajendra Choladeva I (A.D. 1011-43). Built in at the end. Records gift by Alvar Sri Pirantakan Kundavai Pirattiyar while she was in the palace (koyil) at Palaiyaru. (Kundavai Pirattiyar was the king's aunt, i.e. the elder sister of Rajaraja I and the queen of Vallavaraiyar Vandyadevar, who survived

her brother into the reign of Rajendra Chola I. Palaiyaru is probably the place in Tirunaraiyurnadu referred to in No.148 above).

351 of 1907 (Tamil) — On the east wall of the first prakara of the same temple on the right side. A record of the Chola king Tribhuvanachakravartin Sri Kulottunga Choladeva III, 'who was pleased to take Madura and the crowned head of the Pandya,' the date of which is lost. Refers to Vembaru or Edirilisolachaturvedimangalam as the devadana of Rajarajisvaramudaiyar; refers also to a revenue survey of the place.

353 of 1907 (Tamil) — On the same wall. A record in the seventheenth year of the Chola king Tribhuvanachakravartin Sri Kulottunga Choladeva III. Records the sale of land by a woman. Vembarrur is described as above. See *Ep. Ind.,* Vol. X, p.128 where Mr. Sewell shows that the details of the date given in the epigraph (Kumbha Apara I, Saturday Anuradha) indicated January 28th, A.D. 1195, but the nakshatra should be Magha and Purvaphalguni and not Anuradha.

354 of 1907 (Tamil) — On the same wall. A damaged record in the seventeenth year of the Chola king Tribhuvanachakravartin Sri Kulottunga Choladeva III, 'who was pleased to take Madura and the crowned head of the Pandya.' Refers to a revenue survey of the place; seems to register a sale of land.

355 of 1907 (Tamil) — On the second gopura of the same temple, right of entrance. A fragmentary record of the Vijayanagara king Vira Krishnadevaraya Maharaya, the date of which is lost. Records the remission by the king of *jodi* and *arasupera* and other taxes in favour of certain Siva and Vishnu temples. The revenue remitted amounted to 10,000 varahas. See S.A. Nos. 163 and 233.

SWAMIMALAI

Swamimalai to the west of Kumbakonam has a famous shrine on a hillock, dedicated to Subrahmanya, locally called Swaminatha. He is said to have initiated his father into the mysterious significance of the divine *Pranava* mantra, which the latter had forgotton owing to a sin incurred in killing a Rakshasa. To commemorate the incident, the central shrine of Subrahmanya is situated at the top of the hill, while in the same temple, the shrine of Siva is situated below, indicating the fact that the son and the father stood as master and disciple.

PURANIC IMPORTANCE

Indra, the Lord of the celestials, when he was greatly troubled by the Asura Arikesa, is also said to have obtained his blessing here. In commenmoration of Indra presented the deity with a white elephant. An image of an elephant in front of the deity, instead of the usual peacock, indicates this fact. The Vinayaka facing south on the hill is known as Kankkudutta Vinayaka (sight-restorer) and the tradition is that a certain blind man regained his sight by extreme devotion to this deity!

INSCRIPTIONS[8]

The inscritpions that stood in the temple here have been copied by the Madras Epigraphical Department during 1907.

The Subrahmanya shrine, famous as the place where the god instructed his own father in religion and therefore a centre of pilgrimage and vows, has got two inscriptions of the sixteenth century. It has a choultry founded by a principal Sadar Amin who was cured of a disease by taking a vow in the temple! It has, however, no epigraph in it.

496 of 1907 (Grantha and Tamil) — On the first gopura of the Subrahmanyaswami temple, right of entrance. A

damaged record of the Vijayanagara king Virapratapa Krishnadeva Maharaya in S. 1436, expired Bhava. The trisula and a peacock are engraved on the top of the inscription.

497 of 1907 (Grantha and Tamil) — In the same place. A record of the Nayaka king Sevappa Nayaka (1549-72) in S. 1495, expired . . . Refers to the son of Timmappa Nayakkar of the chaturtha gotra, who was a native of Nedungunram in Tondamandalam.

TIRUNAGESVARAM

About four miles to the east of Kumbakonam is a village called Tirunagesvaram, which is said to have been named Jambakaranya. Seikkilar, the author of the Periya Puranam, a masterpiece of Tamil literature, lived here and his figure is found in the temple. The figures of Sankanidhi and Padmanidhi[9] are also seen in the temple.

INSCRIPTIONS[10]

In the second year of Rajakesarivarman[11] the perunagarattar or the merchants of Kumaramattandapuram, perhaps a hamlet of the modoern Tirunagesvaram constructed a verandah around *palli* or the temple of Miladudaiyar, built a gopura for it and assigned a portion of their income for keeping up these structures in proper repair and maintaining some flower gardens. This income was evidently formed of *baravaikal* or the fees which they had the privilege to collect. What the nature of these fees was, we are not told. The name Miladudaiyarpalli, which the merchants of Kumaramattandapuram improved, suggests a Jaina shrine and there is reason for believing that a Jaina temple may have once existed at Tirunagesvaram. Kumaramattanda was the surname of an early Pallava king called Kadupathigal Nandipottarayar. Perhaps the village Kumaramattandapuram owed its existence to this king. The archaic characters of the inscription also suggest that Rajakesarivarman who was ruling at the time may have been Aditya I. Again Miladudaiyar is the name of a famous Saiva saint Meypporulnayanar whose copper image was installed in the Brihadesvara temple at Tanjavur in the third year of Rajendra Chola I. He was connected with one of the Chedi chiefs of Kiliyur in the South Arcot district. It is also possible that Miladudaiyarpalli at Kumaramattandapuram refers to a school or monastery built in honour of the Saiva saint Miladudaiyar. If this were so the date of Meypporulnayanar will have to be sometime prior to Rajakesarivarman Aditya I.

The inscriptions here have been copied during the year 1897 and 1911 by the Madras Epigraphical Department.

The village is now well-known not only for its Naganathasvami temple, but also its Uppiliyappan or Tiruvinnahar shrine referred to in the Prabhandhas.

211 of 1911 (Tamil) — On the north wall of the central shrine in the Naganathasvamin temple. A damaged record in the sixth year of the Chola king Parakesarivarman or Rajendra Chola I. Provides for a gold jewel studded with gems and pearls from the income of a land evidently presented by Adigal Acholan, one of the junior elephant *mahauts* (*ilaiyakunjiramallar*) in the army of Udaiyar Sri Rajendra Choladeva commanded by Solamuvedavelar, to the temple of Tirunagesvaram Udaiyar at Tiruvinnagar Tirunagesvaram in Tiraimurnadu, a sub-division of Uyyakondarvalanadu. (Tiruvinnagar is named after the local god Vishnu or Uppiliyappa. The great Gopala Desika, the founder of the Munitraya cult of Sri Vaishnavism is said to be an avatar of this God).

212 of 1911 (Tamil) — On the same wall. A record in the eighth year of the Chola king Parakesarivarman or Rajendra Chola I. Records gift of 48 sheep for half a lamp to the same

Mahadeva or Siva temple by a palace woman or *pendatti* called Tiran Sattividangi for the merit of her daughter Araiyan Uttamadanti. The latter was a resident of Udaiyar Anaimerrunjinarvelam or Abhimanabhushanatterinda-tiruvandikkappuvelam. Mentions Jananathapuram in Tiraimurnadu.

213 of 1911 (Tamil) — On the same wall. A partly damaged record in the fourteenth year of the Chola king Parakesarivarman or Rajendra Chola I. Built in a Registers jewels, gold and silver vessels owned by the temple, with the permission of the king which was obtained at the request of a temple servant named Kandan Kovalanadan. Tirunagesvaramudaiya Mahadeva is stated to have been situated in Tirukkudamukku in Pamburnadu, a sub-division of Uyyakondarvalanadu.

214 of 1911 (Tamil) — On the west wall of the same shrine. A record in the second year of the Chola king Parakesarivarman or Udaiyar Sri Rajendradeva (1050-63). Records that *mulaparudaiyar* or the assembly of Tirukkudamukku received 100 kasus from Manikkan Mavali or Vikkiramasinga Pallavaraiyan, a native of Marudam in Venkunrakottam, a sub-division of Jayangondasola-mandalam. This money was utilized by them for repairing damages caused by the Kaveri floods to the irrigation channel. For this, interest at the rate one kalam of paddy on each kasu was set apart for providing offerings in the temple of Tirunagesvaram Udaiyar and for expounding the Sivadharma in the assembly hall called Tiruchchirrambalamudaiyan built in the temple by the above-mentioned, Vikkiramasinga Pallavaraiyan.

215 of 1911 (Tamil and Grantha) — On the south wall of the same shrine. An unfinished and damaged record in the ninth year of the Chola king Rajakesarivarman (Gandaraditya). Seems to provide for offerings and mentions

Arinjigai Pirattiyar, a Bana queen and the daughter of prince Arikulakesari, the son of Parantaka I. Mentions the Simhalas, i.e. Ceylon. (The marriage of a Bana king with Parantaka's granddaughter shows the later friendship of the Bana and the Chola houses).

216 of 1911 (Tamil) — On the same wall. A record of the Chola king Rajendra Chola I. Built in at the right end. mentions Pasupatadeva as the name of the image carried about in procoessions.

217 of 1911 (Tamil) — On the same wall. A record in the thirty-second year of the Chola king Parakesarivarman or Udaiyar Sri Rajendra Choladeva I. Built in at the right end. It records gift of land to the temple of Tirunagesvaramudaiya Mahadeva at Tirukkudamukku in Pamburnadu, a sub-division of Uyyakkondarvalanadu by Narakkan Krishnan Raman of Keralantakachaturvedimangalam in Vennadu, another sub-division of the same valanadu. The twenty-fourth and thirty-frist years of the king are quoted in the body of the inscription. Mentions also the coin Rajendrasolankasu (evidently issued by Rajendra Chola I). It seems that the original area endowed was 9 1/8 mas, but according to 'the ma of the twenty-fourth year which contained 128 kulis' it amounted to 7 1/8 mas. Krishnan Raman was the general of Rajaraja I and superintended the building of the enclosure of the Brihadisvarasvami temple. See S.I.I., Vol. II, p.139. He also set up an Ardhanarisvara image in the shrine.

218 of 1911 (Tamil) — On the same wall. A record in the fourteenth year of the Chola king Rajaraja Rajakesarivarman I. Records of sale of 1Ç velis of land to the same temple by the assembly of Madanamangalam, a brahmadeya in Tirunaraiyurnadu. Tiruvinnagar Tirunagesvaram is stated to have been a devadana in Tiraimurnadu. The cost of the land (6 mas and 1 *kani*) viz., 101 kalanjus of tulaipon was the fund

formerly deposited for offerings by the princess Arinjigai
Pirattiyar. An introduction of Rajadhiraja beginning with
tingalertaru is inscribed next to this; but is much damaged and
incomplete. The tulaipon is gold after being 'burnt, cut,
melted, cooled and found current.'

219 of 1911 (Grantha) — On the same wall. A damaged
record which mentions Gandaraditya, the temple (*harmya*) of
Naga, Madurantaka and the latter's mother and two queens.
It seems to be hinted, says Mr. Krishna Sastri, that
Gandaraditya was the builder of the temple.

220 of 1911 (Tamil) — On the north wall of the first prakara
of the same temple. A record in the nineteenth year of the king
Chola Tribhuvanachakravartin Rajarajadeva (II?). Records gift
of land in the hamlet of Sivapadhasekaramangalam which was
a part of Tirunaraiyur or Panchavanmahadevichathur-
vedimangalam in Tirunaraiyurnadu, a sub-division of
Kulottunga Cholavalanadu, to the temple of Tirunagesvara-
mudaiyar at Tirunagesvaram in Uyyakondarvalanadu. Refers
to a *karaiyidu* (lease) given to the tenants, by prince
Kosalarayar.

221 of 1911 (Tamil) — On the south wall of the same
prakara. A much damaged record of the Chola king
Parakesarivarman or Tribhuvanachakravartin Rajarajadeva II,
the date of which is doubtful. Begins with the historical
introduction, pumaruviyapolil, etc., and seems to record a gift
of land.

222 of 1911 (Tamil) — On a pillar lying in a mandapa at
the end of the street in front of the same temple. A record in
the second year of the Chola king Rajakesarivarman. Records
gift of *varavaikal* (?) collecteld by the Perunagarattar of
Kumaṛamattandapuram for the renovation of the gopura
and the *tiruchchuralai* called Kumaramattandan in the
Miladudaiyarpalli of that village, which is stated to have been

situated in Tenkarai Tiraimurnadu. (The Chola king was evidently Aditya I. The name Kumaramattandapuram remains one of the pallava Nandipottaraiyar who had that title (See No. 199 of 1907). The name Miladudaiyarpillai, again suggests a Jaina shrine. This, together with the Jain images round the shrine of the goddess in the Naganathasvami temple, shows that this place must have been an early Jaina centre. Again Miladudaiyar is another name for saint Meypporulunayanar and if we suppose that the palli was a school or matha built in his honour, the present epigraph can be said to give a clue to his date, i.e. he was prior to Aditya I. He was connected with the Chedi chief of Kiliyur, South Arcot district. See also S.I.I., Vol. II, p.166, for a reference to the saint).

81 of 1897 (Tamil) — On the west wall of the central shrine of the Naganathasvamin temple. A damaged record of the Chola king Ko Rajaraja Rajakesarivarman I the date of which is indistinct. Records a gift of land.

82 of 1897 (Tamil) — On the same wall. A record in the fourteenth year of the Chola king Ko Rajaraja Rajakesarivarman I. Records gift of land by a queen.

83 of 1897 (Tamil) — On the north wall of the same shrine. A much damaged record of the Chola king Ko Parakesarivarman or Rajendra Choladeva I, the date of which is doubtful.

84 of 1897 (Tamil) — On the south wall of the second prakara of the same temple. A record in the fourteenth year of Tribhuvanachakravartin Konerinmaikondan. Records gift of land.

TIRUPPURAMBIYAM

Tiruppurambiyam is another village, six miles away from Kumbakonam, where Siva is said to have granted salvation to a Parich[12] devotee by appearing to him in the form of Dakshinamurti, and this deity has a shrine of his own. On the bank of the tank to the east of the temple, there is also a white marble image of Vinayaka, the elephant god, who is said to have saved the world from deluge and is known as Pralayakarta Vinayaka. (Pralaya means deluge.) This place is also historically connected as having been the battlefield of two important kings, the Ganga king Prithivipati I, and Varaguna Pandya in the pre-British period. A record of these incidents is to be found in the inscriptions of the temple. The name of the presiding deity originally appears to have been Adityeswara, but later on it was changed into Sakshiswara, since he incarnated as a witness for a girl of the Chetti caste.

INSCRIPTIONS[13]

The inscriptions here have been copied by the Madras Epigraphical Department during the year 1897.

The Siva temple here is well-known in Saivite tradition. It is said to celebrate the grace of the Lord towards Sunda and Upasunda and the miraculous power of Jnanasambandha in reviving the lover of a Vaniga woman who had died of snake bite. Hence the name Sakshiswara of the deity. The temple is mentioned in the *Devaram*. It is also hisitorically important as the scene of a battle betwteen the Ganga Prithvipati I and Varaguna Pandya, in which the former lost his life. See Udayendram plates of Prithvipati II (S.I.I., Vol. II, p.381). It was in Andattukurram in Rajendrasimhavalanadu.

69 of 1897 (Tamil) — On the south wall of the central shrine of the Sakshiswara temple. A record in the fourth year of the Chola king Ko Parakesarivarman 'who cut off the head of the Pandya.' Records gift of land. Built in. (Was the king Parakesarivarman Sundara Chola the destroyer of Vira Pandya?)

70 of 1897 (Tamil) — On the same wall. A record in the forty-third year of the Chola king Tribhuvanachakravartin Kulottunga Choladevla I. Records gift of land. Built in.

71 of 1897 (Tamil) — On the same wall. A record in the sixteenth year of the Chola king Ko Rajakesarivarman. Records gift of land for two lamps.

72 of 1897 (Tamil) — On the same wall. A record in the tenth year of Chola king Ko Rajakesarivarman. Records gift of gold for a lamp.

73 of 1897 (Tamil) — On the same wall. A record in the fifteenth year of the Chola king Ko Rajakesarivarman. Records gift of a lamp.

74 of 1897 (Tamil) — On the same wall. A record in the seventh year of the Chola king Ko Rajakesarivarman. Records gift of a lamp.

75 of 1897 (Tamil) — On the same wall. A record in the fourteenth year of the Chola king Maduraikonda Ko Rajakesarivarman. Records gift of cows for a lamp. (Was he the same Gangaraditya, the son of Parantaka I, who had the titles of Maduraikonda and Rajakesarivarman ?)

76 of 1897 (Tamil) — On the same wall. A record in the tenth year of the Chola king Ko Parakesarivarman. Records gift of sheep for half a lamp.

77 of 1897 (Tamil) — On the same wall. A record in the twenty-first year of the Chola king Madiraikonda Ko Parakesarivarman (Parantaka I). Records gift of sheep for a lamp.

78 of 1897 (Tamil) — On the same wall. A record in the ninth year of the Chola king Ko Rajakesarivarman. Records that certain gold ornaments and a silver vessel were made out of the savings of the temple treasury between the second and ninth years of the king's reign.

79 of 1897 (Tamil) — On the same wall. A record in the

sixteenth year of the Chola king Ko Rajakesarivarman. Records gift of one and a half lamps.

80 of 1897 (Tamil) — On the north wall of the same shrine. A record in the sixteenth year of the Chola king Ko Parakesarivarman or Rajendra Choladeva I. Records a gift of money for ten lamps to the Adittesvara temple at Tiruppurambiyam.

UPPILIYAPPANKOIL

The famous Vaishnava temple of Uppiliyappankoil is situated about three miles to the east of Kumbakonam. It is said that Visnhu appeared here in the form of an old Brahman called Uppiliyappan. Lakshmi the goddess was born here in a delightful spot called Akasanagara or Tulasivana under the Tulasi[14] (*Ocymum sanctum*) plant and was taken care of by sage Markandeya. It is said that the sage while giving Lakshmi in marriage to Vishnu begged of him to excuse her juvenile faults and to partake even of the saltless food she provided him with. It is in keeping with the legend that there is no mixture of salt in any of the dishes which are offered to the deity even today and they are said to taste well enough within the precincts of the temple!

PATTISVARAM

In the south-west of Kumbakonam, at a distance of four miles, is the sacred place of Pattisvaram, named after the holy cow Patti, a descendant of Kamadhenu (the divine cow), which is said to have worshipped the god in this place. The famous prime minister of the Nayak kings of Tanjore, Govinda Dikshadar, lived here during the latter part of his life and there is a statue of the minister and his wife in the Amman (goddess) shrine of the temple.

At a few yards distance in the north is the temple of Saktimuttam, wherein there are some beautiful carvings, one representing the goddess performing tapas or penance and the other showing her as embracing the Linga.

INSCRIPTIONS

The inscriptions at the temple here have been copied during the year 1920 by the Madras Epigraphical Department.

524 of 1920 (Tamil) — Round the base of the Central shrine in the ruined Gopinatha Perumal Temple. Records gift of land given by Saluva Tirumalayadeva Maharaya for offerings and worship to the god Gopinatha Perumal Tiruchattimurram or Mudikondacholapuram. The name Lakshmipati is engraved in the end in Telugu characters.

525 of 1920 (Tamil) — On the base of the ruined platform in front of the same shrine. Mentions the temple of Araya Perumaltali or Virudarajabhayankaresvaram Udaiyar in Rajarajapuram and seems to record a gift of land for the maintenance of a matha, called the Isaindavarkulali matha.

526 fo 1920 (Tamil) — On two slabs lying in the same temple. Records gift of gold for a perpetual lamp to the temple of Udaiyar Tirunaraimetta of Rajarajapuram in Tirunaraiyurnadu.

527 of 1920 (Tamil) — On the left door jamb of the ruined gopura in front of the same temple. States that the gopura was the gift of Saluva Tirumaladeva Maharaja.

528 of 1920 (Telugu) — On the beam of the ceiling at the entrance of the same gopura. A Telugu verse in praise of Saluva Tippa, sons of Gopaya.

DARASURAM

The Airavateswara temple of Darasuram is at a distance of two miles to the south-west of Kumbakonam, and it is one of the cluster of 18 large temples, situated within a radius of ten miles around the Kumbeswara shrine at Kumbakonam.

PURANIC VERSION

The Puranic story of the temple is that Isvara appeared there in the form of a Rudraksha[15] (Elaeocarpus Ganitrus) 'holy beads' tree. The leaves and branches of the tree were so formed as to bear representations of various deities and Rishis or sages.

Yama, the god of death, who was suffering from a Rishi's curse which caused a burning sensation all over his body, went on a pilgrimage to various shrines, including Darasuram, where he bathed in the tank in front of the temple. The waters of this tank are said to have been got by the casting therein of Siva's *sulam* (trident). After a long penance at the spot, Yama is said to have been cured of his ailment, and he thereupon obtained permission to build a temple and observe a tne days festival or Mahautsavam annually.

The temple is said to have been constructed originally by the celestial architect Visvakarma. The festival begins on the Asvini (b. Arietis) in the month of Avani (August-September) and closes on the Amavasya or new moon day. Isvara also decreed that the tank be called Yama Tirtham (Yama's tank). In proof of this, there is an image of Yama seated on a pitham (pedestal) in an inner shrine, with Rishis in attendance. Yama is said to have made a vow that those who managed the temple would be kings, and those who bathed in the tank would be cleansed of their sins and diseases.

TEMPLE BUILDINGS

The temple is stated to have been of much larger extent than it now is, and to have had *sapta veedhis* or seven streets or courts, similar to those of Srirangam. But all the outer courts have now disappeared and the temple stands in a single court. At some distance to the east of the court is the lower part of a large gopura which stands isolated from the inner main buildings. It was probably the entrance to the third prakara or court; but the courtyard walls which abutted against it are now all gone. It has some fine carved work in the form of plasters and niches in the walls and a perforated window in stone.

The tank is an extensvie square, 228 feet in width, and has a supply of fresh water through a channel from the river Cauveri. It gives the temple its chief claim to religious importance, and is the main centre of attraction for the numerous pilgrims who flock here annually. It was this tank that was miraculously supplied with water by the casting in of Siva's rod for Yama's bath, and here numerous deities, sages and others proved the efficacy of its healing powers. Airavata, the white elephant of Indra, while suffering a change of colour from a curse inflicted by the sage Durvasa[16], had its white colour miraculously restored by its ablutions here, and this incident is commemorated by an image of Airavata with Indra seated on it in an inner shrine. It is from this incident the the temple derives its name.

Proceeding west to the gopura which is to the east of the inner court, the visitor will find just outside it a group of small well-carved buildings; they are only the usual appurtenances of such temples, but unique in design. One of these is the *balipitha*[17] whose pedestal adjoins a small shrine formed like a miniature temple which contains an image of Ganesa. The pedestal has a finely-carved set of steps on the south side entirely cut out of three stones. It is considered a wonder that when these are struck they produce different musical sounds! Immediately adjoining this is a large Nandi under a mandapa. The gopura on the east side of the inner court is entirely built of stone.

The inner court is a large one, surrounded on all sides by a verandah with finely-carved pillars. In front of the main shrine is the Alankaramandapa with a fine colonnade of piers each of which has all the square panels on its sides sculptured with scenes from the Saivaite tradition. On the southern front of this mandapa, each side of the base has large stone wheels and a horse, representative of the mandapa being a chariot or car, wherein the deity is decorated on festive occasions.

In the south-west corner of the court is a mandapa in which there are four shrines. One of these has an image of Yama, the god of death, who has connection with the mythical foundation of the temple. Adjoining Yama's shrine are the large slabs sculptured with a representation of the *saptamathas*[18] or the seven celestial nymphs.

In the centre of the west verandah is a small shrine with the God Subrahmanya and his two consorts. A large number of lingams stand in a row along the west verandah and continue around the north side. There is a shrine dedicated to Sarasvati (the goddess of widsom) in the west verandah. The *vasanta* mandapa or spring mandapa in the north-west corner of the courtyard has a finely sculptured stone-panelled ceiling and some well-carved piers.

Along the east half of the wall of the north verandah, there are sculptured representations of various Saiva devotees extending for a length of 60 feet. They promise a unique experience for the students of Tamil literature. Near the north-east corner of this verandah is a group of eighteen finely-carved statues and the nine planets.

The shrine of the Amman or goddess is a separate and stands to the north of the Airavateswara temple. At one time when the outer courts were complete, it was probably enclosed in them, thus forming a component part of the main temple. It now consists of a single large court enclosing the shrine of the goddess with frontal mandapas attached thereto. There are some fine perforated windows in the front mandapa representing intertwining snakes with openings between them.

The inscriptions of the temple record the renovation of the shrines by Kulottunga Chola III and on the north wall of the verandah there are 108 sections of inscriptions, each containing the name and surname of the Saivacharya, whose image is sculptured below, with the principal events of their lives. Another below the image of the Dvarapala, close to the inner gopura, records that a certain image was brought from Kalyanapura (in the Bombay Presidency) by Rajadhiraja I (1018-52) after his capture of the place.

INSCRIPTIONS[19]

The following interesting account from the inscriptions recorded in the temple attribute the construction of this temple of Kulottunga III:

'By Sri Rajarajesvara may be meant the Brihadesvara temple at Tanjore which in ancient times was called Sri Rajarajesvaramudaiyar. As Sri Rajarajesvara is mentioned along with other ancient temples which Kulottunga III could only have renovated (not built afresh), it is very likely that the Brihadesvara temple at Tanjore benefitted at the hands of Kulottunga III. But as the location of Sri Rajarajesvara is not given, and as the Tanjore temple built by the Chola king Rajaraja I does not bear any traces of having been repaired in later times, it is not impossible that the Airavatesvara temple at Darasuram near Kumbakonam is meant here. The latter is called Sri Rajarajesvara in its inscriptions. In fact it is the name Rajarajesvara that appears to have been corrupted into Darasuram. The former name was in later times written into two abbreviations for raja side by side and the syllable suram affixed. Accordingly, the name became Rarasuram, which occurs in some of othe inscriptions of the place. This form is evidently responsible for the modern Darasuran. The Airavatesvara temple at Darasuran is built in the style of the Kampaharesvara temple at Tribhuvanam and both of them seem to have been copied from the Tanjore temple. It is thus not impossible that the Airavatesvara temple at Darasuran near Kumbakonam, which is called Sri Rajarajesvara in its inscription was either renovated or built by the Chola king Kulottunga III.'

The architectural merits of the two shrines here are far greater than those of the Kumbakonam shrines. See Fergusson's Ind. and East Arch., pp.367-9.

2 of 1915 (Tamil) — On the north wall of the verandah round the Airavatesvara temple. Consists of 108 sections, each containing the name and surname of the Saivacharya whose image is sculptured there.

3 of 1915 (Tamil) — On a pillar of the mandapa in front of the central shrine of the Somesvarasvamin temple in the same taluk. A damaged record in the fifth year of the Chola king Rajarajakesarivarman (Rajaraja I). Records gift of land for sacred bath, offerings and Sribali to the Aivar of Tirusomisvaram at Tirukkudamukku, i.e. Kumbakonam, a devadana of Vadagarai Pamburanadu.)

16 of 1908 (Tamil) — On the walls of the central shrine in the Airavatesvara temple. Contains the names of Saiva devotees with sculptures representing the principal events of their lives. A very interesting epigraph illustrative of the establishment of Saivite saint worship by the tenth century.

17 of 1908 (Tamil) — On the east wall of the first prakara of the same temple. A damaged record in the twenty-first year of the Chola king Tribhuvanachakravartin Sri Rajarajadeva (II?) The temple is called Rajarajesvaramudaiyar.

Arrangements are made for the disposal of fruits grown in the temple garden (This seems to be the same as Ins. S.Dts., No. 119, p.248).

18 of 1908 (Tamil) — On the same wall. A fragmentary record of the Chola king Rajadhiraja II (1171-1186), containing a portion of the the historical introduction beginning with the words *kadalsulnda*.

19 of 1908 (Tamil) — On the same wall. An unfinished record in the twelfth year of the Chola king Rajakesarivarman or Tribhuvanachakravartin Sri Rajadhirajadeva (II?) (This seems to be the same as No. 124 in Ins. S.Dts., p.249, but the reignal year reads thirteenth).

2o of 1908 (Tamil) — On the same wall. A record in the eighth year of the Chola king Parakesarivarman or Tribhuvanachakravartin Sri Kulottunga Choladeva. The temple is called Rajaraja Isvaramudaiyar. The king referred to is evidently Kulottunga III (1178-1216).

21 of 1908 (Tamil) — On the south wall of the same prakara. A record in the third year of the Pandya king Maravarman Tribhuvanachakravartin Vira Pandyadeva. Records gift of land for repairs to the temple of Udaiyar Rajaraja Isvaramudaiyar Nayanar at Rajarajapuram. (Was this king one of the mediaeval Pandyas or identical with Maravarman Vira Pandya Abhiraman Viramaran Seliyan Kaliyugaraman Tirunelvelipperumal who ascended the throne between March and July, 1443, and who was the joint ruler with Arikesari, 1422–64? See Ins. S.Dts., No.118, p.248).

22 of 1908 (Tamil) — On the inner gopura of the same temple, right of entrance, records in S. 1408, expired, Krodhana, gift of land for providing the requirements of worship in the temple of Irarasuram (also Rarasuram).

23 of 1908 (Tamil) — In the same place. A record of the Pandya king Maravarman Tribhuvanachakravartin Sri

Vallabhadeva, the date of which is doubtful. Registers provision made for repairs and for celebrating festivals in the temple of Irarasuramudaiya Nayanar. (Was the king the predecessor of the medieval Pandya Jatavarman Kulasekhara I or identical with the later Irandakalamedutta Srivallabha or the great Ativirarama? It is evidently the former).

24 of 1908 (Tamil) — Below the image of a dvarapalaka set up close to the same gopura, left of entrance. A record of Udaiyar Sri Vijayarajendradeva. Records that the image was brought from Kalyanapuram by the king after capturing the place. (The king was evidently Rajadhiraja I, Jayangondachola (1018-52), the anointer of heroes at Kalyanapura).

. 25 of 1908 (Tamil) — On the west wall of the outer gopura of the same temple. These are small labels containing the names of gods, whose images have, in most cases, since disappeared or have been mutilated.

26 of 1908 (Tamil) — On two stones lying in the courtyard of the same temple. Each of them contains a portion of the historical introduction of Kulottunga I.

27 of 1908 (Tamil) — On a third stone in the same place. The gopura is called Igaimuvendiraiyartirukkopuram.

The following inscriptions have been taken from the Mack. MSS. Their exact places in the temple are not given:

A grant of half panam by each inhabitant of the village to the God in the tenth year of Vallabha Raya Mahadeva.

Grant of 2 mas and 3½ kanis of land for the god by Rajarajadeva in his thirty-first year.

A grant of 3½ velis of land by the same king in his second year at 'Vayeghanelloor.'

A grant of 2½ velis of land at 'Auyenvama Raja Poorum' by Pratapadevaraya in S. 1268, Krodhi. The date is wrong.

A grant of 13½ velis of land at 'Taramala Varatadi Colla' by Rajarajadeva in his twenty-second year.

A grant of 3 velis and 8 mas of land in 'Paninaralliyoor' to the Vrishabavahana festival by Rangapati Udaiyan in the thirty-third year of Rajarajadeva.

A record dated in S. 1199, Bahudhanya, in the reign of Virapratapa Devaraya. Records the erection of a mandapa and tank at Pattisvaram and grant of 4 mas and 3 kanis of land to Pattisvara Nayanar. Ins. S.Dts., No.127, p.250. Date wrong.

A record of Viradeva Maharaya in S. 1137, Dhatu. Records the erection of a pagoda of god Pattisvara and grant of 9½ velis of land at 'Chandole Poorum' for the repair of the temple. Ibid., No.128. Date wrong.

TIRUVALANJULI

This sacred station, wherein the shrine dedicated to the god Kapardisvara and goddess Brihannayagi, is three miles to the south-west of Darasuram on the bank of the Kaveri in the Tanjore district. The sage Herandar, who occupies a prominent place in the shrine, is said to have got inside an underground passage through which the Kaveri, at one time, reached the nether world. He made her re-appear on the earth and proceed further to join the Mahodadi (Bay of Bengal) for the welfare of the Chola country! This accounts for the deification of the sage.

VINAYAKA'S IMPORTANCE

Behind Nandi the bull in front of the original mandapa, there is Vinayaka to whom great sanctity is attached and it is he who is called Svetavinayaka or the white-coloured Vinayaka. In the mandapa on the east of this shrine there are several stone-cut works of a high order. Inside the mandapa, in front of Vinayaka, there is a perforated stone window about 9 ft. high and 7 ft. wide cut out of a single stone. There are also many stone lamps and lamp posts about 7 ft. in height. The cornice of the front mandapa is of a double curve having many carvings. The whole exterior of this shrine, resembling a car drawn by horses, presents an example of high architectural workmanship.

The tradition of Vinayaka of this place is that the Devas ignored the worship of this idol before they churned the ocean of milk for getting amrita (nectar), and that in consequence they got poison instead of nectar. When the Devas were informed of their negligence, they rectified the error by getting an image made immediately with sea sand. Indra, the chief of the Devas, obtained this image of Vinayaka prepared when the ocean was churned. When he was worshipping the deity in the shrine here, he left the image of Vinayaka in the niche, intending to take it back on his return. When Indra did so, the Vinayaka did not allow himself to be removed, but said that he would stay there only and promised to confer on Indra the benefits of the daily worship by his visiting him once a year on the Vinayakachaturdasi day. The Vinayakachaturdasi day festival (in August–September) is in consequence observed in this town with special splendour. There is a fine metal figure of Ganapati in the shrine with his consorts Veni and Kamali and this is intended for being taken out in procession during the festival occasions in honour of this god. Also Vishnu is supposed to worship this form of Vinayaka on all Sukla Sashti day in Margali, i.e., the sixth day of the bright fortnight in Decembe–January.

There are inscriptions relating to Chola king Rajaraja I, which also mention his surname Sivapadasekhara and also the ornaments which 3 relatives of the king dedicated to the shrine of Kshetrapalesvara built by him. The three persons referred to are his queen Dantisakti Vitanki or Lokamahadevi, his dauther Kundavai, the queen of Vimaladityadeva, the ninth Eastern Chalukya king) and his 'middle' daughter Madevadigal.

INSCRIPTIONS[20]

The inscriptions here have been copied by the Madras Epigraphical Department during the year 1902. On the north wall of the mandapa in front of the central shrine, one numbered 628 of 1902 mentions gifts made to Kannappar of Kalahasti fame.

The local temple is well-known for its delicately chiselled stone work. Some of the figures are considered to be of Jaina origin. See Tanj. Gazr., Vol. I, p.223, for details. The place was so called because the Kaveri was prevented from submerging into the nether world by the self-sacrifice of Varaganda muni.

618 of 1902 (Tamil) — On the south wall of the mandapa in front of the central shrine in the Kaparedisvara temple. A record in the thirty-ninth year of the Chola king Tribhuvanachakravartin Tribhuvanaviradeva, who took Madura, Ceylon, Karuvur and the crowned head of the Pandya, Kulottunga II. Records gift of land. The date corresponds to Wednesday, 25th January, A.D. 1217. See *Ep. Ind.,* Vol. VIII, p.5.

619 of 1902 (Tamil) — On the south wall of the mandapa in front of the central shrine in the same temple. A record in the ninth year of the Chola king Tribhuvanachakravartin Rajadhirajadeva (I?). Records gift of two lamps.

620 of 1902 (Tamil) — On the same wall. A record in the seventeenth year of the Chola king Rajaraja Rajakesarivarman or Rajarajadeva I. Refers to a grant made in the thirty-eighth year of Maduraikonda Parakesarivarman (Parantaka I).

621 of 1902 (Tamil) — On the same wall. A damaged record in the eighth year of the Chola king Tribhuvanachakarvartin Rajadhirajadeva (I?) Records gift of three lamps.

622 of 1902 (Tamil) — On the same wall. A record in the fourth year of the Chola king Parakesarivarman or Tribhuvanachakravartin Rajarajadeva II. Records gift of land for lamps. See *Ep. Ind.,* Vol. VIII, p.2, where Dr. Kielhorn shows that the English equivalent of the date is Wednesday, 23rd November, A.D. 1149.

623 of 1902 (Tamil) — On the same wall. A damaged record in the fourth year of the Chola king Parakesariviarman or Tribhuvanachakravartin Vikrama Choladeva (1118-35).

624 of 1902 (Tamil) — On the same wall. A record in the twenty-first year of the Chola king Rajaraja Rajakesarivarman or Rajarajadeva I. Records that while staying at Tiruvallam, the king, who bore (as in Tanjore inscriptions) the surname Sivapadasekharadeva, confirmed a grant of land made in the twelfth year of Parakesarivarman.

625 of 1902 (Tamil) — On the north wall of the same mandapa. A record in the eighth year of the Chola king Vikrama Choladeva (1118-35).Records copy of an inscription of the seventh year of Parakesarivarman or Udaiyar Rajendradeva (1050-63).

626 of 1902 (Tamil) — On the same wall. A damaged record in the sixteenth year of the Chola king Parakesarivarman or Tribhuvanachakravartin Rajarajadeva II. See *Ep. Ind.,* Vol. VIII, p.263, where Dr. Kielhorn discusses the date of this inscription and concludes that it should be assinged to Wednesday, 11th July, A.D. 1162.

627 of 1902 (Tamil) — On the same wall. A damaged record in the eighth year of the Chola king Rajakesarivarman or Tribhuvanachakravartin Rajadhirajadeva II. See *Ep. Ind.,* Vol. IX, p.211, where Dr. Kielhorn points out that the date corresponds to Monday, 10th August, A.D. 1170.

628 of 1902 (Tamil) — On the same wall. A record in the twelfth year of the Chola king Parakesarivarman or

Tribhuvanachakravartin Rajarajadeva II. Records gift of land to the images of Tirunavukkarasudevar, Tiruvadavuradigal, i.e. Manikkavasagar and Tirukkannappadevar. The date corresponds to Wednesday, 26th March, A.D. 1158. *Ep. Ind.*, Vol. VIII, p.3.

629 of 1902 (Tamil) — On the south wall of the second prakara of the same temple. A record in the eighth year of the Chola king Tribhuvanachakravartin Rajarajadeva III. Records gift of land. The corresponding date is Monday, 7th October, A.d. 1224. See *Ep. Ind.*, Vol. IV, p.6.

630 of 1902 (Tamil) — On the same wall. A record in the twelfth year of the Chola king Tribhuvanachakravartin Rajaradeva (III?). Partly built in.

631 of 1902 (Tamil) — On the north wall of the Nandi mandapa in the same temple. An incomplete record in the thirty-sixth year of the Chola king Tribhuvanachakravartin Tribhuvanaviradeva, who took Madura, Ceylon, Karuvur and the crowned head of the Pandya, i.e. Kulottunga III. The date corresponds to Monday, 14th April, A.D. 1214. See *Ep. Ind.*, Vol. VIII, p.5.

632 of 1902 (Tamil) — On a stone set up in front of the inner gopura in the same temple. A record in Saka (year doubtful) Visvavasu. A few syllables of every line are cut away.

633 of 1902 (Tamil) — On the north wall of the Bhairava shrine in the same temple. A record in the twenty-fifth year of the Chola king Rajakesarivarman or Rajarajadeva I. Records gifts of ornaments by Rajarajadeva's queen Dantisakti or Vitanki or Lokamahadevi, his daughter Kundavai, the queen of Vimaladityadeva, the Eastern Chalukyan king, and his middle daughter Madevadigal, to the shrine of Kshetrapaladeva, which had been built by the king.

634 of 1902 (Tamil) — On a stone lying in the garden in the same temple. Records gift of land to the shrine of Svetavighneshvara said to have been worshipped by Indra.

NOTES

1. For the various Yugas that prevail in India please refer to page 3.
2. More detailed information about the importance of the festival could be obtained by referring to Chapter VI of *South Indian Festivities.*
3. In this form the female energy of creation occupies a prominent position.
4. The deity is named so since he appeared then with a Saranga or deer.
5. For further particulars reference may be made to page 80.
6. This figure is from Tadikombu near Dindigul.
7. *Inscriptions of the Madras Presidency,* Government of Madras, 1919, Vol. II, pp. 1235–42.
8. *Inscriptions of the Madras Presidency,* Government of Madras, 1919, Vol. II, pp. 1280–9.
9. *Inscriptions of the Madras Presidency,* Government of Madras, 1919, Vol. II, p.1243.
10. These are deputed to be the presiding deities of the wealth and riches of men. These illumine the property of men. They are generally sculptured over the stone jambs of temple entrances. The former holds a Sankha or conch and the latter a Padma or lotus in accordance with their names.

    Metal figures of both these exist at the outer entrance into the shrine on the Tirupati hill.
11. *Inscriptions of the Madras Presidency,* Government of Madras, 1919, Vol. II, pp. 1252–5.
12. Annual Report of the Madras Epigraphical Department, 1911-12, p.62.
13. For further particulars refer p.212n.

14. *Inscriptions of the Madras Presidency*, Government of Madras, 1919, Vol. II, pp. 1262–3.

15. This holy plant possesses remarkable medicinal properties: it is of a dark purple colour having a great smell. In most Indian houses it is grown in the open courtyard in order that the air inside may get purified. It is also worshipped by the females of the house. Out of its roots beads are made and worn around the neck by both men and women as its contact is quite beneficial to health.

16. The tradition relating to these holy beads is that when Brahma, Vishnu and others complained to Siva about the trouble caused by the Asura Tripura, he grew so angry that drops of tears fell on earth from his three eyes. These transformed themselves into the 38 varieties of Rudraksha trees. The Saivites consider the wearing of the seeds of these trees as an act of religious merit. Over the seeds up to thirteen facets are visible and it is said that the lesser the number of such facets the greater the efficacy.

    At one time in the village of Boochakra there lived a Brahman by name Supradeepa who had a great veneration for these seeds. When an ascetic Yogangan went for alms without wearing these seeds the Brahman refused to give him alms. The matter was taken to the notice of the king, who began to enquire into the matter. Then the Brahman began to tie the Rudraksha to one of the cats in the palace of the king, which act enabled it to bring down from heaven the *Kalpataru,* the tree which can fulfil every wish. The king and all present there learnt the importance of the Rudraksha seeds.

    A Brahman of the Kalinga country died as a result of his great sins. When the corpse was being carried to the cremation ghat a crow carrying away the necklace of Angasundari, daughter of king Chakravahu after mistaking the pearls that stood along with the Rudraksha seeds in the necklace for food, dropped it on this corpse. In consequence of this the Brahman obtained heaven instead of hell in spite of his numerous sins!

17. Particulars relating to the life of sage Durvasa and his figure appear in the chapter relating to Tiruvarur.

18. Bali means sacrifice and Pitham means seat. So Balipitha is the principal seat or spot where offerings of food are made to propitiate the deities. This is the raised circular seat by the side of the dhvajasthamba or flagstaff where worshippers of the temple prostrate themselves before entering into other parts of the temple.

19. Detailed notes relating to the importance of these goddesses appear on page 285 in the footnote.

20. *Inscriptions of the Madras Presidency*, Government of Madras, 1919, Vol. II, pp.1233–5.

21. *Inscriptions of the Madras Presidency*, Government of Madras, 1919, Vol. II, pp.1263–5.

Chapter 13

NALLUR

The Kalyanasundaresa temple in this place stands on an artificial hillock and is three miles to the east of Papanasam Railway Station in Tanjore district.

PURANIC VERSION

The Puranic version of the temple is that sage Agastya witnessed the wedding of Siva and Parvati in Kailasa from here.

The big tank in front of the temple is sacred, and Kunti, the mother of the Pandavas, is said to have had her bath in this tank before she worshipped God. This incident finds a place in sculptures on the tank bund.

ARCHAEOLOGICAL INFORMATION

The central shrine has a lingam on the pedastal with a corresponding lingam on another side. One curious fact connected with the lingam is that it is highly polished, and it is stated that it changes its colour five times in a day! The walls of the interior shrine have many fine sculptural representations of Siva and Parvati on the west, Vishnu on the north, and Brahma on the south. A bronze Sabhapati, another name for the god Nataraja, with eight hands, and dancing on the head of an asura (demon) is a fine piece of workmanship. This is probably one of the *Navatandavam* or the nine dancing aspects of Siva, (nava means nine). Besides the figures mentioned already, the temple has also a few other sulptural and metallic representations of Ganapati, sage Agastya[1] and Sundarar with his consort. God Kalyanasundara had a miracle worked out through Amarneethi Nayanar.

AMARNEETHI NAYANAR

Amarneethi Nayanar was born to Vaisya parents in the village of Pazhayar of the old Chola country. He spent his life in feeding and supplying loincloth to all Siva devotees. One day while thus engaged in this work in Nallur, the presiding god there came in order, to test the devotion of this Nayanar, in the disguise of an aged Brahman. He deposited a piece of rag for safe custody with him. It was lost after a short time. When the god demanded it back, Nayanar was not in a position to return it. He then demanded an equal weight of gold for another piece of loincloth produced. It was accordingly placed on the scale pan, but all the wealth he possessed was not found equal to cover the weight! Then there stood the Nayanar alone with his devoted wife, ready and willing to get into the scale pan. Thereupon the Nayanar obtained the blessings of the Almighty.

EPIGRAPHICAL IMPORTANCE

Of the many Chola inscriptions available in this temple one particularly refers to the general enquiry into the affair of the temple, under the personal orders of the Chola kings. This also signifies the fact that in those days the state controlled the management of the religious institutions.

INSCRIPTIONS[2]

The inscriptions here have been copied by the Madras Epigraphical Department during the year 1911. One of the Saivaite centres of worship south of the Kaveri; it has been sung by Jnanasambandha and Appar.

40 of 1911 (Tamil) — On the south wall of the central shrine in the Kalyanasundaresa temple. A fragmentary record of the twenty-third year of the Chola king . . . kesarivarman. Seems to record a gift of a lamp to the temples of Illangoyil Mahadeva.

41 of 1911 (Tamil) — On the same wall. A fragmentary record of the tenth year of the Chola king Parakesarivarman Madurantaka Uttama Chola. Refers to an enquiry into *srikarya* or the affairs of the temple of Mahadeva at Nallur under orders of the king, by a certain Manakkurrai Viranarayananar.

42 of 1911 (Tamil) — On the same wall. A fragmentary record in the fifteenth year of the Chola king Rajakesarivarman, i.e. Rajaraja I. Contains portions of the historical introduction of Rajaraja I and refers to a mandapa built by a certain Narayanan Ekaviran of Panchavanmahadevichaturvedimangalam which appears to have been another name of Nallur.

43 of 1911 (Tamil) — On the south wall of the second prakara of the same temple. A record in the twenty-third year of the Hoysala king Sarvabhaumachakravartin Vira Ramanathadeva. Records gift of land by a certain Aghoradeva to the temple at Tirunallur or Panchavanmahadevichaturvedimangalam in Nallurnadu, a sub-division of Nittavinodavalanadu. This inscription affords a proof of Hoysala domination over Chola dominion in the time of Vira Ramanatha.

44 of 1911 (Tamil) — On the same wall. An unfinished and damaged record in the fifteenth year of the Chola king

Rajarajadeva (III?). Records sale of a temple land to a certain Ponnan Rajan or Vikkiramasingadeva of Pandimandalam, who was a subordinate of Sola Konar.

45 of 1911 (Tamil) — On the same wall. An unfinished and damaged record in the fifth year of the Chola king Tribhuvanachakravartin Rajarajadeva (III). Records gift of a lamp to the same temple by a certain Vanakovaraiyar.

46 of 1911 (Tamil) — On the same wall. A record in the fourth year of the Chola king Tribhuvanachakravartin Rajendra Choladeva III. Records gift of lands clubbed together under certain specified names. A hamlet called Manukulamedutta Perumal was evidently named after the king who, we know had that biruda.

47 of 1911 (Tamil) — On the same wall. A record in the fifth year of the Chola king Tribhuvanachakravartin Rajarajadeva (III?). Records gift of money for a lamp and of a lampstand by the chief mentioned in No. 45 of 1911 who bore the titles Tundanadudaiyan Ekavachakan and Ulagukanvidutta Perumal.

48 of 1911 (Tamil) — On the same wall. A record in the twenty-fourth year of the Chola king Tribhuvanachakravartin Rajarajadeva (III?). It gives a list of all the tax-free lands enjoyed by a temple, the name of which is not clearly written on the stone.

49 of 1911 (Tamil) — On the same wall. A record in the twenty-fifth year of the Chola king Tribhuvanachakravartin Rajarajadeva (III?). Records gift of a matha to the teacher called Tattanudaiya Isanadeva, by a lady disciple of his, in accordance with the instructions of her dying husband. Later on, the epigraph mentions the grant of an additional land to the same matha. Isana Siva was a teacher of the Mudaliars of Maligai matham at Thiruvidaimarudur and he evidently settled at Nallur. See Tj. 1010, 1012, etc., for similar mathas.

50 of 1911 (Tamil) — On the same wall. A record in the

thirtieth year of the Chola king Tribhuvanachakravartin
Rajarajadeva. Records sale of land to the temple by a native
of Kiliyur in Pandikulasanivalanadu. In continuation of this
inscription is engraved a record of the second year of the
same king which refers to the assembly of Rajakesarichaturvedimangalam in Nallurnadu and to a gift of land for
a lamp to the temple of Tirunallur Nayanar.

51 of 1911 (Tamil) — On the east wall of the same
prakara. A record in the thirty-third year of the Chola king
Tribhuvanachakravartin Rajarajadeva. Records gift of land for
supplying a garland of red lilies (*Sengalanir*).

52 of 1911 (Tamil) — On the same wall. A damaged record
in the twenty-first year of the Chola king Tribhuvanachakravartin
Rajarajadeva. Records gift of land for supplying a garland of
red lilies (sengalunir).

53 of 1911 (Tamil) — On the same wall. A record in the
twenty-ninth year of the Chola king Tribhuvanachakravartin
Rajarajdeva. Records gift of paddy for offerings.

54 of 1911 (Tamil) — On the same wall. A record in the
thirteenth year of the Chola king Tribhuvanachakravartin
Rajadhirajadeva II, who was pleased to take Madurai (Madura)
and Ilam (Ceylon). Records gift of 2000 kasus for two lamps.

55 of 1911 (Tamil) — On the same wall. A record in the
third year of the Chola king Tribhuvanachakravartin
Kulottunga Choladeva. Records gift of land.

56 of 1911 (Tamil) — On the same wall. A damaged and
incomplete record in the eleventh year of the Chola king
Tribhuvanachakravartin Rajadhirajadeva (II?). Records gift of
land for offerings.

57 of 1911 (Tamil) — On the same wall. A damaged record
in the fifth year of the Chola king Tribhuvanachakravartin
Rajarajadeva (III?). Records sale of a house site and a garden
for the temple of Agambadi Vinayaka Pillayar.

58 of 1911 (Tamil) — On the same wall. A record in the fifth year of the Chola king Tribhuvanachakravartin Rajarajadeva (III?). Records sale of a house and eight coconut trees to the same temple which is stated to have been built by the Agambadiyar, i.e. the servants of the temple of Tirunallur-Nayanar. (Was the term Agambadiyar connected with the Agamudaiyar caste?).

59 of 1911 (Tamil) — On the same wall. A record in the twenty-ninth year of the Chola king Tribhuvanachakravartin Rajarajdeva. Records gift of land for offerings to the temple of Tirunallur Nayanar.

60 of 1911 (Tamil) — On the base of the north verandah in the same temple. A mutilated record in the fourth year of the Chola king Tribhuvanachakravartin Rajendra Choladeva. Records gift of lands situated in different villages to the same temple.

61 of 1911 (Tamil) — On the same base. A record in the fifth year of the Chola king Tribhuvanachakravartin Rajendra Choladeva. Built in at the bottom. Records gift of land.

62 of 1911 (Tamil) — On the second gopura of the same temple; right of entrance. A record in the twenty-sixth year of the Chola king Tribhuvanachakravartin Rejarajadeva. Records gift of land for feeding the Mahesvaras.

KAMARASAVALLI

Kamarasavalli is a small village in the district of Trichinopoly, situated within ten miles from Papanasam on the South Indian Railway. It was formerly called Kamakavanam in the Dandakaranyam (a wild forest covering the country lying between the river Krishna in the North and Rameswaram in the South). Siva is known here as Sundareswarar and Vishnu as Varadaraja.

PURANIC VERSION

The Devas or the celestials were unable to defend themselves from the oppression of the demons and they sought the aid of Siva when he was in deep contemplation and could not be disturbed. Thereupon they prevailed upon Kama (Cupid) to shoot his flowery arrows[3] on Siva. This enraged Siva who in consequence opened his Phala Netra (eye of fire) and burnt the insolent Kama to ashes. According to the Puranas this eye is also the eye of wisdom. When Kama was burnt up, Rati (Venus), bemoaning the loss of her spouse, approached Vishnu, who advised her to go to Sundaratirtha, a tank in this place, and offer prayers to Siva. Her husband was restored to her on condition that he would be visible only to her. A bronze figure of Rati, in the act of her appeal to God is preserved here. The full moon day of Phalguna or Panguni (February–March) commemorates the burning of Kama, and the festival is observed all over India.

The Ekambaranatha temple at Conjeevaram contains a sculptural representation of this incident in one of the mandapas within. This form of Siva is known as Kamadahanmurti or Kamantakamurti.

INSCRIPTIONS[4]

The inscriptions here have been copied by the Madras Epigraphical Department during the year 1914.

61 fo 1914 (Tamil) — On the north wall of the central shrine in the Karkotakesvara temple. Records in the seventeenth year of the Chola king Parakesarivarman or Vira Rajendra Choladeva (i.e., Rajendra Chola I) gift of land to the temple of Tirunallur Mahadeva.

62 of 1914 (Tamil) — On the same wall. An incomplete record of the Chola king Rajakesarivarman alias Rajarajadeva I,

dated in his twentieth year, Kanya, Krittika, corresponding to Wednesday 20th September, A.D. 1004. Mentions an assembly of eighty persons.

63 of 1914 (Tamil) — On the same wall. Records in the twenty-ninth year of the Chola king Rajarajakesarivarman or Rajarajadeva I gift of fifteen kalanjus of gold for a lamp to the temple of Tirunallur Mahadeva at Kamarasavalli-chaturvedminagalam, a brahmadeya in Miraikurram which was a sub-division of Vadagarai Rajendrasimhavalanadu.

64 of 1914 (Tamil) — On the same wall. Records in the twenty-sixth year of the Chola king Rajaraja Rajakesarivarman (Rajaraja I) gift of ten kalanjus of gold to the temple treasury for a lamp to Mahadeva of Tirukkarkotakisvaram at Tirunallur in Kamaravallichaturvedimangalam, a brahmadeya in Viraikurram.

65 of 1914 (Tamil) — On the same wall. Dated in the reign of the Chola king Parakesarivarman or Udaiyar Sri Rajendra Choladeva I. Records in his twenty-ninth year, Rishaba, Arudra, corresponding to Wednesday 7th May, A.D. 1041, gift of land by the great assembly of Kamarasavalli-chaturvedimangalam to Sakkai Marayan Vikramasolan for performing the dance (*sakkaikuttu*) thrice on each of the festivals Margalitiruvadirai and Vaigasitiruvadirai. Mr. Swamikannu Pillai points out that the date shows that this king began to rule between 6th May and 7th July, 1012.

66 of 1914 (Tamil) — On the north, west and south walls of the sane shrine. A record of the Chola king Rajakesarivarman or Tribhuvanachakravartin Kulottunga-Choladeva I. Records in his twenty-seventh year, Tula, su. di. 10, Satabhishaj, corresponding to Sunday, 18th October, 1097, gift of land for a flower garden by the assembly of Kamarasavalli-chaturvedimangalam, a brahmadeya, in Viraikurram which was a sub-division of Geyavinodavalanadu. The land had been a

waste and it was now given for the garden tax-free and the assembly resolved to bear the burden in case the tax (*irai*) was levied.

67 of 1914 (Tamil) — On the west wall of the same shrine. Records in seventeenth year (of?) a sale of land in Vannam or Madhurantakanallur, a devadana village belonging to the temple of Karkotisvaram Udaiyar, in Virakurram, a sub-division of Vikramasolavalanadu.

68 of 1914 (Tamil) — On the same wall. Records in the fifteenth year of the Chola king Rajaraja Rajakesarivarman (Rajaraja I) gift of land for the offering of *akkaradalai* on the festival day of Margalitiruvadirai.

69 of 1914 (Tamil) — On the same wall. A record of the Chola king Rajaraja Rajakesarivarman or Rajarajadeva I. Records in his twenty-second year, Dhanus, su. di. 9, Revati, gift of tanks and ponds by the Mahasabha for supplying red lotuses daily during the month of Dhanus to the Mahadeva temple. The date corresponded to Monday December 2, A.D. 1006.

70 of 1914 (Tamil) — On the same wall. Records in the twenty-fourth year of Rajakesarivarman or Rajaraja-Rajadeva I gift of 4 mas of land for sandal paste (1 pala every sandi) to Tirunallur Mahadeva at the temple of Tirukkarkotisvaram in Kamarasavallichaturvedimangalam by a native of Priyadhiramangalam.

71 of 1914 (Tamil) — On the same wall. Records in the seventeenth year and the thirty-seventh day of king Rajarajadeva III a sale of land. The transaction was the same as in No. 67 above.

72 of 1914 (Tamil) — On the west and south walls of the same shrine. A recordo of the Chola king Parakesarivarman or Rajendra Choladeva I, dated in his eighth year, Tula, Sravana, corresponding to Friday October 9, A.D. 1019.

Records gift of land. The assembly is stated to have met at the temple of Sri Kayilasamudaiyar in this village.

73 of 1914 (Tamil) — On the same. A record of the Chola king Rajakesarivarman alias Tribhuvanachakravartin kulottunga-Choladeva I, dated in his twenty-sixth year, Makara, su. di. 13, Arudra (Thursday, January 10, A.D. 1096). The assembly makes provision for festivals and *srilali* in the temple of Sri Kailasa or Rajendrasola Isvaramudaiyar. It resolved that one kuruni of paddy from irrigated fields, one kuruni from lands growing varagu and sesamum, one nut from every *kamugu* and one lamp oil from the owners of every *manai* was to be collected from the village.

74 of 1914 (Tamil) — On the south wall of the same shrine. Dated in the reign of the Chola king Rajakesarivarman. Records in his fifth year, Makara, Friday, Punarvasu, gift of land for sidari by Balasiriya Bhattan Silan Kuttan of Adanur, devadana and brahmadeya in Innambaranadu.

75 of 1914 (Tamil) — On the same wall. Records gift of two stones by Kadan Adigal of Arunallur.

76 of 1914 (Tamil) — On the same wall. Records in the thirteenth year of the Chola king Rajaraja Rajakesarivarman, 'who destroyed the ships at Salai' (Rajaraja I) gift of fifteen kalanjus of gold, the interest on which was to be given to those who recited the Talavakara Samaveda on the day of Tiruvadirai in the month of Margali before the god's bath. Details of the method of recitation given.

77 of 1914 (Tamil) — On the same wall. Records in the seventeenth year of the Chola king Rajaraja Rajakesarivarman (Rajaraja I) gift of gold for the midday offerings by the *madhyastha* of the village on the new moon days. Kamarasavallaichaturvedimangalam is mentioned as a brahmadeya in Vadagarai Rajarajavalanadu.

78 of 1914 (Tamil) — On the same wall. A record of the

Chola king Parakesarivarman ;dated in his ninth year, Dhanus, Thursday, Krittika. Registers gift of land for conducting the services of sribali and tiruppalli eluchchi. Mentions Kodandaramavaykkal.

79 of 1914 (Tamil) — On the north wall of the mandapa in front of the same shrine. Records that the mandapa was constructed by Araiyan Tiruvarangamudaiyan Appaninum-nalla Sembiyadaraiyan of Pudukkudi.

80 of 1914 (Tamil) — On the same wall. A record of the Chola king Tribhuvanachakravartin Vikrama Choladeva (1118–35). Records in his fourteenth year gift of land. Built in at the end. Mentions that Venkadan Pandarangamudaiyan or Neriyudaichchola Pallavaralyar, a native of village in Marudadunadu, a sub-division of Venkunrakottam in Jayangondasolamandalam, was also present in the assembly.

81 of 1914 (Tamil) — On the same wall. A record of the Chola king Parakesarivarman or Tribhuvanachakravartin Vikrama Choladeva (1118–35) in his fourteenth year, relating to gift of ten kalanjus of gold for a lamp to the temple of Tirukkalkodisvaramudaiya Nayanar at Kamarasavalli-chaturvedimangalam in Viraikurram, a sub-division of Vikramacholavalanadu.

82 of 1914 (Tamil) — On the south wall of the same mandapa. An incomplete record of the Chola king Tribhuvanachakravartin Kulottunga Choladeva I, dated in his fiftieth year. Records gift of money for three lamps. States that Kamarasavallichaturvedimangalam was a brahmadeya in Viraikurram, a sub-division of Vadagari Ulaguyyavandasola-valanadu.

83 of 1914 (Tamil) — On the same wall. Records in the tenth year of the Chola king Tribhuvanachakravartin Kulottunga Choladeva III, 'who was pleased to take Madurai (Madura)', a gift of money, for a lamp and midnight offerings

and for betel leaves, areca nuts, a knife (*kilikatti*) and a pair of scissors to the god and goddess by a native of Alangudi.

84 of 1914 (Tamil) — On the same wall. Records in the fiftieth year of the Chola king Rajakesarivarman or Tribhuvanachakravartin Kulottunga Choladeva I, gift of land for worship by the assembly to the temple of Tiruvagattisvaramudaiya Mahadeva at Valavan-Puliyangudi in Vadagarai Ukagyyavabdasikavalanadu. Mentions the irrigation channels Kodandarama-peruvaykkal and Avanigandharva-vaykkal. See No. 78 above.

85 of 1914 (Tamil) — On the same wall. Records in the fourth year of the Chola king Vikrama Choladeva gift of money for a lamp to the temple of Tirukkarkoti Isvaramudaiyar at Kamarasavallichaturvedimangalam in Miraikurram, a sub-division of Geyavinodavalanadu.

86 of 1914 (Tamil) — On the same wall. Records that Araiyan Tiruvarangamudaiyar or Sembiyadaraiyar of Pudukgudi covered his mandapa with flat tiles.

87 of 1914 (Tamil) — On the same wall. Dated in the reign of the Chola king Rajakesarivarman or Tribhuvanachakravartin Kulottunga Choladeva II. Records in his third year, Simha, su. di. 12, Sravana, (Thursday, August 22, A.D. 1135), gift of land for two lamps.

88 of 1914 (Tamil) — On the east wall of the first prakara of the same temple. Records in the tenth year of the Pandya king Jatavarman Tribhuvanachakravartin Vira Pandyadeva assignment of certain custom duties on articles of merchandise for repairs to the temple of Tirukkarkotisuramudaiya Nayanar at Kamarasavallichaturvedimangalam, by the people of the eighteen countries and the seventy-nine valanadus.

89 of 1914 (Tamil) — On the entrance into the gopura of the same temple, right side. Records in the twenty-second year of the Chola king Tribhuvanachakravartin Rajarajadeva

gift of oil by the oil merchants for bathing the god with it, on Saturdays.

90 of 1914 (Tamil) — In the same place. Records in the sixteenth year of the Chola king Tribhuvanachakravartin Rajarajadeva, gift of a silver forehead plate by a native of Tolumur.

91 of 1914 (Tamil) — On the same entrance, left side. A record of the Chola king Tribhuvanachakravartin Rajarajadeva III. Records in his nineteenth year, Vrischika, su. di. II, Satabishaj, corresponding to Wednesday, October 4, A.D. 1234 (Vrischika is wrong for Tula), gift of oil for lamps.

92 of 1914 (Tamil) — On the east wall of the Ganapati shrine in the same temple. Records in the eleventh year of the Chola king Tribhuvanachakravartin Rajarajadeva that the assembly of Kamarasavallichaturvedimangalam arranged to have the village administration (*grama karya*) attended to by those who consented to vacate their seats by the year, according to the old custom.

93 of 1914 (Tamil) — On the north wall of the same shrine. A record of the Chola king Tribhuvanachakravartin Rajendra Choladeva III. Records in his fourteenth year, Vrischika, ba. di. 5, Punarvasu (Thursday, November 6, A.D. 1259), gift of land for maintaining a flower garden to the temple of Kamarasavallichaturvedimangalam in Viraikurram in Vadagarai Vikramacholavalanadu.

94 of 1914 (Grantha and Tamil) — On the same wall. Records in the fifth year of the Hoysala king Pratapachakravartin Vira Somesvara that the king, in settling the dispute between the temple managers and a private individual regarding the ownership of the village Vannam or Madhurantakanallur, decided that it should be enjoyed as a temple property.

95 of 1914 (Tamil) — On the east, north and west of the Chandikesvara shrine in the same temple. A record of the Chola king Tribhuvanachakravartin Rajendra Choladeva, dated in his twelfth year . . . su. di. Friday. Registers gift of land to the Tirugnanasambandantirumadam by Kunrankilan Tirunavukkarasu Devan, a native of Urrukkatttukottam in Jayangondasolamandalam and a devotee of the temple.

NOTES

1. A short life-sketch of this dwarfish sage and his figure appears in the chapter relating to Vedaranniyam.
2. The five arrows of Kama or Manmatha are known as Tapani, Dabani, Visvamohini, Visvamardini and Madini.
3. *Inscriptions of the Madras Presidency*, Government of Madras, 1919, Vol. III, pp. 1609–13.

Chapter 14

TIRUVARUR

The ancient religous town, populrly known as Tiruvarur, is situated 15 miles to the west of Negapatam on the Mayavaram–Arantangi railway line in Tanjore district. At one time it was the capital of the Chola kings, and it also finds mention in the Tamil work Periyapuran.

SRI VALMIKESVARA TEAMPLE

The presiding deity, said to be made of the clay of an ant hill, is called Valmikesvara (Valmika in Sanskrit means an ant hill). On the ceiling of the mandapa, in front of the sanctum, there are the figures of the Ashtadikpalas or the deities of the eight cardinal points and 27 Nakshatra devatas or stars. There is also a shrine and an image of the goddess Kamalambal, in an attitude of performing penance.

The sacred well inside the temple is called Sankha tirtha, and the water of this well is believed to cure several diseases! A bath in this holy well on the Chitrapournami or the full moon day in the month of Chitrai (April–May) is considered very sacred.

The tank of Kamalalaya situated outside the temple has a picturesque appearance with a fine Myya mandapa or a tower on an island in the centre. The tank covers an area of about 33 acres. The Vinayaka on the bank is named Mathuraitha pillayar (Mathu in Tamil means carat); for he is said to have tested the purity of the gold that saint Sundara left in the river at Vriddhachalam in the South Arcot district and applied to the presiding god there for its delivery at Tiruvarur. The temple and a pond called sengalanir *odai* (sengalanir is the name of a red lily flower and odai means a pond), where a species of red lily is grown for the worship of Tyagaraja, have the same dimension.

SRI TYAGARAJA SHRINE

The shrine of Tyagaraja is very famous; the idol is supposed to have been brought down to this mundane world by king Muchukunda, who is said to have obtained it from Indra, king of heaven. A replica of this seems to have been given to the king and this we find in the temple at Tirunallar near Karaikal. Similar replicas are also to be found in the temple at Tirukaraivasal near Tirunattyyattankudi, Negapatam, Thirukkuvalai near Kilvelur, Vedaranyam and Tiruvamur, 4 miles south-east of Madras. Tyagaraja is said to have performed 364 lilas or miracles in this place similar to the 64 sports of god Sundaresa in Madura.

BUILDING RELATING TO THE TEMPLE

The Ayirakkal mandapa or hall with one thousand pillars is a beautiful structure, and some of the Puranic scenes are painted here. Standing in this hall, the famous saint Sundara is said to have recited the *Tevaram* songs.

In the shrine of Hatakesvara there is said to have existed, at one time, an underground passage called nagabila. People in large numbers are said to have ascended to heaven by worshipping god in this place, and to prevent an undue congestion of the heaven Indra is said to have closed this short-cut by a hillock called Arunarasringam.

The Araneri shrine within the temple, also known as Achalesvara, is considered very important on Panguni Uttirama day or the full moon day in the month of Panguni (March–April). Naminantiadiak Nayanar[2] one of the 63 Saiva saints, is said to have made a lamp of water burn here!

King Manu Chola is said to have ordered the crushing of his son under the wheels of a vehicle for his having killed a calf by negligently driving his carriage over it. The mother cow reported the offence to the king by causing the bell in front of his palace to be rung. There are sculptural representations in proof of this incident outside the temple near the northeastern entrance of the temple. This is also supported by the inscriptions in the temple.

In the main street, close by the vehicle, there is a small shrine, the presiding deity of which is said to have drunk the whole water of the sea which once threatened to inundate the town! This forms one of the 364 sports of Tyagaraja. The image of god is said to have a very fine polish. The sage Durvasa[3] is said to have worshipped this idol, and a figure of this sage is in the temple.

SAINTS KALARSINGA AND TANDIYADIGAL

This place is also associated with two other famous saints Kalarsinga Nayanar[4] and Tandiyadigal Nayanar[5] details of whose lives are found in the valuable work Periyapurana.

TIRUVARUR AND CHIDAMBARAM

Tiruvarur is analogous to Chidambaram in several items. God Tyagaraja is in Pushpa-Sabha—Sabha where flowers strewn in abudance over the god while Nataraja is in Chit Sabha. These are the presiding deities in both these places. Yama, the god of death, holds the place of Chandikesvara in Tiruvarur while in Chidambaram this duty of Chandikesvara is performed by Brahma. Sages Patanjali and Vyaghrapada reside in the west of the town in both the places having set up lingams in their own names. There is *rahasyam* (secret which is invisible) in both the places, here in Tiruvarur in the breast of god Tyagaraja himself which could not be seen even by the *gurukkals* (priests) who do the daily service and the Bijakshara (the mystical letters) in the breast of the image which ever remains covered with a plate attached thereto. Herein lies the difference between both these important deiteis—Tyagaraja is always considered divine whether inside or outside the temple as the rahasyam is inseparable from the image while that applies to Nataraja only while he is seated along with rahasyam in the Chit Sabha.

EPIGRAPHICAL IMPORTANCE

There are inscriptions of importance engraved on the gopura of the second prakara or courtyard signifying that this was built for a chief of the Vijayanagar kingdom, who was ruling this part of this country in A.D. 1440-44. There is one relating to the social ideas of ancient days wherein the opinion of Narada, Maskara, Yajnavalkya and other authorities regarding the origin, duties and privileges of certain or mixed *Anuloma* castes are recordoed. Another engraved on the west wall of the second prakara relates to the fifth year of Chola king Kulottunga II, mentioning the 56 festivals that were conducted anually in this temple.

SRI TYAGARAJA LEELAS

Of the 364 miracels said to have been performed by Sri Tyagaraja Swami in Tiruvarur, the following are most generally known:

MANUNITHIKANDA CHOLA

Tiruvarur was one of the five seats of government in the time of the Chola kings. Here reigned a king named Manunithikanda Chola, who ruled over this kingdom with justice and fairplay. He had a son named Vithividangan (Sundara Chola). When this prince came of age, he wished to see his father's kingdom. Hence one morning he set out in his chariot and rode around the city, surrounded by his attendants. While the merry procession was passing through one of the thoroughfares, there suddenly rushed into the crowd a young calf, frisking and skipping about, as young calves would; and before any one could notice it, it came in front of the chariot and got crushed beneath the ponderous swift-moving wheels.

The mother cow, seeing what had happened, bewailed her loss and went and shook with her horns araichimani or the bell in front of the palace which a suppliant had to ring in order to gain the audience of the king. The king came out and learning what had happened, consulted his ministers. They suggested that the prince should perform some expiatory ceremony for his unintended sin. But the king saw this would not satisfy to the bereaved mother and so ordered that his only son be slain. The minister who was both unwilling to execute the cruel order and afraid of disobeying his sovereign, committed suicide. The king thereupon set out himself to see that the act of retributive justice was done. He came in his chariot and drove it over his son's body, very near the place where the calf lay dead. Almost instantaneously, there appeared before him Mahadeva and Parvati mounted on their Vrishabha (bull), followed by their Devaganas (attendants). They extolled the good king's stern sense of duty, recalled to life the calf, the minister and the prince and gave them all a benediction and disappeared! And even today, stone figures of the cow, the calf, the chariot, the king, his son and god Siva himself are seen opposite the temple outside the north-east gopura of the temple. There is an inscription, numbered as 164 of 1894 in the records of the Madras Epigraphical Department, relating to the 5th year of king Ko Parakesarivarman or Vikramacholadeva (A.D. 1118–1135) which refers to this legend.

MANIKKA NACHCHIYAR

There is a temple in the north-eastern corner of the main street of Tiruvarur, which goes by the name of Manikka Nachchiyar temple. This Manikka Nachchiyar was a staid and god-fearing *devadasi*, who had taken a vow to consort each day with the first man that sought her and be faithful to him even as a wedded wife. The Lord, with the intent to test her faith, appeared one morning before her in the guise of an old grey-haired Brahman, bent double with age, toddling along with the aid of a stick. He requested her company for the day. Unhesitatingly, she gave her word, and rejecting many advantageous offers that came later, awaited the arrival of the venerable old man who had with him only a single Rudraksha bead to offer and which however was very humbly and gratefully accepted as a magnificent gift by the woman. When he came late in the evening, she received him respectfully, washed his feet, offered him dainties and cow's milk. The old man pretended to drink, and, as if chocked by it, he struggled for breath and died after a few gasps. The woman sincerely grieved his death and resolved to perform Sati as a dutiful wife. Accordingly, when the Brahman's body was cremated the next day, she too ascended the funeral pyre. But just when the pile was set afire god Siva and goddess Parvati appeared before her, commended her faith and gave her Moksha (salvation). Thus was her faithfulness rewarded. There is a painting of hers in the Neelothpalambal temple here.

THE BARBER OF PERUMBUGALUR

In this village, situated two miles north-west of Tiruvarur, once there lived a barber who was a staunch devotee of Siva and offered free services to all devotees of Siva. One chilly morning in winter, there appeared an aged Brahman, asking to be shaved. He was shivering with cold. His body was marked all over with festering sores. And yet he asked the barber to give him a shave without causing the least pain. The barber gladly consented. The Brahman said that no water, hot or cold, should be used, the wound should be gently licked and that the skin wetted before the razor was applied. Without the least hesitation, the barber carried out his injunctions for the love of the Lord, and lo! When he had done all, the aged Brahman disappeared and instead he saw before him god Siva and his divine consort. The divine pair blessed the barber and granted him Moksha (salvation).

MAHADEVA TIRTHA GHAT

In Kamalalayam, the big tank of Tiruvarur, there are 64 ghats or sacred bathing places, similar to those along the Ganges. Here on Panguni Uttiram day, which falls in the month of Panguni (March–April), a very large concourse of pilgrims flock to this particular Deva Tirtha ghat every year. In the course of an aerial procession of Siva and Parvati the latter questioned her Lord as to whether the whole of the huge crowd gathered at the bathing ghat would reach heaven as she was afraid that enough space may not be found in Svarga (heaven). Siva then put the following test to prove to his consort that only a few, a very few indeed, would attain heaven. On that occasion, an aged Brahman couple came for the sacred bath.

The old Brahman, while bathing in the tank, was hemmed in by the crowd. Thus he lost his footing, and got into the deep water. The old lady, who was sitting on the bank saw her husband struggling for life and cried aloud for help. At this, many rushed forward to save the old man. But the old woman interposed and warned them that, if any sinful person touched her husband, instantly he would die! And so the rescuers turned back and laughed at the old woman asking whether one could be so immaculate. Just then, there came forward a Brahman in the full bloom of youth. The faded flowers in his hair and the scarlet tinge of his lips, due to the pansupari all gave evidence of a revel overnight in a prostitute's house. This young Brahman straightaway plunged into the water, swam across to the old man, and brought him back safely to the shore. While the people were just wondering what had happened, god Siva and Parvati appeared on their sacred bull, blessed the bold Brahman youth, who was no other than saint Sundara, and all the assembled pilgrims, thus pointing to the spiritual efficacy of a bath in that holy ghat on that sacred day and disappeared miraculously.

SOMAYAJI

About a mile east of Punthottam is Tirumahalam. In this village, lived Somayaji, a Brahman well-versed in Vedic lore. Intending to perform a great sacrifice, he conceived the audacious idea of bringing Sri Tyagaraja himself to grace the occasion and receive the *Havirbhagam* at his hands. To achieve this end, he sought the intercession of Sri Sundaramurti in Tiruvalur, who, after a long and persistent requests, agreed to exert himself on behalf of our hero. When the matter was put before the Lord, he, with great hesitation, assented, but he gave a word of caution that he may appear in any form, and that it was the devotee's responsibility look-

out to recognise him when he came. And so, the day fixed
for the sacrifice came. The sacrificial rites were proceeding
apace. The holy Brahmans were chanting the Vedas. When the
Purnahuti was about to be performed, a noise of drums was
heard outside, and in a short time, a procession was seen
approaching. When it drew nearer, the Brahmans recognised
a pariah with the carcase of a calf thrown over his shoulders,
followed by his wife with a toddy pot on her head, and his
two children running after their dogs and a host of others
beating their drums. The pious Brahmans fled precipitately,
crying 'Somayaji, our caste is lost. Warn them not to move
further towards the sacrificial fire.' But Somayaji, true
devotee that he was, saw before him not a crowd of pariahs
but the Lord himself in human form accompanied by Parvati,
Ganesa, Subrahmanya, and the Bhutaganas. The Bhakta at
once offered the chief oblation to the divine one. Instantly,
the scene changed. The pariahs disappeared and instead there
stood god Siva and Parvati on their bull. They blessed the
devotee and gave him a seat in Kailasa, Siva's own abode,
where the devotee could worship him for ever. The Brahmans
who fled at the sight and approach of the so-called pariahs
became Vajasaneyans, otherwise called *Madhyamaparayan*
i.e., mid-day pariah, who had to observe *Panchama*
degradation for an hour and a half at noon daily and follow
the *Sukla Yajur Veda.*

Bestowal of a very large quantity of Grain to Sundarar
from Kundaiyur.

One old man (Vellala) of Kundaiyur near Tirukkuvalai,
hearing of Sundaramurti Nayanar's greatness, was supplying
him with paddy and dhol. Owing to adversity of season he
was being unable to contribute the stipulated quantity. Hence
prayed to God earnestly and in his dream God appeared and
granted his request. There were heaps and heaps of paddy all

over the village and when Sundaramurti was informed about
it, he went from Tiruvarur and sang before the Tirukkuvalai
god to tranship the paddy to his village. After nightfall the
whole quantity was carried there by Bhutaganas (attendants
of Siva). Paravai Nachchiar on seeing the next morning, heaps
of paddy in front of her house and all over the streets, that
announced the people might collect the paddy kept in front
of their houses.

GRANTING OF GOLD AT TIRUPUGALUR

Paravai Nachchiyar wanted money for the approaching
Panguni festival and requested her lover Sundaramurti to get
gold for her. He accordingly went to Tiruppugalur about 8
miles away and prayed to God and fell asleep in the mandapa
using some burnt bricks keptt nearby as his pillow. When after
a short nap he rose to go to the Matha close by he found all
the bricks used for the pillow converted into pure gold which
he brought home!

VIRANMINDA NAYANAR'S AVERSION TO
RESIDENTS OF TIRUVARUR

Viranminda Nayanar, a native of Trichengode, 5 miles to the
east of Sankaridrug Railway Station on the Madras–
Mangalore line, was in the Devasrayan mandapa (the
thousand-pillared mandapa) in Tiruvarur along with other
devotees, when he noticed Sundaramurti Nayanar going to the
temple's inner precincts without the least reverence for the
Saiva devotees. He also learnt that Sri Tyagaraja was
employed by Sundara to propitiate Paravai Nachchiyar's
anger. Viranmindar consequently developed great aversion
not only to Sundara but all residends of the place and lived
outside it in Vandompalai village. As he was feeding several
Saivites in hospitality, he enquired from them about their

village; he would slay them with his *parasu* weapon if it happened to be Tiruvarur. One morning Sri Tyagaraja went to his residence. Viranmindar happened to have gone out and when his wife asked the Brahman as to which village he belonged, the latter replied that he belonged to Tiruvarur. She requested the Brahman to give out a different village when her husband turned in order to avoid being slain by in husband. However, he refused to utter a falsehood and requested her to place the parasu weapon on her hsuband's left side instead of on the right as was usual. The host returned and on being audaciously told by the Brahman to *selva* Tiruvarur (selva means wealthy) looked for his weapon. It was found after some delay and this gave ample time to the Brahman to take to his heels and run. The host ran after him and overtook him only after Tiruvarur entering. His attentiion was drawn to this, and therefore he cut out his own legs with his weapon for having unconsciously broken his word. Sri Tyagaraja appeared to him in his divine form and appeased his hatred for Sundaramurti!

TRANSPLANTATION OF PADDY SEEDLINGS IN TIRUNATTIYATHANGUDI

Sundaramurti Nayanar went to Tirunattiyathangudi shrine to play for, and get gold from the god. He did not find the deity in the temple precincts and was told by Ganesh, that the god and the goddess were out to the fields to transplant some seedings. The devotee paid his visits to them and this festival is celebrated every year in the village.

TIRUTHONDATHOGAI

Viranminda Nayanar, a zealous devotee of Sri Tyagaraja, reproached Sundaramurti Nayanar for not showing respect to the Saivite saints assembled in the Devasraya mandapa (the thousand-pillared hall) whenever he entered the temple. Sundarar wanted to appease Viramindar and prayed to God that he may be inspired to sing in praise of the devotees; and from asareri, i.e. air he heard a few words and beginning with that he sang eleven stanzas in praise of the devotees. This came to be known as Tiruthondathogai. On hearing this Viranmindar became surprised and recognising a great spiritual personage in Sundara began to respect him. It is this Tiruthondathogai that forms the neucleus for the grand Tamil work *Periyapurana* that was written later on.

SUNDARAMURTI'S CURSE AND RESTORATION OF EYESIGHT

Sundaramurti Nayanar was going about to various placels singing psalms in praise of the presiding deity of the place, while at Tiruvottiyur (near Madras) he married Sangili Nachchiyar and promised to her never to leave the place. After sometime he yearned to visit Tiruvarur and left Tiruvottiyur; as a consequence of his breaking his word he immediately lost his eyesight! On his way to Tiruvarur he prayed and sang at various places for the rstoration of his sight; he got his left eye restored at Conjeevaram and the right eye at Tiruvarur!

GOD ACTING AS MESSENGER AT MIDNIGHT TO PARAVAI NACHCHIYAR'S HOUSE

On Sundarar's return to Tiruvarur, Paravai Nachchiyar learnt of his marriage with Sangili at Tiruvottiyur and strictly forbade Sundarar from entering her house. Sundarar prayed to Sri Tyagaraja to intervene. In the guise of a Gurukkal (priest rendering divine service to the temple) Tyagaraja went to Paravai on a dark night and pleaded for Sundarar. But Paravai was unrelenting and Tyagaraja had to return without any success in his mission. Sundarar was unconsolable and offered to give up his life. Paravai slowly began to reflect and discern that the messenger might not be a mere human being. Tyagaraja, ever active in the service of his true devotees, went to her a second time that night and prevailed on her to accept Sundara's company.

ORIGIN OF *OTTU* (JOINT) TYAGAR TEMPLE

Viranminda Nayanar was guarding the temple entrance with an axe in hand, allowing only those to enter who had bathed and wore sacred ashes and Rudraksha beads. He was very much offended at the levity shown by Sundarar in entering the temple without bathing or other purification after spending the night in Paravai's house. Sundarar rushed into the temple while Viranmindar was looking away. When he noticed it he chased Sundarar with axe in his hand and when he was about to overtake him Sri Tyagaraja hid him in the wall of the temple and thus saved him from Viranmindar's axe. Marking this site is a small shrine close by outside the north wall of the second enclosure opposite to the north gopura. This shrine is called Ottu Tyagar shrine where Viranmindar's figure also exists.

VANDAMPALAI VILLAGE

Enraged at the partiality shown by Sri Tyagaraja towards Sundarar and his misdeeds, as they appeared to be, Viranmindar left Tiruvarur for good, solemnly vowing never to set foot at Tiruvarur. He settled down at Tirupungur and made it a point to feed at least one Saivite devotee everyday. But his hatred of Tiruvarur was so much that if any of his guests should say that he belonged to Tiruvarur, Viranmindar would cut his head off with his axe, and when about to feed the guest he always placed at his side for the purpose the axe. One day one such guest turned up and when Viranmindar's

wife learnt that he belonged to Tiruvarur she warned him of
the danger he was in, but this guest insisted on remaining for
dinner but requested the lady to place the axe on the left side
of Viranmindar instead of on the right as usual. When the
guest sat for dinner, he was questioned as to where he came
from. The guest provokingly answered that he was from
'Tiruvarur which abound in wealth.' Viranmindar got furious
and fumbled for his axe and before he could find it the guest
took to his heels and ran for his life towards Tiruvarur hotly
pursued by Viranminder. When the guest entered the
boundary of Tiruvarur he shouted out 'we have come on this
side.' At once Viranmindar found that he had himself set one
of his feet within the abhorred limits of Tiruvarur and true
to his vow he cut off that foot of his. The chased one revealed
himself as Sri Tyagaraja and bestowed on Viramindar eternal
beatitude for his staunch devotion. The temple Vandampalai
is known as Uttara (north) Gokarnam.

KALIKKAMBA NAYANAR'S RESTORATION
TO LIFE AFTER HIS SUICIDE!

Kalikkamba Nayanar of Tiruppangur was another devotee
who took offence at Sundarar's taking liberties with the deity
in engaging the deity for an amorous errand to Paravaiyar and
similar such conduct. Sri Tyagaraja with a view to effect a
reconciliation between the two devotees caused Kalikkambar
to suffer from colic and informed him that he would be cured
of the disease by Sundarar who was directed to proceed to
Tiruppangur for this purpose. Kalikkambar who lay writhing
in pain on hearing of the approach of Sundarar, committed
suicide rather than be treated by such a reprobate. Sundarar
finding what had happened reproached himself and attempted
suicide. The deity appeared on the scene, restored

Kalikkambar to life and made both the devotees close friends for life.

SUNDARAR RECOVERING GOLD IN A TANK AFTER THROWING THE SAME IN RIVER!

Sundarar sang for gold in Vridhachalam (South Arcot district) and obtained 12,000 pieces of gold. He further prayed that they might be transmitted to Tiruvarur. Obeying the deity's direction, he threw them into the river Manimukthanadhi at Vridhachalam and went to Tiruvarur where he searched for the treasure in the Kamalalayam tank. But not finding it and being ridiculed by Paravaiyar for throwing it into a river and seeking for it in a tank, he fervently prayed to the god that he might recover the gold and his prayer was duly granted. It was tested and its purity proved by Vinakaya at the north-eastern corner of the grand Kamalalayam tank and he is called 'Assaying Vinayaka.'

DANDIYADIGAL NAYANAR RESTORED TO SIGHT

Dandiyadigal Nayanar an ardent devotee, was born blind. Desiring to do some religious service he resolved on digging the Kamalalayam tank. Being blind he fixed stakes and tied a rope thereon to guide him and was carrying mud and silt from the bed to the banks. The Jaina residents on the banks were annoyed at the blind man digging earth with the chance of killing many insects and worms and at the mud being thrown near their houses. They removed the guide posts and ropes and taunted him with his blindness. He prayed to god for help in his distress, and recovered his sight. The Jainas on the other hand, were struck blind and left the place in terror!

TYAGARAJA SAVING THE TOWN FROM FLOOD

Once upon a time Varuna, god of water, caused a flood to inundate the place; but the deity consumed the water and saved the locality. The shrine of this deity is located in the East Car street and has been celebrated in the psalms as Paravayumandali. Here Durvasa Rishi worshipped the deity and the shrine is also known as Thuvanainar temple.

KONDIYAMMAL CAUSING THE BIG CAR TO BE DRAGGED

Kondiyammal, a dancing girl of the temple, was very devout and was piously chanting devotional songs and waving *chamaram* in the presence of Sri Tyagaraja during the daily evening service. During the procession of the big car the huge wheels got stuck in the mud and the car would not move in spite of the hard attempts of king Chola to pull it. The king was disconsolate and prayed to god for help; and then he heard a voice to the effect that if Kondiyammal was brought to flourish two chamaras to the deity with both her hands the car would move. The car began to move smoothly when this was done.

DAKSHINAMURTI SUBDUING A DEMON

Once upon a time a demon called Somakasuran walked away with the four Vedas and hid himself in the ocean. God Vishnu incarnated as fish to recover them. However, he could not hold in his hand the four Vedas, which were in the form of four babies, and fight the demon at the same time. He appealed to god Siva for help. God Siva trampled down the demon as muyalahan under his right foot and the four Vedas became his pupils as Sanaka, Sanandana, etc. The deity in this form is Dakshinamurti and his temple is on the north bank of the tank in front of the temple at Pulivalam, a village two miles off Tiruvarur. This is known as Dakshina (south) Gokarnam.

INSCRIPTIONS[6]

The inscriptions here have been copied by the Madras Epigraphical Department during the years 1890, 1894, 1901, 1904, 1918 and 1919.

For an account of the legends, the local shrine and other antiquities of this important Sivasthala see Tanj. Gazr., pp. 248-50.

73 of 189 (Grantha) — Qn the west wall of the second prakara of the Tyagarajasvamin temple. A record of the Chola king Anapaya, i.e. Kulottunga Chola II.

74 of 1890 (Grantha) — On a stone near a well in the first prakara of the same temple.

164 of 1894 (Tamil) — On the north wall of the second prakara of the same temple. A record in the fifth year of the Chola king Ko Parakesarivarman or Vikrama Choladeva (1118–1135). Records gift of land. Refers to the *Periyapurana* legend of king Manuchola and the calf.

269 of 1901 (Tamil) — On the west wall of the second prakara of the same temple. A record in the seventh year of the Chola king Rajakesarivarman or Tribhuvanachakravartin Kulottunga Choladeva II. The concluding portion was copied in 1890 (No. 73 of 1890). The inscription is very important for the information it gives that the Kulottungachola whose inscription begins with the expression Kulottunga II was Anapaya Chola. Also records the 56 festivals conducted annually. This enables us to say at once that Sekkilar, the author of the *Periyapurana*, lived in his reign and not in that of Kulottunga I, as some suppose.

533 of 1904 (Tamil) — On the east wall of the Tyagaraja shrine in the same temple, left of entrance. A record built in

in the twenty-third year of the Chola king Rajakesarivarman or Tribhuvanachakravartin Kulottunga Choladeva (I?) and damaged.

534 of 1904 (Tamil) — On the north wall of the Tyagaraja shrine in the same temple. A mutilated record in the ninth year of the Chola king Parakesarivarman or Rajendradeva (1050–62). Seems to record a sale of land.

535 of 1904 — On a slab built into the floor of the first prakara, to the north of the same shrine. Records in Kali 4818 — and S. 1639, expired, Hemalamba, that the Maratha king Sarfoji (1711–27) of Tanjore made some repairs to the temple. See Tanj. Gazr., p.44.

536 of 1904 (Tamil) — On another slab built into the floor of the same prakara, north of the central shrine in the same temple. A damaged record of the Nayaka king Achyutappa (1572–1614), son of Sevvappa Nayaka (1549–72), in S. 1482, expired, Rudhirodgarin (wrong). See Tanj. Gazr., p.38.

537 fo 1904 (Tamil) — On the east wall of the first prakara of the same temple, right of entrance. A record in the eighth year of the Chola king Parakesarivarman or Tribhuvanachakravartin Kulottunga Choladeva III. Built in at the end. Records gift of land for three lamps.

538 of 1904 (Tamil) — In the same place. A record in the second year of the Chola king Rajakesarivarman or Tribhuvanachakravartin Rajadhirajadeva (II?). Records gift of land by a native of Palaiyanur in Menmalaipalaiyanurnadu, a sub-division of Jayangondasolamandalam.

539 of 1904 (Tamil) — In the same place. A record in the thirty-fifth year of the Pandya king Maravarman Tribhuvanachakravartin Sri Vallabhadeva. Built in at the end. Seems to record a gift of land. (Was the king the predecessor of Jatavarman Kulasekhara I, 1190-1217?)

540 of 1904 (Tamil) — In the same place. A record in the

tenth year of the Chola king Rajakesarivarman or Tribhuvanachakravartin Rajadhirajadeva II, corresponding to Tuesday, 27th February, A.D. 1173. Records gift of land by a native of Palaiyanur different from the donor in No.917. See Ep. Ind., Vol. IX, pp.211-2.

541 of 1904 (Tamil) — In the same place. A record in the forty-fourth year of the Chola king Rajakesarivarman or Tribhuvanachakravartin Kulottunga Choladeva I. Records gift of land.

542 of 1904 (Tamil) — In the same place. A record in the ninth year of the Chola king Rajakesarivarman or Tribhuvanachakravartin Rajadhirajadeva II. Built in at the end. Records gift of land by the donor in No. 540.

543 of 1904 (Tamil) — In the same place. A record in the fifth year of the Chola king Tribhuvanachakravartin Rajadhirajadeva II. Built in at the bottom. Refers to an order issued during the ninth year of Vikrama Chola's reign.

544 of 1904 (Tamil) — On the south wall of the same prakara. A damaged record in the thirty-fourth year of the Chola king Rajakesarivarman or Tribhuvanachakravartin Kulottunga Choladeva I. Registers lands belonging to the shrine of Ulagisvaramudaiyar at Tiruvarur.

545 of 1904 (Tamil) — On the same wall. An incomplete record in the sixth year of the Chola king Parakesarivarman Tribhuvanachakravartin Vikrama Choladeva (1118-35). Seems to record a gift of land.

546 of 1904 (Grantha and Tamil) — On the west wall of the same prakara. Records in the second years of the king a gift of land.

547 of 1904 (Tamil) — On the same wall. Contains an incomplete introduction beginning with the words pumaruviyapolilclum.

548 of 1904 (Tamil) — On the same wall. Records in the

fifteenth year of the king a grant of land to a certain Pungoyil Nambi who sang the Viranukkavijayam in honour of 'our son' Virasola Anukkar.

549 of 1904 (Tamil) — On the same wall. An incomplete record in the fifteenth year of the Chola king Rajakesarivarman or Tribhuvanachakravartin Kulottunga Choladeva I. The inscription stops with the date.

550 of 1904 (Tamil) — On the same wall. A record in the thirteenth year of the Chola king Tribhuvanachakravartin Kulottunga Choladeva II, 'who took Madura and the crowned head of the Pandya.' Records gift of land for the requirements of Tikkunirainda Vinayagapillaiyar set up on the western bank of the fresh water pond.

551 of 1904 (Tamil) — On the same wall. A record in the fortieth year of the Pandya king Maravarman Tribhuvanachakravartin Kulasekhara I (1268–1308). Registers gift of land made in the thirty-second and fortieth years of the king's reign. At the end S. 1229, expired, i.e. 1230, is given as the equivalent of the fortieth year. The date corresponded to Monday, 18th March, 1308. See Ep. Ind., Vol. VIII, pp.276-7.

552 of 1904 (Tamil) — On the same wall. A record in the twelfth year of the Chola king Kulottunga Choladeva. Refers to the sixteenth year of 'the king who abolished tolls', i.e. Kulottunga I and records a gift of land for a flower garden.

553 of 1904 (Tamil) — On the same wall. A record in the tenth year the Chola king Rajakesarivarman or Tribhuvanachakravartin Kulottunga Choladeva. Records that the members of the assembly Rajaraja Brahmamangalam (a brahmadeya in Tiruvarurkurram, a sub-division of Geyamanikkavalanadu) being assembled in the mandapa called Devasriyan, i.e. Devasraya, exempted from taxes certain lands belonging to the Tiruvarur temple. See Ep. Ind., Vol XI, p.289, where it is pointed out that the date

corresponded to Monday, 30th November, A.D. 1142.

554 of 1904 (Grantha and Tamil) — On the north wall of the same prakara. A record in the twenty-fourth year of the Chola king Tribhuvanaviradeva (Kulottunga III). Registers the redistribution of certain temple lands. The king is described as 'the friend of God.'

555 of 1904 (Tamil) — On the same wall. A record in the twentieth year of the Chola king Tribhuvanachakravartin Rajendra Choladeva III. Records a gift of land. The date corresponds to Wednesday, Jaunary 20th, A.D. 1266. See Ep. Ind., Vol. VIII, p.274.

556 of 1904 (Tamil) — On the same wall. A record in the eighth year of the Chola king Parakesarivarman or Tribhuvanachakravartin Vikrama Choladeva, corresponding to Tuesday, 18th August, 1125. Recordos gift of money for a lamp by a merchant of Melai Marayapadi or Koyyakkuru-nadu. See Ep. Ind., Vol. VIII, p. 263.

557 of 1904 (Tamil) — On the same wall. A record in the thirteenth year of the Chola king Tribhuvanachakravartin Rajendra Choladeva. Records gift of land to the shrines of Alagiya Tiruchchirrambalamudaiyar and Porpadikkunayaga Isvaramudaiyar built in the southern street in front of the temple; to the shrine of Tirumaligai Vinayakapillaiyar built in this temple in the twentieth year; and to the shrine of Subrahmanya built in the same temple in the twenty-second year.

558 of 1904 (Grantha and Tamil) — On the same wall. Registers the opinion, Narada, Maskara, Yajnavalkya and other authorities regarding he origin, duties and privileges of certain mixed castes (anuloma). A very interesting epigraph illustrating the social ideas of the age.

559 of 1904 (Tamil) — On the same wall. A record in the thirty-ninth year of the Chola king Tribhuvanaviradeva (Kulottunga III). Mentions the temple of Vikrama-

cholesvaramudaiyar at Sri Mahesvaranallur and records a gift of land by a woman who had a relative at Valaippandal in Palakunrakottam, a sub-division of Jayangondasolamandalam.

560 of 1904 (Tamil) — On the south wall of the second prakara of the same temple. An incomplete record in the third year of the Chola king Parakesarivarman or Tribhuvanachakravartin Vikrama-Choladeva (1118-35). Records gift of land.

561 of 1904 (Tamil) — On the same wall. An incomplete record in the forty-ninth year of the Chola king Rajakesarivarman or Tribhuvanachakravartin Kulottunga Choladeva I. Mentions the mandapa called Devasriyan.

562 of 1904 (Tamil) — On the same wall. An incomplete record in the third year of the Chola king Rajakesarivarman or Tribhuvanachakravartin Vikrama Choladeva. Records gift of land. Vikramachola was a Parakesarivarman. The present epigraph is one of the very few which give the title Rajakesarivarman to him.

563 of 1904 (Tamil) — On the same wall. A record in the fourth year of the Chola king Parakesarivarman or Tribhuvanachakravartin Vikrama Choladeva (1118–35). Built in at the bottom. Records gift of a pond. Dated as in the next record. (But Aparapaksham wrongly given for Purvapaksham. See Ep. Ind., Vol. VIII, p.262.)

564 of 1904 (Tamil) — On the same wall. An incomplete record in the fourth year of the Chola king Parakesarivarman or Tribhuvanachakravartin Vikrama Choladeva. Connected with the previous inscriptions. Same date as that of the previous one, but the details more correct. Corresponds to Wednesday, 10th May, A.D. 1122. See Ep. Ind., Vol. VIII, p.262.

565 of 1904 (Tamil) — On the same wall. A mutilated record containing an incomplete introduction of Vikrama-Chola (1118–35).

566 of 1904 (Tamil) — At the entrance into the western gopura of the same prakara on the right side. A record in S. 1362, expired, Raudri. Records the building of the gopura by Nagarasa, son of Siddharasa, for the merit of the minister Lakkanadannayakka-Udaiyar. See note to the next inscription.

567 of 1904 (Kanarese) — In the same place on the left side. A record in S. 1362, expired, Raudra. A Kanarese copy of the above epigraph. Lakkanadannayakka is here called Dakshina-samudradhipati, while in the above one the portion occupied by the biruda is damaged. For a coin of Lakkanadannayakka see Ep. Rep., 1905, pp.58-9. His position in Madura history has been summarized by me in Ind. Antq., 1914 (January).

568 of 1904 (Tamil) — On the north wall of the Achalesvara shrine in the south-east corner of the second prakara of the same temple. A mutilated record in the eighth year of the Chola king Parakesarivarman or Rajendra Choladeva I (1011–1053).

569 of 1904 (Tamil) — On the same wall. An incomplete record in the second year of the Chola king Rajaraja-kesarivarman or Rajarajadeva I (985-1013). Records a gift of land.

570 of 1904 (Tamil) — On the south wall of the same shrine. An incomplete record in the second year of the Chola king Rajakesarivarman. Records gift of silver vessels by Udaiyapirattiyar Sembiyan Mahadeviyar for the merit of Sri-Uttama Choladeva. She was the queen of Gandaraditya and the mother of Madurantaka Uttama Chola.

571 of 1904 (Tamil) — On the same wall. A record in the seventh year of the Chola king Rajarajakesarivarman. Refers to the building of a shrine of stone in the temple of Tiruvaraneri Alvar by Udaiyapirattiyar Sembiyan

Mahadeviyar and the setting up of two images in it by the same lady and records that she presented 234 kasus for daily requirements, additions to the temple and for repairs.

572 of 1904 (Tamil) — On the west wall of the mandapa in front of the same shrine, right of entrance. A record in the twentieth year of the Chola king Rajakesarivarman. Records a gift of two lamps.

573 of 1904 (Tamil) — In the same place. A record in the thirty-second year of the Chola king Parakesarivarman (905–947), 'who took Madurai.' Records gift of gold for a lamp. The characters are comparatively modern.

574 of 1904 (Tamil) — On the same wall, left of entrance. A record in the sixth year of the Chola king Parakesarivarman. Records gift of gold for a lamp. The characters are comparatively modern.

575 of 1904 (Tamil) — On the north wall of the mandapa in front of the Achalesvara shrine in the south-east corner of the second prakara of the same temple. A damaged record in Kilaka of Virabhupati Udaiyar (1409–22).

576 of 1904 (Sanskrit and Grantha) — On the west wall of the third prakara of the same temple, left of the gopura. A mutilated record. Mentions the shrine of Anandesvara.

577 of 1904 (Tamil) — On the south wall of the central shrine in the Satyavachakesvara temple in the same village. A damaged and incomplete record of the Chola king Rajakesarivarman or Chakravartin Kulottunga Choladeva, the date of which is lost. Mentions Tirumandaliudaiya Mahadevar.

578 of 1904 (Tamil) — On the same wall. A mutilated record in the forty-eighth year of the Chola king Rajakesarivarman or Chakravartin Kulottunga Choladeva I. Registers allotments for the various requirements.

579 of 1904 (Tamil) — On the north wall of the same

shrine. A record mutilated at the end. Contains a portion of the historical introduction of Kulottunga I. Mentions the temple of Tirumandaliudaiya Mahadevar.

553 of 1918 (Tamil) — On fragments in the Nagaraja temple in the Kamalalayam tank at Tiruvarur. Some of the fragments seem to register a gift of land. One of them mentions the name Agaravallaban who was probably the donor of the stone.

669 of 1919 (Tamil) — On the south wall of the Tyagaraja shrine, Tyagarajasvamin temple, Tiruvarur. Begins with a short introduction. Gives the details of the quantity of gold which was used for plating and gilding the different parts of a golden pavilion (ponnintiru mandapa).

670 of 1919 (Tamil verse and prose) — On the south wall of the same shrine. Commences with the introduction. Records that in compliance with the king's order Venkadan Tirunilakantha or Adhikari Irumudisolamuvendavelan utilised certain gold and silver vessels in the temple treasury for the erection of a golden pavilion for the god Udaiyar Vidivitankadeva of Tiruvarur in Tiruvarurkurram, a sub-division of Adhivalanadu. The four verses, engraved in continuation, refer to several gifts of golden ornaments by Kuttan Sembiyan Vendavelan of Pundi.

671 of 1919 — On the same wall. Begins with the introduction. Records gift of 3 kalanjus, 1 manjadi and 1 kunri of gold of standard weight and fineness and equal to Rajarajan madai by Arumoli, Rajendracholan which was invested by the temple assembly in purchasing and leasing out 450 kulis of tax-free land for the expenses connected with the sacred bath of the god.

672 of 1919 — On the same wall. Begins with the introduction. Built in at the end. Gift of 96 sheep for a perpetual lamp to the temple of Mulasthanam Udaiyar of

Tiruvarur, in Tiruvarurkurram, a sub-division of Geyamanikkavalanadu by one Narayana Singalattarayan, a portion of whose full name is obliterated.

000674 of 1919 (Tamil) — On the west and south walls of the same shrine. Registers an order of the king to the managers of the temple of Mulasthanam Udaiyar of Tiruvarur in Tiruvarurkurram, a sub-division of Kshatiryasikhamani-valanadu, making some provision for offerings and scented water to the god on certain festival occasions. Mentions the Arudra of Adi and Sadayam of Arpasi as the rasterisms of the king and his father respectively.

675 of 1919 (Tamil) — On the west wall of the same shrine. Much damaged. Begins with the introduction. Records an order of the king to Velalakuttan or Sembiyan Muvendavelan to cover certain portions of the garbhagriha and Ardha mandapa of the temple with gold plate.

676 of 1919 (Tamil) — On the north wall of the same shrine. Begins with the introduction etc. Records the gift of a wreath of precious stones for the goddess, consort of Udaiyar Vidivitankadevar by Perumakkalurudaiyanvelan Seyyapadam of Gangaikondasolapuram.

677 of 1919 (Tamil) — On the same wall. Begins with the introduction. Records that Kuttan or Sembiyan Muvendavelan of Pundi a hamlet of Pavicherru Pundi a sub-division of Adhirajavalanadu, made tax-free gift of land by purchase for 100 kasus from the asscmbly of Pulivalam, a Brahmadeya of Vijayarajendravalanadu, for the expenses of feeding 12 sivayogins daily at the temple and making two gold ear ornaments for the god.

678 of 1919 (Tamil) — On the same wall. Begins with the introduction. Records deposit of gold by Purakkudayan Surri Adattan or Solavichchadira Vilupparayan of Purakkudi in Ambatnadu, a sub-division of Uyyakonda-valanadu with

certain merchants of Tiruvarur for providing offerings and oil for bath to the god and further gifts for gold for supplying clothes to the images and fees to temple songsters and servants.

679 of 1919 (Tamil) — On the north and west walls of the same shrine. Incomplete. Begins with the introduction. Records the details of the quantities of paddy accruing from the several bits of temple devadana lands in the villages of Tiyyankudi and Menmangalam which were bought over by the king and Anukkiyar Nakkan Pavainangaiyar for expenses incurred in making offerings and worshiping the god Tiruvaraneriyudaiyar.

680 of 1919 (Tamil) — On the same walls. Incomplete. Begins with the introduction. Gives a detailed list of the gifts of Rajendra Choladeva and his servant Anukkiyar Pavainangaiyar for plating and gilding certain portions of the temple of Arumolikuttan or Lokarayan of pearls and coral wreaths and of several other gifts of precious stones and ornaments and lamps to the god. Rajarajankasu niraikal is mentioned as a standard weight of gold.

681 of 1919 (Tamil) — On the west wall of the Valmikinatha shrine, same temple. States that the jewel chests of the big temple at Tiruvarur and Valmikinath, which were in the custody of one individual, were now left in the joint charge of two men Brahmarayar and Viluppadarayar and lays down what ought to be done when any discrepancies arise in the jewel accounts if the seals of the Ponpandavaravasal were mishandled.

NOTES

1. Sundaramurti Nayanar: As the foremost of the Saiva devotees
he holds a place amidst the four Nayanars. He was a Brahman
by birth belonging to Tirunavalur, otherwise known as
Tirunamanallur, 12 miles west of Panruti Railway Station. His
former name was Nambiyarurar. He was brought up by
Narasinga Muniyar of Tirumunaipadi the ruler of the country
at that time, who was attracted by his extraordinary intelligence.
At the time of his proposed marriage Isvara is said to have
appeared in the form of an old Brahman and by the evidence
of document supposed to have been executed by the grandfather
of the Nayanar, claimed possession of him as a slave, and
prevented the marriage. This he is said to have done with a view
to cause the doctrines of Salvism to be preached more freely
to the world. Thenceforth he is reported to have toured round
the country visiting various Saiva shrines and singing songs in
praise of the presiding deity of the place. While at Tiruvalur
he married a lady named Paravaiyar, with his lord's sanction.
On one occasion he was presented with some gold as a reward
for his songs, which he is said to have thrown into a river at
Vriddhachalam, with an appeal to the deity of the place to
deliver it at the tank at Tiruvalur. On reaching Tiruvarur he
received his gold through the god Ganesa whose image is still
installed on the banks of the tank and is called Mathuraitha
(*mathu* means carat) Pillayar, i.e., the Pillayar who tested gold.
In Tiruvottiyur near Madras he married another woman named
Singiliyar, and promised to remain with her forever. Tempted
by a desire to visit other shrines he left the place and in
consequence of breaking his vow became blind! He pursued his
pillgrimage, however, and regained his sight gradually at the
famous places of pilgrimage—his left eye in Conjeevaram and
the right eye in Tiruvarur. On returning to Tiruvalur, his first wife
refused to receive him on account of his second marriage, and
the god had to arbitrate between them to effect a reconciliation.

On the flagstaff or dhvajastambha in front of the temple at Avanasi in the Coimbatore District, there is a representation of a crocodile disgorging a Brahman child. The tradition connected with this is that a corcodile in a tank swallowed a child while his mother was bathing therein. When Sundaramurti visited the place the mother appealed to him to recover the child in order that she might perform the upanayanam ceremony (the investiture of the sacred thread) along with that of his co-mate, which was then being performed. Sundara is said to have sung a song in prase of the presiding god, and brought back the child safely and satisfied the parents! While he was staying as the guest of the Chera king at Tiruvanjikalam the god of the place considered his mission was over and took him to heaven.

2. Naminantiadikal Nayanar was a Brahman belonging to the village of Emapperur, 6 miles south of Tiruvarur, in the Chola country. He used to worship the deity daily in the temple at Tiruvarur. One evening, while getting out of the Araneri shrine, the idea of lighting the temple came to him. As darkness was setting in, he requested the inmates of a nearby house for ghee not knowing that they were Jainas. They refused as the tenets of their religion were antagonistic to those of the Saivites. Not only did they refuse ghee but they further slighted Nayanar by saying, 'If you are so particular to light the temple of your god do so with water.' Vexed at this he prayed to the god in Araneri shrine, and lighted the lamp with water and to the wonder of the Jainas the light did burn! At another time, when he thought that by following a procession he was polluted, god appeared in his dream and made him understand that for those born in Tiruvarur there was no such thing as pollution and that they were equal to Saiva ganas. Appar has also praised this devotee in his poems.

3. 'The Sage Durvasa was born of Anusuya, the model of chastity, and the wife of the sage Atri as a portion of Rudra, impregnated with the quality of darkness. By his fearful looks, thoughts and words, he burnt down those who insulted him. He is said to have worshipped the linga in this shrine. The Nataraja in the temple

at Tirukkalar near Tirutturaipundi, on the Mayavaram-Arantangi Railway line, is said to have danced to please this sage, and so the figure of the sage is depicted in front of Nataraja there. A sculptural representation of this sage with tuft of his hair tied in a peculiar fashion, characteristic of sages, exists in the matha close by the temple of Anantesvara on the west of Chidambaram town.

4. Kalarsinga Nayanar was one of the Pallava kings who reduced to subjugation several of the kings in the north. When on a visit to the temple at Tiruvarur he noticed his wife smelling the flower intended for the god. This displeased him to such an extent that he disfigured her limbs as a sort of punishment. After reigning his kingdom righteously for a long time he joined the attendants of god Siva.

5. Tandiyadigal Nayanar was born in Tiruvarur. To widen the tank attached to the temple he had a peg planted with the aid of a rope, he was removing earth from the tank. While he was removing earth the Jainas remarked about the sin of causing the death of living worms and insects and forcibly removed the spade in his hand and threw it away. They also taunted him for his blindness. To favour him, god appeared in his dream and gave him sight and made his opponents—Jainas blind! The Chola king, who resided at the place, was also made to drive out the Jainas who displeased Nayanar.

6. *Inscriptions of the Madras Presidency*, Government of Madras, 1919, Vol. II, pp. 1349–54.

Chapter 15

NEGAPATAM

This is an important seaport of the Tanjore district, being the terminus of the Tanjore–Negapatam railway line, and is famous for the temple of Kayarohanasvami and his consort Nilayathakshi. The deity of the temple Tyagaraja is considered very important. The metallic figure of Panchamukha Vinayaka, the five-faced elephant god), also known as Heramba Ganapati and that of Sattayappa in a separate shrine on the west are of great sanctity. The stone work of the Ashtadikpalas[1] or the guardian angels of the eight cardinal points, is also a fine piece of workmanship, and occupies a prominent place over the sanctum of the deity.

SAINT ADIPATHAR

This is the place where the fisherman saint Adipatha Nayanar[2] lived and obtained the god's blessing.

BUDDHIST SHRINES

Negapatam formerly seems to have been an important Buddhist or rather Jaina centre. According to the inscriptions, it is seen that two Buddhist shrines flourished here about 11th century A.D. These were the Rajarajaperumpalli and the

Rajendracholaperumpalli and from these names it would appear that the Chola kings tolerated Buddhism or Jainism to a large extent in their region. It is said that the Vaishnava saint Tirumangai Alwar carried away a golden Buddhist figure and utilised the metal for covering the vimana of Sri Ranganatha at Srirangam. About 15th century A.D. a king from Pegu is said to have visited this shrine.The Puduveligopuram or the Chinese pagoda, subsequently demolished by the Jesuit priests, might have been one of the important Buddhist shrines of the ancient days.

According to the Leyden[3] grant the building of this Buddhist temple was commenced by Chulamanivarman, the king of Kataka or, in Tamil, Kidaram, who was apparently a feudatory of the Chola king before the 21st year of the reign of Rajaraja I. It was completed during the reign of his successor Madurantaka Rajendrachola or by Maravijayottungavarman, the son of Chulamanivarman. Kataka[4] repetition over which Chulamanivarman and Maravijayottungavarman ruled, appears to have denoted some portion of lower Burma or of the Indo-Chinese peninsula, as Rajendra Chola I, in his war against Samgrama-vijayottungavarman of Kidaram, is reported to have despatched many ships in the stormy ocean and to have taken possession of the Nicobar (Nakkavaram) and Papphala (Mappapalam) which, according to the Mahavamsa, is a sea-port in Ramannadesa, the ancient name of Burma.

This building[5] was a four-sided tower of 3 storeys constructed of bricks, with an entrance for doorway in the middle of each side. In 1867 it was demolished and the present St. Joseph's College was built on it. One of the figures presented to the then Goveornor of Madras, Lord Napier, by the Missionaries, bore an inscription having the name Agamapandita, which might refer to Umapatisivacharya or

Sankalagamapandita of Chidambaram Dikshadars and not the name of any Buddhist monk as inferred by some.

PORTUGUESE CONNECTION

Negapatam was one of the earliest Portuguese settlements on the east coast. It was subsequently acquired by the Dutch and became their headquarters. There is an old Dutch cemetry in the town, containing many antique tombs, surmounted with heavy stone slabs bearing inscriptions cut in large letters in high relief and said to have been imported from Holland. Thereafter it passed into the hands of the Nawab. The Raja of Tanjore held it till 1778 when it passed into the hands of the English.

INSCRIPTIONS[6]

See Mr. Sewell's *Antiquities* Vol. I, p.281 and Tanj. Gazr., p.243 f., for detailed accounts of the *antiquities* of this place. Dr. Hultzsch mentions in the ancient Kayarohanasvami temple (called Karona in inscriptions and in the Periyapurana), a number of epigraphs allegedly belonging to 'Rajaraja, Rajendrachola and other Chola kings,' but he gives no details about these. See Mad. Ep. Rep., June 1891, p.3, para 6. The following have been taken from *antiquities* and Tanj. Gazr.:

In a stone in the wall of the Kailasanatha temple. Records in Dutch the death of a gentleman in A.D. 1777.

On a bronze image discovered near the demolished tower of the ancient 'China pagoda.' A record, according to Dr. Burnell, belonging to the twelfth or early thirteenth century.

On a stone in 'a small temple.' A Dutch record saying that it was built in 1777 under the auspices of the Governor Reynier Van Vlissingen.

On a drum in the hands of Mr. C.E. Crighton. 'A short

inscription in ancient Tamil and Grantha characters.' No details given.

A Telugu silver plate grant (now in the Batavia Museum). Records that Vijaya Raghava, the last Naik king of Tanjore, gave Negapatam to the Dutch.

A Tamil silver plate grant in the same place. Records the confirmation of the above grant by the Maratha king Ekoji in A.D. 1676.

On a stone in the old Dutch Church. Records its foundation in 1774.

NAGORE

Nagore, known in former times as Punnagavanam, is a town situated close by. There is a fine Mohammedan mosque here which is a famous place of pilgrimage and both Hindus and Mohammedans visit this annually.

INSCRIPTIONS[7]

Over the tomb in the local mosque. Records that the mosque was built by Pratapa Singh of Tanjore in eleven days in H. 1171 (A.D. 1757). *Antiquities*, Vol. I, p.281.

A C.P. grant in the same place. Records the grant of fifteen villages to the mosque by the same king. Ibid., p.281.

THE FAMOUS MINARET

The minaret is 125 feet in height and is an example of exquisite workmanship. It was constructed by the Raja of Tanjore over the *darga* (tomb) of Mohammedan saint Miran Sahib who performed several miracles some four centuries ago. The construction of the minarets is attributed to the then king of Tanjore and the largest of the fine minarets is nearly 100 feet in height. In the building brick and plaster have been used. The interior consists of two irregular cloistered courts inclusive of the central tomb. It stand under a dome which is approached through seven high doorways plated with silver.

The annual festival takes place in autumn when a large concourse of pilgrims of all castes including Brahmans gather at the place. The festival lasts for 12 days and most of the ceremonies take place in the night especially from the ninth day.

HISTORICAL REFERENCE

The place has its own connection with the modern history. Lally, on his expedition to Tanjore in 1758, plundered its wealth. In 1773 the Dutch obtained the place from the Rajah of Tanjore in consideration of the money they had advanced.

VEDARANYAM

Vedaranyam or Adi Setu or Kodikkarai is another famous place of pilgrimage on the Tirutturaipundi Vedaranyam Railway in the Tanjore district. Rama is said to have expiated in this place the sin of having killed Ravana. The Vedas also worshipped God here, and this fact accounts for the great sancity attached to this place.

VINAYAKA'S IMPORTANCE

The Vinayaka (the elephant god) found at the west entrance of the temple (Fig. 88), named Virahatte Vinayaka who is considered to have got rid of the ghosts of the Rakshasas slain by Sri Rama, whom they haunted, is said to be very powerful.

A bath in the temple tank Manikarnika is said to expiate sins.

EPIGRAPHICAL INFORMATION

The epigraphical records of this place show that, on recovery of his health, a ruler of this province ordained a great festival. The famous Tamil saints, Appar and Sambandar, performed several miracles in this place.

INSCRIPTIONS[8]

The inscriptions recorded in this temple have been copied by the Madras Epigraphical Department during the year 1904.

In literary history Vedaranyam is known as the native place of Paranjoti Munivar, the son of Minakshi Sundara Desika, and the author of the monumental *Tiruvilayadalpurana*. For his life history see *Abhidhana Chintamani*, (p. 637). His date is controvers, but he evidently belonged to the thirteenth century.

415 of 1904 (Tamil) — On the south wall of the central shrine in the Vedaranyesvara temple. A record in the fourth year of the Chola king Tribhuvanachakravartin Kulottunga Choladeva, corresponding to Thursday, 11th March, A.D. 1182. Records gift of gold for a lamp by a certain Gangaikondar Rajarajadeva or Pottappichcholan to the temple at Tirumaraikkadu in Kunrurnadu, a sub-division of Umbala-nadu. See Ep. Ind., Vol. VIII, p.264.

416 of 1904 (Tamil) — On the same wall. A record in the twenty-ninth year of the Chola king Tribhuvanachakravartin Kulottunga Choladeva III, 'who took Madura, Ilam (Ceylon) and the crowned head of the Pandya'. Records gift of money for a lamp.

417 of 1904 (Tamil) — On the same wall. A damaged record in the fifteenth year of the Chola king Tribhuvanachakravartin Kulottunga Choladeva III, 'who took Madura and the crowned head of the Pandya'. Records the gift of a lamp.

418 of 1904 (Tamil) — On the south wall of the mandapa in front of the same shrine. A damaged record in the ninth year

of the Chola king Tribhuvanachakravartin Rajendra Choladeva
III. Records gift of land for a lamp. Dr. Kielhorn calculates the
date to be Tuesday, 12th January, A.D.1255. See Ibid., Vol.
VIII; p.273.

419 of 1904 (Tamil) — On the same wall. A record in the
fourth year of Choladeva. Records gift of money for a lamp
by a certain Virasingapanmar.

420 of 1904 (Tamil) — On the same wall. A record in the
fifth year of the Chola king Tribhuvanachakravartin
Rajarajadeva. Built in at the beginning. Records gift of money
for lamps. At the bottom is an inscription of Kulottunga III,
which is also partly built in.

421 of 1904 (Tamil) — On the same wall. A record in the
sixth year of the Chola king Tribhuvanachakravartin Rajendra
Choladeva. Records an order of Vanadarayan.

422 of 1904 (Tamil) — On the north wall of the same
mandapa. A record in the second year of the Chola king
Rajakesarivarman or Tribhuvanachakravartin Kulottunga
Choladeva (I?). Records that the king granted to a certain
individual the privilege of singing the Tiruppadiyam hymns
in the temple and the emoluments connected therewith.

423 of 1904 (Tamil) — On the same wall. A record in the
fourth year of the Chola king Tribhuvanachakravartin
Rajendra Choladeva III, corresponding to Wednesday, 5th
January, A.D. 1250. Records gift of land for a lamp. The Saiva
Brahmans of the Muppaduvattam of the temple took charge
of the land. Ibid., p.272.

424 of 1904 (Tamil) — On the same wall. A mutilated
record in the seventeenth year of the Chola king
Tribhuvanachakravartin Rajarajadeva. Records gift of jewels
to the temple.

425 of 1904 (Tamil) — On the same wall. A damaged record
in the twenty-third year of the Chola king Rajakesarivarman or

Tribhuvanachakravartin Kulottunga Choladeva (I or II?).

426 of 1904 (Tamil) — On the same wall. A record in the twentieth year of the Chola king Tribhuvanachakravartin Kulottunga Choladeva III, 'who took Madura, Ilam (Ceylon) and the crowned head of the Pandya.' Built in at the end. Records gift of fifty sheep for a lamp.

427 of 1904 (Tamil) — On the same wall. An incomplete record in the thirty-second year of the Chola king Tribhuvanachakravartin Tribhuvanaviradeva (1178–1216), 'who took Madurai, Karuvur and the crowned head of the Pandya and performed the anointment of heroes and victors,' i.e. Kulottunga III. The date corresponds to Monday, 21st December, A.D. 1209. Ep. Ind., Vo. VIII, p.266.

428 of 1904 (Tamil) — On the north wall of the mandapa in front of the central shrine in the same temple. A record in the thirty-fifth year of the Chola king Tribhuvanaviradeva (Kulottunga III). Records gift of money for a lamp.

429 of 1904 (Tamil) — On the same wall. A record in the twenty-seventh year of the Chola king Tribhuvanachakravartin Rajarajadeva (III?). Records gift of land for a lamp.

430 of 1904 (Tamil) — On the same wall. A record in the twentieth year of the Chola king Tribhuvanachakravartin Kulottunga Choladeva III, 'who took Madurai, Ilam (Ceylon) and the crowned head of the Pandya.' Records gift of money for a lamp. At the bottom is an incomplete and damaged inscription of the twentieth year of the same king. The date corresponds to Sunday, 3rd May, A.D. 1198. Ibid., p.265.

431 of 1904 (Tamil) — On the same wall. A record in the twenty-seventh year of the Chola king Tribhuvanachakravartin Rajarajadeva. Records gift of land.

432 of 1904 (Tamil) — On the same wall. A damaged record in the twenty-second year of the Chola king

Tribhuvanachakravartin Rajarajadeva. Records gift of land.

433 of 1904 (Tamil) — On a pillar within the same mandapa. An incomplete record in the thirty-third year of the Chola king Maduraikonda Parakesarivarman (905–47).

434 of 1904 (Tamil) — On the same pillar. A record in the thirty-fifth year of the Chola king Maduraikonda Parakesarivarman (905–47). Records the gift of ninety sheep for a lamp.

435 of 1904 (Tamil) — On another pillar in the same place. A record in the thirtieth year of the Chola king Maduraikonda Parakesarivarman (905–47). Records the gift of six *ilakkasu*⁹ for a lamp.

436 of 1904 (Tamil) — On the same pillar. A record in the ninth year of the Chola king Parakesarivarman. Records gift of ninety sheep for a lamp.

437 of 1904 (Tamil) — On the same pillar. A record in the fifteenth year of the Chola king Rajaraja Rajakesarivarman I (985–1013). Records gift of ninety sheep for a lamp.

438 of 1904 (Tamil) — On the same pillar. A damaged record in the eigth year of the Chola king Parakesarivarman.

439 of 1904 (Tamil) — On the same pillar. A record in the twenty-second year of the Chola king Rajakesarivarman or Rajarajadeva I. Records gift of land.

440 of 1904 (Tamil) — On the same pillar. A record in the sixth year of the Chola king Rajarajakesarivarman (985–1013). Records gift of ninety sheep for a lamp.

441 of 1904 (Tamil) — On the same pillar. A record in the ninth year of the Chola king Rajarajakesarivarman (985–1013). Records gift of money. Mentions Mutturrukurram in Pandinadu.

442 of 1904 (Tamil) — On the same pillar. A damaged record in the sixth year of the Chola king Rajakesarivarman.

443 of 1904 (Tamil) — On the same pillar. A damaged

record of the Chola king Parakesarivarman, the date of which is lost.

444 of 1904 (Tamil) — On the third pillar in the same place. A record in the twentieth year of the Chola king Maduraikonda Parakesarivarman (905–47). Records gift of gold.

445 of 1904 (Tamil) — On the same pillar. A record in the twenty-eighth year of the Chola king Maduraikonda Parakesarivarman (905–47). Records gift of ninety sheep for a lamp by Arunidi Kaliyan of Marudur, an officer of Sri Parakesarivarman.

446 of 1904 (Tamil) — On the same pillar. A record of the Chola king Maduraikonda Parakesarivarman (905–47), the date of which is lost. Records gift of ninety sheep.

447 of 1904 (Tamil) — On the same pillar. A record in the twenty-fourth year of the Chola king Maduraikonda Parakesarivarman (905–47). Records gift of land.

448 of 1904 (Tamil) — On the same pillar. A record in the sixth year of the Chola king Parakesarivarman. Records gift of ninety sheep for a lamp.

449 of 1904 (Tamil) — On the same pillar. A record in the twenty-seventh year of the Chola king Maduraikonda-Parakesarivarman (905–47). Records gift of sheep for a lamp.

450 of 1904 (Tamil) — On the fourth pillar in the same place. A record in the twentieth year of the Chola king Maduraikonda Parakesarivarman (905–47). Records gift of ninety sheep for a lamp.

451 of 1904 (Tamil) — On the fourth pillar in the same place. A record in the eighteenth year of the Chola king Maduraikonda Parakesarivarman (905–47). Records gift of ninety sheep for a lamp.

452 of 1904 (Tamil) — On the fourth pillar in the same place. A record in the twenty-fifth year of the Chola king

Maduraikonda Parakesarivarman (905–47). Records gift of ninety sheep for a lamp.

453 of 1904 (Tamil) — On the fourth pillar in the same place. A record in the thirteenth year of the Chola king Maduraikonda Parakesarivarman (905–47). Records gift of gold.

454 of 1904 (Tamil) — On the fourth pillar in the same place. A record in the eighteenth year of the Chola king Maduraikonda Parakesarivarman. Records gift of ninety sheep for a lamp.

455 of 1904 (Tamil) — On the fourth pillar in the same place. A record in the thirtieth year of the Chola king Maduraikonda Parakesarivarman (905–47). Records gift of ninety sheep for a lamp.

456 of 1904 (Tamil) — On the fourth pillar in the same place. A record in the twenty-seventh year of the Chola king Maduraikonda Parakesarivarman (905–47). Records gift of 180 sheep for two lamps.

457 of 1904 (Tamil) — On the fourth pillar in the same temple. A mutilated record in the thirty-second year of the Chola king Maduraikonda Parakesarivarman (905–47).

458 of 1904 (Tamil) — On the fourth pillar in the same place. A damaged record in the thirteenth year of the Chola king Maduraikonda Parakesarivarman (905–47).

459 of 1904 (Tamil) — On the fourth pillar in the same place. A record in the fifth year of the Chola king Parakesarivarman. Records gift of ninety sheep for a lamp.

460 of 1904 (Tamil) — On the south wall of the Tyagaraja shrine in the same temple. A record in the sixteenth year of the Chola king Tribhuvanachakravartin Rajendra Choladeva III, corresponding to Monday, 1st May, A.D. 1262. Records gift of land for meeting the expenses of two festivals called Tiruvikkiramansandi. See Ep. Ind., Vol. VIII, p.273.

461 of 1904 (Tamil) — On the pillar in the mandapa in front of the same shrine. A mutilated record in the sixteenth year of the Chola king Rajaraja Rajakesarivarman I (985–1013).

462 of 1904 (Tamil) — On the same pillar. A damaged record in the nineteenth year of the Chola king Rajakesarivarman or Rajarajadeva (985–1013).

463 of 1904 (Tamil) — On the same pillar. A damaged record in the fourteenth year of the Chola king Parakesarivarman.

464 of 1904 (Tamil) — On the same pillar. Records in the sixteenth year of the king a gift of land.

465 of 1904 (Tamil) — On the second pillar in the mandapa in front of the Tyagaraja shrine in the same temple. A record of the Chola king Maduraikonda Parakesarivarman (905–47), the date of which is lost. Records gift of ninety sheep for a lamp.

466 of 1904 (Tamil) — On the third pillar in the same mandapa. A partly damaged record in the year of the Chola king Rajakesarivarman. Records gift of ninety sheep for a lamp.

467 of 1904 (Tamil) — On the same pillar. A record in the eighth year of the Chola king Rajakesarivarman. Records gift of a lamp.

468 of 1904 (Tamil) — On the fourth pillar in the same mandapa. A partly damaged record in the seventeenth year of the Chola king Maduraikonda Parakesarivarman (905–47). Records gift of a lamp.

469 of 1904 (Tamil) — On the same pillar. A partly damaged record in the twenty-eighth year of the Chola king Maduraikonda Parakesarivarman (905–47). Records gift of ninety sheep.

470 of 1904 (Tamil) — On the fifth pillar in the same mandapa. A mutilated record in the fifteenth year of the Chola

king Rajakesarivarman (985–1013). Records gift of 180 sheep for two lamps.

471 of 1904 (Tamil) — On the sixth pillar in the same mandapa. A damaged record in the twentieth year of the Chola king Rajakesarivarman.

472 of 1904 (Tamil) — On the same pillar. A record in the sixth year of the Chola king Parakesarivarman. Records gift of ninety sheep for a lamp.

473 of 1904 (Tamil) — On the seventh pillar in the same mandapa. A record in the nineteenth year of the Chola king Maduraikonda Parakesarivarman (905–47). Records a gift of two lamps.

474 of 1904 (Tamil) — On the same pillar. A record in the sixth year of the Chola king Parakesarivarman. Records gift of ninety sheep. Damaged at the end.

475 of 1904 (Tamil) — On the same pillar. A damaged record in the ninth year of the Chola king Parakesarivarman.

476 of 1904 (Tamil) — On a pillar in the mandapa in front of the Ramanathesvara shrine in the same temple. A record of the Chola king Maduraikonda Parakesarivarman (905–47), the date of which is doubtful. Records gift of ninety sheep for a lamp.

477 of 1904 (Tamil) — On the same pillar. An incomplete record in the twenty-seventh year of the Chola king Rajakesarivarman.

478 of 1904 (Tamil) On the same pillar. A record in the thirtieth year of the Chola king Maduraikonda Parakesarivarman (905–47). Records gift of 180 sheep for two lamps.

479 of 1904 (Tamil) — On the same pillar. A record in the fifteenth year of the Chola king Maduraikonda Parakesarivarman (905–47). Records gift of ninety sheep for a lamp.

480 of 1904 (Tamil) — On the same pillar. A record in the fifteenth year of the Chola king Maduraikonda Parakesarivarman (905–47). Records gift of 180 sheep for two lamps.

481 of 1904 (Tamil) — On the second pillar in the same mandapa. Records the gift of ninety sheep for a lamp by a certain Kalikesarin.

482 of 1904 (Tamil) — On the same pillar. A record in the thirteenth year of the Chola king. Maduraikonda Parakesarivarman (905–47). Records gift of ninety sheep for a lamp by the same donor.

483 of 1904 (Tamil) — On the same pillar. A record in the tenth year of the Chola king Rajakesarivarman. Records gift of ninety sheep for a lamp.

484 of 1904 (Tamil) — On the same pillar. A record in the eighth year of the Chola king Parakesarivarman. Records gift of ninety sheep for a lamp.

485 of 1904 (Tamil) — On the same pillar. A record in the seventh year of the Chola king Maduraikonda Parakesarivarman (905–47). Records gift of a lamp.

486 of 1904 (Tamil) — On the same pillar. A record in the thirty-second year of the Chola king Maduraikonda Parakesarivarman (905–47). Records gift of ninety sheep for a lamp.

487 of 1904 (Tamil) — On the same pillar. A record in the twenty-sixth year of the Chola king Rajakesarivarman. Records gift of 180 sheep for two lamps.

488 of 1904 (Tamil) — On the same pillar. A damaged record of the Chola king Parakesarivarman (905–47), 'who took Madurai and Ilam (Ceylon),' the date of which is indistinct.

489 of 1904 (Tamil) — In the second gopura of the same temple, left of entrance. A record of the Vijayanagara king

Prabhushi (for Praudha) Devaraya Maharaya (1449–65) in S. 1386, expired, Tarana. Records sale of land.

490 of 1904 (Tamil) — In the same place. A mutilated record of the Vijayanagara king Virapratapadeva Maharaya (date lost), cyclic year (doubtful). Seems to record a gift of land.

491 of 1904 (Marathi) — On a slab built into the floor in front of the same gopura. Mentions the Maratha kings Pratapasimha Maharaja and his son Tulaja Maharaja (1763–87) of Tanjore. See Tanj. Gazr., Vol. I, p.49.

492 of 1904 (Tamil) — On the south wall of the first prakara of the same temple. A partly damaged record in the thirty-third year of the Chola king Tribhuvanachakravartin Rajendra Choladeva (III?). Records gift of land.

493 of 1904 (Tamil) — On the same wall. A partly damaged record of the Chola king Tribhuvanachakravartin Rajarajadeva (III?) the date which is lost. Records gift of land for a lamp.

494 of 1904 (Tamil) — On the west wall of the same prakara. A record in the eighteenth year of the Chola king Tribhuvanachakravartin Rajendra Choladeva III. Records gift of land. Dr. Kielhorn discussing the details of the date, points out that Apara paksha is a mistake for Purva paksha and that the English equivalent is Wednesday, 2nd January, A.D. 1264. See Ep. Ind., p.274.

495 of 1904 (Tamil) — On the same wall. A record in the twenty-seventh year of the Chola king Tribhuvanachakravartin Rajarajadeva III. Records gift of land. An irregular date. Ibid., p.271.

496 of 1904 (Tamil) — On the west wall of the first prakara of the same temple. A record in the nineteenth year of the Chola king Tribhuvanachakravartin Rajarajadeva III. Built in at the beginning. Records gift of land for a lamp.

The date corresponds to Sunday, 11th June, A.D. 1234. Ibid., p.269.

497 of 1904 (Tamil) — On the north wall of the same prakara. A record in the twenty-first year of the Chola king Tribhuvanachakravartin Rajendra Choladeva (III?). Records gift of land.

498 of 1904 (Tamil) — On the same wall. A record in the fourteenth year of the Chola king Tribhuvanachakravartin Rajadhirajadeva (II?). Records gift of land for a lamp.

499 of 1904 (Tamil) — On the same wall. A record in the third year of the Chola king Tribhuvanachakravartin Rajarajadeva III. Records a sale of five men and five women and their relatives (*vargattar*) for 1,000 kasus by a certain Ariyan Pichchan or Edirilisola Gangainadavaln who was evidently the police officer of the district. He says that the five men were his slaves and 'had been made over to the temples as slaves by his master (mudaliyar).'

500 of 1904 (Tamil) — On the same wall. A record in the eighth year of the Chola king Tribhuvanachakravartin Rajarajadeva (III?). Records gift of land for a lamp.

501 of 1904 (Tamil) — On the same wall. A partly damaged record in the thirtieth year of the Chola king Tribhuvanachakravartin Rajarajadeva (III?). Refers to an invasion of Singanna Dandanayaka and to the rebuilding of the temple of Kodikkulagar. See 498 of 1902 at Tiruvannamalai where a Simhana Dandanatha is referred in the fifth year of Rajendra Chola III (i.e., 1250–51), but it is doubtful whether the two are identical.

502 of 1904 (Tamil) — On the same wall. A damaged record in the twenty-fourth year of the Chola king Tribhuvanachakravartin Rajarajadeva III. Records a sale of two women by the same man who is mentioned in No. 499 above.

503 of 1904 (Tamil) — On the same wall. A record in the

twelfth year of the Chola king Tribhuvanachakravartin Rajendra Choladeva (III?). Records gift of land.

C.P. N.40 of Mr. Sewell's List (Tamil) — Records a document in S. 1418 (A.D. 1496), Krodhi, by which the temple authorities at the Vedaranya temple of the god Chandisvara granted certain privileges to a priest.

AGASTYAMPALLI

Agastyampalli is another small village near Vedaranyam. At the wedding of Siva and Parvati at Mount Meru all the Devas (minor deities in the Hindu pantheon) were present and as the weight became heavier, it began to sink. Thereupon Siva ordered the sage Agastya (the dwarf sage) to proceed to the south to keep the equilibrium, where he presented himself to this sage in his marriage robes.

Agastya is also known as Kumbhamuni. The latter name is in consequence of his having been born from a pot (*kumbha* means pot), or rather from his having been escaped from a jar during a pralaya or deluge. It is in connection with the latter story that his representations are made with a pot in hand. The Pandyan kings held this sage as their *kulaguru* (family priest).

He is also represented as a star. It is somewhere near in the sky situated in the apex of an obtuse angle. There is a saying that as soon as this Agastya star brightens the waters on earth get purified. The mountain of Agastyamalai or Potiyamalai in the district of Tinnevelly is named in memory of this sage. It is somewhere near this mountain at Shermadevi or thereabouts that he is said to have devoured the demon Vatapi, who with his brother was causing much annoyance to the Brahmans of the locality under the pretence of performing ceremonies for deceased manes. At one time, to expose an Asura who was causing trouble to Indra by hiding himself in the ocean, this sage drank the whole water in the ocean and thus gave relief to Indra!

His name is also associated with medicine, astronomy, chemistry, alchemy and several other sciences. The Tamil language claims him as its commentator and his Tamil grammar *Tolkappiyam* is still a standard authority. He helped the spread of Saivism to such an extent that his work is called *Agastya Jnanam*, (Agastya's wisdom), and teaches the highest form of monotheism to the Saivites In the work *Agastya Muppadu* (Agastya's 30 stanzas), he condemns the differentiation in gods as Brahma, Vishnu and Siva, and instructs the worship of one as Parabrahman.

INSCRIPTIONS[10]

The inscriptions recorded in this temple have been copied by the Madras Epigraphical Department during the year 1904.

504 of 1904 (Tamil) — On the south wall of the central shrine in the Agastyesvara temple. A damaged record in the fifteenth year of the Pandya king Maravarman Tribhuvanachakravartin Vira Pandyadeva. Seems to record a giift of land. [Was he the king who ruled from 1253 to 1278?]

505 of 1904 (Tamil) — On the south base of the same shrine. A record in the second year of the Chola king Tribhuvanachakravartin Rajarajadeva III. Records gift of 1,500 kasus for a lamp. The date corresponds to Monday, 29th January, A.D. 1218. Scc Ep. Ind., Vol. VIII, p.267.

506 of 1904 (Tamil) — On the north wall of the same shrine. A record in the thirty-first year of the Pandya king Maravarman Tribhuvanachakravartin Kulasekharadeva (1268–1308). Records gift of land for celebrating a festival in the temple for the recovery of the king from some illness.

507 of 1904 (Tamil) — On the north base of the same shrine. A record in the fifth year of the Pandya Maravarman

Tribhuvanachakravartin Kulasekharadeva (1268–1308).
Records gift of money.

TIRUCHCHENGATTANGUDI

This religious centre, lying at a distance of a few miles from
Nannilam Railway Station, is famous for its Vinayaka shrine.
It is also intimately connected with the life of a Saiva devotee
called Siruttonda Nayanar. The deity Vinayaka appears in the
form of a human being instead of the usual elephant form.
It was Vinayaka of this place who killed a powerful demon,
Gajamukhasura and the place is only a few yards away from
the temple.

VINAYAKA'S IMPORTANCE

Vinayaka has a precedence of worship, because of his
capability of removing all obstacles. In view of this, Siva is
said to have placed him in command of an army and to have
proclaimed that unless Vinayaka had the precedence of
worship all undertakings would end in disaster. Vinayaka is
said to have been vitalised out of clay by Parvati and the event
is observed annually on the Vinayaka Chaturthi day, in the
month of Avani (August-September).

There is also another shrine dedicated to Vatapi Ganapathi
in the same temple.

SIRUTONDAR'S STORY

Sirutondar, one of the 63 Saiva devotees, is said to have served
as a *paranjodi* or a military officer under a small chief in his
earlier days, called king Kadavar Kone, at Vatapi (Badami)
in the Bombay Presidency. To test the devotion of Sirutondar,
Siva appeared in the form of an ascetic and demanded an
offering of the cooked flesh prepared out of the body of the

devotee's only son. The youth, when informed of this queer request of the stranger, quietly consented to give up his life. When the flesh of the body was being cooked and offered to the sage quite a strange thing happened. To the surprise of the parents the boy was restored to life and the parents were blessed by the god Siva! This accounts probably for the existence of two central shrines in this place.

One of them is called Ganapatisvara[11] and the other Uttarapatisvara.[12]

INSCRIPTIONS[13]

The inscriptions of this temple have been copied by the Madras Epigraphical Department during the year 1913.

This place is well known as the native place of saint Siruttonda who was a contemporary of Jnanasambandha, who figures in *Periyapurana* and who was present in the battle of Vatapi about A.D. 642. See S.I.I., Vol. II, p.172, for his idol set up at Tanjore. Saivite tradition connects it which god Ganapati's victory over a demon, thereby giving rise to the name of the shrine Ganapatisvaram. It has been sung by Jnanasambanda and Appar.

'51 of 1913 (Tamil) — On the north wall of the central shrine in the Uttarapatisvara temple. An unfinished record of the Vijayanagara king Vira Viruppanna Udaiyar II, i.e., Virupaksha I, son of Vira Ariyaraya (Harihara II) in S. 1306, Raktakshi. Seems to record a gift of land to the shrine of Ganapatisvaram Udaiyar Nayanar and Uttarapati Nayaka at Tiruchchengattangudi, in Marugalnadu which was a sub-division of Geyamanikkavalanadu by the chief Somaya Dannayakkar.

52 of 1913 (Tamil) — On the wall to the left of the dwarapala images in front of the same shrine. A record of the Vijayanagara king Vira Bhupatiraya Udaiyar (1409–22) in S.

1332, Khara. Records gift of a lamp to the temple of Uttarapati Nayaka at Tiruchchengattangudi by a native of Palaiyur or Malaikilanvalam in Urrukkattukottam, a district of Tondaimandalam.

53 of 1913 (Tamil) — On the south wall of the mandapa in front of the same shrine. A damaged record in Visvavasu. Registers a gift of land and houses to certain merchants connected with the treasury of Uttarapati Nayakar, on their having presented a throne to the temple.

54 of 1913 (Tamil) — On the west wall of the same mandapa. A damaged record in Plavanga. Seems to provide for a festival in the same temple by the merchants of the Chola country.

55 of 1913 (Tamil) — On the west wall of the Ganapatisvara shrine in the same temple. A record in the thirty-second year of the Chola king Rajakesarivarman or Udaiyar Sri Rajadhirajadeva (I?). Records sale of land as iraili to the temple of Ganapatisvaram Udaiyar Mahadeva at Tiruchchengattangudi by the assembly of the village Tirukkannapuram, a brahmadeya in Marugalnadu which was a sub-division of Kshatriyasikhamanivalanadu. The assembly is stated to have met together in the temple of Paramisvaramudaiya Mahadeva of their village.

56 of 1913 (Tamil) — On the same wall. A record in the third year of the Chola king Rajakesarivarman Rajarajadeva I. Records gift of land for two lamps to the shrine of Siraladeva at Tiruchengattangudi by a certain Velialan Ulagan or Tappilla Muvendavelan. Sirala was the son of Siruttonda who was sacrificed to Siva when the latter came as a guest of Siruttonda. The price of 2,450 kulis or 1 3/8 *nilas* has been given as 115 kasus.

57 of 1913 (Tamil) — On the same wall. A record in the ninteenth year of the Chola king Rajaraja Rajakesarivarman

or Rajarajadeva I. Records gift of land for feeding the devotees attending the festival of Sittirai Tiruvadirai when the god Siraladevar of Tiruchchengattangudi in Marugalnadu a sub-division of Mummudisolavalanadu was taken in procession to the mandapa of Siruttonda Nambi in that temple.

58 of 1913 (Tamil) — On the same wall. A record in the third year of the Chola king Parakesarivarman or Tribhuvanachakravartin Rajendra choladeva I. Records gift of land at Ikkadu or Perumur to the temple of Ganapatisvaram Udaiyar to Tiruchchengattangudi by a certain Tayan Tiruchchirrambalamudaiyar, for holding the same festival.

59 of 1913. — (Tamil.) On the north wall of the same shrine. A record in the nineteenth year of the Chola king Rajaraja Rajakesarivarman or Rajarajadeva I. Records gift of 3 mas of land for the festival *tiruvila* of Siruttonda Nambi, who was a devotee of Siraladevar of Tiruchchengattangudi, by two residents of Marugal. Refers to the 'revenue survey' made in the seventeenth year of Rajaraja.

60 of 1913 (Tamil) — On the same wall. A record in the fifth year of the Chola king Parakesarivarman. Records gift of land by purchase to the temple of Paramesvara at Tiruchchengattangudi by the assembly of Maruganadu in order to provide for two lamps in that temple.

61 of 1913 (Tamil) — On the same wall. A record of the Chola king Rajadhiraja I. Fragment containing portions of the historical introduction beginning with *tingalertaru*.

62 of 1913 (Tamil) — On the same wall. A record in the eleventh year of the Chola king Parakesarivarman. Records sale of land for a lamp by the assembly of Marugal.

63 of 1913 (Tamil) — On the west base of the mandapa in front of the same temple. A record of the Chola king Tribhuvanachakravartin Rajarajadeva III in his third year,

Karkataka (wrong for Rishabha) su. di. II, Attam, corresponding to Monday, 7th May, A.D. 1218. Built in at the right end. Records gift of land to the shrines of Uttarapati Nayaka and Siruttondadeva in the temple of Uttarapati Nayaka by two residents of Marungur or Rajanarayana-chaturvedimangalam.

64 of 1913 (Tamil) — On the north wall of the same mandapa. A record in the forty-fifth year of the Chola king Tribhuvanachakravartin Kulottunga Choladeva III. Records gift of land for providing garlands of red lilies to the two shrines of Ganapatisvaram Udaiyar and Uttarapati Nayaka by the residents of Tiruchchengattangudi, a village in Marugalnadu which was a sub-division of Geyamanikkavalanadu.

65 of 1913 (Tamil) — On the same wall. A record of the Chola king Parakesarivarman or Tribhuvanachakravartin Kulottunga Choladeva III, 'who took Madurai (Madura) and was pleased to take the crowned head of the Pandya,' in his eleventh year and 175th day, Vrischika, ba. di. 14, Friday, Anilam. Registers that a document connected with the temple of Tiruviramandisvaram Udaiyar at Tirukkannapuram, a brahmadeya village of Marugalnadu in Geyamanikka-valanadu, was engraved on the walls of the temple at Tiruchchengattangudi, as the former was evidently not constructed of stone. The record refers to the fifth and tenth years of Periyadevar Kulottunga Choladeva in whose time the Tirukkannapuram temple came into existence. Mr. Swamikannu Pillai points out that eleventh is an error for twenty-second year; that the date corresponds to Friday, 19th November, A.D. 1199, and that the 175th day shows that the reign began on the 23rd May, A.D. 1178.

66 of 1913 (Tamil) — On the same wall. A record of the Chola king Tribhuvanachakravartin Kulottunga Choladeva III, 'who took Madurai (Madura) and was pleased to take the

crowned head of the Pandya' in his eighteenth year and 330th day. Records gift of land by purchase for laying out a road to carry in procession Siralapillaiyar from the mandapa of Siruttondadevar at Tiruchchengattangudi to the village of Tirumarugal. Refers to the land survey made in the sixteenth year of Kulottunga Choladeva I who abolished tolls.

67 of 1913 (Tamil) — On the same wall. A record in the eighteenth year and 330th day of the king Tribhuvanachakravartin Kulottunga Choladeva III, 'who took Madurai (Madura) and was pleased to take the crowned head of the Pandya.' Registers the remission of taxes in favour of the temple, for maintaining the worship of Siralapillayar. Refers also to the eleventh year of Kulottunga Choladeva, 'who abolished tolls.'

68 of 1913 (Tamil) — On the same wall. Records, that the grants registered in the above two inscriptions were caused to be made by Savannachakravartin of Velichcheri, by the lady devotee, Alliyangodaiammai and Andar Vilangudaiyar Siruttondar.

69 of 1913 (Tamil) — On the north base of the same mandapa. A record of the Chola king Tribhuvanachakravartin Rajarajadeva III, in his twenty-fourth year, Simha, ba. di. 13, Saturday, Pusam. Records gift of land by Arasurudaiyan Tiruchchirrambalamudaiyar or Tiruchchirrambala Pallavaraiyan for providing offerings in the mandapa called Tirumuttuvaneri to the god Uttarapati Nayaka on the occasion when he was to give salvation to his devotee during the festival of Sittirai Barani (Bhairava was the form in which Siva came from the north and gave salvation to Siruttonda).

70 of 1913. — (Tamil.) On the same base. A record of the Chola king Parakesarivarman or Tribhuvanachakravartin Kulottunga Choladeva III, 'who was pleased to take Madurai (Madura),' in his tenth year and 123rd day. Built in at the

beginning. The king is called Tribhuvanachakravartin Konerinmaikondan. Seems to record the grant of landed property to a certain Rajendrasola Achariyan, who was perhaps the temple architect. The royal secretary (*tirumandira olai*) was Rajendrasinga Muvendavelan.

71 of 1913 (Tamil) — On the same base. An unfinished record of the Chola king Tribhuvanachakravartin, the date of which is lost. Seems to record a gift of land in the villages Tiruvittaikattalai and Dinachintamanichaturvedimangalam for providing offerings on each day of Bharani to the god Uttarapati.

72 of 1913 (Tamil) — On the east, north and west walls of the Vatapi Ganapati shrine in the same temple. A much damaged record of the Chola king Tribhuvanachakravartin Kulottunga Choladeva III, 'who was pleased to take Madurai (Madura), Ilam (Ceylon), Karuvur and the crowned head of the Pandya,' in his twenty-second year and 130th day. Seems to register a number of lands acquired for constructing the third prakara of the temple and a street around it. Reference is also frequently made to the reign of Kulottunga Chola I, 'who was pleased to abolish tolls,' and to the temple of Vikrama Cholesvara.

73 of 1913 (Tamil) — On the east wall of the same shrine. This wall is the gift of Vattavarsadaiyan Rajasuryapallavaraiyan of Puduvur.

74 of 1913 (Tamil) — On the second gopura of the same temple, right of entrance. A record in Ananda of Pattukkattari Konerideva Maharaja. Records gift of taxes to the temple of Uttarapati Nayaka at the request of Maluvachakravartin for celebrating certain festivals.

75 of 1913 (Tamil) — In the same place. A much damaged record of the Vijayanagara king Viruppanna-Udaiyar II, i.e. Virupaksha I, son of Vira Ariyappa Udaiyar, Harihara II or

in S. 1306, Raktakshi, Kumbha, ba. di. 10, Mula, corresponding to Sunday, 5th February, A.D. 1385. Seems to record a gift of land.

76 of 1913 (Tamil) — In the same place, left of entrance. A record in the seventh year of the Pandya king Tribhuvanachakravartin Parakrama Pandyadeva. Records gift of two velis of land at Marungur for repairs in the temple of Uttarapati Nayaka. Refers to the Siralan Siruttondanmadam, in the temple of Ganapatisvaramudaiyar Nayanar.

77 of 1913 (Grantha and Tamil) — In the same place. A damaged record of the Chola king Parakesarivarman or Rajadhirajanarapati Rajendra-Chola III (1245–67), 'who cut off the heads of two Pandya kings.' Supplies a long list of the Sanskrit birudas of the king.Seems to record a gift of land to the god Uttarapati Nayaka in the temple of Ganapatisvaram Udaiyar for the purpose of the Bharani festival in the months of Chittirai and Arpisi. Among the achievements of the king are mentioned his capture of Uttara Lanka the stronghold of Vira Rakshasa, which Mr. Krishna Sastri surmises to be a place near Rajahmundry in the Godavari delta; his victory over two over Pandyas, and his powering of the Karnataka king Somesvara of the Hoysala dynasty. Vira Rakshasa is said to be the sole hero of the Vadugas, and Rajendra's campaign against him was perhaps due to a general war against Kopperunjinga whose territory extended as far as Draksharama and who had given a good deal of trouble to Rajaraja III. Rajendra Chola's time was thus one of genuine attempt to revive the Chola greatness. For the relations between Rajendra and Somesvara see 49 of 1913 at Sivayam (Trichinopoly district?).

78 of 1913 (Tamil) — In the same place. A damaged and unfinished record of the Vijayanagara king Vira Virupanna Udaiyar II, i.e. Virupaksha I, in S. 1322, Pramadi, Mesha, ba.

di. 12, Uttirattadi corresponding to Friday, 2nd May, 1399. Seems to provide for certain festivals in the temple of Uttarapati Nayaka.

79 of 1913 (Tamil) — In the same place. A fragmentary record in S. 1394, Nandana, Simha, su. di., Monday, Attam. Seems to record a gift of land by purchase of Palur in Vadagal Marugalnadu which was a sub-division of Geyamanikka valanadu, for offerings to the temple of Uttarapati-Nayaka by a native of Nandisvaram in Tondaimandalam.

80 of 1913 (Tamil) — On the west wall of the mandapa in front of the Chulikamba shrine in the same temple. A record of the Chola king Rajadhirajadeva II 'who was pleased to take Madurai (Madura) and Ilam (Ceylon),' in the thirteenth year, Simha, ba. di. 9, corresponding to Wednesday, 24th July, 1174. Some stones are missing. Seems to record the sale of four women as devaradiyar to the temple of Tiruvalangadudaiya Nayanar for 700 kasus.

81 of 1913 (Tamil) — On the main gopura of the same temple, right of entrance. A damaged record in Prajapati. Seems to record the fees on looms, etc., fixed by an agent of Vira Narasingara Ayyan.

82 of 1913 (Tamil) — On the same gopura left of entrance. A record of the Chola king Rajakesarivarman or Tribhuvanachakravartin Rajadhirajadeva II, the date of which is lost. Begins with the introduction kadalsulnda, etc. Refers to a certain Kaduvangudaiyan Araiyan Atkonda Nayakan who was perhaps the donor.'

NOTES

1. Vide p. 141, n.1.

2. Adipatha Nayanar was born in a fisherman's family in Negapatam. He was a staunch devotee of the presiding Siva deity in the temple of the place. The best of the fish he got from the sea he gave to the god by leaving it back in the sea in the name of the Almighty. To test his devotion, Siva made him get only one fish for a number of days. Even then he left the only fish got on those days to god, to the annoyance of his relatives. On one day when a golden fish was caught he dedicated even that to the God though he and his relations were then in a miserable condition. Satisfied at this conduct of Nayanar, and in recognition of his devotion, Siva gave him a place in the midst of his attendants.

3. This is a copper plate so named as it is now preserved at the University Museum of Leyden in Holland. A translation of this inscription appears in the *Archaeological Survey of Southen India,* Vol. IV, pp. 204.

4. *Annual Report* of the Madras Epigraphical Department for 1898–99, p.12.

5. A plan of this as it stood in 1846 is illustrated in the *'Indian Antiquary',* September 1878, p.224.

6. *Inscriptions of the Madras Presidency*, Government of Madras, 1919, Vol. II, p. 1346–47.

7. *Inscriptions of the Madras Presidency*, Government of Madras, 1919, Vol. II, p. 1346.

8. *Inscriptions of the Madras Presidency*, Government of Madras, 1919, Vol. II, p. 1434–42.

9. The currency of Ceylon coins in the mainland need occasion no surprise when we remember the position of Vedaranya and the commercial intercourse between the mainland and the island. A later poet Ganapati Kurukkal, who had a number of disciples in the surrounding district, took advantage of this to sing the whole *Skandapurana* in songs which could be sung by the sailors.

10. *Inscriptions of the Madras Presidency*, Government of Madras, 1919, Vol. II, p. 1429.
11. This name is given on account of Ganapati having worshipped the deity here.
12. As the god is said to have came from the North, to satisfy the devotee Siruthondar, the deity is so named (*Uttara* means north).
13. *Inscriptions of the Madras Presidency*, Government of Madras, 1919, Vol. II, pp. 1323–28.

Chapter 16

TANJORE

Tanjore is the headquarters of the district bearing the same name on the South Indian Railway and from the train a good view of the great Brihadisvara temple can be had. This was a famous centre of the later Chola kings.

ORIGIN OF THE CITY

There is a story that once there lived a powerful Rakshasa[1] (demon) named Tanjan who was a descendant of the famous demon Madhu. This demon was very a scourge to the peaceful inhabitants and, to overcome him, god Vishnu appeared as Nilamegaperumal at this place. The temple constructed in honour of this aspect of Vishnu is situated about two miles to the north of Tanjore. It was after this incident that the place came to be known as Tanjore (Tanjai in Tamil). It was for a long time the capital of the famous Chola kings.

TEMPLE CONSTRUCTION

It was during the reign of Chola king Rajaraja that the temple of Brihadisvara with its high tower of stone, and other architectural beauty was constructed. Tradition has it that the mason in charge of the construction, who came from Conjeevaram, had an inspiration regarding the different dynasties and nations that would rule this part of the country, and put up next to the Chola, the Naik and the Mahratta, a European figure on the Vimana (tower).

THE PALACE

The palace in the heart of the town within the fort covers an extent of about 30 acres of land. The structure of the arsenal is like that of the gopura or the tower of the temple. There are other fine works of art and curious devices to note the hours of the day. The bathing tank at Krishna Vilas with its fine statues is another object of attraction. There are two Darbar Halls, one known as the Naick's Darbar Hall and the other as the Mahratta Darbar Hall. Of these, the former should have been constructed prior to 1614 A.D. as Vijayranganatha Naick is said to have been enthroned in the 'Lakshmi Vilas' now known as the Naick's Darbar Hall. There is mention of this fact in the Sanskrit work *Sahitya Ratnakara* by Yagyanarayana Dikshitar, son of the famous Govinda Dikshitar,[2] prime minister of the Naik Kings.

EPIGRAPHICAL IMPORTANCE

Large endowments both in land and money were made to the temple by the Chola king. The several incidents connected with the founding of the temple find place in a drama called *Rajarajeswara Nataka* that was written in A.D. 1055. King Rajarajeswara's conquests extended over almost the whole of the Madras Presidency and included also Ceylon, portions of the southern districts of Bombay, and several islands, the names of which cannot be identified. He is said to have permitted a feudatory of his to build a Buddhist shrine at Negapatam and also to have granted the village of Anamangalam for its maintenance.

[3]The inscriptions on the north and west walls (upper tier)

of the great temple mention that the temple was built by Rajarajadeva and was called after him as Rajarajesvara, i.e., the Isvara (temple) of Rajaraja; a list of gold images, vessels and ornaments, which he presented to the temple and to the image of Dakshinameru Vitankar; a number of gold trumpets and flowers weighed by the stone called after 'adavallan.' The west wall inscription describes 11 gold vessels to the goddess Umaparamesvari. The north wall (lower tier) records mention of 30 sacred ornaments; the south wall (second tier) the extent of the land given by this king and those of his elder sister Kundavaiyar. Those over the main entrance mention the images set up by this Kundavaiyar.The images set up by him and the endowments made for their worship are narrated as having been issued from his palace at Gangaikondasolapuram. The other important items mentioned are the chemicals used for scenting the bathing water of the chief idol and Nataraja; camphor which had to be burnt before the images; the life Chandesvara represented in two successive scenes.

TIRUVALANGADU PLATES RELATING TO CHOLA KINGS

Tiruvalangadu near Madras between Madras and Arkonam is an important religious centre. The Siva temple here is intimately connected with the famous Saintess Karaikalammai. The Nataraja (Siva in his dancing aspect) here, is next in importance of Chidambaram and large number of pilgrims visit the temple daily.

The Madras Epigraphical Department discovered in this temple a set of 31 copper plates containing both Sanskrit and Tamil writings which narrate the history of the early Chola Kings. The Sanskrit plates consists of 271 lines and is mostly Puranic, tracing the origin of the Cholas to the Sun and Manu, the later of whom is ascribed to have been produced by concentration of mind.Then follows the names of kings that ruled in mythical ages of Krita, Treta and Dwapara Yugas. This is followed by a series of historical Chola kings of the present Kali Yuga. The plates are illustrated in the South Indian Inscriptions[4] recently issued by the Government of Madras.

Of the Chola kings Karikala is spoken of as having renovated the town of Kanchi (Conjeevaram) with gold and established his fame by constructing flood-embankments on the river Kaveri. A sculpture of this king is available in the temple of Ekambaranatha at Conjeevaram. King Kochenkannan (red-eyed), one of the Nayammars (Saiva devotees) of Periyapurana, is said to have constructed many Siva temples.To king Vijayalaya (the abode of victory) is attributed the founding of the capital Tanjore. Aditya is narrated to have conquered the Pallava king, Aparajita and to have taken possession of the then Tondaimandalam country. Parantaka, the next king, drove the Pandya King of his time into the sea and carried his conquest up to Ceylon. It is he who renovated the golden hall at Chidambaram. Rajaditya is said to have defeated the Vijayanagara king Krishnadevaraya in the battle of Takkolam near Arkonam. The next king Gandaraditya was succeeded by Arindama whom Sundara Chola (Parantaka II), who ruled justly and charitably, followed. Arumolivarma defeated the Andhra king Bhima and performed the tulabhara. Lastly Madurantaka (Uttama Chola II), who defeated the Keralas while camping at Mudigondapuramis, is said to have granted the village of Pazhaiyar (Tiruvalangadu) at the request of one Terukklathi Pichchan to the temple at the place. The *Srimukha* or the royal order conveying this grant was composed by poet Narayana and written by the king himself. A detailed description of the boundary line of the village is also given. The conditions and privileges with which the village was granted to the temple as well as the names of the architects—Aravamudu with his two brothers Ranga and Damodara and his son Purushothama born in Conjeevaram and belonging to Ovi family are also given.This royal writ was taken round the village in a procession headed by a female elephant.

INSCRIPTIONS[5]

The inscriptions here have been copied by the Madras Epigraphical Department during the years 1888, 1890, 1891, 1897, 1911 & 1918.

C.P.No. 5 of Mr. Sewell's List (Tamil) — Records grant by Andavarayar Vanangamudi Tondaman to certain members of his family. (They belonged to Papanadu.)

C.P.No. 6 of Mr. Sewell's List (Tamil and Telugu) — Records grant by seventy-four artisans in S. 1640 (A.D. 1718), "while Rajadhiraja Ekoji's sons, Sarfoji and Dukkoji, were reigning as kings" to a Ganesa temple "on the west road from Ramesavaram" — the other boundaries being very vaguely given.

C.P.No. 7 of Mr. Sewell's List — Records a deed of sale of some lands in S. 1581 (A.D. 1659) by Vijaya Arunachala Vanangamudi Tondaman, son of Andavarayar Vanangamudi Tondaman to Andoni Muttu Tevar, son of Kotta Rayappa Tevar.

The Tanjore Sanskrit and Kanarese spurious plates of the W. Ganga Ari Varma Maharajadhiraja are now in the British Museum. Ari Varma was the son of Madhava I, who was the son of Konganivarma of the Jahnaveya family and Kanvayana gotra. The date is given, but irregular, according to Dr. Kielhorn. See *Ind. Antq.*, Vol. VIII, p.212; Ibid., Vol. XXIV, p.10, No.166, and Kielhorn's Souther List No. 108.

65 of 1888 (Tamil and Grantha) — On the north and west walls of garbhagriha of the Brihadisvara temple, second tier. A record in the twenty-sixth year and twentieth day of Ko Rajakesarivarman or Rajarajadeva I. The king issued orders that the gifts made by him, his elder sister (Kundaviyar) and his queens should be recorded on the walls of the temple he built. See S.I.I., Vol. II, No.1, p.1–14.

66 of 1888 (Tamil and Grantha) — On the west wall of garbhagriha, second tier. A record in the twenty-fifth year of Ko Rajakesarivarman or Rajarajadeva. Ibid., No.2, pp.14–20. Enumerates the gifts of gold vessels and ornaments by Kundaviyar.

67 of 1888 (Tamil and Grantha) — On the south wall of garbhagriha, first and second tiers. A record in the fifteenth year of Ko Parakesarivarman or Udaiyar Rajendra Choladeva I (1011–43).

68 of 1888 (Tamil and Grantha) — On the south wall of garbhagriha, first tier. Records dated in the sixth and tenth years of Ko Parakesarivarman or Udaiyar Rajendra Choladeva regarding the interest to be paid to temple by certain villagers for a sum of money contributed by several donors and by the temple treasury. The inscription is valuable for throwing light on the prices and rate of interest in that age. Ibid., Nos. 9, 10, 11, 12, 13, 14, 15, 16, 17, 18 and 19, pp.90–105.

69 of 1888 (Tamil and Grantha) — On the south wall of garbhagriha, second tier. A record in the twenty-ninth year of Ko-Rajakesarivarman or Rajarajadeva I. Specifies the revenue in paddy, in gold and in money which a number of villages had to pay to the temple. These had been assigned by the king

till the twenty-ninth year of his reign. The inscription is of value for the construction of the fiscal history of the land. See Ibid., No.4, pp.42–53.

70 of 1888 (Tamil and Grantha) — On the east wall, second tier. A record in the third year of Ko Parakesarivarman or Udaiyar Rajendra Soladevla I (1011–43).

71 of 1888 (Tamil and Grantha) — On the north wall, second tier. A record of Ko Rajakesarivarman or Rajarajadeva I, the date of which is lost. Contains a description of thirty ornaments made partly of gold and jewels from the temple treasury and partly of pearls given by the king. See Ibid., No.3, pp.21–42.

72 of 1888 (Tamil and Grantha) — On the north wall, third tier. A record in the fifth year of Tribhuvanachakravartin Konerinmaikondan. Records an order of the king by which certain lands which had been wrongfully sold during the third and fourth years of his reign were restored to the temple. S.I.I., Vol. II, No. 21, pp.109–112.

73 of 1888 (Tamil and Grantha) — On the south wall, first tier. A record of Saluva Tirumalaideva in S. 1377, expired, by which a number of villages are exempted from taxes (e.g., pradhanijodi, karanikhajodhi, talayarikkam, dues on animals, tanks, etc.). See Ibid., No. 23, pp. 117–9.

74 of 1888 (Tamil and Grantha) — On the south wall, first and second tiers. A record in the thirty-fifth year of Tribhuvanachakravartin Konerinmaikondan. Records the grant of the village of Sungamtavirttacholanallur (suburb of Tanjore) in 108 shares to Brahmans and the local deity by a feudatory Samantanarayana. The inscription is singularly valuable for the fiscal terms it uses. See Ibid., No.22, pp.112–7.

75 of 1888 (Tamil and Grantha) — On the south wall, second tier. A record in the twenty-ninth year of Ko Rajakesarivarman or Rajarajadeva I, describing the gifts made

till that year by Alvar Parantakan Kundavaiyar. See Ibid., No.6, pp.68–77. The inscription, like the others of the series, is of incalculable value in the light it throws on currency, weights and measures, rate of interest, price, etc.

76 of 1888 (Tamil and Grantha) — On the south wall of Chandesvara shrine. A record in the second year of Udaiyar Rajendra Soladeva I (1011–43). Records the weight of the four water-pots of gilt copper presented by Adititan Suryan Tennavan Muvendavelan of Poygainadu. See Ibid., No. 60, pp.246–7.

77 of 1888 (Tamil and Grantha) — Round the base of Chandesvara shrine. A record of Ko Rajakesarivarman or Rajarajadeva I, the date of which is lost. See Ibid., No.59, pp.236–45. Describes the diadem and girdles of god Rajarajesvara.

78 of 1888 (Tamil and Grantha) — Inside gopura, left of entrance. A record in the twenty-ninth year of Ko Rajakesarivarman or Rajarajadeva I, to the effect that two sums of money were deposited by Kadan Ganapati, a sirudanam servant of the king, with the inhabitants of a bazaar at Tanjore and of certain villages for supplying (for the cost of the interest) cardamom seeds, champaka buds and khaskhas roots for scenting the abhisheka water of two deities. Ibdi., No.24, pp.121–4. Also No. 25, pp.125–6.

79 of 1888 (Tamil and Grantha) — Inside gopura, right of entrance. A record in the twenty-ninth year of Ko Rajakesarivarman or Rajarajadeva I. Records two deposits of money by Adittan Suryan Tennavan Muvendavelan, the srikarya of the Rajarajesvara temple, with the people of a village, the interest of which, paid in paddy in the first case and in money in the second, was to be devoted for certain needs. *S.I.I.*, Vo. II, No. 27, pp.126–31.

80 of 1888 (Tamil and Grantha) — Inside gopura, right

of entrance. A record in the twenty-ninth year of Udaiyar Rajarajadeva I. Records that an officer of the king (Karayileduttapadam) deposed 50 kasus with the sabha of a village (Perunangaimangalam) the interest on which (6 1/4 kasus) was to be used for purchasing camphor for a sacred lamp. Ibid., No. 27, pp.131–2. Also No. 28 Ibid.

81 of 1888 (Tamil and Grantha) — Inside prakara, east, first niche. A record in the twenty-ninth year of Udaiyar Rajarajadeva I. Records that an officer of Rajaraja named Irayiravan Pallavayan or Mummadicholapuram set up a copper image of Chandesvaradeva and presented ornaments. Ibid., No. 56 pp.224–7.

82 of 1888 (Tamil and Grantha) — Inside gopura, east, second pillar. A record in the twenty-ninth year of Udaiyar Rajarajadeva I. Records the setting of the image of Suryadeva by a sirudanam servant Kovan Annamalai or Keralantaka Vilupparayan, and presentation of ornaments. Ibid., No. 56, pp.224–7.

83 of 1888 (Tamil and Grantha) — Inside gopura, east, second pillar. A record in the twenty-ninth year of Udaiyar Rajarajadeva I. Describes a number of copper images made by the king till his twenty-ninth year to represent scenes from the life of Chandesvara and the Lord of his heart. Ibid., No. 29, pp.134–7.

84 of 1888 (Tamil and Grantha) — Inside gopura, east, third pillar. A record in the twenty-ninth year of Udaiyar Rajarajadeva I.

85 of 1888 (Tamil and Grantha) — Inside prakara, south, first pillar. A record in twenty-ninth year of Rajarajadeva I. Gives the dimensions of a copper image of Panchadeha (Siva with five bodies) set up by the king. Ibid., No.30, pp.137–8.

86 of 1888 (Tamil and Grantha) — Inside gopura, south, third pillar. A record of Udaiyar Rajarajadeva I. Ibid., No. 31,

p.139. Records that the enclosure was built by the order of the king under the superintendence of the General Krishna Rama.

87 of 1888 (Tamil and Grantha) — Inside gopura, south, fourth pillar. A record in the twenty-ninth year of Udaiyar Rajaraja-deva I. Describes a group of copper images of Siva, Parvati, their two sons, etc., set up by Velan Adittan Parantaka Pallavaraiyan, a perundanam servant of the king. *S.I.I.,* Vol. II, No. 32, pp.139–41.

88 of 1888 (Tamil and Grantha) — Inside gopura on the south, sixth pillar. A record in the twenty-ninth year of the king, whose name is lost (evidently Rajaraja I).

89 of 1888 (Tamil and Grantha) — Inside gopura on the south, eighth pillar. No details given.

90 of 1888 (Tamil and Grantha) — Inside prakara on the south, ninth pillar. A record in the twenty-ninth year of Udaiyar Rajarajadeva.

91 of 1888 (Tamil and Grantha) — Inside prakara on the south niche. A record in the twenty-ninth year of Udaiyar Rajarajadeva. Ibid., No. 33, pp.141–2. Same as 84 above.

92 of 1888 (Tamil and Grantha) — Inside prakara on the south, tenth pillar. Records that Lokamahadevi, a queen of Rajaraja, set up a copper image of Pichchadevar and presented a number of ornaments. Ibid., No. 34, pp.142–5. Also No. 35 which records a deposit of money in favour of Pichchadeva by certain officers of the king.

93 of 1888 (Tamil and Grantha) — Inside prakara on the west, first pillar. A record in the twenty-ninth year of Udaiyar Rajarajadeva I. Records that Aravanai Malari Kesava, the *srikaryakankani* Nayaka of the temple, gave an Ilaparisu spittoon (padikkam), weighing sixty-nine palas and costing three kasus. Ibid., pp.149–50.

94 of 1888 (Tamil and Grantha) — Inside prakara on the

west, second pillar. A record in the third year of Udaiyar Rajendracholadeva I (1011–43).

95 of 1888 (Tamil and Grantha) — Inside prakara on the west, third pillar. A record in the twenty-ninth year of Udaiyar Rajarajadeva I.

96 of 1888 (Tamil and Grantha) — Inside prakara on the west, fourth pillar. A record in the twenty-ninth year of Udaiyar Rajarajadeva I.

97 of 1888 (Tamil and Grantha) — Inside prakara on the west, first niche. A record in the twenty-ninth year of Udaiyar Rajarajadeva I.

98 of 1888 (Tamil and Grantha) — Inside prakara on the west, first niche. A record in the twenty-ninth year of the king, whose name is not mentioned. Records that Aravanaimalari Kesava, the *srikarayakangani* Nayaka, gave a spittoon weighing sixty-nine palas and costing three kasus. Ibid., No. 36, pp.149–54. Also No.37 recording Rajaraja's deposit of 360 kasus with four bazaars at Tanjore for paying out interest, one hundred and fifty plantains daily (54,000 in a year.) The cost of the plantain is one kasu for 1,200. So the total cost would be forty-five kasus, which is the usual interest on three hundred and sixty kasus. Also No. 38 of Ibid. which describes the setting up of seven images, among which were those of Gananasambanda, Appar and Sundaramurti, pp.152–61.

99 of 1888 (Tamil and Grantha) — Inside prakara on the west, fifth and sixth pillars. A record in the twenty-ninth year of Udaiyar Rajarajadeva I. Records that Krishna Rama, the commander who built the enclosure, set up an image of Ardhanarisvara and presented ornaments. *S.I.I.*, Vol. II, No. 39, pp.161–6.

100 of 1888 (Tamil and Grantha) — Inside prakara on the west, seventh and eighth pillars. A record in the third year Ko Parakesarivarman or Rajendra Choladeva I. Records the

setting up of a copper image by Adittan Suryan (see No. 79 above). The image represented Miladudaiyar or Meypporul-nayanar whose career (narrated in the *Periyapurana*) is referred to.Ibid., No.40, pp.166–9.

101 of 1888 (Tamil and Grantha) — Inside prakara on the west, second niche. A record in the third year of Udaiyar Rajendra Choladeva I, which describes gifts of two lamps and one stand for sacred ashes made to the four images of Gananasambanda, Appar, Sundaramurti and Periya Perumal (Brihadisvara). See No. 98 above. Ibid., No. 41, p.169.

102 of 1888 (Tamil and Grantha) — Inside prakara on the west, second niche and ninth pillar. A record in the twenty-ninth year of Udaiyar Rajarajadeva I. Says that Rajaraja's queen Lokamahadevi set up the images of Adavallar and his consort, and presented ornaments. Ibid., No. 42, pp. 169–72.

103 of 1888 (Tamil and Grantha) — Inside prakara on the west, tenth pillar. A record in the tenth year of Udaiyar Rajaraja-deva, saying that his queen Abhimanavalli set up the images of Siva, Brahma and Vishnu as a boar to illustrate the Arunachalamahatmya, Ibid., No. 44, pp.174–7.

104 of 1888 (Tamil and Grantha) — Inside prakara on the west, third niche. A record of Udaiyar Rajarajadeva I. Ibid., No. 45, Same as 84 and 90.

105 of 1888 (Tamil and Grantha) — Inside prakara on the west, third niche, eleventh and twelfth pillars and fourth niche. A record in the twenty-ninth year of Udaiyar Rajarajadeva I, saying that queen Chola Mahadevi set up images of Siva, Uma and Ganapati, and presented ornaments. Ibid., No. 46, pp.178–90.

106 of 1888 (Tamil and Grantha) — Inside prakara on the west, thirteenth pillar. A record in the twenty-ninth year of Udaiyar Rajarajadeva I. Records that an officer of the

king set up a copper image of Bhringisa. *S.I.I.*, Vol. II, No. 47, pp. 190–93.

107 of 1888 (Tamil and Grantha) — Inside prakara on the west, fifth niche and fourteenth pillar. A record in the twenty-ninth year of Udaiyar Rajarajadeva I. Records that queen Trailokya Mahadevi set up the images of Kalyanasundara, Uma, Vishnu, Brahma, etc., and presented ornaments to the first two. Ibid., No. 48, pp.193–98.

108 of 1888 (Tamil and Grantha) — Inside prakara on the north, first pillar.A record in the twenty-ninth year of Udaiyar Rajarajadeva I, regarding the setting up of a copper image of Subrahmanya. Ibid., No. 49, pp. 198–99.

109 of 1888 (Tamil and Grantha) — Inside prakara on the north, second pillar. A record in the twenty-ninth year of Udaiyar Rajarajadeva I. Describes the images of Dakshinamurti and other deities set up by the king. Ibid., No. 50, pp.199–202.

110 of 1888 (Tamil and Grantha) — Inside prakara on the north, third pillar. A record of Udaiyar Rajarajadeva I.

111 of 1888 (Tamil and Grantha) — Inside prakara on the first niche, fourth and fifth pillars and second niche. A record in the twenty-ninth year of Udaiyar Rajarajadeva I, saying that queen Panchavan Mahadevi set up the images of Tanjayalagar, Uma, and Ganapati and presented ornaments. The inscription has been edited in Ibid., No. 51, pp. 203–17. An elaborated document on the jewellery of the age.

112 of 1888. — (Tamil and Grantha.) Inside prakara, north, sixth pillar. A record in the twenty-ninth year of Udaiyar Rajarajadeva I. Ibid., No. 52, pp. 217–18. Records the setting up of a copper image of Maha Vishnu.

113 of 1888 (Tamil and Grantha) — Inside prakara on the north, seventh pillar. A record in the twenty-ninth year of Udaiyar Rajarajadeva I. Records the erection by queen

Panchavan Mahadevi of a copper image of Patanjalideva (half—— man and half-snake). See Ibid., No. 53, pp. 218–20.

114 of 1888 (Tamil and Grantha) — Inside prakara on the north base. A record in the tenth year of Ko Parakesarivarman or Rajendra Choladeva I (1012-53). Records that a sum of 120 kasus was deposited with the assembly of Perumakkalur by a number of officers in favour of Chandrasekhara and his consort and that the sabha undertook to pay 15 kasus every year as interest. Ibid., No. 54, pp. 220–22.

52 of 1890 — On the north wall of the garbhagriha of the same temple. A record in the twenty-ninth year of the Chola king Ko-Rajakesarivarman or Rajarajadeva I.

53 of 1890 — In the base of the west verandah of the same temple. *S.I.I.*, Vol. II, No. re, pp. 172–74. Records the setting up of the images of Kshetrapaladeva, Bhairava, Siruttonda and his wife and son.

35 of 1891 (Tamil) — On the east wall of the grabhagriha of the Tanjore temple. A record of the Vijayanagara king Devaraya II in S. 1368, expired, Kshaya. The beginning of every line is built in. Describes a few gold and silver ornaments which were presented to the temple by a certain Vallabhadeva, apparently a military officer of the king. Ibid., No. 71, pp. 338–40.

36 of 1891 (Tamil) — On the west wall of the Brihannayaki shrine. A record on the three-hundred and thirty-fourth day in the second year of Konerinmaikondan, saying that he built the shrine of Ulagamulududaiya Nachchiyar and presented to it eleven velis of land at Kottagarkudi or Ulagandanayaki-nallur. Ibid., No. 61, pp. 246–47.

37 of 1891 (Tamil) — On the outside of the north wall of the enclosure of the Tanjore temple; first inscription. An obliterated record in the fifteenth year of the Chola king Ko

Rajakesarivarman or Kulottunga Choladeva I—the only record of this king in the Tanjore temple. Unfinished inscription. The donor was apparently Arumolinangai, the queen of Vira Rajendra (1064–70). Ibid., No. 58, pp. 229–36.

38 of 1891 (Tamil) — On the west wall of the Brihannayaki shrine in the Tanjore temple. Records gift of the remnants of sacred offerings to the inhabitants of Puliyur, who, at the instance of Mallappa Nayakkar, constructed the Murtiamma mandapa adjoining the Brihannayaki shrine. Ibid., No. 62, pp. 247–48.

39 of 1891 (Tamil) — On the outside of the north wall of the enclosure of the Tanjore temple, second inscription. A record in the twenty-ninth year of the Chola king Ko Rajakesariviarman or Rajarajadeva I. First two lines only copied. Contains a list of shepherds who had to supply ghee for temple lamps from the milk of cattle either presented to the temple or purchased from its funds. Ibid., No. 63, pp. 249–51.

40 of 1891 (Tamil) — On the outside of the north wall of the enclosure of the Tanjore temple, third inscription. A record of the Chola king Rajarajadeva I. First two lines only copied. Ibid., No. 64, pp. 251–52.

41 of 1891 (Tamil) — On the outside of the north wall of the enclosure of the Tanjore temple, fourth inscription. A record in the twenty-ninth year of the Chola king Ko Rajakesarivarman or Rajarajadeva I. End not copied. Records an order of the king assigning a daily allowance of paddy to each of 48 persons appointed to recite the Tiruppadiyam in the temple and to two persons who had to accompany the others on drums. *S.I.I.*, Vol. II, No. 65, pp. 252–59.

42 of 1891 (Tamil) — On the outside of the north wall of the enclosure of the Tanjore temple; fifth inscription. A record in the twenty-ninth year of the Chola king Ko

Rajakesarivarman or Rajarajadeva I. End not copied. A very long inscription, recording the king's order assigning the produce of a certain land to a number of men who performed various services in the temple and 400 women (evidently dancing girls) transferred to the Tanjore temple from other temples in the Chola country. Each received one or more shares, each of which consisted of a veli of land, which was calculated at 100 kalams of paddy. The inscription is of great interest and value as the names of those figuring in it are of historical importance and as a good knowledge of temple establishments is given. Ibid., No. 66, pp. 259–303.

43 of 1891 (Tamil) — On the outside of the east wall of the enclosure of the Tanjore temple, left of entrance. A record of a Chola king (whose name is not clear). Professes to be the continuation of an inscription to the right of the entrance, which is now obliterated. Gives a list of villages which had to supply watchmen for the temple. Ibid., No. 57, pp. 227–29.

55 of 1893 (Tamil) — On the outside of the north wall of the enclosure of the Tanjore temple. A record in the sixth year of the Chola king Ko Parakesarivarman or Rajendradeva (1050–63). Invasion of Irattapadi and conquest of Ahavamalla is mentioned. (Records that the king assigned a daily allowance of paddy to a troop of actors who had to perform the drama Rajarajesvaranataka on the occasion of the Vaikasi festival. Ibid., No. 67, pp.303–7.)

56 of 1893 (Tamil) — On the outside of the north wall of the enclosure of the Tanjore temple. A record in the fourth year of the Chola king Ko Parakesarivarman or Vikrama Choladeva (1118–35). Records that the king assigned an allowance to a person who used to check and measure the supplies of paddy which, according to the numerous

inscriptions, were delivered into the temple stores. Refers to the king's viceroyalty in the north in the earlier period. Ibid., No. 68, pp. 307–12.

57 of 1893 (Tamil) — On the outside of the east wall of the enclosure of the Tanjroe temple, right of entrance. A record in the twenty-ninth year of the Chola king Ko Rajakesarivarman or Rajarajadeva I. Consists of a list of villages which had to supply treasurers, servants and accountants to the Rajarajesvara temple in accordance with the king's order. Ibid., No. 69, pp. 312–28.

58 of 1893 (Tamil) — On the outside of the east wall of the enclosure of the Tanjore temple, right of entrance. A record in the twenty-ninth year of the Chola king Ko Rajakesarivarman or Rajarajadeva I, giving a list of the villages in the Chola country which had to supply watchmen for the temple. *S.I.I.*, Vol. II, No. 70, pp. 328–38. This is the earlier part of No. 43 above.

20 of 1897 (Tamil) — On the outside of the north enclosure of the Rajarajesvara temple.A record in the twenty-ninth year of the Chola king Ko Rajakesarivarman or Rajarajadeva I. Records gift in the form of money, she-buffaloes, cows and ewes by the king's officers, and other invididuals and groups of men for burning lamps in the temple. Ibid., No. 94, pp. 436–58.

21 of 1897 (Tamil) — On the same wall. A record in the twenty-ninth year of the Chola king Ko Rajakesarivarman or Rajarajadeva I. Records gift of cattle to various shepherds by Rajarajadeva for the supply of men for burning lamps in the Rajarajesvara temple. Ibid., No. 95, pp. 458–97.

22 of 1897 (Tamil) — On the second gopura of the same temple, right of entrance. A record of the Nayaka king Achyutappa-Nayaka (1572–1614), son of Sevvappa Nayaka in S. 1499, expired, Bahudhanya. Records grant

of exemption from taxes to the goldsmiths of Tanjore. Ibid., No. 97, pp. 498–9.

23 of 1897 (Tamil) — In the same place. A mutilated record in the third year of the Chola king Tribhuvanachakravartin Rajarajadeva III. Records a political pact entered into by three chiefs of the Chola country to be faithful to the king and to stand by each other. Ibid., No. 96, pp. 497–98. The pact shows that the country was disturbed by internal dissensions and Tanjore was not free from them.

24 of 1897 (Tamil) — In the same place. A record in the twenty-ninth year of the Chola king Ko Rajakesarivarman or Rajarajadeva I (985–1013). Records the gift, by the priest Isanasiva Pandita, of eight copper pots and one receptacle for sacred ashes, in the second year of Rajendra Chola I (1011–43). A ninth pot was presented by Pavana Pidaran,the Saivaacharya of the temple, in the third year of Rajendra Choladeva. The tulakkol is mentioned. Ibid., No. 90, pp. 413–5.

25 of 1897 (Tamil) — On the pillar of the south enclosure of the same temple. A record in the twenty-ninth year of the Chola king Ko Rajakesarivarman or Rajarajadeva. Records a gift. Published in Ibid., No. 32.

26 of 1897 (Tamil) — On another pillar of the same enclosure. A record in the twenty-ninth year of the Chola king Ko Rajakesarivarman or Rajarajadeva I. Records that a native of Nallur or Panchavanmadevichaturvedimangalamin Nallurnadu, a district of Nittavinodavalanadu, set up a copper image of Durga-Paramesvari and presented a number of ornaments to it. *S.I.I.*, Vol. II, No. 79, pp. 395–400.

27 of 1897 (Tamil) — On another pillar of the same enclosure. A record in the twenty-ninth year of the Chola king Ko Rajakesarivarman or Rajarajadeva I. Records that Prithvimahadeviar, a queen of Rajarajadeva, set up a copper

image of Srikanthamurtigal, and presented some ornaments to it. Ibid., No. 80, pp. 400–1.

28 of 1897 (Tamil) — On another pillar of the same enclosure. A record in the twenty-ninth year of the Chola king Ko Rajakesarivarman or Rajarajadeva I. Records that the son of an officer of Rajarajadeva set up a copper image of the goddess Kala Pidari. Four different varieties of Pidari are mentioned, namely Punnaitturainangai, Poduvagaiurudaiyal, Kuduraivattamudaiyal and Tiruvaludaiyal. Ibid., No. 81, pp. 401–2.

29 of 1897 (Tamil) — On the base of the same enclosure. A record in the seventh year of the Chola king Ko Prakesarivarman or Rajendra Choladeva I (1011-43). Records an endowment in money in favour of the image of Srikanthamurtigal set up by Prithvimahadeviar, queen of Rajarajadeva. Ibid., Nos. 82 and 83, pp. 402–5.

30 of 1897 (Tamil) — On a pillar of the west enclosure of the same temple. A record in the twenty-ninth year of the Chola king Ko Rajakesarivarman or Rajarajadeva I. Records the setting up of seven copper images of the god Ganapati by king Rajarajadeva viz., two in the dancing posture, one big and the other small; three of varying heights comfortably seated; and two in the standing posture. Ibid., No. 84, pp. 405–7.

31 of 1897 (Tamil) — On another pillar of the same enclosure. A record in the third year of the Chola king Ko Parakesarivarman or Rajendra Choladeva I (1011-43). Records the gift of copper, zinc and bell metal vessels to the image of Ganapatiyar set up in the principal temple. The image was known as Alaiyattu-Pillaiyar. Ibid., No. 85, pp. 407–9.

32 of 1897 (Tamil) — On another pillar of the same enclosure. A record in the twenty-ninth year of the Chola king Ko Rajakesarivarman or Rajarajadeva I. Records gift to the

shrine of Ganapatiyar in the parivaralaya made by king
Rajaraja and by Adittan Suryan, of ornaments to the same
image. Ibid., No. 86, pp. 409–11.

33 of 1897 (Tamil) — On another pillar of the same
enclosure. A record in the twenty-ninth year of the Chola king
Ko Rajakesarivarman or Rajarajadeva I. Records gift of
ornaments made to the Ganapatiyar shrine in the principal
temple by a servant of king Rajarajadeva named Madhurantakan
Parantakan, a native of Marudur in Serrurkurram in Kshattriya
Sikhamanivalanadu. *S.I.I.*, Vol. II, No. 87, pp. 411–12.

34 of 1897 (Tamil) — On another pillar of the same
enclosure. A record in the twenty-ninth year of the Chola
king Ko Rajakesarivarman or Rajarajadeva I. Records the
gift of a bell-metal dish to the shrine of Ganapatiyar in the
enclosure hall by a servant of Rajarajadeva. Ibid., No. 88,
p. 412. The donor was a native of Kamadamangalam in
Purakkiliyurnadu and evidently employed in the
department for assessing tax on endowments (tinaikala-
nayakam).

35 of 1897 (Tamil) — On a niche of the same enclosure.
A record in the twenty-ninth year of the Chola king Ko
Rajakesarivarman or Rajarajadeva I. Records gift of
ornaments to the same image. Ibid., No. 89, pp. 412–13.

36 of 1897 (Tamil) — On the north wall of the mandapa
in front of the central shrine of the same temple. A record in
the twenty-ninth year of the Chola king Ko Rajakesarivarman
or Rajarajadeva I. Records gift of silver vessels. This is the
only inscription which records gift of silver and not gold
vessels. Ibid., No. 91, pp. 415–25.

37 of 1897 (Tamil) — On the south wall of the same
mandapa. A record in the twenty-ninth year of the Chola king
Ko Rajakesarivarman or Rajarajadeva. Records the
assignment to the Tanjore temple of certain villages in

Tondainadu Pandinadu, Gangapadi, Nulambapadi, Malainadu and Ilam (Ceylon). Ibid., No. 92, pp. 424–28.

38 of 1897 (Tamil) — On the same wall. A record in the twenty-ninth year of the Chola king Ko-Rajakesarivarman or Rajarajadeva I. Records the jewels and ornaments presented by the king out of the treasures seized from the Cheras and Pandyas and out his own treasures. Ibid., No. 93, pp. 428–36.

39 of 1897 (Tamil) — On the gopura in front of the Toppul Pillaiyar temple. A record of the Vijayanagara king Achyutadeva Maharaya in S. 1454, expired, Nandana. Records gift of land by Tattapa Nayaka, son of Konappa Nayaka.

40 of 1897 (Tamil) — On the west and south walls of the shrine of the Rajagopala Perumal temple. A record of the Vijayanagara king Achyutadeva Maharaya in S. 1461, expired, Vilambin. Records the foundation of the temple.

41 of 1897 (Grantha) — On the north wall of the same shrine. An incomplete genealogy of the Vijayanagara kings.

274 of 1911 (Tamil) — On a pillar of the kitchen in the Brihadisvara temple. The beginning and end of this inscription are lost. Gives the measurements of certain images made of alloy (called tara) and set with jewels. These were evidently meant to be placed in the temple.

275 of 1911 (Tamil) — On another pillar built into a wall of the same kitchen. A record of the Chola king Udaiyar Sri Rajarajadeva I. The face now exposed refers to one of the five bodied images (panchadehamurti) of copper, placed in the temple of Rajarajesvaramuedaiyar by the king, until his twenty-ninth year.

VALLAM

Vallam, a few miles to the west of the town, was the seat of government of the Naik kings, who were a branch of the Vijayanagara dynasty in the 16th century. The most famous

of these was Sevappa Naik with his famous prime minister
Govinda Dikshitar. A statue of this king with his queen still
exists in the temple of Srimushnam in the South Arcot district
showing that his territory extended to that distant place.

The fort at Vallam has almost disappeared now. There is
a tank called Varja Tirtham where a bath on the occasion of
Masimagha, in February-March is considered sacred. It was
these Naik kings that built the fort which surrounds the great
temple in Tanjore and which might have been intended to
ensure its safety.

TIRUVADI

Tiruvadi stands on the left bank of the Kaveri and is seven
miles to the north of the Tanjore Railway Station. The Puranic
version is that Tiruvadi is the chief of the *sapta sthalams* or
seven holy places and great sancity is attached to the place.

THE SEVEN HOLY WATERS

Tiruvadi, or Tiruvaiyaru in Tamil, represents the five sacred
rivers, viz., Suryapushkarani, Ganga, Amritha or
Chandrapushkarani, Palaru and Nandivainorai or Nandi.
These are said to have been created for Nandi's (Siva's bull)
abishekam or bath. All these are supposeod to have an
underground flow into the Kaveri on the west of
Pushyamandapam.

PURANIC VERSION

The Puranic version of the temple is that god
Panchanadisvara, who resided in the form of
Swayambulinga (self-created) at one time, ordered the
sage Neymesa to build a temple. When the sage was in
a perplexity regarding funds, the presiding God is said

to have told him that treasure and building materials lay below the ground close by and that he would find them under the footprints of His bull (Nandi). The oval-shaped pits now seen are said to relate to this incident. On completion of structures over the lingam, other additions are said to have been made by several devotees including the great Saiva saint Appar.[6]

A Brahman named Darmasethu of Godavari, who took the bones of his dead father to Rameswaram, is said to have seen them converted into flowers at this place, and on this account many people even today throw the bones of deceased relatives in Kaveri here!

TEMPLE BUILDINGS

The Panchanadisvara temple is the chief shrine. Sage Ghorathapasi prayed here to expiate himself from the sin of having thrown a stone into the vessel of a begger while he asked for alms. On this account Tiruvadi is also called Jappiyeswaram.

On entering the first courtyard of the temple by the eastern gopura or gate, there is on the south a shrine called Dakshina Kailas, and another on the north known as Uttara Kailas.

The original construction of both these buildings was carried out, according to Puranas, by Suratha Maharaja of the Lunar race, during his pilgrimage from Hastinapur. A few marble-cut pillars lend a beautiful appearance to the Dakshina Kailas. The Periyamandapam in the second courtyard is a subsequent addition, but the original Garbhagriham (central shrine) is said to date from the time of the sage Neymesa. The famous Govinda Dikshitar, prime ministeir of the Tanjore Naik kings and the great philanthropist Pachaiyappa Mudaliar, also carried out many improvements in the temple.

The third prakara has in the south three large oval footprints of a bull, with a Puranic version.

EPIGRAPHICAL IMPORTANCE

Inscriptions exist all over the temple buildings. The erection of this temple appears to date back to a very early period. The Vengi king Vimaladitya made gifts to this temple in 1013–14 A.D. The Uttara Kailas shrine was renovated by Lokmahadevi, the chief queen of king Rajaraja of Tanjore. Uttara Kailas, or 'the Northern Kailas' was founded by Dantisakti Vitanki, a queen of the great Rajaraja and was called Lokamahadevisvara after the queen's title Lokamahadevi which means 'the great queen of the world'. She gave to this shrine a number of gold flowers and appointed a gold-smith to work for the temple.The shrine of Dakshina Kailas, i.e. "the Southern Kailas", bears inscriptions recording a gift of gold ornaments by Rajendra Chola's queen.

SCULPTURES

There is a beautifully sculptured Brahma figure in the temple. The Kshetrapala God is locally known as Alkondar. People attach much importance to this deity, who appeared here in this form to overcome Yama, the God of Death, on behalf of a devotee.

INSCRIPTIONS[7]

The inscriptions recorded on the walls of this temple have been copied during the year 1908 by the Madras Epigraphical Department.

For an account of this most important stronghold of Saivitism, see Tanj. Gazr. Vol. I, pp. 276–9.

213 of 1894 (Tamil) — On the east wall of the Dakshinakailasa shrine in the Panchanadesvara temple. A record in the third year of the Chola king Ko Parakesarivarman or Rajendradeva (1050–63).

214 of 1894 (Tamil) — On the same wall. A record of the Chola king Parakesarivarman or Rajendra Chola (1011–1043).

215 of 1894 (Tamil) — On the east wall of the mandapa in front of the Uttarakailasa shrine in the same temple, right of entrance. A record in the twenty-ninth year of the Chola king Ko Rajakesarivarman or Rajarajadeva I.

216 of 1894 (Tamil) — In the same place, left of entrance. A record in the fourth year of the Chola king Ko Parakesarivarman or Rajendra Choladeva I.

217 of 1894 (Tamil) — On the south wall of the same shrine. A record in the twenty-second year of the Chola king Ko Rajaraja Rajakesarivarman or Rajarajadeva I. Records gift of a lamp.

218 of 1894 (Tamil) — On the same wall. A record in the twenty-first year of the Chola king Rajarajakesarivarman or Rajarajadeva I. Records gift of two lamps.

219 of 1894 (Tamil) — On the base of the same wall. A record in the twenty-first year of the Chola king Ko Rajakesarivarman or Rajarajadeva I.

220 of 1894 (Tamil) — On the west wall of the same shrine. A record in the third year of the Chola king Ko Parakesarivarman or Rajendra Choladeva I.

221 of 1894 (Tamil) — On the north wall of the same shrine. A record in the thirty-second year of the Chola king Ko Rajakesarivarman or Rajadhirajadeva I (1018–52).

222 of 1894 (Tamil) — On the base of the north, west and south walls of the same shrine. A record in the twenty-fourth year of the Chola king Ko Rajarajakesarivarman or Rajarajadeva I. Records gift of gold ornaments and vessels.

223 of 1894 (Tamil) — On the base of the south wall of the Panchanadesvara shrine in the same temple. A record in the twenty-first year of the Chola king Madirakionda Ko Parakesarivarman (905–47). Records gift of a lamp.

224 of 1894 (Tamil) — On the west wall of the same shrine. A record in the tenth year of the Chola king Ko Rajakesarivarman. Records gift of land.

225 of 1894 (Tamil) — On the base of the same wall. A record in the twenty-second year of the Chola king Kadiraikonda Ko Parakesarivarman (905–47). Records gift of a lamp by a queen.

226 of 1894 (Tamil) — In the same place. A record of the Chola king Maduraikonda Ko Parakesarivairman (905–47), the date of which is lost. Records gift of a lamp by queen Cholasikhamani.

227 of 1894 (Tamil) — On the north wall of the same shrine. A record in the sixteenth year of the Chola king Maduraikonda Ko Parakesarivarman (904–57). Records gift of a lamp.

228 of 1894 (Tamil) — On the same wall. A record of the Chola king Ko-Rajakesarivarman, the date of which is lost. Records gift of land for a lamp.

229 of 1894 (Tamil) — On the same wall. A record in the ninth year of the Chola king . . . sarivarman. Records gift of gold for a lamp.

230 of 1894 (Tamil) — On the same wall. A record in the ninth year of the Chola king Ko Rajakesarivarman. Records gift of a lamp.

231 of 1894 (Tamil) — On a stone built into the mandapa surrounding the same shrine. An incomplete record in the fourth year of the Chola king Ko Farakesarivarman. Records gift of land by a merchant of Tanjavur.

232 of 1894 (Tamil) — On another stone in the same place. A fragmentary record in the fortieth year of the Chola king Ko Parakesarivarman (905–47), "who took Madurai and Ceylon."

233 of 1894 (Tamil) — On the same stone. An incomplete record in the thirty-ninth year of the Chola king Ko-Parakesarivarman (905–47), "who took Madurai and Ceylon." Records gift of a lamp.

234 of 1894 (Tamil) — On the south wall of the mandapa in front of the same shrine. A record in the third year of the Chola king Ko Parakesarivarman. Records gift of land for three lamps.

235 of 1894 (Tamil) — On the same wall. A record in the seventeenth year of the Chola king Ko Rajakesarivarman. Records gift of land for two lamps.

236 of 1894 (Tamil) — On the same wall. A record in the twenty-first year of the Chola king Ko Rajakesarivarman. Records gift of land for a lamp.

237 of 1894 (Tamil) — On the same wall. A record in the twenty-sixth year of the Chola king Ko Rajakesarivarman. Records gift of a lamp by an inhabitant of Tanjavur.

238 of 1894 (Tamil) — On the same wall. A record in the nineteenth year of the Chola king Ko Rajakesarivarman. Records gift of a lamp by a queen.

239 of 1894 (Tamil) — On the same wall. A record in the nineteenth year of the Chola king Ko Rajakesarivarman. Records gift of a lamp by a queen.

240 of 1894 (Tamil) — On the same wall. A record of the Chola king Ko Parakesarivarman "who cut off the head of Vira Pandya." Records gift of a lamp. The king was evidently Parantaka II, Sundara Chola, the son of Arinjaya and father of Aditya II Karikala.

241 of 1894 (Tamil) — On the same wall. An incomplete

record in the thirty-first year of the Chola king
Maduraikonda Ko-Parakesarivarman (905–47).

242 of 1894 (Tamil) — On the same wall. A record in the
fourteenth year of the Chola king Ko Maduraikonda
Parakesarivarman (905–47). Records gift of gold for a lamp
by a queen.

243 of 1894 (Tamil) — On the same wall. A record in the
twenty-fifth year of the Chola king Ko Rajakesarivarman.
Records gift of gold for a lamp.

244 of 1894 (Tamil) — On the same wall. A record in the
seventeenth year of the Chola king Ko Rajakesarivarman.
Records gift of gold for a lamp, by a dancing girl of the king.

245 of 1894 (Tamil) — On the same wall. A record of the
Chola king Ko Rajakesarivarman, the date of which is
doubtful. Records gift of land for a lamp.

246 of 1894 (Tamil) — On the same wall. A record in the
second year of the Chola king Ko Parakesarivarman.
Records gift of a lamp.

247 of 1894 (Tamil) — On the same wall. A record in
the twenty-fifth year of the Chola king Ko
Rajakesarivarman. Records gift of gold for a lamp by a
merchant.

248 of 1894 (Tamil) — On the same wall. A record in the
thirty first year of the Chola king Maduraikonda Ko
Parakesarivarman (905–47). Records gift of a silver lamp and
of land by a queen.

249 of 1894 (Tamil) — On the same wall. A record in the
sixteenth year of the Chola king Ko Rajakesarivarman.
Records gift of land for lamp.

250 of 1894 (Tamil) — On the same wall. A record in the
twelfth year of the Chola king Ko Rajakesarivarman. Records
gift of lamp by a queen.

251 of 1894 (Tamil) — On the same wall. A record in the

twentieth year of the Chola king Ko Rajakesarivarman. Records gift of land for a lamp by the nurse of Kannaradeva (Krishna III of the Rashtrakuta dynasty?).

252 of 1894 (Tamil) — On the same wall. A record of the Chola king Ko Parakesarivarman, the date of which is indistinct. Records gift of lamp.

253 of 1894 (Tamil) — On the east wall of the second prakara, left of entrance. A record of Vira Savana Udaiyar, son of "Vira Mukkana Udaiyar" (Bukkana Udaiyar or Bukka II), dated S. 1303 (expired), Durmati. See Ins., S. Dts., P. 267, No. 209. The latter says that 19 velis of land were granted for the Pushya festival.

254 of 1894 (Tamil) — On the south wall of the third prakara. A record of the second year of Ko Jatavarman Sundara Pandya I, making a gift of land. The exact date was Thursday, 27th March, A.D. 1253. See *Ep. Ind.*, Vol. VI, p. 306.

255 of 1894 (Tamil) — On the west wall of the same prakara. A record of Devaraya II (1422–49) of Vijayanagar, dated S. 1351 (expired), Saumya.

256 of 1894 (Tamil) — On a stone north of the Uttara Kailas shrine. A record of Sadasiva Raya, dated in S. 1480 (expired), Siddhartin. Ins., S. Dts., p. 267, No. 208.

135 of 1918 (Tamil) — On the south wall of the central shrine in the Panchanadesvara temple. Gift of 25 kalanjus of gold for half a lamp to the temple of Tiruvaiyarrupara-mamahadeva. The gold was deposited with the merchants (nagarattar) of Sivapuri.

136 of 1918 (Tamil) — On the same wall. Gift of gold for lamp.

137 of 1918 (Tamil) — On the same wall. Gift of 96 sheep for a lamp by Nakka Namban of Irungandapuram on the southern bank of Pennai in Vanagappadi.

138 of 1918 (Tamil) — On the west wall of the same

shrine. Seems to record a gift of land to the temple.

139 of 1918 (Tamil) — On the north wall of the same shrine. Gift of gold for a lamp. Mentions Malainattuchchaliya.

140 of 1918 (Tamil) — On the south base of the verandah of the second prakara of the same temple. Seems to register that the dancing girls were to enjoy the lands given to them for service in the temple of Tiruvaiyarru Udaiyar in Polgainadu, a sub-division of Rajarajavalanadu, of which they had been dispossessed.

141 of 1918 (Tamil) — On the same base. Records a transaction similar to that in 140 above.

142 of 1918 (Tamil) — On the west base of the same prakara, seems to refer to Carpenter's rights and privileges in the temple of Tiruvaiyarru Udaiyar, Aludaiyar, Nachiyar, Ulagamadevi Isvaramudaiyar and Tribhuvanamadevi Isvaramudaiyar.

143 of 1918 (Tamil) — On the stone built into the east wall of the Sokkottanmandapa in front of the same shrine. Seems to record a gift of land.

144 of 1918 (Tamil) — On another stone in the same place. Seems to register a gift of land for feeding a Brahman with sumptuous meal daily in the temple by queen Arinjigai, daughter of Iladarayar.

145 of 1918 (Tamil) — On the north wall of the third prakara of the same temple. Appears to make provision for conducting the tiruppallieluchchi (rising from bed) service.

146 of 1918 (Tamil) — On the same wall. Gift of the Brahman village Gyanasamudrachaturvedimangalam in Vikramacholavalanadu to the Brahmans of the temple for various services and to a number of temples.

147 of 1918 (Tamil) — On a stone built into the western gopura of the same temple. Gift of a chauri by Panchavanmadeviyar, queen of Mummudi Chola.

148 of 1918 (Tamil) — On the east base of the Dakshina Kailas shrine in the same temple. Records in detail the various ornaments given to the temple.

149 of 1918 (Tamil verse) — Records that Vanavan Marayan of Vevasal set up the images of Panchanadivanan and Anjalai Umaiya in Ayyaru.

150 of 1918 (Tamil) — Gift of 20 kasus for a lamp by Ammangai Nachiyar or Puvanamulududaiyal of Vadasathamangalam to the temple of Tenkailayamudaiyar at Tiruvaiyar in Poingainadu, a sub-division of Tirupuvanamulududai-valanadu.

151 of 1918 (Tamil) — Gift of 20 kasus for a lamp in the same temple.

152 of 1918 (Tamil) — On the south base of the Uttara Kailas shrine in the same temple. Gift of 7 bronze lamp-stands to the temple of Ulagamahadevi Isvaramudaiyar Manadeva by Dandisaktivitankiyar or Ulagamahadeviyar, queen of Rajarajadeva.

153 of 1918 (Tamil) — On the same base. Built in at the bottom.

154 of 1918 (Tamil) — Gift of gold ornaments set with jewels to the same temple by the same queen as mentioned in 152 above.

155 of 1918 (Tamil) — Records the gift of various ornaments, one of which is said to have been presented in the 25th year of Rajarajadeva.

156 of 1918 (Tamil) — On the north, west and south wall of the same shrine. Gift of land to the stone temple of Ulagamahadeviyar Isvaramudaiyar built by Dantisakti-vitankiyar or Ulagamahadeviyar, queen of Rajarajadeva at Tiruvaiyarru.

157 of 1918 (Tamil) — On the west base of the Darmambika shrine in the same temple. Gift of 10 velis

of land in addition to the existing devadana which was found insufficient for conducting worship and offerings to the goddess Ulagudaiya Nachiyar of the Tirkkamakkottam in Tiruvaiyarru. Mentions Anapayanallur.

NOTES

1. Rakshasas or Demons are always dangerous to the Devas or celestials and to men on earth. To destroy them God incarnates in one form or another.

2. A famous Saivite prime minister of the Tanjore Naik kings, over whom he wielded his influence, and obtained immense wealth for repairing Saiva temples. A statue of him and his wife are found in the temple at Pattisvaram near Kumbakonam.

3. For detailed information reference may be made to *South Indian Inscriptions*, Vol. II, part 5.

4. Vide Vol. III, Part III, pp. 383 to 439.

5. *Inscriptions of the Madras Presidency*, Government of Madras, 1919, Vol. II, pp. 1400 to 1412.

6. Appar was born in Amur village of a Vellala family with the name Marulnikkiyar. Through study he began to acquire knowledge. While in Pataliputra (Patna) he became a convert to Jainism, assuming the name Darmasenar. When suffering from a bad stomachache he could not get relief from the medical men of the Jain faith and on the advice of his sister in Tiruvadi near Panruti in South Arcot District, he reverted to his original Hindu faith and visited several temples, repairing most of them. His images are, on this account, represented with a spade.

7. *Inscriptions of the Madras Presidency*, Government of Madras, 1919, Vol. II, pp. 1425 to 1428.

Chapter 17

TRICHINOPOLY

Trichinopoly or "Dakshina Kailas," on the Madras Danushkodi line of the South Indian Railway, which is believed to form a part of Mount Kailas, derives its name from Tirisirasu, a three-headed demon who worshipped the God here and obtained all his boons. This rock, situated in the centre of the town, is conspicuous all over the town, especially when viewed from the sacred river Kaveri which flows through the town. Besides having been the capital of the Cholas who had their palace at Uraiyur close by, the Nayak kings of Madura also removed the capital from Madura to this place erecting a palace near the rock.

PURANIC VERSION

Once upon a time a lady of a pious family was coming the mother of from a distant village to meet her daughter who was in labour. She was prevented from performing the journey owing to heavy floods in the river Kaveri at that time. To avoid disappointment and uneasiness to the daughter, the God transformed himself into the mother and acted as a midwife! Later on, when the true mother came, the Divinity disappeared! This aspect Siva is known as Tayumanavar (*Tay* in Tamil means 'mother').

Hanuman, the favourite disciple of Sri Rama, is said to have visited this place; and there is a mark in the temple signifying this event.

SAINT TAYUMANAVAR

Tayumanavar was also the name of a son of a minister of the Vijayanagar dynasty who ruled over this place. The boy then became one of the greatest Saiva saints of southern India.

TEMPLES ON THE ROCK

The image in the central shrine on the hill faces the western direction while the minor deities face the eastern direction, as is generally the case everywhere. The reason put forward is that Parantaka, a haughty king of the Chola dynasty, in the suburb of Uraiyur, robbed the god Tayumanavar of flowers intended for his worship and utilised them for the worship of the deity at Uraiyur. This annoyed Tayumanavar, and in token of his anger he destroyed Uraiyur and the deity there.

The Vinayaka in the hill shrine, known as Uchchi Pillayar, has a depression on the forehead. The belief connected with this image is that on his return to Ayodhya (Oudh), Sri Rama presented Vibhishana (the brother of Ravana) with an image of Vishnu, strictly enjoining him not to place it on the ground. While Vibhishana was carrying the image to the south, he found Vinayaka in the disguise of a Brahman youth standing near the modern site of the Sirarangam temple. Vibhishana, who had to ease himself, entrusted the image temporarily with the youth, telling him not to place it on the ground. But the boy inadvertently placed it on the ground. On his return Vibhishana found that the image had been installed at Srirangam and could not be removed. This is the origin of the god Ranganada of Srirangam. Vibhishana, in his fit of anger, chased the boy to the summit of the Trichinopoly rock, but he found the boy was none other than Vinayaka. Vibhishana, who was still more enraged at this sight, struck Vinayaka on the forehead, and when his temper cooled down begged the deity for forgiveness. This incident accounts for the depression referred to previously.

EPIGRAPHICAL IMPORTANCE

[1]"The oldest monument of this place seems to be a rock-cut cave not far from the top of the famous rock. The whole of the back wall of the cave is occupied by a much defaced inscription in old Tamil, in which I have hitherto failed to discover a king's name or date. On the left side there are two pillars with somewhat worn inscriptions. Each of the two pillars contains four Sanskrit verses which record that a king Ganabhara, who bore the birudas Purushottama, Satrumalla and Satyasamada, built a temple of Siva on the top of the mountain and placed in it a linga and a statue of himself. Both inscriptions mention the river kaveri i.e., the Kaveri on whose banks Trichinopoly is situated, and refer to the Chola country. On the left pillar the Kaveri is called "the beloved of the Pallavas"; this means in prose that a Pallava king ruled at that time over the banks of the Kaveri river. This allusion and the fact that the characters of the two pillar inscriptions remind of those of the Pallava inscriptions at Mamallapuram and Kanchipuram, make it very probably that Gunabhara was a Pallava prince who ruled over the Chola country."

INSCRIPTIONS[2]

The inscriptions here have been copied by the Madras Epigraphical Department during the years 1888, 1890, 1904 & 1905.

411 of 1904 (Pallava, Grantha and Tamil) — On the outer row of pillars in the upper rock-cut cave. A partly damaged record. The inscription contains a number of birudas in Sanskrit, a few in Tamil and the rest apparently in Telugu. This inscription seems to have been continued on the pillar forming part of the outer wall of the central shrine to its left, but a few letters only of the first line can now be seen on it. See *Ep. Ind.*, Vol. I, pp. 58-60, where Dr. Hultzsch edits the two inscriptions on the pillar, and also *S.I.I.*, Vol. I, Nos. 33 and 35, pp. 28-30.

412 of 1904 (Tamil) — On the third pillar of the same row. A partly damaged record of the Chola king Rajarajakesarivarman (985-1013) dated in his sixteenth year. Records sale of waste land for five Kalanjus to a person to be reclaimed for cultivation, so as to feed Brahmans and devotees in the nine-day Chitrai festival. The shrine is called Tiruchchirappali at Sirrambur in Uraiyur Kurram.

413 of 1904 (Tamil) — On the last pillar of the same row. A much damaged record of the Pandya king Maranjadaiyan, dated in his fourth year. Mentions the Pandyadhipati Varaguna and the temple of Tirumalaipperumanadigal (the king was the same as the invader of Idavi and Vembil, the enemy of Aparajita and Western Ganga Prithvipati I in the battle of Tiruppirambiyam, who ascended the throne in A.D. 862. See *Ep. Ind.*, Vol. IX, p. 84 ff. Also Ambasamudram and Tillaisthanam inscriptions.)

414 of 1904 (Grantha and Tamil) — On the east wall, right of entrance into the same cave. A record of the Pandya king Maranjadaiyan, dated in his fourth year. Records gift of gold by the king who is called the Pandyadhiraja Varagunadeva in the grant portion. (See note to the above.)

134 of 1904 (Tamil) — On a rock in Matribhuteswara temple. A damaged record of the Vijayanagara king

Venkatadeva Maharaya, dated S. 1539, expired, Pingala. Records a gift for the merit of Virappa Nayaka. [The Government Epigraphist surmises that Venkatadeva was Venkatapati I (1586-1616.) Virappa was evidently the Madura Naik who ruled from A.D. 1609 to 1623. For the relations between himand Venkata I, see *Ind. Antq.*, 1916, pp. 133-34].

62 of 1888 (Tamil) — On the back wall of a rock-cut cave near the top of the Trichinopoly rock.

63 and 64 of 1888 — On the pillars on the left side of the same cave. "Each of the two pillars contains four Sanskrit verses which record that a king Gunabhara who bore the birudas Purtushotthama, Satrumalla and Satyasandha, built a temple of Sive on the top of the mountain and placed in it a linga and a statue of himself." The river Kaveri is called "the beloved of the Pallava." This together with the palaeographical similarity of this epigraph with the Pallava inscriptions of Mamallapuram and Conjeevaram, made Dr. Hultzsch recognise in Gunabhara, a Pallava king who ruled over the Chola country; and the later researches of Venkayya and others have decided that Gunabhara was the famous Mahendravarman I.

C.P. No. 41 of Mr. Sewell's list — Records grant in S. 1714 (A.D. 1792) Kaliyuga 4893, Paridhavi, by "Sri Muttu Virappa Nayakkan, grandson of Sinna Lakka Nayakkan and son of Chokkanatha Lakkaya Nayakkan," conferring certain lands and an annuity on a Mussalman priest.

C.P. No. 42 on Mr. Sewell's list (Tamil) — Records an agreement by four private people, bearing the surname "Nayakkan," to conduct the religious ceremonies of their village temple in S. 1602 (A.D. 1680), Raudri.

C.P. No. 43 of Mr. Sewell's list (Tamil) — Records grant of lands to a Mussalman priest for the maintenance of a Pallivasal or place of worship, by Kamakshi Nayakkan, in S.

South Indian Shrines

1661 (A.D. 1739), Prabhava, Kaliyuga, 4841. The grant states that Rama Raya was then ruling over the world.

C.P. No. 44 of Mr. Sewell's list (Tamil) — Records grant by the Madura Nayakkan, Vijaya Ranga Chokkanatha, here called "Vijaya Chokka Ranganatha Nayakkan"—mentioning his father Muttu Virappa and grandfather Chokkanatha to a Pandaram (Sudra priest), for worship at a Durga Kali temple at the south gate of the Trichnopoly Fort, in S. 1649 (A.D. 1727), Kaliyuga 4828, Prabhava. The grant states that Venkata Vema Maha Raya was then reigning at Kannakama. For a detailed account of Vijaya Ranga's reign see *Ind. Antq.*, 1917, p. 186 ff. Nothing is known about Venkata Vema of Kannakama.

C.P. No. 47 of Mr. Sewell's list (Telugu) — Records grant of land to a Brahman in S. 1613 (A.D. 1691), Kaliyuga 4792, Prajotpatti, by Mangammal, widow of Chokkanatha of the Madura Nayakkan dynasty. See *Ind. Antq.*, 1917, p. 156 for a detailed account of Mangammal's administration.

C.P. No. 49 of Mr. Sewell's list (Telugu) — Records grant of land for a charitable object, at the gate of Trichinopoly Fort, in S. 1654 (A.D. 1732), Kaliyuga 4833, Pramadicha, by Minakshi, widow of Vijaya Ranga Chokkanatha, the son of Ranga Krishna Muttu Virappa and grandson of Chokkanatha. For Minakshi's reign and the downfall of the Madura Naik dynasty, see *Ind. Antq.*, 1917 (October-November).

C.P. No. 1 of 1908 — A forged plate, dated in S. 1098, K. 4421, Sarvadhari (wrong), referring to the defalcation of Rs 4 lakhs by two Acharis and its recoupment by the community, to which they belonged.

C.P. No. 2 of 1911–12 (Tamil) — A record dated in S. 1272, Bhava (which is inconsistent) recording the gift of two bullocks to the temple of Subrahmany at Ayipalayam by an agent of Nallappa Kalatka Tolar named Muttu Vaidyanatha Pillai who made them tax-free wherever they were taken, carrying loads. Records also the gift of a cow for a lamp to the same temple by a certain Vaduganatha Pillai.

C.P. No.3 of 1911–12 (Tamil) — Dated in S. 1600, K. 4779, Kalayukti. Records gift of the village of Amutarangota to the temples of Krishnesvara and Arunachalesvara at Sritalavanam or Tiruppanandal by Kachchikalyana Rangappa Kalaka Tola Udaiyar, in the Palayasima between the Uttara Kaveri and Svetanadhi.

C.P. No. 4 of 1911-12 (Telugu) — Dated in S. 1706, K. 4885, Krodhin. Records gift of land in the village of Sendora to the temple of Sabhanayaka at Chidambaram by Muduvijaya Rangappa Kalaka Tola Udaiyar, son of Nallappa Kalaka Tola Udaiyar.

C.P. No. 1 of 190-11 — This plate is dated S. 1643, Subhakrit (wrong by two years), in the time of Vijaya Ranga Chokkanatha Naik of Madura (1704-31). It is in Telugu and records a gift of rent-free land to a certain Narasa Pantulu. Mr. Krishna Sastri surmises that he was a doctor, as he was to offer prayers to Dhanvantri. (*Mad. Ep. Rep.*, 1911, p.90). For Vijaya Ranga's reign see *Ind. Antq.*, 1917, p.186 ff.

C.P. No. 2 of 1910-11 — It is a grant by a Raja Viajaya Raghunatha Tondaman, son of Tirumalayappa Raya Tondaman and grandson of Tirumalairaya Tondaman in S. 1727, K. 4906, Krodhana (A.D. 1805). It records the gift of the village of Orandikodkkodi to a certain Irasappa Mudaliyar of Devanampattanam, for maintaining a feeding house at Trichinopoly (Vijaya Raghunatha was evidently the Pudukottai chief who ruled from 1719 to 1807).

A C.P. in the hands of a resident of Trichinopoly named Chaik Hussain, records grant of lands to a mosque in S. 1655 (A.D. 1733) by Queen Minakshi to the Naik dynasty. See *Ind. Antq.*, Vol. I, p.268. See No. 784 above.

URAIYUR

The ruined temple of Uraiyur, also known as Tirumukkisvaram in Vilvaranyams is at a short distance from Trichinopoly. The deity in the temple is knwon as Panchavarneswara, and he is so called because he appeared in five colours to Brahman (pancha means five). Nagaraja, the head of the serpents, who was carrying 5 lingas from Patalloka (nether region) to install them in various places found that all of them joined the central Linga here and became united into one! The image is also said to have been worshipped by a serpent, a Garuda (kite), the sage Kadhiru and also by the wife of the sage Kasyappa.

INSCRIPTIONS[3]

This is the well-known ancient Chola capital referred to by Ptolemy. See Antiquities, Vol. I, p. 269.

181 of 1907 (Tamil) — On the south wall of the central shrine in the Panchavarnesvara temple. A fragmentary record, dated eleventh year of some king.

182 of 1907 (Tamil) — On the same wall. A damaged record of the Chola king Rajakesarivarman, dated in his third year. Mentions Kirtimarttanda Brahmadhirajan.

183 of 1907 (Tamil) — On the same wall. A damaged record of the Chola king Parakesarivarman, dated in his sixteenth year. Seems to provide for the daily requirements of the temple of Tiruvudaitalai Perumal at Uraiyur.

184 of 1907 (Tamil) — On the same wall. A record of the Chola king Rajakesarivarman, dated in his second year. Built in at the end.

185 of 1907 (Tamil) — On the west wall of the same shrine. A record, dated in the fourth year (of?), relating to the village of Atigunakarpaganallur. A few words of the

historical introduction of the Chola king Rajendradeva can be traced at the beginning of the inscription. See No. 188.

186 of 1907 (Tamil) — On the north wall of the same shrine. A record of the Chola king Parakesarivarman or Udaiyar Sri Rajarajadeva, dated in his seventh year, mentioning Rajasrayachaturvedimangalam in Uraiyur-kurram, a sub-division of Keralanatakavalanadu. The temple is called Udaiyar Tirundaitalai-Mahadeva at Tiru Uraiyur.

187 of 1907 (Tamil) — On the same wall. A record of Tribhuvanachakravartin Konerinmaikondan, dated in his thirty-second year, registering a gift of land to the temple of Vendan Mukkisvaramudaiyar at Uraiyur in Rajagambhiravalanadu. Mentions Atigunakalpaganallur.

188 of 1907 (Tamil) — On the south wall of the central shrine in the Panchavarnesvara temple. A damaged record of the Chola king Parakesarivarman or Udaiyar Sri Rajendradeva (1050-63), the date of which is doubtful.

51 of 1890 — On a rock, called Cholamparai, close to Uraiyur near Trichinopoly. A record of Tribhuvanachakravartin Tribhuvanavira Vikramadeva.

JAMBUKESWARAM

This small but famous place, more popularly known as Tiruvanaikkaval or Tiruvanaikka i.e., the sacred elephant grove, is two miles away to the north of Trichinopoly. The deity is known as Appu linga or the water linga, and it is so called because the image in the Garbhagriha (sanctum) is always in water, a phenomenon quite curious and inexplicable! It is stated that an arrangement has been made so that even if the water around the linga is pumped out, it is soon again surrounded by water! The place derives its name from the fact that at one time there was an extensive plantation of Jambu trees (Eugenia jambolara.)

PURANIC VERSION

There is a tradition to the effect that, in ancient days, the elephant living in the neighbouring forest was in the habit of worshipping the local God and would offer a profuse shower of water through its trunk. A spider is also said to have worshipped the deity and to prevent the fall of leaves from trees, it constructed a canopy over the linga with its web; and when the elephant saw this he tore it down, for he thought that the existence of cobwebs over the deity was an act of sacrilege. After this they became violent opponents, and one day the spider found its way into the trunk of the elephant and bit him badly. The elephant then dashed his trunk on the ground as a result of which both died. The God admiring their devotion to him, is said to have given them salvation. The dead spider was in consequence born as king Kochchengan.[4]

It is said that one of the Chola kings, who had his capital at Uraiyur close by, lost his pearl necklace while bathing in the Kaveri one day, and that he was much grieved at the loss of the jewel. In order to please his bhakta (devotee) the God caused the jewel to be found in a pot of water intended for the bath of the linga, and the king saw it falling from the pot and adorn the deity!

TEMPLE BUILDINGS

The temple measuring 2400' by 1500' has five prakaras (courtyards) and the outermost is called Tiruneethi prakara. It is so called because the God in the form of a mason supervised the construction of the temple and contributed a packet of holy ashes towards the wages of the workmen and when the packets were opened they are said to have contained their daily wages (Tiruneeru means holy-ash)! Inside this court, there is a finely carved hall with thousand pillars called Ayirakkal mandapa.

The mandapa (hall) in front of the goddess Akilandesvari contains many carvings depicting the scene of the elephant's worship. In commemoration of the goddess' worship to God, it was ruled that the priests of the temple were to appear in the garb of a lady and offer the midday puja! This continues even today. There is also a fine sculpture of an Ekapada Tirumurti$_5$ (the Trinity on one leg) in a pillar. Siva stands in the middle with Brahma and Vishnu to the right and left respectively with their vahanams—Bulls, Swan and Garuda (Kite). It is said that, at one time, the deity was so powerful that devotees who were not pure in mind and body met with some kind of mishap and that to mitigate the fury of the deity, Sri Sankaracharya placed a *tatanka* or *todu* (ear-ring) with a discus (chakra) in her ears. An image of Vinayaka (elephant god and son of the deity) was also installed in front of the deity.

Rajarajeswara temple is another small shrine in the neighbourhood and in one of the cells there is a fine linga with the sculptural carving of Panchamuka or the five faces of Siva, viz., Satyojata, Vamadeva, Tatpurusha, Agora and Isana, and the last face occupies a higher place than the first four.

INSCRIPTIONS[6]

The inscriptions recorded on the walls of the temple have been copied by the Madras Epigraphical Department during the years 1891, 1903, 1905, 1908 & 1910.

See Mr. Sewell's Antiquities, Vol. I, p.267, Fergusson's *Ind. and East Arch.*, p.365; Moore's *Trichinopoly Manual*, pp.341-2 and *Trichinopoly Gazr.*, pp.321-3, for the religious and architectural importance of the place.

61 of 1903 (Tamil) — On the east wall of the third prakara of the Jambukesvara temple. A record in the twentieth year

of the the Chola king Tribhuvanachakravartin Rajarajadeva (III?). Records sale of land.

62 of 1903 (Tamil) — On the same wall. A record in the twenty-ninth year of the Chola king Tribhuvanachakravartin Rajarajadeva IIII. Recorods gifit of land. The date corresponded to Monday, 6th February, A.D. 1245. See *Ep. Ind.*, Vol. IX, p.216.

63 of 1903 (Tamil) — On the same wall. A record in the twenty-sixth year of the Chola king Tribhuvanachakravartin Rajarajadeva (III?). Records sale of land.

64 of 1903 (Tamil) — On the north wall of the same prakara. A record in the twenty-sixth year of the Chola king Tribhuvanachakravartin Rajarajadeva (III?). Records sale of land.

65 of 1903 (Tamil) — On the same wall. A record in the twenty-second year of the Chola king Tribhuvanachakravartin Rajarajadeva. Records sale of land.

66 of 1903 (Tamil) — On the north wall of the Akhilandanayaki shrine in the same temple. Records in S. 1500, Bahudhanya, gift of land.

67 of 1903 (Tamil) — On the south wall of the same shrine. A record of the Saluva king Tirumalairaja, son of Gopparaja in S. 137 . . . Srimukha. Records gift of an ornament. (Poet Kalamegha visited the court of this king and had his famous controversy with Atimadhura and others. Kalamegha's date is thus determined.)

499 of 1905 (Tamil) — On the east wall of the third prakara in the Jambukesvara temple. Records in the twentieth year of the Chola king Tribhuvanachakravartin Rajarajadeva, sale of land.

500 of 1905 (Tamil) — On the same wall. Records in the twenty-ninth year of the Chola king Tribhuvanachakravartin Rajarajadeva III, gift of land. See *Ep. Ind.*, Vol. IX, p.216,

where it is shown that the date corresponded to Monday, 6th February, A.D. 1245.

501 of 1905 (Tamil) — On the same wall. Records in the twenty-sixth year of the Chola king Tribhuvanachakravartin Rajarajadeva III, sale of dry land. Ibid., Vol. IX, p.215, where it is shown that the date corresponded to Tuesday, 4th October, A.D. 1244.

502 of 1905 (Tamil) — On the same wall. A record of the Chola king Tribhuvanachakravartin Rajarajadeva. Records in his twenty-sixth year, sale of dry land. See Ibid., where it is shown from the details of the date that it is the same as that of the previous epigraph.

503 of 1905 (Tamil) — On the same wall. A damaged record of the Chola king Tribhuvanachakravartin Rajarajadeva, the date of which is lost. Appears to record a sale of land.

504 of 1905 (Tamil) — On the same wall. A damaged record of the Chola king Tribhuvanachakravartin Rajarajadeva, the date of which is lost. Appears to record a sale of land.

505 of 1905 (Tamil) — On the same wall. A record of the Chola king Tribhuvanachakravartin Rajarajadeva. Mentions sale of land. The date of the record is lost.

506 of 1905 (Tamil) — On the same wall. Records in the twenty-ninth year of the Chola king Tribhuvanachakravartin Rajarajadeva, sale of dry land.

507 of 1905 (Tamil) — On the west wall of the kitchen in the same temple. A record of the Chold king Tribhuvanachakravartin Rajarajadeva in his twentieth year; mentions sale of land.

508 of 1905 (Tamil) — On the same wall. A record of the Chola king Tribhuvanachakravartin Rajarajadeva in his twenty-fourth year; sale of land. See *Ep. Ind.*, Vol. IX, p.215.

18 of 1891 (Tamil) — North wall of the third prakara of

the Jambukesvara temple. Records of the Hoysala king Vira Somesvaradeva, dated in his second year. Mentions the image of Poysalelsvara set up by him at Kannanur or Vikramapura, and four images named after his grandfather (Ballala II), grandmother (Padmala), father (Narasimha II) and his queen (Somala) at Jambukesvaram.

19 of 1891 (Tamil) — On the north wall of the third prakara of the same temple. A record of the Hoysala king Vira Somesvaradeva.

20 of 1891 (Tamil) — On the north wall of the third prakara of the same temple. A record of the Hoysala king Vira Somesvaradeva, dated in his twenty-seventh year.

21 of 1891 (Tamil) — On the north wall of the third prakara of the same temple. A record of the Hoysala king Vira Ramanathadeva, dated in his fourth year.

22 of 1891 (Tamil) — On the north wall of the third prakara of the same temple. A record of the Hoysala queen Somaladevi, dated in the twenty-fifth year of Vira Somesvaradeva.

23 of 1891 (Tamil) — On the north wall of the third prakara of the same temple. A record of the Chola king Ko Rajakesarivarman or Rajarajadeva III, dated in his sixteenth year. See *Ep. Ind.*, Vol. VI, pp.281-2.

24 of 1891 (Sanskrit) — On the west wall of the third prakara of the Jambukesvara temple. A fragmentary record of the Pandya king Ko Jatavarman or Sundara Pandyadeva; as far as the text goes, it agrees with No. 32 of 1891.

25 of 1891 (Tamil) — On the west wall of the second prakara of the Jambukesvara temple. A record of the Pandya king Ko Maravarman or Kulasekharadeva, dated in his tenth year. See *Ep. Ind.*, Vol. VI, p.309, where it is pointed out that the date is Wedensday, 5th January, A.D. 1278. The inscription refers to a street called after the God who

transformed a spider into a Chola king, a distinct allusion to the local story given in the Periyapurana!

26 of 1891 (Tamil) — On the west wall of the second prakara of the same temple. A record of the Hoysala king Vira Ramanathadeva, dated in his seventh year. Mentions his queen Kamaladevi, the daughter of a certain Ariya Pillai.

27 of 1891 (Tamil) — On the west wall of the second prakara of the same temple. A record of the Saubhana queen Jakhadevi, queen of Rahutta Jajaladeva, son of Bhimadeva.

28 of 1891 (Tamil) — On the west wall of the second prakara of the same temple. A record of the Hoysala king Vira Somesvaradeva, dated in h is twenty-first year. Mentions the same queen as in the above inscription.

29 of 1891 (Telugu) — On the west wall of the second prakara of the same temple. A record of the Kakatiya king Pratapa Rudradeva. *Ind. Antq.*, Vol. XXI, p.200.

30 of 1891 (Tamil) — On the north wall of the second prakara of the same temple. Records grant of one veli by the Chola king Valakamayar or Akkalarajar, dated S. 1403 (expired), Plava, to the God of Tiruvanaikka. See *Ep. Ind.*, Vol. III, pp.72-3, where the inscription is edited. (The date, according to Dikshit, corresponded to Sunday, 3rd February, 1482.)

31 of 1891 — On the east wall of the second prakara. A record of the forty-seventh year of Rajakesarivairman Kulottunga Chola I. A certain Villavarayan makes a bull vehicle and endows land purchased by him. See *S.I.I.*, Vol. III, No. 76, pp.168-72.

32 of 1891 (Tamil) — On the south wall of the second prakara. A record of the tenth year of Jatavarman Sundara Pandya I (1251-64). See *Ind. Antq.*, Vol. XXI, p.121; Ibid., Vol. XXII, p.221 and *Ep. Ind.*, Vol. VI, p.307, where Dr. Kielhorn points out that the date corresponded to Wednesday,

28th April, 1260. See also *Ep. Rep.*, 1892, p.8, paragraph 8.

480 of 1908 (Tamil) — On the west gopura of the Jambukesvara temple, right of entrance. A damaged record of the Chola king Tribhuvanachakravartin Kulottunga Choladeva III, "who was pleased to take Madura and the crowned head of the Pandya", dated in his nineteenth year. Seems to register a political compact between Siyan Udaiyapillai or Pillai Akalanka Nadalvan and Tondon Seman or Rajarajamuvarayan.

481 of 1908 (Tamil verse) — On the west gopura of the same temple, right of entrance. Records the gift of the Chola country by Sundara Pandya to the Bana king. See *Ind. Antq.*, Vol. XXI, p.122.

482 of 1908 (Tamil and Grantha) — On the west gopura of the same temple, right of entrance. A verse in the Vamsatha metre in praise of the Bana king, evidently called Viramagadan as indicated by the single. Tamil line at the top. Another damaged inscription of two verses refers to the same Bana king.

483 of 1908 (Tamil) — In the same gopura, left of entrance. A damaged record of the Chola king Tribhuvanachakravartin Kulottunga Choladeva, dated in his eighteenth year. Renewal of a political compact between Rajarajadeva Ponparappinan Vanakovaraiyan and Siyan Udaiyapillai or Akalanka Nadalvan.

484 of 1908 (Tamil) — In the same place. A damaged record of the Chola king Tribhuvanachakravartin Rajendracholadeva, dated in his sixth year. Records gift of land for a flower garden.

485 of 1908 (Tamil) — On the walls of the Ganesa shrine in the same temple. A fragmentary record of the Hoysala king Vira Ramanathadeva, dated in his fourteenth year. Refers to the temple at Tiruvanaikkaval in Tenkarai Pandikulasanivalanadu.

486 of 1908 (Tamil) — On the west wall of the

Samkaracharyasvami matha in the same village. A record of Tribhuvanachakravartin Konerinmaikondan. Refers to the building of the matha called Narpattennayiravan madam by Avurudaiyan Solakon, on the northern side of the temple at Tiruvanaikkaval and provides for the feeding of the ascetics.

487 of 1908 (Tamil) — On the same wall. A record of Tribhuvanachakravartin Konerinmaikondan. Refers to the building of the same matha.

92 of 1910 (Tamil) — On the gopura of the Rajarajesvara temple. A damaged record of the Hoysala king Pratapachakravartin Vira Ramanatha, the date of which is doubtful. The signature of the king at the end, viz., Malaparoluganda, is in Kanarese characters. Seems to record a gift of land by a servant of Nagala Mahadevi to the shrine of Prasannisvaram Udaiyar or Rajakkal Nayanar situated on the western side of the temple of Tiruvanaikkavudaiyar and mentions Kiliyurnadu in Pandyakulasanivalanadu.

TIRUVASI

Tiruvasi is another small place of pilgrimage close by. Nataraja in the temple here has a knotted lock of hair, and the Muyalaga or the image of Rakshasa on his bend stands near the deity instead of the God dancing on the prostrate body of Muyalaga, which is the usual form.

KANNANUR

Close by is Kannanur or Vikramapura, which has formerly the capital of a royal family in the South—the Hoysala[7]. The remains of a palace, once great, are nearly traceable now, and the mighty capital is now a crumbling heap of ruins in the neglected corner of a hamlet. The inscriptions of this place are very important and they afford an insight into the civilization of the people in the past.

INSCRIPTIONS[8]

The inscriptions at this place have been copied during the years 1891 & 1905 by the Madras Epigraphical Department.

For an excellent historical account of the place see *Trichinopoly Gazar.*, Vol. I, pp.315-6. Its ancient name was Vikramapura.

509 of 1905 (Tamil) — On the south wall of the central shrine in the Bhojesvara temple. Records in Ananda gift of money by certain merchants of Conjeevaram. [Bhojesvara is evidently a corruption of Poysalesvara, the Hoysala king who founded the temple of this place (as he made it his capital). See inscription (189 of 1891) at Jambukesvaram and Bangalore C.P. quoted in *Trichinopoly Gazr.*, p.316, *Ep. Rep.*, 1892, p.7.]

510 of 1905 (Tamil) — On the same wall. A mutilated record in the third year of Tribhuvanachakravartin Konerinmaikondan. Records gift of land to the temple of Posalisuramudaiya Nayanar at Kannanur for celebrating a festival called Ranamukharaman sandi after the king. (Vira Ramanatha, the son of Somesvara, is evidently the king referred to.)

511 of 1905 (Tamil) — On the gopura of the same temple, right of entrance. A record in S. 1439, Isvara, of the Vijayanagara king Virapratapa Krishnadeva Maharaya. Records remission of certain taxes in favour of a number of temples. The Sanskrit verse *Namastunga*, etc., is written mostly in Tamil. The taxes amounted to 10,000 gold pieces and consisted of four items, viz., "jodi, sulavari, piravari and arasuperu." See also S.A. 435, 233 and Tp. 608 below.

33 of 1891 (Tamil) — In the Poysalesvara temple at Kannanur, five miles north of Srirangam. A record of the Hoysala king Vira Ramanathadeva, dated in his seventeenth year, Prajapati (A.D. 1271).

NOTES

1. *Madras Epigraphical Report* for the year 1888.
2. *Inscriptions of the Madras Presidency*, Government of Madras, 1919, Vol. III, pp. 1602 to 1606.
3. *Inscriptions of the Madras Presidency*, Government of Madras, 1919, Vol. III, pp. 1605 to 1606.
4. Kochchengan was born to the Chola king Subadeva by queen Kamalavadi in the sacred city of Chidambaram. This birth was the fruit of the worship the spider made to the linga in Jambukesvaram. As soon as the pains of confinement approached, the State astrologers, who were consulted, said that if delivery could take place after a *naligai* (equal to 24 minutes) the child would rule over the universe. The queen, with the usual motherly affection, ordered her being tied up with the legs upward till the auspicious hour fixed neared. The child was born red eyed as the result of forced stay in the womb; hence he was so named (*ko* means king; *che*, red; and *kan*, eye). The queen also died after a short time. In due course the prince assumed charge of his kingdom. He ruled the country priously, renovating several Saiva shrines.
5. This form is also known as *Ekapadamurti* and it is one of the various forms of Siva.
6. *Inscriptions of the Madras Presidency*, Government of Madras, 1919, Vol. III, pp. 1559 to 1603.
7. The circumstances under which the Hoysalas settled in this part of the country are mentioned in the inscriptions recorded in the temple of Jambukeswaram.
8. *Inscriptions of the Madras Presidency*, Government of Madras, 1919, Vol. III, pp. 1525 to 1653.

Chapter 18

SRIRANGAM

The picturesque island of Srirangam, the scene of the annual Ekadasi pilgrimage, is situated 3 miles to the north of Trichinopoly. The island lies between two branches of the river Kaveri, one running to the south and the other to the north. The great temple lies in the centre of the island and it is here that the great festival of Vaikunta Ekadasi is observed.

EKADASI FESTIVAL

The Ekadasi festival which is observed in Srirangam takes place on the 11th day of each fortnight in the year and there are thus annually[1] some 24 of these celebrations occurring alternately in the darker and brighter phases of the moon. The festival is said to commemorate the victroy of the Ekadasi goddess who overcame the asuras (demons).

VARIOUS FORMS OF VISHNU

Among the numerous avatars of Vishnu — those of the reclaining Anantasayin, the Lotus-navelled Padmanabha, and the lord of the assembly hall, Ranganada — it is to the last mentioned Avatar that the temple at Srirangam is dedicated.

In the assembly hall, as is generally the case in such temples, Mahavishnu resides with his attendants Ananta (the serpent), Sankha (the conch), and Chakra (the discus).

PURANIC VERSION

The myth related to the temple is an interesting one. At the end of the Mahapralaya (the deluge of Hindu Puranas) when the whole world was in deluge, Sri Narayana lay on the bosom of the waters. Then he meditated the act of creation. Thereafter arose first, *Brahmandam* (the universe) from which arose space, atmosphere, fire and water in order. From his navel came out a golden lotus which gave birth to Brahma. To him Sri Narayana taught the Ekaksharam[2] and Pranavam.[3] Repeating these sacred mantras, Brahma was able to evolve the Vedas and create men and animals. Accomplishing creation, Brahma, now initiated into the *Jyotisha Sastra*, the Hindu system of astrology, was perplexed at the anomalies of life. Puzzled by this problem he prayed to Sri Narayana; and He thereupon appeared to him in the aspect of Sri Ranganada, recumbent on the coils of Adisesha, his attendant serpent with his consorts,[4] Sri Bhu and Sri Neela, worshipping at his feet, and with the whole of creation attendant. The Vimana on which Sri Narayana thus appeared, was symbolic of Pranavam, the four Vedas, while the serpent god on whom Naravana lay, was the symbol of Brahma in the aspect of the Rudra, the destructive power. Thereafter Brahma prayed to Sri Narayana, that He should appear unto him thrice daily, in the aspect of Sri Ranganadha and also bless with longevity, wealth and health, the worshippers of the deity in that aspect. His abodes are three, viz., the sea of milk, the orb or disc of the Sun or the heaven, and the invoked Vigrahams and Saligrams (sacred stones). Thus honoured, Sri Ranganada blessed Brahma and his other worshippers. The Vimana so consecrated was brought from the high heavens to this capital

Ayodhya (at modern Oudh) by Ikshvaku,[5] king of Ayodhya, and thereafter Sri Ranganada was worshipped at Ayodhya by the Solar line of kings. Sri Rama, one of this illustrious house, gave Vibhishana,[6] the prince of Lanka (Ceylon), permission to remove the Vimana to his country. While Vibhishana was on his way to Ceylon he is said to have dropped the great Vimana near Chandrapushkarani on the island of Srirangam. While giving the Vimana to his disciple, Sri Rama had especially cautioned the latter not to put it down anywhere on the way, lest it should become rooted to the ground. Vibhishana, however, was forced by circumstances to entrust it for a few moments to the god Vinayaka in the disguise of a Brahman lad. As Vibhishana exceeded his allotted time of absence Vinayaka cuased the Vigraha to become rooted to the ground. When Vibhishana returned he could not remove it. Enraged at the trick, he chased Vinayaka and threw a stone which hit the god on the head. Hence the sculptured representation of Vinayaka at Trichinopoly is made with a dent on the head, and the shrine of this Vinayaka on Trichinopoly rock is this day known an Uchchipillaiyarkoil.

REMOVAL OF THE IMAGE

The Guruparamparaprabhava relating to the Vaishnava Alvars (saints), as well as the inscriptions on the east wall of the second prakara of the temple, mention that when the Muslims captured Trichinopoly, the priests of the temple at Srirangam stealthily took away the Alagiyamanavalan to Tirupati.

Subsequently Gopannarayar, a Brahman minister of Kampa II, who resided at Senji (Gingee), is said to have brought the image from Tirupati to Singavaram near his place, where it was duly worshipped and thence taken back to Srirangam, where he reconsecrated the God and his two consorts—Lakshmi and Bhudevi (Earth).

The route used for taking images is also mentioned, viz., Tirunarayanapuram in Mysore State where it was kept for many days and then taken to Tirupati. But subsequently the Muslims left the Trichinopoly country and went to conquer the Pandya country. Finding that the figure of Alagiyamandavalan could be safely restored to the temple at Srirangam, Gopanna, chief of the Gingee country belonging to the Vijayanagar kingdom, took the image from Tirupati to Singavaram, near Gingee, kept it there for a few days in Saka Samvatsara 1293 (A.D. 1371-72), and then in Paridhapi Samvatsara on the 17th solar day of the month of Vaigasi (May-June) restored it to the temple at Srirangam after performing the consecration ceremony on a grand scale.

TOWN PLANNING

The houses in the place in ancient days have been planned in accordance with the Hindu Silpa Sastras (Indian science of architecture), which combined the essential principles of hygiene and convenience with those or religion. The temple contains seven prakaras (the nucleus of a complete temple), which measure follows:

Central Shrine	... ...	240	feet by	181	feet.
2nd prakara	... ...	426	feet by	295	feet.
3rd prakara	... ...	767	feet by	503	feet.
4th prakara	... ...	1,235	feet by	849	feet.
5th prakara	... ...	1,653	feet by	1,270	feet.
6th prakara	... ...	2,108	feet by	1,846	feet.
7th prakara	... ...	3,072	feet by	2,521	feet.

The second enclosure is a little more magnificent enclosing the 1,000-pillared hall. The piers of this hall are of a single block of stone bearing at the same time elaborate carvings. The jambs of some of the gopuras on the court walls measure more than 40 feet in height and the roofing slabs about 25 feet.

ARCHITECTURE

Architecturally the temple of Srirangam is unique among the great temples of south India. The architectural buildings therein have all been constructed according to ther Silp Sastra. The amount of earnestness with which the Hindu kings constructed these buildings, especially the temples for Gods, is well known to all. Even modern European authorities on the subject like Fergusson, Burgess, Havell, Rea and Geddes have praised these buildings in no ordinary measure. Most of the stone pillars contain fine carvings.

HYMNS BY THE ALVARS

The Alvars[7] have praised the Gods presiding over the various shrines in India. They have composed hymns about one or other of the different shrines. But all these have taken up in their works only the temple of Ranganada at Srirangam and no other place out of the Nutteltuttirupads — 108 holy Vaishnava shrines — have been praised by all. This accounts for the special importance and sacredness of the shrine at this place. The praise by these Alvars about the various shrines are contained in the Tamil work *Nalayiraprabhandam*. It may be interesting to know what each of these Alvars says about the presiding Lord at the sacred Srirangam.

Poigai Alvar[8]: "The blue-coloured Lord Mahavishnu is worshipped here in the name of Sri Ranganada. Even the sacred Vedas could not properly mention the merits of this deity. Let me ever be thinking of Him to save me from a re-birth again".

Bhutattalvar[9]: "It is you Lord that during your avatar as Sri Krishna tore to pieces the Bakasura[10] who disguised himself as a crane and troubled your devotees. You preside over the shrines at Srirangam, Tirukkoshtiyur, Tirupati, Tirunirmalai, Tanjore, Tiruthankal and Mahabalipuram to bless the devotees".

Peyalvar[11] : "O Lord, it is to save the sufferings of your devotees on earth that you incarnated as Vamana and begged of king Mahabali three feet of land...".

Tirumalisai Alvar[12]: "Who could know properly the merits of this Lord, who alone at the time of destruction of the whole world, floats in the Ocean of Milk. In Anbil near Srirangam you are much praised and worshipped. I feel insensible while concentrating my thoughts on you. It is to save the world that you preside at Kumbakonam, Kanchipuram, Tiruvellore, Srirangam and Anbil".

Nammalvar[13]: "After coming in sight of you, O Lord! I feel restless. During the deluge you kept the earth in your belly and thus protected the universe. Wherever I turn my eye I feel you. It is to protect the virtuous you incarnated on earth as Sri Rama. To distribute amrita (ambrosia) to Devas you incarnated as kurma (tortoise); you saved Prahlada by slaying Hiranyakasispu. To remove the pangs of a mortal you shine at this spot. By uplifting the mountain Govardhana in your Krishnavatar you made the people understand what you were. You, at times, appear as Siva, Brahma and so forth in various forms. Even the Tulasi[14] (*Ocymum sanctum)* plant at your feet saves all from their sufferings by their accepting it heartily".

Kulasekaralvar[15]: "The gem on the hood of the serpent, over which you preside, gives special attraction to the place. I am ever anxious to stand by the side of the stone pillars close by your garbhagriham and to be adoring you. Sages Tumburu, Narada as also Brhama, Siva, Indra and other Devas are ever meditating on you at this place. The Panchayudha, i.e., five weapons—Sankha, Chakra, Saranga, Gada and Danda with all powerfull Garuda—guard you on all sides. To save Arjuna, you by Chakra hid the Sun during the day and thus caused night to previal. By sucking, you overcame the disguised Bhutaki in your Krishnavatar."

Periyalvar[16]: "At one time, to enable the virtuous Pandava Kings long by saved King Parkshit. To please the ardent devotee Vibhishana, you remain you here facing the south, wherein his kingdom lay. You saved Gajendra[17] when he cried for your help I also entreat you thus to save me in times of my distress. You represent the Panchabhutam (five elements) at this sacred place."

Tondaradipodi Alvar[18]: "I feel the greatest pleasure in praising you, O Lord! As during the life of a mortal, major part is covered by sleep, childhood, old age, etc., I do not pray for a re-birth as thereby my time to think of you is shortened. All Hindus except the Buddhists and Jains, who act contrary to the Vedic dictates must, to get themselves free from their human birth, worship you. Sri Rama who, by the mere despatch of a solitary arrow made the vast ocean[19] disappear, blessed Vibhishana in this form of your almighty. The prescribed daily rites of one could also be neglected provided he is before you always."

Tirumangai Alvar[20]: "... You made Brahma, the God of Creation, appear in your navel. You shine at this spot like the most precious gem."

Tiruppanalvar[21]: "... Being the first that appeared in creation it is you only, Lord, that could save the whole world"

EPIGRAPHICAL IMPORTANCE

For a proper comprehension of the inscriptions in the Srirangam temple and the significance of their existence there, it is necessary to know a little of the history of the various dynasties of chiefs who have left their memorials in the great temple and who swayed the destinies of the *Trichinopoly* country. For this purpose a short extract has been prepared from the political history of the Trichinopoly *District Gazetteer* dealing mainly with the kings mentioned in these inscriptions.

The inscriptions in the Ranganatha temple at Srirangam belong to the Chola, Pandya, Hoysala and Vijayanagara dynasties who successively swayed the destinies of the Trichinopoly district. They range in date betwteen the 9th and 16th century A.d., and are registered as Nos. 45 and 46 of the Epigraphical collection for 1891 and Nos. 51 to 74 of 1892. Of these five have been published in the *Epigraphia Indica* and *South Indian Inscriptions* where also other kings or chiefs who were in any way connected with the people mentioned are discussed. The contents of the inscriptions as made out by the Madras Government Epigraphist are given below:

THE CHOLAS — The early kings of this family whose inscriptions we find in the temple are Rajakesarivarman, Parakesarivarman and Parakesarivarman "who took Madura." We do not know for who the first two names stand. They may perhaps be referred to Vijayalaya and his successor Aditya I. Parakesari 'who took Madura' is Parantaka I, the powerful early Chola sovereign whose conquests extended as far as Ceylon. These early Chola inscriptions refer to the temple as Arangattu Perumanadigal. Kulottunga I and III and Rajendra Chola III, the later kings finish the number of the Chola princes represented in the inscriptions.

RAJAKESARIVARMAN — Two inscriptions (69 and 70 of 1892) belong to this king and are dated in his 4th and 26th years. The first registers a certain decision arrived at by the assembly of Srirangam about the affairs of the temple. The second provides for feeding a fixed number of Brahmans in the temple of Sri Arangattupperumanadi out of the interest accruing on a sum of money.

PARAKESARIVARMAN — Parakesarivarman is represented only by one inscription (73 of 1892) dated in his second year. The inscription records a gift of money by a certain Pusaragan Piranderuman, son of Talikkottur Devanar of Nenmalinadu (?) for daily feeding a Brahman versed in the Vedas in the temple.

PARANTAKA I — Nos. 71 and 72 of 1892, dated 24th and 17th years. Both of them record a gift of gold for a lamp in the temple of Sri Arangattupperumanadi by a certain Taruvagaichchangaran Iranasingan of Tennadu.

RAJAKESARIVARMAN or KULOTTUNGA CHOLA I (A.D. 1070-1118) — Of this king there are two inscriptions (61 and 62 of 1892) of which the latter has been published (*South Indian Inscriptions*, Vol. III, p.148 f). It is important for the history of Tamil literature since it gives us the lower limit of the date of one of the Vaishnava Alvars. The inscription records a provision made for offerings on three nights during which the text beginning with Tettarunthiral was recited before the God. The text is the second chapter of the sacred hymns of Kulasekhara one of the 12 Alvars whose work is incorporated in the *Nalayiraprabhamdam*. No. 61 (dated in his 15th year) records a gift of money to provide for the recitation of the Tiruvoimozhi during the Tiruppalli Ezhuchchi in the temple of Tiruvarangattalvan.

PARAKESARIVARMAN or KULOTTUNGA CHOLA III (A.D. 1178–1215) — Nos. 63 and 66 of 1892 are of this king. The latter has been published (*South Indian Inscriptions*, Vol. III, p.216 f) and the former in which the king is given the epithet "who took Madura and the crowned head of Pandya" is dated in his 18th year. It records a gift of money for a lamp to Alagiya Manavalapperumal (Ranganathasvamin) by a certain Madavan Ayirkadan of Malaimandalam.

RAJENDRA CHOLA III (A.D. 1246-1267) — The last powerful king of the dynasty, of whom it is stated that he defeated the Hoysalas in 1252. Both his inscriptions (64 and 65 of 1892) dated in his 7th and 8th years mention his defeat of Vira Somesvara. In the former he is called the "hostile rod of death to the Karnata king." The inscription registers that two merchants of Kulottungasolapattinam reclaimed a certain land belonging to the temple which had been silted up by the overflow of the river and brought it under cultivation. The other records a gift of land by purchase by a certain Narasimha Nayaka (son of Latadeva Nayaka who had the title Mahavadda Vyapari) for a flower garden to the temple of Sriranganatha, who had to be supplied with 9 garlands every day.

CHENNAYYA BALAYADEVA — No. 56 of 1892 belongs to this chief who is called the "Lord of Uraiyur" and records certain gifts made by him in A.D. 1530. He calls himself a Maharaja and "an ornament of the Chola race." It thus appears that as late as the 15th and 16th centuries descendants of the Chola dynasty with the hereditary title "Lord of Uraiyur" ruled as vassals of the Vijayanagara kings. The inscription refers to Krishnaraya who must be the great Vijayanagara sovereign.

THE PANDYAS — The kings of this dynasty mentioned in the Srirangam inscriptions are Maravarman Sundara Pandya I and Jatavarman Sundara Pandya I. The former is the contemporary of the Hoysala Narasimha II. His accession has been fixed at A.D. 1216 from his Srirangam record (No. 53 of 1892) which is dated in his 9th year. The king boasts of having conquered the Chola country and to have restored it to the king. The inscription records that the various people of the temple met in the street called Rajamahendirantiruveedi and took away the management of the temple from certain individual who had been misusing the temple properties and left its affairs in confusion. The name of the street suggests that it might have been called after the Chola prince of that name who shared his throne with Rajendradeva (A.D. 1052-64).

JATAVARMAN or SUNDARA PANDYA I — The other king represented in the inscription is Jatavarman or Sundara Pandya I. His date of accession has been fixed as A.D. 1250 from his Jambukesvaram inscription (No. 32 of 1891). His Srirangam inscriptions are two in number (Nos. 45 of 1891 and 609 of 1892) of which the first has been published (*Epigraphia Indica*, Vol. III, p.7 f). It describes in Sanskrit verse a large number of gifts he made to the temple and states that he took Srirangam from a king called in the inscription "the Moon of the Karnata" whom he killed. This is the Hoysala king Vira Somesvara whose defeat and death took place in A.D. 1253-4, the year of accession of Ramanatha.

The other inscription of this king (No. 60 of 1892) also celebrates his victories over the Cholas, Keralas and Hoysalas from whom he carried a large booty and from which he performed the tulabhara ceremony and presented the gold to the temple. The inscription alludes to his victories over the kings Simhana and Rama who appear to be the Hoysala Narasimha III and his half brother Ramanatha (both sons of Vira-Somesvara).

THE HOYSALAS — There are a number of inscriptions of this dynasty in the Tamil country. Their capital was at Dvarasamudra in Mysore. Narasimha II, who is called the "Establisher of the Chola country", was the first among the Hoysalas who possessed a portion of the Trichinopoly district. His attention must have been drawn to the south by the frequent wars between the Cholas and the Pandyas. His conquest of Srirangam seems to have taken place between A.D. 1222 and 1224 (*Epigraphia Indica*, Vol. VII, p.162). It is stated of him that he again started on a victorious campaign in about 1231 hearing that the Chola king had been captured as prisoner by a prince of Pallava descent Perunjinga by name and released the former (*Epigraphia Indica*, Vol. VII, 160 f) from his enemy's hands. This shows that his first conquest of the south was only of a temporary nature. There is a mutilated inscription of this king at Srirangam (No. 54 of 1892) dated in Vijaya corresponding to A.D. 1233, which records a grant by a female relation (?) of Bhujabala Bhimakesava Dandanayaka, the great minister of Pratapa-chakravartin Posala Sri Vira Narasimhadeva.

SOMESVARA — His son Somesvara is represented by only one inscription (No. 68 of 1892). This records a gift of money for a flower garden to the temple by a certain Irai Annan one of the Devaram group of the temple instituted by Somaladeviyar queen of Somesvara. This king had built his southern capital at Vikramapuram which is identical with the modern Kannanur near Srirangam and had established himself there. He died in 1253 in a fight with the Pandya king Jatavarman Sundara Pandya I and was succeeded by his son Ramanatha whose inscriptions are also found at Srirangam.

RAMANATHADEVA — He is represented by five inscriptions in the temple which range in date between his 2nd and 15th years. Two of his inscriptions (Nos. 51 and 52 of 1892) mention a gift of some ornaments to the temple by a person named Sokkavalli Bhatta or Mudaliar Kariyamati Sakalavidyachakravartigal to whom they had been presented by Perumal Vira Pandya. The donor, to judge by his name, was probably a very learned man and a spiritual teacher of Vira Pandya. This Vira Pandya again must have been one of the two princes of that name who are known to have been ruling about this time, one of them as a co-regent of

Jatavarman Sundara Pandya I. (*Historical sketches of Ancient Dekhan*, p.169). From another inscription (No. 57 of 1892) we learn that Ramanatha was the son of Somesvara by the western Chalukyan princess Devala. The record registers a gift of two pieces of garden land for offerings and worship to the god (Periya Perumal) on the Karthika festival in that month by princess Ponnambaladevi, the sister of Ramanatha. The other inscriptions belonging to this king are Nos. 67 (2nd year) and 74 (15th year). The purport of the former is a gift of land by purchase for a flower garden to the temple by a certain Tuppa Nayakan of Nallur, and of the latter is a gift of money for offerings etc., in the temple by a native of Ranadhirachaturvedimangalam in Viyanurnadu.

RAVIVARMAN OF KERALA — No. 46 of 1891 which is the only inscriptions of this king found in the Srirangam temple has been published (*Epigraphia Indica*, Vol. IV, p.148 f). It records that the king after subduing his opponents worshipped his tutelary deity Vishnu at Ranga, set up an image there and celebrated the festival of lights in his honour and provided for the annual payment of 1800 panas each to 50 learned men. The king had the other names Sangramadhira and Kulasekhara. He is stated to have defeated a certain Vira Pandya twice and made the Cholas and Pandyas his subordinates. Jatavarman Vira Pandya the illegitimate son and successor of Maravarman Kulasekhara I. This seems, as already stated in the history extract, to have been facilitated by the fact that the power were prostrated at the time by the sudden invasion of Malikkafur on the south.

HARIHARA II, HIS MINISTER MUDDAYA DANDANAYAKA — Three more inscriptions finish the list of records secured from the temple. They belong to the Vijayanagara dynasty and the allied Saluvas. No. 58 of 1892 is of the time of Harihara II, with however no date. It is in Sanskrit verse and eulogises at length the greatness of Muddaya Dandanayaka, the minister of Harihara.

No. 55 (in Sanskrit), which is dated in Saka 1293, is an inscription of Goppana and has been published in *Epigraphia Indica*, Vol. VI, p.322 f. This Goppana was a Brahman minister of Kampa II and seems to have taken part in his master's wars against the Mussalman chiefs of Madhura, as the Ranganatha inscription alludes to his conquest of the Tulushkas. It would appear that the authorities of the Ranganatha temple learning about the Muhammadan capture of Trichinopoly, had secretly removed the image of the God to Tirumalai. Subsequently when Harihara II had reconquered the Tondamandalam country, one of his officers, this same Goppana Udaiyar who resided at Senji (modern Gingee), took the above-mentioned image from Tirupati to Singapuram where it was duly worshipped. In Saka 1293 after completely vanquishing the Mussalmans he brought back image of Perumal to Srirangam and reconsecrated the God and his two consorts. It is this fact of the images being brought back and reconsecrated at Srirangam which is celebrated in the inscription under reference.

The next and the last inscription (No. 59 of 1872) which is dated in Saka 1385 and is the time of Tirumaladeva or Gopa-Timma I. The double name Gopa-Timma which must mean Timma, son of Gopa may suggest that he has to be identified with Timma, son of Gopa, in the pedigree of the Saluvas given at page 168 of *Archaeological Survey Report* for 1908-9. This king is identical with the Saluva chief Timma, the elder brother of Saluva Narasinga (*Epigraphia Indica*, Vol. VII, p.77, note 2). The object of the inscription is to record the gift of taxes derived from several specified villages accruing to the king, to the temple of Srirangaraja.

TIRUVELLARAI

This sacred station wherein is the shrine dedicated to Pundarikakasha Perumal lies at a distance of about 12 miles to the north of Trichinopoly. There is also a rock-cut temple to Siva called Jambunatha. This cave consists of a cell cut into the rock into two niches on either side. Of the two to the right, the first contains an image of Vishnu, while the second enshrines the god Ganesa. In the two niches on the left side are several sculptures. The front part of the cave is verandah supported by four pillars carved out of the main rock itself.

EPIGRAPHICAL IMPORTANCE

The inscriptions in the Vishnu temple mention the gifts made to the god Sri Krishna and his consort Rukmini though these images are not any more available in this temple. There is a big well close by these temples with inscriptions therein naming it as Marppiduguperunginaru and stating that its construction was commenced in the 4th year of the Pallava king Dantivarman and completed in the next year. There are four entrances leading into the well with steps going down. In the portals midway between the entrance and the bottom of the well are sculptures of various Gods. The inscriptions records is that no object in this world is permanent, that life is sure to decay and therefore if one commands wealth, he may keep what is required for his maintenance and utilise the remainder in doing works of charity. Another record therein says that during the reign of Hoysala king Vira Ramanatha (A.D. 1262-63) a merchant (vaniyan) repaired this well as it had suffered considerable damage from floods and other causes.

NOTES

1. There may be one in excess in every year and sometimes two.
2 & 3. These represent symbolically the full blown creation.
4. Vide Figure 109 on pge 452.
5. The descendants of Ikshvaku who settled in the south of India were known as Gangas as they trace their name to the river Ganga or Ganges. Their chief city at the beginning was Kuvalala (Kolar in the Mysore State) and during the 3rd century it was removed to Tolakad at the source of sacred river Kaveri in the south-east of the Mysore district.
6. Sculptural representation of this prince worshipping Sri Ranganada exist to this day at Srirangam and votive offerings placed before him on a particular night in the year are said to disappear miraculously the next morning!
7. The lives of these Alvars, the greatest of the Sri Vaishnava saints, whose figures are worshipped in most of the Vaishnava shrines, are detailed in the work *Guruparamparaprabhava.*
8. He first appeared in the tank attached to the temple of Tiruvekkha at Conjeevaram as an *Amsa* (form) of *Panchajanya*. Being the first of all Alvars he was named as Mudalalvar (*mudal* in Tamil means the first). His contemporaries were Bhutattalvar and Peyalvar who all chanced to meet at Tirukoilur and who for the sake of the good of the people composed various works.
9. This Alvar first appeared in a Kurukkathi tree in Mahabalipuram on Avitta star (*delphini*) day.
10. There is a sculptural representation of this Asura in the gopuram at Tirukkuvalai near Kilvelur, Negapatam taluk.
11. In a *Sevvali* flower in the tank attached to a Vishnu shrine in Mylapore he first appeared. He had renounced the world and led an indifferent sort of life; hence he was named Peyalvar. Even now the well is pointed out and it is held in much reverence by the Vaishnavites.
12. He was born as an *Amsa* (form) of Sudarsana and had a very keen contention with Rudra. Though neglected by the sage

Bhargava to whom he first appeared he fared well and visited Triplicane and lastly ended his days in Kumbakonam.

13. He was born and brought up under the Tamarind tree in Alvar Tirunagari. It is on a Vaigasi Visaka day he was born. For ten years he prayed under this tree. His original name was Maran.

14. The legend in connection with this holy plant is that the Asura Jalandara, who immensely troubled the Devas, had in his wife Brinda such a chaste and pure woman that her virtue guarded him against all his wrongs. It is her good qualities that prevented even the Gods from overcoming him. At last, Vishnu promised to bring slur on her modesty by engaging Himself with her while the Devas were fighting with him. Accordingly in the disguise of her husband he approached her as though he came out victorious in the fight while she was fasting and praying for her husband's success. When she went out to extend her arms to embrace Him she detected the fraud played by the Lord; thereafter she entered the funeral pyre immediately.

The lord Hari atoned for the wrong done to this innocent woman by causing her premature death and He intended to give her salvation; but this course he had to adapt for the good of the Devas, who were much teased by this wretched Jalandara. While thus in his anxious moments his tears fell over the ashes of Brinda, up arose a pretty little plant which he called in joy Tulasi (*tula* means 'equal' or 'like' and *asi*, 'thou art').

From that time this plant became the chief object of worship to Vishnu. Even the most fragrant flowers are not equal to this plant in the eye of the Lord. The place where Brinda died was called Brindavana or the garden of Brinda. (Vide footnote 1 on page 29). Later on even the pots and spots where this plant was reared began to be named accordingly. This salvation to Brinda at the hands of the Lord took place on the 12th day in the light fortnight of the month of Kartika (November-December) which in consequence was called Brindavana Dvadasi and the worship to Vishnu under this plant then is said to secure special merits.

15. He was king of Quilon and as a strong devotee of Mahavishnu, relinquished his government, went to Srirangam and remained

there worshipping the Lord. He worked a miracle when he was charged to prove his innocence of theft, by dipping his hand in a pot containing a snake and coming out unscathed!

16. He was born at Srivilliputtur as an amsa of Garuda. Being a strong devotee of Sri Krishna he composed hymns in His honour. He demanded large wealth from king Vallabhadeva of the Pandya country and out of it renovated the temple at Srivilliputtur. To him appeared the famous Andal as daughter from the earth on a *Adi Puram* day. He was first named Vishnusittar. He spent his last days in Srirangam.

17. It is said that this incident, which has been copied in most of the sculptural representations at all places, originally took place in the mountain of Trikuta and the details thereof are mentioned in *Bhagavatam*.

18. Born at Tirumandankudi, he proceeded to Srirangam while young, raised flower gardens and worshipped Sri Ranganada daily with the flowers therefrom. He is always sculptured with a basket (*kudalai*) on hand containing flowers.

19. The details of this incident are narrated in Ramayana and the place where this incident occurred is identified as Tiruppullani in Ramnad district.

20. He had his birth in a low caste as an amsa of Saranga in Tiruvali Tirunagari near Shiyali and was Commander-in-Chief of the Chola army. He is always represented in sculptures with a sword in hand. It is he that renovated most of the Vaishnava shrines. He had a keen contest with the famous Tamil saint Sambandar at Shiyali and it is he that defeated the Buddhists in Negapatam, removed the golden Buddha figure and out of it had the Vimana at Srirangam covered with gold plate.

21. He appeared in a field at Uraiyur near Trichinopoly and was picked out by a low caste man. While hesitating to approach the Lord in the temple he was carried on shoulder and the Lord ordered his being freely admitted to his presence.

Chapter 19

KARUR

Karur or Tiruanilai, called after its presiding deity
Tiruanilai Mahadeva or Pasupathisvara (Lord of the Cows),
lies on the Trichinopoly-Erode line of the South Indian
Railway. The town stands on the left bank of the river
Amaravati, 6 miles to the south-west of its confluence with
the Kaveri. It was at one time the capital of the Chera kings,
and was also known as Vanji on account of the large quantity
of fodder available there. The capital appears to have been
removed from this place to Tiruvanjikulam, the modern
Cranganore, on the west coast (Malabar).

ANTIQUITY

The town is said to have been a flourishing mercantile centre
at one time, as will be seen from the several Roman coins that
are frequently obtained on digging the earth. The temple
inscriptions mention its having formed a principality of the
Kongu country, and also having been once under the sway of
the Chola dynasty.

Karur is also known as Bhaskarapura or Bhaskara Kshetra,
and the name was probably given to it by the Chola kings who
traced their origin to Bhaskara or the Sun. The Chola king,

Veera Rajendra I (A.D. 1050–1070), fought with the Chalukyas and gained a decisive victory over them a third time at Kudalsangamam,[1] probably Kudali, at the junction of the Tunga and the Bhadra rivers in the Mysore State.

Old Tamil works mention that Karur was a strongly fortified city, that it had drainage and water supply, and was surrounded by deep most full of different varieties of lotus grown in them. Several old machines of war were mounted over the walls of the fort to throw stones and boiling oil at the enemy in times of war.

SAINTS PUGAZHCHOLA AND ERIPATHAR

The Saivia devotee, Sivakami Andar, who was carrying flowers to the temple, was one day attacked by an elephant of the Chola king Pugazh at this place.[2] Eripatha Nayanar[3], another staunch devotee of Siva, obtained his salvation.

EPGRAPHICAL IMPORTANCE

One of the inscriptions of the temple refers to the royal warrant issued to the Kammalars, or artisans of the temple, permitting them the use of double conches and drums on the occasion of marriage or funeral and the construction of two-storeyed houses with chunam plaster, double door entrance, and the decoration of houses with festoons and water-lilies. A duplicate of this warrant can be seen inscribed in the temple at Perur, near Coimbatore.

The Madras Government epigraphist in his annual report for the years 1891 & 1896–97 remarks:

"In the inscriptions of the Karur temple, the town is called Karuvur or Mudivalangu Cholapuram. It belonged to Vangalanadu, a division of Kongu country. The old name of the temple, which is preserved in the inscriptions and in the Tamil *Periyapurana*, was Tiruvaninalai Mahadevar, 'the lord of the sacred cow-stable'. The modern designation Pasupatisvara is a Sanskrit rendering of this Tamil name. The two earliest inscriptions of the Karur temple belong to the 9th year of the reign of the Chola king Koparakesarivairman or Rajendradeva or Rajendra Choladeva, who seems to have been the successor of his namesake, the great Rajendracholadeva of the Tanjore inscriptions.

... In this (next) inscription, dated in the 3rd year of Ko Rajakesarivarman or Vira Rajendradeva or the king claims to have conquered Ahavamalla. The new inscription further reports that he defeated Vikkalan, the son of Ahavamalla at Punal kudal Sangam (the junction of the rivers), and drove him out of Gangapadi, beyond the Tungabhadra river and that he killed the Mahadanda Nayaka Chamundaraja. As he bore the surname Rajakesarin, Vira Rajendradeva must be distinct both from the great Rajendracholadeva and from Rajendradeva, whose surname was Parakesarin, and he was probably a successor of the last mentioned king, as he continued to fight with Ahavamalla and was also at war with Ahavamalla's son Vikkalan, who might be identified with the Western Chalukya Vikramaditya VI (Saka 997 to 1048). The Mahadandanayaka Chamundaraja is perhaps identical with the Mahamandalesvara Chavundaraya who was a tributary of Ahavamalla II... The king is said to have conferred the title of Rajaraja on his elder brother, the title Chola Pandya and the soverignty over the Pandya country (Pandiamandalam) on his son Gangaikonda Chola, and the title of Sundarachola or Mudikonda Chola, now a ruined city in the Udayarpalayam taluk of Trichinopoly district. The remaining Karur inscriptions belonged to Vira Chola to Vikrama Choladeva, to "the emperor of the three worlds Kulottunga Choladeva, who was pleased to take Ilam (Ceylon), Madurai (Madura), the crowned head of the Pandya king, and Karuvur" and to

Konerinmaikondan. The last name signifies he who has assumed the title 'the unequalled among kings' and occurs elsewhere as the surname of various Chola and Pandya kings.

An inscription at Karuvur gives a graphic account of the historical events during the reign of the Chola king Vira Rajendradeva I, who ruled in the period between 1050 and 1070 A.D. and fought three times with the Western Chalukya king Abavamalla Somesvara I and his two sons Vikramaditya VI and Jayasimha III, or, as they are styled in the Chola inscriptions, Vikkalan and Singanan. The Chola king claims to have gained a decisive victory over them at Kudal-Sangamam, which is perhaps the modern Kudalai at the junction of the Tunga and Bhadra rivers in the Mysore State. Among the vassals of the Chalukya king, the Karur inscriptions mention Chamundaraja, Kesava and Marayan. These three persons appear in the records of the Western Chalukyas as Chavundaraya, Kesavaditya and Marasimha.

One of the inscriptions gives a graphic account of the historical events during the reign of the Chola king Virarajendradeva I (A.D. 1050–1070) and the introduction given on pages 2 and 3 of the report of the Epigraphical Department for 1896–97 reads as follows:

"While the goddess of fortune was prospering; while the circle of the great earth rested on the king's round arm as lightly as his bracelet of jewels, and while the shadow of his royal white parasol set with numerous jewels protected the living beings of the circle of the earth more tenderly than the mother that bore them; while all other kings wearing sounding ankle-rings took shelter at his feat; and while the Kali age, in despair, retired to the abyss to dwell in — the king duly bestowed a splendid crown of jewels on his incomparable elder brother, Alavandan, along with the title 'Rajaraja who is praised on the great earth.' He was pleased to grant the

Pandi Mandalam, whose crown of jewels is exalted in this world, to his royal son Gangaikondasolan, along with the title 'Sola Pandyan, the leader of an army of very tall elephants.' He bestowed a brilliant crown on Mudikonda Solan, whose hand held the sword and whose spear had a sharp point, along with the title Sundarasolan, and conferred endless great distinctions on him. Thus he granted to each of his numerous relations suitable great riches. He drove from the battle-field in Gangapadi into the Tungabhadra the Mahasamantas, whose strong hands wielded cruel bows, along with Vikkalan, who fought under a banner that inspired strength. He attacked and destroyed the irresistible great and powerful army which he (Vikkalan) had again despatched into Venginadu; cut off the head of the corpse of the Mahadandanayaka Chamundaraja; and severed the nose from the face of his (Chamundaraya's) only daughter, called Nagalia, who was the queen of Irugayen, and who resembled a peacock in beauty. The enemy, full of hatred, met and fought against him yet a third time, hoping that his former defects would be revenged.

The king defeated countless Samantas, together with these two sons of Ahavamalla, who were called Vikkalan and Singanan, at Kudalsangaman on the turbid river. Having sent the brave vanguard in advance, and having himself remained close behind with the kings allied to him, he agitated by means of single mast elephant that army of the enemy, which was arrayed for battle and which resembled the northern ocean. Surrounded by the furious elephants of his vanguard, he cut to pieces at the front of the banner troop Singan, the king of warlike Kosali. While Kesava Dandanayaka, Kettarasan, Marayan of great strength, the strong Pottarayan and Irechchayan were fighting, he who was named Porkodai Muvendi cut to pieces many Samantas, who were deprived of weapons of defence. Then Maduvanan, who was in command, fled; Vikkalan fled with dishevelled hair; Singanan fled, his pride and courage forsaking him; Aunalan and all others descended from the male elephants on which they were fighting in battle, and fled; Ahavamaka too, who had joined them, fled before them. The kings stopped his fast furious elephants, put on the garland of victory, seized his (Ahavamalla's) wives, his family treasures, conches, parasols, trumpets, drums, the meghadamba drum, white chauris, the boar banner, the ornamental arch (makara torana), the female elephant called Pushpaka, and a herd of war elephants, along with a troop of pransing horses, and, amidst general applause, put on the crown of victory, set with jewels of red splendour."

The king (Virarajendra I 1050–70) is also said to have defeated the Chalukyas at Kudalsangamam which probably refers to Kudali at the junction of the Tunga and Bhadra and captured the wives of the enemy, the boar banner, and the female elephant Pushpaka. It is also mentioned that Ceylon, or at least a portion of it, was in the possession of king Rajendra. Tribhuvanachakravartin Konerinmaikondan granted certain privileges to the Kammalars (artisans) and it is recorded as follows in Tamil :

"We have ordered that, from the month of Adi, of the 15th (year of our reign), at your marriages and funerals, double conches may be blown and drums, etc. beaten, that sandlas may be worn (on the way) to places of visit, and that your houses may be covered with plaster. On the authority of this written order (olai), this may be engraved on stone and on copper (in all places desired by you so as to last as long as the moon and the sun). It is learnt from another inscription in the temple that the actual names of this king was Vira Chola and the Tribhuvanachakravartin and Konerinmaikondan are titles of his."

This place has got inscriptions of Vira Rajendra, Rajendra,

Kulottunga III and Virachola. But it is a very ancient city and was evidently the celebrated Vanji of Tamil literature. It is referred to by Ptolemy. Of late a controversy has been raging as to whether Vanji should be identified with Karur or Cranganore, but the question in favour of Kaur has been unanswerably settled by the able and erudite Pandit Raghavaiyanagar in his *Vanjimanagar* published a few months back. According to some inscriptions it was later on included in Adhirajarajamandalam (Kongu), and according to the others in Solakeralamandalam. In the time of Rajendra I and Rajaraja it was in Keralantakavalanadu. The local epigraphs mention the two sub–divisions of Kongu, Vengalanadu and Tattaiyurnadu.

NOTE

1. The Kudalsangamam referred to herein is Bhavani, 9 miles to the north-west of Erode. It formerly belonged to the ancient Kongu kingdom and was known as Mukkudal and Tirunana at the confluence of the rivers Bhavani and the Kaveri and not Tungabhadra as inferred by the Madras Epigraphical Department. The three bodies of water implied in the name Mukkudal are the Bhavani, the Kaveri and the holy water at the feet of the presiding deity in the temple at Bhavani, viz., the Sankakukanatha. There is also a shrine to the Vishnu god Adikesava within the temple of Sankamukanatha.

2. King Pugazh Chola was ruling in Uraiyur. He was so powerful a king that he received homage at Karur from the Chera and Kongu kings. Being a great devotee, at last he entered the sacrificial fire and joined the ranks of Nayanmars.

3. Eripatha Nayanar, was a native of Karur in the Kongu country. He used to with anyone or anything that did the least harm to the god of the place or His devotees. Sivakami Andar, a Saiva

devotee, was knocked down by a State elephant belonging to the Chola king on his way to the temple with flowers. The Nayanar observing this killed the elephant, which enraged the king, who proceeded thither to punish him. At this moment the God appeared, explained the matter to the king and conferred salvation on both of them!

Chapter 20

PALANI

Palani or Palani, at a distance of about 40 miles from Dindigul on the Madras Dhanushkodi railway line, is the most important hill shrine dedicated to the god Subrahmanya, an aspect of Siva.

PURANIC VERSION

Palani is also called Tiruvavinangudi in the Puranas, probably because a herd of cows was collected there. Goddess Lakshmi, the Sun, the Earth and the Fire are said to have worshipped the Lord here.

Sundaresa, another incarnation of Siva, is said to have transformed himself into a sow[1]! The object was to feed the youngs of another sow that died immediately after birth. This was in a forest round the hill, and this part is therefore known as Varahagiri (boar hill).

TEMPLE BUILDINGS

The temple stands on a picturesque hill which is a continuation of the Kodaikanal range, and the image Palni Andavar is the infant aspect of Subrahmanya. The hill is said to have formed part of the Meru[2] mountains, which forms a

couple of the hillocks called Sakti and Siva. These hillocks
are said to have been given by the god to sage Agasthya to
be installed in the south. The sage in turn entrusted the task
to his disciple Idumbasura, a demon, and he carried them on
his shoulders in the shape of a kavadi.[3] On the way the kavadi
dropped down and the hills installed themselves. It was
subsequently discovered that Subrahmanya or the presiding
deity, who chose this place for his abode, was responsible for
this miracle.

SUBRAHMANYA GOD

Siva is said to have made his son Subrahmanya, commander
of the celestial army. He is called by many names, such as
Kartikeya, Tarakajit, Shanmuga, Saravanabhava, Senani,
Kraunchabith, Gangaputra, Guha, Agnibhu, Skanda and
Swaminatha. His favourite vehicle is peacock or goat, and
they are found in all temples dedicated to Subrahmanya.

In the grant[4] belonging to this temple the following
description of god Subrahmanya appears:

"The son of Sri Paramesvara, who burned the Tribhuvanas;
the God of Gods; the Lord of the Daiva (divine) world; the
Lord of the vast universe which has many karors of worlds
under it; the Kumara, who argued with the Lord of the Swans
(Brahma), and, after cuffing him on his head and pushing him
out by his lock, gave him his Brahmaship[5]; the brave
commander who comes riding on his peacock, which is as
terror-striking as the battle-field of the Asuras, where the
horse chieftains whirl amidst the tumultuous cry of trumpets,
and the Asura's blood collects in pools, turning the place into
a burning ground; the Kumara of the cock-banner, who,
shouting in the battle-field, tore (to pieces) the bodies of the
Asuras without falling into the hands of the many by-standers;
the warrior that has (commands) the shining army of the

Kulis[6] that are howling and the Kukais[7] and other devils that are brawling; the brave solider that has taken up the beautiful javeline in the cause of the weak and the old; the Commander of the Devas who liberated Indra that cut the mountains, the trees of which extended to the skies; the possessor of the emerald-coloured peacock—which shines as it were the ill-luck of the Tisira—as his vehicle; the moon (Subrahmanya) born in the yagya (sacrifice) which Narada bred up (kindled), and who came to burn Tiripurakodu; he who taught Agastya the pure classic Tamil, the Agamas and the truth of the six letters[8]; he who by his power gave happiness to the Dehnu (cow); he who acted so that the Sun might see his path; he who granted the promised boon to the Vani (Sarasvati); he who gave life and happiness to the mountain daughter (Parvati); the salughterer of the Asuras; the guard of Amaravati; he who has for his vehicle the peacock of the flowing tail which shines like gold; the nephew of Sridhara (Vishnu); Sivasubrahmanya; the fierce destroyer; the exceedingly fierce (god); the clamorous (god); the bold Kumara; the Lord of the 600 holy places of Pattamangalam, Avinangudi, Palani (and others); he who is fond of devotees; the possessor of the mountain on which live the devotees; the son of Parvati; the son of Siva-Ganapati himself; the Lord (breaker) of all obstacles; the brother of all the Gods; the supreme javelin-armed god (Velayudhasvami), the God of all the gods, and the javelin-armed god Subrahmanya of the Palani mountain, who sits amidst worship, in the holy places celebrated in songs—in Tiruppurankunram, Siralavay, Avainankudi, Erkalam, and Palamudir Solai, among the mountains, the six Tiruppatis, otherwise called Yagapati, Tillai, Tiruvannamalai, Tirukkalattiri, Tiruttani, Tiruvenkatam, and Tirupadi."

ORIGIN OF KAVADI

God Siva, at one time, gave sage Agastya[9] the two hillocks called Siva and Sakti that were in Mount Kailas with the permission to remove them to the south that he could worship both of them as the God and Goddess. But the sage left them there in a forest called Burchavanam and returned to the south. When at another time he was about to start for the north to bring these hillocks, Idumban, the guru (preceptor) of the Asuras, undertook to bring them himself. To enable Idumban to carry them with ease the sage initiated him to certain mantras and also acquainted him with the route to go through. Accordingly Idumban proceeded to the forest where the hillocks were then located and offered puja (worship) to them. He was however feeling anxious as to how to lift them. Then the danda or stick of Brahma, the God of creation, stood over the hillocks and the snakes of the earth stood there to serve the purpose of a rope to enable Idumban to carry them by tying to the rod. So Idumban did, and bore them on his shoulders in the form of a Kavadi and returned to the south. While nearing the forest at Palani, he kept them on the ground to rest a while. On attempting to lift them again, he found them fixed to the ground! To know the reason thereof he got over the higher of the two, viz., Sivagiri, and on it he noticed a youth with stick in hand and wearing only loincloth. This was no other than god Skanda in disguised form, who then attempted to work out a miracle. On being asked as to why the hills would not move, he claimed them as his own when an altercation between the lad and Idumban ensued and the latter fell senseless in the scufle. When the wife of Idumban appealed to this boy Skanda for redressal Idumban was restored to life. Then Idumban prayed to Skanda that he should be made to stand at his portal for ever as the Dvarapala (gate-keeper) and also that whoever should offer vows in this

Kavadi form, similar to the process adopted by him in bringing these hillocks, should be blessed fully. These boons were granted and it is from then that the temple over the hill was put up with the deity in the form he appeared to Idumban and with the figure of Idumban at the portal. From that time this Kavadi worship was resorted to by denotees who were in trouble. It is being done not only in this place, but also in most of the places where the god Subrahmanya is worshipped.

NOTES

1. One of the stone pillars of the Pudu mandapam at Madura bears a sculptural representation of the event.
2. The Olympus of India. This is supposed to be the central part of Jambudvipa within which is situated the sacred India.
3. This is worn on the shoulder to propitiate the God for the vow taken to cure ailments in the body and other troubles. Wooden pieces, one on each side over which Gods Vinayaka and Subrahmanya are carved, are fixed to a shaft to which small pots filled with milk or sugar are tied and taken round the temple. When the deity is satisfied milk is supposed to overflow!
4. Vide page 129 of the *Archaeological Survey of South India*, Vol. IV, by Burgess and Natesa Sastri.
5. It is said in the *Skandapurana* that Bhrama came to pay a visit to Siva when Subrahmanya was very young and playing outside the mansion of Siva on the Kailasa. Brahma did not know who the boy was and hence did not behave respectfully to him. Subrahmanya was greatly enraged, and, calling Brahma, asked him whether he knew the Vedas; Brahma replied that he was the author of the Vedas. Subrahmanya then asked Brahma to explain him the meaning of "Om". Brahma was not able to do it and hence Subrahmanya imprisoned him; after long captivity Paramesvara interfered, and by his kind recommendation

Brahma was released. This story is alluded to in the above passage.

6&7. Kulis, Kukais, dwarfish imaginary demons. They form part of Siva's *gana.*

8. The *Shadakshara* mantra is sacred to Subrahmanya, like the *Panchakshara* is to Siva.

9. For the figure of Sage Agastya and other particulars relating to his life refer to page 461.

Chapter 21

MADURA

Madura, which was once the capital of the ancient Pandya kingdom, on the Madras Dhanushkodi line of South Indian Railway, was originally known as Kadambavanam or the forest of Kadamba (*Nauclea kadamba*). A part of this tree still exists in the northern prakara of the shrine of Sundaresvara. The legend goes that this is one of the four holy trees that grew on Mount Meru; the other three being Naval (*Eugenia fambolana*), Banyan (*Ficus indica*) and Arasu or peepal (*Ficus religiosa*). These trees grown in luxuriance in Southern India affording a cool shade.

Madura has been famous as the seat of Tamil literature in southern India and conferences of scholars called Sangams were held from ancient times. In one of those gatherings of scholars, God Sundaresvara is said to have played the part of a poet!

The history of the place is described in detail in the *Halasya Mahatmya* in Sanskrit and in the *Tiruvilayadalpurana* in Tamil. This place is also famous for the representation of the god Siva dancing as Nataraja with the right foot on the ground, while in all other representations, he stands with the left foot below. The hall where Nataraja is said to have danced here, is known as Velliambalam or the silver hall.

PURANIC VERSION

The discovery of the sacred place is originally attributed to a merchant by name Dhananjaya of Manavoor, a few miles to the east of the present town of Madura. The merchant was returning from the West Coast where trade had taken him, and as he reached the douse forest, the sun set. The day was Somavara (Monday) and the merchant observed Indra worshipping the Swayambku (self-created) linga. He reported the fact to the king who, at once cleared the forest and built the temple and the beautiful city around it, as laid down in the Silpa Sastras or the science of architecture. The town is planned in the shape of a coiled serpent (Halasya in Sanskrit or Alavoi in Tamil) and it is said that the design of the town was suggested to the king by the god Sundaresvara Himself. At the earnest desire of the king, a serpent is said to have been sent out to mark the boundary of the town, and it curled itself bringing its head and tail to the centre and pointing by its outermost coils the circumference of the city to be constructed.

In ancient days Indra incurred the displeasure of his preceptor Brihaspathi and committed various sins. To expiate them he visitied the God at Madura on the day of Chitra Pournami (full-moon day in the month of Chitrai—April-May). In honour of this event the shrine of Sundaresvara is supported by the *ashta gajas* or the eight elephants Airavata, Pundarika, Vamana, Kumuda, Anjana, Pushpadantha, Sarvabhauma and Supradipa, and the festival of Chitra Pournami is considered highly important here. It was in this place that the goddess incarnated herself as Meenakshi, the daughter of the Pandya king, and god Sundaresvara is said to have sought her hand in marriage.

BUILDING RELATING TO THE TEMPLE

The Ayirakkal or thousand-pillared mandapa within the temple is a beautiful structure with sculptures on its stone pillars executed in accordance with the directions in the Sastras.

Virappa Nayaka of Tanjore, who was a contemporary of Varatunga and Srivallabha of Madura, is reported to have erected a beautiful mandapa with stone pillars in this great temple and presented the goddess Meenakshi a *kavacha* (armour) made of gold and set with jewels.

The porch leading to the Meenakshi temple is named "Ashta Sakti mandapam" on account of the eight sakties being figured therein. There is also a shrine of the female saint Karaikkal Ammai,[1] who by her staunch devotion to Siva and very severe penance, became famous as one of the 63 devotees of Siva. Murtinayanar's[2] fame is also connected with this place.

Opposite to the temple of Sri Sundaresvara is a finely sculptured mandapa 33 feet by 105 feet, that goes by the name of Pudumandapam or new mandapa that was put up long after the other important buildings in the town as a summer resort of the God and hence it is also called the "Vasanta mandapam." In the middle row of pillars are the statues of ten of the Nayaka kings of Madura together with their wives. The pillars on the outer rows contain elaborate sculptures of the various forms of Siva. Amongst these one relate to the marriage scene of Parvati-Kalyanasundara, one relate to an elephant eating sugarcane and one depicting Sundaresvara as a sow feeding a number of young pigs are worthy of admiration.

In the corridor round the tank within the temple the 64 Sundara leelas of the God are painted on the walls.

(These paintings stand on the north-east wall around the

tank within the temple. This is one panel of the complete series relating to all the 64 sports of god Sundaresa.)

VANDIYUR TEPPAKULAM

To the east of the temple, at a distance of about three miles, is a picturesque tank of about 1,000 feet square known as Vandiyur Teppakulam, with a square island in the middle wherein is a small shrine. This is close to the river Vaigai and a channel connects this tank with the river. The sanctity is attached to this tank as when it was excavated for removing earth to build the Tirumal Naick's palace, the huge Vinayaka now in the temple is said to have been found buried therein. On this account the spot was considered holy and it was converted into a Teppakulam, i.e., a tank wherein the floating festival is celebrated.

MANIKKAVACHAKAR

Manikkavachakar was a Brahman born in Tiruvathavur during the reign of the Pandyan king Arimardhan. At birth, he was named Vadhavoorar. As he was proficient in all Sastras even when quite young, the Pandyan king not only made him his minister, but he also graced him with the title 'Brahmarayan'. He was ably conducted the government of the country, receiving divine inspiration in critical moments.

Though he was discharging his duties as the minister of the king, he was ever in search of a guru (preceptor) and despairing of securing a suitable master to learn from and get the proper initiation to obtain Mukti, he sought Lord Siva himself as his guru and began worshipping him as such.

The king once sent him on an errand to purchase horses for his army. When he arrived at Tirupperundurai, otherwise call Avadayarkoil, Iswara, with a view to give him the initiation he was in need of, assumed the role of a preceptor and was seated under a Kuruitha tree, with his followers in front as his disciples. Seeing him, the minister of Pandyan, advanced towards him and prayed for initiation, who forthwith, on a day auspicious for the ceremony of initiation under the influence of the Star Arudra in the month of Margali when the Sun was in the archer, gave him the necessary instructions to attain Moksha. By virtue of the initiation from Iswara, he began to sing wonderful songs in his praise. Pleased with him, Iswara called him 'Manikka Vachakar' i.e., one dropping gems from his mouth.

Enriched with the new name conferred on him, he in lieu of the reward called 'Guru Dhakshina' which every disciple is expected to give to his preceptor, built a big temple with fine porticos and corridors for circumambulation, with the money brought by him for the purchase of horses for the king's army.

Finding that his minister did not return with the horses at the appointed time, the king sent men in search in all directions. They found him at Avadayarkoil and him gave the king's message. He thereupon prayed to Iswara for help and was directed to go to the king in advance and represent to him that the horses were coming. Accordingly, he returned to the king and told him that the horses had been purchased and were on the way and he might expect their arrival in his capital the next day. Lord Iswara, to save his devotee and disciple from the dilemma in which he found himself, gave to the king and thus to the world the Aswa Sastra or the science of the horses.

The king, displeased with the minister on account of the delay caused by him in procuring the horses, punished him in diverse ways. To teach the king a lesson, Lord Siva converted the horses—given to the king in return for the money advanced to the minister for the purchase of horses and which was utilised by him in building a temple—into jackals, which again in the morning when the stable doors were thrown open, ran into the woods through the streets of his capital city after having devoured the real horses of the king at night! All these happened in a day presided over by the Star Jyeshta in the month of Avani when the Sun was in the Lion (Leo). The next day presided over by the Star Moolam, the king sent his servants to punish his minister for the trick played upon him by passing metamorphosed jackals for real horses. Lord Iswara drove back the servants by causing heavy floods in the river Vaigai in Madura.

The king, having come to know subsequently that everything had transpired by the will and pleasure of Lord Siva, praised Manikkavachakar and his devotion to Iswara. Unmindful of the king's regard for him, he proceeded again to Avadavarkoil and after having visited several places of pilgrimage, he at last, arrived at Chidambaram and there by his wonderful powers, restored speech to a girl dumb from birth invoking in metre the assistance of the super-physical agencies, and at last merged himself in god there!

At Avadayarkoil, a famous temple of Manikkavachakar has come up. There he shines as one of the foremost Bhaktas (devotees) of Siva. An annual festival is celebrated up there in the month of Margali when the Sun is in the archer, on the day presided over by the Star Arudhra. It was Tirukkalukkunram near Chingeput that god Siva gave him initiation appearing before him as a teacher giving instruction to his disciples. In Ceylon he defeated the Buddhists and invited them to Chidambaram for a controversy. While in sight of Sri Nataraja at Chidambaram he is said to have disappeared and thus united with the omnipresent. Madura is the place famous for his administration as the prime minister of the king.

EPIGRAPHICAL IMPORTANCE

The inscriptions in the temple record a curious incident. In the reign of king Vijayaranga Chokkanatha of the Naik dynasty the officers of the palace levied unauthorised taxes on certain sarvamanya or rent-free lands of the temple servants. Unable to endure the unjust measure the servants made up their minds to commit suicide in a body and one of them actually climbed up the eastern gopura of the temple, jumped down and died. This tower is considered as haunted and even to this day people do not enter the temple for worship by this gate. Visvanatha Naik granted a plot of land near Tribhuvanam for maintaining and lighting a mosque for the use of Fakirs on 17th April, 1560. The Pandya king Maravarman or Nedunsadayan is said to have conquered the Cholas, Pallavas and Keralas and constructed the walls of the city of Karavandapuram. The ways and means adopted with the unanimous consent of the members of the Padayachi caste in Madura for financing the Dharma temple constructed by Nachiyan Padayachi in the waste land situated between the Maravan mandapa and the mosque in the East Masi Street near the north gopura are also recorded. This Dharma temple was constructed on 31st January, 1762, with the permission of the Nawab who then ruled Madura. Muhammad Ali was the Nawab of the Carnatic at the time. According to an inscription in the Panchanadesvara temple at Tiruvandarkoyil near Pondicherry dated the 10th year of Chola king Rajendra I, it is evident that this king constructed at Madura a huge palace (maligai) "by whose weight even the earth became unsteady" and anointed his son Chola Pandya as the Viceroy of the Pandyan kingdom at Madura.

MAHAL OR THE PALACE

The palace known as Tirumalnaik's Mahal, said to have been

constructed during the reign of Tirumala Naik between A.D. 1623–1645, is on the south-east of the town at a distance of about a mile. The stucco work in the dones and arches herein is splendid and attracts the admiration of all visitors. The portion in the front goes by the name of Swarga Vilasam or the "celestial pavilion". To the north of this building stand 10 huge stone pillars known as "The Ten Pillars," and they are said to have been intended for the elephant stables. This structure known for its exquisite design and perfection of workmanship, deserves a short account of the circumstances under which it was built.

About the middle of the 16th century Muthu Tirumala Naik of the Naik dynasty reigning then at Trichinopoly, was suffering from a bad catarrah and all medical aid proved unavailing. When he was resting during his journey to Madura god Sundaresvara and goddess Minakshi appeared in his dream and told him that if he changed the seat of his government from Trichinopoly to Madura, and renovated the temple with all grandeur, he would be cured of his disease. They also offered him some ashes, with directions for use both internal and external. When he got up from his sleep, he narrated the vision to the Brahman priests and his court officials, vowing that if he was cured he would endow large sums of money for the construction of the hall. He was soon after cured of the disease and in fulfilment of his vow, he built the hall, and settled at Madura. This magnificent building was shorn of its splendour by Tirumal Naik's grandson Chokkanadha, who changed his court from Madura back again to Trichinopoly. In order to provide himself with a suitable palace, Chokkanatha removed the best part of his grandfather's residence, to Trichinopoly. Today we see only one block of the splendid residence, with its ten pillars and a small dome and the site of the old Noubat Khana (band stand). The surviving building consists of two oblong portions running east to west. The smaller of these measures about 140 feet long and 70 feet wide and 70 feet in height, "possessing all the structural propriety and character of a Gothic building." The larger building is more architectural in style and character. It measures about 252 feet x 151 feet x 40 feet, connected with well-designed brick arches. At the back of the arcade runs a line of cloisters 43 feet wide, and supported by rows of huge pillars. The portico is splendid and has a height of over 50 feet.

M. Langles speaks of this Swarga Vilasam (heaven) in these words: "This pavilion is so constructed as to cause it to be said that in no other country is there a court equal to it by reason of its splendid ornaments, their excellence, number, extent, curious workmanship and great beauty. To the west in the midst of a great dome-shaped hall is square building of black stone, inside which is a chamber made of ivory. In the middle of this is a jewelled throne, on which the king is accustomed to take his seat at the great nine nights festival surrounded by all his banners or ensigns of royalty, and before which all kings are accustomed to do homage."

This building was taken over by the government during the administration of Lord Napier, Governor of Madras, the Governor himself taking a personal interest in the matter of its restoration. Though it will take a very long time to restore it to its original grandeur, it has now been considerably improved. Most of the public-offices are located in the building today.

The Mangammal Palace, built during the days of queen Mangammal between A.D. 1689 and 1704 is an edifice which has not been preserved in full. Only parts now remain with some beautiful polished stone pillars and plaster domes. This queen was celebrated for her acts of virtue among which was the making of roads and the planting of avenue trees for the shelter of the travellers.

VISHNU TEMPLE

There is a shrine of Vishnu called Kudal Algar (Kudal being one of the former names of the town) and it is said that Vishnu came down to this place to give away Meenakshi in marriage to the god Sundaresvara. The Vimana or tower of the god in the temple is of a very fine workmanship and is known as the Ashtanga Vimana. The marriage of Meenakshi is to have been celebrated on the day of Panguni Uttara, generally occurring on the full-moon day of the month of Panguni (March-April) and an important festival is still held to mark the event.

ANAMALAI

From a distance this huge hill, about 6 miles to the north-east of Madura, appears as an elephant in a reclining posture with its face turned to the west and tail to the east. On the northern side of it are 3 caves, of which one is natural and on a slightly detached rock while the other two are cut into the hill. On the rock overhanging the natural cave are the sculptures of Saptakannimars with inscription below each. Another cave is popularly known as Shamanalkovil with the mention of the name Ajjanandi.

The central shrine of Narasingaperumalkovil is also a rock-cut cave. Here is an inscription relating to the time of king Parantaka I (907 A.D.) when in the month of Karnataka there was a eclipse of the Sun on Friday and the Nakshatra was Aslesha. The village itself is named Narasingam. According to Tevaram, saint Sambandar drove out the Jainas from its vicinity after converting the king Nedumaran to the

Saiva faith. God Vishnu was set up, according to inscriptions, in Kali 3871 (A.D. 770) in this cave.

TIRUPPARANKUNRAM

To the south of Madura, at a distance of about 7 miles, is the celebrated cave temple dedicated to god Subrahmanya. He is said to have married Devasena, daughter of Indra, in this place and performed several of his miracles. Great sanctity is attached to the hill as a whole and people circumambulate it on that account on all important days.

THE HILL

The famous hill here is about 1050 feet above the sea and it is also named Skandamalai on account of its connection with the god Subrahmanya. Many sculptures of the Hindu Gods are available within the temple for students of iconology. Great sanctity is attached to the whole hill and people in large numbers go round it on all Kartigai and other important days of special worship to Subrahmanya.

EPIGRAPHICAL IMPORTANCE

According to the inscriptions engraved on the inner gopura in Saka 1714 a regiment of Europeans came and destroyed the Sokkanatha temple and even the temple of Palaniandavar, seized the town, took into their hands the asthana mandapa, broke the gates of the aksha gopura and were approaching the kalyana mandapa. The bhattars or priests seeing that the town and its god would be destroyed, and the festivals would be discontinued, asked one Kutti to ascend the tower and jump down; and as the regiment went away as soon as he fell, they gave him a written document as a favour for the blood that he shed by his fall whereby he and his ancestors are to enjoy perpetually certain lands.

Mohammadans have also put a mosque near the temple and they claim the place as their own.

NOTES

1. Karaikkalammaiyar was born in Karaikkal with the name Punitavatiyar. She was married to one Paramadatta of Negapatam and he lived with her in her native village. Admiring her devotion God made a mango fruit, which she had already disposed of, to reappear in order that she may satisfy her husband thereby! The husband went abroad trading and at last settled in Madura, whither she proceeded to join him. But realising her devotion he used to worship her as a saint. There is a shrine in the Sundaresvara temple at Madura dedicated to her. She had the rare merit of having witnessed the dancing of Nataraja in Tiruvalangadu near Madras.

2. Murtinayanar was born in Madura in the Vaisya caste. He was in the habit of supplying sandal for the daily worship of the presiding God of the place. At that time the country was overrun by Jainas, consequent on its having been taken by the king of the Carnatic. Then this Nayanar found it impossible to secure even sandal wood as he did not want to encourage Saivism. In consequence of this trouble this Nayanar attempted to make use of his elbows, when the God blessed him!

Chapter 22

RAMESVARAM

Ramesvaram is an island in the Bay of Bengal, and it is connected with the main land by the Madras Danushkodi Railway line.

The town of Ramesvaram derives its name from Sri Rama, and the sanctity of the place is due to the installation of a lingam by Sri Rama himself. Its sacredness has been recognised from the earliest times by all sects of the Hindu community.

PURANIC VERSION

Puranas have it that to purge himself of the sin of Brahmanicide committed by Sri Rama by killing Ravana, who was the son of a Brahman married to a Rakshasa woman, Rama was advised by the Rishis to establish a lingam/on the Gandhamandhana hill on which Ramesvaram stands. For fulfilling, Hanuman was this purpose by Rama to get a lingam from the sacred river Narmada. As Hanuman did not return by the auspicious time fixed for the event, Sri Rama installed a lingam made of sand, and called it Ramalinga or Ramanathalinga. Hanuman, on his return, heard of this and got angry. Rama assuaged his grief by to instal the linga aduising him brought by him, a little further to the north of the sand linga. He called it 'Hanuman linga' and also gave to his linga the precedence of worship. Not satisfied with this, Hanuman tried again to displace Ramalinga by his linga, but he failed in his attempt. The marks on the Ramalinga speak of the above incident.

According to the *Sthalapurana* 24 Tirthas or sacred waters bodies exist within the small island; of which 14 are in the form of tanks and wells within the temple precincts and great sanctity is attached to them Setumadhavar shrine is another important shrine and it is sacred to the god Vishnu, who is said to have appeared in the form of a Brahman called Setumadhavar and seduced Gunanidhi, daughter of the Pandyan king. Gunanidhi, who is supposed to be another aspect of the goddess Lakshmi, was married to Setumadhavar; but before the marriage could take place Setumadhavar was said to have been imprisoned by the king, who was, however, informed of the god's incarnation. The shrine of Setumadhavar is visited by pilgrims all the year round. A bath in the sea at Rameswaram at the junction of the Indian Ocean and the Bay of Bengal, is considered to be considered to be very sacred. The junction itself is ascribed to Sri Rama, who is also said to have destroyed the invincible bridge with his Kothanda, when the people complained that Rakshasas from Lanka might come across the bridge and do harm to them. The eleven important lingas especially important to this temple are those founded by Hanuman, Sri Rama himself, Sitadevi, Lakshmana, Sugriva, Nala the builder of Setu bridge, Angada, Neela, Jambavan, Vibhishana and Indra.

According to Hindus Sastras only on particular occasions people could bathe in the sea but this general rule has an exception in case of places like Setu, the junction of the Indus and the Ganges, Trivandrum, Gokarna and Jagannath. Further, Sunday, Tuesday and Friday are forbidden in case of the other places whereas on all days one could bathe in Setu. Again while the bath in the other seas propitiates the spirits of the deceased Setu alone is recommended for the prosperity of the living ones.

TEMPLE BUILDINGS

The temple consists of three prakaras. The original walls were constructed of limestone which in the course of renovation were replaced by black granite. The colonnades in this temple are a source of attraction to all visitors and the piers bear statues of the various Setupatis who constructed parts of this temple and also made generous endowments. About these colonnades[1] it is said, "The glory of this temple resides in its corridors. These extend to nearly 4000 feet in length. The breadth varies from 17 to 21 feet of free floor space, and their height is apparently about 30 feet from the floor to the centre of the roof. Each pillar or pier is compound, 12 feet in height, standing on a platform 5 feet from the floor, and richer and more elaborate in design than those of the Parvati porch at Chidambaram, and are certainly more modern in date. The painting on the ceilings and the colonnades are either fading away or have faded altogether. As the corridors run for the most part round open spaces, and have light admitted to them through the back walls, they have none of the mysterious half-light of those of Madura and will perhaps strike some visitors as less impressive."

SETUPATIS

The Setupatis or the Rajas of Ramnad, who are the lords of Setu, have long been worshipping the god Ramanatha here, and they have made large endowments to this shrine. Statues of the Rajas are sculptured on the pillars of the mandapas and prakaras (Courtyard).

EPIGRAPHICAL IMPORTANCE

In Appendix A, [2]'Nos. 11 and 12 belong to the time of Dalavay Setupati Kattadevan and record grants made by him of 13 villages to the temple of Ramanathaswami and the shrine of Parvatavardhiniamman at Ramesvaram. However, No.10 belongs to the time of Tirumalai Raghunatha Setupati Kattadevar who is elesewhere stated to have successfully averted an invasion of Madura by the king of Mysore. The inscription under reference states that he was the son (perhaps an adopted son) of Tirumalai Dalavay Setupati Kattadevar and bore the title 'Hiranyagarbhayaji', i.e. the performer of the Hiranyagarbha sacrifice). Another king who bore the title 'Hiranyagarbhayaji' was Maddu Vijia Ragunatha Setupati Kattadevar who was ruling in Saka 1635, Vijaya (A.D. 1711–14). Maddu Ramalinga Vijaya Raghunatha Setupati Kattadevar mentioned in No. 7 of Appendix A, is stated to have been 'the elevator of the family of Hiranyagarbhayaji Raghunatha Setupati Kattadevar'. The record is dated in Saka 1692, Vikrita (A.D. 1770–71) and gives a long list of fanciful titles to the king some of which, viz. 'the lord of Tevainagara', 'the ornament of the solar race' and 'the bearer of the Hanuman-flag' be shared in common with other kings of the Setupathi family who also bore the surname Hiranyagarbhayaji. That he defcatcd the Tulukkar, i.e. the Mohammedans and performed the 16 great gift ceremonies commencing with the tulapurusha, viz. weighing oneself against gold, are, perhaps, significant enough and account in a way for the defeat inflicted on this chief whose power was evidently growing, by the combined forces of the Nawab of Trichinopoly and the English, in A.D. 1773. This is the very Setupati whose capture by Hazrat Nawab, his imprisonment in Trichinopoly, and the confiscation of his country around Trichinopoly are referred in No. 14 of Appendix A, the date of which is Nandana (A.D. 1771–73).

'There are several inscriptions in the temple, which relatle the exploits of various kings. One of them relates that Raghunatha Setupati who ruled a small principality near this place about 1669 A.D., defeated the armies of the Raja of Tanjore in a battle, and annexed the towns of Mannargudi, Pattukottai, Arantangi, Devakottai and Tiruvarur. Another inscription mentions that the mighty Thirumalai Setupati (1645–1670) assisted the Madura king and defeated the Raja of Mysore who invaded Madura. In appreciation of his services the king of Madura gave to Tirumalai Setupati the villages of Tirupuvanam, Tiruchli and Pallimadai. The copper plates relate (1) that Dalavay (Commander-in-Chief) Kattadevar made a gift of five villages to the temple of Ramanatha on 20th November, 1606 for worship and offerings and again on the 8th July, 1607, eight villages near Pamban. (2) Hiranyagarbha Ravikula Setupati ordered that Muthuvijayan Servai should get food every day from the temple in appreciation of his having dragged the king's elephant by its tail on 8th June, 1627. (3) Sri Tirumalai Raghunatha Setupati performed Hiranyagarbhadanam at Danushkoti on 12th January, 1659. (4) Sasivarna Periya Udaya Tevar or Vijaya Raghunatha constructed a matha (monastery) on the bank of the Vaigai, and gave a plot of land for its maintenance to Satyavasagaswami, who came from Chidambaram on the 26th November, 1734. Jaffna was also brought under his control. An agreement was entered into between the Darmakartha Ramanatha Pandaram and 512 Mahajanas of Ramesvaram on the 29th August, 1722, consequent on the resumption of certain temple villages, by Nawab Hazrat, who confined the Setupati at Trichinopoly.

The temple servants went to Chennapatnam, paid homage to Nawab Hazrat and his Dewan Rayar, and redeemed the villages.'

NOTES

1. Fergusson, *Indian & Eastern Architecture.*
2. *Report* of the Madras Epigraphical Department for the year 1910–11, pp. 88–89.

Chapter 23
=========

TINNEVELLY

Tinnevelly or Tirunelveli, denoting the sacred hedge for paddy, formerly formed part of the Pandya country. The inscriptions in the temple speak of the deity Vrihivritesvara's assumption of the form of a hedge and a roof to save a devotee's store of paddy from rain.

PURANIC VERSION

Tinnevelly is also called Venuvaxa (a forest of bamboo) from the fact that there was an extensive growth of bamboos in the temple and the deity is said to have appeared under this. Nataraja's shrine in the temple is known here as Tambra Sabha or the copper hall and there are many sculptural representations in it. Some of the pillars in the temple produce a musical sound on being struck.

IMAGES IN THE TEMPLE

Vishnu, who is said to have given away the Goddess Parvati in marriage[1] to Siva is here represented in a metallic figure with a Gindi (a vessel with a spout), in his hands. The stone Somaskanda and the metal figure of Isvara here are of very fine workmanship.

PANDYA CAPITAL

Manalur, for some time the Pandya capital, is within easy reach from Tinnevelly. The existence of several mounds around the place represents the relics of the ancient grandeur of the place.

SUBRAHMANYA TEMPLE

God Subrahmanya's shrine situated in the middle of the river Tambraparani is known as Kurukkuthorai temple, and it remains submerged in the river during floods. The representation of Subrahmanya with his consorts shows fine workmanship.

TIRUCHCHENDUR

Tiruchchendur, meaning a sacred and beautiful town, is a coastal town 18 miles to the south-east of Srivaikuntam in Tinnevelly district, The temple dedicated to god Subrahmanya, who represents the warrior aspect of Siva, is built on a small rock.

PURANIC VERSION

The town was so small when god Subrahmanya came here with his army that he ordered Visvakarma, the celestial architect, to extend and improve it. Since then it assumed the names Tiruchchendur or Jayanthipuram or Tiruchchiralavay and Srisandhinagaram. The second name signifies the conquest of the demon Surapadma by god Subrahmanya, the third a fertile sea-coast, and the last was a rendezvous for god Subrahmanya prior to His going to war and after return. Tradition is that god Subrahmanya's ganas desired to select a place for his worship which was to be a mountainous tract by the side of a river and the sea.

Tiruchchendur was selected for the purpose as it had all having these advantages.

DATTATREYA SHRINE

There are some rock-cut temples and natural caves by the seaside and in close proximity of the temple with sculptural representations of god Subrahmanya. The image of Dattatreya[2] in the cave close by is also an object of worship.

SCULPTURES IN THE TEMPLE

The temple is said to have been constructed by Ugrapandyan, the fifth descendant of the Pandya dynasty of Madura. The sculptures on the right wall represent Subrahmanya sitting on a peacock and engaged in war with Surapadma. On the left wall Subrahmanya and his consort are seated on an elephant.

EPIGRAPHICAL IMPORTANCE

The early inscriptions of the Pandya king Varaguna speak of his monthly grant of 1,400 gold kasus or coins to the temple, and the injunction that this sum should be invested as a permanent loan among village assemblies, so that the interest therefrom might be spent on the temple. There is also mention of a shrine to Narkiradeva Nayanar, which speaks highly of the literary advancement of the period when famous poets were deified and worshipped. Narkira was the author of *Tirumurugaarruppadi*, the first of the ten idyls commentator of *Iraiyanaragapporul.*

CAPE CAMORIN

Cape Camorin is the anglicised name for Kanyakumari or Kumari, the virgin goddess. In some inscriptions it is called kalikkudi. It lies in 8' 4" North latitude and 77° 36' 45" East longitude. This is the southern extremity of India. The sea here has a holy connection and religious importance.

The temple stands on the mainland at the sea-shore and it is dedicated to the goddess Bhagavati. The legendary version connected with the goddess Kanyakumari is that god Siva at Suchindram wanted to wed her and that the same fell through.

The axe of Parasurama, when he reclaimed this land, is said to have fallen here.

The inscription recorded in the temple relating to the 9th year of the reign of Parantakapandya alias Jatavarman relating to the checking of the inroads of the sea, similar to the 52nd *tiruvilayadal* or divine sports of god Siva wherein Ugra Pandya is reported to have hurled his spear and curbed the fury of the sea, and to the engraving of the family crest on the Malaya mountain. This king is also said to have fought a battle at Vilinam. The place also known as Kulotungasolappattınam subsequent to the place having been captured by Kulottunga Choladeva I in the 13th century. This king also paid his attention to the standardisation of the prevalent weights and measures, which were stamped with his royal totem, the carp. He set up 10 golden lamps for the deity of the temple at Ananthasayanam (Trivandrum) and also arranged for the feeding of those attended the grand annual festival of the goddess here on Tai Pusam day or the day on which he was born. The boundaries of land belonging to the goddess Kanyakumari are also mentioned.

There is another temple here by name Guhanathaswami at a distance of about half-a-furlong from the other shrine. This temple was called Rajarajesvaram, according to the inscription found here, evidently called after Rajaraja the Great of the Chola dynasty.

SUCHINDRAM

The famous temple here dedicated to Stanamurti contains very fine carvings. Indra, according to tradition, was absolved of his sin and freed from its effects by worshipping the presiding deity this temple. Hence the name of the place which means 'Indra purified.'

PADMANABHAPURAM

This was the capital of Travancore state for a very long time prior to Trivandrum. The temple is an important one and is well fortified. Close by this place is Keralapuram. Here inscriptions in the Siva temple found record the fact that king Ravivarman reconstructed the temple and made the 16 great gifts. It also mentions that he was master of all sciences and arts.

NOTES

1. On the occasion of this divine marriage the two consorts of Vishnu (Lakshmi and Bhumidevi) are also said to have been present. Siva stands with his right leg forwards holding in his right hand the right hand of Parvati in the act of *panigrahana* a part of marriage rituals wherein the bridegroom holds the hand of the bride accepting her as his life partner. The face of Parvati reveals feminine modesty with her eyes down cast. Brahma is seated in front of a square sacrificial pit with blazing fire in it. Menaka attends on Parvati. Sages Sanaka and Sanandana are on the left of Siva. It is to satisfy Agastya (the dwarfish sage) that Siva is said to have appeared in this marriage form Kalyanasundara.

2. Dattatreya is an *amsa* of the god Vishnu. At one time sage Animandavya cursed the leper Kausika, that before the next

sunrise, he should die. His chaste wife feeling this curse upon her husband, prayed to the Sun not to rise the next day. So it happened and the Devas approached Anasuya, the wife of sage Atri, for redressal. Anasuya appealed to the wife of Kausika to give up her prayers to the Sun and promise to spare the life of her husband. Besides granting this boon, Kausika's wife was also blessed with three sons, one as the amsa of Brahma, another of Vishnu and the third of Siva. It was the son of Vishnu's amsa who was named Dattatreya. He is represented as a wandering mendicant with ashes rubbed over his body. He is also followed by the four Vedas in the form of four dogs. He personified goodness and destroyed the wicked demons. Engaged in yoga (meditation) he began to enjoy the worldly pleasures. He was always encircled by the sons of ascetics. For some time he lived within the water of a lake and came out of it with a woman to disassociate himself thereafter from the ascetic clan. Still they did not leave him. He is said to have lived in a valley of the Sahya mountain. There is a special temple to this god in Narasohawadi, about nine miles from Shirol Road Station in the Poona-Bangalore-Mysore Railway line, where on full moon days and Saturdays pilgrims flock in plenty.

3.   This figure is from Kolappallur, North Arcot district.

Chapter 24

TIRUCHCHENGODE

This place, famous for the Ardhanariswara (the half woman aspect of the god Siva) situated on a hill, 7 miles away from Sankaridurg Railway Station in the Salem district. The idol in the form of, half-man and half-woman, signifying the truth of the universal soul and its creative power, is said to have been made out of a mixture of some powders by the ancient sages. Goddess Parvati is said to have done penance at Devatirtham. This place has a good supply of water.

PURANIC VERSION

The hill is traditionally said to be a part of Mount Meru split up from another mount in a conflict between Adisesha (the god of serpents) and Vayu (the god of wind) and hence named as Nagachala. The ascent to the rock, on which the temple is located, is by a flight of steps with mandapams built at intervals on the north east of the hill. The deity stands within a hollow. There is a five-hooded serpent about 35 feet in height carved on the way to the temple. The Nritta mandapa in front of the shrine has well carved piers with outstanding equestrian figures, one of which represents Pratyangira, popularly known as Bhadrakali; and in the ceiling are lotus flowers on the petals of which parrots are sitting. The bressummers are full of carvings representing scenes from the *Skanda Purana*. The Kalyana mandapa in the hall in front of the central shrine is supplied with a mechanical clockwork arrangement in the roof for the falling of Vilva (*Aegle marmelos*) leaves on the head of the idol dating as early as the construction of the mandapa.

SUBRAHMANYA SHRINE

The god Subrahmanya is supposed to have obtained initiation at the hands of Siva at this place. He also performed several miracles here. The dwarapalas (door-keepers) are so finely sculptured that even the smallest needle could pass throught the holes over the body for affixing ornaments on occasions. The mandapa in front of the shrine dedicated to Subrahmanya has similar well-carved piers, bressummers and ceilings with figures.

There is the rough sculptural work of Mr. Davies, Collector of Salem in 1823, with hat in hand to commemorate his replacing two broken stone lintels in two of the mandapas. There are also minor shrines dedicated to Vishnu, and to the famous Tamil poet saints Appar, Manikkavachagar, Sundarar and Sambandar.[1]

The granite bull in this shrine is said to have proved its divinity by eating Bengal gram offered by a saint on a particular occasion which finds a place in the *Sthala purana*! This forms one of the miracles[2] by god Subrahmanya on the hill here.

EPIGRAPHICAL IMPORTANCE

The inscriptions of Chola, Pandya, Vijayanagar and Konga kings on both sides of the path can be seen. They speak not only about the gifts of the temple, but also about the construction of the various parts of the buildings themselves. One of the records dated the 9th year of the Pandya king Jatavarman or Tribhuvanachakravartin Sundara Pandya (A.D. 1251–64) refers to the breach of a tank and states that the land irrigated by it was lying fallow for a long time. This place formed part of the old Kongu country which was later on called Cholakeralamandalam.

NOTES

1. These appear as Figs. 95, 133, 83 and 6 respectively.
2. There lived a Tamil poet named Gunaseela in this place who was a faithful devotee of the deity of the place, Subrahmanya. Once he learnt that a poet of the Pandya region proposed to defeat him in a competition and thus establish his superiority. This terrified the local poet Gunaseela who appealed to the god. To save this devotee, god Subrahmanya appeared as a boy cowherd before the Pandya poet at the outskirts of the town. By engaging in talk he gave that poet him the impression that he was the disciple of the local poet. He talked all about the importance of tending the cows, and convinced the poet about the superiority of his master. This made that poet retrace his steps. Thus Gunaseela was saved!

Chapter 25

TIRUPATI

This range of the Eastern Ghats, which consists of seven peaks, lies in 13° 41' North Latitude and 79° 24' East Longitude on the Katpadi Gudur Railway line. The top of the hill is about 2,000 feet and the world famous temple of god Srinivasa is on the topmost peak. These seven peaks are said to represent the seven hoods of the king of serpents— Adisesha. The consort of this famous deity is not along with Him; but in another village at the foot of the hill that goes by the name Alamelumangapuram. The founding of this temple is attributed in the Puranas to king Parikshit of the Mahabharata fame. This deity is said to free his devotees from all kinds of diseases, troubles.

The shrine is said to stand over a cluster of seven hills which forms a part of Mount Meru. The reason assigned for its distant location is that a dispute arose between Adisesha, the god of serpents, and Vayu, the god of wind, when the latter blew out the 1,000 peaks of Mount Meru; and the former covered them with his thousand heads. Vayu being disappointed in his attempt to destroy them pretended exhaustion and discontinued his blowing. Adisesha, thinking that all was safe, raised his head, when Vayu once again blew out the peaks, one of which fell at Venkatachala or Tirupati, and this accounts for its connection with the holy Mount Meru.

The Hindu conception regarding the chain of these hills is that they represent the body of the serpent Lord Adisesha, on which the god Vishnu, the protector of the world, is said to rest. The seven hills of Tirupati are said to represent the seven heads of the serpent, on which Venkatachalapati stands; the centre of the serpentine body is the seat of Ahobala Narasimha; and the tail end is the abode of Mallikarjuna of Srisaila. The beginning, the middle and the end of the vast creation, presided over respectively by the Trinity—Brahma, Vishnu and Siva, have thus been ingeniously conceived and perpetuated in popular tradition. The serpent with its several coils denoting limitless time is a cosmic conception current amongst several nations of the world.

GILDING THE VIMANA OF THE GOD

According to an inscription on the east wall of the central shrine in the temple of Varadaraja at Conjeevaram we learn that one Tatacharya gilded the vimana of god Venkatesa on the Phanipatigiri, i.e. Seshachala Tirupati with gold in the year Promoduta corresponding presumably to Saka 1492. This Tatacharya was the Manager General of the temple affairs (*Srikaryadurandhara*) during the time of the Vijayanagara king Venkatapatideva Maharaja. He was the spiritual guru, who officiated on his coronation. The latter admiration for his acharya is said to have offered the whole kingdom to him. He was also known as Lakshmikumara and Kotikanyadanam Tatacharya. He spent the latter part of his life in Conjeevaram.

OTHER SHRINES

Varahasvami or Vishnu in the incarnation of a boar, was the original deity of the Tirupati hills, and his shrine is on the bank of the Svamipushkarani tank. When Srinivasa Perumal came there, Varahasvami resented his residence; but the former promised the latter precedence of worship and offerings, and this is followed even today.

Lower Tirupati dedicated to Govindaraja Perumal is at the foot of the hills in contradistinction to Venkatachalapati's shrine on the top of the hills.

EPIGRAPHICAL IMPORTANCE

"The inscriptions below the images in the northern wall of the gopura in front of Sri Govindaraja Perumal state that the gift of the gopura was made by Anantarajayya, son of Matli Tiruvengadanatharajayyadevachola Maharaja and that certain figures cut on the stone walls of the same gopura are those of Matla Tiruvengadanatharaja and his queen Chennamma. Evidently these figures were cut on the walls by the son in honour of his parents. There is reference to this Matli chief Ananta in Sidhout (Cuddapah district), in an inscription recorded on the east wall of the fort there, according to which 'while Vira Venkataraya, i.e. Venkata I, the sovereign of the whole Hindu kingdom was ruling the Chandragiri country in the Saka era 1527, Anantaraja of the Solar race and of the Devachoda family, who killed in the battlefield Veligonda Venkatadri of the Ravela family, who was victorious at the battle of Jambulamadaka (Jammalamadugu), who devastated Katakapuri, i.e. Cuttack, who threatened Nandyela Krishnama by the strength of his arm, who was the right hand of the Karnata emperor (Venkata I), who defeated Kondraju Venkatadri, captured Chennuru, composed Telugu, works of

high literary merit such as *kakusthavijaya*, built the tank
called Yellamarajacheru (in the name of his father), who led
the campaign against Dravida king of Madura, who displayed
his herosim in humiliating the Mohammedan sovereign
(Padusa) in the battle of Penugonda and was the son of
Rangamamba, who held the birudas—Aivaraganda,
Mannehamvira and Rachabebbuli, who was the father of
Matla Tiruvengadanath, built a tank in his own name at
Siddhavattan (Sidhout) which was won by his father Yella at
the point of his sword after crushing Kondraju Tirupatiraju at
the battle of Utukuru and who constructed as a complemental
protective wall of Siddavatesvara, the fort round the town to
last as long as the Sun and the Moon endure."

Midway between these two hills there is a tower called Gali
Gopura, or the tower of wind (Gali in Telugu means wind). The
hills on which this is situated form part of the Eastern Ghats.
These hills were called by different names in different eras viz.
Rishabhadri in the Krita Yuga, Anjanachala in the Treta Yuga,
Seshachala in the Dvapara Yuga and Venkatagiri in the present
Kali Yuga.

In the same place there is a minor shrine dedicated to
Sudarsana[1] or Chakrathalvar, the fire deity. He has 16 hands,
holding in each a weapon. The flame in this shrine assumes
the form of a shatkona or hexagon.

SCULPTURES

In the gopura or tower downhill several Puranic legends are
commemorated in sculpture. Also the statues of king
Krishnadevaraya of Vijayanagara and his consorts Chinnadevi
and Tirumaladevi are installed in a separate shrine on the top
of the hill within the temple proper. An inscription of their
visit and endowments made to this shrine is engraved below
the figures. A little further to the left of the gopura, there is

a figure of Venkatapati Raya (A.D. 1586–1613), who removed the seat of the Vijayanagara dynasty to Chandragiri. The important scenes stating the capture of the Udayagiri fortress could be seen in the second courtyard of the temple.

CAMPHOR ANOINTMENT

The custom of anointing the body of this god has its origin in the fact that, at one time, an old Brahman devotee made a vow to dig a tank near this temple. Being too poor to pay the wages he began to engage his pregnant wife to carry the excavated earth. When the woman felt the pangs of labour the god himself in the guise of a Brahman youth began to help her by carrying the earth half-way! On noticing this the old man grew jealous at a third man sharing the virtues of his service to the god and so hit him with his crowbar. To his utter surprise he found blood pouring out from the same spot in the body of the idol where he had hit the body of the youth! Thus finding that it was no other than the Lord himself who worked this miracle he immediately began to dress the wound with camphor. From that time people began the custom of applying camphor to the body of the deity.

TONSURE CEREMONY

The principal part of the vow in the uphill consists in shaving completely the heads of men and women. how and when this custom began nobody is able to give a satisfactory account.

EPIGRAPHICAL IMPORTANCE

The Chola inscriptions in the temple prove the fact that they were written in the time of Vira Narasimhadeva Yadavaraya on the occasion of a removation of the temple. The originals seem to have contained grants to Tiruvengadadeva, the deity of Tirumalai, thus showing that the temple was already in existence at the time of Chola king Rajaraja and Rajendra Chola. Most of the inscriptions belong to the second Vijayanagar dynasty; two of them mention gifts made by Chinnaji Amma and Tirumala Amma, two queens of Krishyaraya and one speaks of Krishnaraya's attacking Prataparudra Gajapati, his pursuing him as far as Kondavedu and capturing the fort of Udayagiri.

The Madras Government Epigraphist's Report for the year 1903–04 on page 4 says:

'The interior of the Tirumala temple contains no inscriptions whatever. Perhaps the repairs made during the time of king Vira Narasimhadeva Yadavaraya, to which reference is made in one of the records on the north wall of the first prakara (*Epigraphia Indica*, Vol. VII, p. 25), are answerable for the absence of lithic records in the interior of the temple. But I have been assured by respectable gentlmen at Tirupati that there are inscriptions in that portion of the interior which is open to the public only once during the year in the Mukkotti Ekadasi day.

'At Tirumala there are three groups of statues of royal personages close to the first gopura from outside, of which two are made of copper and third of stone. The group, which is founded to the right as one enters the temple, consists of Vijayanagara king Krishnaraya and his two consorts Chinnadevi (to his left) and Tirumaladevi (on his right side) whose names are engraved on the images. These two queen are frequently mentioned in inscriptions as making donations to temples along with the king. They seem to have accompanied him on his tours of conquest. Of course we have no means of ascertaining if what we have here is an accurate representation of Krishnaraya.

'The accounts of the Portuguese chronicler Domingo Paes show that Krishnaraya was a strong man fond of out-door sports and physical exercise (Mr. Sewell's *Forgotten Empire*, p. 121). Paes informs us that the king used to drink a three-quarter pint of gingelly oil before sunrise and then to take exercise until he sweated out all the oil (Ibid, p. 249). If these statements are true, the statue cannot altogether be a conventional representation of Krishnaraya. To judge from the characte in which the names are engraved (on the right shoulder in each case) the images must have been set up during the lifetime of the king. To the left of the same gopura is a statue of Venkatapatiraya made of copper and containing his name. This must be Venkata I (A.D. 1586-1613) who removed the seat of government to Chandragiri. The third group is also to the left but made of stone and there is nothing to show whom the two images—a king and his consort—represent.

[2]"The Venkatesa Perumal temple in the Tirupati hill bears four Chola inscriptions on the north wall of its first prakara, which were copied from their (now lost) originals; when the temple was rebuilt in the fortieth year of Vira Narasimhadeva Yadavaraya. The second and third of these four copies (Nos. 62 and 63 of 1888–89) are dated in the 14th year of Parakesarivarman. These two inscriptions record gifts by Samavai or Kadavan Perundevi, the daughter of Pallava Perkadaiyar, and the queen of Sattividangan or Sri Kadappattigal. It is not imporabable that this Pallava king Sattividangan, i.e. Sakti Vitanka, who was a contemporary of the early Chola king Parakesarivarman is the same person as the Pallava king Satti, i.e. Sakti, (in the second half of the ninth century).'

ICONOLOGY[3]

Idols are no mere toys, that the temples are not mere museums or repositories of artistic images, the places of pilgrimage are not holiday resorts but they are all centres of powerful activity and have both attractive and repulsive forces. Starting for a place of pilgrimage must be preceded by devotional sublime objects by a mental preparation to formulate the higher desires and aspirations and to receive the fulfilment thereof and the pilgrimage must be conducted in a religious spirit. If in these centres your evil thoughts overpower you they will be repelled with a redoubled force on your self but if the desire to conquer the lower nature in you predominates on the occasion you are considerably helped by the ready response which the magnetism of the place accords to you. Hence you will find that the pilgrim coming from a distance becomes the recipient of greater blessings than the vicious man on the spot who makes himself impervious to the good influences as is truly said: "The nearer the Church the farther from God." The process of pilgrimage conducted on the right lines is bound to earn for you the attainment of your higher aims but at least through an obstinate pursuance of it. Every time you make a pilgrimage you are made better and though you may start with Bhoga you will end in Yoga.

The idol worship is of paramount importance, and let us not be misguided by the enemies of our religion if they deride or scorn our idolatry.

Hindu iconography is therefore not a mere secular science of fine art but a science of religion and as such it is a very vast science dealing with the location and structure of our temples, the form and constitution of our idols, both the principal and the subordinate deities, the ceremony of installation and perpetuation of the spiritual magnetism in these centres etc.

God's manifestation in the idols is the essence of our religious life. Alien religionists have been deriding this form of worship in very strong terms which have been appealing to those who never cared to enquire or study the underlying significance of the much condemned idolatry.

To take an ordinary common sense point of view an idol represents or symbolises the deity and even if it did nothing more than that it need not be a subject of decision. It is a common practice prevalent in all countries to commemorate a hero of history, politics or science by a statue wherein the prominent features of the hero are best manifested. An equestrian statue in a coat of armour represents a great military hero. An impressive statue with a book in the hand represents a great educationist. The unveiling of statues and their decorations form a regular puja. If these be appropriate to the human heroes may we not with force claim for the divine statue a continuous puja as knowledge of and reverence to the deity form, the essence of every portion of our existence. but the idols enshrined in the holy places of worship are more than mere symbols. The initial object of setting up images before us is no doubt to facilitate our mediation, to fix a definite object before us for concentration and when our thoughts are so concentrated they help us in taking the thoughts over to an object beyond and behind the actual phenomenon and that is the noumenon thereof. This power of translation and transportation exists in the Holy Idols by the amsa of god that has been invoked both at the initial pratishta as well as the daily puja of these idols made by the appropriate mantras. The chanting of the appropriate mantras concentrate in the the image an amount of spiritual magnetism by the power of the mantras and the highly developed faculties of those who chant the same. Hence we find that pratishtas made by those who have been in themselves an amsa or avesa of god like Sri Sankara, Sri Ramanuja, or Lord Gauranga bring in an imperishable and ever-growing magnetism. Hence it is essential too that the Archakas entrusted with the daily worship must be also men

of high and unimpeachable character. The Paramatman infuses
his amsa in such images and shrines in graded proportions and
is ever present with us in this form. It is upon the strength of
the initiation and worship and upon the extent of the God's
amsa that has entered into and pervaded these images depend
the varying greatness of our religious centres.

It is also to be noted that in some centres the Paramatman
makes a manifestation suo moto without an initial invocation
and that is known as Swayam Vyaktam or self manifestation
of God in an image. The foremost instance of this is that of
Sri Venkateswara in Tirupati. Thus we speak of the Tirupati
shrine occupying the foremost place, the shrines at Srirangam,
Conjeeveram, Badri Narayan, Kalahasti, Rameswaram,
Tiruvannamalai, Kasi, etc., being more important than the
lesser shrines elsewhere and so on in varying gradations.
Though from one standpoint the shrine of even the least
importance is an object of veneration for its own religious
efficacy yet in the determination of the relative religious objects
to be attained the varying importance cannot be lost sight of.
The Agamas both *Vaighanasa* and *Pancharatra* which are
treatises prescribing the particular forms of idol worship have
been intended on literally by some authors on iconography and
the situation and significance of idols have been judged from
the standpoint of the rules referred to in these agamas; but in
my humble opinion they do not afford infallible tests in our
study of the ancient temples. These Agamas have become
interpolated and interspersed with sectarian prejudices while
the inherent features of the ancient temples are not in
consonance with these narrow regulations.

There then are spread all over the country numerous idols
some of which are of very recent origin, some older still but
whose installations are borne but by the *Sthalapuranas* while
some yet are of an age out of calculation. In the case of these

last, attempts are often made by the archaeologists to fix their age by inscriptions and forms surrounding the idols, many of which certainly came into existence on various occasions to glorify the acts of those who have periodically rendered some service or *kainkaryam* to the temples. On the whole it is futile to attempt the fixing of the age of shrines like Tirupati.

"The Parabrahman is omnipresent and omnipenetrative. Still there is what is known as the seat of the Parabraman which the Visishtadvaitins call the Srivaikuntham. *Indira cuncta nec incluses; extra cuncta nec exclusus.* God exists in his universe, but he transcends it also. By whatever denomination it may be known it stands to reason and is in accordance with the Puranas that there is a centre where everything is good and nothing bad, where there is all knowledge and no ignorance, where there is all virture and no vice. The Brahman has, according to one school, one of six supreme attributes i.e., Shadguna and according to another he is Nirguna. But both are synonymous as in the one case it is based on relativity and in the other on absolutism or positivism. This centre of centres, this sanctum sanctorum of the divine realm is the noumenon of the Tirupati hills. if you have any trust in those accredited agents of god, who now and then performed on earth their mission of unravelment of the divine mysteries, then trust me when I say that their writings locate the Sri Vaikuntham in the place manifested as the Tirupati hills and Parabrahman in the idol manifested as Sri Venkateswara.

The first Archa form therefore which the Supreme being divulged in for the benefit of human meditation was in the Tirupati shrine. Hence therefore the Dhruvaberam of the Mula Vigraham presents itself to us as a combination of the Trinity in the Unity though two alone are visible in the manifested form. The Brahma aspect representing the creation was not at any time supposed to be an object of meditation for the created because it is an aspect not concerning them in their development. Hence the two aspects of Vishnu and Siva alone are made manifest to us in the Dhruvaberam. The Tata in the Kritam, the Nagabaranam on the right forearm recall to us, whenever we worship this idol, the great Siva while with Mahalakshmi on the right breast the general features of the image present to us the protector.

In other words there are in this idol the Vyakta Vishnu, the Avyakta Brahma and the Vyakta Vyakta Siva. In one view this idol may also be described as the Vyuha form of the Paramatman. This idol therefore is just the Paramatman becoming manifest without any initial invocation by any particular sage or saint. The subsequent avatars great and small, the later sages and saints who had the amsa or avesa of God in them have all contributed by their magnetism or will power to keep up the full manifestation of God in this idol. Hence this is to this day and will ever be at least as long as the Archa form is willed and permitted by the Paramatman, the foremost shrine on the earth. The spiritual influence is further kept up here by the daily worship not of the human Archakas we find there but by that of the Nityasuris. You will find here that every night when the temple is closed for us the vessels used for worship are filled with fresh water. Early morning when the doors are re-opened that water is distributed to us as the one used for Brahmaradhanam during the preceding night, i.e., the worship conducted by Brahma with the Nityasuris! It is by these that the spiritual power of the shrine is daily sustained. Hence the Dhruvaberam of this temple commands unique power and exercises a very unique influence. The idol here is in the standing posture, i.e. the Stanaka form with the left hand extended to the left thigh and placed on it. This is called the Kati or Yoga. Be your aim what it may, whether the attainment of pleasure, prowess or salvation that is the one which can give

it to you. The right hand is with the fingers pointed forwards
and downwards. It is known as Varadahastam, the hand
assuring you a gift of what you seek in good faith and
earnestness; viewed in the Yoga aspect, the posture of the two
hands together demonstrates the Charama sloka. The khadga
or the sword and shield that extends from the waist and
proceeds between the two legs is the ruling power, the symbol
also of the dispeller of ignorance. This idol is a complete
representation of the Supreme being in all aspects. At the feet
of this Dhruvaberam you will find the small silver idol of the
Kautuka or Bhoga which is used for the daily bath. The daily
bath of this emblem of purity represented symbolically by the
whiteness of the silver renders water and all the elements pure.
Water is the most important of the elements as from water
evolved all the creation and as everything is reduced to water
at the dissolution of the universe. There is between the
Dhruvaberam and the Kautukaberam a connecting link known
as Sambandhakoorcham which is clearly exemplified on
occasions of Sahasra Sankhabhishekam. This is a grand
ceremonial bath or *tirumanjanam* for this idol in the mandapam
outside the golden gate. On this occasion a long silk cord is
made to commence from the feet of the Moola Vigraham and
extend up to the Kautukaberam when this small idol is taken
out to the mandapa. Thus the purification of the elements really
proceeds from the Dhruvaber. This as the Bhogaberam
discharges the functions of all Bhogam, i.e., the enjoyment by
God of all the pleasures of his creation. The idea is the animate
and the inanimate world—The Chetana and the Achetana are
all for the Leela and Bhogam of the Supreme being and by
symbolising those pleasures which mortals consider valuable
this Bhogamurti manifests the supreme aspects of the pleasure.
There is next to this idol the Snapana Srinivasa Murti which
is said to be an embodiment of the anger as the facial expression

will show. It is not that low passion of anger which we detest but that higher aspect of it which punishes sinners only to protect them. This Murti is taken out only once in a year i.e., on the Kausika Dwadesi day at 4 a.m., and is taken back to the temple before sunrise. In connection with the Snapanaberam of Tirumalai there is a tradition that if this idol is taken out on any other day or after sunrise even on that day the world will be annihilated! The idea is that the Parabrahman represented in the Dhruvaberam in constant conjunction with Purusha (Kautukaberam) and Pradhana (Snapana) is the cause of the creation and sustenance while the separation of this combination means destruction or Pralaya. It is only the supreme kindness of Iswara in another form. There is on the right side the Utsavaberam called Malai Appan. The Lord of the hills who is taken out for all festivals and processions, who fulfills the desire of devotee who wishes to offer all his personal sacrifices to the deity in this shrine and who gives the acquittance to them and for the discharge of their vows.

In this temple unlike the other Vishnu temples you will find no minor shrines or idols representing the Vaishnava saints—the Alwars and the Acharyas. These have their temples in the places where they were born or lived in their incarnations and also wherever their influence has been exerted whereas here they all exist in their primaeval form on par with the Nityasuris and the Muktas because they proceeded from and returned to this place. but you find a temple only for Sri Ramanuja who is said to have added the visible Sankha (conch) and the Chakra (discus) to this idol. It is said that originally these were not in the idol and when a dispute arose as to whether the idol was a Vaishnavite or a Saivite one Ramanuja proposed that both the emblems should be placed before the deity during night after worship and the idol might choose between the two and declare what he is. It is added that during night Ramanuja, an Avatar of Adisesha, took the form of a cobra and went in through the opening intended for passing out the abhishekam water from the grabhagriha and prayed to the deity whereupon he took up the Vishnu emblems! Thereafter that opening was closed, and to this day you will find all the water being taken out in the vessels.

Give this tradition what it is worth. This later introduction of a temple for Ramanuja does not alter the supreme significance of the initial shrine. The temple of Sri Venkateswara is one of perfection. The spiritual influence wielded by it is unique. I can give you instances of strong-minded atheists and sceptics who went into it after being pressurised by their wives and children and came out of it as completely transformed theists devoted to god more than their fellow theists. All this cannot be accomplished by a mere statue-like representation of the Iswara but by the pervading amsa of god in the intensest form in this particular shrine. The hills underlying and surrounding this shrine are the manifest Vedas. This Vedic environment cannot but maintain the spiritual magnetism of the place intact.

In the Lower Tirupati or Tirupati proper you have the temple of Sri Govindaraja Swami and Sri Kothandaramaswami. In the former the Dhruvaberam is in a reclining posture known in the Agamas as Virasayanamurti. At the feet there are the Sri Devi and the Bhu Devi. The demons Madhu and Kaitabha stand at the feet in an act of supplication, Brahma is seated on a lotus issuing from the navel of the image. The idol is thus reclining on Adisesha. The right hand is bent towards the head while the left hand is extended up to the knee. There is also the khadga here. These in a reclining posture are the indications of a Viramurti. This was the posture of Bhagavan Sri Krishna just before the commencement of the great war of Kurukshetra when he was taking his firm resolve. The head of this idol is placed on the south. This position indicates the grant of victory (Jayadana) to the worshipper. The Utsava Vigraham here is in Virasana form, is seated as Arjuna's Charioteer. The left hand hold, the reins while the right hand presents what is known as Chinmudra or Vyakyana mudra also known as Sandarsan mudra. This mudra consists in the tips of the thumb and the forefinger being made to touch each other so as to form a circle, the other fingers being kept straight; the palm of the hand faces the front. This is a mudra adopted when an explanation or exposition is given. Here in this idol it represents Bhagavan Sri Krishna dictating Bhagavatgita to Arjuna. The devotees will attain both knowledge and victory by worshipping idols of this form.

I referred to the temple of Sri Kothandaramaswami in Tirupati. Sri Rama was one of the Dasavatars, but the peculiarity of this Avatar was that it was wholly humanised and the unique symbols of Vishnu, viz., the Sankha and Chakra are not associated with idols of Sri Rama. Hence Ramamurtis are two-handed and hold only the dhanusha. The group of idols in a shrine of Sri Ramachandra if complete will present an ideal an ideal king and man, and ideal womans and wife, an ideal brother and an ideal Bhakta. The bow and the arrows are ever ready for action to destroy evil force.

In Tiruchchanoor you have the goddess in Padmasana exercising highest form of that motherly affection which makes you sure of your father's love for you. Devi worship is a distinct factor in Hindu religion and there is a volume of literature on the Devi icons. Among the Hindus there are some known as Saktas who assign a greater place to Devi than to the male god. But others assign a subordinate position to Devi. The goddess in Tiruchchanoor represents Devi according to the Vaishnavite conception of the female factor at the head of the divine realm; she is the consort of Vishnu and known as Mahalakshmi. When in conjunction with a Vishnu idol she takes the place of Sri Devi represented with two hands, one holding a lotus. When she is installed as an independent icon with a separate shrine as in Tiruchchanoor she is represented with four hands, two holding each a lotus and the front hand protecting the Bhaktas and assuring them the fulfilment of their desires. Among the shrines allotted to goddesses, this temple at Tiruchchanoor for Padmavati occupies as prominent a place as the shrine of Venkateswara with this difference that I class the temple at Tiruchchanoor among the secondary Archas. About 'Sri' the *Vishnupurana* says "that mother of the universe—Vishnu's energy is enduring and undeteriorating—O foremost of the twice-born ones, even as Vishnu is omnipresent, so this one also. Vishnu is the sense and she is the word. She is morality, Vishnu is justice, Vishnu is perception and she the power thereof : he is merit and she is the act of piety. Vishnu is the Creator and she the Creation. Sri is earth and Hari the supporter thereof."

'Connected with this group of shrines is a Kshetram—the temple of Kapaliswaraswami in Lower Tirupati relating to the appearance of Parama Siva in response to the penance of Kapilamahamuni.'

TIRUCHCHANUR

This holy village wherein stands the temple dedicated to Alamelumangai, the consort of the god at Tirupati, lies at the foot of the hill at Tirupati. It is also known as Chiratanur and Padmasaras. Some of the inscriptions mention the locality as Tiruchchoganur, Tiruchchoginur or Tiruchchuganur.

It is doubtful if this goddess was the presiding deity of the place in early times as well. The most ancient shrine of the temple, which is said to have been called Sundararaja-perumal, was pulled down a few years ago and the ancient inscriptions which it contained were all scattered. Some of the inscribed slabs are found at the entrances of private houses. A few have been built into modern structures and others are lying uncared for in the temple and its neighbourhood. In some of the fragments the village is called Tiruchchoganur or Tiruchchoginur, while the form Tiruchchuganur occurs in later inscriptions found at Yogi Mallavaram, which is quite close to Tiruchchanur. Thus the connection which is claimed for the village with the sage Suka is not warranted by earlier records. The temple, or, at least the shrine which has been pulled down, was apparently known in ancient times as Ilangoyil. In one of the Tanjore inscriptions of the Chola king Rajaraja (*S.I.I.* Vol. II, No. 66) reference is made several times to the Tiruvilangoyil temple at Kadambur. Here there is nothing to prove absolutely whether Tiruvilangoyil was a Siva or a Vaishnava temple. The Tamil work *Periyapurana*, which gives an account of the sixty-three devotees of Siva, mentions the Ilangoyil at Miyachchur, which must be Saiva. Again, in the Nallur grant of the Vijayanagara king Harihara II, published by me (Ep. Ind., Vol. III, p. 126, verse 24) Yalangovil, which is a popular form of Ilangoyil, occurs as the name of a Saiva temple. The word Ilangoyil itself means 'the house of the young king' and may be taken to denote a shrine of Subrahmanya. Thus there is reason to suppose that the shrine in the Tiruchchanur temple which has been pulled down was originally called Ilangoyil and was therefore Saiva. From the earliest hitherto described inscription of the place (No. 262 of 1904) it appears that this shrine was built as accompaniment of the temple at Tirupati, known at the time as Tiruvengadattu Perumanadiyal. Perhaps this can be taken to support the popular belief that the deity at Tirumalai was originally Siva. In the temple at Yogi Mallavaram, which was known in ancient times as Tippaladiswara were found a number of Chola inscriptions."

THE 108 VAISHNAVA HOLY PLACES
(NUTTETTU TIRUPATI)

On account of the importance of this place amongst the Vaishnava shrines it is held in much esteem. There are 108 such places in the whole of India, and they are:

1. Tiruvarangam — (modern Srirangam) — The temple faces the south as from here the Lord Ranganatha is supposed to guard Lanka (Ceylon) to satisfy his devotee Vibhishana, a faithful devotee of Sri Rama.

2. Kozhiur or Nichulapuri (Modern Uraiyur) — The name is due to the fact that a fowl (kozhi Tamil) and an elephant had a fight at this place at one time and the former came out successful. The Lord here is named Manavalapperumal by Tirumangai Alwar. Also king Ravivarmaraja worshipped the Lord here. The temple faces the north.

3. Tanjaimamanikkoil — (modern Tanjore) — This temple is situated on the bank of the Vennar. To sage Parasara, the god is said to have first appeared here; close by there are nine other places relating to these 108 places.

4. Anbil (two miles north of No. 8) — The deity here first appeared to sage Valmiki and Brahma.

5. Karambanur (Uttamarkoil, three miles north of Srirangam) — There are shrines of Brahma and Siva also within this temple and thus is unique as the temple for the Tirumarti. The Lord here appeared to sage Sanakar etc. Plantain is the Sthala Vriksha or the local tree.

6. Tiruvellarai (ten miles north of Srirangam) — The

birthplace of Uyyakondan. For the goddess earth and king Sibi, god appeared here on the hill known as Svetagiri.

7. **Pullabudangudi** (four miles north of Sundaraperumalkoil) — This is famous for Sri Rama's having visited this shrine. Also king Krita worshipped the Lord here.

8. **Tiruppernagar** (otherwise known as Koviladi, ten miles north-west of Budalur) — The god has a pot near him in his right hand and this is in keeping with the name of the god Appakudaththan (kudam means pot in Tamil). Sages Upamanya and Parasara worshipped the Lord here.

9. **Adanur** (five miles west of No. 14) — Here appeared the deity to the holy cow Kamadhenu and Tirumangai Alwar.

10. **Tiruvazhundur** (Terazhundur, four miles south-east of Kuttalam, near Mayavaram) — The god here is said to have appeared for the river Kaveri.

11. **Sirupuliyur** (three miles north-east of Peralam) — Here the temple faces the south. For sages Vyasa and Vyagramar the Lord appeared here.

12. **Tiruchcherai** (six miles south-east of No. 14) — The river Kavei is said to have worshipped the deity here and he granted a boon that during Tula (October–November) month, she should be considered as superior even to Ganga.

13. **Talaichchangananmadiyam** (Thalaichangadu, ten miles south-east of Shiyali) — Chandra, the moon, is said to have worshipped the god here. It is on the southern bank of the sacred Kaveri river.

14. **Tirukkudandai** (modern Kumbakonam) — Sage Hemarishi is said to have prayed to the god here who appeared with 'Saranga' (deer) in hands, in the temple of Sarangapani. There is a sculptural representation of this sage in the west of the temple on the northern bank of Pottamarai tank.

15. **Tirukkandiyur** (six miles north of Tanjore en route to

Tiruvadi) — It is here that Vishnu removed the sin of Rudra who had severed one of Brahma's heads. Sage Agastya has also worshipped the deity here.

16. Tiruvinnagar (modern Uppiliyappankoil near Kumbakonam, three miles east of No. 16) — The goddess earth worshipped the Lord here. A votive offering without salt neither spoils the taste nor makes the dishes unpalatable! This is Tirupati to the Tamil country. Marriages on vows are performed here. The Lord here is in a standing posture.

17. Tirukkannapuram (five miles south-east of Nannilam) — Sage Kanvar is said to have worshipped the deity here, who is in a standing posture.

18. Tiruvali Tiruanagiri (six miles south-east of Shiyali) — The temple faces the south. In Tiruvali there is a shrine for Narasimha and in Tirunagiri for saints Manavalan and Tirumangai Alwar.

19. Tirunagai or Nagapattanam (modern Negapatam) — Serpent Nagaraja prayed to the god here, in the temple of Soundararajapperumal. This is an important place of saint Tirumangai Alwar.

20. Tirunaraiyur (Nachchiyarkoil, six miles south east of No. 16) — Sage Medava who lost his daughter got her back by praying to the deity here. Tirumangai Alwar had his *samasrayanam* (initiation) here. There is a sculptural Garuda here which is taken out only on two occasions in Margali and Masi months on the prescribed dates; and as he is taken out the bearers are said to feel the weight in varying grades!

21. Nandipuravinnagaram (Nadankovil, three miles south of No. 14) — The temple faces the west. Nandi (the holy bull) worshipped the god here and the place where he prayed, is named as Nandivanam. Also king Sibi worshipped the Lord here.

22. Jndalur (Tiruvazhuntur, three miles north-east of

mayavaram) — Chandra, the moon, is said to have worshipped the Lord here on the bank of the Kaveri.

23. Tillai-Tiruchchitrakutam (modern Chidambaram) — The shrine to the deity Govindaraja perumal is within the famous Siva temple of Nataraja. The Lord here appeared to sage Kanvar and the 3000 dikshadars of Chidambaram.

24. Kalichiramavingaram Sirkali (Shiyali) — The temple is named as Thadalankoil and it is within the town quite the railway station. This is in honour of the Tiruvikrama form, and the Mula Vigraha or the deity fixed in the central shrine is of this form. The Lord here appeared to sage Ashtakona.

25. Kudalur (Aduthurai Perumalkoil in Tanjore district, four miles north of Iyyampet) — The Lord here is known as Vaiyagam Kathaperumal (i.e.,) the protector of the world. The Lord here appeared to sage Nandaka.

26. Tirukannamangai (two miles east of Kilvelur) — Sage Gautama is said to have worshipped the deity here.

27. Tirukannamangai (five miles west of Tiruvarur) — Varuna, the guardian deity of the west, and Romasa Rishi are said to have worshipped the god here. There is a beehive in the temple to which 'puja', i.e. worship, is done as Devas (celestials) are said to be worshipping the god here in this form.

28. Kapistalam (two miles north of Papanasam) — Both Gajendra and Anjaneya worshipped the deity here. Close by at a distance of four miles on the north-east is Tirumandankudi, the birthplace of Tondaradippodi Alwar.

29. Tiruvelliyangudi (six miles to the north of Tiruvidaimaruthur) — Sukra worshipped the deity here. Also sage Parasara visited this place.

30. Manimadakovil (Tirunagur, four miles north-east of Vaithiswarankoil) — Ekadasa Rudras (eleven Rudras) and Indra worshipped the deity here. Six important shrines lie close by and it should have been an important centre at one time.

31. Vaikundavinnagaram (in No. 30) — Sage Uthankar and king Uparisaravasa worshipped the god here.

32. Arimeyavinnagaram (in No. 30) — Sage Uthankar worshipped the Lord here.

33. Tiruttevanartogai (Kizhaichalai, two miles north of No. 30) — The Temple faces the west. Sage Vasishta worshipped the god here.

34. Vanpurushottamam (in No. 30) — Sage Upamanyu worshipped the deitry here.

35. Semponseikovil (in No. 30) — Rudra worshipped the god here who gave out the importance of the Dvadasanamams or the 12 Vaishnava marks to be worn at particular parts of the body.

36. Tirutterri Ambalam (in No. 30) — Ananda worshipped the god here.

37. Tirumanikkudam (Annankoil, a few furlongs west of No. 33) — King Swetaraja of Ikshvaku line worshipped the Lord here.

38. Tirukkavalampadi (eight miles south-east of Shiyali) — The Lord Gopalakrishna is worshipped here.

39. Tiruvellakkulam (Annankoil, a few furlongs west of No. 33) — King Swetaraja of Ikshavaku line worshipped the Lord here.

40. Parthanpalli (two miles south east of No. 39) — Partha (Arjuna), Varuna and Ekadasa Rudra worshipped the god here, who stand facing the west.

41. Tirumalirumsolaimalai (modern Alagarkoil near Madura, twelve miles north-east of Madura) — The hill on which the Lord stays is known as Rishapagiri. The waterfall Nupuragangai on the hill is a sacred one. King Malayadhvaja Pandya worshipped the Lord here.

42. Tirukkoshtiyur (thirty miles north of Manamadura) — This is the birthplace of saint Nambi. The lord here is named

Saumiyanarayana and sage Kadambar worshipped the Lord here. Here the Lord is depicted in all the forms—sitting, standing, lying and dancing.

43. Tirumeyyam (twelve miles south of Pudukotta) — The temple faces the south and for the Devas the Lord here appeared under a jackfruit tree.

44. Tiruppullani (Darbaisayanam, five miles south of Ramnad) — This is also known as Puttaranyam where Sri Rama is seen in his reclining posture! Varuna, the god of ocean, prayed to Sri Rama here. The Aswatta (*ficus religiosa*) tree is considered sacred here.

45. Tiruppullani (Tiruththangal, fifteen miles north-west of Sattur) — The Lord here appeared unto a lion. King Salleya Pandya and Sri Vallabha also worshipped the Lord here.

46. Tirumohur (seven miles north-east of Madura) — The Rudras worshipped the god here.

47. Tirukkudal (ten Madurai, modern Madura) — The shrine is known as Kudalalagarkoil and the vimana over the central shrine is known as Ashtangavimana. The Lord here appeared to sage Brigu.

48. Srivilliputtur (twenty-five miles north-west of Sattur) — This is the birthplace of Perialvar and Andal. Sage Mandukar worshipped the god here. Here the Nayak kings had a palace and it is the Tirupati for Pandya country.

49. Tirukkuruhur (modern Alwar Tirunagari, twenty miles east of Tinnevelly) — Brahma and Nammalwar worshipped the god here. There is a sacred tamarind tree in the temple which is said to be possessed of supernatural powers! This is on the Tampraparni river and there is a shrine Nammalwar. There are nine important shrines here lying closely inclusive of this and hence they are known as Nava Tirupatis (nava means nine).

50. Rettai Tirupati (Tolaivillimangalam, close to No. 49)

— Vayu, god of Wind, prayed to the god here. There are two separate shrines here and hence thename Rettai Tirupati (Rettai in Tamil means two).

51. Srivaramangai (Vanamamalai or Todadri, modern Nanguneri twenty miles south of Tnnevelly) — The god here with all his attendants appeared to sages Markandeya, Bhrigu and Romasa. There is a well, the water of which is said to cure several diseases!

52. Tiruppulingudi (close to No. 49) — Niruti, guardian of the south-west, worshipped the lord here. Here Ranganatha was worshipped by king Tondaman.

53. Tirupperai (two miles south of No. 50) — Sukra and Esana, god of the north-east, worshipped the god here.

54. Srivaikuntam (three miles west of No. 49) — Indra, the god of the east, worshipped the god here. There is a sculpture of Sri Rama embracing Hanuman in a mandapa here. It is on the Tamparaparani river.

55. Varagunamangai (close to No. 49) — Agni, god of the south-east, worshipped the god here.

56. Tirukkulanthai (Perungulam, four miles north-east of No. 92) — Brihaspati worshipped the god here.

57. Tirukkurungudi (ten miles south-west of No. 51) — Siva worshipped the god here and he stands the god Vishnu.

58. Tirukkolur (close to No. 49) — Kubera, the God of the north, worshipped the god here. Also Madurakavi Alwar. It is on the Tamparaparani river.

59. Tiruvanandapuram or Anantasayanam (modern Trivandrum, capital of Travancore state) — Chandra, the moon, Indra and Rudra worshipped the lord here who is named Padmanabha.

60. Tiruvanparisaram (Tirupatisaram, twenty-five miles south-east of No. 57) — To Vindai, Kari and Odayanangai, the lord here apeared. The sea-bath here is sacred. Twelve

miles on the south of this is the sacred Kanyakumari (Cape Comorin).

61. Tirukkatkarai (two miles east of Edapalli in Shoranur line) — The temple faces the south. Sage kapilar worshipped the god here.

62. Tirumuzhikkalam (five miles east of Ariganidi on the Shoranur line) — The lord here appeared to sage Hareda.

63. Kuttanadu or Tiruppuliyur (Puliyur, three miles west of No. 64) — To the Sapta Rishis (the Seven Sages), the god appeared here.

64. Tiruchchenmgannur (modern Trichur, twenty miles north-east of Quilon) — Siva fearing Padmasura worshipped the lord here who faces the west.

65. Tirunavai (close to Eddakkolam station on the Mangaloare line) — The temple faces the south. Lakshmi and Gajendra worshipped the god here.

66. Tiruvallavazh (Tiruvallai, five miles north of No. 67) — The lord here appeared to Kandakarna.

67. Tiruvanvandur (Tiruvamundur, five miles west of No. 64) — The temple faces the west and he lord appeared here to Narada.

68. Tiruvattaru (twenty miles north-east of No. 60) — Parasurama worshipped the god here.

69. Vittuvakkodu (ten miles south-east of Edapalli on the Shoranur line) — To king Ambaresha, the lord here appeaed facing the south.

70. Tirukkadittanam (three miles north of No. 66) — The lord here appeared to king Rukmangada.

71. Tiruvaranvilai (Arummulai, four miles east of Sengannur to be approached from Quilon) — The god appeared unto Brahma facing the north.

72. Tiruvahindrapuram (three miles west of Tiruppapuliyur

— Cuddalore) — To Garuda, the lord appeared here on the bank of the river Gadilam.

73. Tirukovalur (Tirukoilur) — This is the famous place for the Trivikrama form. The lord here appeared to king Bali and sage Mrikanda, father of Markandeya. It is on the southern bank of the river.

74. Kanchipuram (Hastigiri, modern Conjeevaram) — There is the famous Arulalapperumal or. Varadaraja temple in little Conjeevaram. The temple faces the west. Besides, there are 27 other shrines dedicated to the various forms in this town scattered throughout the town. It is on the river Vegavati. The deity here appeared to Brahma, Gajendra and Narada.

75. Attabhuyakaram (Ashtabujam a few yards to the south of No. 82) — The temple faces the west. Gajendra worshipped the lord here.

76. Tiruttanga (Vilakkolikoil, close to No. 75) — The temple faces the west. Saraswati, the goddess of learning, worshipped the lord here.

77. Velukkai (south of No. 17) — Sage Bhrigu prayed and worshipped the lord here. The original shrine on the lake is said to have been washed away in a flood.

78. Padagam (Pandavathutharsannithi, west of Ekambaraswami Sannithi street) — This is the temple of the famous Krishna who acted as tudar (messenger to the Pandavas). The god appeared unto King Janamejaya.

79. Neragam — Sage Akrura worshipped the lord here. By neglect the shrine is no longer under worship and the deity is now in No. 81.

80. Nilatingaltundam — Siva and Parvati worshipped the god here. The shrine went into ruin and the deity is now on the first prakara of Ekambara temple.

81. Uragam (Ulakalanthaperumalkoil, west of Kamakshiamman temple) — This is the temple dedicated to

the famous Trivikrama form. To Uraga of the serpent species, the lord appeared here facing the west.

82. Tiruvekka (Yathothkarisannithi, few furlongs on the west of Varadarajaswami temple) — This is the birthplace of Poigai Alwar. The god here is known as 'the Truth sayer' and Brahma and Saraswati worshipped him here.

83. Karagam — The temple faces the south and the lord appeared unto sage Garha. The shrine was neglected and the deity is now in No. 81.

84. Karvanam — The temple faced the west. The lord met goddess Parvati here. The shrine has been neglected and the god is now under worship in No. 81.

85. Tirukkalvanur — The temple that faced the west went into ruins and the deity is now on the north-east of the tank within the Kamakshi temple. There are shrines over the vimana.

86. Pavalavannam (Pavalavannar temple, a few furlongs to the east of Ekambareswara temple and a few furlongs to the north of Kamakshiamman temple) — The temple faces the west. The twin Aswins worshipped the lord here.

87. Paramechchuravinnagaram (Vaikunthaperumal temple) — The temple faces the west and is named Vaikunthaperumal temple. The lord here appeared to king Pallavaraya. There are sculptures on the inner walls and shrines over the central vimanas of the temple.

88. Tiruppukkuzhi (seven miles west of Conjeevaram) — Jatayu worshipped the lord here who appeared as Vijiaraghava. The figure of Jatayu is also here.

89. Tiruninravur (modern Tinnanur) — The lord appeared unto Varuna here.

90. Tiruvevvul (modern Tiruvallur near Madras) (fig. 174) — This is also called Vesharanniem. Sage Salihotra worshipped the lord Viraraghava here.

91. Tirunirmalai (three miles off west of Pallavaram) — The temple faces the south. God Ranganatha here was worshipped by king Tondaman.

92. Tiruvidavendai (Tiruvidanthai, six miles north of Mahabalipuram) — Markandeya worshipped the lord here.

93. Tirukadalmallai (modern Mahabalipuram or the seven Pagodas, Mallapuram, some twenty miles south-east of Chingleput) — This is the birthplace of Bhutatthalwar. Sage Pundarika worshipped the Lord here. This is the famous place of sculptural representation near Madras.

94. Tiruvallakkeni (modern Triplicane in the city of Madras) — The god in the temple is known as Parthasarathi, i.e. Krishna as charioteer to Arjuna. He is in the central shrine with his family consisting of brother Balarama, consort Rukmani etc. The lord was installed by sage Vyasa here and worshipped by sage Atreya. The temple has also four other shrines dedicated to Ranganatha, Narasimha, Sri Rama and Varadaraja.

95. Tirukkadigai (modern Sholingur) — This is the famous Narasimha temple. Lakshmi worshipped the lord here. There is a powerful Anjaneya on a hillock here.

96. Tiruvengadam or Venkatadri (modern Tirupati) — This is so very famous that no remarks need be offered.

97. Singavelkunram (Ahobilam, thirty miles off Nandyal) — The famous Narasimha temple. There are the nine forms of Narasimha. To save Prahlada, the lord appeared in this form.

98. Ayodhya (modern Oudh) — The famous Sri Rama temple is here. It faces the north. The Hanuman shrine is important. It is on the river Sarayu.

99. Naimisaranyam (Seven miles off Nimisar) — Sudharma and the Devas (celestials) worshipped lord here. Suthar, the author of 18 Puranas, lived here and presented to

the sages his sayings. The lord presided over the forest here, and hence puja is done to the forest.

100. Salagramam (hundred miles off Gorakhpur) — The temple faces the north. The lord here was worshipped by the river Gandaki that flows from here and wherefrom Saligrama stones are taken out.

101. Badirikasramam (nearly two-hundred miles off Katgoodani Station) — The lord himself here initiated his bhaktas (devotees) under an Elanthai tree. Being in the snowy country on the Himalayas "puja" is done only for six months and during the other six months the temple is closed. It is then that the Devas are said to be worshipping the Lord. In proof of this, the flowers laid out when closing the temple are seen to be unfaded when opening it after six months! There are two tanks known as Naradakunda of cold water and Taptakunda of hot water and after bathing in the former, people bathe in the latter.

102. Kandam (Kadinagar, modern Prayag, fifty miles off Hardwar) — For Sage Bharathwaja, the Lord here appeared.

103. Tiruppiriti (modern Josimadam, hundred and sixty miles off Hardwar) — The Lord here appeared to Parvati. It is on the Manasarova lake.

104. Dvaraka (modern Dwarka, some two hundred miles off Bombay) — The Lord here facing the west appeared unto Draupadi, wife of the Pandavas, and it is on the sacred river Gomati.

105. Vada Madurai (modern Mutira) — The Lord Sri Krishna was born here on the south bank of the Yamuna at Brindavanam and the mountain Govardanagiri which he uplifted is also nearby.

106. Tiruvaippadi (Gokulam, three miles south-east of Muttra) — To Nandagopala, the charming Krishna appeared

here on the banks of the river Yamuna. Here Lord Krishna lived for a long time.

107. Kshirabdhi (otherwise called Tiruppakkadal) — North Pole.

108. Paramapadam or Srivaikuntam — Heaven where the Lord is ever present with all His attendants!

Chapter 26

KALAHASTI

This religious centre, picturesquely situated between two steep hills, widely known for its temple dedicated to Vayu (air), and surrounded by two sacred hills, is said to have formed part of the celestial Mount Meru in ancient days. It is also known as Sripuram and Mummudichcholapuram. The flickering light in the interior sanctum is said to prove the existence of the Vayu linga which is also said to have been worshipped by a spider by spinning a web over it, a snake by placing a a gem upon the linga and an elephant by washing the linga with water, all of them obtained salvation. The marks of these animals can be found on the central linga. which together with the ancient bull in front, are whilte in colour and are *svayamban* (natural).

The river Svarnamukhi takes a northernly course at this place and it was he almost the west wall of the temple which is situate in the valley between the two hills referred to above and on the slope of the Kannappa hill. The main entrance of the temple is on the south though the God faces the west.

PURANIC VERSION

There is a story that as a result of an altercation between

Adisesha (the serpent lord) and Vayu (lord of the air) three blocks separated themselves from Mount Meru and fell to the earth. One of these fell at Kalahasti; one at Trichinopoly; and another at Trincomalee in Ceylon.

TEMPLE BUILDINGS

Of the two hills mentioned above, one in the north has the temple of Durgamba and the other in the south has the shrine of Kannapeswara and owes its name to the hunter sage Kannappa,[1] who sacrificed one of his eyes to the deity and when he was offering the other eye, the God prevented him and gave him salvation!

The temple of Kalahastiswara is situated to the west of the Kannappa hill. The two entrance gopurams (towers) of this shrine are imposing. In the second court is an underground cell where a Vinyaka called Patala Vinayaka is lodged at a depth of about 30 feet and this is said to mark the level of the river that passes by. The sculpture of Kannappa, Sakti Vinayaka, as well as the metal figures of the 63 Nayanars, snake, spider, elephant, sage Bharadvaja and Mahishasuramardhini in the inner court are of very ancient date.

OTHER SHRINES

Further south on the slope of the Kannappa hill is a small shrine dedicated to Brahma in which the linga carries figures with four faces on the different directions. Close by on the boulders are seen figures of Saiva mythology engraved and these are of high workmanship. The Manikantesvara shrine close by of a very ancient date, though now in a much neglected condition, has an important inscription in the entrance gate referring to Kannappa the famous Saiva devotee of this place.

The rock-cut mandapa to the south-east of the temple goes

by the name of Maniganniagattam in memory of a woman having been blessed with the holy "Taraka" mantra by Siva's whispering it into her right ear, similar to the incident relating to Benares. In proof of this even nowadays the bodies of the superstitious and pious are brought here at the time of death and placed upon their right side with the ear resting upon the ground. At the moment of death the body is said to turn round upon its left side while the spirit escapes cut of the right ear of the body leaving the corpse!

[2]"The Manikantesvara temple at Kalahasti, which was called Tirumanikkengaiydaiya Nayanar in ancient times, was built during the reign of Tribhuvanachakravartin Virarajendra Choladeva, who is probably identical with Kulothunga III. The building of the temple may, therefore, be assigned roughly to the last quarter of the 12th century A.D.

An inscription at Tiruvannamalai states that Krishnaraya had built the mandapa of 100 pillars and the big gopura at Kalahasti. Another on the west wall of the second prakara dated in the same year as the Tiruvannamalai record, fig. A.D. 1516–17 confirms but differs from that of Tiruvannamalai in giving details about the king's war in Kalinga and in furnishing a list of places and forts which he captured in Telingana. The king returned to Vijayangara after these wars. He then set out for Kalahasti and this was the occasion when the mandapa of 100 pillars and the "big gopura of the last gate" were built. The object of the Kalahasti inscription is to record the construction of these two buildings. "The big gopura of the last gate" probably means the tower which is now called Gali gopura, but which has at present no connection with the temple.

The inscription dated Saka-Samvat 1289, Plavanga, corresponding to A.D. 1367–68, is engraved on a cylindrical pillar set up near the recordroom in the Kalahastisvara and must have belonged to a local family, which probably acquired some territory during the confusion which prevailed in southern India prior to the rise of the Vijayanagara dynasty. Kalahasti and its vicinity, in the 14th century, must have suffered very much from the ravages of wild beasts and it is not altogether impossible that the position gained by Valli Arasar and his predecessors was, to certain extent at least, due to their markmanship.

EPIGRAPHICAL IMPORTANCE

Inscriptions of the place reveal that ravages of wild animals were quite common in the country in the 14th century and kings often came there for sport.

TONDAMANAD

In the Tondamanad temple at a distance of about 6 miles, where once stood a fort surrounded by a most still visible, there are writings in stone relating to the periodical festival in this place in honor of Indra, of which nobody hears today. The Tamil work *Silappadigaram* mentions similar festival in honor or Indra at Kaveripattanam which was a capital of the Cholas situated at the junction of the Kaveri and the Bay of Bengal. The approximate date of the composition of the well-known Tamil grammar "Nannul" could be gathered from one of the inscriptions. Pavanandi the author or this work is said to have prepared at the request of the Ganga king Siya Ganga Amarabharana whose daughter endowed the temple here.

NOTES

1. In the village of Uduppur, Kannappa Nayanar was born with
    the name of Tinnan but he was subsequently named Kannappan
    by the God at Kalahasti. He went for hunting as a boy chasing
    a pig near the hill at Kalahasti. being carried away by the
    sanctity of the place, he began to worship the linga there, and
    also offer to the god there the meat got by hunting. On finding
    that the place had been profaned and defiled by the offerings
    of meat, the priest hid himself within the sanctun to detect the
    culprit. To prove to the priest the devotion of the boy made
    blood come out of the linga's right eye. Pained at this the boy-
    hunter took out his right eye and fixed it on to the linga and
    thus prevented the blood from coming out. To test him further,
    immediately He made blood come out of the left eye also; when
    he began to take out his left eye too. The God was much pleased
    at his devotion, called him "Kannappa," restored his sight and
    made him remain on the right side!

2. The Madras Epigraphist's Report for 1903–1904, pp. 11, 12
    and 16.

Chapter 27

PUSHPAGIRI

This sacred place, which takes its name from a hill, situated on the river Pennar, is ten miles to the north-west of Cuddapah. Pushpagiri, which also means 'the hill of flowers,' having a mythology of its own, is sacred to both Vishnu and Siva. The Vaishnavites say that it is the Tirumala Madhya Ahobilam (midway between Tirupati and Ahobilam) while the Saivites call it as the Madhya Kailasam (midway between Benares in the north and Chidambaram in the south).

PURANIC VERSION

The tradition is that, once upon a time, when Garuda1 the divine kite, was carrying a pot of nectar from the kingdom of heaven, to relieve the sufferings of his mother, he was attacked by Indra, the celestial king. In the course of the fight at a drop of nectar fell into the tank this place. As result the water of the tank acquired the property of causing rejuvenation and immortality and thereby discredited Brahma the creator. Thereupon, sage Narada advised Hanuman to drop a hill to cover the tank. When he did so, the hill instead of sinking floated on the water like a flower! This accounts for the significance of the place. It is also said that both Siva and Vishnu claimed the hill jointly. Another story is that once a Brahman, en route to throw the bones of his deceased father into the Ganges rested here. To his surprise the bones were converted into flowers!

SHRINES IN THE PLACE

There are eight temples on the hill, viz., Kasi Visvanatha, Raghavaswami, Vaidyanatha, Trikotisvara, Bhimesvara with several sculptured panels, Indranatesvara, Kamalasambhavesvara, and Siva and Kesavaswami in one court, usually named as Pushpagiri temple. Of these eight temples, four are enclosed by court walls. Besides these, there are dozens of other small temples at the foot of the hill and the construction of these is attributed to a Chola king who had them put up to avert the evil effects of a curse on him.

EPIGRAPHICAL IMPORTANCE

The inscriptions in the temple of Santana Malleswara mention the existence of five shrines dedicated to Vejanatha (Vaidyanatha) bearing several interesting sculptural representations, Kamalasamara, Durga Devi, and Rudrapadamu Rameswara. The Chenna Kesava temple has a lofty gopuram. The carvings therein include one that depicts the gift of arrow Pasupatastra, by Siva to Arjuna and also one that partrays the interpretation and delivery of the Gita by Parthasarathy to Arjuna. These are fine works of art. Some scenes from the Ramayana and the Mahabharata are depicted well in sculpture. The Bhimewara shrine, close to that of Vaidyanatha, has also several mythological scenes shown in it.

NOTES

1. The Brahmani kite, Garuda, was born to sage Kasyapa and his wife Vinata. Aruna, the hipless, was his elder brother and in consequence of his mother's breaking open the egg before it was ready to be hatched, he had a strong body only above the hip. Having learnt a lesson from this incident the mother fully waited for the development of the egg out of which Garuda emanated. So is it that he was dubbed with immense strength, beautiful wings and also became a veritable foe of the serpents, who were born to his stepmother. The ill-feeling between his mother and stepmother resulted in the former being enslaved unjustly. To free his mother from the bondage of slavery he boldly undertook to procure the nectar from heaven. As this was no easy task, he was advised to eat tortoise and elephant to gain the required strength for this purpose. This he did and with his powerful wings even overcame the thunderbolt of Indra. It is also said that Sri Krishna was none other than this Garuda who was in reality Vishnu born on this earth to establish righteousness.

Chapter 28

HAMPI

This place, at a distance of about seven miles from Hospet in the Bellary district, that once played an important part in the history of India, is now kin ruins.

Nimbapura is a hamlet close by Hampi, and it is believed that the remains of Vali exist in a mound.

IMPORTANACE OF THE PLACE

The sanctity of Hampi rests on the fact that it was the capital of the kingdom of Kishkinda which flourished during the period of the Ramayana, and was ruled over by the powerful brothers Vali and Sugriva of the monkey clan. Later, the Vijayanagar dynasty was established here, and the ruins bear evidence to the ancient civilisation and the glory of the city.

Nearby there is a sacred hill called Matanga Parvata where the sage Matanga did penance. It is to this sage that Sugriva, with his chief Hanuman, is said to have fled for protection when driven out of the kingdom by his brother Vali. The sacred Rishyamuka hill is on the bank of the Pampa river now called Tungabhadra. It was here that Rama is said to have sought the aid of Sugriva for the recovery of Sita from Ravana. Close by this, is the Malyavatha hill where Hanuman communicated to Rama the happy tidings of the discovery of Sita in Lanka or Ceylon.

VIJAYANAGAR DYNASTY

The kingdom of Vijayanagar was established probably after the Chalukyas, who had the boar (Varaha) as their emblem, and this was adopted by the former also. Virupaksha, the lord of the Nagas (snakes), was the tutelary deity of the Vijayanagar dynasty. Even Jainism was tolerated during the reign of King Bukka Raya, who allowed the Jainas to have their shrines in Hemakuta near the Hindu temple of Pampapati. King Harihara is recorded to have made large gifts to several distant places of sanctity extending from the river Krishna in the north to the town of Kumbakonam in the south. In A.D. 1397 pillars of victory appear to have been planted by the king in all the 56 states into which India was divided then. Krishnadevaraya, the most enlightened of the Vijayanagar dynasty, was a patron of Sanskrit and Telugu literature. His successor Achutha Raya made huge gifts to the Brahmins. In A.D. 1565 the Mohammedans took possession of this city which brought about its ruin. The Vijayanagar princesses thereafter fled to various places.

BUILDINGS IN THE PLACE

The existing buildings, though many, are all in ruins. The stone aqueducts, traces of which still remain, were constructed for the supply of water from a large tank to the principal buildings of the city. The Mahaarnavami Dibba (throne) consisting of a stone platform was the seat of the kings during the festival of Navaratri, and when they received homage from their minor nobles and chiefs. There is a terraced wall all around the platform. The intervals between the different rows of plinth mouldings have bas-reliefs representing the infantry, the cavalry, etc., of the ancient times, and these are splendid specimens of the art of the period.

SCULPTURES

The outer walls of the Hazara Rama temple contain several bas-reliefs depicting scenes from the Ramayana and the Mahabharata, inclusive of a figure of Bhima. The Kalki Avatar incarnation of Sri Vishnu, is represented in splendid style. The incarnation represents a figure mounted on a horse holding a drawn sword in his hand.

The stables for the elephants face the west and contain 11 spacious stalls with lofty domed roofs, characteristic of Indian architecture. There is also a square turret over the stalls with a flight of steps at the side.

The fine statue of Narasimha measuring about 25 feet in height is said to have been cut out of a single stone. There is an inscription in the Narasimhaswami temple dated Saka 1450 stating that Krishnaraya asked Arya Krishna, who had placed himself under his protection, the consecration of Lakshmi and Narahari (Narasimha) at Krishnapuri part of Hampi.

VITTALA TEMPLE

The Vittala temple, though less important, contains a few pieces of architectural work. The Kalyana mandapa and the stone care are of exceptionally fine workmanship.

KRISHNA TEMPLE

The Krishnaswami temple of fine workmanship was constructed during the days of Krishnadevaraya.

THE GLORIES OF VIJAYANAGAR[2]

"Hampi, the site of the city of Vijayanagar, metropolis of the great empire of that name which flourished from 1336 to 1565, is rich with memories going back to the days of Sri Rama. Legend says that it was the capital of the kingdom of Kishkindha; and it was on the banks of the lake Pampa that the great epic hero made friends with Sugriva, slew Vali and secured for ever the service of Hanuman. Later, it was the seat of a thriving Hindu kingdom; and still later, before its final ruin, it became the rallying centre for the forces of Hindu national life. The rise of Vijayanagar may truly be characterised as the visible representation of the first birth of nationalism in southern India. It embodied the first great protest that Hindu patriotism made against the onslaught of alien barbarism. Combining all the might and all the resources of the decadent and dispirited Hindu principalities of the south for a new grand effort of national uprising, it stood as an impenetrable barrier against the flood of Moslem invasion from the north for a period of two centuries and a half. Vijayanagar was not the outcome of mere military ambition. It was not the work of dynastic rivalries or of greed for territorial conquest. It was, in truth, an edifice erected for the enshrining of the "Hindu Dharma." Learned men and great religious leaders played as important a part in laying its foundations as mighty warriors and generous princes. The patriot who conceived the plan of bringing this new kingdom into being—to absorb within itself all the weak and warring Hindu principalities of old and to act as an effective check against the reckless hordes from the north and of making it the nursery for a new Hindu aspiration leading to a splendid renaissance of letters and arts — was not a soldier or a prince or a court intriguer or a local chieftain, but a scholar and sage whose name has come down in the history of Sanskrit literature as well as in that of the great Hindu pontificate of Sringeri as Madhava Vidyaranya. The success of this gifted and broad-visioned sanyasin in the task of national regeneration was rendered possible by the work, in other fields, of the celebrated Vaishnava teacher, Sri Vedanta Desikar, and his worthy contemporary, Sri Akshobhyateertha, an exponent of the Dwaita philosophy. Besides making ample contributions to Sanskrit and the vernacular literatures, these saints brought about a wonderful moral and religious awakening in the land by their incessant preachings and discourses and by the austere and earnest lives they led. The result was that the great masses were aroused and energized for a new life of collective self-assertion and self development. The monarchs that led the mighty movements were of course men of noble spirit and heroic mettle. The ruins of Hampi stand today to remind us of all the noble idealism, the purposefulness and the organised enterprise of the people of southern India four centuries ago. They are a visible proof, to those who may need it, of the great traditions behind us which entitle us to cherish great aspirations for the future. They are a living inspiration for noble endeavour to all who have an eye for historical truth and a heart for patriotic pride."

EPIGRAPHICAL IMPORTANCE

The inscriptions in the Pampapati temple give a geneological account of the second Vijayanagar dynasty down to Krishnaraya. It consists of both a mythical and a historical part. From the latter it is learnt that the founder of the second Vijayanagar dynasty was a native of Tulu or Northern Malayalam, the country of Tuluvas and that he must have been a usurper as he claims only a mythical relationship to the princes of the first dynasty of Vijayanagar. King Kishnadeva Maharaja gave the village of Singanayakanahalli to the Siva temple called Virupaksha (the old name of the

Pampapati temple) and built the Ranga mandapa (assembly-hall). The image of Lakshmi-Narasimhadeva in the Ugranarasimhasvami temple at the western extremity known as Krishnapura was consecrated on Friday, the 15th of the bright half of Vaisakha of Saka 1451, Virodhi Samvatsara when there was an eclipse of the moon. The inscription on a lamp pillar in front of the Jaina temple named Ganigitti temple or the temple of the oil-woman "commences with an invocation of Jina and of his religion followed by a pedigree of the spiritual ancestors and pupils of the head of a Jaina school, who was called Simhanandin." The epithets of the teachers given are acharya, arya, guru, desika, muni and yogindra. The pedigree of the Jaina teachers is followed by a short account of two kings of the first Vijayanagara dynasty viz. Bukka, who descended from the race of the Yadava kings, and his son Harihara, whose hereditary minister was the general Chaicha or Chaichapa. His son, the general or prince Iruga or Irugopa, adhered to the doctrine of the above-mentioned Jaina teacher Simhanandin. In Saka 1307 Iruga built a stone temple Kunthu Jinanatha at Vijayanagara. This city belonged to Kuntala, a district of the Karnata country. Near the wall of the temple of Anjaneya at Sankalapura stands an inscribed stone taken Saka 1455 (A.D. 1513) bearing a seated Vinayaka in the top recording the grant of this village to a temple of Ganapati, which was called Kota Vinayaka i.e., 'the Vinayaka in the fort.' In honour of this temple the village Sankalapura received the surname Kota Vinayakapura or Vinayakapura and this is a mile east of Hospet adjoining the ruins of Hampi.

NOTES

1. *Avatar* or incarnation means manifestation in form. Such manifestations of God are treated as avatars and these are required for the religious advancement of all human beings for the express purpose of getting over the conglomeration of wordly ideas.
2. The *Hindu* dated 17th April, 1922.

Chapter 29

AHOBALAM

This religious centre of great antiquity, also known as Singavelkunram, dedicated to Narasimha, the lion aspect of the god Vishnu, is 30 miles from Nandyal railway station in the Kurnool district. Of all the places dedicated to Narasimha Ahobalam stands pre-eminent, for it is only here that the nine forms (Nava Narasimham) of the deity are enshrined.

PURANIC VERSION

It is here that god Vishnu, in his lion aspect, killed the demon king Hiranyakasipu who, prohibited worship His.

Ukkustambam, a pillar in the shrine, is the place through which the deity is said to have come out into the world, and Jwala was the place where Hiranya was caught hold of.

The deity in the upper Ahobalam hill is called Swayambhu or self-created and has ten arms, standing on a natural cleft of the rock tearing upon the abdomen of the demon. This form of Narasimha is called Ugra (terrible) Narasimha. The deity in the lower Ahobalam is named Lakshmi Narasimha or Prahlada Varada. Siva lingas exist both here as well as in the upper Ahobalam shrines.

The Bhavanasi river, which rises in the Jwala hill, settles

in a hollow named Rakthakundam. The water of this hollow is reddish supporting the popular belief that there was a river of the demon's blood or that the deity after killing the demon, washed his hands in the pool.

PLACES OF IMPORTANCE

The milder aspect of Narasimha is called Lakshmi Narasimha or Prahalada Varada who is enshrined in the lower Ahobalam. Locally these shrines are called Eguva or Pedda (upper) Ahobalam and Digua or Chinna (lower) Ahobalam and the former is considered more sacred.

Lanja Koneru is a natural spring about two miles to the north-east of the shrine, en route to Bhargavam. The spring has its own sanctity. It is said that once upon a time a *lanja* (harlot) constructed this with a view to expiate her sins in selling herself for the satisfaction of the carnal desires of men.

The Kanchu Kumbham or the interior tower and the monolithic Tayasthamba (victory pillar) in the lower Ahobalam are objects of interest.

RAMATIRTHAM

Ramatirtham, a tank sacred to Sri Rama, is five miles from lower Ahohalam. There is an ant-hill called Puttalamma (in Telugu), which has its own sanctity. Garuda (kite) did penance here to invoke the blessings of Vishnu who appeared in the cave near Jwala when he cried 'Aho: Bilam,' which accounts for the name of the place. Vedadri which corresponds to the preceding Garudadri is sacred for the fact that the Vedas were granted their superiority over the *Ithihasas*.

EPIGRAPHICAL IMPORTANCE

During the days of Vikramakedu, the great western Chalukya

King (1076-1106), reigning at Kalyan in the Bombay Presidency, only the mula *vigrahams* (fixed sculptures) were worshipped. Later on Prataparudradeva, a powerful Kakatiya King (1300-1325), installed the *utsava vigrahams* (metal images intended for being taken out). On his return from Srisailam he halted at a place called in later times Rudravaram, 10 miles from Ahobalam, when he ordered the vigraham of Narasimha to be cast, and installed it at Ahobalam. To commemorate his devotion a famous poem entitled *Prataparudriyam* was composed.

The ancient records of the temple reveal that king Krishnadevaraya of the Vijayanagar dynasty visited this shrine on his return from the conquest of the Kalinga country, and presented the deity with a diamond necklace, an emerald wristlet, a gold plate and thousand pieces of gold.

NOTES

1. Hiranyakasipu obtained the boon of immortality from the God. Strengthened by this boon he began to tyrannise over the lesser gods and his subjects and issued a mandate that nobody including his son Prahladha, should worship God. As the boon was such that the demon could not be killed either by man or beast neither in day or in night or by any weapons of war either in earth or in the heavens, Vishnu assumed the form of a man and a beast at twilight (immunity from these the demon did not claim) and placing Hiranya on his lap tore him into pieces with his claws. Prahladha was then crowned king in the place of the wicked Hiranyakasipu.

Chapter 30

SRISAILAM

This important religious shrine is on the Rishabhagiri hill on the southern bank of the river Krishna and is famous for Srisaila or Sriparvata, one of the several aspects of the god Siva. Its sanctity is claimed by the Hindus and the Buddists as well. There is reference to this place in the Mahabharata and the *sankalpas*, i.e. recitations on occasions of religious bath. Almost in every Hindu epic poem or Purana,[1] mention is made of this place, while the Chinese travellers Fa-Hian and Huin Tsang refer to it in their anecdotes on the Buddhist saint Nagarjuna, who is said to have lived in the first century A.D. All these go to show the sanctity attached to the shrine from time immemorial.

PURANIC VERSION

The mythological relevance of the place exists because Rishabha or the sacred bull of the god Siva is said to have performed penance here, and that to bless him god Siva with his wife Parvati appeared in the form of Mallikarijuna and Brimharambha. The river Krishna, called Patalaganga in this part, is abundant in lingams for worship.

EPIGRAPHICAL IMPORTANCE

Local belief is that one of the provincial officers of Srisailarajya which was under the Vijayanagar sway made presentation of a bull, and of an idol of the sage Bhringi both in gold to this shrine. This sage is said to have been reduced to a mere skeleton by the goddess Parvati for his devotion partiality to Siva, who is subsequently said to have mended matters, and as a sign thereof Bhringi obtained an additional leg to stand. The sage is thus seen standing on three legs!

Vijayanagara kings Narasingaraya and Harihara visited this place. The latter in Saka 1326 presented the Mukha mandapa. The Kalyana mandapa on the northern side of the temple was built in Saka 1451 by a servant of Krishnaraya who also set up a golden pinnacle on it and built a shrine for the linga called Demesa. In Saka 1438 Krishnadevaraya had *mandapas* constructed in the Car Street.

From a copper plate grant available in the Madras Museum it is seen that during the 15th century there was a dispute between the Brahmans and the Kshatriyas belonging to the upper classes and the Vaisyas, regarding certain rights and privileges in this temple, and that it was decided in favour of the Vaisyas on the 13th February, 1416 A.D.

NOTES

1. The first or lowest row bears figures of elephants harnessed in different ways as if let in procession, many of them twisting up trees with their trunks as is characteristic of them; the second row represents horses and hunting scenes; third row hunting tigers, etc.

2. The Puranas and *Itihasas* are elaborate commentaries on the Vedas, explaining the details, in a very simple style, for the

724 South Indian Shrines

benefit of the lower orders of society not sufficiently gifted with the necessary intellectual capacities comprehend the importance of the Vedas. The style adapted in these is simple with a view to convey more easily and more impressively to the ordinary public, the highly abstract and philosophical ideas which could not otherwise be so easily grasped.

Chapter 31

BEZWADA

Bezwada, or the mythological Vijayavata, mentioned in inscriptions as Rajendra Cholapuram, is a famous place of pilgrimage on the river Krishna, and dedicated to Siva in the local aspect of Malleswara or Jayasena. Sage Agastya is said to have been the greatest devotee of this deity, and an admirer of the deity's several *lilas* (sports).

PURANIC VERSION

The place is surrounded by many hillocks and the most important of them is called Sitanagaram, while the less important being Kanaka Durga[1] or Kanaka Konda. Traditionally these hills were continuous and at the command of god they went apart making enough space for the river Krishna to flow through. It is on one of these hills known as Indrakila where the Pandava hero Arjuna[2] obtained from Siva the most powerful weapon called "Pasupatastra". The aspect in which Siva appeared unto Arjuna for bestowing the boon, is known as kirata (hunter). The shrine has the representation of this and many other events of the Mahabharata, commemorated in sculpture.

[3]"The origin of Malleswara, the name of the Siva temple

at Bezwada: It is recorded that prior to the Kali age sage Agastya had named the god (at Bezwada) Jayesana. The Mahabharata hero Arjuna whose capabilities in wrestling (*mallayuddha*) are well-known, called him Malleswara. Siva, says the record, graces with his presence the blessed town Vijayavata 'the ornament of which is the river Krishna.' In the Kali age, early as the Saka year 117, there was a king by the name of Madhavavarman. The son of this king killed a child of the woman 'who eked on her livelihood by selling shoots of the tamarind tree. The king sentenced him to be hanged in order to meet the ends of justice. On seeing this, god Malleswara was pleased and rained (on him) a shower of gold which brought back to life the deceased prince and the dead body of the woman's son! Thus the Malleswara established in this world the fame of that great king (Madhavavarman). Later on, came a pious devotee of Siva named Panditaradhya who proclaimed to the world that the devotees of Siva were superior to the divine sages (perhaps Brahmans?) and illustrated the truth of it by bundling up burning coal in a piece of China muslin, with the tender twig of a *sami* tree without burning the cloth! God Mallesvara was pleased and manifested himself in the presence of his devotee. Such is Mahadeva Malleswara 'the endless one, the lover of his devotees worshipping whom the lords of the earth prospered of old.'

EPIGRAPHICAL IMPORTANCE

The temple inscriptions relate also to the prayer of Arjuna to Indra in the forest of Dvaitavana, to provide him with the means to overcome Duryodana, the cousin of Arjuna. Indra directed Arjuna to pray unto god Siva. Also the temple of Kanakadurga with prakaras etc., is enumerated. Besides the details of village constructions, festivals, repairs to gopuras, *mukha mandapa* of the Mallesvara temple etc. are recorded.

HISTORICAL REFERENCE

Besides having been a religious centre Bezwada was also the capital of the Vengi kingdom.The Chalukyas who reigned at Kalyan in the north conquered the place about the beginning of the 7th century A.D. and created a separate province. The famous Chinese traveller Huin Tsang visited this place about A.D. 639 when Buddhism was at its zenith. The Chola king conquered this part of the country known as Venadesa and ruled it until A.D. 1228, after which it fel into the hands of the Mohammedans who established their capital at Kondapalli, a hill fortress, near Bezwada.

There is said to have stood a fort here at one time but it has since been dismantled. In digging for the canal many remains were exposed. The caves connected with the Buddhists are all hollowed out of the east side of the big hill, at the foot of which the town stands.

NOTES

1. On the south side of the Kanaka Durga temple is a rock with sculptures bearing labels indicating the names of Gods and Goddesses cut below them. Most of the figures are forms of Durga, the very popular deity of Bezwada at present. These figures are illustrated in the anual report of the Madras Epigraphical Report for the year 1917–18. The fantastic forms goddess Durga was capable of assuming are detailed in the books *Mantra Sastra.*
2. The various names of Arjuna are generally repeated by pious Hindus whenever there is thunder to avoid the evil effects thereof. These names are: Arjuna, Phalguna, Partha, Kirita, Svetavahana, Bibhatsu, Vijiya, Krishna, Savyasachi, and Dhanamejaya.
3. Page 81 of the *Annual Report of the Madras Epigraphical Department* for the year 1910.

Chapter 32

DRAKSHARAMAM

This religious place, formerly called Takshatapovana or Takshavatika in the Godavari district, is five miles to the south-east of Ramachandrapuram. The historicity of this place is attributed to sage Vyasa, who is said to have installed a linga in this place, and this event is commemorated by an annual festival in February-March.

PURANIC VERSION

The puranic version regarding the place is, that the demon Taksha, whose daughter was married to god Siva, was quite annoyed at the niggardly way in which he was treated by Siva. In revenge Taksha performed a yaga sacrifice) to which Siva was not invited. However, the daughter was present at the ceremony and Taksha resented it. In the end, she burnt herself in the sacrificial fire. It is locally believed that the sacrifice is still on, and the Siddhi Vinayaka (Elephant God) at Ayinavalli, eight miles away to the north of Amalapuram, is supposed to bring the sacrifice to a successful end.

THE TEMPLE

The temple of Bhimeswara is the principal shrine of the

place. The linga in the sanctum is said to be one of the five bits worn by Taksha round his neck. The other four bits are said to have fallen in Bhimavaram in Cocoanada, in Amaravathi in the Guntur district, in Palakollu in Kistna district, and Kumararama yet to be identified. The construction of the temple is said to have originated with the Sun. The seven sages Kasyapa, Atri, Gauthama, Bharadwaja, Viswamitra, Jamadagni and Vasishta—are said to have worshipped the God here and also caused the seven mouths of the river Godavari. The tank here called Sapta Godavari, is named after the seven sages and great religious efficacy is attached to a bath in this.

EPIGRAPHICAL IMPORTANCE

Inscriptions in the temple indicate the antiquity of the shrine dating as early as the eleventh century, when the Chola king Rajaraja was reigning at Rajahmundry.

Of the numerous inscriptions available in this ancient temple, most of which refer to gift of lamps, there are others relating to king Parantaka's setting up images of Siva and Parvati and making gifts of villages to them, detailing the names of some of the geographical divisions of the olden days, the gifts of golden bulls and the construction of a golden pinnacle and the erection of several mandapas and other parts of the buildings within the temple.

The famous Muslim saint Saiyid Shah Bhaji Aulia is said to have come here from Medina. As he was very hungry he slaughtered a cow, and this led to a violent dispute between the Hindus and the Muslims the latter came out successful, and as agreed upon, he was given a matha which was subsequently converted into a Mosque where there is also the tomb of the saint. The tomb is said to be five hundred years old and the saint was contemporary of the famous Mira Sahib of Nagore, near Negapatam.

HISTORICAL REFERENCE

There are also two Dutch tombs called "Ollandu Dibba" erected in A.D. 1675 and 1728 containing some fine works of sculpture.

Chapter 33

SIMHACHALAM

This religious on the Bengal-Nagpur railway in place Vizianagaram, is sacred to Narasimha, the lion aspect of Vishnu.

The shrine is built on the hill, about 800 feet above the sea, and gateways are observed en route to the shrine. A broad flight of steps run all through and on the top is the Hanuman gate. In the Hunuman gate there is a bastion showing the presence of ramparts used earlier to protect the shrine.

PURANIC VERSION

The foundation of the temple is attributed to Hiranyakasipu, who, furious at his son Prahlada's devotion to Vishnu, threw him into the sea and placed this hill on his head. Narasimha went to his rescue, stood by the side of the hill and tilted it up so that the boy might escape from the weight of the hill. Later on the pious Prahlada is stated to have founded the shrine.

One of the pillars in the Mukha-mandapa is named Kappam Stambam or "the tribute pillar" and attracts large number of crowds on account of its power of curing cattle diseases and granting children to barren women! There is also a stone car with stone wheels and stone horses.

THE DEITY

The body of the deity Narasimha in the principal shrine is perpetually covered with a thick coating of sandal paste, which is said to have appeased the fury of the God after his destruction of Hiranyakasipu, the demon athiest. The coating is renewed annually on the Vaisakha (the day in the month of May-June on which the asterism Visakhal (libra) has sway) day in May, which is considered very sacred, and people from all over the country visit this shrine.

SARABHA GOD

As the terrific nature of Narasimha (man lion) incarnation continued even after the destruction of the demon Hiranya Kasipu and this caused trouble and fear to Devas, Siva assumed the Sarabha (bird-like) form and pacified Narasimha by trampling him under his feet. The consecration of this image is supposed to destroy enemies, secure success in battles, cure all ailments and procure every good. There are fine sculptures of this form in the temples at Chidambaram and Darasuram near Kumbakonam. The metal figure in the temple at Tribhuvanam close to Kumbakonam is very inviting.

EPIGRAPHICAL IMPORTANCE

The temple inscriptions record the history of the Kalinga country, the conquests made by the Chola king Kulottunga (A.D. 1010–1118), the construction of the central shrine with its several mandapas, and the victory pillars of King Krishnadevaraya of Vijayanagar (A.D. 1515–1516).

Chapter 34

SRIKURMAM

This place is important for the incarnation of Vishnu as a tortoise *Kurmavatar*. It lies at a distance of 16 miles on the south of Chicacole station.

PURANIC VERSION

The presiding deity of the temple facing west goes by the name of Kurmeswara and there are several sacred water bodies within the temple. The Lord is said to have first appeared here to bless king Svetamaharaja. It is said that the bones of the deceased, if thrown into the Svetapushkarani tank within this temple, get converted into tortoises! Outcastes and women in menses are forbidden to touch the waters of this tank and if they do so the moss accumulations are supposed to he formed which when sprinkled with the holy water of the god disappear!

EPIGRAPHICAL IMPORTANCE

In this temple there are inscribed pillars relating to the three descendants of the Eastern Chalukya king Vimaladitya (A.D. 1015–1022) and of his son Rajaraja (A.D. 1022–1063) who resided in Rajamahendrapattanam. He is also said to have translated with the help of scholars the history of Bharata race into Telugu and this is said to be the essence of all *smritis*. It was this king who ordered Nannayabhatta to translate Mahabharata into Telugu.

According to the *Epigraphica Indica* "In one of the pillars in the hall in front of the temple is a Telugu record relating to the setting up of images of Rama, Sita and Lakshmana in Saka 1215 and to Naraharitirtha having ruled the Kalinga country and also defended this holy place against an attack of the Sabaras who are the savage inhabitants of the forests of the Ganjam district. This Naraharitirtha is also said to have built a shrine of Yogananda Narasimha in front of this temple. The life of this Naraharitirtha is recorded, in *stotra* entitled 'Narahariyatistotra', which is included in the work *Stotramahodadhi*. It states that, before conversion to the Madhva faith, this tirtha was called Samasastrin or Ramasastrin, and that he was styled Naraharitirta after receiving his initiation at the hands of Purnaprajna who commanded his going to the capital of the Gajapati king and ruling that country. Naraharitirtha, who had learnt the true import of the Bhashya from his teacher, preferred to remain a Sanyasin and said Lord; 'What do I gain by ruling a kingdom'? The master replied: 'There in the Gajapati kingdom are the images of Rama and Sita, which you must try to acquire with great skill, in order that I may worship them.' Accordingly he did and ruled that country for 12 years during the time of the infant king. When the prince attained his majority, he handed back the kingdom to him and, as a present and compensation for the services rendered, applied to the king for the images of Rama and Sita that remained in the royal treasury then. On return to Srikurmam he handed the images to his master who at a later period gave them to Naraharitirtha himself. While on tour on a preaching mission he dreamt at a certain place that an image of Vishnu merged in a tank in that town. The next day he had the image taken out, consecrated it, and called the town in consequence of this incident Narayanadevarkere the tank of the god Narayana which is now in the Hospet taluk of Bellary district. Having made over the charge of the images to his pupil, Naraharitirtha retired to the bank of the Tungabhadra and there died in Srimukha year A.D. 333."

Chapter 35

MAHENDRAGIRI

The famous Mahendragiri Ganjam district lies at a distance of 20 miles on the north-west of Mandasa Road railway station on the Madras-Calcutta line. It is situated in 18°58' north latitude and 84°24' east longitude. The place is about 16 miles from the sea. The mountain is nearly 5,000 ft. above the sea-level and it is one of the sacred hills that find mention in the epics—Ramayana, Mahabharata, Puranas and the Kavya literature.

PURANIC VERSION

The *Vishnu Purana* mentions it among the *Kulaparvatha* i.e., the chief mountain of Bharata Varsha (India). The famous poet Kalidasa describes this place in the course of his narrative of the victorious conquests of Solar king Raghu. From the summit of the hill a delightful view of the surrounding country and the sea could clearly be had.

THE TEMPLE

Bhima's temple has its summit over the sanctum made out of a single block of stone. The dressing and fitting of stones are of high finish. At a short distance from this place, on the eastern slope of the hill, is the temple of Yudhisttira which is known for its architectural beauty.

At a little distance further down the eastern slope is the temple of Kunti, mother of the famous Pandavas, in the midst of grove. Fine sculptures are seen on the niches of the temple walls. Over the entrance of the porch is a carved representation of Navagraha or the nine planets. This temple is also mentioned as Gokarnesvara temple.

EPIGRAPHICAL IMPORTANCE

The inscriptions recorded here mention the conquest of Kalinga by Rjendra Chola I in the 11th century and the fixing of Jayastamba or pillar of victory here.

HISTORICAL REFERENCE

During the 10th, 11th, and 12th centuries, this place was the seat of god Gokarneswara, the tutelary deity of the Ganga kings of Kalinga country. Subsequently this part of the country is said to have formed part of the Andhra domains.

Chapter 36

SIVAGANGA

Sivaganga is a holy place of pilgrimage in the Mysore State and is called the Southern Kasi. The hill here command a fine view all round and is named Kakudgiri. It is about 5000 feet above the sea-level.

PURANIC VERSION

The stalapurana of the place is named Kakudgiri Mahatmya. The temple stands on the northern slope. As we ascend the flight of steps, figures of Ganapati, Virabhadra, Subrahmanya and others are met with. Following there, is the temple of Gangadharesvara and a huge Nandi called Erumebasava or she-buffalo.

THE TEMPLES

The temple, proper having two entrances on the north and east with gopuras, is a huge cave protected by overhanging boulders. It faces north. Besides various forms of God, there is a peculiar Chandikesvara in the form of brahma with four faces and four hands, holding a trident, an axe, a water vessel and a rosary. The inner walls of the Mukhamandapa bears images of *sapta matrikas* or the seven mothers, ashta dikpalas

739739

739739739

739739739

or the regents of the eight directions, navagrahas or the nine planets, sages, musicians, etc., who are supposed to have gathered together to witness the marriage of Parvati with Siva, which forms the chief subject of composition. The structural vimana or tower over the shrine is a fine piece of workmanship.

The Honnadevi temple faces the east. The terrific goddess tramples the demons, Chanda and Munda. The name Honnadevi or Honnamma is the Kannada form of the Sanskrit Svaranamba. The Utsava Vigraha of his Goddess is also similar to the stone sculpture in the sanctum.

The Santesvara temple founded probably in memory of Santala-devi, queen of Vishnuvardhana, who died at Sivaganga in A.D. 1139, has in front a peculiar carving in the shape of a circular disc with a lotus in the centre and creepers round it. The stone parapet above the steps of Kalyanitirtha or Kamalatirtha pond has a freeze of figures all round illustrating scenes from the Ramayana and the *Bhagavata Purana*. The story of Sri Ramachandra is completely delineated from his birth to his coronation. The carrying of Rishyasringa from the forest to Ayodhya (Oudh) by dancing girls is also represented here. The steps here have their front faces carved with figures of animals etc. at intervals.

EPIGRAPHICAL IMPORTANCE

On the summit is a hill known as Kodugalbasava (peak-bull) on account of its location on the peak and an inscription at the spot traces its execution to A.D. 1388. A little higher over this is the srine of Virabbadra and in one of the stone pillars close by, water is said to ooze out on the day of the winter solstice of Makarasankranti. The pillar is in consequence named as Tirthalakamba which is octogonal bearing an

inscription recording its erection during the reign of King
Narasimha I (1141–1173 A.D.).

THE HOLY WATERS

Some of the important tirthas on the hill are the Kanva, the
Kurubhavati, the Patala Ganga, the Chakra tirtha the
Sankaracharya tirtha on account of Sri Sankaracharya having
performed penance here, the Maitreya tirtha, the Mandalya
tirtha, the Ganga tirtha and the Agastya tirtha.

Chapter 37

NANDIDROOG

Nandidroog in the Kolar district is at a height of about 5,000 feet above sea level at a distance of about three miles from Nandi railway station. The summit commands a fine scenery of the surrounding Kolar and Bangalore districts and the droog consists of Kalavara durga of Skandagiri on the north, Brahmagiri or Varahagiri on the south-west, and Chennakesava or Chennarayanbetta on the north-west. Several rivers such as the north Pennar (*Uttara Pinakini*), the South Pennar (*Dakshina Pinakini*), the Arkavati, the Palar, the Papagni and Chitraavati start therefrom. There is an extensive plateau at the top, sloping to the west, in the centre of which is a hollow containing a well-constructed tank called Amritasarova fed by perennial springs.

FORTIFICATIONS

The fortifications on the hill are attributed to Tipu Sultan and some parts bear his name also. There is also the palace occupied by Tipu still preserved. This is fully described in Meadows Taylor's *Tippo Sultan*. According to the local tradition this hill is named Sringiparvata and Kushmanda parvata. The former name has given rise to a square pond in the temple at the village Nandi at its foot named Sringitirtha and there is a sculpture of sage Kushmanda in the hall attached to the Yoga Nandisvara temple on the hill.

TEMPLES

In the village Nandi at the foot hill are two temples, one dedicated to Bhoga Nandisvara and another to Arunachalesvara. The construction of the former is attributed to Ratnavali, wife of the Bana King Bana Vidyadhara, who also made gift to it in A.D. 810. Also a grant in A.D. 806 by the Rashtrakuta king Govinda III (794-814) has been noticed in a copper plate inscription found in a well in the place. The latter temple appears to have been founded by one Kesava, who might have been a sculptor judging from the excellent sculptures available here. Some of the works relating to birds, beasts, foliage, and human figures are accurately sculptured and a few of these are illustrated in the *Mysore Archeological Report* for the year–ending 30th June, 1914. The ceiling of the Bhoga Nandisvara temple has the cardinal deities cut in the proper directions with Siva and Parvati in the central panel. In the *navaranga* (hall) of the Arunachalesyara temple is a peculair Vinayaka, about three feet high with a small lion face and a lean proboscis. The ceiling over the pillars, about five feet deep, has the cardinal deities carved on the different tiers. There are also the sculptures of Hanuman playing on the lute (*veena*), pulling up the *saikatalinga* made of sand worshipped by Rama, fish incarnation (matsyaavatar) of Vishnu killing Somaka, sage Narada playing the flute, Sri Krishna removing butter from the pot, and the great seven sages (Sapta rishis).

EPIGRAPHICAL IMPORTANCE

Regarding the inscriptions relating to this place the *Mysore*

Archaological Report says: "The Chikballapur copper plates, which are dated in A.D. 810, give the interesting information that the temple at Nandi was caused to be erected by Ratnavali, the queen of the Bana king Bana Vidyadhara. The Ganga genealogy given in these plates is of a singular interest, as it is not found in any grant of that dynasty so far published."

Chapter 38

SOMANATHAPUR

Somanathapur, or Vidyanidhiprasanna Somanathapura according to inscriptions, is situated at a distance of about 20 miles to the south-east of Seringapat of the Mysore State. It lies on the left bank of the river Kaveri. From inscriptions we learn that Soma or Somanatha, prime minister of king Narasimha III (A.D. 1254–1291), founded this village and named it after him.

THE TEMPLE

The Kesava[1] temple built by Somanatha three-celled structure; the main cell facing the east and the other two, which are opposite to each other, facing north and south respectively.

The railed parapet of these shrines bear bas reliefs of elephants, horseman, scenes from the epics and the Puranas, with various scrolls. The story of Prahlada, as narrated in the Puranas, is sculptured. The other Gods, relating to the Hindu pantheon that are well-depicted here are Narasimha, Varaha, Hayagriva, Venugopala, Vasudeva, Brahma, Siva, Ganapati, Indra, Manmatha, Surya, Garuda, Lakshmi, Sarasvati and Mahishasuramardini. The south cell contains scenes from the Ramayana, west cell Bhagavatham and north cell Mahabharata. The original image of god Kesava in the central shrine is not available now and in its place wall has been put in. From the large number of Saivite figures within this temple we are to infer that Vaishnavite people then were tolerant towards Saivites. The *prabha* or halo over some of them bears the *dasavatars* or the ten incarnations of Vishnu.

Some of the images bear on their pedestals the names of the artists who executed them and these are of value to the historians of art. From the fact that the Garudakamba (flagstaff bearing the figure of the divine kite Garuda) is not exactly opposite the entrance as usual, but a little to the north-east, it is said that when the temple was completed it looked so grand and beautiful that god, thinking it was too good to be on earth, attempted to transport it to heaven. Accordingly the building began to rise from the earth, when the artist in his anxiety to prevent it, set about mutilating some of the images when it descended and settled in its present situation!

EPIGRAPHICAL IMPORTANCE

The inscriptions mention the Gods that were set up and the provision made for their services. The *Varaha* or the boar incarnation is praised. The geneology of the Hoysala kings down to Narasimha III is detailed. We are also informed therefrom that when king Narasimha was one day seated in the council chamber in his capital Dorasmudra or Halebid, Somanatha made obeisance to him and applied for grant for the worship of the temple founded by him.

An inscription of A.D. 1497 tells us that of Saluva king Immadi Narasinga ordered the restoration of the ruined Agrahara here which is also said to have been the hermitage of sage Vasishta. The geneology of Soma is also recorded in the inscription at Harihar. The Agrahara is said to have been so full of learned men that even the parrots there were capable of holding discussions in *Mimamsa, Tarka* and *Vyakarana.*

Soma is said to have borne several titles a jewel of ministers, a *Chanakya* in policy, Yugandhara in business, champion over traitors to their lords.

NOTES

1. Fergusson praises the elegance of outline and marvellous elaboration of detail in this temple. Workman in his *Through Town and Jungle* says that the towers absolutely captivate the mind by their profession of detail and perfection of outline; and there is no suggestion of superfluity in the endless concourse of figures and designs.

Chapter 39

NUGGIHALLI

There are three temples of importance at this place dating from the reign of Somesvara (A.D. 1249) and these go by the names of the Lakshminarasimha, the Sadasiva and the Somesvara.

THE TEMPLE

The main temple of Lakshminarasimha is a three-called one with the figure of Kesava in the centre, Lakshminarasimha in the left and a beautifully carved Venugopala in the right. On the top is represented the ten avatars or incarnations of Vishnu, while at the sides are sculptured figures of cows, cowherdesses, sages and gods. Though Lakshminarayana occupies a subsidiary cell, He is the chief deity. The ceilings of the *Navaranga* or hall have on the flat under-surface figures of Brahma and Surya.

SCULPTURES

The Utsava Vigrahas or metallic figures intended for being taken out on procession are highly attractive. The *Bhagavata Puranic* is carved on the walls. So are the 24 *murtis* or forms of Vishnu: (1) Kesava, (2) Narayana, (93) Madhava, (4)

Govinda, (5) Vishnu, (6) Madhusudana, (7) Trivikrama, (8) Vamana, (9) Sridhara, (10) Rishikesa, (11) Padmanaba, (12) Damodara, (13) Sankarshana, (14) Vasudeva, (15) Pradyumna, (16) Aniruddha, (17) Purushottama, (18) Adhokshaja, (19) Narasimha, (20) Achyuta, (21) Janardhana, (22) Upendra, (23) Hari and (24) Krishna. Amongst the splendid sculptures is one of a rocking cradle with the god and goddess seated therein and another of Garuda bearing on his shoulders Kasyapa and Kadhru; Balarama with his attributes the plough and the pestle; Hayagriva killing Somaka under his feet.

SADASIVA TEMPLE

The Sadasiva temple has a large number of perforated screens though sculptures are missing. The linga faces the east. The ceilings abound with lotuses. The Mahishasuramardhini figure is 3 ft. high, with 8 hands, 6 of them holding a discus, a trident, a sword, a shield, a bow and a bell, one placed at the head of the Asura and the eighth in the act of taking out an arrow from the quiver. Brahma here is seated on the swan, in the natural posture of riding, unlike most others, with a noose, an elephant goad, a fruit and a rosary for his attributes.

Chapter 40

ARSIKERE

Arsikere, known also as Arasiyakere, is situated in the Mysore state and it lies in 13°19' north latitude and 76°19' east longitude. The approach to the place is from Hassan in the Bangalore–Poona line of the Southern Maratha Railway and the distance therefrom is about 25 miles on the north-east. The place takes its name after a large tank called Arasiyakere or princesses' tank, which appears to have been constructed by the Hoysalas in the 11th century. There are a number of ruined temples to the north of the town and amongst these the Siva temple, with a large number of inscriptions is of considerable importance.

The object of worship in the nearby mountain is a Sahasrakuta Jinalaya or the 1000 Jaina figures.

THE TEMPLE

The Isvara temple faces the east and has plenty of architectural beauty. The doorway to the sanctum is beautifully sculptured with geometrical patterns amd lions standng one over the other. The ceiling bears the dancing form of Siva or Nataraja at the centre with attendant musicians all around. The stone beams contain beads and scroll work. The

Mukhamandapa or the front hall is circular, supported by 21 pillars, of which eight are in the middle and 13 in the surrounding verandah. Below each of the outer pillars are 2 elephants facing different directions. Most of the sculptures bear labels giving their names. The presiding god is called Kattamesvara.

EPIGRAPHICAL IMPORTANCE

The temple was constructed in A.D. 1220 and to its left stands a double shrine called Halavakalludevastana. The jamb of the dcorway of the south shrine contains the figure of Manmatha, the Indian Cupid or the god of love.

Chapter 41

SERINGAPATAM

Seringapatam (Sri Ranga Pattanam) in the Mysore state, lies in an island formed by the sacred Kaveri, in 12°25' north latitude and 76°45' east longtitude. This is distinguished from the important Srirangam, also an island formed by the same Kaveri river in the district of Trichinopoly, by being known as Paschima or western Ranganatha Kshetra while the other is named as Purva or eastern Ranganatha Kshetra. The founding of this place is attributed to sage Gautama. According to the inscriptions, the Ranganatha temple here was founded by the Ganga king Tirumalaiya in A.D. 894.

PALACE

The Dharya Daulat Bagh, a summer palace of Tipu Sultan just outside the east side of the fort, is distinguished for its graceful proportions and the arabesque work in rich colours. The west wall is painted with a representation of the victory of Hyder Ali over Colonel Baillie at Polilore, near Conjeevaram, It had been defaced prior to the seige of 1799, but the Duke of Wellington, then Colonel Arthur Wellesley, who made this garden his residence, had it restored. It was afterwards whitewashed and almost obliterated, but Lord

Dalhousie, having visited the spot during this tour in Mysore
got it painted again by an Indian artist who remembered the
original.

LALBAGH

The Lalbagh is a garden 2 miles east of the fort on the other
side of the Ganjam suburb, which intervenes between it and
the Darya Daulat. It contains the mausoleum of Hyder Ali and
Tipu Sultan, a square building surmounted by a dome with
minarets at the angles, and surrounded by a corridor which is
supported by pillars of black hornblende, a stone remarkable
for its beautiful polish. The double doors, inlaid with ivory,
were given by Lord Dalhousie. Each of the tombs is covered
with a crimson pall. The whole is kept up by the Mysore state.
The epitaph on the Tipu's tomb is in verse — The light of Islam
and the faith left the world, Tipu became a martyr for the faith
of Muhommad; the sword was lost and the son Hyder fell a
noble martyr. The inscription gives the date 1213 A.H. (1799
A.D.) In front of the Lalbagh is a simple memorial to Colonel
Baillie, who died in 1782, as a prisoner of Tipu Sultan. On the
way to the garden, on a rising ground near the road, there are
interesting memorials of the officers and men of the 12th and
74th regiments killed in action in 1799.

EPIGRAPHICAL IMPORTANCE

There is an inscription in the Pampapati temple at Hampi
which says that king Narasa (Saka 1404–18), father of
Krishnadeva Maharaja of Vijayanagara bridged the Kaveri
crossed it, straightaway captured the enemy, brought his
kingdom and the city of Srirangapattanam under his power
and set up a pillar of fame—his heroic deeds being praised
in the three worlds, which appear to be the palace of his glory.
(*Epigraphia Indica*, Vol I, page 361.)

THE TEMPLE

The Ranganatha temple here is the largest in the state with a high gopura in front. The central deity Ranganatha, reclining on Adisesha, is said to have been worshipped by sage Gautama, who had his asrama or hemitage in the north-west on the northern bank of the river Kaveri. That is why this place is also known as *Gautama Kshetra*. There is an image of the sage in the sanctum near the feet of the lord. It is at the request of the river Kaveri that the lord is said to have taken his seat here. Unlike most other figures of Ranganatha, there is neither a lotus springing from the navel nor are there the figures of his consorts, Sri Devi and Bhu Devi, at the feet. There is however a figure of the goddess Kaveri sitting at the feet of the lord with one of her hands holding a lotus.

In the second courtyard there are shrines of the Alvars. Two pillars in front of the inner entrance are called *Chaturvimsati* pillars as the twenty-four Murtis or forms of Vishnu are depicted with labels giving their names.

The temples of Ranganatha on the three islands of Seringapatam, Sivasamudram and Srirangam, are called respectively Adi Ranga, or the first Ranga, Madhya Ranga, the middle Ranga, and Antya Ranga or the last Ranga. Tipu Sultan has made several gifts to this temple.

Besides this temple, there are also temples Gangadhareswara and Narasimaha here. The Utsavavigraha — the metallic image for taking out in procession—of the Gangadhareswar temple is a very handsome figure of Dakshina Murti. In the Siva temple there are the flgures of some of the *Saiva devotees*. The labels on them give their names and their castes.

The temples at Nanjangud and Chamrajnagar contain the figures of all 63 Saiva devotees. Another shrine in this locality

contains a pretty figure of Ambegal Krishna or baby Krishna
in the attitude of crawling on his hands and knees. Near the
temple are now seen remnants of mud walls and a small
granary the relics of an ancient palace.

Chapter 42

HALEBID

Halebid, the famous capital of the Hoysala line of kings between the 11th and 14th centuries of the Christian era, lies at a distance of about 20 miles south of the Banavar railway station in the Mysore state. It was founded in the 11th century and was known as Dorasamudra, Dwarasamudra or Dvaravatipura. The old palace is said to have stood to the east of the present town where now stands a small hill called Benne-gudda. Traces of Anigundi or 'the elephant pit' and the ancient aqueduct from yagache are still visible near this hill.

HOYSALAS

The importance of this indigenous family of kings which ruled over the whole of the olden Karnata kingdom is detailed in the *Epigraphia Carnatica* volumes issued by the Government of Mysore. The birthplace of Hoysalas or Poysalas was sosevur or Sosavur, the Sasakapura of Sanskrit writers, now identified with Angadi in the Western Ghats. They claimed to be Yadavas and of the lunar race, and bore the title 'the lord of Dvaravatipura' (applies both to Dvaraka, the reputed capital of Sri Krishna, the hero of the Yadavas, and to Dorasamudra, their own capital). They were originally

Jainas, and the progenitor of the family was Sala. On a certain
occasion when he went to worship at the temple of his family
goddess at Sosevur and was receiving instruction from the
Yati (sage) there, a tiger is said to have bounded out of the
forest, glaring with rage. The Yati hastily snatched up his rod
(the usual stout rod of an ascetic, made of solid or male
bamboo) and handed it to the chief, saying *Poysala* which
means 'strike Sala'; whereupon Sala hit at and killed the
tiger, finishing it off perhaps with his dagger. Moreover, from
the Yati's exclamation he assumed the name Poysala, of which
Hoysala is the more modern form. This story is repeated in
all the accounts of the origin of the dynasty.

About the inscriptions of the Hoysalas, it is stated in the
Quarterly Journal of the Mythic Society, Bangalore, July 1911,
page 111: 'One characteristic feature of the Hoysala records
is their fine execution in charmingly proportionate Kannada
characters drawn out here and there where convenient into
fantastic floral devices so as to decorate the margins of the
granite slab, pillar or other material on which they are engraved.
The style of the language too, written more often in poetry than
in prose, is so highly polished and learned that one cannot help
being carried away by conviction that Kanarese literature must
have made considerable progress under the patronage of the
Hoysala kings, as it certainly appears to have done under the
western Chalukyas and probably also under the Kalachuryas,
the Yadavas and other Karnata families of about the same
period.'

After thus settling for a long time on a firm basis the
Hoysalas of the Karnata country (Mysore), according to the
Report of the Archceological Survey of India for 1909-10,
entered the Chola domain to quell the rebellions there and also
free the Cholas from the troubles they had at the hands of the
neighbouring Pandyas and others. It is Vira Narasimha II (A.D.

1220-1234) that came into closer contact with the Chola country in the south. Thus the real history of the Hoysalas in the south may be said to have actually begun with this king. In A.D. 1222 he marched against Srirangam and acquired the name 'the founder establisher of the Chola kingdom.'

Leaving his capital Dorasamudra, Narasimha II is stated to have marched first against the Mahara (also mentioned as Makara or Magara) kingdom and halted at Pachchur from where he despatched two of his military officers, Appanna and Samudragoppaya, to compel the Pallava king Kopperunjinga to release Rajarajadeva whom he had imprisoned at Sendamangalam, South Arcot district, and to invade his dominions. These latter passed through the enemy's country from Pachchur and reaching Sendamangalam, released the Chola emperor and reinstated him. The route followed by these officers is also detailed in the inscriptions recorded in Tiruvendipuram. At Srirangam he seems to have built a mandapa in the temple during his halt there on the march against the Pandya. The *Koyilolugu* which records the history of the Srirangam temple mentions the name of a king of the Kanarese people, Vira Narasingaraja, to have built one of the mandapas in that temple. He is also said to have set up a pillar of victory at Setu (Rameswaram).

Someswara, son of Narasimha, who was then only Yuvaraja, was placed in independent charge of the Hoysala possessions in the south in A.D. 1228-29, and so occupied Kannanur in the Chola country. The southern capital of Someswara, Vikramapura founded in the Chola country which he had acquired by conquest, has been identified with the modern Kannanur near Trichinopoly, five miles north of Srirangam.

In 1237, three years after his coronation, he granted 11 villages to his two able generals—Bogayya and Mallaya, who, on their turn, conferred the same on Brahmans in the presence of Ramanatha at Setu. Someswara is said to have uprooted Rajendra Chola and to have reinstated him after the latter begged for protection. Vikramapura, the modern Kannanur near Trichinopoly, was founded by him after he obtained that place by conquest. His records are found at Srirangam, Jambukeswaram, Tiruvasi, Ratnagiri and Tirumalavadi in the Trichinopoly district; at Mannargudi in the Tanjore district where once seems to have existed a palace, the ruins of which are still mentioned; and at Tingalur and Adhamankottai in the Salem district. The Srirangam inscriptions mention him as '*Soma* (the moon) of the Karnata who had reduced this lotus pond of Srirangam into a pitiable state' and this shows that he was a staunch Sava and therefore neglected the Vaishnava temple at Srirangam and mainly supported the Siva temple of Jambukeswara, on the same island. In A.D. 1236-37 he put up several minor shrines of Siva within the Jambukeswaram temple, called Vallaliswara, Padumaliswara, Vira Narasingeswara, and Somaliswara which were evidently so named after his grandfather Ballala II, grandmother Padmaladevi, father Viranarasimha and aunt Somaladevi whom he loved like a mother. The front gopura of seven storeys of the Jambukeswaram temple might have also been constructed by Someswara. The Bhojeswara (Posaliswara) temple at Kannanur was raised in the name as Malaparoluganda (lord among the Malepas, i.e. the hill tribes in the Western Ghats), a family title of the Hoysalas from the very commencement of their career in bold Karnata (Kannada) characters. He assumed the imperial title *Sarvabhauma* and performed the rites of Tulapurusha and Ratnadhenu at Kannanur.

Someswara's son Veera Ramanatha's accession to the Tamil districts took place about A.D. 1255 and his inscriptions of the 12th, 15th and in 17th years, which correspond to A.D. 1267, 1270 and 1271, are found at Srirangam and Kannanur. This king attended to the checking of the revenue accounts in the 4th year of his reign; the communal repairs made to the Vanigan's well, now known as Nalummulaikkeni at Tiruvellarai, whose walls, it is stated, had sunk in on the four sides probably on account of heavy rains in the 8th year of the reign of the king, and exempted the tax on salt dealers at Tirumalavadi. He made to the temple of Ranganatha at Srirangam, a gift of a gold crown embedded with jewels, two flywhisk with handles of gold and a kalanji (betel-pot). He was succeeded by his son Vira Viswanatha in A.D. 1293-94; after which the kingdom merged into the then rising power of the Vijayanagara empire Subsequent to this, during the time of Ballala III, the Hoysalas had Tiruvannamalai in the district of South Arcot for the seat of government as in A.D. 1323 Umamalaipattanam, i.e. Tiruvannamalai is stated to have been his permanent capital.

HOYSALESWARA TEMPLE

The Hoysaleswara temple at Halebid has four doorways two on the east, one on the north and one on the south with beautifully sculptured lintels. The figure of Nataraja, or the dancing form of Siva, is sculptured in the centre of the lintels flanked by Makaras, on which Varuna, the god of sea, with his consort is seated. The south doorway displays the best workmanship and this might be due to the fact that the king had his palace in the south-west and he must have been using this entrance for entering the temple.

KEDARESWARA TEMPLE

The Kedareswara temple bears at the corners of its terrace the figures of elephants facing outside. The friezes of this temple contain figures of horsemen very finely sculptured. There are shrines dedicated to the Sun and the Moon by the sides of the

Nandi or the bull in the temple of Hoysaleswara. The usual figure of a man stabbing two tigers on both his sides, which is characteristic of the Hoysalas, is seen everywhere. The sculptures of both these temples are one of the best and the steatite or potstone used for the purpose is said to have been quarried from the hill nearby called Pushpagiri or 'the hill of the flowers.'

OTHER SHRINES

Of the several hundreds of Jaina *basties* that once adorned this place, only a few now remain, and amongst these, those of Adinatheswara, Santeswara and Parsanatheswara are important. There is a Brahma pillar in front of the Adinathabasti, the front face of which has a caparisoned horse galloping to the east, the emblem of Brahma according to Jaina iconography.

Chapter 43

BELUR

Belur, on the right bank of the river Yagaeher, is in the state of Mysore. It lies on 13° 10' north latitude and 75°55' east longitude at a distance of nearly 30 miles from Banavar railway station in the Bangalore Poona line. In Puranas and inscriptions the place is known as Beluhur, Velur and Velapura. On account of the high religious importance it was also called as Abhinavakshoni vaikuntha or the earthly vaikuntha (the abode of Vishnu in heaven) and Dakshina Varanasi or the southern Benares.

THE TEMPLE

The Kesava temple is the most important at this place and the god Kesava is known in inscriptions as Vijaya Narayana.

The temple court measures nearly 444" by 396" and the sanctum proper 178' by 156'. The temple has two gates on the east; of which the one on the north is surmounted by a lofty gopura and the other is called Anebagilu or the elephant gate. It was constructed by Vishnuvardhana to comemorate his conversion by the celebrated Vaishnava consecrated on one and the same occasion the five images of Narayana—*Pancha Nayana Partishte* at different places viz., Belur, Talkad, Melakote, Tonnu and Gadag.

SCULPTURES

It is an ideal place for the study of Iconology as the temple is full of sculptures. The story of the great epic Mahabharata up to the Salyaparva is illustrated on the railing to the right of the east entrance. There are on the side scenes from the Ramayana. On the right of the east doorway the darbar of king Vishnuvardhana, who built the temple in A.D. 1117, is sculptured. Also the story of Bali, the demon king who made the gift to Vamana, the dwarf incarnation of Vishnu, is depicted various scenes like the pious Prahlada undergoing various kinds of torture at the hands of his father Hiranyakasipu; the darbar of king Narasimha I, son of Vishnuvardhana; a female figure stripping herself on noticing a lizard in her cloth are all well-executed in stone. In one of the beams of the temple are sculptured the 24 murtis of forms or Vishnu.

The main deity Kesava or Vijaya Narayana is very hardsome and is about six feet in height with *prabha* or halo having on it the Dasavatara or the ten incarnations of Vishnu. The image said to have been brought from the Baba Budan Hills. While removing this god they tried but failed to remove the goddess also. This provoked the ire of the goddess who in consequence refused to be removed to the latter place and preferred remaining at the original place itself. This accounts for the god's being taken to the former place once during the annual festival in the month of April.

In some of the pedestals the names of many other sculptors artists, besides the famous Jakanachari to whom the execution of this temple is attributed and who prepared the sculpture over them, are inscribed. It is interesting to note that many of the labels furnish details about their native place, parentage, characteristics, titles and the like. One other historical fact elicited here is that Belur belonged to the Kuntala country, one of the 56 older divisions of India.

EPIGRAPHICAL IMPORTANCE

According to the inscriptions recorded in the temple the affairs of the temple were managed by a committee of 88 Sri Vaishnavites. Also an account of the rise of the Yadu race and the Hoysalas and their genealogy down to Vishnuvardhana is given and these are of great historical value.

NOTES

1. About the architecture of this temple Fergusson says that it combines constructive propriety and exuberant decoration to an extent not often surpassed in any part of the world and that there are many buildings in India which are unsurpassed for vividness of detail compared to any other in the world; but this one surpasses even those known for their richness of fancy.
2. This is also known as Vayu Parvata or Marut Saila. It is the loftiest range on the Mysore table land wherefrom the rivers Veda and Avati take their rise. In form it resembles a horse-shoe with the the opening in the north-west. The hill is over 6,000 feet above the sea-level.
3. The falling of lizard on the various parts of the body is said to augurs good or evil according to the established Sastra on the subject. Anyhow it is considered impious the moment the lizard happens to fall on the body and to ward off this impurity, bath in the sacred water at the place followed by the worship of the presiding god of the place, is prescribed.
4. The one special feature then is that for a period of three days during this festival *Panchamas* or outcastes have the privilege of entering the temple to pay homage to the god. This is on

account of the fact that the renewal of the slippers, which the god is supposed to make use of while going to the hills to visit the goddess, is done by the cobblers of the place. The few other temples where outcastes secure admission on occasions of the annual festival, are the Narayanaswami temple at Melkote and the Ranganathaswami temple on the Biligirirangan hills.

5. This famous architect and sculptor Jakanachari was born in Kaidala near Tumkur, which was once a capital known at that time as Kridapura. The tradition relating to an incident in his life is that immediately after a son was born to him he left his native village entered the service in another court. The son, who could not even recognise the father, went in search of his father. While at Belur, though a youth, being a chip off the old block, he remarked that one of the images was sculptured in a block of stone condemned in the Silpa Sastras (the science of architecture) and as such it was objectionable. To test the matter, a paste as suggested in the Sastras, was applied to the sculpture. When it was in the process of drying a defeet was noticed at a particular part. When it was opened a frog with some sand and water was seen living there! Realising his mistake, pointed out by a young critic, Jakanachari cut off his right hand. Then the mutual relationship between both was recognised. On his return with his son to Kaidala, Jakanachari is said to have constructed another Kesava temple in accordance with the dictates in the Sastras. On its completion the god installed therein miraculously restored to him his right hand!

Chapter 44

DODDAGADDAVALLI

The sacred station of Doddagaddavalli, dedicated to Lakshmidevi, is situated at a distance of about 12 miles to the north-west of Hassan. The prefix 'Dodda' which means 'Big' is intended to distinguish it from the other place bearing the same name which is called 'Chikka' or 'Little' Goddavalli. In inscriptions it is named 'Gaddumvalli'. The other name 'Abhinava Kollapura' or the modern Kolapura is in consequence of the temple here being dedicated to goddess Lakshmi similar to the famous shrine the same goddess in Kolhapur in the presidency of Bombay.

THE TEMPLE

The temple has four cells and was founded in A.D. 1113 during the reign of Hoysala king Vishnu by a merchant Kullahana Rahuta and his wife Sahajadevi. It measures nearly 120 square feet. The west gate supported by 16 pillars has ceilings containing fine architectural workmanship.

Of the four cells three are in the south and one in the north. In one is lodged the Lakshmi Goddess in the western Linga and named Bhutanatna. The northern cell bears a Kali with 8 arms seated on a demon. In the prabha or halo are carved

9 seated preta or ghosts armed with swords. There are also vetalas or goblins scculptured here and there.

EPIGRAPHICAL IMPORTANCE

According to an inscription in Hassan, Malloja is the architect who built this temple. The other details of the structure are also narrated therein. Other grants also mention the provision made for garland makers and weavers who were to supply flowers and looms to the goddess Lakshmidevi.

Chapter 45

AMRITAPURA

Amritapura lies at a distance of about 6 miles north-east of Tarikere in the state of Mysore which has splendid specimens of Hindu architecture.

THE TEMPLE

The Amritesvara temple here is said to have been built in A.D. 1196. There are entrances in the east and west. The ceilings in the Mukhamandapa and the Navaranga halls bear excellent sculptures. Of these the former front hall is supported on the east by 44 well-polished stone piers and has 20 splendidly carved ceilings. It has porches on all the four sides; the north one has figures carved on the four sides of the central lotus bud, while the rest show only lotus buds. It is said that on the Sivaratri day in February–March, the rays of the rising sun used to fall directly on the linga before and that on account of the badly managed repairs effected to the east gate, the rays now only partly fall on it.

SCULPTURES

Over the rails, the story of the *Bhagavata Purana*, primarily the 10th Skanda which deals with the boyish sports of Sri Krishna ending with the destruction of Kamsa, are sculptured.

The representation of Vasudeva as falling at the feet of an ass shown here has no bearing in the book but it has been given out traditionally that Kamsa had kept an ass near the room where Devaki, the wife of Vasudeva, was confined, with instructions that he should bray as soon as the child was born, so that Kamsa might be apprised of the event and thus kill the child. Vasudeva fell at the feet of the ass entreating him not to bray. To the right of the north entrance begins the story of the Mahabharata ending with the acquisition by Arjuna of the *Pasupatastra* from Siva. On the south of the hall the Ramayana incidents are fully delineated.

In front of the tower we have the Hoysala crest adjoining which there is a very fine figure of Gajasuramardana with a prabha or halo containing the figures of the deities of the cardinal directions.

OTHER SHRINES

Shrines to Bhairava and Saraswati are found within the temple. This is in fact one of the best temples from an architectural point of view as there is ample scope for one to learn everything leading to a complete study of Hindu Iconology.

Chapter 46

SRINGERI

The sacred city of Sringeri[1], in the Kadur district of the Mysore state is situated on the left bank of the river Tungabhadra[2] which originates in the Varaha Parvata of the Western Ghats and flows in a north-easterly direction. The origin of the name is associated with the Rishi Sringa who, according to tradition, dwelt here during the period of the Ramayana. Hence the name Rishasringagir, popularly known as Sringagiri or Sringeri. Some of the local inscriptions also refer to the place as Sringapura, the city of Sringa, commemorating the birth of the Rishi at the hermitage of his father Vibhandaka Rishi, whose penance here is highlighted in another tradition.

PLACES OF INTEREST CLOSE BY

Other important sacred places in the neighbourhood Sakkarepatna, believed to have been the capital of Rukmangada, a king whose exploits figure in the Mahabharata and whose name is commemorated with the Ekadesi festival. He is believed to have constructed the Ayyankere or Dodda Madagakere reservoir, about four miles off Heremagaluru[3] and Chikamaguluru in the neighbourhood which, by tradition, are the estates Rukmangada bestowed on his elder and younger daughter respectively, by way of dowry. The former of these, known earlier as Bhargavapuri, is said to have been the scene of the Sarpayajna[4] (serpent sacrifice) performed by king Janamejaya to avenge the death of his father who died of snake. A stone pillar with a spear or flame-shaped head is said to have been the sacrificial stone used for this sacrifice and to this day Hindus believe that a ceremonial circumambulation of this pillar and a bath in the neighbouring Sidha Pushkarani expiate their sins. Copper plate inscriptions record grants made to Brahmans who performed the Sarpa Yajna. Khandeya, on the rignt bank of the river Bhadra, contains a temple dedicated to the sage Markandeya.

Tradition records that Mrikandu Rishi, the father of the sage, lived here and by observing austerities sought and obtained from the god Siva the boon of a son. The god, however, gave him the option of having a son who would be foolish but would enjoy a longlife, or one who would die at the age of sixteen. Mrikandu chose the latter, but his son, Markandeya, by his indefatigable *kshetratanam* (visiting holy places), austerities and mantra siddhi, won from Siva victory over Yama[5], the god of death.

BIRTH OF RISHYASRINGA

Vibhandaka, son of Kasyapa, consulted his father as to the choice of the best place for tapas (penance); he was directed to the spot in which the river runs in three directions (Tungabhadra flows north-east past Sringeri, then it turns to north by west and again to north-east). Starting from the source of the river the sage proceeded in search of such a place. After passing through various tirthas and holy spots, he came to Sringapura and identified the place to be the one mentioned by his father, as the river branched off in three directions in this locality. There the Rishi settled and did his penance so rigorously that it began to shake even Indra's region. Indra thereupon, to save himself from this situation, caused the divine nymph Urvasi to disturb the Rishi's penance (tapas). When Vibhandaka was engaged in performing his sandhya (evening ablutions), this celestial nymph appeared before him. At the same time a deer came to drink water from the river and unconsciously took in the washings of the ascetic. The animal, in consequence, gave birth to a human male child with the unusual addition of a horn like that of a deer. The child thus acquired the name Rishyasringa[7] and grew up to be a man without having ever seen a woman!

The Mallikarjuna temple on the hill here was founded in memory of this sage. And in the centre of the town of Sringeri stands the temple[8] of Mallikarjuna, founded in memory of the sage Vibhandaka.

During the regime of Romapada over Anga Desa (somewhere to the west of Bengal proper) the country was by an unusual drought of twelve month struck duration. The Brahmin priests advised him that this catastrophe might be overcome if you could somehow induce the young Rishyasringa to visit Anga-Desa. This was done by sending fair damsels who managed to allure the Rishi into visiting the country of Anga. The manner in which they brought Rishyasringa[9] is significant. They joined hands and formed a living palanquin for him. The origin of the idea of the modern palanquin is to be traced to this incident. This vehicle is still in vogue and is used often in marriage procession!

The moment he set his foot on the soil of Anga it started raining heavily! Romapada, the barefooted was so pleased with this young sage that he gave his daughter in marriage to him. About this period Dasaratha, the king of Ayodha (Oudh), was in deep distress by reason of the absence of an heir to the throne.

The sages advised him to bring down Rishyasringa from the Anga Desa. Dasaratha started out to the land of his friend Romapada and requested him to send Rishyasringa with his wife Santa to enable him to fulfil his object. Rishyasringa acted as Dasaratha's priest for the *Asvamedha*[10] yajna or horse sacrifice wherefrom a divine *payasa* (literally a drink made of milk) or sweet drink was obtained which, on being distributed to the queens of the royal household, four sons Rama, Lakshmana, Bharata and Satrughana were born. While returning to his country he worshiped the god Chandrasekhara, at the foot of the Sahya mountain. He attempted to see the diety in the darkness with half-closed eyes whereon he was absorbed in the linga in the temple at Kigga which is close to the eastern base of the Weatern Ghats. It is said that at this holy spot no drought will ever approach within 1 *gavadas* of the god here (one gavada equals 1 English miles).

ADI SANKARA

Later on, this place became connected by tradition with Adi Sankaracharya who, while returning to the south from his northern tour, went to the river Tunga, whose water is pure for drinking (the saying is: Ganga Snanam and Tunga panam), to perform his Madhyamika or midday ablutions. There he observed the unnatural phenomenon of a frog being protected from the heat of the sun by its inveterate enemy, a serpent, which omen induced the swami to found a matha there.

VIDYASANKAR TEMPLE

Though Sringeri contains over two scores of temples the best of those from an architectural view point is that of Vidyasankara, founded in memory of Vidyasankar in Saka 160, Bahudhanya (A.D. 1338). The temple is Dravidian in style and is apsidal at both ends. It faces the east, as is the case with most of the temples and consists of a sanctum with a mandapa (hall) in front of the sanctum. Surrounding these two connected structures is the passage for pradakshina (circumambulation) around them. Again there is what is called a Navaranga or a central hall of about 18 feet in height. This hall bears a ceiling, the centre of which is 8 square feet with a panel of 4 square feet in the middle, and 2 feet deep having a lotus bud of 5 tiers of concentric petals, with parrots pecking on the four sides, pointing their head downwards. The flooring slabs of this hall are 9 feet by 4 feet with the central one of 9 square feet. It has 3 entrances, one on the east, the other on the south and yet another on the north.

SCULPTURES

Against the entrances facing the outer walls of the garbhagriha or sanctum are three niches having in them the figures of Brahma with Sarasvati on the south, Lakshminarayana on the west, the Umamahesvara on the north. Between the east and south entrances are the figures of Indra, regent of the east; Yama, regent of the south with two dogs seated at sides, and several others including Sri Rama, sage Vyasa, Durga and Sani (Saturn). In the space between the south entrance to the pradakshina are Garuda, Hanuman, Lakshminarayana and Brahma with Saraswati. Between the south and west entrance are Kalki, the tenth avatara of Vishnu, seated on a horse holding a sword, Venugopala, Balarama and Parasurama. Between the west and north entrances are Vamana and Bali, Kurma, Matsya, Harihara, Markandeya embracing the linga while being dragged by a noose by Yama, Ardhanarisvara, Tiruparasamhara and Manmatha (Cupid) aiming arrows at Siva. Between the pradakshina north entrance and the north entrance are Chandra (Moon), Hayagriva, Annapurna with a pot and a ladle, and Sarasvati; between the north and east entrance walls and these afford for a study of Hindu iconography. At an angle on the right of the front entrance Vyasa is shown in an attitude of imparting instruction to Sankaracharya, who holds a palm leaf manuscript in his hand. The friezes contain figures of the animal kingdom. Chains of stone rings, which are a source of admiration for Europeans, hang from the caves at the corners of the hall.

The Navaranga hall is supported by 12 sculptural pillars bearing on them lions with riders. Stone balls are placed in the mouth of the lions and these can be rolled about, but not taken out, thus showing the workmanship of the architects of those days. Each of these 12 pillars bear on their back a sign of the zodiac and the pillars are so planted that the rays of the sun fall on each successively in the order of the solar months. This is another admirable piece of workmanship in this hall. Not to speak of these each pillar has an individual graha on it, similar to the zodiacal arrangement of, the various Navagraha or the nine planets; the Sun alone being the lord of all the rasis is shown on the top panel.

On the right of the Mahamandapa, in the place of the Ganapati figure is now placed a miniature Saturn fashioned out of steel. To ward off the evil effects of this powerful planet, people get the figure bathed in oil, as it is believed that nothing else pleases this god more. Besides this steel Saturn, there is a metallic figure of Harihara[11] (half Siva-half Vishnu) which is not commonly found.

The linga in the central shrine is named Vidyasankara installed in memory of Vidyatirtha. It was set up under the supervision and guidance of Bharatitirtha, a devotee and true disciple of Vidyatirtha, who made gifts to several Brahmans on the auspicious occasion of Kumbabisheka or the opening ceremony.

On the west of the Vidyasankara temple are several small shrines of samadhi gudis or tomb temples (samadhi means tomb, gudi means temple) built over the tombs of the various heads of this matha. In the midst of these samadhi gudis is the one dedicated to one Malayala Brahma whose figure is about 5 feet high with a curious story related to it. It is said that this Malayala Brahma was a Brahmarakshasa (evil spirit) who was brought down to this place by Vidyaranya who promised to feed the spirit to his satisfaction. In memory of this incident Hindus worship him on all occasions of feasts and other important ceremonies, in order that such occasions may have a successful termination.

Amongst the idols here, the Sarada goddess is cast in pure gold. Venugopala and Srinivasa with their consorts are cut out of rubies. There is a Nandi (bull) worked in a single pearl. A miniature mandapa has been carved out of a block of emerald.

OTHER SHRINES

On the north of Vidyasankara temple is a small shrine dedicated to Janardana, an aspect of Vishnu, and a little further off, on the very same northerly direction, one to Sakti Ganapati and another to Vagisvari, both of whom are said to have been the favourite deities of Vidyaranya.

EPIGRAPHICAL IMPORTANCE

The old records available in this matha are said to throw much light from a social and historical point of view. The swamis in charge of the matha had complete power to order enquiries into the conduct of the disciples, punish the offenders and direct the local officials to extend facilities to the matha representatives to carry out these duties. Even the letters addressed to the swami by the iconoclastic Mohammedans like Hyder and Tipu, were couched in reverential language.

There is a reference to an attack on the country by three groups of enemies whose destruction the swami had been requested to effect by celebrating what are known as Satachandi Tapa[12] and Sahasrachandi Tapa[13] for a period of one mandala or 48 days. In another instance Varuna Tapa[14] and Rudrabisheka[15] for half-a-mandala or 24 days were performed to ward off certain calamities.

A few copper-plate grants noticed in the *Annual Report* of the Mysore Archaological Department mention a grant by the Gnaga king Konkanivarma, son of Madhava II in the second year of his reign. They also refer to another grant by his senior queen, as well as a grant by his son Durvinita in the twentieth year of his reign. These records go back to the fifth century. Another record furnishes the information that Vidhyaranya died in A.D. 1386. There are many other records of historical and social interest, testifying at the same time to the high esteem in which the presiding priests of the matha were held by various rulers and chiefs. There are the letters addressed by Hyder and Tipu couched in reverential language for the holy personages, though they belonged to an alien faith. Tipu entreats the swami in several letters to have certain Hindu ceremonies performed at his expense in the prescribed manner for the success of his aims against the English, the Marathas and the Nizam; and requests him to pray to god for his welfare and to send him his benedictions. In another letter he sympathises with the swami for the great loss sustained by the matha in consequence of a raid by the Marathas under Parasuram Bhau, during which the raiders not only plundered the matha of all its property worth 60 lakhs; but also committed the sacrilege of displacing the sacred image of the goddess Sarada, and orders the grant of requisite money and things for reconsecrating the image.

In one of the copper plates Vidyaranya's feats are stated to be more wonderful than those of Brahma seeing that he can make the eloquent dumb and the dumb the most eloquent; Bharatitirtha is described as the refuter of the doctrines of Bhatta (Kumarila), Buddha, Jaina, Guru (Prabhakara), the logicians and the Charvakas, and the establisher of the Advaita doctrine. Of Bukka it is said that his excellent qualities were worthy of admiration by the past, present and future kings of the solar and lunar races, that he was truthful, munificent, kind of Brahmans, a treasure to dependents, protector of pure dharma, and a sun in destroying the masses of darkness hostile kings; and finally, Harihara is described as the destroyer of tricks of the kali age, as the head jewel of the good, as the traveller in the path of dharma and Brahma, as converting Kaliyuga into Kritayuga by his pure conduct, and as possessed of the fire of prowess which, blown into flames by the fan of the constantly moving ears of the elephants of the cardinal points, caused the leaf ornaments or the wives of hostile kings to wither: and a wish is expressed that he may live happily for a thousand years.

Another interesting fact brought to light is that at about A.D. 1356 Vidyaranya was at Benares and that he came to Sringeri by order of Vidyatirtha and at the request of Bukkal. From the mention of a grant to the linga at Simhagiri, the front face of which is carved with a figure of Vidyatirtha, the Linga named Chaturmurtimadyhesvara, must have been set up in memory of Vidyatirtha before A.D. 1380. Vidyaranya died at Hampi in 1386 and his Samadhi (tomb) was situated behind the Virupaksha temple there. The existence of the Janardana temple and the Bharatiramanatha and the Vidyavisvesvara, which evidently represent two of the Samadhi temples near the Vidhyasankar temple before 1386 could be made out from these copper-plate grants.

NOTES

1. The city lies in 13°25' north latitude, 75°19' east longitude, 2439 feet above the sea.

2. A legend associated with the river Tungabhadra (the confluence of the Tunga and the Bhadra) says that the Tunga represents the left and the Bhadra the right tusk of Vishnu in the aspect of a boar. With the left tusk the bored into the earth, and on the right he held it up.

3. Kanarese *here*=elder; *chikka*=younger; *magal* = Daughter; *uru*=town.

4. This rite is performed for the destruction of these wild animals. by reciting the mantras related to this sacrifice, the snakes all around are drawn to the spot and made to fall a prey to the sacrificial fire!

5. This scene is said to have taken place in the village of Tirukkadayur near Mayavaram where there is a highly inviting metal figure—Kalasamharamurti with Siva in the act slaying Yama for the sake of Markandeya.

6. Bath in running streams, besides removing the dirt over the body, relieves also the pains in the body and aids the circulation of blood, whenever such rivers have a retrograde course from the natural one, special merits are attributed to the water of such spots.

7. The story is not unlike the Roman myth of Leda and the Swan.

8. The stone pillar in the courtyard of the temple has the crude figure of Ganapati (the elephant-headed god) said to have been designed by Abhinava Narasimha Bharati, who presided over the Sringeri matha (monastery) between A.D. 1589 to 1622 A.D. It is believed that the outlines of the figure grow clearer with the passage of time!

9. The Sringesvara temple at Kigga, also known as Marukalu, has sculptures showing an ingenious combination of men, animals, etc., One of them is noteworthy as representing the incident of the sage Rishyasringa being carried by dancing girls to king

Romapada's capital. The palanquin formed by the women themselves is shown here as being supported by two antelopes. Such sculptures without the antelopes are available at Devanhalli and Sivaganga.

The linga in the temple is called Sringesvara, a shortened form of Rishyasringesvara; because it was set up in the name of the sage Rishyasringa. According to another account, he was absorved into the linga. It is said to have Santa, wife of Rishyasringa at the left side and has two horns over the head like those of the sage. The puranic account of the place describes the linga as the remover of famine which spread over 12 yojanas of the earth, as rejoicing to have Parvati on his left thigh, as the fulfiller of the desires of devotees, as being worshipped by all the gods and as having the shape of a Rudraksha, i.e. the berry of the Rudraksha tree (*Elaeocarpus ganitrus*); and Rishyasringa as being in company with his wife Santa; as dwelling on the bank of hte river Nandini and as being adorned with Rudraksha berries.

10. This sacrifice is performed for the prosperity of the king and his people. The benefits conferred thereby are said to be numerous; a horse is let loose on an auspicious day and it goes round and returns to the same place.

11. In the district of Ramnad there is a temple specially dedicated to Harihara of Sankaranarayana; the figure is said to be 3 1/2 feet high with four hands, the upper right holding a trident and the lower a rosary, the upper left a discus and the lower a conch. Lakshmi and Parvati, Nandi and Garuda, are also sculptured on the pedastal.

12. Sata=one hundred, Chandi=goddess kali, Satachandi fapa is a repetition of certain mantras invoking the help of Chandi probably with one hundred hands the goddess Kali, for the distruction of the enemy.

13. Sahasra=one thousand, *Chandi*=goddess Kali.

14. Varuna fapam is performed to invoke the help of Varuna, the god of rain, and it is performed by the observer, immersed to a certain depth in water, especially praying for rains.

15. Rudrabhisheka is performed for god Rudra to propitiate him in various forms, eleven in number, and the abkisheka or bath is made especially of panchakavya, the five different forms of cow's milk, and other things for bath. Rudra is the god of destruction in his lower aspect and is the protector from all evils. He is called Siva or Sankara in his high aspect of conferring all sorts of boons and comforts.

Chapter 47

PURI JAGANNATH

The famous religious centre, Puri Jagannatha, has a branch railway line from Khurda road station on the Madras-Calcutta line. It is on the coast of the Mahodadi or the Bay of Bengal where the sea bath on important occasion is considered highly sacred. Pilgrims in large numbers flock to the place all the year round.

THE TEMPLE

Within the famous temple, dedicated to Jagannath or the Lord of the universe, which applies to Sri Krishna, whose figure exists with those of his elder brother Balarama and his sister Subhadra; there are also various other minor shrines. It is said that during the iconoclastic Mohammedan period this image was often thrown into the water of the Chilka Lake on the south as well as in the forest on the west and that on the deity appearing in the dreams of devotees and acquainting them of the place, they carried it back to the shrine and began to worship him as usual!

THE TEMPLE

The shrine in which these idols are lodged is named Sri

Mandir which has three entrances. The first entrance has on its sides huge lion dvarapalals or gatekeepers. After passing 22 steps there is a raised hall, Sabha mandapa, or hall behind which there is the sanctum sanctorum having a conical tower nearly 200 feet high, surrounded by a chakra or wheel.

THE IMAGES

The images are made of wood and some of the limbs do not have perfection their hands; the reason being that the lord Mahavishnu himself who was engaged in carving these figures in the disguise of a sculptor, was asked by the queen of the king Indradyumna of Malwa to open them a few days prior to their completion and that in consequence they are imperfect in the formation of certain limbs. There is highly valuable diamond on the forehead of the deity.

According to a paper read before the Literary League, Chittoor, 'The idols are crude, nay hideous. All the same the importance of this shrine is of a very high order. Here there is a special reason for the crudeness. The tradition here is that the idol represent the half-cremated, mutilated body of Bhagavan Sri Krishna after the cremation of whose physical body there was a heavy downpour. It is said that the half-burnt body was washed away to Jagannatham where the essence of it is still preserved inside the crude figures which are replaced every thirteenth year.'

CAR FESTIVAL

The grandest festival here is Ratha Yatra or the car festival that takes place in the month of Ashada, Adi (July-August). During this time the god, after having a bath in the sea on the full moon day, remains privately for a fortnight. Thereafter the god is taken in a car which has 16 wheels, to a place in the north at a distance of about 6 furlongs named Indratumna, after the king of that name at whose orders the images in question were made. There in a picturesque garden, the god stays in a small shrine for eight days and thereafter he is taken back to the temple. A large number of people flock on this occasion to drag the car.